Ulf Pillkahn Using Trends and Scenarios
as Tools for Strategy Development

Acknowledgements

I would like to express my gratitude to the many individuals who contributed to the successful completion of this book. I particularly wish to thank the following people for their invaluable support:

Sofia Benevides
Bruno Díaz
Anne Gelas
Marion Günther
Jacques Helot
Stefanie Maurer
Nathalie Morisset-Bouchard
Eleonora Peis
Renate Pillkahn
Martina Richter
Natascha Römer
Steffi Schulz
Gerhard Seitfudem
Heinrich Stuckenschneider
Claus Weyrich
Willfried Wienholt

And the friendly support staff at the libraries of the Siemens Corporation

Ulf Pillkahn

is a Strategy Consultant at the Siemens Corporation in Munich, Germany. Born in 1967 in Gera, Germany, Pillkahn earned a degree in Electronics and Information Technology at Chemnitz Technical University before going on to work in the development of telephone exchange systems and at the Siemens Corporation in Norway. A holder of numerous patents and patent registrations, Pillkahn's most recent work has centered on innovation management, the strategic, technical and economic aspects of technologies in the areas of information management and communication, strategy development, and future studies.
Contact: ulf@pillkahn.de

Using Trends and Scenarios as Tools for Strategy Development

Shaping the Future of Your Enterprise

by Ulf Pillkahn

Publicis Corporate Publishing

Bibliographic information published by Die Deutsche Nationalbibliothek

Die Deutsche Nationalbibliothek lists this publication in the Deutsche Nationalbibliografie; detailed bibliographic data is available in the Internet at http://dnb.d-nb.de.

This book was carefully produced. Nevertheless, author and publisher do not warrant the information contained therein to be free of errors. Neither the author nor the publisher can assume any liability or legal responsibility for omissions or errors. Terms reproduced in this book may be registered trademarks, the use of which by third parties for their own purposes may violate the rights of the owners of those trademarks.

www.publicis-erlangen.de/books

Contact: Dr. Gerhard Seitfudem, gerhard.seitfudem@publicis-erlangen.de

ISBN 978-3-89578-304-3

Editor: Siemens Aktiengesellschaft, Berlin and Munich
Publisher: Publicis Corporate Publishing, Erlangen
© 2008 by Publicis KommunikationsAgentur GmbH, GWA, Erlangen

This publication and all parts thereof are protected by copyright. All rights reserved. Any use of it outside the strict provisions of the copyright law without the consent of the publisher is forbidden and will incur penalties. This applies particularly to reproduction, translation, microfilming or other processing, and to storage or processing in electronic systems. It also applies to the use of extracts from the text.

Printed in Germany

The Future is Partly Made of Clay

Globalization, fierce competition, and the growing complexity of products, technologies and processes of change have become all-pervasive. They force us to think ahead to the medium and long term while we simultaneously concentrate on our day-to-day business activities. This task demands an ever greater degree of flexibility and adaptability on the part of managers at enterprises throughout the world.

Niels Bohr, the recipient of the Nobel Prize for Physics in the year 1922, once quipped, "Prediction is hard, especially if it's about the future." Indeed, we are not in a position to make precise predictions about future events, let alone plan these events. This, however, does not free us from the task of considering the future.

Considering the future is largely a matter of understanding the present and the past. Strangely enough, we live in a time of too much information and too little information. This predicament arises from the fact that growing complexity virtually bars us from fully comprehending our environment and all of the emerging changes. In light of these limitations, individuals and teams of individuals face a more demanding task when it comes to converting ideas into true innovations and viable market solutions. This task requires effective decision-making support.

The development of many innovations today is not only determined by what is technologically feasible, but by what creates the greatest benefits for the consumer, what is economically feasible, and what appears to be acceptable in societal terms. Despite this, science and technology remain the strongest drivers of progress and wealth in the modern world. Scientific discoveries and new technological developments, i.e. innovations, have an impact on our lives and change our behavior. Innovations arise from knowledge. Ikujiro Nonaka confirms this suggestion, "Successful companies are those that consistently create new knowledge, disseminate it widely throughout the organization, and quickly embody it in new technologies and products." Knowledge has become the most important raw material of our time: knowledge about technologies, knowledge about markets and consumers, knowledge about the complex relationships among the variables in our environment, and knowledge about relevant future trends.

It has become indispensable for enterprises today to have the means of detecting trends – which may signal risks or opportunities – at an early stage and to use this knowledge for strategic purposes. This book makes a valuable contribution in this regard by offering a systematic account of how one can create "pictures of the future." Such pictures offer various coherent views of the future – the future of individual markets, technologies, and other segments of society. While there is naturally no guarantee that what is depicted in the pictures (scenarios) will actually occur in the future, they nonetheless offer a basis for playing an intelligent and more active role in developments – not least when it comes to communicating with one's internal and external partners.

While it is obviously not possible (or even desirable) to precisely plan the future, it is equally obvious that the future does not simply happen. Partly made of clay, the future is shapeable – and that is what matters. Enterprises have considerable responsibility in the shaping of the future. This book will be a companion to all decision makers who have a share of this responsibility and will help them to systematically detect opportunities in the future. Visions, perspectives, fantasies, and curiosity are matter of inspiration. Given that curiosity about the future is in all of us, this book should be of interest not only to researchers, strategic planners and innovators.

I wish all the readers of this book an enjoyable read – and much success in giving shape to their own ideas.

Prof. Dr. Claus Weyrich

Former member of the Management Board
at the Siemens Corporation and
Director of Corporate Technology

Contents

Introduction 13

CHAPTER 1 Venturing a Look into the Future
Moving from the Past into the Future via the Present

1.1 Reflections on the Future 23
1.2 Changes in Our Environment 41
1.3 Enterprise Development 45
1.4 Present and Future Challenges 50
1.5 Enterprise Intelligence Test 72

CHAPTER 2 Detection
Detecting and Recording Changes in the Enterprise Environment

2.1 A Plea for Foresight and Prior Action 81
2.2 The Enterprise Environment 82
2.3 Information as a Basis for Decision Making 86
2.4 How We Can Learn to Understand Our Environment ... 95
2.5 The Future of Television (I) 104

CHAPTER 3 Reflection
Sorting and Structuring Information

3.1 Changes in the Environment 115
3.2 Stability – Paradigms and Assumptions 120
3.3 Changes – Trends 122
3.4 Uncertainty 142
3.5 Contradictions 142
3.6 Indeterminate Elements – Chaos and Wildcards 143
3.7 From Hypothesis to Future Element 144
3.8 The Future of Television (II) 147

CHAPTER 4 **Understanding**
Anticipating the Future

4.1 Memories of the Future 155
4.2 The Possibilities and Limits of Foresight 158
4.3 Origins and Development of Foresight 162
4.4 Pictures of the Future 174
4.5 Demarcation and Focus 177
4.6 Selecting Future Elements 179
4.7 The Actual "Look" into the Future 179
 4.7.1 Principles and Methods of Analyzing the Future 181
 4.7.2 Methods of Analyzing the Present 194
 4.7.3 Methods of Opinion Formation and Decision Making .. 194
 4.7.4 Selection of Foresight Methods ("Looking into the Future") 198
 4.7.5 Developing Hypotheses 198
4.8 Development of Scenario Frameworks and Scenarios 200
4.9 Creating Pictures of the Future 206
4.10 Evaluation of Scenarios 208
4.11 Pictures of the Future 209
4.12 The Future of Television (III) 211
4.13 Lessons Learned 227

CHAPTER 5 **Planning**
Seizing Opportunities and Avoiding Hazards

5.1 Planning for the Future: An Insurance Policy 233
5.2 Strategy Review 234
5.3 Developing Strategies in Turbulent Environments 240
5.4 Enterprise Analysis 243
5.5 Strategy Synthesis 253
 5.5.1 Basic Understanding of Strategy and Strategic Goals ... 254
 5.5.2 Strategic Options and Strategic Fit 257
 5.5.3 Developing Enterprise Scenarios 259
 5.5.4 Developing Strategic Options 260
 5.5.5 Strategic Fit 262
 5.5.6 Robust Strategies 263
5.6 Strategic Decisions 265
5.7 Examining the Future in the Context of Strategy Development 266
5.8 The Future of Television (IV) 272

CHAPTER 6 **Implementation**
Managing Change

6.1 The Dimensions of Change ... 287
6.2 The Logic of Change ... 289
6.3 The Reality of Change in Enterprises ... 290
6.4 Elements of Change ... 294
   6.4.1 The First S: Strategy ... 297
   6.4.2 The Second S: Structures ... 298
   6.4.3 The Third S: Systems ... 301
   6.4.4 The Fourth S: Style ... 305
   6.4.5 The Fifth S: Staff ... 307
   6.4.6 The Sixth S: Skills ... 309
   6.4.7 The Seventh S: Shared Values – Visions ... 310
   6.4.8 F – Foresight ... 316
   6.4.9 E – Entrepreneurship ... 317
   6.4.10 I – Innovation Management versus Innovation ... 317
6.5 Orientation in the Process of Change ... 321
6.6 Including the Results of Analysis ... 325
6.7 Reflection, reflection, reflection 326
6.8 The Future of Television (V) ... 327

CHAPTER 7 **Learning**
Applications and Examples

7.1 Dealing with Uncertainty in Practice ... 335
7.2 The Future of Petroleum – Introduction ... 335
7.3 The Future of Petroleum – An Information Base ... 338
7.4 Compression and Operation ... 358
7.5 Generating Environment Scenarios ... 364
   7.5.1 Scenario 1: "Empty" ... 368
   7.5.2 Scenario 2: "Transition" ... 371
   7.5.3 Scenario 3: "Fight" ... 374
   7.5.4 Scenario 4: "Independence" ... 377
7.6 Generating Enterprise Scenarios ... 381
   7.6.1 Scenario 1: Cautious Innovation ... 384
   7.6.2 Scenario 2: No Experiments ... 386
   7.6.3 Scenario 3: No Plan ... 387
   7.6.4 Scenario 4: Aggressive ... 389
7.7 Strategic Implications ... 392
7.8 Example Summary ... 394

CHAPTER 8 **Homework** 397
What You Should Do

CHAPTER 9 **Appendix I** 403
100 Sources of Information

CHAPTER 10 **Appendix II**
Short Profiles of Selected Methods

    10.1 Macro Environment Analysis 419
        10.1.1 Environment Analysis (STEEPV) 419
        10.1.2 Trend Analysis 420
        10.1.3 Issue Management 421
    10.2 Micro Environment Analysis 422
        10.2.1 Stakeholder Analysis 422
        10.2.2 Customer Profile Analysis 423
        10.2.3 Industry and Market Analysis 424
    10.3 Enterprise Analysis 426
        10.3.1 The 7S Model 426
        10.3.2 Value-chain Analysis 427
        10.3.3 Benchmarking 428
    10.4 Foresight 429
        10.4.1 Morphological Analysis 429
        10.4.2 Forecast 430
        10.4.3 Weak-signal Analysis 431
    10.5 Strategic Analysis 431
        10.5.1 BCG Matrix 431
        10.5.2 SWOT Analysis 433
        10.5.3 Ansoff Matrix 434
    10.6 Change Management 435
        10.6.1 Eight-phase Model According to Kotter 435
        10.6.2 Balanced Scorecard 436

References 437
Index 450

Introduction

A typical scene at the supermarket: three of eight cash registers are open. Around five people are waiting in each line to pay for their groceries. You want to avoid having to wait, so you select the line that you hope will be the fastest. Experience shows, however, that you will probably not be in the fastest line. People sometimes forget to weigh their fruit, price tags get lost and the rolls in the register have to be changed. You are often forced to wait longer than you had hoped and experience it as a nuisance – for one because of the delay and for another because you didn't pick the other line, the one that is so much faster.

In the world of business, the consequences of waiting too long are far more dramatic for customers, enterprises and employees, and the circumstances themselves are far more complicated.

It is a matter of the future. When facing the need to make a decision, who hasn't already desired to know exactly how the future will develop. This book cannot help you to make exact predictions about the future, but it can help you to deal with uncertainty.

In recent years, we have seen the following developments:

- Trends used as instruments
- Trend research and trend management

These are always used in the hopes of improving one's ability to detect future events and to thereby make uncertainty more manageable.

"But what exactly is a trend?"

For me, everything began with this question. Around three years ago there was a point at which it occurred to me that the use of the term "trend" had become inflationary. Everything was a trend, or related to a trend. The mystique of the "trend" seems to come from the fact that the things that are labeled such do not thereby become more comprehensible. On the contrary, they become more nebulous. My hunch back then was that the excessive use of the word actually came from the fact that most people didn't really want to concern themselves more closely with what was being referred to. Complex situations were reduced to "trends" and appeared therefore to have been explained. But it is precisely this hope for simplicity that is deceptive.

In the 1990s, we were informed, "The trend is going towards home offices." In the 1980s, we heard, "The trend is going towards the paperless office." Once a subject has been labeled a trend and blown up by the media, it takes on a life of its own and has to be reckoned with by nearly everyone. Added to this is the fact that the labeling of certain phenomena as "trends" is often rather plausible. They quickly find their proponents and market criers and appear in *Time*, *Newsweek* and *People*.

"The trend is going towards ..." Such statements tell us the direction of a development, and include a claim about what will happen in the future. In short, such statements cross a metaphysical barrier. Clarity as to whether what is claimed is a supposition, a belief or a fact can only be established by a careful investigation. But who goes to such lengths? One assumes that the messengers (the trend scouts) have done careful work and know what they're talking about. And evidence to the contrary is also not always apparent.

The paperless office was a vision – drafted by technicians and formulated by theoreticians – or it was exactly a trend, depending on the source. Home offices – even when outfitted with modern office equipment – cannot replace the conventional workplace. We know that today. Although it was no more than a temporary appearance in the wake of the Internet boom (home and office workplaces are actually complementary), it was hyped into a trend that ultimately fizzled.

The examples offer a view of the gray zone one enters into as soon as one examines trends more carefully. One is faced with claims, conjecture, suspicions, wishes, conviction, and the search for security and orientation. Trends turn complex phenomena into something that looks simple. The wish to reduce the world to trends is understandable, but it is no replacement for knowledge.

The inspiration for this book was a desire for greater clarity in the trend fog. Linguistic precision and clear analysis are important prerequisites when it comes to an examination of the future. The same applies to scenarios. The referential scope of the term "scenario" is broad, ranging from A as in "assumption" to I as in "idea" to P as in "picture of the future."

The day-to-day business of enterprises is fraught with problems, and we are confronted by new challenges every day. As shown in Figure 1, we can use a matrix to represent the problems and possible solutions as known and unknown realms of possibility.

Solutions may already be available for known problems. These are then applied (below left) or a search is conducted for yet unknown solutions (upper left). For instance, when a customer complains about a service, the problem is clear – it is only the solution that is missing. The further development of technologies also belongs in this category: the problem is known and a search is conducted for the solution to it.

The situation is far more difficult when a problem remains undetected or cannot be represented or demarcated (below right). This situation occurs when new physical effects or technologies are discovered. The potential wrapped up in laser technology, for instance, was only realized gradually. In the beginning, there was a solution – but no problem (the push effect of technology). The search for applications essentially is a matter of searching for and detecting possibilities of improvement.

The area in the upper right corner of the matrix is reserved for "problem unknown/ solution unknown." This area is essentially characterized by uncertainty. Traditional

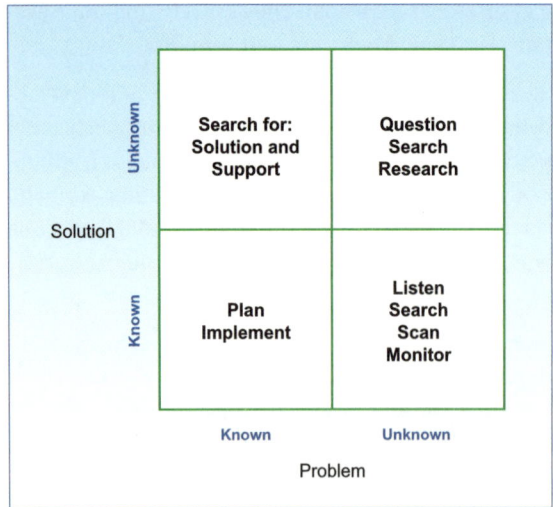

Figure 1   The problem-solution matrix: what one should do given various constellations

approaches to solving problems fail here because there is no known and clearly demarcatable problem. We do not yet know what the problems of tomorrow will be. No one would have hit upon the problem of global warming one hundred years ago. It is clear that the approaches and answers of today and yesterday do not present a solution.

We can only approach these types of problems and solutions relating to the future playfully. Clear answers will remain exceptions. In the beginning, there will be questions. One will approach the problem and its solution, although without ever really reaching them, via research, establishing hypotheses, and trial and error.

Dealing with uncertainty is something new for many enterprises. These enterprises have to first learn that it is no longer possible to contain uncertainty and to keep everything entirely under control. Ignoring such factors or sticking one's head in the sand is also a kind of solution, but it is a high-risk solution given the nature of competition. If, on the other hand, one accepts the fact that the future is uncertain and shows a willingness to cope with it, then there will be plenty of room to maneuver. In the present book, I am concerned to present ways of understanding uncertainty, broadening and sharpening our view of the future and learning to deal with uncertainty.

The future and investigations of the future are multifaceted. Chapter 1 of this book is devoted to an assessment of the current situation, a sketch of the use of trends and scenarios, and the provision of a thematic framework for the subsequent chapters.

Chapter 2 is concerned with an observation of the events taking place in the environment: What do we observe? What information is important for the enterprise? How do we manage this information?

Chapter 3 is concerned with the ways in which we analyze information. This discussion provides a basis for the subject of Chapter 4 – namely, looking into the future.

The strategic consequences of scenarios are treated in Chapter 5 and Chapter 6 offers a number of approaches to implementing the lessons learned in one's own enterprise.

This ideal sequence – from the gathering of information to informed decision making and execution – is shown in Figure 2. The application of this sequence is then illustrated in Chapter 7 with the use of a concrete example.

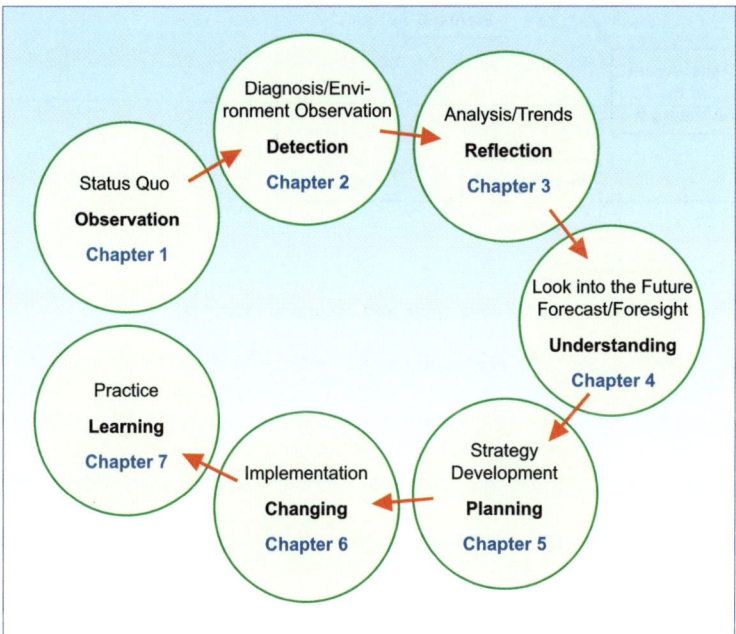

Figure 2 The structure of the book: the ideal way to develop and use scenarios

Figure 3 offers a guide from the perspective of strategic management for navigating one's way through the book.

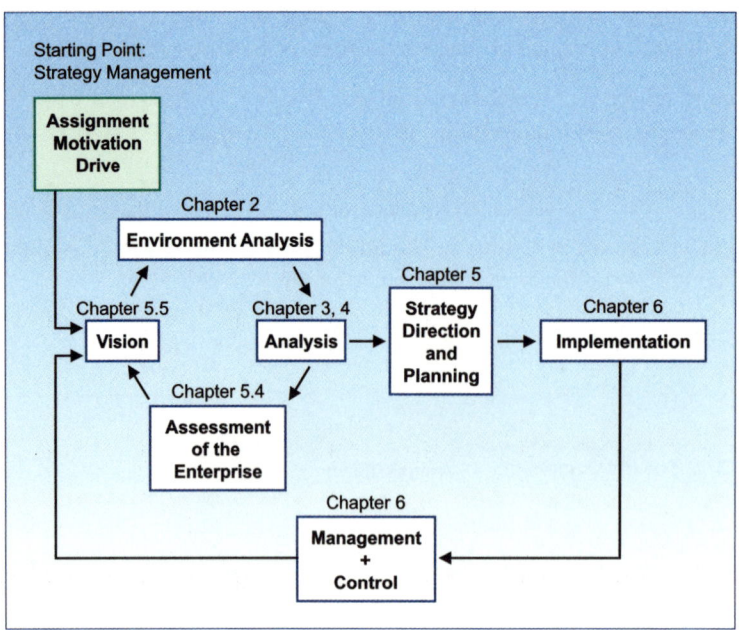

Figure 3 Flowchart: the real sequence for developing and using scenarios

Chapter 1

Venturing a Look into the Future

Moving from the Past into the Future via the Present

There once was a very ambitious city mayor who wanted nothing so desperately as to know how his city would develop in the future. A number of major projects had been planned, elections were coming up, and the city and its inhabitants were simply not flourishing as he had hoped.

No longer able to contain his curiosity, the mayor sends for old man, a wanderer of sorts, who was known throughout the land for his ability to see into the future. When summoned by the mayor, the clairvoyant says that he can indeed offer a very clear and, if need be, detailed description of the city's development for the next 25 years, but that his special service would cost a considerable sum of money. Now, although the mayor is a man of unmistakably rational persuasion, there is something about the clairvoyant's demeanor that he finds truly captivating, and he agrees to have the future of the city told – despite the steep cost.

The clairvoyant begins his account as follows, "The city will develop magnificently in the coming years. The investments will pay off handsomely, new enterprises will spring up, and talented and hardworking people will come to the city from far and wide to take part in and help to further expand its prosperity. With its generous funding, the city college in particular will become prominent. And the mayor will be reelected."

The mayor beams. For this is exactly what he wanted to hear. He is content and congratulates himself for having consulted the clairvoyant. The pending decisions were to be made exactly as he had planned.

But as the clairvoyant continues with his account, the mayor's ecstatic vision becomes clouded, "A global crisis will be upon us in nine years, triggered by speculation on the stock market. Your city, too, dear mayor, will be hit rather forcefully. The rate of inflation will skyrocket and many companies will not survive the crisis. Unemployment will increase dramatically, and with it a certain misery will prevail in the city."

The mayor stops short. This was not what he had in mind.

"After a few years, the situation will more or less return to normal. The city, too, will gradually recover and return to its former prosperity."

The mayor is instantly relieved, but before he has a chance to gain his bearings, the clairvoyant continues his tale, "The 13th year is the year of grave political change, and you will be powerless to do anything about it. A dictatorship will emerge at the highest level of the republic whose proponents will have no qualms about achieving their political ends by force. Despite the constraints of the political order, however, material development in the city will remain good. The mayor, however, will be forced to step down."

The mayor is devastated – and then it gets even worse.

"In the 19th year, all semblance of political life will have vanished, replaced by the iron rigidity of military rule. All of the city's resources are channeled into the arming of the country. And at the end of the year, the military regime will thrust the country into a war."

The mayor turns pale.

"The war lasts for a harrowing 6 long years. At its end – in the 25th year – your city will be destroyed in an aerial bombing."

Was it really such a good idea to let his curiosity about the future get the better of him? The mayor is no longer sure. He takes a seat and begins to brood. What should he do? What should he tell the others at city hall? Will they even believe him? Is the clairvoyant's tale a "true" vision of the future?

After a time, the mayor rose of a sudden and summarily dismissed the clairvoyant. He had resolved not to say a word about the unusual encounter.

The story of the curious mayor and the clairvoyant is, of course, not without a historical parallel. The mayor's city might have been the German city of Dresden in the year 1920, which has been bombed and destroyed during World War II.

This thought-provoking anecdote, drawn from a presentation by Arie de Geus [Burmeister 2004], raises a host of questions that will be the focus of my attention throughout the book. One such question is: How much sense does it make to concern ourselves with the future when it is clear that things will occur over which we have no control, and that precisely these things will have a profound impact on society. In the present chapter, I address this and other questions as I seek to establish a point from which to embark. After all, attempts to study the future are largely a matter of dealing with a lack of clarity, half-truths, facts, models, opinion, prospects and a lot of emotion. It will be helpful to establish a set of assumptions, a foundation, as it were, for the remaining chapters.

1.1 Reflections on the Future

Imagine that you could look into the future. What information would you find especially interesting and what would you do with this information?

The Motivation for Considering the Future

While curiosity, anxiety and uncertainty provide an obvious incentive for considering the future, there is also a desire to use the information available for purposes of more informed action, in particular, to use the information to gain strategic and tactical advantages – as well as personal advantages. The exact motivation behind our interest in acquiring knowledge about the future is likely to vary from person to person, with the spectrum ranging from caution or a protective instinct to a consideration of advantages such as power, wealth, influence and fame.

From time immemorial, human beings have been fascinated by the notion of looking into the future – probably because such a capacity would allow them to use information about the future to inform their decisions today, and thereby establish certain advantages, whatever these advantages might be:

- The interest of a scientist might be focused primarily on the question *how*?
- The interest of a philosopher might be focused on changes in accepted notions of consciousness, being and truth.
- The interest of a politician might be focused on constellations of political power.
- The interest of private individuals is likely to focus on their own well-being.
- The interest of an environmentalist might be focused on the state of various ecosystems and that of the environment in general.
- The interest of an economist might be focused on overall economic development, expressed in terms of buying power, consumer behavior, wealth, GDP, currency stability and the state of the world's stock markets, etc.
- The interest of a company executive is likely to focus on the well-being of the enterprise, i.e. its market positioning and capacity to outperform its competitors.

While the perspective in this book is largely that of a company executive, the methods outlined could just as well be applied to societal issues. **Questions about how one should respond to change and which methods are the most promising form the focal point of the discussions in this book.** To begin, we might ask ourselves what motivates entrepreneurs and company executives to consider the future.

Successful enterprises tend to want to build upon their success. They are on the uptake for investment opportunities promising the greatest returns at the lowest risk. Less successful enterprises place their hopes in positive market developments and are oriented towards short-term success.

Given that enterprises are not self-sufficient and are not only exposed to micro and macroeconomic developments, an interdisciplinary point of view will prove to be essential when it comes to answering these questions. Changes occur in all areas of an enterprise's environment, and this makes it necessary to broaden one's perspective.

One can observe of late that the acceptance of the discipline of future studies is closely correlated to economic development. This is why our interest in examining the future fluctuates – ranging from the implementation of a scaled-down strategic planning to the implementation of a broad based and long-term program of "corporate foresight."

In the last few years, future studies have enjoyed a kind of renaissance. This can be seen in increased budgets for strategic consultation and an increased interest in the notion of foresight. As a development, it can probably be traced to an increased uncertainty in the corporate world. The term "foresight" refers to any attempt to establish a long-term orientation. In the corporate world, one speaks of "corporate foresight."

The Past of Future Studies

A concern with the future and an interest in predicting future events was common in ancient civilizations. Such supernatural powers were attributed to druids and shamans. The carcasses of animals and other natural occurrences were analyzed to arrive at a reading of the future. Well-known instruments for generating predictions – back then and now – include the crystal ball and the stars and other heavenly bodies. Many personal decisions and even decisions made at a political and societal level are based on superstition and prophesy, despite their utter lack of a scientific foundation. But however dubious the methodology, the advantage of such decision-making aids lies in the momentum they generate. Predictions – even if they are misguided – ensure some sort of response, and thereby allow us to overcome an intolerable state of merely waiting and wondering.

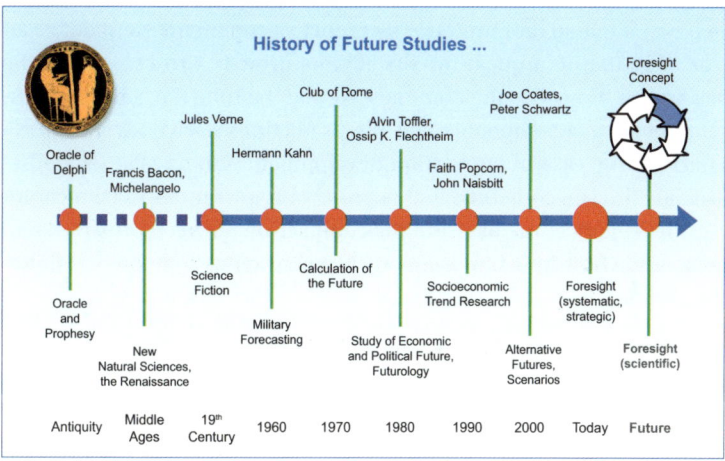

Figure 4 From oracles to future studies

Random action was supplemented in antiquity by an examination of concrete evidence and an evaluation of information. The history of Delphi can be traced back to well before 2000 BC. The fact that Apollo spoke through the Pythia – a priestess – and not through a priest at Delphi goes back to the ancient cult of Gaia. The Pythia sat on a tripod over a chasm. According to the myth, vapors arose from out of this chasm and put the Pythia in a trance. Although it has been handed down that the oracle answered correctly when asked by King Croesus what he was doing at the moment – namely, cooking lamb and turtle – one has to suspect that the oracle worked with spies. Nonetheless, the oracle in ancient Greece had tremendous significance for a period of more than a thousand years [Orrell 2007]. Politics was at work here – and kingdoms could be made to fall apart on account of an oracle.

Historical records indicate that the two expressions "Know thyself" and "Nothing in excess" were inscribed near the entrance to the ancient temple of Apollo at Delphi. The first, and more well-known of the two sayings, is particularly indicative of the actual intent of the cult (i.e. the deity that was the object of worship), namely, the resolution of problems and questions via an examination of one's inner self. Knowledge of the inner self thus served as the key to solving problems in the outer world. This approach has retained its validity to the present day – as we will see in the chapters to come.

The first attempts to take a systematic approach to studying the future go back to 1946 when the Stanford Research Institute (SRI) began to develop forecasts. The RAND Corporation and Hermann Kahn, who developed the scenario method, followed in 1948. These investigations, whose focus at the time was military-strategic planning, were later developed by the Royal Dutch Shell Corporation into a formalized method of supporting its corporate strategies.

The Club of Rome was founded in 1968. This non-commercial organization concerns itself with global development and gained much attention in 1970s when it published its *Limits to Growth* report, a book whose scope extends to the year 2100 and whose main tenet is that current rates of technical development, progress and resource consumption cannot be maintained indefinitely. The report's proponents viewed it as an argument in favor of initiating a quest for sustainable growth. Critics accused the Club of undue pessimism. However, the dominant view at the time (i.e. a belief in linear societal development) is questionable and the predictions derived from it have proven – particularly in the case of population development – to be false. Nonetheless, the note of social criticism contained in this projection warrants special recognition. Moreover, this brief look at the past and the comparison between projected and actual development also show how important such scenarios were in our examination of societal development.

The so-called trend researchers appeared on the scene later (in the 1990s) when societal development came to be regarded as rather uncertain or non-linear.

Futurists and Trend Forecasters

The need for reliable predictions is extremely high. Pressure to generate growth and unrealistic expectations make the situation even more difficult for enterprises, and tend to have an impact on risk behavior. Individuals and institutes whose work is devoted to future studies and trend forecasting promise to help.

With his book *Megatrends*, John Naisbitt [Naisbitt 1982] heralded a new epoch. Guidelines like, "It's a tremendous strength not having to be right" marked the beginning of a less absolute and much more flexible view of the future. While Naisbitt focuses on political and societal developments, Faith Popcorn [Popcorn 1991, 1996] devotes her attention exclusively to the customer and generates trends in the area of marketing. Cocooning, clicking and evaluation (eva-lution – the new power of the feminine) are examples of the models she introduced. Whether it is really a matter of trends or, as in the case of cocooning, a creative re-labeling of something much more commonplace ("my home is my castle") is an open question. The fact is: Popcorn ranks as the highest paid trend forecaster in the United States and she has left her imprint, with her theories and predictions, on the marketing departments of many corporations.

A further exponent of trend research is Gerald Celente who founded the Trends Research Institute in 1980 and gained a degree of recognition for his book *Trends 2000* [Celeste 1997]. In the book, he introduces what he refers to as the Globalnomic® Method – a term that is left rather loosely defined – and claims, "Our trends and our forecasts are based upon a synthesis of all the available information. The secret lies in putting together the relevant evidence and coming up with the correct big picture." While the Trends Research Institute regards itself as "the world leader in trend forecasting," one cannot help but wonder what synthesis is at work when one reads a few pages later in the book that China is likely to collapse in the year 2000 with "a billion people and millions of problems spilling over her borders – with none of her neighbors strong enough to stop her, especially Russia."

The question indeed arises as to the legitimacy of the methodology and whether trend researchers are really in a position to provide the guidance for the future that is demanded by enterprises. The methods that such forecasting institutes use to acquire and structure knowledge remain largely in the dark. Even if, for instance, scanning and content analysis are often referred to as methods – for instance by Naisbitt and Horx [Horx 1996] – the rather nebulous descriptions of these fail to dispel the considerable doubt. It follows that it is primarily those in need of guidance who – capable of no more than a limited and uncritical questioning of the methods – are inclined to give credence to the forecasts.

However, the discussions that are published in study reports and monthly trend newsletters are indeed a matter of keen interest for enterprises. One is given a quick overview of specific issues and one learns something about new or emerging phenomena. Moreover, one also learns the very latest terms of reference for events and products. Such naming [Horx 1996] of heretofore unknown things makes a decisive contribution to our understanding of new phenomena. That being said, it is important to avoid making the future of enterprises dependent on theories that are based on trend speculation. A willingness to do this is regrettably often evident when enterprises have already taken the step of outsourcing the task of reflection, or have lost the capacity to observe their environment, or when the critical thinkers and smart analysts within an enterprise fail to convey their important messages to the deciders (this issue will be addressed further in Chapter 5).

Given that trend research institutes make the results of their investigations available to a large circle of customers, such information is little helpful from a strategic point of view because the lack of exclusivity prevents any one enterprise from gaining a competitive advantage.

It is clear that most futurists have taken up their investigations of the future because they either hope or believe that it is possible to accurately project what will occur in the future so long as one has access to the right data, the right theories, the right methods and, naturally, the right amount of money.

Sadly, the approaches taken by trend forecasters tend to be just as unclear as the course of change itself. These approaches include pure fiction, whereby trends are simply postulated in the absence of empirical or theoretical explanation, compilation, whereby an attempt is made to combine facts, deductions, speculation and fantasy into a coherent whole, and reduction, an attempt to abstract clear and concise (or even bite-sized) trends, megatrends, or metatrends from the chaotic and unfathomable world we live in. Here especially, the "weak signals" and signs of trend breaches are often sacrificed in the name of clarity – to the point of triviality.

Trend research conducted in the 1980s and 1990s has been criticized for its lack of a scientific basis and for the deployment of farfetched methods. Naisbitt speaks of content analysis, and Horx and Popcorn speak of scanning while championing themselves as revolutionaries: "Trend research sees itself as an interdisciplinary metascience. It is less concerned with fulfilling the requirements of the traditional definition of science than with generating something new that is beyond the current thought horizon." [Horx 1997] Rust – one of the fiercest critics of trend researchers – describes their approach as nothing more than voodoo, "It involves a presumptuous disregard of all the criteria that are essentially linked in the academic world to the notion of research, including a clear statement of the subject of inquiry, clearly formulated hypotheses, and verifiability. None of these remain, and what is left is voodoo." [Rust 1997] Rust describes trend research as pre-scientific and concludes that such intellectual investments in intuition, conjecture and speculation lead to a certain arbitrariness. This can be seen in Popcorn's description of the utility of her clicking trend, "If you pay attention in the case of today's trends to where it clicks, then you will also learn how you can profit from it tomorrow." The question is whether trend analysis conducted at the level of popular science and its conclusions – dressed up for maximum media impact – represent appropriate sources of support when it comes to developing strategies and managing change in a corporate environment. From the point of view of the executive team, it would clearly be advantageous to be able to draw a sharper distinction between what qualifies as market research, trend analysis and futurology and what qualifies as a scientifically-based solution that can be integrated into the enterprise.

An intact and independent capacity for reflection and an ability to draw one's own conclusions is essential to the survival and flourishing of enterprises. The Delphic oracle admonishes us to rely on our own strengths. This admonishment has become more relevant than ever. In writing this book, it is not my intention to publish a manual or predict the next megatrends. On the contrary, my intention is only to encourage the development of a capacity to reflect (i.e. a certain posture that is geared to learning and discovery) as well as to sketch ways of interpreting signals in our environment, managing uncertainty and responding to change as it happens. An excessive concern with external phenomena is the wrong approach, and will sooner or later lead to a lack of orientation. Cultivating and developing of one's own strengths and simultaneously avoiding a myopic approach to the external world will lead to long-term success. But all our efforts to establish foreknowledge by which to orient ourselves and make wise decisions hinges on a single question:

Can we predict the future?

"No," says the chaos theorist.

"Yes," responds the astrophysicist.

"To an extent," says the economist.

"Usually," says the meteorologist.

It is apparently not an easy question. Let's carefully attempt to arrive at an answer to the question, and thereby also establish a foundation for the chapters to come.

Somehow all of the respondents are right. The chaos theorist makes a plausible case for degrees of freedom, complexity and the unfathomable dependencies of events. The astrophysicist can predict within a tenth of a second when a solar eclipse will occur one hundred years from now. The economist submits projections (e.g. of GNP growth) that exhibit more or less high rates of accuracy. The meteorologist regularly issues weather reports that are often, or usually – to put it more charitably – right, despite the occasional occurrence of rather surprising weather developments.

While the answers to our question may appear rather convincing when viewed from the perspectives of the various experts, all of the answers seem not to suffice when it comes to a final settling of the issue.

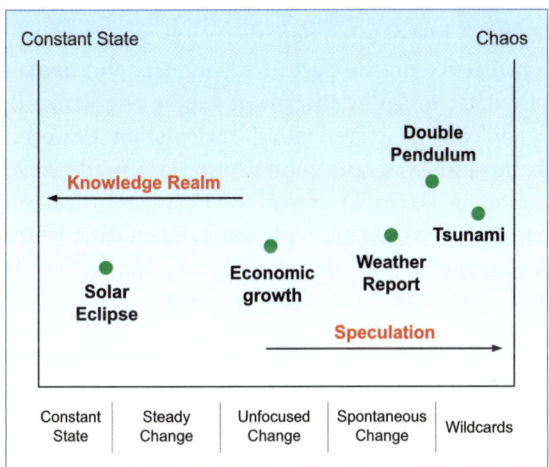

Figure 5 Moving from a constant state to chaos: the continuum of change

As shown in Figure 5 above, the types of possible change can be effectively illustrated by transposing the examples described above to a continuum of change that ranges from a constant state to chaos. The examples differ in terms of their structure and in the manner in which they are observed. There are phenomena on the constancy side of the spectrum that exhibit little or virtually no change and there are phenomena on

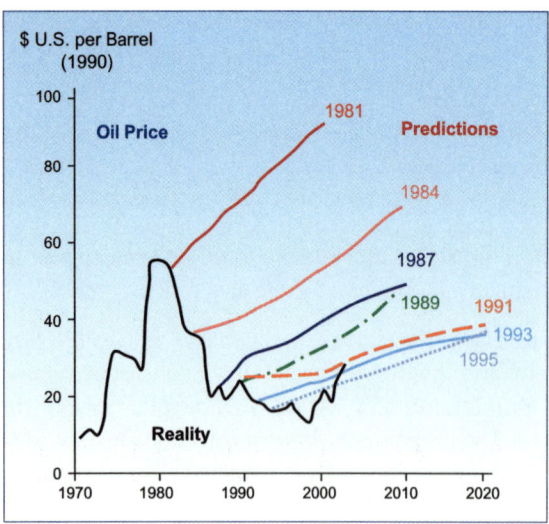

Figure 6 Oil price development: projection and reality

the chaos side of the spectrum whose spontaneous occurrence is virtually unpredictable (e.g. tsunamis).

Figure 6 shows a comparison of real oil price development and projections. The fact that the projected development and the actual development diverge as greatly as they do is astonishing in light of the insistence on the part of economists and market experts that the price is essentially determined by the law of supply and demand. Both of these variables are known and can be factored into the calculation. However, the human reactions involved, both emotional and political, are less predictable. Human reactions introduce a gigantic uncertainty factor to the business of looking into the future and making projections. The assumption that human behavior is ultimately rational – an assumption that forms the basis of many investigations – is highly questionable and has often enough led to inaccurate projections.

The Scientific Integrity of Future Studies

The term "science" comes from the Latin "scientia" and refers to a state of having knowledge as distinguished from a state of ignorance. As such, it has a certain normative character, with scientific endeavors and conclusions being seen as having a secure foundation and enjoying our respect, while also tending to dispel doubt.

However, given that knowledge tends to accumulate and areas of inquiry tend to expand, scientific points of reference cannot remain static. In discussions in the area of the philosophy of science, an area that shows few major developments since the contributions of Popper, Kuhn and Lakatos and in which the past enjoys far more respect than the future as an object of scientific inquiry, there is little room for the notion of a science of the future. This is perhaps on account of the fact that the future of knowledge appears unfathomable: "It comes down to the simple fact that we are not in a position to anticipate the evolution of knowledge in any truly appreciable sense." [Rescher 1985]

Even before Socrates, Xenophanes, Alcmaeon and Ekphantos came to the conclusion (500 years BC) that it is not possible to acquire certain knowledge of the real world. The aim of the early proponents of natural philosophy was to arrive at an understanding of the real world in the framework of empirical theories [Mansfeld 1983]. Xenophanes is reported to have said: "There is no such thing as certain knowledge. Even if we were to know something exactly, we could not know that we knew it. In all matters, we have no more than assumptions."

After reaching such a self-critical view at such an early stage in our history, how did such a rigidly deterministic world view ever become so ascendant in the natural sciences? The apparent limit to acquiring knowledge in the area of philosophy and the natural sciences was naturally not satisfactory for the speculative mind. This apparent contradiction was soon resolved by Parmenides who introduced formal terms – variables – for things in the real world.

This then gave rise, in what was known as the Pythagorean school, to formal mathematics and later, thanks to Plato and Aristotle, formal logic. The claim of absolute truth and validity can be traced to the fact that the subjects of the theory are defined in a manner that ensures that the theory remains free of contradiction, which, however, is only possible using abstract entities and not real entities. This epistemological nuance was pushed aside in the wake of the broad correspondence between theory and experiment at the beginning of physics. However, the correspondence was more a result of investigations limited to extremely simple systems. Complex, real occurrences can either not be modeled at all or can only be modeled in approximation. For instance, chaos theory assumes that even complex and dynamic systems are subject to the deterministic laws of classical physics, but that practical predictability is only possible for short spans of time.

Philosophers of science such as Sir Karl Popper regard physics as the starting point for reflections on the nature of science. "But, with Galileo and Newton, physics began to leave all other sciences far behind, and since the time of Pasteur, the Galileo of biology, the biological sciences can claim to have proceeded on a similar path. The social sciences, however, have not yet found their Galileo. In these circumstances, scientists who work in one of the social sciences are greatly interested in problems of method, and much of their methodological discussion is conducted with an eye upon the methods of the more flourishing sciences, especially physics." [Popper 1965]

Physics gained the status of a role model because physical processes (e.g. the oscillations of a string pendulum in the gravitational field of the earth) can be exhaustively explained in terms of differential equations. Given a knowledge of the starting conditions and the relevant laws of change, it becomes possible to make concrete predictions about the future behavior of the physical systems – as seen in the notion of a determined system mentioned above. However, this calculability applies only to laboratory conditions or ideal circumstances. When it comes to real physical processes, the calculability forms an exception, i.e. it applies only a minimal part of the processes.

In physics class, we learn that there is a big difference between theory and practice, for instance, when the physics teacher explains that, except for the influence of wind resistance, the time that objects spend in free fall depends only on their height and weight, when in reality a feather is longer underway than a ball of the same weight.

Bifurcations represent an example of a practical and theoretical inability to predict events (e.g. our inability to determine the ultimate trajectory of a pinball shot out of a slot and onto the arched surface of the pinball machine). This exact determinability cannot be maintained as the complexity of the system involved – manifested by a high degree of freedom and independent variables – increases.

The aim of science can be seen as the attempt to establish general propositions about the world that permit us to both explain events and predict events. Chalmers suggests that the problem of underpinning such generalizations must be solved in light of the fact that our world is so complex and unordered that it scarcely seems possible to detect regularities on the basis of which to derive scientific propositions that can be apppplied to the world [Chalmers 1999].

General validity, reproducibility, context independence, verifiability and an absence of formal contradiction are the main criteria used to assess scientific claims [Rescher 1997]. The lack of their application in the sort of trend forecasting described above unveils such forecasting a kind of pre-scientific activity. Moreover, the use of the term "research" (as in "trend research") in connection with such forecasting is indeed misleading. The practice of compiling observations and generating forecasts by way of extrapolation will lead to nothing more than a collection of hypotheses.

Strictly speaking, the term "future studies" implies an attempt to acquire knowledge of the future using scientific means. As a would be scientific discipline, however, future studies is confronted by a major problem right from the outset in that the subject of investigation – the future – has no more than a virtual existence. Moreover, the possibility of intervening in or preconditioning the future prevents reproducibility. In the run-up to the year 2000, for instance, warnings were issued that computer-generated chaos and with it, unforeseeable consequences, were in store. While nothing of the sort took place and while the warnings may have been exaggerated, these warnings did indeed lead to the implementation of measures designed to prevent a catastrophe. This example underscores the disadvantaged status of predictions, in particular when our responses (intervention) can lead to their fulfillment or non-fulfillment. Propositions about what will occur in the future trigger responses, and these responses may make the propositions appear (in retrospect) to be accurate or inaccurate.

This introduces the issue of how we evaluate propositions about the future.

Technically speaking, the warning about the computer chaos that was supposed to be touched off by the changeover from year 1999 to the year 2000 was false. However, when one considers the overall situation, it is possible that it was precisely this warning that prevented the occurrence of considerable problems on January 1, 2000. This aspect was succinctly described by Friedrich August Lutz in 1955 in a remark about the unavoidable predicament economic forecasters find themselves in: "Forecasts that are, in and of themselves, accurate are destined to become false if they are published, believed and acted upon while forecasts that are, in and of themselves, false tend to become true." [Lutz 1955]

This suggests that it will not be sufficient to evaluate forecasts solely in terms of their scientific status. In what follows, we examine forecasts as instruments of empirical research in economics and other social sciences.

Predictions and Forecasts

The term "forecast" comes from the Middle English and means to scheme or plan beforehand. The principle behind forecasting is to analyze past events, identify regularities (laws), and then use these as a basis for drawing conclusions about future events. Past observations are represented using time series. In order to apply what one learns from the time series to the future, one must assume that the conditions that prevailed in the past will continue to prevail in the future. This premise is referred to as the stability-time hypothesis. "Strictly speaking, the condition is never entirely met in economic reality, and this essentially rules out any forecast." [Hansmann 1983] This admonition can be found in a guide on forecasting procedures. This problem is then circumvented when we assume (i.e. in the absence of an alternative) that the stability-time hypothesis is essentially fulfilled. Here, however, it warrants bearing in mind that even as our methods and models become ever more sophisticated and appear to deliver better results, all forecasting procedures are subject to this basic flaw.

Figure 7 shows a forecast (made in the year 1950) of population development in Germany for the period from 1950 to 1980. With a variance of around 20% by 1980, the

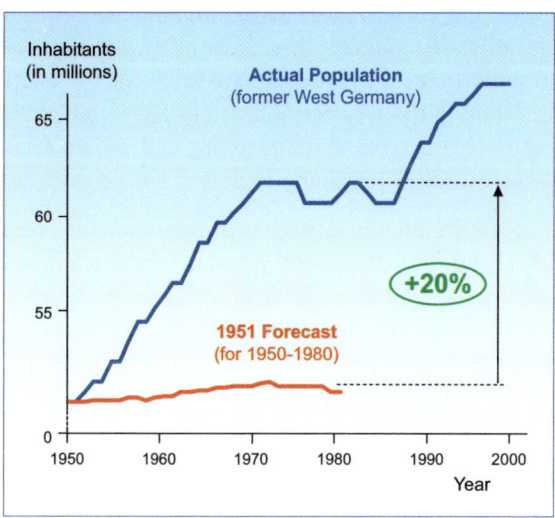

Figure 7 Forecast of population development in Germany: a poor basis for planning [Bretz 2001]

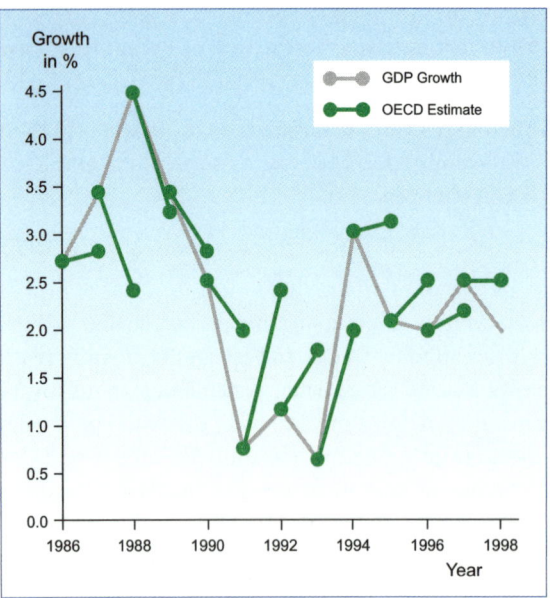

Figure 8 One-year forecast versus actual growth in GDP in the G7 countries from 1986 to 1994: considerable inaccuracy despite presumed scientific merits [Orrell 2007]

forecast is very imprecise when one considers that the variable involved tends to develop relatively slowly.

An even more telling example is illustrated in Figure 8. The OECD drafts growth forecasts for the OECD countries on an annual basis. As is apparent, the forecasts are virtually useless given the fact that even slight differences in growth entail significant changes in the overall economic situation of a country. This can be evaluated in retrospect. However, it is unsettling to think that these forecasts are the basis for many political and economic decisions. Although the degrees of acceleration, complexity, and uncertainty continue to increase in many areas of the economy and society, forecasts are based on theories that assume static conditions.

Despite the scientific merits of the investigation, the forecast is useless from the point of view of the user. We can conclude that despite the scientific nature of the empirical research involved, the findings are as little reliable as those of the futurists. Science should therefore concern itself with the basic principle behind forecasting instead of seeking to improve the models and procedures.

Figure 9 offers a more or less accurate sketch of the overall situation. Corporate foresight is deployed as a form of support for decision making. The need for improved guidance is given. Support provided by both trend researchers and scientists is welcome. As mentioned above, the discipline of future studies lacks a theoretical basis – expanding the scientific framework would seem to represent a prerequisite for a higher degree of acceptance.

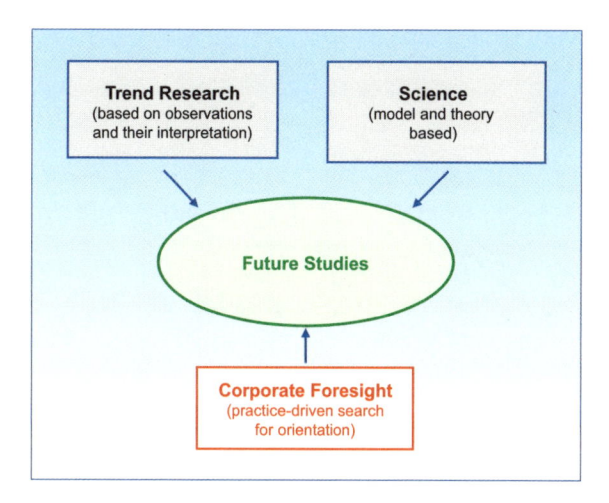

Figure 9 Classifying future studies: neither trend research nor science have proven suitable for lowering or eliminating uncertainty in the business environment

Degrees of Probability

One often comes across attempts, both in practice and in the literature, to assign degrees of probability to future events. For instance, the market research company Gartner, Inc. assigns probabilities to the occurrence of various events in the future. Weather reports commonly indicate the probability of rain for the coming days. However, the probability of precipitation – expressed as a percent – merely informs us that similar weather conditions (air pressure, temperature, etc.) were followed by precipitation at a certain frequency. This value is given as the probability of rain for the coming days. Such statements concerning the probability of rain only make sense when we assume that the number of parameters will remain constant. In contrast, assigning degrees of probability in the case of market observations, as is practiced by Gartner, Inc., makes little sense. Such statements are based on the assumption that the market in question can be demarcated and all intervening factors either remain constant or can be calculated. One deliberately assumes that no substitute products will enter and have an impact on the market during the period in question and no social or economic changes will affect the dynamics of the market. In short, one assumes that no market development will take place at all – a false assumption. This is a good example of conveying a sense of security by suggestion.

Figure 10 offers an illustration of the development of knowledge. The one coordinate shows knowledge itself, ranging from knowledge to the absence of knowledge. The other coordinate more or less represents our awareness of knowledge. It reaches from "the knowledge that one knows something" to non-self-reflective knowledge. The inner segment represents codified knowledge (e.g. of an enterprise) in the form of books, presentations and digital files. The next segment represents half-knowledge and hidden knowledge in the form of unwritten laws, undocumented process knowledge and even personal contacts. Everything beyond these two segments con-

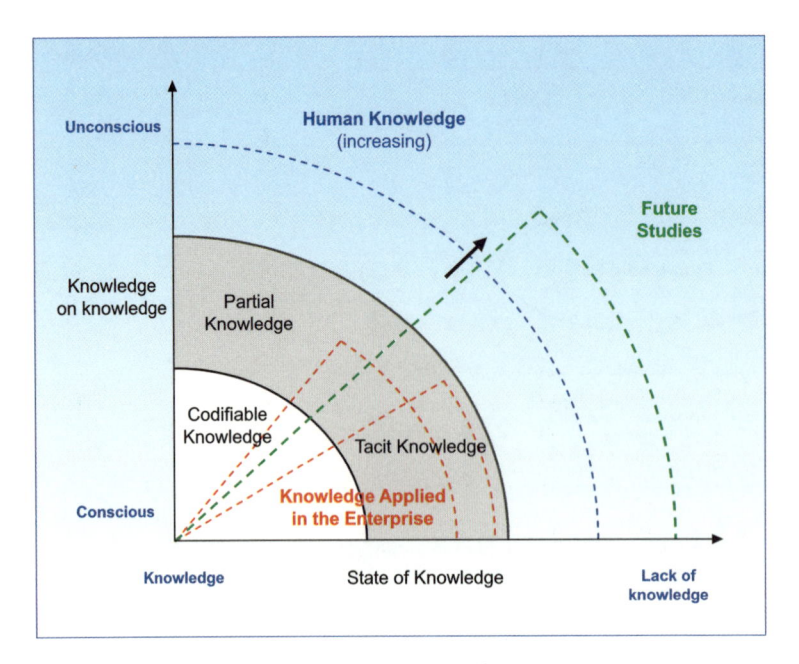

Figure 10 Knowledge development: a never-ending space

stitutes the absence of knowledge (business and worldly). The broken blue line is intended to mark the knowledge of humankind, which grows daily. Nonetheless, the absence of knowledge is unending. The philosopher of science Karl Popper [Popper 1969] puts it this way, "There is one thing that is impossible for us to know, namely what we will know in the future. Because otherwise, we would already know it." We can thus assume that the future will include novelties that are presently in the realm of the absence of knowledge of an unknown order. Assigning probabilities to values of an unknown order makes little sense. And assigning probabilities to future developments does not make sense on the assumption of non-closed systems. The exceptions here are trivialities of the following sort formulated by Keynes: "In the long run, we are all dead." [Keynes 1936]

Figure 11 offers an illustration of transferring this notion to the problem-solution matrix shown in Figure 1.

Known problems and solutions are covered by current markets and standard product development programs. The search for solutions to known problems is market induced (market pull). New technologies for which there are (on the face of it) no corresponding problems often arise in research-intensive areas. Here, the task at hand is to identify applications that establish the technology's utility (technology push). Our attention in the particular case of future studies is focused on the "New Territory" quadrant. Neither the problems nor the solutions are known. One enters – as it were – new territory. This starting position applies to most conceivable and inconceivable situations in the future.

"In a world of constant change," write Watts Wacker and Ryan Mathews in *The Deviant's Advantage*, "good questions are the real scarcity." [Wacker 2002] No problem-solving or marketing strategy can help here. Only asking questions, researching, experimenting, establishing hypotheses and looking for evidence can help us to get closer to the unknown.

"Anyone who is technically proficient can solve a problem that is already formulated, but it takes true originality to formulate a problem in the first place." (Albert Einstein as quoted by [Sternberg 1999])

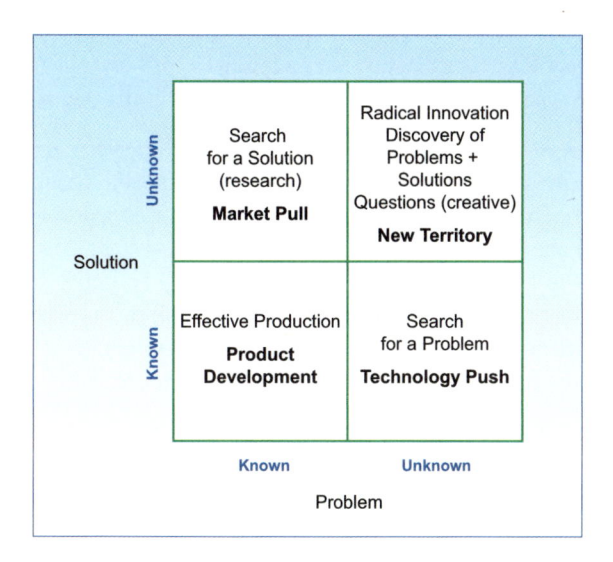

Figure 11 Problem-solution matrix: searching for problems and solutions

It follows that the attempt to assign degrees of probability to future events is misconceived. For instance, try to imagine what the probability of a terrorist attack in the near future is (something that is often discussed in political contexts). Compare this value to what the estimated probability would have been BEFORE September 11, 2001. The degree of probability that we would assign to the occurrence of a terrorist attack is presumably far higher today than it would have been before the striking attack in New York. Objectively speaking, the probability of such an occurrence is unknown to us today as it was back then. The difference is that we are much more aware today of the existence of acts of terror. Factoring the increased efforts to prevent such attacks into the equation, it becomes clear that the opportunities to carry out terrorist attacks are fewer today than back then. The risk can thus be expected to be lower than back then.

Consider the mathematicians' joke: if you fear your plane will be brought down by a suicide bomber, then take a bomb on board yourself. The probability of there being two bombs on board must be dramatically lower, even negligible.

Making Decisions in the Face of Risk and Uncertainty

Having concluded that assigning degrees of probability to future events is not a suitable form of support when it comes to uncertainty and the need to make decisions concerning the future, the question arises as to whether risk assessments represent a more appropriate form of support. Risk management, the aim of which is to assess emerging risks and to propose any necessary countermeasures, has become a fixed institution in many enterprises.

In 1921, the economist Frank Knight outlined the difference between risk and uncertainty in his book *Risk, Uncertainty and Profit* [Knight 1921]. He describes risk as randomness with known degrees of probability. For instance, the tossing of a coin will result in either heads or tails. In contrast, uncertainty is randomness with unknown degrees of probability – as in the case of the mayor and the clairvoyant at the beginning of the chapter [Cleary 2006].

Applied to business practice, this means that investment bankers are exposed to risk (profit or loss) while enterprises face uncertainty (i.e. a multiplicity of possible developments). When the degree and the extent of the uncertainties increases continuously, enterprises are simply not in a position to manage it – the many attempts to resolve the uncertainties via the instrument of risk management are an indication of this helplessness. New concepts are needed for dealing with future uncertainty. These should either allow us to minimize uncertainty or accept it and come to terms with it.

In this connection, Rosenzweig argues that security as something that is pursued and achieved is an illusion "because it leads us to overlook the essential unpredictable nature of business." [Rosenzweig 2007]

In the present book, I devote my attention exclusively to dealing with uncertainty. In chapters 2, 3 and 4, I discuss its analysis. In chapters 5 and 6, I discuss the corresponding synthesis, i.e. the concrete actions that can be derived from the latest findings.

Despite the numerous serious reservations on the part of scholars, the bell curve (or Gaussian curve) developed by Carl Friedrich Gauß in the nineteenth century established itself in the social sciences as an important tool for calculating degrees of probability and as a basis for many other calculations, coefficients and terms. The Gaussian model assumes that the average is the rule, i.e. that a normal distribution will apply. Exceptions do not contradict the average. An example – paradoxically from the world of finance – shows that these exceptions – the 10 trading days with the greatest exchange volume within the last twenty years – account for almost 50% of the value of the S&P 500 index. The assumption of a normal distribution of statistical fluctuations in the price of stocks is therefore catastrophically misguided (Figure 12).

Particularly in light of the increasing dynamic nature and complexity of economic activity, the question arises as to whether the framework has been properly set when it comes to considering risks and whether risk estimates ultimately have a negative impact on decisions (i.e. risk is used only as a relative component).

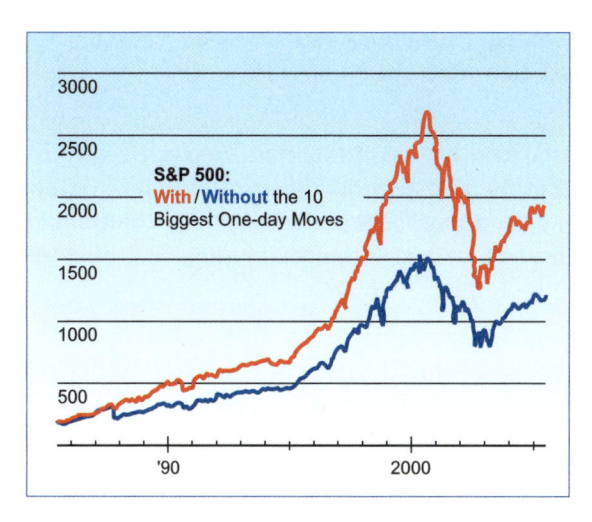

Figure 12 Statistical disobedience: the exceptions account for the effect [Fortune 2005]

The utility of risk management as an instrument for dealing with uncertainty is limited because it does not cover the (possibly highly relevant) portion of unforeseen events, and "risk" in this connection refers merely to what is known and calculable.

The Phenomenon of Time

Among the fundamental philosophical categories, the category of time is the one that is central to future studies. Any form of reflection aiming beyond the present, any prediction, forecast or act of planning presupposes the future as an aspect of time and will entail models of the course of time that are reflected in expressions and terms such as "the future is open," "shaping the future," "foresight," and "trend."

Having asked the question, "What is time?" the philosopher Saint Augustine went on to explain that he knew what it was until he was called upon to explain it [Baeriswyl 2000]. The human perception of time is always tied to change – consciousness of change is a condition for perceiving time. The philosopher John Ellis McTaggart claimed that a universe in which absolutely nothing changed (including the thoughts of the conscious being existing inside of time) would be a timeless universe [Zimmerli 1993]. Beyond this organic world view, which is based on our daily experience of time (boredom, stress, aging, etc.), a conception of time based on natural science has developed since the Middle Ages. This has concerned itself mainly with the exact measurement of time and has, in its cold, sterile and merciless approach advanced to the measure of all things.

The attempt on the part of humans to decouple themselves from the cyclic time of nature is also characteristic of the epoch in which future studies have become a societal and business necessity. The result of industrialization, measurement, operationalization and rationalization is that we human beings no longer orient ourselves on natural cycles. Instead it is civilization and technical advances that set the pace. Speed, shortage of time and acceleration are the result.

In our day-to-day lives, we accept it as self-evident and incontrovertible that time runs only in one direction, revealing itself in an endless stream consisting of the past, the present and the future. In contrast to things in space, we cannot perceive time via our senses. It remains curiously beyond our grasp. The past is no longer, the future is not yet. The present appears to be a small, immeasurable moment linking the past to the future.

We live in the now, our experience is based on the past, but the decisions we have to make are exclusively about the future. While the course of time is irreversible, it nonetheless leads us to project our knowledge of what we have experienced onto the future. Given these circumstances, Mark Twain took it upon himself in the year 1883 to forecast the future length of the Mississippi River: "In the space of 176 years the Lower Mississippi has shortened itself 242 miles ... therefore any calm person who is not blind or idiotic can see ... that in 742 years from now the Mississippi will only be a mile and three-quarters long." [Twain 1984]

While the future is largely indeterminate for us, facts were established in the past. Actions, however, are exclusively reserved for the present. "If life were oriented solely on past experience, any form of innovation would be impossible. Conversely, if we had no memory, every situation would be new." [Brockhaus 2000]

Strictly speaking, every action is brought to completion under unique circumstances that will never be exactly reproduced. It follows that the utility of applying what we have learned, our experience, to each new situation is limited. Our ability to act in the present is characterized by the capacity to distinguish between what has been and what is emerging, and to develop new options for action when facing that which is new in the emerging situation.

When applied to a specific moment in the future, this means that any capacity to act depends on the ratio of the new to the known. Unpredictability derives from the fact that we cannot know now – in the present – what we will know at that moment in the future, i.e. what part of the new will have become a part of the known. This constitutes a formulation of the fundamental problem of any quest to examine the future.

It follows that the best preparation for the future consists of gathering knowledge – i.e. learning as stockpiling – and increasing our intelligence and capacity to respond in order to be able to respond intelligently (and appropriately) to the new and unknown.

Conceptual Basis

We tend to think and argue in accordance with very simplified models. World views differ from person to person and are based to a large degree on our previous experience, cultural backgrounds and personal and social values. The vastly complicated nature of the real world prevents us from using it as a point of reference for our daily reflections. We would otherwise soon be confronted by the philosophical dilemma that everything depends on everything else.

I therefore assume in what follows that only very simple, clearly demarcated events that are subject to no dependencies (or only a few dependencies) can be predicted. Conversely, I also assume that highly complex problems and issues cannot be solved with simple approaches and that the business of making predictions is viable only for extremely simple systems, for instance, as illustrated in classical physics. As we will see in greater detail in Chapter 5 below, it is surprising that the complexity of situations is often underestimated when it comes to developing corporate strategies.

The following assumptions also apply to the discussions below:

1. Time is the interesting and pivotal component of future studies. The future is always fraught by uncertainty.
2. Uncertainty will increase and possibilities of control decrease as the relevant degrees of acceleration and complexity increase.
3. While assigning degrees of probability to the occurrence of future events is popular among futurists, it is a misguided approach.
4. It only makes sense to devise risk estimates for closed systems.
5. Knowledge plays a major role in our reflections on the future. It forms the basis of the models we use, and is thus the basis for imagination.
6. Changes are temporary, finite processes.
7. Personal impressions and views influence our view of things.
8. Luck, misfortune and pure chance may have a decisive impact on developments. Foresight hardly yields starting points for a systematic, methodical approach.
9. The tendency to draw conclusions about the future based on the past is daring at best, dangerous at worst, and usually too superficial.
10. The basic structure of change is detectable. Classifying the parts of this structure as necessary, possible, and desirable can help one to shape the future.

1.2 Changes in Our Environment

We all notice the change. There is much written and reported about it. But what is it exactly that is changing in our environment, i.e. in the world beyond the borders of an enterprise.

The notion of a universe that is subject to constant change and that nonetheless follows certain laws goes back to Heraclitus of Ephesos (also a pre-Socratic thinker). The works of Heraclitus represent an elementary basis for the distinctively Western world view – even Hegel sees Heraclitus' theory about the interrelatedness of opposites as the basis of his own dialectic philosophy. Plato later famously summarized the world view of Heraclitus with the words "panta rhei" or "everything flows." All things are ceaselessly in flux. The only certainty is endless change. Permanence is an illusion. Plato uses Heraclitus' example of the man who cannot enter the same river twice because the river and the man will have changed in the meantime. Even if it may sound trivial, we are indebted to Plato for reminding us that we are all too easily subject to the illusion of continuity and fail to take notice of the changes – just like the frog that dies while sitting in a container of water when the temperature is gradually increased to the point of boiling. Had the temperature increased of a sudden, the frog would have leapt out of the container. In our world, flooded by information and stimulation, we have grown accustomed, like the frog, to concentrating on what we regard as the essentials and fail to take notice of the gradual changes (see Chapter 2).

The nature of changes can vary significantly. In light of the fact that the proposition "everything changes and nothing is permanent" is of little practical help to an enterprise, it may prove helpful to attempt to classify various types of change. We might, for instance, draw a distinction between structural and gradual change.

Table 1 Classifying Change

Area	Types of Change	
	Structural	Gradual
Nature	Hurricane	Climate change
Society	Knowledge community	Declining birth rates
Technology	Internet	Miniaturization
Economy	Globalization	Currency exchange rates
Politics	Democratization	Household debt
Humans	Puberty	Education
Values	Awareness of time	Individualization

Moreover, one can break down the overall environment into various areas that are subject to specific kinds of change. As shown in Table 1 the overall environment can be broken down into various areas that, despite being interrelated, tend to change independently of one another. Each area is subject to different laws and the change within these areas proceeds according to different cycles. Nature tends to change very slowly. However, the impact of humankind on nature has "forced" nature to change more quickly (e.g. global warming and melting glaciers). In contrast, those areas that are strongly influenced by humankind can also exhibit mercurial change.

Humankind Propels Change

Humankind is the main cause of change. This makes change largely incalculable. Political influence and military action can cause major and surprising changes (e.g. the fall of the Berlin wall in the year 1989). Consumer behavior is also subject to change. Analyzable economic change (also people-driven) is comparatively slow in coming while change on financial markets can be both mercurial and profound (e.g. the collapse of the New Economy in the year 2000). Such change can be traced to the simultaneously resolute and panic-driven behavior of the market participants. The ratio of reason and emotion in decision making determines the profundity of the changes generated by people.

The leeway humans have when making decisions or behaving makes humankind the great unknown variable in reflections on the future. The mistaken assumption of rationality (e.g. as reflected in economic models that assume complete rationality and a market that is determined solely by supply and demand) often leads to mistaken projections. It is safe to assume that the unpredictability of human decision making will increase because electronic networks now enable us to transfer information (and money) around the world in fractions of a second. Once a sluggish component in the overall environment, humankind and individual humans have become unpredictable.

Figure 13 illustrates the dynamics and complexity of change. While much will remain as it is, increasing dependency will cause increasing vulnerability.

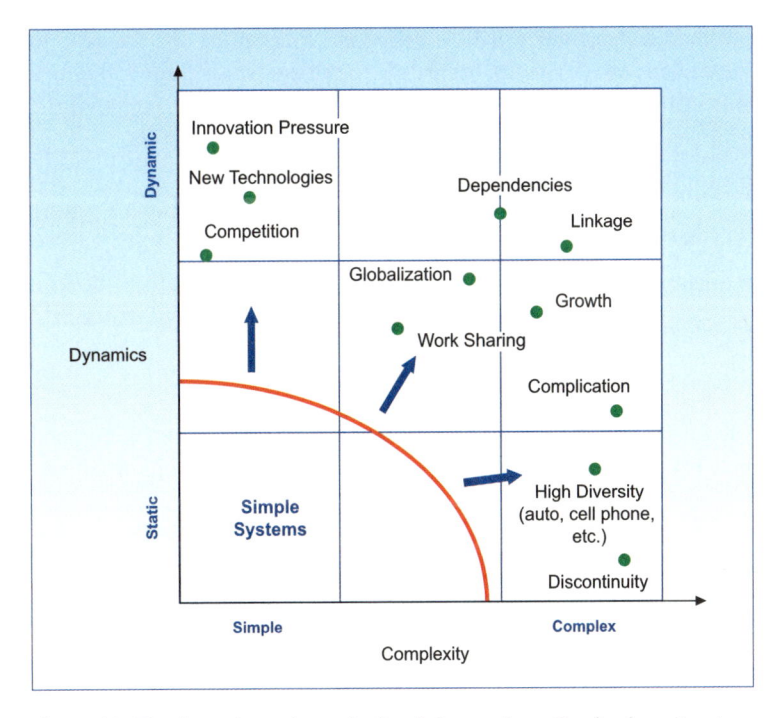

Figure 13 The dynamics and complexity of change: from the simple system to unpredictability

1.2 Changes in Our Environment

The world of the future will largely resemble that of today. However, while much will remain the same, and some things will change only marginally, we are virtually certain to also witness cases of radical change. However, what is it that will change and what will remain the same? We don't know the future, but we will have to shape it. Casting a careful and reflective look into the future is one of the conditions for preventive action. Thinking as a kind of stockpiling will turn the destructive path of "learning after the crash" into "learning before the crash."

A number of approaches to explaining the processes of change are well-known. Depending on their form, we can distinguish among linear, exponential, spiral, and other models. What all approaches have in common is their high degree of abstraction. In what follows, we present two models that offer partial and retrospective explanations of change.

Theory of Evolution

Evolution does not proceed in a linear and determined fashion in the direction of a hypertechnical future. On the contrary, it proceeds in fits and starts, it takes detours, and it is subject to breaches, contradictions, and setbacks. Only seldom in the history of the world is the one completely detached from the other. Events that conform to laws collide with events born of chance. All emerging is a matter of recombination and all future solutions emerge from a realm of possible future solutions [Röß 1993].

Wave Theory

Nikolai Dimitrijewitsch Kondratieff (1892 to 1938) is regarded as the founder of what is referred to as Long Wave Theory. According to the model attributed to him, a basis innovation is introduced every 30 to 50 years. These have so far included the following:

1. Kondratieff cycle (K1): steam machine, cotton
2. Kondratieff cycle (K2): steel, railroad
3. Kondratieff cycle (K3): electrical engineering, chemistry
4. Kondratieff cycle (K4): automobile
5. Kondratieff cycle (K5): information technology, computer

One characteristic of the Kondratieff cycles is that existing, but unexploited (and unknown) resources suddenly become a subject of general attention and broad significance. In the case of cycles 1 through 4, these resources were (material) energy. Ever since cycle 5, the resource has been (immaterial) information and knowledge. Enterprises usually do not recognize the opportunities that are associated with the use of the new resources until signs of instability emerge (e.g. during the transition to computer technology). This is likely to remain the case in the future owing to the fact that the duration of a Kondratieff cycle is longer than the economic horizons of most enterprises.

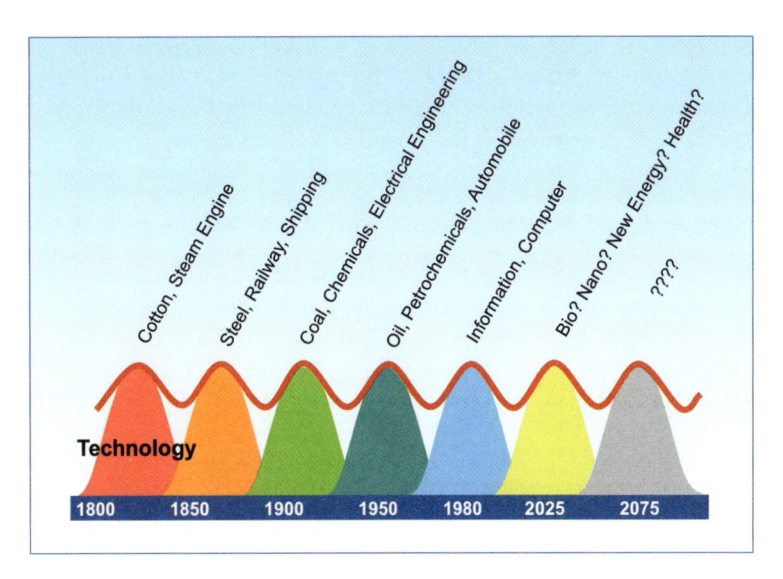

Figure 14 The Kondratieff cycles: what will come next?

As illustrated in Figure 14, the focus of speculation concerning the successor cycle K6 (i.e. the cycle that follows the information technology cycle) is broad and includes such items as biotechnology, nanotechnology, health, and knowledge management. This also reveals the disadvantage of the model: one is able to positively ascertain the subject of the next Kondratieff cycle only in retrospect or only after the cycle has long since begun.

Given that the development of enterprises and the development of their environments generally do not conform to the same rules, the mechanisms and the changes themselves will also differ. While environments do not need to take enterprises into consideration, enterprises do indeed face the task of surviving in their environments!

1.3 Enterprise Development

In his book, *The Company*, John Micklethwait describes the success story of the commercial enterprise as an institution. Next to the family, he sees companies as the most important organizational unit of our times and highlights, in particular, their value for societal and economic development. The success of enterprises lies in the ability to adapt to changes [Micklethwait 2003]. The origin of every company is that someone sees an opportunity or a threat earlier than others. Micklethwait uses innumerable examples to support his view, including the example of Henry Ford who saw the potential of automated automobile production.

In the course of an enterprise's lifetime failures result from risks and threats that were detected too late and every success results from opportunities detected at an early stage. It is not always the enterprise from which one would expect it most that it is predestined to detect risks and opportunities on time. It is often the case that stable industry structures are challenged by outsiders to the branch. For instance, the electric light bulb was not discovered and introduced to the market by a manufacturer of gas lamps, and the digital camera was not developed and introduced by a traditional camera maker. These events threatened existing business or replaced it altogether.

Consider the following thought experiment: an enterprise's decision makers are given an opportunity to select or shape their own environment. What would they do?

- We assume that the aim of the enterprise is to make a profit. The customer is the means to an end because the customer supplies the money in exchange for a product or service. The ideal customer would be rich and easy to please. This would allow the enterprise to command high prices for simple products and little service.

- Only a giant marketplace can promise giant profits. The term "marketplace" in this context refers to any demand that can be expressed in terms of sales units and volume. Competition has a negative impact on the price one can command and the volume one can supply. It follows that a monopoly would be ideal.

- Furthermore, risk (i.e. business uncertainty) in our present scenario would be negligible, and the marketplace itself would exhibit long-term stability.

- All uncertainty factors would be eliminated, there would be no competition, the marketplace and demand would be giant, and customer wishes would remain largely constant.

Table 2 offers an outline of the difference between a market environment that is ideal for enterprises and a market environment that is real. While many will continue to

Table 2 The Ideal Enterprise Environment vs. the Real Environment

	Ideal Environment	Real Environment
Market	Infinitely extensive and protectable	Finite and open to competitors
Risk	Zero, negligible	Present
Competition	Zero, controllable	Unpredictable
Customers	– Undemanding – Constant demand – Rich and inclined to purchase	– Demanding – Ambivalent – Spontaneous
Environment	Stable	Unstable
Future	Predictable	Unpredictable
Surprises	None	Possible at any time
Product	Value chain automation (economy of scale)	Partial value chain automation

dream of ideal market conditions, such monopolies have existed only in part or very temporarily (e.g. before deregulation, a number of railway companies in several countries and air carriers throughout the world). Enterprises that have achieved long-term success under real market conditions therefore deserve much praise.

On the other hand, when we examine the corporate planning and the stated goals of some corporations, we are inclined to ask ourselves whether the managers involved have made the mistake of assuming ideal market conditions.

"We clearly underestimated Boeing!" This is what Tom Enders, the former joint CEO of the EADS Corporation, said on July 11, 2006, by way of describing the real situation in which Airbus found itself at the time – an exceedingly typical situation in the world of business where competition is real and the situation in which nearly all enterprises find themselves in today.

Are we to suppose that managers know things that other market participants do not (yet) know? Are enormous corporate resources (still) being left unexploited? Or has one simply fallen prey to wishful thinking and assumed ideal market conditions? How realistic are such statements at all? We can only speculate about the reasons why managers sometimes resort to such explanations. Perhaps it is a blend of ambition, vanity, ignorance, overestimating one's own abilities or blindness, lack of foresight and illusion.

We'll find out only after a few years, if at all. This is because the act of formulating and communicating goals awakens ambition.

If such goals are drafted on the assumption of ideal conditions, then it usually does not last long until the real environment makes itself felt and reveals the absurdity of the plan. It soon looks advisable to cut costs, and there we see the contradiction between ideal and real market conditions (Table 3). In their book, *Competing for the Future*, Hamel and Prahalad refer the strategy of cutting costs as a no-brainer. A frequently observed phenomenon in the history of corporate development is that enterprises initially attempt to cut costs (often in the form of staff reduction) only to discover shortly afterwards that they have become too small to be competitive. The consequence is then a merger with another enterprise (e.g. Alcatel and Lucent).

Table 3 The Gap between Ideal and Real Enterprises

	Ideal Enterprise	Real Enterprise
Costs	Minimal, on the decline	Appropriate to excessive
Motivation	High, on the rise	Dependent on leadership style and culture
Employees	Human capital	People
Maintenance costs	Minimal	Dependent on respect towards employees and corporate policy

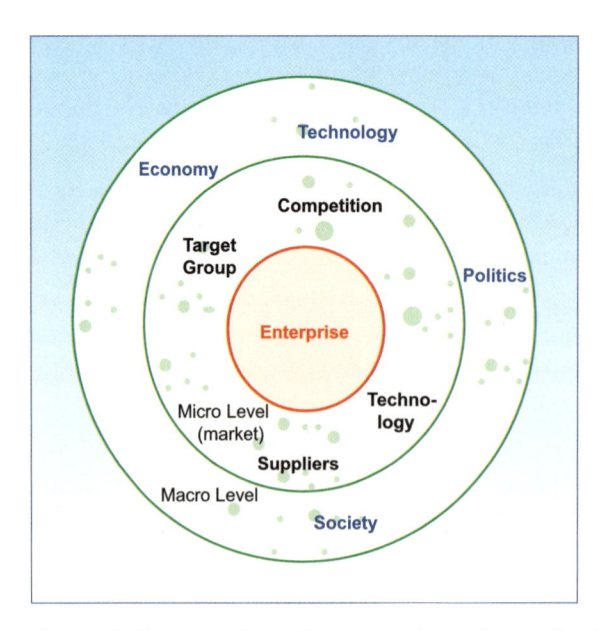

Figure 15 The enterprise environment: micro and macro levels

Enterprises must respond to the changes in their environments. Market laws demand that they do. Figure 15 illustrates the position of an enterprise within its environment. The micro level includes all areas of its environment that are within immediate striking distance of the enterprise. Non-adjacent areas are subsumed under the macro level. As shown in the previous section, this environment is subject to constant (more or less significant) change. The capacity to anticipate changes and developments and to detect the opportunities and threats associated with them earlier than one's competitors and to account for these in one's business strategy will become one of the most important enterprise success factors in the 21st century.

As shown in Figure 16, the number of published and applied management concepts has reached record levels in recent years. The demand for ever new concepts appears to be quite healthy and this is an indication of increased corporate uncertainty when it comes to facing greater competition, changing markets, etc. Instead of rushing to follow the latest concepts, it would be far more useful to take stock of one's strengths. Indeed, the inner, organic strength of enterprises is often not fully understood. I address this topic in greater detail in Chapter 5.

The average lifespan of a corporation – Fortune 500 and the like – is between 40 and 50 years. In a number of countries, as many as 40% of all newly founded companies do not celebrate a tenth anniversary. A third of the corporations listed in Fortune 500 in the year 1970 did not exist in the year 1983 – having been bought out or gone bankrupt. Foster [Foster 2001] makes a similar comparison: Of the corporations listed in the Forbes 100 in 1917, only 17 still existed in 2001! How can it be that the average life expectancy for individuals of 75 years is higher than that of our major corporations?

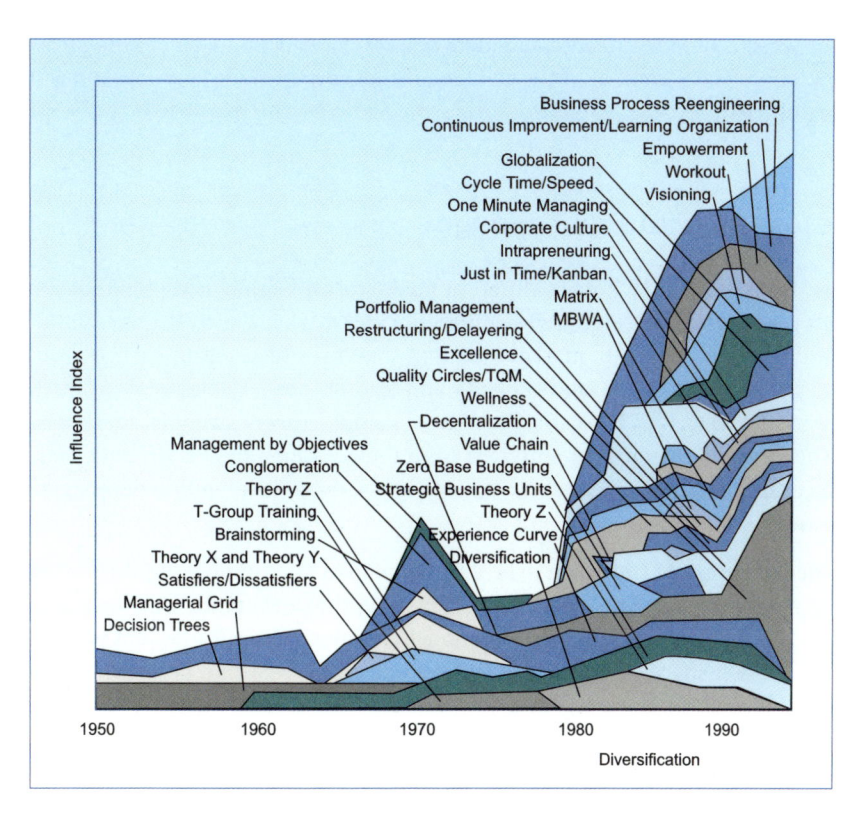

Figure 16 A flood of management concepts: a history of permanent diversification [Pascale 1990]

While this may appear to be a mere academic question, it is of great interest from the perspective of foresight.

It warrants pointing out in this context that some enterprises are older than 700 years. The origins of Stora (a Swedish enterprise that started in copper mining and is today active in the paper industry) can be traced back to the year 1300 and Sumitomo (a Japanese enterprise that began trading in medicines and books and is today one of Japan's largest corporations) can be traced back to 1590. The Weihenstephan brewery in Germany is said to have been founded in the year 1000 – long before Adam Smith introduced his theory on the wealth of nations. With common sense and without management concepts, these enterprises survived for hundreds of years, weathering wars, epidemics, periods of radical inflation, financial crises, and more. Was it a matter of chance? How else might we explain the difference? In documenting a study they conducted together, Collins and Porras [Collins 1994] have identified so-called "visionary companies." The two Stanford professors suggest that these distinguish themselves primarily by their capacity to learn from the changes in their environment, to adapt to these changes and to place greater value in retaining ideals than in increasing shareholder value.

1.3 Enterprise Development

The gap between real marketplaces and ideal marketplaces is immense. In the pages that follow, I describe a number of the challenges that corporations face now and will face in the future.

1.4 Present and Future Challenges

Although corporations may pursue different goals, it is generally accepted that the main goals center on increasing their profitability and market share. The shareholders demand financial strength; market dominance secures future profits. The problem is that these two goals are contradictory and lead to conflict. The times in which markets were characterized by scarcity are gone. Manufacturers struggle to win customers. They try to distinguish themselves from their competitors via product characteristics, branding, price, service, etc. so as to better draw the attention of prospective customers.

As illustrated in Figure 17, the drive to be different and to offer unique products often contravenes attempts to reduce costs (e.g. via outsourcing and standardization). The right balance would lead to a win-win situation. Customer satisfaction would prevail, increases in market share would follow, and the stakeholders would be content with the profits. It is seldom, however, that such situations last long: customers change and along with this change come changes in their needs. If the enterprise is not capable of anticipating these changes, then the win-win situation will sooner or later turn into a lose-lose situation. Customers become unsatisfied and switch to competing products, with the result that the enterprise's market share and profits decline.

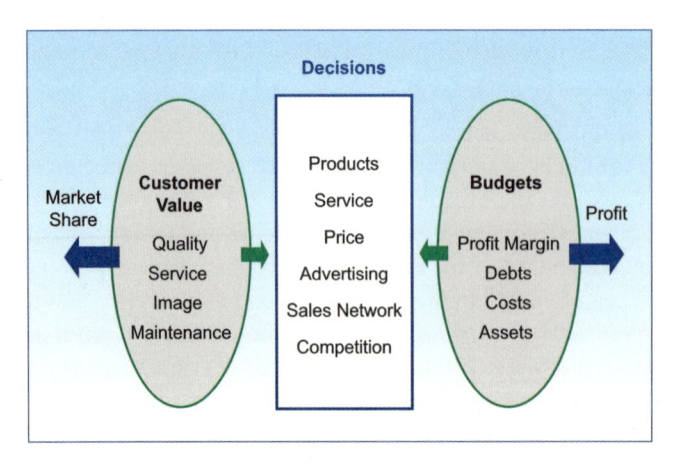

Figure 17 Profit maximization versus market share: contradiction or balance?

It is much more common that stakeholders are discontent with the profit situation. The typical response of the management is to introduce cost-cutting measures. As an exception, product and innovation campaigns may be initiated. However, cutting costs is a two-edged sword. Despite being widespread, the assumption that one can push through significant staff cuts and continue to offer customers the same or an improved degree of service is naive. The result of such moves is often greater strain, employee overload, decreased quality and increasing error rates. Reducing costs is important, but it has to happen continuously and not abruptly! Cost-cutting programs seldom lead to the expected increases in profit and often lead to dissatisfied customers [Hamel 1995].

Nowhere is the contradiction between customer orientation and cost cutting/profit maximization so clear as in the case of service hotlines.

Consider the store of a cell-phone network operator in Munich. You enter an appealing, futuristic-looking environment. You are greeted in the reception area by a brace of young, attractive women who are clearly willing to help. New customers are really treated like kings! However, if you've already signed a contract and you have some questions or wish to air a grievance, you are invited to go down the stairs to the cellar (no joke). The first thing you notice once you get downstairs is the long line. Next you notice that the turnover is slow. After a considerable wait, you consider bailing out. Then you do bail out. As you leave the store, you notice the abundance of attractive young women helping the new customers.

Among the company's business principles, we find the following promise, "We stand for outstanding work and the highest degree of customer satisfaction. You can rely on our service." [O_2 2006] Reading this, we feel like we are being derided. The gap between aspiration and reality, between the top management and the nature of the work at the basis is immense. The contradiction between profit maximization and customer service is insurmountable.

In what follows, I formulate a number of the challenges and dilemmas facing enterprises. In the course of the book, it should become clear that dilemmas, strategy, success and understanding of the future are all related to one another and that a better understanding of the future will issue in a better understanding of how to master current challenges.

The Dilemma of the Underestimated Future

As noted at the beginning of this chapter, enterprises are keenly interested in the future. They long for security. Investments are to pay off and the success of the enterprise is to be as predictable as possible.

"Today's CEOs, Boards, and senior managers often report that they feel stuck ... they have no time to think about the future because of the pressing nature of today's problems. The pressure from market analysts for the next quarter's prospects creates a constant need to deliver short-term performance. The paradox is that these CEOs know that unless they also look ahead continuously, there may be no future for their organizations. Often the future looks so different from the present that CEOs may be apprehensive about discussing it with their Boards and management. Many feel that long-term future is either too complex or too uncertain to be planned for. They rely instead on traditional strategic planning, which appears to them to ensure survival, but which may in fact condemn the organization to its own extinction by failing to properly understand the future of its markets." [Marsh 2002]

Departments that concern themselves systematically with questions about the future and long-term developments have been established in surprisingly few companies. The author of one study of the role of future studies in enterprises concludes, "... future studies units in enterprises represent an exception to the rule ... and fewer than 7% of the enterprises surveyed venture a look into the future that extends beyond ten years." [Kreibich 2002] It looks as if there is a need for foresight activities and that this necessity is recognized in the upper echelons of enterprises. When it comes to the implementation of concrete proposals, however, it turns out that enterprises are more inclined to devote attention to the preferred issues of rationalization and increased efficiency. This effect is also seen among overweight individuals who are willing to lose weight. The desire to lose weight is there, but there is a lack of willpower and follow-through, with the result that everything – except for the low fat milk – stays the same.

Recent developments in the music industry show just how deceptive this tranquilizer can be. The music industry was faring exceptionally well in the 1990s. The CD had established itself as a medium. The typical business model was directed towards signing contracts with the right artists and keeping the CD production and marketing costs as low as possible. The planners and strategists in the branch were generally well-informed, and clever besides, but they were still broadsided by the technological developments of the time, developments that pushed the music branch into the biggest crisis of its history.

Declining CD sales and declining profits led to the usual reactions. What follows is a list of measures that either were or might have been implemented by the music industry at the time.

Restructuring	Restructuring and job cuts to improve the cost situation, with the aim of establishing greater efficiency.
Reengineering	Improvements in sequences and internal processes, with the aim of cutting costs and increasing efficiency.
Quality	Initiation of a program to increase the quality of sound media and sound quality, with the aim of increasing competitiveness.
Customer focus	Trend scouts redouble their efforts to analyze the zeitgeist and trend setters, with the aim of better capturing musical tastes.
Benchmarking	Examine and evaluate the business concepts of one's competitors, with the aim of detecting potential for improvement.

Research	Intensify one's research efforts in the area of copy prevention, with the aim of preventing customers (e.g. with a sophisticated digital rights management system) from participating in the illegal forwarding of music, i.e. to "force" the purchase of music.
Balanced scorecard	Beginning with one's corporate strategy, ascertain critical success factors (CSFs) and use these as a basis for establishing key performance indicators (KPIs) and a scorecard. Use the scores to quantify the degrees to which the strategic goals are reached. Monitor and control goals and goals achievement via corrective measures in a continuing process. The aim of perfecting the existing system presupposes that the basic system conditions will not change – a risky assumption, as the example shows.

As is now clear from later developments, none of this would have helped because the rules of the game were rewritten and the music industry essentially lost the leverage it once had with respect to the end customer. Enterprise blindness led to a situation in which a technological development (MP3 data compression) was overlooked. While it proved possible to temporarily limit the P2P (peer-to-peer) data exchange that emerged and that revolutionized the dissemination of music (Napster) via legal means, Apple was the one to think the concept through and create a new and simple method of selecting, managing and, not least, experiencing music with the combination of iPod and iTunes.

The (hypothetical) question remains as to whether the music industry, equipped with an appropriate foresight system, would have been able to overcome its own enterprise blindness and use the digitalization of music in the framework of its own business concept five years before Apple. The question may be academic, but when you consider how the entire entertainment sector changes and how enterprises magnify their enterprise blindness and simply refuse to accept the changes, then one can expect to see surprises in the coming years on the order of those that broadsided the music industry in the 1990s.

Table 4 shows the degrees to which foresight is accepted.

An understanding of alternative future prospects or futures is necessary to reach Level 2. One of the aims of this book is to help its readers grasp this understanding and offer them support when it comes to its implementation.

"On average senior managers devote less than 3 percent ... of their time to building a corporate perspective on their future." [Hamel 1995] Hamel goes on to point out that some companies devote even less, and suggests that such efforts are far too little to generate helpful projections about the future." Achieving Level 2 requires more than motivation and willpower. Indeed, for serious efforts to change, one will also have to devote more than the 3 percent of the work time mentioned by Hamel.

Table 4 Corporate Foresight Maturity

	State	Principle
Level 0	Enterprise blindness: daily business matters, sales and quarterly profit determine everything. There is no acceptance or knowledge of the benefits of foresight activities and, accordingly, neither money nor time is wasted on foresight activities.	*Hope*
Level 1	General acceptance of the necessity: however, the focus is on minor adjustments and continuing in autopilot mode. There is a belief that one can conduct an investigation to locate the important screws and levers for success, i.e. which can guarantee future success – virtually automatically. The scope of investigations is largely restricted to the enterprise's immediate environment.	*Leverage*
Level 2	The principle of foresight and the opportunities it creates have been understood and put into practice. The continuous monitoring of environments prevents enterprise blindness and supports the development of future strategies.	*Radar*

The Acceleration Dilemma

It is widely accepted that the world is changing at an accelerated pace, that the clock is somehow ticking faster. Where does this notion come from? Is it only a feeling?

The feeling of acceleration and the race to establish competitive advantages are largely driven by technical advances. The theory that the predictability of the future declines along with modernity is no mere rhetorical claim. The declining predictability of future living circumstances is much more a consequence of innovation density, i.e. the measurable increase in scientific, technical, organizational and cultural innovations per unit of time.

A shrinking of the present occurs – the length of the periods of relatively constant living, work and production circumstances declines. The unknown future encroaches upon the present. The growing proximity of the unknown brings uncertainty. While the incalculability of known events was a source of worry ("Will A occur or B?") in the past, today it is the unpredictability of the new ("What will come?").

Telephone, Internet and broadcasting services permit us to transmit information at the speed of light throughout the world. The high-speed worldwide exchange of data and documents is also no problem thanks to broadband networks. Electronic stock exchanges and electronic banking permit us to invest or transfer extensive assets and securities in the shortest amount of time. The real-time sensation extends from our immediate living environment to a global level – the world is growing together. More information presented at shorter intervals – media presence – conveys a sense of acceleration.

Personal mobility and the transport of goods have also accelerated, although less rapidly when compared to the digital world, i.e. information and finances.

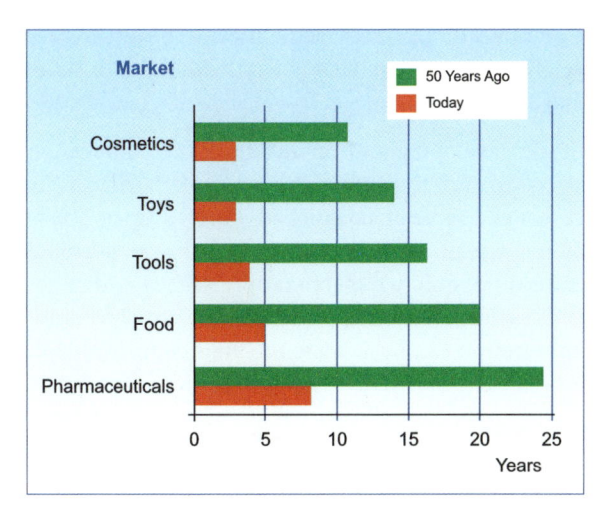

Figure 18 Shortening product life cycles: no time to design new products [Little 1997]

The varying speeds of financial, data, and commodities markets lead to market warping, volatility and insecurity. A temporal disconnect has emerged between the real and the virtual world (cyberspace). This leads to increased expectations and pressure in the real world. This infinite spiral was once manifested in the hype of the New Economy. Slogans such as "the slow are eaten by the fast" tend to increase the pressure on business processes. Product development times and innovation cycles are becoming ever shorter, but still fail to keep up with changing customer needs. Figure 18 is derived from a study conducted by Arthur D. Little, demonstrating the shortening life cycles of products in various branches.

The life expectancy of a pig used to be around three years. Today, it is ready for the slaughterhouse in six months. Will pigs soon be slaughtered before they are even born? Or can we expect to bump up against the limits of acceleration at some time in the near future?

"Time is money" is a truism whose real-life adherents undermine attempts to take a careful look at problems and situations, promote fast solutions over optimal solutions and otherwise do their part to create hectic environments. The future will show that time is more than money.

The Complexity Dilemma

The phenomenon of complexity is also something like a feeling. It can be described as a combination of complication, a multiplicity of options and dynamic development, and is thus the opposite of simple. The intensity of each of the three components grows continuously – which can be observed daily.

Technical gadgets offering an ever broader range of functions tend to increase the complexity surrounding us, as do efforts to establish regulation and their associated exceptions. The buzzword for low complication is "user friendliness." The aim here is not to bring the user to the point of understanding what is happening, but to spare the user the irritations of operating a gadget.

Figure 19 offers an illustration of the development of the means of communication ever since the introduction of the first written characters. Beginning with exclusively personal contacts, a vast array of means has been established – driven by technical progress – including the telephone, e-mail, fax, SMS, MMS, letter and personal exchange. In addition to the technical possibilities, personal preference and situation-specific criteria play a role in the selection of an appropriate channel of communication. Further means of communication can be expected to emerge, probably in even shorter intervals.

Uwe Schimanek describes the complexity of the polycontextual society as follows, "The societal reality is thereby not the only one, but often exists in another form, i.e. as often as there are diverging subsystem perspectives on society." [Ahlemeyer 1997]

Complexity allows for ambivalence. Owing to their diversity, societies that are based on the ideal of freedom tend to generate a tremendous realm of possibility. In contrast, dictatorships, strict religious communities and other less developed societal

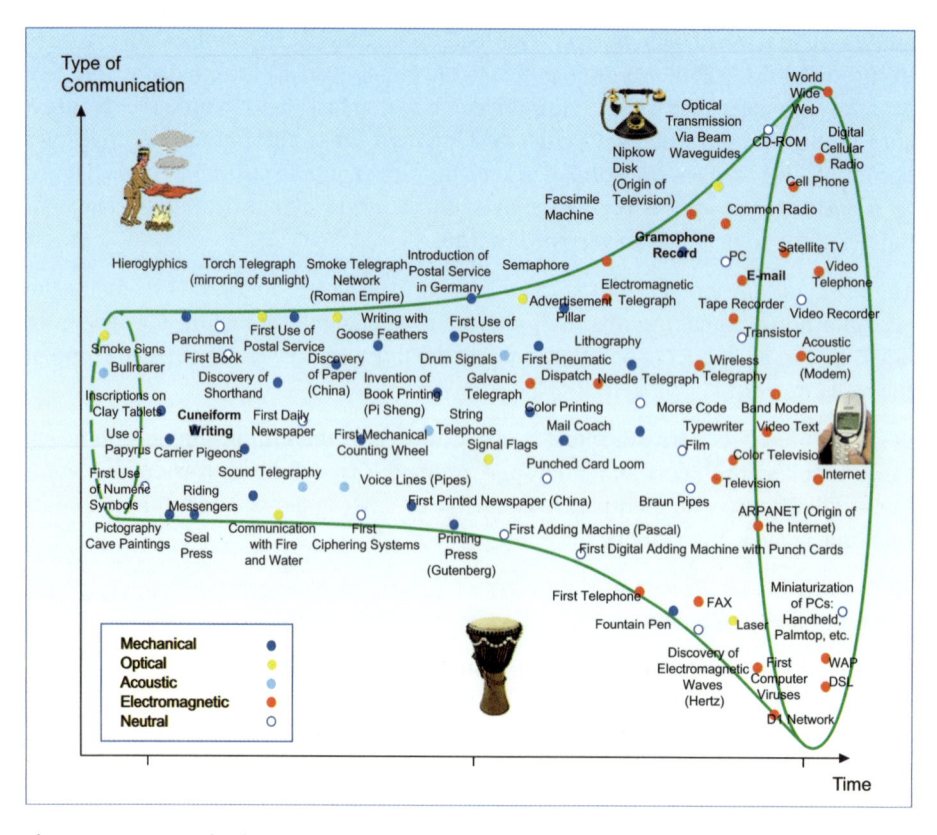

Figure 19 Communication media: rapid increase in complexity in the 5th Kondratieff cycle

forms are characterized by a low potential for differentiation. However, diversity and opportunities can be seen from more than just a societal perspective. They are also reflected in increasing product variety. There were times when the options on the automobile market – including luxury, midsized and compact cars – were very clear. With convertibles, SUVs, roadsters, vans, minivans, etc., today's market is much harder to sort through. And this applies to almost all areas of our daily lives – bicycles, sneakers, jeans, and so on.

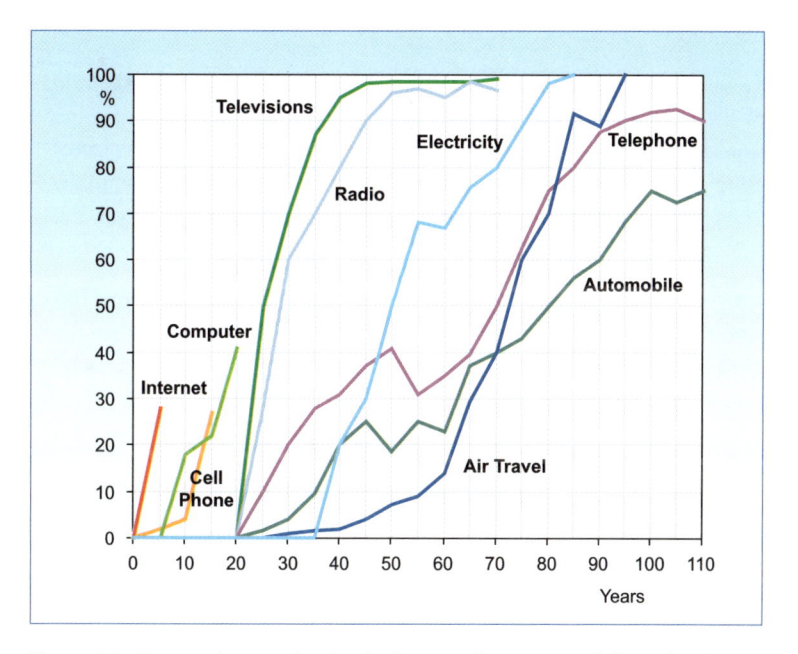

Figure 20 offers an illustration of acceleration in the spread of new technologies.

Figure 20 New products and technologies: ever faster rates of dissemination

This not only influences markets and customers – the capacity to accept novelty is limited – but also corporate management. A sense of familiarity is lost, the need to accustom oneself again and again to new situations increases the feeling of turbulence. It therefore seems naive when the authors of management guides suggest that the complexity and turbulence can be managed by following a three to ten-point action manual. For instance, in his book, *Seven Steps to Nirvana*, Sawhney [Sawhney 2001] declares that senior managers can place their enterprises on the path to the future by simply following his seven steps.

If strategic plans can be reduced to a short list of instructions, then these will either be too general to be of any real help or they will only partially account for the situation. The fact that Sawhney was described in *Business Week* as the John Maynard Keynes of the cyber era doesn't change the situation – it becomes more a matter of embarrassment.

Further causes of increased complexity are competition and regulation.

The introduction of the deposit for disposable containers in Germany in 2004 succeeded in converting a simple, proven system consisting of standard returnable bottles and special disposable containers into an enormously complicated, impractical and time-consuming system.

Consumers who prefer not to forfeit the deposit are forced when shopping to distinguish between disposable and returnable containers and between real disposable containers and essentially disposable containers that qualify as returnable. For a time, consumers were also required to have a grasp of the different disposable-returnable policies of the various grocery chains.

The purchasing and return of containers rapidly turned into a challenge. However, the consumer is not the only victim of the increased complexity associated with buying food and beverage containers. The grocery chains are burdened by the time and effort required for sorting, transporting and storing the containers (in the meantime, many stressed consumers have taken to simply forfeiting their deposits, which gives the retailers additional income).

If one considers the motivation two years ago for introducing the new system, one has to ask whether the added time and effort is at all justified. The goal was to reduce the share of disposable containers to an arbitrary value. It may be that the goal has been reached, but at what cost? Is this really in keeping with the notion of sustainability?

Antoine de Saint-Exupéry is said to have remarked, "Technology develops from the primitive to the complicated to the simple." It is no surprise that gadgets that effectively reduce complexity (i.e. such as the iPod, which distinguishes itself for simple operation) are so successful and that technologies like WAP – which is described by users as stressful – are flops.

Douglas C. Engelbart – the man who invented the computer mouse – says the following about complexity, "The Complexity and Urgency of the world's problems are just going to snowball. And unless we can do something effective about improving our collective abilities to deal with such complex, urgent things, humanity is doomed. Humanity has never, ever had to deal with such complex and rapid change. So we have no history of how to accommodate to it. If we just go on what used to be the way of incorporating improvements, it's not going to work. There is both a threat and an opportunity." [Fouke 2000]

Complexity leaves us with a sense of powerlessness. Optimal decisions are no longer possible in highly volatile societies and markets. The belief that we can master situations without understanding them appears to be becoming commonplace. However, it is not really possible to simply reduce complexity. The reduction of outer complexity merely increases inner complexity. Figure 21 shows an attempt (derived from Graf, 2005) to systematize complexity.

Complexity entails a certain instability and thus unpredictability. While the future never was and never will be predictable, we are today exposed to something new, namely, rapid and abrupt changes that are often a matter of chance, or are of an

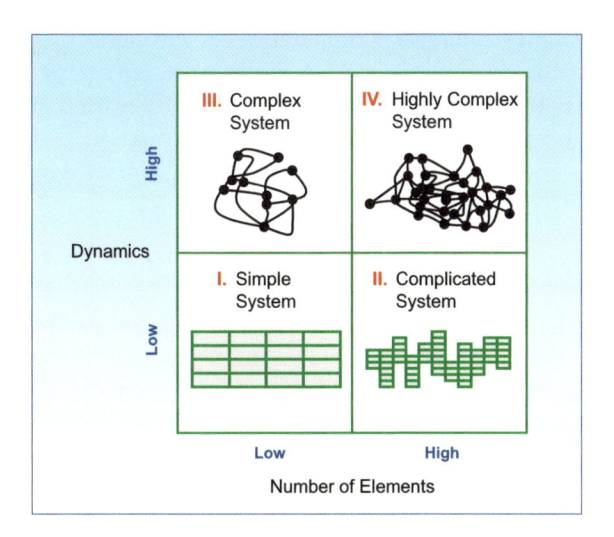

Figure 21 The complexity of systems: a systematization

uncertain nature. Given these circumstances, the search for a hypothetical and sustainable state of balance, or for predictable and controllable trends, is destined to be in vain.

The dilemma of complexity consists in our tendency to demand and strive for simple solutions at the same moment that we perceive the nature of our environment becoming more complex.

The Growth Dilemma

Why are enterprises pressured into growing?

It is a paradigm that is so deeply anchored in our heads that calling it into question tends to trigger a degree of incomprehension. The various reasons include the following:

- There is an obligation to the shareholders who want their stake in the enterprise to develop positively.
- There is the nature of competition which includes striving for a greater share of the market.
- There are personal reasons, including vanity and the pressure felt by the management to succeed.
- There is the fact that striving for higher profits via expanded business activity is an accepted societal norm.
- There is the fact that growing systems are regarded as healthy.

Growth as a goal is based on the assumption that growth equals or is an integral part of success. The task of securing growth, however, becomes more difficult as an enterprise grows. The possibilities are limited. Markets become saturated. Price increases in the face of stiff competition are not viable. New business venues represent a possibility, but lucrative markets tend not to last indefinitely, as seen in our discussion of ideal market conditions above. While the creation of brand new markets – as Sony created with its Walkman and Starbucks with its cafes – is certainly costly and harbors the greatest risk, it also promises the greatest profit.

The struggle to grow forces enterprises to devote greater attention to big and lucrative business (key accounts). This results in the neglecting of what are regarded as mere niche markets, this despite the fact that mass markets always arise out of niche markets! While searching for the growth markets that will permit our enterprises to grow, we also tend to neglect the fact that all markets will at some point begin to contract. The task of achieving corporate growth on contracting markets introduces special challenges. In the future, these challenges can be expected to become the usual challenge.

> The smallest bank in Germany is the Raiffeisenbank in Gammesfeld. The bank director's name is Fritz Voigt. The bank has an eight-member, largely voluntary board of directors. "The Raiffeisenbank in Gamesfeld is not only the smallest bank in Germany, it is probably the most successful bank in Germany." wrote Germany's foremost daily newspaper, the *Frankfurter Allgemeine Zeitung* on December 24, 2006. The bank's conditions: 2.5% on savings accounts, 3.5% for long-term loans, and 4.5% for consumer loans.
>
> Now compare this to the conditions offered by Germany's largest bank, the Deutsche Bank, with 836 offices and 26,336 employees as of the end of 2005: 0.5% on savings accounts (2.8% on accounts with € 5,000 or more), 7.9% for long-term loans, 9.84% for short-term loans, 10.25% and more for credit line cash (conditions as of 1/1/2007). (Source: "Gier nach Größe," Spiegel 11/2006)

This shows that while the perceived need to grow may prove advantageous for enterprises, it is not necessarily so for customers.

The Capital Dilemma

This dilemma arises between the inner and outer reality of capitalism, i.e. between the short and long term.

In economic terms, capitalism is based on the power of capital. The main drive and motivation is to increase one's possessions. The total amount of money available in the world today is 50 times larger than it was in the 1950s. Now, however, there is some indication that this development has reached its limits. The ever increasing capitalization of corporate decisions has led to a situation in which the value of those areas of life that cannot be expressed in monetary terms (e.g. raising children) is perceived as questionable. If families were run according to the tenets of a market economy – exactly as the world of private enterprise and the state (opaque tax policy) seem to be encouraging citizens to consider – it would be more worth it to raise pigs than kids.

The tragic part of this is that the inherent tension radiates beyond the corporate environment and has an impact on broader parts of society. The rate of birth is on the decline in all of the developed industrial countries. While the reasons may be multi-faceted and no signs of change are in sight despite a recognition of the problem, the fact remains that children represent a financial risk for the family. In monetary terms, motherhood is a kind of down time and has also come to be treated as such at a societal level. The same is happening with the economy. The focus on the short-term and intense competition on capital markets have led to a situation in which entire market segments are neglected. The result is a lot of "unborn market segments."

The availability of capital leads almost necessarily to the desire for its increase, an increase that can be expressed and measured in the form of return on equity. However, it now appears that opportunities for continued increases are not being restricted by an absence of capital, but by an absence of investment opportunities born of inspiration and ingenuity. This is evidenced, for instance, by the share buyback programs implemented by many major corporations.

The talent enterprises have shown for earning money in the past will be no compensation when ideas are in short supply.

The problem with ideas and knowledge, however, is that they are uncomfortable, difficult to handle and – in contrast to money – neither countable nor interest-bearing. They also cannot be collected, for instance, at a bank. On the contrary, employees are the sources and the vessels of knowledge, and they cost money and walk through the gates of the factory on a daily basis. The dilemma is that enterprises will only have a chance in the long run if they rise to meet the challenge of regarding their employees as a source of ideas and not as cost factor.

The Competition Dilemma

We often hear that "the competition has become more fierce" as a lead-in to announcements of new cost-cutting measures or as an argument in favor of new research activities. How does competition arise?

New enterprises and new markets always begin with an idea, i.e. as a result of the opportunity that is seen to establish a foothold on a market by offering added value to prospective customers. For the most part, competitive advantages arise when we see opportunities before anyone else does and when we also succeed in using the head start to prepare the market.

The dilemma here consists in the perceived lack time, in the perceived need to work at the lowest possible cost, and in the perceived need to determine exactly what consumers want.

Porter's five-forces framework is an instrument that allows us to analyze the intensity of competition. The criteria that are used include entrance barriers for new market participants, substitution possibilities, existing competitors, and leverage with respect to buyers and suppliers (see Appendix II, Section 10.2.3). The procedure, also referred to as branch structure analysis, gives us an idea of how attractive a branch is likely to be. The upshot of the analysis is that we should avoid intensely competitive industries and concentrate on attractive branches. However, examples such as Dell on the intensely competitive PC market and Aldi on the intensely competitive grocery market suggest that market environment is not a sufficient litmus test. Foresight, strategic skills and entrepreneurial thinking are the more decisive factors for market success.

The comparison of ideal and real enterprise environments in Section 1.3 above has already shown that favorable – ideal – market conditions cannot be expected to prevail for long. It follows from this that the search for "easy" markets (e.g. via portfolio analysis) essentially undermines an enterprise's competitiveness and capacity for innovation.

The Consumer Dilemma

If one follows what the experts say, it should be obvious what the consumer really wants. Customer relationship management (CRM) systems, milieus studies (Figure 22) and surveys of consumer opinion are only a few of the instruments available in the marketing department that seek to convey this impression. In reality, however, manufacturers and consumers are often tuned into different channels.

The problem is that the drive for greater efficiency also has an impact on how one deals with the consumer, with the result that it is less a matter of attempting to understand the consumer and the consumer's needs (which, in and of itself, does not bring added value and is not measurable), but of selling something to the consumer. Development times and product lifecycles are becoming ever shorter. This is only going to

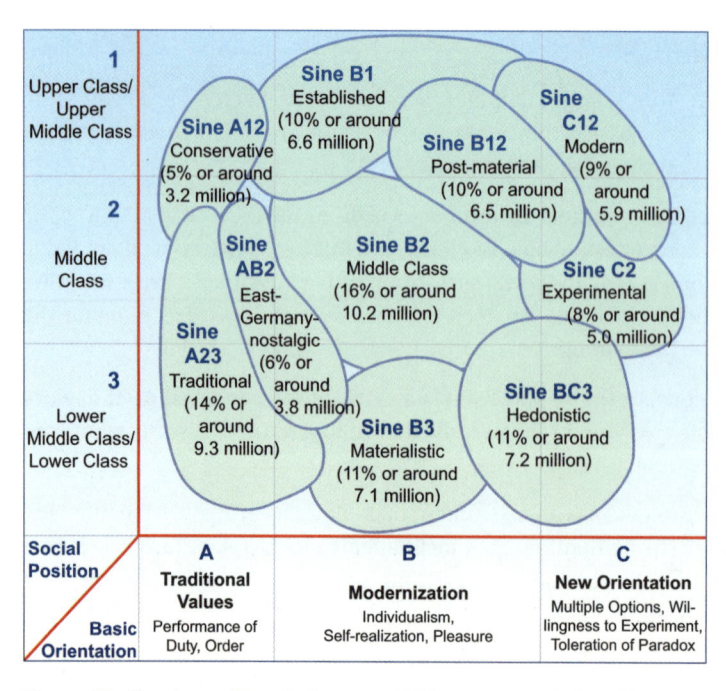

Figure 22 The sinus milieus in Germany 2006 as an example for milieus studies (potato diagram): to what extent does this clear world apply? [www.sinus-sociovision.de]

succeed as a strategy, however, if preferred deployment times also decrease because it assumes that consumers will willingly exchange the old for the new more often. However, consumers may very well ruin the party by not conforming to the manufacturer's expectations.

CRM promises have led many to believe in the transparent consumer as opposed to the unpredictable consumer. This is where something comes into play that certainly can be referred to as a trend (see Chapter 3 for more on the subject of trends): approaches to customers are becoming increasingly automated. Most of our daily errands can be easily handled via machines. Tickets, airport check-in, gasoline, beverages, bottle returns, banking, stamps, DVD rental – virtually everything is possible today and corporations are hard at work on fully automated shopping.

This has led to a formalization and partial standardization of the sales process. The consumer is left only with the option of shopping or not shopping (service or no service). Consumers who decide in favor of this scheme accept the consequence that they as consumers will shoulder the burden if there is a hitch. This dissolving shopping culture, however, contrasts with new concepts in adventure shopping, for instance, at Starbucks that recently succeeded in recasting the traditional coffeehouse experience [Pine 1999].

A further long-term problem that is emerging for service providers is that they no longer know anything about their customers because they no longer have any contact with them. Banks are already faced by this problem. Most banking business is handled electronically and anonymously – via machines or call centers. But who are the customers? What do they want? In order to understand customers, it is necessary to seek contact with them and not lock them out!

In any case, it is safe to assume that consumers want to be taken seriously. But when we consider mass marketing and customer relationship management approaches, we can legitimately begin to wonder whether this wish is being met – for both of these are instruments conceived to better "address" and "persuade" consumers, as one often hears in marketing departments.

Using target groups to address consumers is a further attempt at getting a handle on the stubborn consumer. The traditional class model has been supplemented by lifestyles, and these two criteria – classes and styles – are used to define milieus. These target groups – or milieus – are supposed to represent (as far as possible) homogeneous groups exhibiting similar life patterns and preferences. The success of the milieu notion is based on the simplicity milieus convey. The message is clear: consumers are not nearly so complicated as one might think. In fact, there are roughly ten different groups of them, with ten different sets of needs. But precisely this simplicity is the problem. Attempts to arrive at individual evaluations or classifications quickly turn into a challenge. Is one middle class because one owns an espresso machine or an experimentalist because one is single? Does one belong in the established milieu because one prefers to do one's own travel planning or is one post material because one prefers organic food? Various milieus will match depending on the situation. It is simply not as clear cut as one had hoped. The question now arises as to the sense of it all and whether the approach isn't rather obsolete for assuming that the world is clear-cut and stable [Raschke 2005].

This suggests that the consumer will remain a considerable uncertainty factor well into the future. It remains an illusion to assume that the consumer is a controllable variable that can be "managed" with the help of certain data (given the popularity of management courses in "customer satisfaction," it would appear that this misconception is rather stubborn). Analyses of consumer behavior are fraught with uncertainty, as are voter opinion polls, which can be seen in many elections. Despite the intensive surveys, voters do not behave according to the projections made by the election researchers.

The traditional assumption that consumers essentially act rationally has often been discredited. For instance, in his book, *The Paradox of Choice*, Barry Schwartz presents a number of selected challenges that are faced by consumers today [Schwartz 2004]. So many factors play a role – price, customer utility and functionality, comparison, and product variety – that it would appear to be impossible to understand, model and influence them all.

The consumer will remain an unknown entity in the future because all people are different and the most sophisticated attempts at classification will always involve a compromise. When we come to appreciate the fact that our capacity to understand the consumer is limited, a look into the future can be frightening. How will consumers develop? They, too, will learn a thing or two – and are likely to again pay greater attention to product quality and service.

"But often the customer does not really know, what she wants or needs. Indeed, the customer may have no perceived preexisting needs at all." [Lester 2004] While enterprises specialize in solving problems efficiently, how are they to even formulate a

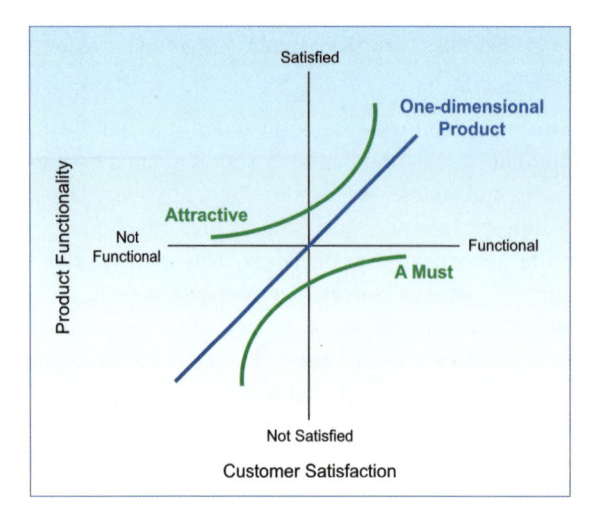

Figure 23 Kano diagram: the potential for increasing customer satisfaction is especially high in the case of novelties.

problem if consumers are not in a position to describe their needs? Greater attention will be given in the future to finding problems, not solutions (cf. Figure 1).

Figure 23 shows an example of a model developed by Kano [Kano 1984] in 1984 that illustrates the connection between customer satisfaction and product functionality. Product properties that are thought to be surprising and compelling and that have a positive impact on customer benefit contribute disproportionately to customer satisfaction. While this may sound trivial, it shows that new product properties represent an especially decisive factor. This is at least an approach to maintaining some sort of influence on the uncertainty factor known as the customer in the future.

The Measurability Dilemma

Our faith in numbers is unshakeable. Numbers suggest accuracy and security – they convey the feeling that everything is under control. The notion that "less is often more" and the philosophy according to which only measurable things are good tend to have fatal consequences for enterprises.

The ability on the part of enterprises to convert new knowledge and inventions into new products and to present and position these on the market is referred to as innovation capacity. Even the ambition of the economists has not yet put us in a position of being able to represent this capacity – as a measurable variable – in the form of a meaningful number. Many investigators have instead taken to using the number of patents and the R&D budget of enterprises as an indicator of innovation capacity. This, however, illustrates the sheer extent of the dilemma. A patent does nothing more or less than protect an invention. Just how suitable the invention is as a source of new products and new business is an open question.

This tendency to cling to numbers and our desire to measure and control everything, as well as the linking of measured values to the criteria of evaluation, can cause one to lose sight of the actual goal. In a thought experiment, Roger D. Pollard [Fouke 2000] assigns himself the task of identifying technologies we would be better off without, i.e. we would be better off today if they had never been invented. He arrives at an astonishing example: spreadsheet software and Microsoft Excel in particular.

"Spreadsheet software has led practitioners in the humanities, social sciences, and liberal arts to believe that to be numerically literate, complete, and accurate; all you need to do is feed data into rows and columns of a spreadsheet. Many decisions taken by managers who have no scientific training are based on erroneous conclusions drawn from such analysis."

This remark is not in need of elaboration. The popularity of numbers in general and matrices in particular among senior managers is presumably owing to the appearance of simplicity they convey. Complex matters are reduced to numbers, or quadrants, and these appear to be complete and absolute. Factors that are not amenable to quantification simply do not make their way into the equation and remain hidden. Both quantitative and qualitative methods and instruments (e.g. as presented in the Annex) play a supporting role when it comes to the visualization, structuring and evaluation of a situation. They are no substitute for an intelligent interpretation.

Remaining with our example of the patents, I would suggest that even if a large number of patents is evaluated as a success, it does not tell us anything definite about innovation capacity and it is certainly no guarantee for successful innovations. However, given that there is no established measure of marketed inventions, it is likely that increasing the number of patents will remain a goal. Unfortunately, patents are completely unsuited as measures of future development. How can we express uncertainty and risk in numbers? In quite general terms, the following applies:

All of the important aspects of life or of an enterprise cannot be categorized and represented in numbers. For instance, how would one measure motivation or entrepreneurial quality in the case of employees?

Norbert Bolz [Bolz 1997] summarizes the dilemma as follows "Statistics are so well loved because they suggest that one can understand complex matters without structural insight, simply on the basis of numbers."

The Information Dilemma

While knowledge acquisition is continuous and is a motor of change, the capacity of an enterprise to take up and process this knowledge is limited.

If one assumes that information and knowledge are the raw material of tomorrow's innovations, then technical progress in the form of the Internet, electronic databases and archives offers us a simple access route. While access to information used to be significant, the situation has now changed. As an easily accessible commodity, information is no longer a suitable means of gaining competitive advantages. The surplus of information leads automatically to a scarcity of information because it is the "right and important" information that becomes crucial, i.e. the information that introduces a knowledge head start. But what is the right and important information? This depends upon the enterprise's context and can therefore only be determined by the enterprise itself. The degree to which information technology can help is limited – as is shown in detail in Chapter 6.

The management of information is and will remain an important competence: understanding, reflecting upon, evaluating, filtering, combining, and generating new information. However, in the wake of the euphoric reception of IT, many enterprises neglected their own capacity to develop in this regard. This may also stem from the fact that no value creation is attributed to activities such as reading for comprehension, i.e. the absorption and processing of information.

The advantage enjoyed by larger enterprises with larger budgets will become less crucial. The intelligent management of information – quality and interpretation instead of quantity – is becoming ever more important.

The Ignorance Dilemma

President Eisenhower charged the Paley Commission to investigate the subject of energy. The objective was to secure a sufficient energy supply for the United States, and thereby ensure the country's continued development. In its report, the Paley Commission indicated that the country would be confronted by a scarcity of energy by the beginning of the 1970s at the latest and recommended an accelerated development of "new" sources of energy (e.g. solar energy) to meet demand. The Paley Commission was right on target with its assessment. Only, it was largely in vain. Eisenhower decided in favor of nuclear technology. Solar technology was "too expensive" compared to the "cheap" petroleum available at the time. (Chapter 7 is devoted exclusively to the subject of petroleum as a utilizable form of energy and future scenarios with or without the coveted black gold.)

This example shows us the extent of the gap that often exists between decision makers and thinkers. Either the thinkers fail at the task of properly communicating their ideas or the deciders understand the message (at least in part), but ignore it, refuse to consider it or consider it to a limited degree.

Making decisions based on a gut feeling can, for a variety of reasons (these are discussed in Chapter 2), quickly lead to problems, especially in times that are becoming more turbulent.

The Efficiency Dilemma

Projects are considered efficient if the desired goal is reached at the least possible effort and expense. Efficiency essentially describes the cost-benefit ratio.

While the desire for efficiency is understandable from an economic point of view, it is not sufficient from the point of view of the enterprise. Efficiency alone – without effectiveness – can have a catastrophic effect on an enterprise. Consider the case of the gas lamp manufacturers who concentrated on efficiency in the production of gas lamps at the beginning of the last century and overlooked the development of the electric light bulb.

Securing effectiveness – or "doing the right thing," as Drucker suggests – is a strategic task and can never be replaced by efficiency.

Hamel and Prahalad are fairly critical in their treatment of the subject of efficiency [Hamel 1995]. They accuse managers of preferring to concentrate on costs (efficiency = benefit/expense) because it appears to be the easiest approach, "... aggressive denominator reduction under a flat reverse stream is simply a way to sell market share and the future of the company. Marketing strategists term this a harvest strategy and consider it a no-brainer."

Arie de Geus [Geus 1997] goes one step further. He describes how one can succeed in ruining an enterprise within 12 months. The starting point according to de Geus is the conclusion on the part of the management that the enterprise is not profitable enough and that this is to be changed.

The message is clear: ambitious growth objectives can only be realized via investments.

The Opportunity Dilemma

Like physical systems, organizations strive to achieve a state of balance or, as Nicolis and Prigogine [Nicolis 1989] put it, a state of temporary stability. The reasons here are satisfaction with what has been achieved and a certain aversion to change. On the other hand, the relationship between employees and management also contributes to stability and consensus.

Managers generally promote those workers who fit in, i.e. those who have similar views and opinions as the majority and who are generally accepted. From the bottom-up perspective, employees are taught that it will pay off career-wise if they do not cause trouble, i.e. refrain from endorsing opinions that are not widely accepted in the organization. Consensus-based organizations move forward in a kind of comfort zone. This tendency is especially pronounced in uncertain and turbulent times.

This is reinforced by the usual practice of honoring excellent performance in the past with promotions. The considerable drawback here is that it effectively leads to a recycling of past recipes for success and curtails the influence of future-oriented employees. The result is that new, heretofore unknown problems, are approached with old solutions. The negative consequences can be considerable. [Pfeffer 2000]

Fit organizations with a low tendency towards opportunism are capable of adapting rapidly to new market conditions, or they are capable of shaping these conditions themselves.

The subject of future-oriented organizations as learning organizations will be addressed again in Chapters 5 and 6.

The Innovation Dilemma

The claim that innovations are important for enterprise success is uncontroversial. It is not only senior managers and authors who regularly point out the significance of innovations. Even the German government has recognized the extent to which this is true and is making an effort to boost the level of its support. However, the problem with the situation is that attempts are being made to "manage" innovations, as if it were a matter of a cut-and-dry process. For instance, innovation projects have been initiated in the framework of innovation management. Evaluations of project applications – and only the *best* are to be promoted – are strongly influenced by the mandatory statement of the expected results. The collective assumption is that we first have to know exactly what is to be created before such a project can be initiated.

The notion that the creative processes that lead to innovation are often open-ended is not widespread. We are advised here to again recall what Popper had to say about future knowledge, "There is one thing that is impossible for us to know, namely what we will know in the future. Because otherwise, we would already know it." [Popper 1969] Traditional approaches to innovation, for instance, as described by Hauschild [Hauschild 2004], focus instead on the process itself and see innovation primarily in new approaches to existing problems.

Figure 11 offers an illustration of the problem-solution space. The unknown problem/unknown solution area is almost never shown for the subject of innovation. The result is that innovations are located almost exclusively in the incremental area.

Table 5 Innovation at the nexus of promotion and expectation (figures in percent) [Berth 2003]

Innovation Type	Manager Esteem	Rate of Return Expected by Managers	Actual Rate of Return	Flop Rate	Average Share of Budget for R&D
Old products	High	7.3	5.2	–	19
Product maintenance	Medium	6.8	3.7	–	31
Improvement	High	14.9	6.9	69	22
Renewal	Medium	15.1	11.8	67	16
Breakthrough	Low	9.1 ⎫ 12.3	14.7 ⎫ 34.6	61	7 ⎫ 12.0
Vision/Mission	Low	3.2 ⎭	19.9 ⎭	64	5 ⎭

In the context of a study of innovation projects conducted by Rolf Berth of the Düsseldorf-based *Akademie Schloss Garath* [Berth 2003], managers were requested to answer a series of questions on 432 innovation projects from 32 branches. The alarming result is presented in Table 5. The highest share of R&D budgets goes into minor innovation and improvements, which also enjoy the highest recognition on the part of managers. Breakthrough innovations are unpopular despite promising the highest rate of return. Berth summarizes his results as follows: "An overwhelming majority of managers are afraid of precisely those innovations that enjoy the greatest degree of general recognition (up to Nobel Prize level) and promise the greatest rate of return at a moderate degree of risk. This offers a compelling explanation for the fact that the number of truly visionary breakthroughs as a percentage of all innovations has been on the decline for 25 years."

The results of a study conducted by the IFO Institute are similarly alarming [IFO 2003]. It was found that in the year 2002 products in the so-called contraction phase – at the end of their lifecycles – outsold products in the market introduction phase by 6% – the poorest result in 20 years. In addition to taking a snapshot, Christensen goes a step further in his book, *The Innovator's Dilemma*, [Christensen 2000] and arrives at the diagnosis that, among other things, a fixation on the consumer contributes to the dilemma. The consumer is not even in a position to articulate radical innovations (e.g. the airbag). Christensen goes on to claim that managers neglect important matters because they have to concentrate on urgent matters or, in other words, they "manage" the important matters only after they have become urgent. This quickly turns innovation management into crisis management.

Hamel and Prahalad [Hamel 1994] see corporate foresight and innovation as important means of preparing enterprises for the future. Long-term commitment to a business area and the will to secure resources and competencies are the basic conditions for successful innovations.

Gassmann [Albrecht 2005] estimates that two innovations that lead to business success remain for every one thousand ideas. This shows that while innovations are difficult to "manage" and entail certain risks, it is illusory to think one can concentrate on low hanging fruits instead. For instance, Sony created the music market for its Walkman, but missed the bus on the transition to digital music (MP3). Clinging to existing (allegedly secure) business turned the market leader into a niche supplier.

It follows that one should do more than expect innovation, one should also promote it.

The Dilemma of Planning without a Compass

What do we use to orient ourselves? Usually the average and our competitors. But when we have no ideas, we implement such things as share buy-back programs, which may even make economic sense in the short term. These represent clear evidence for a lack of ideas for other investments.

Situations are assessed inaccurately. Whether this applies to consumers, competitors, partners, the government, the cost of raw materials – it is ever more the case that assumptions and estimates miss the mark. The exception becomes the rule, "Complexity creates uncertainty. Uncertainty turns into fear. We want to protect ourselves against this fear. Our brains therefore block out all that is complicated, unfathomable, and unpredictable. What remains is an extract – that which we already know. However, given that this extract is linked to the whole that we don't want to look at, we make a lot of mistakes – failure is logically programmed." [Dörner 2003]

Then what do we need plans for?

Even Rumpelstiltskin had a plan: "Today I bake, tomorrow brew, the next I'll have the young queen's child." A good plan, but thankfully a failure because the rigid assumptions about what would transpire proved inaccurate.

"Planning is a matter of reflecting on what one could do." [Dörner 2003]

Once a plan has been devised, it often qualifies as sacrosanct, even when it becomes clear that something was not considered while devising the plan. Doubt, complexity, surprises and uncertainties are the biggest enemies of the planner. This can lead to fabrication, as the world, consumers, competitors, etc. are tailored to fit the plan.

Mere suggestions for modifying the plan are like heat-seeking missiles. They threaten the plan's entire composition and are interpreted as personal defeats by the planners. As amply suggested in our previous discussions, the market is a dynamic, complex system that is capable of changing spontaneously. For planners, changing needs, unforeseeable problems and a variety of options are assumptions that have not been considered. However, if plans rule (i.e. when a system forces all of its parts into the plan's scheme), then the success of the whole will depend on the fortune of each part. The success of the plan thus depends on its individual parts – the basic conditions and those who carry it out – far away from the planners. If we consider the complexity, dependencies and dynamic nature of the world, it will become clear that only unscripted independent action will permit one in the future to adapt to changed situations.

A Way Out of the Dilemmas?

The dilemmas outlined above represent no more than an excerpt of all relevant dilemmas. I hope, however, that they suffice to show that steering an enterprise on cruise control – as described by Berner [Berner 2004] – is the wrong approach. Complex situations cannot be mastered using the simple tools in the standard management toolbox. The problems, challenges and dilemmas confronting enterprises today are unusually multifaceted, interconnected, unclear and not capable of demarcation. They can only be solved in a future-oriented manner together with many different stakeholders who have different points of view and opinions. We are in need of individual solutions that account for capacities of analysis and synthesis.

The task faced enterprises can be divided into routine tasks and non-routine tasks. Routine tasks can be programmed and automated, under given conditions they always proceed in the same manner. In contrast, non-routine tasks such as strategy development and innovation cannot be automated. Attempts to do so tend to focus on the formalization of the procedure – which leads to process manuals instead of renewal.

The future of enterprises is not decided in the area of routine. The intelligence of enterprises will be a decisive success factor in the struggle to survive and outperform one's competitors. This can be seen in the capacity to recognize signals and changes and, even more importantly, in the capacity an enterprise has to reflect upon, interpret and understand the fast and slow change processes and to be in a position to respond accordingly, i.e. proactively or reactively.

In his book, *What's Your Corporate IQ?*, Underwood examines the various capacities of enterprises and proposes a corresponding evaluation in the form of an IQ score. He asserts, "I have never found a high IQ Company that was in trouble." [Underwood 2004] The following test was conceived to allow stakeholders to estimate the state of their enterprises. The test differs from the test proposed by Underwood in being oriented towards an enterprise's future and not its present state. The question is "How intelligent is your enterprise?" The intelligence of an enterprise refers to its capacity to assert itself on the market, respond quickly to change and, essentially, to survive. The test result offers one an idea of how well the enterprise is prepared for the future.

It warrants pointing out that the test was designed as a source of guidance, diagnosis and suggestions for improvement. It is not meant to serve as a substitute for comprehensive analysis and an individual, situation-specific evaluation.

Notes

- To obtain a meaningful evaluation, please offer candid assessments of your enterprise and do not let your notion of where you think your enterprise ought to be creep into your answers. Choose the answer that best reflects the real situation!
- Choose only one answer per question.
- Answer the questions on the basis of that part of your company you know well. If you have a good view of the entire organization, then answer the questions from the point of view of the entire enterprise.

1.5 Enterprise Intelligence Test

This test can be applied to a broad array of organizations.

1. **What are the means used by the enterprise to keep itself informed of developments in its environment?**
   a) These means are systematic and institutionalized; data from many sources are analyzed by a single department. ☐
   b) Information makes its way more or less by chance to the decision makers. ☐
   c) Partial systems are in place with varying points of focus and cost and various methods. ☐
   d) There is too little time. ☐

2. **How is information handled in the enterprise?**
   a) Information is power, the release of information is a loss of power. ☐
   b) There are various platforms and systems of information and knowledge management. A lack of user friendliness and a lack of time prevent greater use of the platforms and systems. ☐
   c) Employees are encouraged to transfer information in accordance with enterprise policy so as to promote its exploitation. ☐
   d) Little exchange of information takes place within the enterprise. The management pays little regard to the subject. ☐

3. **How are strategic decisions made?**
   a) Strategy management is essentially crisis management. ☐
   b) Strategy is developed once a year and is based on budget planning. ☐
   c) A long-term approach is taken, based on continual analysis and the tactical measures derived from it. ☐
   d) The strategy is declared by the senior management and planned accordingly. ☐

4. **How is employee performance assessed?**
   a) The annual planning and control includes the complete measurability of the results. ☐
   b) Given that teamwork is promoted and expected, the team is also evaluated. Outstanding individual performance is honored separately. ☐
   c) Superiors evaluate the performance of their employees once a year. In addition to this, individual employee meetings take place. ☐
   d) No evaluation of performance is made. Salary is determined on the basis of the time one has spent with the enterprise. ☐

5. **What criteria are used for purposes of hiring and promotion?**
   a) Outstanding performance in the past and compelling self-presentation are decisive. ☐
   b) Strategic thinking and future orientation are decisive. ☐
   c) Promotions are always of a temporary nature so as to prevent hierarchical inflexibility. ☐
   d) Individual performance and the right connections are important. ☐

6. **What motivates employees to work in the enterprise?**
   a) The motivation derives from the assigned goals and their achievement. Goals and the means of their fulfillment are established once a year. ☐
   b) The enterprise is concerned to inculcate a sense of intrinsic motivation. Monetary rewards are regarded as obsolete and ultimately counter-productive. ☐
   c) Motivation derives from a dependence on an income. Deep down, a majority of the employees have already handed in their resignation slips. ☐
   d) The desire to climb the latter quickly is the biggest motivator. ☐

7. **How does the enterprise handle innovations?**
   a) Innovations are expected, but hardly promoted. ☐
   b) Innovation means: idea meets money. Fast. ☐
   c) An innovation management system has been implemented and most adhere to it. ☐
   d) We don't talk much about innovations. If we have an idea, we go to the boss, or directly to those we believe will be able to offer support. We have the freedom to explore ideas. ☐

8. **One of your competitors introduces an ingenious product to the market. How long does it take for your enterprise to respond and, if appropriate, introduce a comparable product to the market?**
   a) One of our strengths is the capacity to respond quickly. We observe markets and our competitors carefully and continuously. Our product development is specialized in imitation. ☐
   b) Our strategic planning leaves little room for surprises. It is likely that we will respond only after we have lost our market. ☐
   c) The budget planning for this business year is settled. An application for product planning can be submitted for the next business year. ☐
   d) We first examine the development on the market. If necessary, we will be able to respond quickly. ☐

1.5 Enterprise Intelligence Test

9. **You have an interesting idea and you are convinced that it would be very valuable for the enterprise. What opportunities do you have to gain support for and develop this idea?**
   a) An online innovation management tool is available. The response time is around 6 months. ☐
   b) An invention report can be drafted. Such reports usually receive little attention within the enterprise. ☐
   c) The budget does not account for such exceptions. It is therefore not possible until the next business year. An application has been submitted. ☐
   d) The idea is presented to managers, investors and other interested parties at the enterprise's internal innovation fair "Idea Meets Money." Decisions are made promptly. The aim is to quickly find a promoter for good ideas. ☐

10. **Is your enterprise in a position to bring about changes on the market?**
    a) The management sees our enterprise as a trendsetter, but in reality we are saving ourselves to death and have trouble keeping up with our competitors. ☐
    b) Market changes take place too quickly for our enterprise. The management is mainly concerned with key financial data. ☐
    c) Thanks to our innovative capacity we continuously generate new markets and attempt to gain competitive advantages via market novelty. ☐
    d) Our philosophy is "We shape the market!" That applies to products, speed, and marketing. ☐

11. **What views of the future does your enterprise have?**
    a) The future looks quite similar to today – only much better. ☐
    b) The enterprise takes a very systematic approach to future studies, keeps itself informed of various contents and methods. This preliminary work is used to actively shape enterprise strategy. ☐
    c) Our goal is to increase the value of the enterprise and to double profits in the coming years. A way will present itself. ☐
    d) Somewhere in the enterprise there are people responsible for considering the future. However, little notice is taken of the results – neither at the management level nor elsewhere in the enterprise. Implementation seems more or less random. ☐

12. **How are administrative tasks handled in your enterprise (e.g. vacations, travel planning and accounting, payroll, human resources issues, work and project planning)?**
    a) We have a specialist for everything, or a contact partner who supports employees so as to ensure fast processing. ☐
    b) The enterprise is strict when it comes to keeping overall costs as low as possible. Saving time takes precedence over saving money. ☐

    c) The enterprise is making an effort to gradually have the employees themselves handle the bulk of the administrative tasks (e.g. electronically). While this increases the load for the employees, it reduces costs for the enterprise. ☐

    d) Everything is strictly regulated and very bureaucratic. Nothing happens without a signature. ☐

13. **Does a certain managerial style prevail at your enterprise?**

    a) An authoritarian management style prevails. This ensures clarity and speed. ☐

    b) A decision weakness is prevalent throughout the enterprise. Everyone is afraid of making the wrong decision. Better no decision at all than the wrong decision. ☐

    c) The boss has the function of a coach. Owing to the high degree of responsibility the employees have in performing their work, the boss is focused more on difficult decisions and budget questions. ☐

    d) There is no prevailing management style. The managers are geared instead to meeting objectives. How they do this is left up to them. ☐

14. **How does your enterprise show that it is capable of learning?**

    a) Cross-functional teams have been assigned to manage knowledge transfer within the enterprise and beyond department borders. ☐

    b) The capacity to learn is stymied by cost-center structures and department borders. ☐

    c) Learning cannot be represented in the project structure of the enterprise. There is no evidence of a monetary benefit. ☐

    d) Lessons-learned activities and best-practice initiatives are used as part of an attempt to better learn from enterprise mistakes and successes. ☐

15. **How would you characterize the culture at your enterprise?**

    a) While respect, openness and fairness are written down in the enterprise guidelines, reality shows that quite a bit is sacrificed in the name of the enterprise or personal success whenever it appears necessary. ☐

    b) Respect, openness and fairness are written down in the enterprise guidelines and the managers are generally concerned to be role models in this regard. ☐

    c) The culture is one of power and power structures. The struggle for power and influence makes its mark on day-to-day enterprise affairs and prevents the enterprise from achieving a greater degree of success. ☐

    d) A "culture of consensus" would best describe it. But reaching a consensus costs time and money. ☐

Evaluation

Question	Answer	Foresight	Reaction Speed	Question	Answer	Foresight	Reaction Speed
1	A	3	2	9	A	1	1
	B	1	2		B	1	0
	C	1	1		C	2	2
	D	0	0		D	3	3
2	A	0	1	10	A	1	0
	B	1	0		B	0	0
	C	2	3		C	2	1
	D	0	1		D	2	3
3	A	0	1	11	A	0	0
	B	1	0		B	3	3
	C	3	3		C	2	0
	D	1	2		D	2	1
4	A	0	1	12	A	2	3
	B	3	3		B	3	3
	C	2	2		C	0	1
	D	0	0		D	0	0
5	A	0	2	13	A	1	3
	B	3	3		B	0	0
	C	2	2		C	3	2
	D	1	0		D	1	1
6	A	2	1	14	A	3	2
	B	3	2		B	0	1
	C	0	0		C	0	0
	D	1	3		D	2	2
7	A	1	1	15	A	0	2
	B	2	3		B	3	2
	C	2	0		C	0	0
	D	2	2		D	2	0
8	A	1	3	Overall score			
	B	0	0	Maximum score		40	40
	C	2	0				
	D	2	3				

Evaluation

The table shows the scores for each answer. These are added together to arrive at an overall score for "Foresight" and "Reaction Speed." The overall scores are then transposed onto the diagram shown in Figure 24. The final evaluation for your enterprise is defined by the point of convergence in the diagram.

Proactive: The enterprise attempts to understand, and to some degree, anticipate the changes in its environment. However, it lacks the full capacity to convert the knowledge it gains into competitive advantages. Room for improvement is seen primarily in the area of communication and the integration of the relevant units in the strategy process.

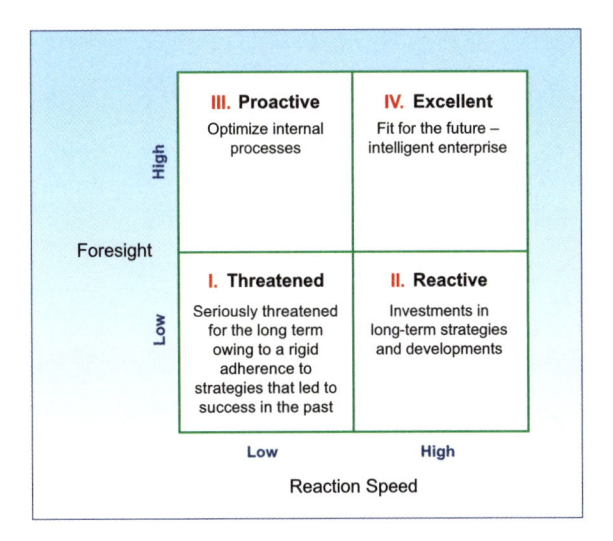

Figure 24 Your enterprise's IQ: indicator of future fitness

Reactive: Changes on the market and in the enterprise's general environment are recognized very quickly by the enterprise. Moreover, the necessary measures are addressed and implemented swiftly. However, the rapid changes and adjustments within the enterprise require considerable increases in staff and bind enormous resources. The enterprise could prepare even better for the future by improving its foresight and capacity to anticipate developments.

Excellent: The enterprise is fully aware of the signs of the times and is well prepared for the future. It has come to the realization that efficiency alone will not bring long-term success. However, depending on the exact point of convergence in the diagram, there may be room for improvement.

Endangered: You prefer to do the things that you have done so far even better. While your enterprise may be quite successful at the moment, it is about to miss the bus into the future. A consideration of changes in the enterprise's environment at the level of strategy development has not been secured, nor are the internal processes geared to fast changes. The smallest changes in the currently stable market are likely to trigger massive problems for the enterprise.

In the chapters that follow, various possibilities for improving the situation will be discussed.

1.5 Enterprise Intelligence Test

Chapter 2

Detection

Detecting and Recording Changes
in the Enterprise Environment

At the beginning of the last century, a team of researchers discovered a heretofore unknown tribe in Papua New Guinea on the island of New Guinea.

After a period of observation, the researchers came to the conclusion that while their manner of living was characteristic of the Stone Age, the indigenous tribe was altogether peaceful. The chief in particular turned out to be friendly, curious and intelligent. And so the researchers decided to take up more complete contact with the tribe. Despite the obvious difficulties in communicating with the natives, a relationship of trust was gradually established. Aware of the scientific significance of their discovery, the researchers proposed a certain experiment to the chief.

In the context of this experiment, the chief is given an opportunity to travel to a "new" world. Together with the researchers, he travels to Singapore for a brief stay. Once in Singapore, the researchers spend a day with the chief, showing him everything that Singapore had to offer at the time, including modern seaports with giant oceangoing steamers, multi-story houses, streets full of traffic, bicycles, automobiles, carriages, marketplaces, money as a means of payment, cultural centers, and museums. The chief witnesses people wearing elaborate clothing, eating with knives and forks, wearing glasses to help them see, and otherwise contending with the general stress of a modern life.

The chief observes everything with a surprisingly blank facial expression. The researchers are unsure whether it is a matter of disinterest or astonishment.

Full of impression from another world, the chief returns to his tribe on the next day. Following the experiment's design, the researchers are now very intent on observing what the chief will relate to the other members of the tribe about his journey.

Here, however, their disappointment is great as they discover that only a single detail from the journey has really captured the chief's imagination, while all of the other novelties, things he can scarcely have been expected to comprehend, have simply been blocked out. With great excitement, the chief reports to the members of his tribe that in the other world he has witnessed a different way of carrying things, a way that allows people to carry more things, such as bananas, on their heads.

How are we to interpret the experiment? The chief seems either to have simply blocked out the things he was unable to explain to himself or perceived and classified them as uninteresting. He presumably did not even have the words to intelligibly describe a seaport or a ship. Our knowledge and our theories about the world shape the way we perceive the world.

Nothing has changed in this regard.

We see the world through the filter of our knowledge and experience. We tend to perceive only those things that we understand. This often leads us to overlook things or refuse to recognize them. The crucial task, however, is to keep our sensors active and to remain alert. Successful enterprises in particular tend to take success for granted and overlook various dangers.

Our perception of things is generally determined by our experience. In the present chapter, I address this and other matters.

2.1 A Plea for Foresight and Prior Action

It is just as important for enterprises to be prepared for the future and to avoid being surprised by change as it is to manage uncertainty. Both require a precise knowledge and understanding of the enterprise's environment.

As we will see in the chapters to come, the activities of individual enterprises can lead to developments that have a considerable impact on the overall enterprise environment. On the other hand, from the perspective of any given enterprise, most developments and changes will come flooding in from the outside. This will remain the case in the future. To ignore these developments would mean to put the future of the enterprise at risk. The enterprise's environment will continue to develop – either with or without the enterprise. The causal connection here is compellingly illustrated by Henry Kissinger in his famous remark, "There can not be a crisis next week, my schedule is already full."

Permit me now to make a few general observations before moving on to outline what an enterprise's environment is made up of and how one can take its measure.

Although enterprises differ in many respects they are unified by a single common goal – the creation of added value by transforming input into output. These activities take place in the face of external changes that are often complex, volatile and very dynamic. It is absolutely essential to consider these changes when analyzing the enterprise's activities and strategy.

The environment of most enterprises has become increasingly subject to dynamic change. The globalization of world markets and increased rates of change have forced enterprises to continuously adjust their strategic behavior to new conditions. Given that products and services are being replaced in many sectors by ever newer products and services at ever shorter intervals, foresight and prior action are becoming ever more important. The ability to anticipate changes and developments and to detect the opportunities and risks associated with them faster than one's competitors will be one of the most important success factors for enterprises in the 21st century [Reher 2001].

An enterprise can develop only as well as it has understood its environment.

2.2 The Enterprise Environment

Everything that does not exist or take place within an enterprise can essentially be regarded as its environment. If you take a look outside your office window, you will probably already have your enterprise's environment in view – and with it, the main problem of enterprise analysis directly before your eyes. The sheer volume of the information available – it is essentially a matter of the rest of the world – will clearly outstrip the processing capacity of any enterprise.

"The capacity of firms to deal with market situations in a cognitive sense, their capacity to process information and turn it into knowledge, is small compared to the sheer scale of problems which confront them. Companies can never deal completely with the complexity of the real world." [Ormerod 2005]

The task at hand is therefore to concentrate on the most important information. The crucial question in this regard is:

What is the important information in the present case?

The summaries of extensive investigations on the subject of the enterprise environment are available in the literature. Their utility for enterprises in general and for strategic analysis in particular, is a matter of debate. [Quinn 1988, Johnson 1988] The results of various studies and investigations support the conclusion that enterprises with functioning programs devoted to the continuous analysis of their environments perform better than those without such programs. [Choo 1995] Fahey & Narayanan [Fahey 1986] suggest that enterprises are especially successful when the strategies they implement account for the changes in their environment.

The starting point for strategic analysis (and thus also an analysis of an enterprise's environment) is the SWOT analysis, which is a measure of *strengths, weaknesses, opportunities* and *threats* and which is explained in greater detail in Chapter 5 and in Section 10.5.1 [Andrews 1971]. The basic idea behind the SWOT analysis is to arrive at an assessment of the strategic fit of an enterprise, i.e. the degree to which the enterprise has adapted its strengths and weaknesses to the opportunities and dangers in its environment.

The Structure of the Enterprise Environment

It is advisable to begin any analysis by first sketching the structure of the enterprise's environment from the viewer's perspective. When it comes to demarcating the boundaries between an enterprise and its environment, a distinction is often drawn between the enterprise's immediate environment (micro level or micro world) and its broader environment (macro level or macro world) [Fahey 1986; Bea 2001] or between context environment and operational environment [Worthington 2003].

Drawing upon the distinction between micro and macro environments, Figure 25 shows the types of possible interaction – managing, influencing and reacting – while hinting at their strategic significance. More information in this regard is offered in Table 6.

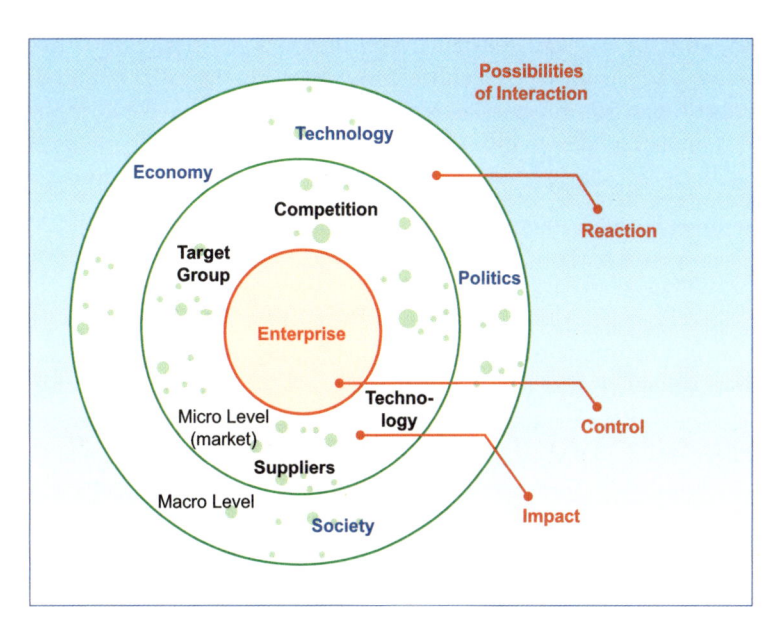

Figure 25 The enterprise environment: micro and macro levels

Table 6 The Focus of Environment Analysis and its Significance for Enterprise Strategy

Perspective	Components	Strategic Significance
Enterprise	Organization, structures, strategy, culture, style, etc. (7S Model -> Chapters 5 and 6)	*Managing and influencing* For instance, planning, strategic measures, initiatives
Micro environment	Branch and industry, competitors, markets, customers, suppliers, partners, etc.	*Direct influence* For instance, via products, marketing, lobbying, partnerships, mergers & acquisitions, agreements
Macro environment	Society, economy, political system, science, etc.	*Indirect Influence* Lobbying, research, revolutionary innovation, sponsoring

The Micro Environment

The enterprise interacts with its micro environment. Dedicated methods of analysis have been established for the individual elements of the micro environment (customer segmenting, competitor analyses, industry analyses, etc.). For instance, marketing and sales represent two operational units that concern themselves with the customer and markets and that use tools such as segmenting, surveys and focus groups to compile and make information available to the relevant decision makers in the enterprise.

Owing to the daily contact with this component of the overall environment as well as the possibility of directly influencing it, the micro environment is generally a subject of intensive observation and information gathering. When viewed from a perspective that is holistic enough to encompass the entire enterprise, it is clear that a centralized program for providing this information is necessary and must be secured. Information is usually handled in quantitative formats and with quantitative methods of analysis.

A number of instruments and methods are presented in the Annex (Chapter 10).

The Macro Environment

In contrast, the macro environment consists of all those areas over which the enterprise has no direct influence. The term "macro environment" refers to the enterprise's general context – that component of the overall environment with respect to which the enterprise is required to adapt itself. Interaction here takes place either to a minimal degree, or not at all. However, it is precisely this predicament of not being able to intervene that gives enterprises a kind of duty to observe, and to make sure that they are in a position to respond quickly to any relevant changes.

In contrast to what is the case for the micro environment, there are no established ways of observing the individual components of the macro environment. Many observers take the STEEP approach (see Section 10.1.1). The origins of this approach go back to Rhynne [Rhynne 1971] who developed the field-anomaly-relaxation method or FAR and later published the method in the context of a project for the United States National Research and Development Center in 1971. Other researchers later adopted and modified the method to fit their needs [Schwartz 1974].

STEEP stands for the following areas of the macro environment:

- S – Society
- T – Technology
- E – Economy
- E – Ecology (this term is sometimes replaced or supplemented by the term Ethics)
- P – Politics

Modifications of the original STEEP include STEEPL ("L" being for Legal or Law and Order) and STEEPV ("V" being for Values).

This rough-and-ready sketch of the macro environment's structure (including five areas) is presented for the sake of efficient discussion. It can also be broken down further. Each area can be investigated according to the notes found in Table 7.

Once we determine the structure of an enterprise's environment, we can move forward and conduct an efficient search for information about the various segments. Before I address the issue of how one arrives at a homogeneous compilation of information in Section 2.4, I examine the issue of information processing in Section 2.3.

Table 7 Using STEEPL to Analyze the Macro Environment

STEEPL Elements	Some Key Questions
Society Societal changes, shifting values	What impact will the societal changes have on product demand and our workforce? Do the educational and social-security systems support the planned investments?
Technology	What technology drivers are at work? Are there any technological breakthroughs and developments that must be taken into account? What possibilities of technology transfer exist?
Economy	How stable is the overall economic environment? How are individual industries developing? To what extent are financial markets actively supporting further development?
Ecology	How stable is the ecological environment? Can certain industries be seen as a threat to the ecological environment?
Political	How stable is the political environment? What impact of international and global developments?
Legal	What are the effects of the tax laws on business? What impact will existing or emerging laws have on business and employment?

Other Approaches to Studying the Enterprise Environment

In the interest of offering a thorough account, it warrants mention in the present context that there are also other approaches to structuring the enterprise environment that allow one to use information more effectively in the context of considering the future and developing strategies.

In his book *Sex, Ecology, Spirituality: the Spirit of Evolution*, Wilber [Wilber 2000] introduces the so-called Four Quadrants Model (Figure 26). Wilber uses this model to distinguish between the individual and the group and between internal and external in an attempt to illuminate several aspects of the environment. Here, he rightfully points out that it is primarily "unclear" or "ambiguous" information that is crucial to the future livelihood of enterprises. He also concedes that the method is very time consuming, which is certainly one reason for its relatively low acceptance.

Another model which focuses primarily on "how" people view their environment instead of focusing only on the content of what they see was introduced by Graves in 1974 [Graves 1974]. This model was developed into its current form by Beck and Cowan who refer to it as Spiral Dynamics [Beck 1996]. Beck and Cowan use a kind of color-coded double helix to juxtapose the conditions of life and cognitive capacities. This unusual, but intensive way of representing the environment has found only sporadic use.

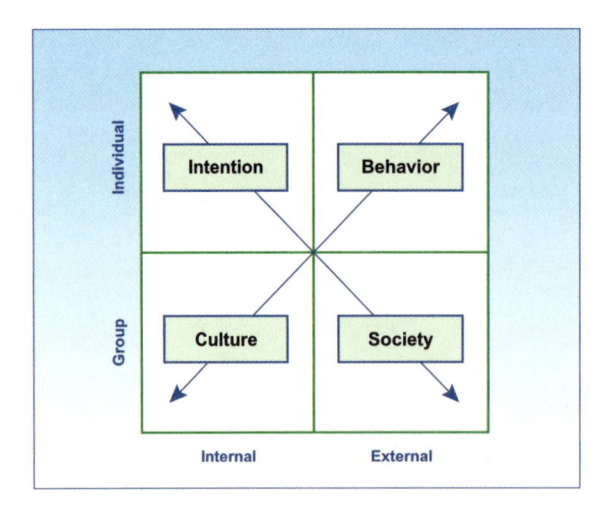

Figure 26 Keeping an eye on the enterprise environment: Wilber's four quadrants model [Wilber 2000]

The STEEP model probably owes its popularity to its simple structure and application. However, this simplicity is also the model's main drawback, i.e. because its application often fails to generate a satisfactory degree of precision and comprehensiveness. In times of heavy workloads and tight schedules, one often comes across STEEP analyses that address no more than the usual surface phenomena.

In addition to the structure of the various models – STEEP, for instance, breaks down the enterprise environment into segments – the content of what is represented is of crucial significance. We expect an analysis of the environment to offer us a feeling for the changes that have occurred or are emerging so that we will be in a position to prepare the enterprise for them. Before we devote ourselves to a consideration of the future, we have to be in the clear on how the present works. One major challenge consists of properly determining the scope of the analysis. Will it be sufficient to take a look out the window? Or should we commission separate studies for each segment? Experience has shown that important findings are gained by independent and intensive research. Experience is usually a more reliable basis for estimating the costs than arbitrarily set budgets and deadlines.

2.3 Information as a Basis for Decision Making

We live in an environment that is rich in information. Estimates indicate that the total volume of information increases annually by more than 30 percent [Lyman 2003] and that the annual increase in new information – as stored in memory media – has reached 5 exabytes ($5 \cdot 10^{18}$ bytes). The problem is no longer a lack of information, but an inadequate capacity to select the right and crucial information.

Today, those who neglect to continually keep abreast of the latest developments in the enterprise environment run the risk of becoming obsolete in terms of their knowledge about their own businesses. Strategic information available at the right point in time together with its proper management and use have an enormous impact on the economic success of enterprises.

"While intuition is often looked upon favorably as a source of information, it is important to make clear that our intuition is essentially a function of our experience. Knowledge based on experience can be very limiting when the task is to gain an unobstructed view of the future."[Micic 2000] This remark offers a good description of the challenges faced in the area of information processing and logistics.

The strategic work is essentially a matter of information processing and depends to a crucial degree on the information used. The main problem is making the necessary information available to the decision makers in a more or less digestible form. As described in Chapter 1, the dilemma is that decisions are usually made by a small group of individuals, or a specific office, while the information itself is gathered throughout the enterprise by virtually all of the enterprise's employees and others external to the enterprise. The flow of information is limited in time and space by the capacity of the information receivers and those who use the information to process it and by the dedicated demand on the part of the management.

In their book, *Invisible Advantage: How Intangibles Are Driving Business Performance*, Low and Kalafut [Low 2002] describe how managers admitted to having the wrong information with which to make decisions. The questions arises as to why this is the case. Furthermore, are decisions really made on the basis of insufficient information or are the managers responsible for making decisions based on insufficient information? A tendency to react to situations can lead to information gaps, while the implementation of proactive policies ensures a continual and systematic gathering of information.

Enterprises invest a lot of money in obtaining the *right* information. The assumption reflected here is that more information and a more comprehensive description of the situation at hand will lead to a greater degree of security when it comes to making decisions. However, this assumption can easily lead to a climate in which decisions are postponed or simply not made. As described in the quote from Ormerod at the beginning of Section 2.2, and as has been amply confirmed by experience, it would be impossible to condense all of the relevant information into a simple statement of facts. The question (or the uneasy feeling) will always remain as to whether the available information is complete. Is it the right information? Does it provide us with the right indicators for the future? Is it helpful when it comes to making a decision? (I address the phenomenon of *paralysis through analysis* again in Chapter 5.)

As already mentioned, situations can change rapidly, especially in light of the fact that the environment itself is dynamic (Figure 27). The information available at a given time t_1 is the basis for decision "A." The relevant information at time t_2 may have changed. The new situation yields a different decision "B" with the following result, "If I had only known that, then I would have decided otherwise." Who hasn't heard this sentence coming out of his own mouth? When we look back upon time t_1 at time t_2 and reconsider our decision, we might have decided otherwise if we had only

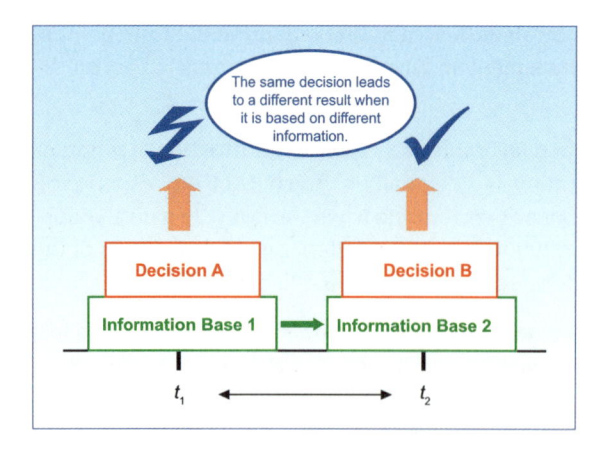

Figure 27 Decisions as a function of time: a changing situation

been aware of the new information. Although this is an essentially banal and insignificant conclusion, it could rapidly turn into a problem, or even a serious threat, for the enterprise.

Figure 28 offers an illustration of the path taken by a news item about an event outside of the enterprise to the receiver inside the enterprise. We can see that there are many barriers and hindrances to clear before the information about the event makes its way to the right person in the enterprise.

When the proverbial sack of rice in China falls over, it is very likely that it won't be noticed in Europe. The media or other channels of information will filter the event out

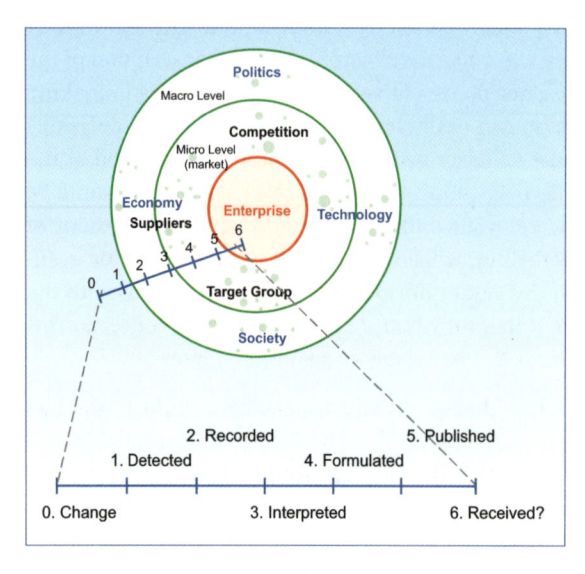

Figure 28 The path of information into the enterprise: what actually arrives?

of the flood of other information – probably on account of its insignificance. The media focus on what are supposed to be interesting events, with "interesting" largely being defined by media perception of consumer interests. For internal reasons or business-political reasons, some information is suppressed and some information is amplified.

As illustrated in Figure 28, it may take several steps before news of a particular event (i.e. an event heralding change) makes its way to an enterprise. Information brokers, or the various media, first have to detect the event on their radar screens, and then process and forward the relevant information. Access to a diverse array of media sources will therefore increase the likelihood that news of an event or a particular interpretation of an event will make it to the enterprise where it can be analyzed.

If we can safely assume that certain information – important or unimportant – will be brought to the enterprise (Figure 29), then we will have cleared the first hurdle. If the information qualifies as relevant, then it may be used to support a decision. However, in order to ensure that it is recognized as relevant and available for decision-making purposes, the information will have to have jumped the gap to level 3.

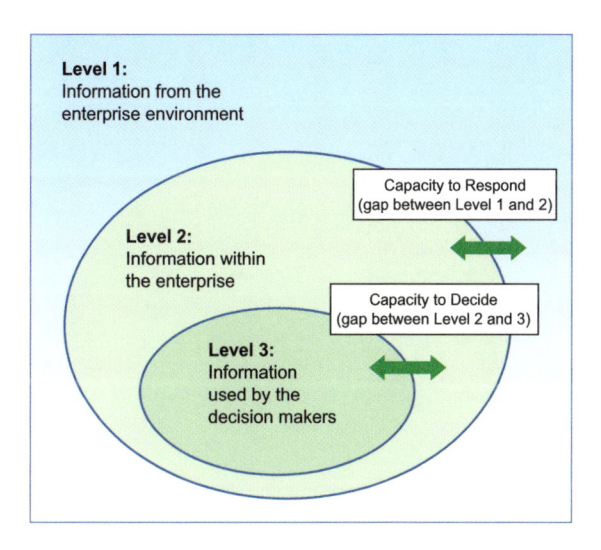

Figure 29 Responding to an unwelcome surprise: the path information takes on its way to supporting a decision [Kunze 2000]

If we assume that the falling down of a sack of rice in China is an event of strategic importance, then it is clear that the path taken by the news of this event on its way to the enterprise for decision-making purposes will be long and full of filters. This thought should encourage decision makers to play an active role in the process of information procurement and to have a hand in determining the balance between what is too much and what is too little information.

2.3 Information as a Basis for Decision Making

Filters

Human beings represent one of the most significant uncertainty factors in this process. The analysis and evaluation of information is largely handled in the realm of the subjective, as was seen in the Singapore experiment. So-called perceptual filters make the task of selecting and disseminating information on an objective basis far more difficult [Weick 1985]. Furthermore, human factors such as ambition, egoism and a thirst for power can play an important role when it comes to making information available [Krystek 1993].

The Need for Information

Figure 30 illustrates the distinction between objective and subjective needs for information and demonstrates how it is not always possible at the moment we become aware of certain information to distinguish clearly between "interesting, but not necessary" and "necessary, but surprising." A lot of information is new and surprising. Some information is interesting, but not directly necessary. The optimal solution would be to concentrate on interesting and necessary information, as represented by the convergence of the circles in the figure. Attempts at delimiting our need for information proceed incrementally owing to the iterative nature of knowledge acquisition.

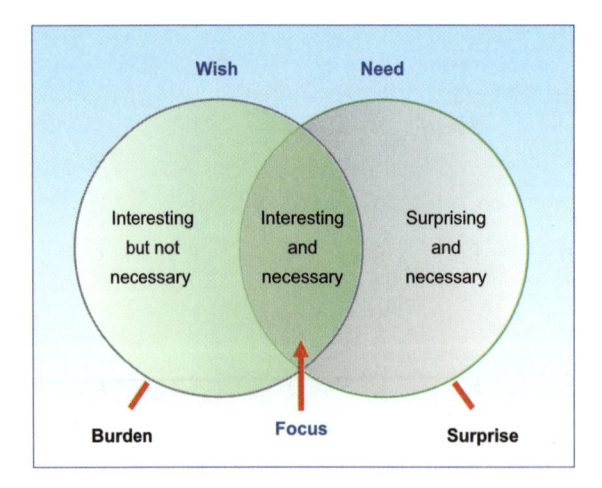

Figure 30 Information need and supply: interesting and necessary is optimal [Marti 1996]

While obtaining information at all was crucial years ago, the task at hand today is to reduce the volume of available information to the amount that is both interesting and necessary. We are therefore called upon to increase and enhance our capacity to intelligently process information.

Knowledge Management

Enterprises depend on the internal identification and availability of data, information and knowledge (i.e. within their own walls) to more effectively generate new core competencies and strategic resources, and to ultimately enable the generation of new knowledge. Information is the raw material used to produce knowledge and to consider the future. Our view of the future begins and ends with the information that is available to us and our ability to combine and stretch this information. However, it must be clear at each stage of the process that the result of every consideration of the future – whether this is effectively a trend, scenario, vision or strategy – is always dependent on the input information.

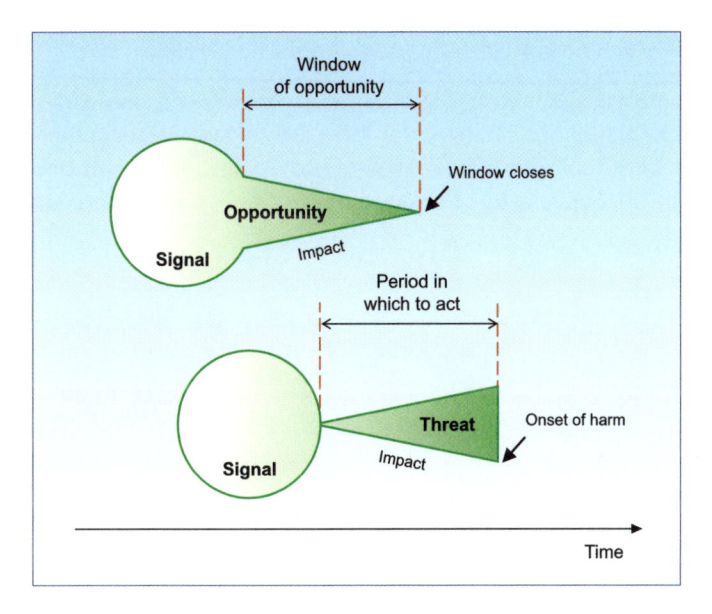

Figure 31 Signals and reaction times: opportunities disappear, threats mount

Knowledge and information are very special goods. They are time-dependent, i.e. their value and strategic significance increases or decreases with time (Figure 31). On the other hand (Figure 10, Chapter 1), neither knowledge nor information are purely objective. They are largely available in subjective form. Knowledge ranges from pure facts to half-truths and speculation, with the distinction between these categories not always being clear. As I point out in what follows, there are thus many barriers and traps to be mindful of when attempting to process knowledge and information.

Information Pathologies

The sheer magnitude of available information represents a serious problem for enterprises. While we are confronted on the one hand by a lack of information, we are forced on the other hand to devise ways of more effectively managing the available flood of information. The subject of information pathology concerns the problems that can arise when we gather, compile and exchange information. Discussions here center on distortion in the transmission of information, the erroneous interpretation of information and the misguided use of information.

Hierarchy-related information pathologies arise in connection with the nature of the communication that takes place between members who occupy different levels of an enterprise's hierarchy, as well as in connection with their dependence on one another. In an effort to secure rewards or avoid penalties, employees and managers might suppress or alter critical information, for instance, information that would otherwise jeopardize the reaching of an immediate goal – before forwarding it to the next level in the hierarchy. This can lead to a degree of distortion in any assessments based on the information – especially if the flow of information involves multiple stages – and ultimately to bad decisions and negative consequences for the enterprise.

Owing to overload, remote sources, a need for consensus, compression, inaccurate assessments and abstraction, highly centralized units that are responsible for gathering and interpreting information are often confronted by an inability to process information fast enough. This can lead to a slowdown in the flow of information and an inability to use it.

In addition to this, there are doctrine-related information pathologies. A reality doctrine can be said to obtain whenever established ways of regarding developments continue to prevail although their validity is questionable. In contrast, an enlightenment doctrine can be said to obtain whenever certain expectations gain the upper hand, with the result that only that information that meets the expectations is forwarded.

Information that defies our attempts to label it according to the accepted categories is often regarded as a threat and suppressed. Complexity, in particular, is a challenge for our capacity to take up and process information. Such complexity can lead to incomplete information records and the misinterpretation of information.

Communication Barriers

In addition to enterprise-specific observations relating to a deficient supply of information, many authors discuss communication barriers that are to be avoided at all costs and no matter what organizational structures are in place. These include [Frank 2001]:

- *Overload*

    Those responsible are expected to handle too much information in too short a time.

- *Stereotyping and interpretation of causes*

    Given that different types of organizations have different needs for information, the recipients of information are often prejudiced by their prior experience when it comes to the task of comprehending the information.

- *Filters*

  Given that different individuals may comprehend new information differently, the content of certain information (e.g. a news item) may be altered as it is communicated from station to station.

- *Rumors*

  Rumors spread when information is released in the absence of official confirmation, for instance, as a result of deficient information policies.

- *Inadequate feedback*

  The senders of a news item never learn whether it has been understood.

- *Unintelligible communication*

  Communication may be rendered unintelligible by the excessive use of abbreviations and technical terms.

- *Poor presentation of information*

  A poorly presented report may lead to an inadequate understanding of the information it contains.

Bounded Rationality

The theory of bounded rationality, which concerns itself with the subject of our limited capacity to process information and the various factors that influence decision making, was introduced by Simon [Simon 1972].

The basic idea is that our insufficient capacity to process information leads us to search for alternatives in a sequential manner, and that this gives us an inclination to accept the first satisfactory solution. Whether an alternative solution is regarded as satisfactory depends on the number of possible alternatives. We tend to lower our expectations when the task of coming up with alternatives is difficult. In contrast, our expectations are raised when there appear to be many alternatives.

This predicament often leads to suboptimal choices.

Mindset and Mental Maps

Our human senses are limited in terms of their capacity to detect or process things in our environment. There are far more phenomena all around us than we are capable of registering. We select the things that interest us (a fish has no understanding of the concept of wetness because it is not familiar with dryness). We essentially perceive according to a model of reality that allows us sort through an overwhelming mass of events. This is necessary in that it enables us to reduce complexity and develop an understanding of our environment. The model itself, however, is relatively static. This introduces the risk that what we "see" is what conforms to our expectations and not necessarily what is actually there.

While managers tend to re-deploy proven solutions, it warrants bearing in mind that it is just as important to be on the uptake for new ideas and approaches. Communication, discussion and the exchange of information and knowledge help in this regard; they promote the regeneration of "mental models."

"Mental models are invisible in the corporation. They are neither explicit nor examined, but they are pervasive. When a company's mental models become out of sync with reality, management makes forecasting errors as well as poor decisions." [Foster 2001]

As we will see in Chapter 4, scenarios are a good means of opening up our thoughts and ridding ourselves of mental blocks. They are a kind of fresh-cell culture for our mental models.

IT Support

The rapid development of the Internet has opened up entirely new ways of gaining access to information. We now have quicker and more intense access to information (from a broad array of sources) about customers, markets, competitors, branches and technological developments [Kunze 2000].

However, with no means of processing the available information, we run the risk of simply being inundated by it. Someone will have to evaluate, classify and determine the ultimate significance of the information on behalf of the enterprise. This task requires a sophisticated level of intelligence and cannot be handled by IT support. This is the reason why precisely this area is prone to bottlenecks.

While gaining access to information was both a challenge in the past and sufficient to establish a competitive advantage, the challenge today inheres in the intelligent selection and compilation of information. It is easy to gain access to large amounts of data and information of questionable quality. The challenge is to convert the available information into meaningful strategic knowledge – and to do it without IT. This means that the available material will have to be read and recorded, reflected upon, understood, thought through and processed. Only then will it make sense to look for answers to the question "So what?"

Despite all of the euphoria about the new options enabled by progress in information technology, one cannot call attention often enough to the following: IT is no more than a form of support. This support can be rendered primarily when it comes to the researching of, the searching for and the meaningful storage of data. Automated finding of truly relevant information that offers an enterprise a crucial advantage over others and automated compilation of corresponding documents will remain an illusion into the foreseeable future.

Attempts have been made at automating the processes of news and trend detection via the Internet. The systems – which are also referred to as "search agents" – are fed with search words and criteria and then turned loose on the web. However, if a situation or an event is so new that it cannot be represented using search words and criteria, then the agent won't be able to find anything. Again, it is helpful to consider Popper in this context, "There is one thing that is impossible for us to know, namely what we will know in the future. Because otherwise we would already know it."

Such a test system would have detected neither SARS nor "tsunami" as important new events, although both phenomena are without doubt important events. It is safe to conclude that while the use of programmed search agents makes sense for routine tasks, they are not helpful when it comes to detecting real novelties for which we simply lack the necessary terms of description.

It is not a matter of efficiently processing as much information as possible, but of having comprehended the right information and then using it to draw intelligent conclusions or to conduct relevant research at a deeper level.

2.4 How We Can Learn to Understand Our Environment

In order to make sure that the gathering of information from our environment is not left to pure chance, enterprises have begun to consider appropriate systematic approaches and are seeking a compromise between costs and benefits – this also applies to the information that is important and necessary for strategic decisions.

Focusing

Systematic approaches begin with a definition of the object of investigation. When it comes to providing an answer to a specific question, the need for information and the approach taken to obtain that information are very different from the needs and approaches relating to a program aimed at a continuous scanning of the environment as a means of preparing the enterprise for change (Figure 32).

	Known	New
Broad	**Overview** Many subject areas and contexts	**Scanning** Many subject areas, developments and surprises
Restricted	**Research** Specific questions and a focused search for information and details	**Monitoring** Selected topics, examination of development, surprises

Scope / Degree of Maturity

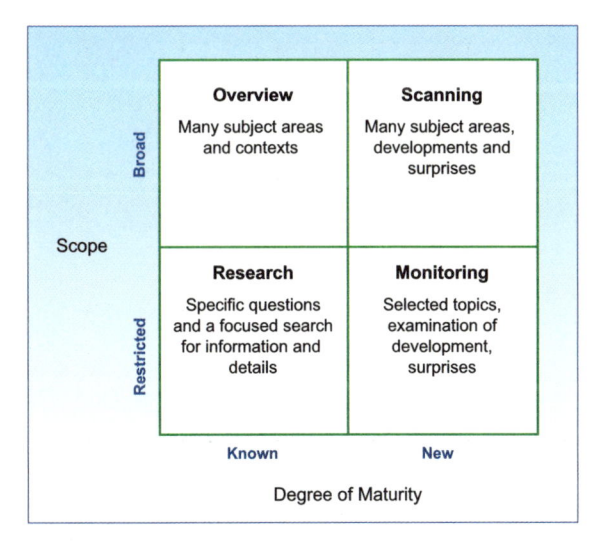

Figure 32 Gathering information: focus and degree of maturity determine the method

A practice of observing our environment leads to information that one can gather, compress, process, validate, structure, represent, and make available. Ideally, the value of the information will increase with each processing stage. In practice, we start at a very general level and then begin to focus (Figure 33).

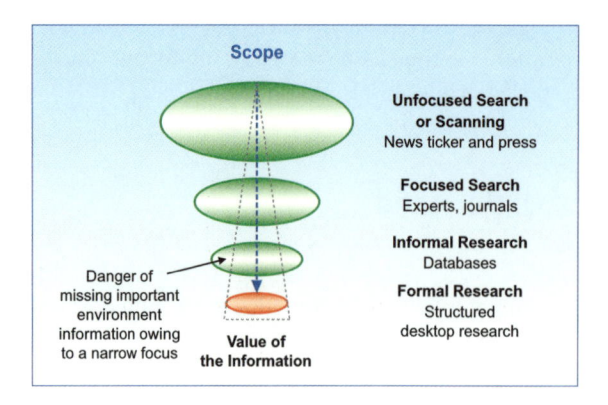

Figure 33 Narrowing the focus: from general sources of to targeted research

Table 8 shows a list of approaches to environment observation – beginning with relatively aimless approaches to and ending with very focused approaches. In general, we can observe our environment without a specific aim. We simply set our sensors to "new." This type of information gathering is usually referred to as "scanning."

Table 8 Approaches to Environment Observation

	Goal	Application	Cost	Number of Sources	Procedure
Unfocused observation – scanning	General observation directed towards areas of interest	Discovery	Minimal	Many	Broad, superficial searching
Focused observation – monitoring	Selection of new and important items	Comprehension	Minimal	Few	Skimming of selected sources
Informal research	Formulating questions and unclear matters	Learning	Medium	Few	Focused search for answers
Formal research	Specification of concrete goals	Basis for decision making	High	Many	Systematic gathering of information in order to answer specific questions
Focused search and study	Reaching an understanding	Learning and development	Medium	Few	General knowledge and search for connections, dependencies and mechanisms

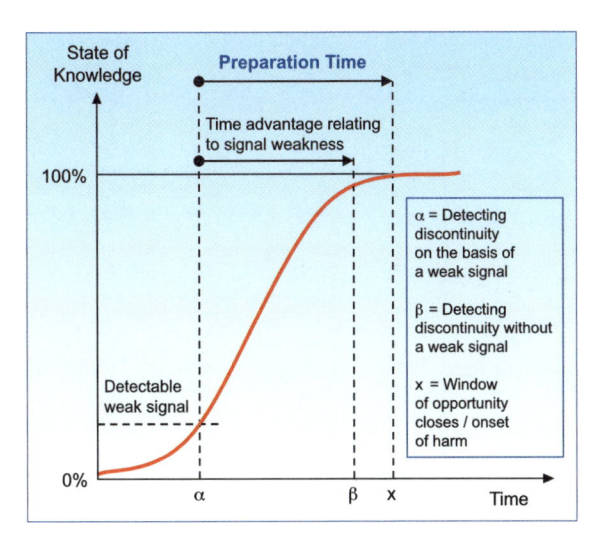

Figure 34 Detecting weak signals at an early stage: head starts generate opportunities

- Scanning

    We use a relatively wide angle when looking for early warnings and signals. The focus of our scanning is on the amount of information we cover, and less on specific requirements. What changes do we detect in the environment? What is unusual? What is new and could be significant? The curious, unfocused view is broad. Its scope encompasses nearly everything that is related to the environment. However, it may ultimately be weak signals that bring the crucial competitive advantages (Figure 34). If the enterprise's preparation time is too long, then the window of opportunity may close, and the opportunity itself may rapidly turn into a threat (see Analyzing Weak Signals in Section 10.4.3).

    While looking for information, enterprises scan the general enterprise environment. Incomplete, contradictory, unclear and ambiguous information is gathered in order to detect the emergence of changes and trends. Scanning can be of special strategic significance particularly for enterprises whose environments are very dynamic and volatile. It is a matter of isolating the crucial information from the mass of information.

    In Figure 35, the focus is specified in relation to the degree of novelty and detail. Here, it is helpful to bear in mind that new signals can indeed be analyzed (detail knowledge) and new items will soon lose their novelty for having been detected.

- Monitoring

    In contrast to scanning, monitoring involves a specific issue and the observation of interesting developments with respect to it over a longer period of time. In the case of monitoring, the scope of the investigation has already been set. One conducts a focused search for information and commences to

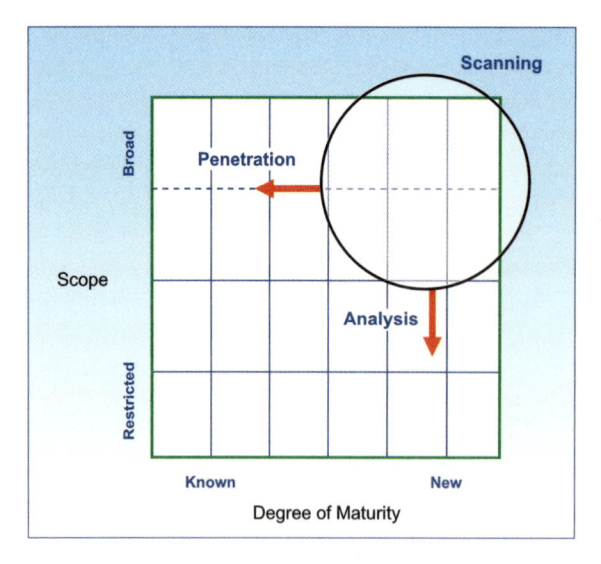

Figure 35 Scanning: the focus is on "new" and "unspecific"

research in a certain area. Topics and changes are observed. What is most important for the enterprise is the ability to interpret specific developments.

- Formal and informal research

  The object of the search is even more concrete when we look for answers to any questions that arise. The research involved may be classified as formal or informal depending on the nature of the questions and the current state of our knowledge.

- Study

  We usually begin by seeking to establish an overview when opening up a new area of inquiry. Very generally, it is a matter of questions about the status quo and the prominent exponents. What is the motivation that is leading to change? What can be seen as influencing the topic, and what connections and interrelations exist with respect to other topics?

Once we have established an overview, the next task is to keep the state of our knowledge up-to-date (e.g. via scanning), monitor the further development of individual aspects, and find answers to specific questions via focused follow-up investigations.

Gathering Information

The list of possible sources of information is long. In general, we can draw a distinction between information that is available internally and information that is available externally (i.e. information in primary and secondary form). Our consideration of the content of the information will depend on the focus and the manner in which it is gathered (in writing, personal, storage media, data formats, costs, etc.).

Table 9 shows a selection of information sources. A list of specific and useful information sources can be found in Chapter 9.

Table 9 Sources of Information on Scanning and Monitoring

External Source of Information	Gathering Method / Medium	Focus
Newspapers/magazines	Read/paper	General
Professional journals	Read/paper/electronic	Specific
Analyses, studies, reports	Read/paper/electronic	Specific
Interviews	Conversation/personal	Specific
Discussions	Conversation/personal	General/specific
Conferences	Conversation/audiovisual	Specific
Patents	Read/paper/electronic	Specific
Notes	Read/paper/electronic	General/specific
News	Read/paper/electronic	General/specific
Papers	Read/paper/electronic	General/specific
Books	Read/paper/electronic	General
Specialist books	Read/paper/electronic	Specific
Press releases	Read/paper/electronic	General/specific
Blogs	Read/electronic	General/specific
Experts/professors	Conversation/personal contact	Specific
Companies	Conversation/personal contact	Specific
Internet	Read/anonymous/electronic	Very general/specific
Internal source of information	**Gathering Method / Medium**	**Focus**
Existing knowledge/employee knowledge	Conversation/documents, repository	General/specific
Internal documentation: notes, data, reports	Read/paper/electronic	General/specific
Internal market research	Read/paper/electronic	Specific
Employees and communication	Conversation/personal contact	General/specific
Databases/Wiki	Research/electronic	General/specific
Statistics	Read/paper/electronic	General/specific
Archives	Read/paper/electronic	General/specific
Reports	Read/paper/electronic	General/specific
Analyses	Read/paper/electronic	General/specific
Presentations	Read/paper/electronic	General/specific

The sheer number of sources and the diverse formats and types of representation make the task of processing more difficult. We need only look as far as the formatting possibilities that are specified in the table to gain a sense for the volume of work that can arise in connection with a study of various input sources. In order to make information available and utilizable, it is necessary to codify it (in a preferred format), structure it, compile it and compress it. It is especially crucial to take account of any contradictions, uncertainties, and dubious information, and conduct research with respect to these if necessary.

It is not enough to treat the detection process as a purely (unstructured) gathering of information. The researched information might otherwise be processed and visualized so that an overall view is generated as a model of reality [Pörner 2000].

Taking a Careful Look at Information

The establishment of a solid information basis presupposes a capacity to tackle contradictions and divergent statements. We are forced to make decisions. These decisions can be made on the basis of the reliability of our sources or by questioning and researching.

However, in order to avoid getting lost in details, we can label information as ambiguous. For instance, statements regarding the future availability of petroleum differ greatly. Even experts offer very different estimates of the situation, with opinions about the secure future availability of petroleum ranging from thirty to several hundred years. It is academic, however, to question such details. It is more important to recognize that the available information is ambiguous.

Compressing Information

This step is the most time consuming and requires experience, patience, focus, and a good basic grasp of the material in question. The aim is to prepare manageable units of information for the sake of further analysis. Being clear here with respect to the structures involved and issues of demarcation allows one to more easily avoid being forced to return to information-validation stage.

The more we work with the information in question, the more versed we become with the subject area. The material becomes more comprehensible, the pieces of the information puzzle begin to fit together, our thoughts flow in a more structured manner, and we begin to formulate and discuss ideas more intelligently. While this occurs, new questions arise that are directly answered or intentionally left open. Our grasp of the subject in question matures only after we have worked with the information. Experience and a good general understanding of the subject area are necessary for effective compilation, a fact that is often underestimated. The intelligent compilation of information means more than just converting it to a higher level of abstraction. Selecting, homogenizing, filtering, asking questions, second-guessing, extending, expanding, reducing, combining, structuring, understanding and clustering all require great concentration and special mental skills.

Without this step (or if it is poorly executed), we will not be able to process the material, we will merely remain on the surface and will not be able to comprehend the information. Even if the temptation is great to avoid the task, or have it done by others (owing, for instance, to a perpetual lack of time and stress), it will pay to meet the challenge. Reflecting on the future is primarily a matter of understanding the past.

GetAbstract is an enterprise based in Switzerland (www.getabstract.com) that summarizes the content of books and supplies its summaries to its customers in various structured forms. This commercial form of information compression has proven to be quite valuable. One is given an overview of books – from the perspective of relevantly knowledgeable reviewers who have read and studied the books and have highlighted important sections and have culled the crucial information according to their understanding of the matter. The advantage is obvious. Instead of reading hundreds of pages, we read roughly 5 pages and we are able to arrive at a view of the whole based on a prepared evaluation and core statements. If we would like to find out more, then we buy the book and take a closer look.

The idea is astonishingly simple and can serve as a model for the compression of information. The content is compiled in a structured form:

Take-aways:	A book's core statements
Rating:	Overall rating / applicability / degree of innovation / style
Review:	Recommendation and learning material
Abstract:	Summarized content
About the author:	Information about the author

It is indeed possible to summarize books of hundreds of pages in the space of five to eight pages. When using this information, however, it is necessary to bear in mind that – and here we return to the notion of information filters – the person who summarized the book has a certain personal background, certain personal opinions, certain background information and a certain educational background. Then there are the specifications used by the enterprise that derive from the requirements of the broad masses of users and readers.

When we consider the sheer number of books that are published – in Germany alone it is nearly 300 a day (including fiction) – then we begin to understand that we would not come close to being able to take account of all of them. If we assume further that half of the published books are specialist and nonfiction books, then we realize that it would be impossible to even read a significant fraction of all the available books – even if we were to concentrate only on the relevant among them and were to ignore the international literature. This is where GetAbstract comes into play. We are given an opportunity to comprehend the books and take their core messages with us. Before reading a book, we are otherwise only able to orient ourselves using the cover and the advertising texts on the inside cover – title, subtitle, info text and, particularly in the case of American books, published quotes about the book – which does not really offer much help in the case of a lot of books. We have all had the experience of buying the wrong book, the book that we put aside after reading a few pages. The GetAbstract summary represents a successful compromise.

However, the summarizing of information is – in a certain way – an art. It is an activity that demands considerable cognitive skills and overall intelligence. Just like other sources, books do not qualify as homogenous suppliers of information. One chapter might be regarded as exceedingly important and in need of further explanation, while other chapters or sections might be void of any important information, however much they contribute to the plot.

I have already emphasized that an arbitrary budget is the wrong criterion to use when setting the scope of one's analysis of the enterprise environment. It is conspicuous that the significance of such analyses is often underestimated. This leads to unpleasant surprises. We read about it in the newspaper, "Company XYZ totally missed the trend." The list of XYZs is a very long one – whether it be a matter of MP3 players, carving skis, the digital camera or political developments.

If we compare scanning, monitoring and drafting analyses of the environment to a health insurance policy – we save without one, but at a significant risk – the necessity and the benefits of such activities become clearer. Just as in the case of the fire department or insurance company, analysis of the enterprise environment should be a continuous undertaking. There are two main reasons. First, once one has established a basis, one can concentrate on the changes. Second, the time taken to identify change is shorter.

While a careful and elaborate analysis of an enterprise's environment alone is naturally no guarantee for a surprise-free future, it can convey a sense of security. It is clear that merely taking a look out the window is not enough, and that it would be impossible to examine all of the available information. The compromise offering the right cost-benefit ratio is likely to lie somewhere in the middle. As a rule of thumb, we can assume that we have reached a reasonable point of saturation (i.e. a state of information that can only be improved upon by significantly increasing cost and effort) when our efforts to research, scan and monitor begin to turn up repeats, i.e. citations involving the same information. More challenges and hazards are associated with the further processing of the information. Still, a content-dependent decision on the scope of one's investigations is better than a budget-dependent decision on the costs.

It may be helpful here to recall that the quality of our strategic decisions will be directly dependent on the care with which an analysis of the enterprise's environment has been carried out.

Information Representation and Access

Once one has moved beyond the gathering stage and has begun the task of editing the information gathered, the question arises as to how it can best be represented and stored so as to secure further access. Information is usually compiled thematically in the form of presentations and reports. These are either made available upon specific request or are stored for general access. Given their clear limitations, neither

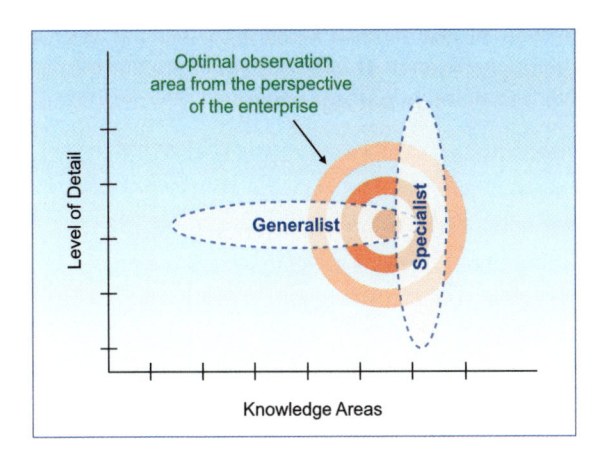

Figure 36 The breadth and depth of investigations: always a compromise

of these forms can be regarded as optimal. I address this issue in greater detail in Chapter 5.

How do we discern change and how is information kept up-to-date? The general answer is: via observation and comparison. Observation leads to the recording of a certain state of things. Change can be said to have taken place whenever a comparison of a current state with a past state yields a discrepancy, for instance, when new phenomena have emerged.

The difficulty we face when it comes to fully recognizing change results from the need to frame its impact as precisely as possible in the context of the enterprise. It is the possible effects of change – these are broken down later in the book into opportunities and risks – that are of special interest. This represents the challenge and difficulty associated with our efforts to observe the enterprise's environment: from the point of view of the enterprise, observation of the environment is necessarily a compromise between a broad, but superficial investigation of a subject area and a deep, but narrow investigation (Figure 36).

Tips for Effective Environment Observation

- Observing the enterprise's environment is a basic task. It enables one to secure a proper orientation with respect to one's branch and the world in general.

  Strategic considerations and decisions are largely based on the information generated by observation. We should therefore not underestimate the significance of such activities. However, given that they are indeed neglected by many enterprises (i.e. those that implement no measures or only sporadic and haphazard measures), it warrants pointing out that the implementation of a fixed, institutional, systematic, and continuous program will help to ensure that the issue of the future is not forgotten on account of the demands of daily operations.

- It always makes sense to work from the general to the specific, i.e. in order to avoid research efforts that are too focused and that fail to account for a lion's share of the relevant information, including important novelties.

- No state of information with respect to a particular subject or problem qualifies as complete.

- However, a state of information that is relatively full will better help one to arrive at an understanding of a situation, to detect connections and to draw intelligent conclusions.

- An assessment of information during the detection and gathering stage entails a certain preliminary filtering. Evaluation only makes sense after all of the relevant information is available for viewing (Chapter 3).

- One should never allow the question "What has changed or is changing in the enterprise's environment?" to be transformed into the question "What arguments are available to support the conclusion that we do not have to change."

- Diversity is crucial. Diversity means the availability of various arguments and points of view.

- Security in discourse on a particular subject can only be achieved by understanding other perspectives.

2.5 The Future of Television (I)

In the interest of shoring up our findings so far, let us consider "the future of television" as an example. The entire development of the entertainment and media industry is characterized by uncertainty, a turbulent environment, dynamic markets and innovative technologies. The example of change in the music industry presented in Chapter 1 (Dilemma of the Underestimated Future) offers a good initial impression of the dramatic changes that could be triggered.

The use of the present example is geared to achieving three aims:

- To illustrate the ideas and concepts presented so far

- To continue to develop the subject of our inquiry by starting with an incomprehensible compilation of information and proceeding to the point of making a strategic decision and establishing a plan for action

- To substantively illustrate the processing of a particular subject of interest, i.e. especially for broadcasters, consumers, technology suppliers, producers, etc.

Figure 37 offers an overview of the development of our subject.

This investigation – which basically works for any topic and any region – is to provide a general assessment of possible developments. We begin with the general question, "What will television look like in the future?" The broad scope of our inquiry gives us a lot

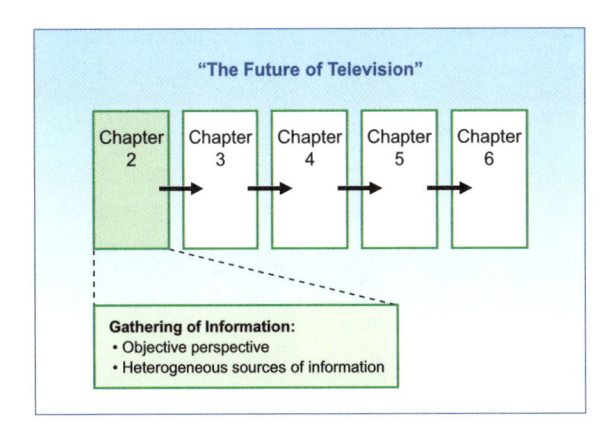

Figure 37 Research project "The Future of Television": the first step is to gather information

room for maneuver and allows us to look at the matter from various points of view. The subject of our investigation can be defined as follows:

Subject: "The Future of Television"

- Focus: Entertainment industry/media industry
- Region: Germany/Europe
- Timeframe: Up to 2020

The first goal is to generate a structured overview of the situation – a situation characterized by much uncertainty and exposed to many different sources of influence – out of a staggering amount of available information (Chapter 2 and Chapter 3). This overview will then be used to develop plausible views of the future in the form of various scenarios (Chapter 4). Finally, the derivation and implementation of a strategy will be discussed (Chapter 5 and Chapter 6).

The present chapter is concerned with the task of gathering information on the subject from as many different sources as possible. In approaching this task, the focus is on maintaining a high degree of both objectivity and diversity. Preconceptions ("That won't work!" "Never!" "That sounds exciting!") are to be avoided as far as possible and a broad array of sources are to be considered so as to secure a variety of perspectives and the insight that comes with doing so. The evaluation will be carried out after we have established an overview of the available material.

Table 10 contains a compilation of the 22 different sources of information used. Separate lines were reserved in the table for each source, with each line containing a space for the following categories: "information source," "core statements," "evidence and signals," and "references and remarks."

The task of gathering of information here is taken an important step towards compression in that the core statements and findings have been abstracted. The table serves as a reference guide. The big picture takes shape while the information is being gathered

2.5 The Future of Television (I)

Table 10 Information Gathered on the Future of Television

No.	Information Source	Core Statements	Evidence and Signals	References and Remarks
1	Magazine: Technology Review Article: Gregor Honsel, "Unrestricted Viewing" Article: Wolfgang Blau, "I-TV on the Air" September/2006	New means of transmission • Market researchers suggest that IPTV (internet protocol television) offers consumers no significant price advantages. • Projections indicate 1.3 million IPTV connections by 2010 (comparison: 20 million households currently outfitted for cable). IPTV startups such as ClickTV offer functions that boost the information and entertainment value of a TV program.	• The conventional means of transmission will sooner or later be replaced by innovative possibilities of TV reception. • It is questionable whether IPTV (as a niche offer) will cause a TV revolution.	
2	Online document: B.A.T Recreation Research Institute, Opaschowski: "Germany 2010 – Scientific Predictions Concerning the Future of Our Society," Hamburg 2001	Trends in TV viewer behavior • Owing to their limited time budgets, media consumers demand a more compact presentation of information: "Where," "What?" and "Why?" • TV viewers want to be entertained while they concern themselves with other things. • "Experience more at the same time" is becoming a paradigm of TV viewing. There is simply no time for patient and reflective broadcasts. Television Program Development • As a consequence of changes in the recreational habits of viewers, TV programs are becoming ever shorter. • More emphasis is being placed on the visual framework of programs than on their content and value as sources of information. • The entertainment value of programs is gaining in significance.	• The entertainment value of watching television is becoming increasingly important for TV viewers. • Watching television is developing into a form of unconscious consumption (television as a passive medium). • Event culture is displacing the knowledge culture.	• "The skyrocketing number of different entertainment programs is undercutting the value of any given program." • "Afternoon programs in particular have the status of fast-food TV." • "There is no idle time anymore." On the subject of television as a background medium: "Ever fewer people are actually watching while the television is on in German households. Television has become a secondary focus for two-thirds of the population. The overwhelming majority of viewers turns away from the screen to attend to other things: reading, eating, ironing, conversing, and talking on the telephone with friends."
3	Online document: Matthias Kremp, "The Future of Television" Spiegel Online, www.spiegel.de August 29, 2006	Technological Innovation and Television • The trend among consumers is towards bigger displays. • The market research company Display Search forecasts that almost half of all television sets sold in the year 2010 will have a screen size of at least 37 inches (94 cm). • Owing to increased capacity and the rapid expansion of production facilities, LCD technology is on the rise and is soon expected to drop in price to the level of plasma technology (i.e. for screen sizes larger than 42 inches) • Owing to the high costs involved, the transition to HDTV programs is expected to proceed slowly.	• The new display technology can be regarded as a driver of the new infotainment society.	
4	Online document: nanoVision, "Your Question Addressed to the Future"	Visions on the Future of Television • 2010: Multifunctional technologies will offer users a diverse range of options: ordering videos, chatting, telephoning, shopping, etc. • 2025: Consumers will be able to choose from hundreds of pay-TV channels and specialty broadcasters.	• The TV landscape is becoming more fragmented and differentiated.	"The living room is turning into a command and control center. Internet and television have tied the media knot for life."

Table 10 Information Gathered on the Future of Television *(continued)*

No.	Information Source	Core Statements	Evidence and Signals	References and Remarks
5	Online document: Holger Dambeck: "Television is Dead" Spiegel Online, September 1, 2006	• Suppliers are outcompeting one another when it comes to ever new TV standards and means of transmission • Broadcasting technologies are becoming ever more complex and sophisticated. This is leading to higher costs for consumers and uncertainty. • Having been replaced by Internet and computer games, television viewing among younger consumers is on the decline.	• The complexity of the technologies could lead to consumer rejection. • In light of changed media behavior, classical TV viewing could be replaced in the long run by computer and Internet activities.	"Yes, what we are facing is a case of TV chaos." "And if those in the young generation retain their habits as they grow older – to let's say 50% – and continue at the age of 30 or 40 to show a preference for the computer game console and the Internet over television, then television is dead."
6	Online document: Brigitte Baetz, "The Future of Television: What is Made Possible by Digitalization" Spiegel Online, July 29, 2006	• Triple-play arrangements (Internet, telephone, television) are associated with high costs for consumers.	• The possibilities of TV broadcasting are becoming ever more complex and expensive for consumers.	"The television of the future might resemble a newspaper kiosk, with hundreds of different and individually payable offers – and even accessible from everywhere."
7	GfK study on entertainment electronics markets in Western Europe August 31, 2006	• In the first six months, consumers paid an average of € 676 (GBP 450, USD 1014) per TV set (25% more than in the previous year).	This consumer behavior is reflective of the trend to higher quality products.	
8	Interview with ZDF director Markus Schächter: "Triple Play Shifts Market Weighting" March 3, 2006	• The digital antenna television (DVB-T), cell phone TV and HDTV are among the most important developments in television. • Private broadcasting is increasingly becoming a matter of pay TV. • The basic encryption of advertisement-financed channels would result in a monthly digital flat rate.	It is not at all clear whether television viewers will be prepared in the future to pay fees for encrypted television channels.	
9	Online document: Dr. Uwe Hasenbrink, "The Future of Television Use" Hans Bredow, Institute for Media Research at Hamburg University	• Television users see themselves confronted by an increase in the number of special-theme channels, the growing significance of pay-per-view offers and new program forms.	The development of television reflects the current societal and cultural processes of change: individualization, demographic development, increase in one-person households, and shifts in the relationship between public and private.	"Television will cease to be what it once was."
10	Book: Münchener Kreis, "2014 – the Future of Information, Communication and Media"	• The experts forecast that local stations will begin broadcasting via cable and satellite within 10 years. • The terrestrial network will be used for mobile reception. • Experts forecast that daily program schedules will be replaced by repeatable program segments broadcast parallel to one another. • Experts forecast that Internet-capable TV sets will be a self-evident feature of German households no later than 2014. • Experts anticipate that, on average, 24% of our time budgets will be accounted for by electronic communication.	• Flexible program design supports growing mobility and customized daily routines.	

Table 10 Information Gathered on the Future of Television *(continued)*

No.	Information Source	Core Statements	Evidence and Signals	References and Remarks
11	Magazine: Sales Economy No. 7 from July 1, 2006 Dirk Ziems/Thomas Ebenfeld, "The Viewers Will Determine the Future of Television"	• With respect to new technological standards, we are witnessing the emergence of an innovation drought -> The complexity of the systems involved has alienated consumers. • Technological progress will only continue when it brings a psychological benefit for consumers. • The flood of new programs runs the risk of overburdening and alienating TV viewers.	• Consumers lack a clear indication as to which developments are really going to survive in the future. • The program alone is what counts for TV viewers, no matter whether a broadcast is received by a satellite antenna or a telephone cable.	"They first want to see which of the hyped innovation developments will have established itself at the end of the day – and then they will come aboard."
12	Magazine: Media Perspectives No. 3 / 2006	• Television use and the range of television showed virtually no change in 2005 compared to the previous year.	• An indication of the slowly advancing fragmentation of television use is a result of the fact that the market share of the six leading programs dropped from 81 to 71%.	
13	Zukunftsinstitut GmbH: Dr. Eike Wenzel et al., "Medialution – from the Mass Media to Digital Individualization"	• Departure of mass media • Publishers and broadcasters must establish a cross-medial presence. • Media on offer will be media according to demand. • Stronger inclusion of situation-based needs • Ubiquitous communication and media consumption has captured users.	An uncompromising battle for the following items reigns: • Attention • Time • Money	"In the year 1988, Germans had comfortable access to 8 TV programs. Today it is 308." "The number of magazines on the market increased between 1970 and 2000 from 850 to 1,942."
14	Siemens AG, Internal Report: Ulf Pillkahn, "Voice, Data and Media Convergence," 2004	Three media platforms will develop: • Lean forward: PC and computer game consoles for interactive individual users, with an emphasis on interaction and exchange, TV (DVB) and communication (VoIP) is also possible • Lean back: TV group experiences, with an emphasis on image and sound quality (home cinema); Internet and communication is also possible • Mobile: Cell phone/laptop individual use, with an emphasis on communication; TV and Internet is also possible (UMTS/EDGE/GPRS) • Each of the three platforms will accommodate multimedia applications, while specializing on one application (Internet, television, or communication)!	See Figure 38.	Internal Report
15	Euroforum, The Conference Company	• The TV market is currently in a fundamental process of transformation and has presented the key players of the TV landscape (producers, marketers, network operators, etc.) enormous challenges.		
16	Article: Welt am Sonntag "Apple Executive Steve Jobs Breaks with Tradition" September 17, 2006	• Apple has conceived a device that enables the wireless transmission of PC contents such as music, photos and movies to the television.		

Table 10 Information Gathered on the Future of Television *(continued)*

No.	Information Source	Core Statements	Evidence and Signals	References and Remarks
17	Online document: Reinhard Mohr, "Television 2067" Spiegel Online, December 29, 2006	Three gigatrends in sight: • Bullshit factor: banality, dumbing down • Vanity effect: unbridled self-PR and self-adulation • Distinction drift: own production and niche broadcasters		"The amount of television trash will reach epic proportions."
18	Jean-Claude Bisenius; Wolf Siegert Multi Media Mobile. Mobile Services in Digital Radio and Telecommunication Networks, Analyses & Perspectives of the MABB Letters Series, 2002	• Overview of multimedia technologies, networks, structures, devices, applications • Investigation of the value-creation chain of the key players in the media landscape and entertainment market • Reference to social setting and event worlds	Competing technologies on the network and device side. New key players will enter the scene in the wake of the new mobile world; new business models and changes are possible.	
19	"Archive TV on the Verge of a Breakthrough" Future Letter 07/2004	• BBC has installed a freely accessible online archive. • The user is no longer just a consumer, but a creator. • Internet archives are made available via a central server and P2P.	Live aspect of digital production will lose significance. Archives develop into key resources.	"The television of the future will be transformed into the personalized demand medium and integrated into the info-highway."
20	"The Future of Television" Newsweek May 30th	Ironic article about the future of television	Media dependence will increase.	"As reality television becomes ubiquitous, being unknown becomes cool."
21	Manfred Spitzer: Caution Screen!	• Examination of the subject of television, video, Internet • Based on scientific findings (Spitzer is professor and medical director of the University Psychiatric Clinic in Ulm) • Consequences of excessive screen exposure: obesity, reading and attention disorders, abnormal social behavior, increased aggression and violent behavior, and immensely disturbed mental development	The effects of high rates of television viewing are immense, especially in the case of children.	
22	Online document: "Goodbye television. Hello Joost." http://www.joost.com/about.html	• Joost announcement • Like Skype, video and TV content is exchanged in P2P procedure. • Pilot project (Beta test) with test users is underway.	The manner with which we watch television will change completely. Technology and platform development will drive change.	"Joost™ is a new way to watch TV, free of the schedules and restrictions that come with traditional television. Combining the best of TV with the best of the internet, Joost™ gives you more control and freedom than ever before – control over what you watch, and freedom to watch it whenever you like."

(e.g. by reading). This is one reason why it is best to gather information on your own (unfiltered) and attempt to comprehend it on your own. **This prepares the brain for the next steps in the process, which are essentially more important than filling in the table.**

In the next chapter, I will move on to the task of editing and structuring the information.

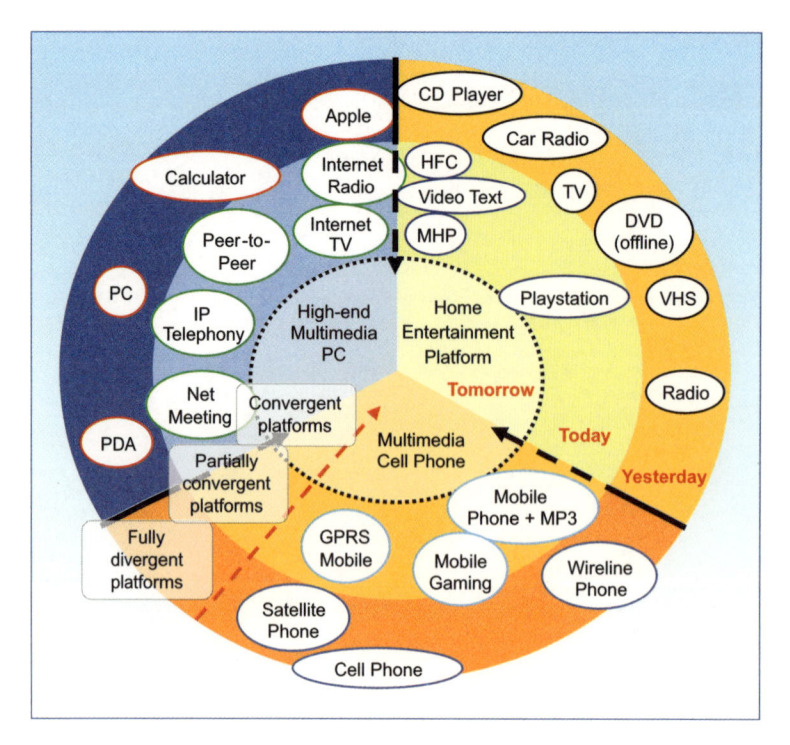

Figure 38 Media convergence: the way into the future

Chapter 3

Reflection

Sorting and Structuring Information

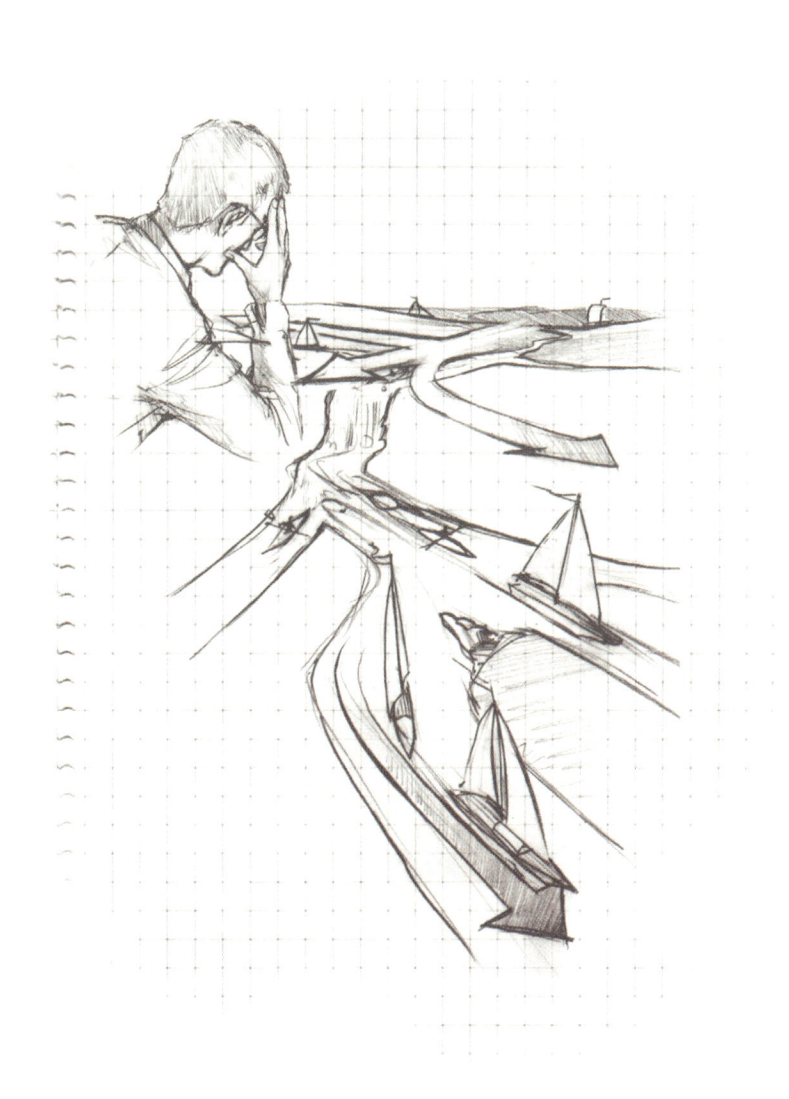

A tribe of Neanderthals has a problem and the leader of the tribe is very concerned. If things continue as they have, the tribe will sooner or later face extinction. It is a matter of offspring – ever fewer children are being born! Having convened a meeting, the leader of the tribe and his councilors are discussing ways of changing the situation. The problem is that they do not fully grasp the connection between sexual intercourse and offspring. The situation has become precarious, particularly for the leader. His position will be threatened if he fails to offer a solution. As a leader, he has gained considerable experience, and has learned to value the opinions of others. Before making a decision, he would like to know what his councilors think.

One of the councilors proclaims that the gods are displeased, and that the tribe will have to offer yet greater sacrifices. Others disagree and attribute the decline in offspring to the poor weather conditions in recent years. Yet another voices the bold theory that sexual intercourse is somehow related to pregnancy and offspring. Is this latter councilor right? The tribe's leader has learned to be careful. Rash decisions have only made situations worse in the past. Wanting to avoid this, especially in the case of a proposition that sounds almost absurd, he proposes an experiment.

An agreement is made according to which 100 pairs are to be allowed to continue to have sex over a certain period of time. The members of another group of 100 pairs are to refrain from having sex altogether during the same period. Once the specified period of time has elapsed, a meeting will be convened for the sake of evaluating the results and considering other responses.

The proposal passes narrowly. The duration of the experiment, however, remains a matter of uncertainty. One suggestion is to wait until summer, or the appearance of 6 new moons. Another suggestion is to wait for the appearance of 12 new moons, which would mean waiting until winter – a long time for a primitive people. After much heated discussion, an agreement is reached on waiting for the appearance of 10 new moons, with the experiment to begin immediately!

The months pass, and the moon appears for the tenth time. The time of reckoning has come. The following result is recorded: the sex-as-usual group shows 11 children and 5 pregnancies. The no-sex group shows 5 children and 5 pregnancies.

An atmosphere of perplexity reigns at the appointed meeting as the councilors struggle to assess the results of the experiment? From a statistical point of view, a slight correlation is evident.

Owing to the lack of a clear difference, the leader and his councilors decide not to pursue the experiment. Sexual intercourse has apparently been shown to have nothing to do with offspring. The hypothesis was not confirmed.

(Note: the idea behind this story derives from a textbook by Einhorn and Hogarth [Einhorn 1987].)

The fact that the no-sex group also shows children and pregnancies can be explained in terms of a measurement error, namely, the failure to take account of clandestine behavior – a factor that continues to vex certain studies today. We now know about the connection between sexual intercourse and offspring, and we also have the capacity to develop theories over a period of 9 months – both with respect to the past and the future. However, changes in our environment – whether they are represented as a trend or not – are often rather complex phenomena. Approaches that involve simple, more or less obvious solutions, often fail to account for the problem.

3.1 Changes in the Environment

As our daily experience reminds us, our environment is complex, chaotic and unpredictable. Material and immaterial things such as supply and demand, technologies, lifestyles, consumer behavior and political constellations are subject to rapid change. Change in one area has an impact on other areas. All areas of life are connected.

The present chapter addresses the issue of how we should manage information. Information alone does not qualify as knowledge. How can we prepare the available information in a manner that ensures that the enterprise can put it to good use, for instance, as form of support when drafting analyses and making decisions?

Our findings from the first two chapters can be summarized as follows:

- The world is subject to constant change.
- We are not able to detect everything that changes.
- Our world view is characterized by stable basic structures and less stable features.
- Changes have causes and tend to fill vacuums.

This connection can be illustrated using the iceberg model (Figure 39). The relatively stable systems and structures, such as values, traditions, consciousness, belief and religion, as well as monetary structures and evolutionary and scientific laws are located below the surface of the water, i.e. at a level that is not at first detectable for the beholder.

The parts that are subject to considerably more rapid change are located on top of this foundation, or above the surface of the water. Technological developments, consumer behavior, changes on capital markets, economic cycles, as well as factors such as lifestyle and fashion trends belong to this group. As we will see later, trends are an instrument that enables us to record, describe and evaluate current changes in this area.

The tip of the iceberg is formed by events and wildcards. These are easy to detect. They usually appear prominently in the media and they draw a great deal of attention. Nonetheless, they are unpredictable and – in cases of surprise – they may be suppressed.

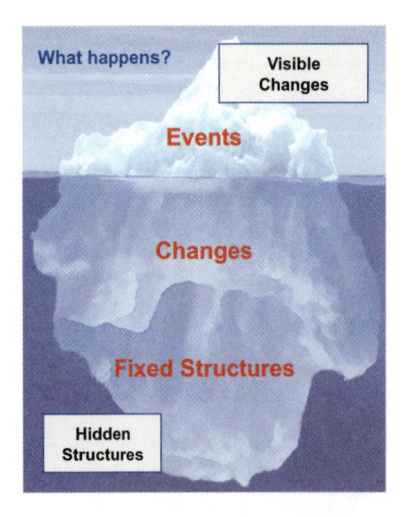

Figure 39 The iceberg model: visible events, hidden trends and structures

The fire department as an institution is a good example of active prevention, or of how one can prepare for surprises. Many environmental desasters and their consequences (New Orleans, Katrina!), which sometimes could have been avoided, show that the exercise of foresight and the implementation of knowledge are often undermined by bureaucratic hurdles, political calculations, or timidity. And even predictable weather phenomena can lead to surprises and threats. Surprises also occur quite often in the economy. Who would have thought a year ago that Airbus and EADS would be facing such a crisis? Orders galore and a real innovation – the prestigious A380 – gave cause for optimistic projections. And today? A crash of equally surprising and unusual character. Even if some might claim to have seen the Airbus disaster coming, there has been no shortage of absolutely unpredictable events, including terrorist attacks, volcanic eruptions, epidemics, and the collapse of Enron in 2001.

Table 11 offers a list of future scenarios whose emergence depends on four categories of uncertainty. We can see a continual shift from the surprise-free future to a future of numerous significant changes. Uncertainty arises as a result of highly dynamic events and a large number of innovations. The high degree of interconnection and the causal dependencies make it increasingly more difficult to clearly assign a situation to one of the four proposed segments.

Table 12 shows a similar breakdown – although with a focus on the environment – proposed by Ansoff and McDonnell. [Ansoff 1990] They assume that the environment will change more dramatically in the future than it did in the past. The possibilities range from recurring changes (degree of turbulence: 1) to surprising changes (degree of turbulence: 5).

How are we to describe events in a turbulent environment? While the two proposed approaches to evaluating the environment (Courtney / Ansoff and McDonnell) as well as the iceberg model are very helpful when it comes to ordering circumstances that

Table 11 Four Types of Uncertainty [Courtney 1997]

	Surprise-free Future	Alternative Futures	Range of Various Futures	Uncertainty
Situation	The situation is stable and no surprises are to be expected.	A number of separate options and alternatives exist.	Uncertain situation with many factors and dependencies	Highly dynamic and complex circumstances associated with a lack of settled knowledge
Examples	Minimally dynamic societal changes (e.g. demographic aging)	Parliamentary election, technology development	Entry into emerging markets, political situation in the Middle East	New technologies and innovation trigger hype.

Table 12 Classification of Turbulence According to Ansoff and McDonnell [Ansoff 1990]

Environment turbulence	Recurring	Expanding	Changing	Unsteady	Surprising
Complexity	National, economic		Regional, technological		Global, sociopolitical
Similarity of events	Similar	Capable of extrapolation		Similar to unsteady	New and unsteady
Speed of change	Slower than reaction	Minimally slower than reaction	Similar to reaction	Minimally faster than reaction	Faster than reaction
Visibility of the future	Periodically recurring	Predictable	Forecastable	Partially forecastable	Not forecastable
Strategic assertiveness	Stable, based on precedence	Reactive, based on experience	Anticipatory, based on extrapolation	Exploratory, based on expected future	Creative, unsteady, based on creativity
Turbulence level	1 (low)	2	3	4	5 (high)

generate uncertain information, they do not go far enough. Situations seldom lend themselves to clear classification. However, we can take a step back and consider the factors and forces that lead to the situations in question.

The situations can be broken down into their elements and each element can be examined in terms of the degree of change involved and the extent to which it can be observed.

Figure 40 shows the result of transferring these criteria to a diagram, with three different situation types representing the "speed of change." These situations include an area of "stability" encompassing paradigms, constants and other elements that are subject to very little change. The other extreme is represented by chaotic circumstances about which we can do no more than speculate (events, wildcards).

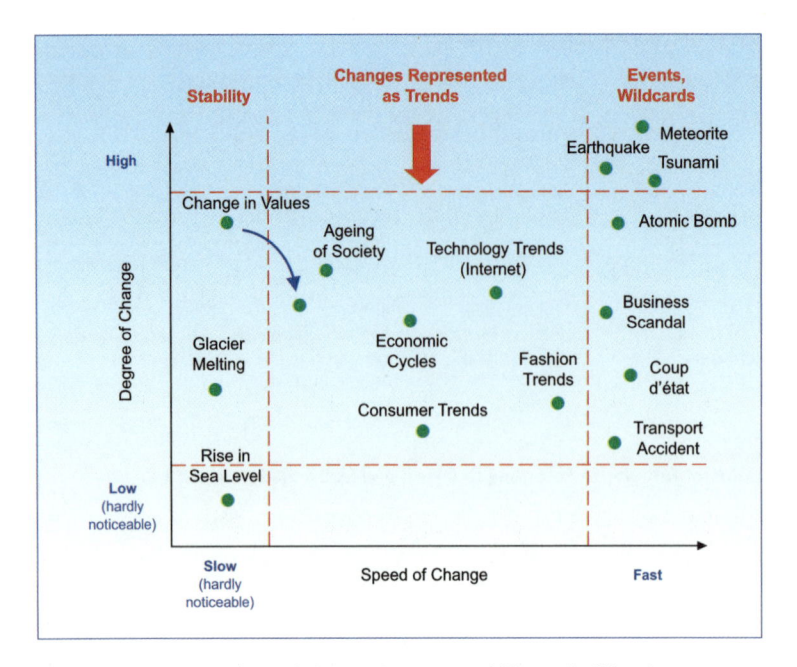

Figure 40 Trends as signs of change: between stability and wildcards

We can also imagine a situation type that is neither stable nor chaotic. Such situations are characterized by focused, continual types of change and can be represented in the form of trends. A trend can thus be regarded as an instrument or model – one of many used to describe changes – that is distinct from the methods we have considered so far.

Given that Figure 40 represents a kind of snapshot, the shift in the "value change" category is depicted using a curved arrow.

We have already demonstrated in Chapter 2 that findings in general and findings about the future in particular can differ considerably in terms of their nature and quality. Using the analogy of the divided line, Plato sought to make a distinction between the visible and the intelligible. For his part, Kant examines the nature of individual convictions. "Belief" and "knowledge" do not differ in terms of the personal degree of conviction involved, but in terms of whether the conviction qualifies as certain or can be objectively proven. It follows from this that, in certain special cases, belief can be even more subjectively reliable than knowledge [Kant 2005].

These considerations allow us to expand upon our existing understanding of the future, which, based on our discussions of the future so far, is essentially oriented towards trends and does not consider various forms of knowledge. I will presently define the various elements of the future, and thereby establish their meaning for the discussions that follow.

Definition of the Future Elements

Figure 41 shows the elements of the future in a matrix representing the criteria "knowledge spectrum" and "change spectrum." In the framework of the present general discussion, this representation largely serves the purpose of establishing a general classification of the terms and their subsequent use.

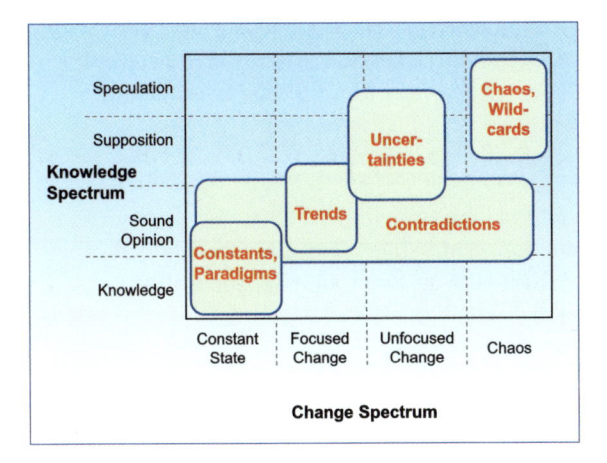

Figure 41 The elements of the future: in the spectrum of change and knowledge

Change spectrum:

- *Constant state: the area of paradigms*

    This state is characterized by virtually stable conditions, as typified by physical constants and cycles in the universe (tides, seasons).

- *Focused change: the area of trends*

    These are foreseeable (e.g. cyclic, wave-shaped or evolutionary) changes.

- *Unfocused change: the area of uncertainty*

    These are typified by economic and financial systems, or scientific discourse in the absence of clear answers.

- *Wildcards: Chaos*

    This area includes surprises that cannot be foreseen.

Knowledge spectrum:

- *Knowledge: corresponds to the state of science and is demonstrable by facts*

    For instance, the law of conservation of energy makes for a good starting point for many discussions.

- *Sound opinion: enough evidence available to make for a safe assumption*

  While there is no exhaustive explanation or proof, the evidence speaks in favor of its veracity. Moreover, it is subjectively sufficient. Example: smoking is hazardous to one's health and tends to shorten life expectancy.

- *Supposition: we can arrive at a conclusion by compiling the evidence and assumptions.*

  This represents an attempt to clear up uncertainty via a logically compelling linking of facts. Example: Assuming that the avian flu virus can be transferred to humans, pandemic circumstances may arise with an untold effect on civilization.

- *Speculation: this level is characterized by hopes, beliefs, wishes and fears.*

  We can speculate, for instance, on the long-term impact of genetic engineering on human beings and the environment. While many place their hope in a technology without side effects, there is as yet no proof that genetically modified crops are really necessary and sensible.

Table 13 offers a list of future elements. These will be explained in following chapters.

Table 13 An Overview of the Future Elements

Future Elements	Explanation	Section
Constants and paradigms	Knowledge that qualifies as certain as well as stable circumstances	3.2
Trends	Focused changes that are partially based on facts and partially based on convictions and subjective opinion	3.3
Uncertainty	Uncertainty about new phenomena and circumstances that are subject to possible developments, i.e. objects of supposition and intuition.	3.4
Contradiction	Opposing, mutually exclusive views or opinions that are possible about all stages of change.	3.5
Chaos and wildcards	While this element is not subject to calculation and can lead to sudden change, it can be subsumed under the area of speculation.	3.6

3.2 Stability – Paradigms and Assumptions

Philosophically speaking, Plato was right when he described the world as being in a state of constant change – "panta rhei" or "everything flows." From the point of view of an enterprise, however, this suggestion offers little help – in particular in the face of the avalanche of information we are confronted by on a daily basis.

We usually assume implicitly that many things in our daily lives are uniform, i.e. that they will recur in more or less the same fashion as they always have.

When it comes to analyzing the enterprise's environment, it is helpful to first call these implicit assumptions and paradigms to mind. Doing so represents a good starting point for reflections on further developments because it narrows the realm of possible changes, and thereby also reduces the magnitude of the overall task as well as the need for discourse. Examples of elements in our environment that either change very little or not at all include physical constants, natural cycles and sequences (tides, seasons) as well as paradigms. The term "paradigm" in this context refers to prevailing theoretical frameworks of scientific inquiry. According to Thomas Kuhn, paradigms remain accepted as valid until phenomena appear that cannot be satisfactorily explained by them [Kuhn 1962].

Current paradigms include, for instance, "growth will spur job creation" or "a modern IT infrastructure will lead to increased efficiency" or the belief in the information society as the beneficent successor to the industrial society.

While paradigms are firmly anchored in the current frameworks of scientific inquiry, and are thus not typically called into question, assumptions are more context specific, relating to the overall conditions, which are thought to be stable. For instance, when investigating the subject "The Future of the Automobile," one (implicit) assumption is that there will be automobiles in the future that are, in certain important respects, similar to those of today, and will therefore still warrant being referred to as automobiles. While explaining such assumptions may seem pedantic, recognizing them and being aware of them can lead to greater clarity. Moreover, in the process of analysis – which is usually marked by uncertainty – it is helpful to have fixed points of reference. Although it is certainly not the main reason why we undertake to examine the future, the discussion about the overall conditions and assumptions represents a valuable contribution.

However, it is not always possible to draw a line between assumptions and paradigms. Terminological clarity is often only given in a specific context. Detailed discussions can run aground in gray areas, given that it may be a matter of dispute whether a certain broad assumption is really a paradigm. It is advisable in cases that seem not to permit final clarification to use the opinion of the group as a point of reference, or to proceed along multiple tracks so as to avoid gridlock.

Examples of Paradigms and Constants

Physical constants: the speed of light c is constant within a given medium, electron charge e, π

Physical laws: propagation of light, gravity

Society: the notion of the family as the smallest organizational unit

Technology: miniaturization and capacity increases in the area of semiconductors are represented by Moore's Law [Moore 1967].

Economics: prices are regulated by the law of supply and demand.

Ecology: public transportation systems are more environmentally friendly than the automobile.

Politics: democracy is the most modern and advanced societal form.

While paradigms are usually assumed to provide a solid basis for inquiry, calling them into question or calling their continued validity into question is indispensable when it comes to a thorough examination of the future. On the other hand, it is important and advantageous, particularly in situations marked by uncertainty and turbulence, to get in the clear on what assumptions qualify as secure. This introduces the following crucial question: What factors qualify as secure even if the course of developments cannot be foreseen?

Paradigm Changes as Fundamental Trends

While paradigms are not necessarily true, they represent generally accepted views in a (scientific) community and imply a host of basic assumptions. In the context of daily communication, paradigms often serve as a shared implicit basis for discussion.

The term "paradigm change" generally refers to an important qualitative change in a pattern of thought. It follows that a paradigm change amounts to a radical change in a personal belief, in complex systems or in organizations. The original way of thinking about a subject or organizing something is replaced by a radically different way. Such changes are triggered by new scientific findings (e.g. Darwin's theory of evolution and the discovery of the laws of planetary motion by Johannes Kepler) or by revolutionary technologies such as the Internet. The dissemination of the associated changes proceeds according to the usual mechanisms of trend dissemination (e.g. as compellingly described by Malcolm Gladwell in his book *Tipping Point*) [Gladwell 2001].

Equipped with the notion of a paradigm change, we can now proceed to a general discussion of change.

3.3 Changes – Trends

We are confronted by uncertainty when we attempt to look into the future. As illustrated in Figure 10 in Chapter 1, our view of the future depends on the current state of our knowledge. The establishment of various elements of the future (cf. Figure 41) encompasses an area of trends that is represented in the transition between "sound opinion" and "supposition."

Trends

What are trends?

Although there are dozens of possible definitions, the term "trend" in the present context is used to refer explicitly to a kind of instrument. The term is commonly used today to refer to something that is "in" or to describe a certain direction in which things seem to be going. The "something" or the "things" are usually matters of current taste or types of consumer behavior. Here, the term "trend" refers generally to the temporally measurable course of a certain development in a certain direction.

When we look in the dictionary, we find the following definition of the term "trend": "... the general movement in the course of time of a statistically detectable change. Encompasses long and longer periods of time, always represents a cross section and is thus limited in terms of its validity. With respect to the past, a trend possesses no more than a certain ascertainment value. It cannot be extended into the future on account of the unpredictability of external factors." [Meyers 2003]

This definition is not a sufficient description of the term "trend" as an instrument. As illustrated in Figure 42, we can think of a trend as a change over a period of time. In retrospect, statistically correlated data yield a trend and can be examined. Using these recorded data as a basis, we can generate hypotheses about the future while making sure to account for any inherent conditions and other assumptions. This naturally includes uncertainty about the exact course of development, and thus presupposes a range of possible developments.

In addition to these more or less general definitions of the term "trend," we can also find definitions that are typical for individual scientific disciplines, although even here we do not necessarily find uniform usage. For instance, in economics and other social sciences, trends represent changes in the moral and behavioral fabric of society. Trends in the area of market research refer to changes and developments in consumer and user behavior. It is precisely here that an independent area of scientific inquiry has emerged, namely, trend research.

A note of caution is warranted at this juncture. For just as in the case of future studies, attempts to establish a scientific basis for the methods used in the area of trend research are often condemned to fail, for instance, when they involve no more than the extrapolation of observed changes. "Strictly speaking, trends amount to nothing more than certain observations that are new enough or sensational enough to grab

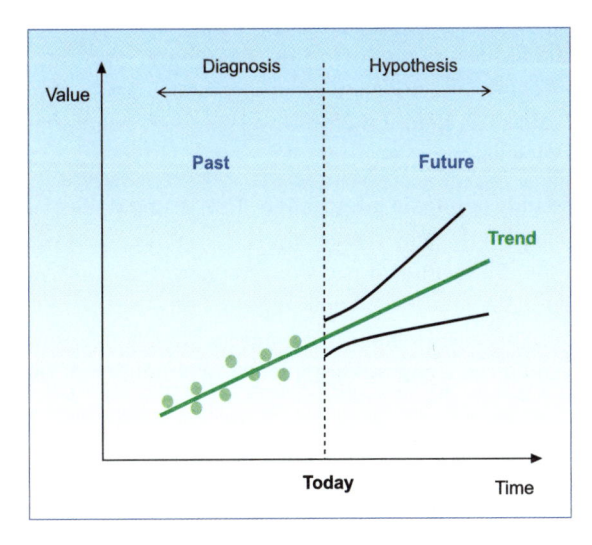

Figure 42 Trends: movement of statistically detectable changes in the course of time

3.3 Changes – Trends

attention." [Rust 2002] While such observations may appear plausible from case to case, and may admirably simplify our view of things, they do not take us where we want to go in our present inquiry. In light of the temptation to skew information as well as the many stumbling blocks along the way to an accurate interpretation of information, it warrants recalling a point we have already addressed:

When seeking to come up with verifiable, solid and reproducible analyses, it is crucial to work carefully across the entire process. This entails taking a neutral approach to information, seeking to eliminate doubts and avoiding preconceptions.

Trends are also ideally suited to the deliberate skewing or concealing of information. As mentioned above, it has become very common to speak of trends in the absence of any real knowledge. One postulates a trend on the assumption that "things will somehow continue to develop in roughly the same direction." "The current trend is towards eLearning!" we read in an Internet publication. "Really?" we may be inclined to ask ourselves. But how does this trend manifest itself? We read in a book, "The trend among managers is towards a reliance on basic instincts." Is that one right, too, or is it no more a momentarily perceived change? Even our serious daily economic journals tend to be fast and loose when it comes to the word trend. This makes clear, however, that trends are not the same as facts. Trends are constructions that are based on the assumptions held by those announcing them and those hearing them. This also makes it so difficult to deal with them and underscores the importance of a capacity to call them into question! We do not prove the existence of a trend merely in virtue of claiming its existence.

Classifying Trends

Owing to the implied novelty or news value, the term "trend" is used all too readily in many different contexts. It is self-referential, i.e. trends are the latest trend. The use of the term is sometimes so imprecise that we could essentially label any given event in the present a trend without eliciting any sort of objection. Regrettably, this rampant postulating of trends does not contribute to clarity. For this reason, I now turn to taxonomy of trend phenomena (Table 14), before then moving on to an attempt to establish a helpful classification of trends.

Trends consist of facts, figures and documentable information. They also consist of a projection into the future that is characterized by visions, personal opinions, suppositions, wishes and pure speculation. The points of transition remain very much in flux and represent a breeding ground for superficial knowledge and misconceptions, as well as for deliberate speculation and manipulation. Trends can be very different in nature, difficult to grasp and difficult to compare owing a lack of suitable criteria for doing so.

Arriving at a sound description and demarcation of trends will provide a common understanding of their nature and help us to use them constructively. In what follows, I make a number of proposals as to how we can record and structure the complex and heterogeneous information that is available about trends so as to secure a

Table 14 Taxonomy of Trend Phenomena

	Explanation	Example
Signal	Information and news that could trigger significant change	"Baby Boom in Hamburg" (newspaper headline)
Trend	Change that can be observed and that permits one to suppose its continuation over time	Fewer children among the college-educated
Emerging trend	Emerging trend whose further course is difficult to foresee	Men accept more responsibility in matters of family planning
Microtrend	Small changes seen in specific regions, or hardly noticeable changes	Increase in the number of one-child families leads to behavioral changes at a societal level
Megatrend	Large, profound and sustained changes	Aging populations
Metatrend	Compilation of trends and/or megatrends	Demographic change
Pseudotrend	A phenomenon is described as a trend although it is not a trend	Companies increase their commitment to families (as a matter of fact, we face a lack of daycare options in many countries)
Trend breach	A development that has been characterized as a trend is suddenly interrupted	Slump in the birth rate caused by the pill
Key trend	Trends that are judged to be especially important	Marketing focus shifts to more mature consumers

deeper analysis and the possibility of arriving at a an evaluation of trends that is differentiated and that permits comparison. I first propose a substantive distinction before moving on to a classification according to trend-specific criteria.

Trends can be classified according to a broad array of criteria, including content, dynamic development, form, dissemination, strength, influence, predictability, projection, risk, etc. I have selected a number of these criteria for further consideration.

Following the STEEPV segmentation (cf. Chapter 2), a substantive demarcation of trends for the macro environment might look as follows:

S	Society	Societal trends
T	Technology	Technological trends
E	Economy	Economic trends
E	Ecology	Environmental trends
P	Politics	Political trends
V	Values	Value trends

- *Societal trends*

    The first signs of new trends can be found primarily in societal groups that are exposed to the conflicts between our notion of traditional values and societal realities (a sense of family versus rugged individualism).

    Example: the aging of society

- *Technological trends*

    These are essentially a matter of new technologies that could generate new consumer needs or replace existing technologies. The evaluation of several competing technologies is significant in this connection:

    – Which technology will establish itself on the market?

    – Do any lobby groups, commissions, syndicates or industry associations support specific technologies?

    Examples: polymer electronics as an inexpensive alternative to silicon; LED as a new kind of light technology

- *Economic trends*

    Such trends essentially arise via changes in types of business processes and value-creation chains. These are often a matter of new business models or changed perspectives with regard to enterprise processes or goals.

    Examples: eBusiness, outsourcing, off-shoring, shareholder-value orientation

- *Environmental trends*

    These encompass changes in nature and the environment.

    Example: global warming and climate change

- *Political trends*

    Political decisions and elections have an impact on lawmaking and lead to extensive change.

    Example: implementation of stricter security measures

- *Value trends*

    Shifting societal values and private values have a profound impact on the shaping of societies.

    Example: individualism leads to a society of singles

The following trends can be defined for the micro environment:

- *Market trends*

    Markets and segments emerge on the basis of actual and projectable demand for applications and products. Trends are generally recorded via extrapolation from current and historical values.

    Example: increasing demand for flat-panel displays

- *Consumer trends*

    These trends are related to the following questions:
    - Are consumer structures changing?
    - Are consumer interests undergoing a shift?
    - What needs are arising and how can these be accounted for in the form of concrete products?
    - Can consumers be represented in segments?

    Example: trend towards online shopping

- *Product trends*

    Products change in more ways than in terms of their design and function. Other criteria that play a role in purchasing decisions and that are subject to change include product cycles, security requirements, size, weight, conditions of warranty and quality.

    Example: increasing share of diesel-powered vehicles

- *Supplier trends*

    Improvements in value creation within an enterprise also lead to new forms of cooperation with suppliers.

    Example: just-in-time delivery, personal leasing and outsourcing

- *Competition trends*

    Changes in the nature of competition can also be characterized using trends.

    Example: increased competition as a result of new market participants, consolidation

Classification of Trends in Time

As outlined in Chapter 2, changes and trends are linked to one another. Patterns of human migration, for instance, have an impact on climate and the environment. The reaction times of the various "systems" affected are very different in this regard. Environmental and societal trends are generally longer than those of other systems, while technology, product and application trends tend to be more dynamic, a fact owing to the interaction between drivers and market participants. Just as between dynamic and sluggish processes, a distinction can be drawn between dynamic and sluggish trends. Megatrends distinguish themselves in terms of their longevity (e.g. the melting of glaciers) and emerging trends in terms of their ephemeral or indeterminate lifecycles (e.g. Tamagochi and kick boards).

Classification of Trends According to Strength

Trend strength is usually analyzed in terms of dissemination and the potential to trigger change. A lack of strength indicators, however, can make it very difficult to arrive at an estimate. For instance, an emerging trend could develop into a key trend or promptly disappear as a pseudo trend.

If we assume, for instance, that the need to transmit increasing volumes of data has led to a trend towards technology offering greater bandwidth (Trend 1), and if we assume further that the proliferation of broadcast services is also a trend (Trend 2), we will see that the two trends exhibit different degrees of strength. Trend 1 encompasses Internet users around the world, while Trend 2 encompasses only the users of digital broadcast services.

In the case of self-contained or quantifiable trends, the number of users, and development with respect to this number, may qualify as a good indicator of trend strength.

In the case of trends that are not immediately quantifiable (e.g. increasing individualism), it becomes necessary to identify specific indicators. Increasing individualism might be indicated by a more diverse offer of vehicle types, ranging from the traditional economy, middle and luxury class vehicles to models such as vans, convertibles and SUVs. In contrast, the strength of the trend can only be estimated, and is based on observations and information about the trend's manifestation.

The Formal Structure of Trends

All changes have their causes. The change itself is manifested in the trend. As our understanding of a trend improves (i.e. our knowledge of its background, driving forces, and anatomy), so too will our capacity to make predictions about its further development (Figure 43).

Trends are generally represented in terms of a certain reference or benchmark. For instance, the trend "increased dietary awareness in the German population" can be represented using the "sales of organic products" as a reference.

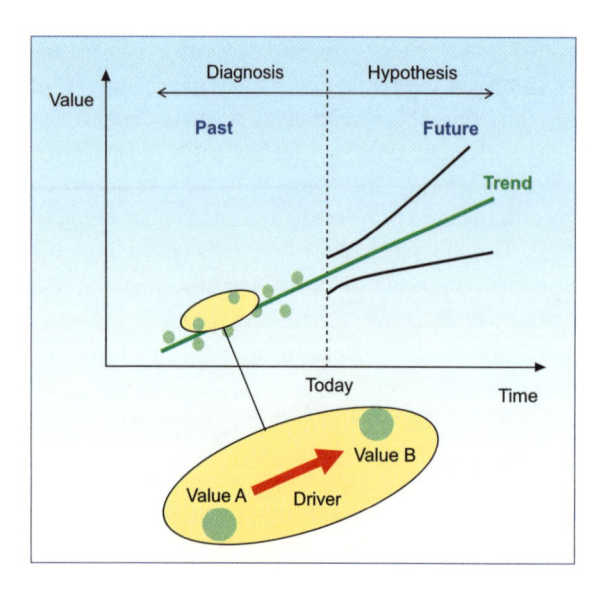

Figure 43 Trend drivers: the effects of drivers

In order to understand a trend one is required to investigate its causes. What is driving the trend, i.e. the change? Drivers for the present example include the following:

- Mistrust directed towards the food industry
- Promotion of regional organic food producers
- Tainted meat scandals
- Other scandals in the food processing and packaging industry
- Availability of better information
- Lifestyle and "Zeitgeist"

Here, we could continue to research the causes (referred to as "forces") of each one of these drivers. The driver of mistrust directed towards the food industry, for instance, arises in connection with the following forces:

- The aim of the food corporations is to maximize profit.
- Higher degrees of industrialization lead to a further compromising of foodstuffs in the form of additives.
- The mechanisms of food quality control are inadequate.

As shown in the example, drivers (level 1 in the hierarchy) and forces (level 2 in the hierarchy) can be identified for each change that is manifested in the form of a trend and that can be represented using a reference or benchmark. Trends can thus be seen as being carried by drivers and forces. These determine the direction and strength of trends. Counter forces also exist (or emerge in the course of trend development) that have the effect of weakening or even blocking trends.

Trends and Countertrends

Most trends generate countertrends or other reactions. For instance, increased globalization has led to an array of counter initiatives. Regionalization is a countertrend to globalization. Its proponents seek to demonstrate that we can pursue goals other than profit maximization and that we can avoid a situation in which work and resources decline worldwide (lower prices) while markets increase (high profits) by instead focusing on the achievement of sustainable economies.

In light of the fact that one can influence development by supporting driving forces and hindering counter forces (or vice versa) it is very important to consider both trends and countertrends in the context of devising enterprise strategy.

In the case of the trend towards increased dietary awareness in Germany, we can also make out the countertrend of "discount food stores" by drawing upon statistics showing increased food sales in the lowest price segment as a reference.

Changes are characterized by driving and inhibiting forces. If certain forces prevail (e.g. in the case of market trends) and a critical mass has been achieved, then certain trends will be carried by their momentum. One example of this is the introduction of

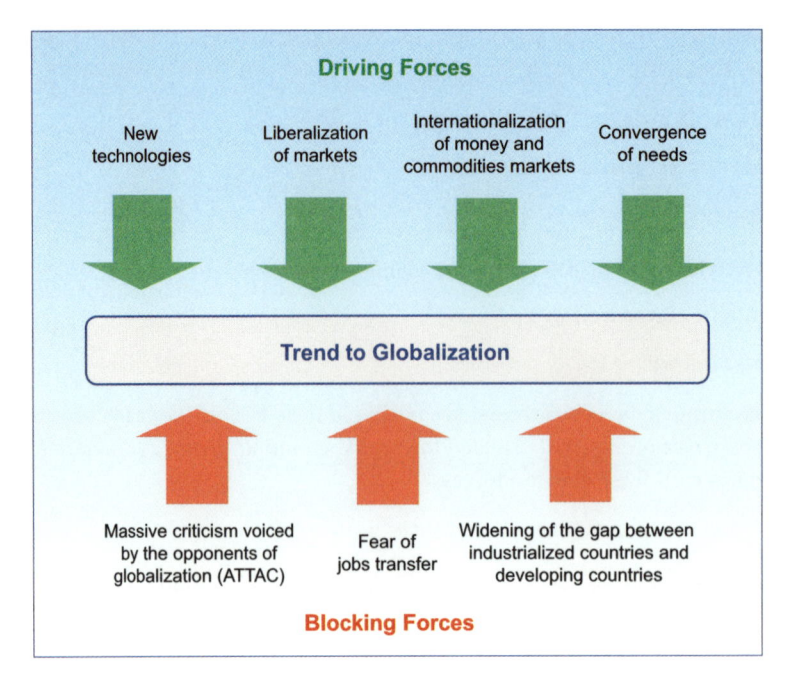

Figure 44 Force field: driving and inhibiting forces in the case of globalization

new product generations. The force-field diagram shown in Figure 44 also offers a good illustration.

The Substantive Structure of Trends

It is not always possible to precisely demarcate and graphically represent a trend as an expression of a change. On the contrary, trends are in fact components in networks of interrelated trends. When it comes to understanding a trend, it can therefore be very helpful to know its position in the overall network.

Figure 45 offers an illustration of the structure of the trend towards the exhaustive penetration of technology into all areas of life. The increasing drive towards miniaturization, the increase in network density and digitalization, as well as increasing complexity, contribute to the propagation and strengthening of the trend. For its part, miniaturization is also being driven by other forces. This interrelatedness can be illustrated in dependency diagrams that make an important contribution to an understanding of the shape and properties of trends.

The Emergence and Propagation of Trends

All of those who regard themselves as "trendsetters" are well aware of just how hard it is to generate a trend.

In his book, *The Tipping Point*, Malcolm Gladwell [Gladwell 2000] offers a very compelling description of how trends emerge, how they are influenced and how they

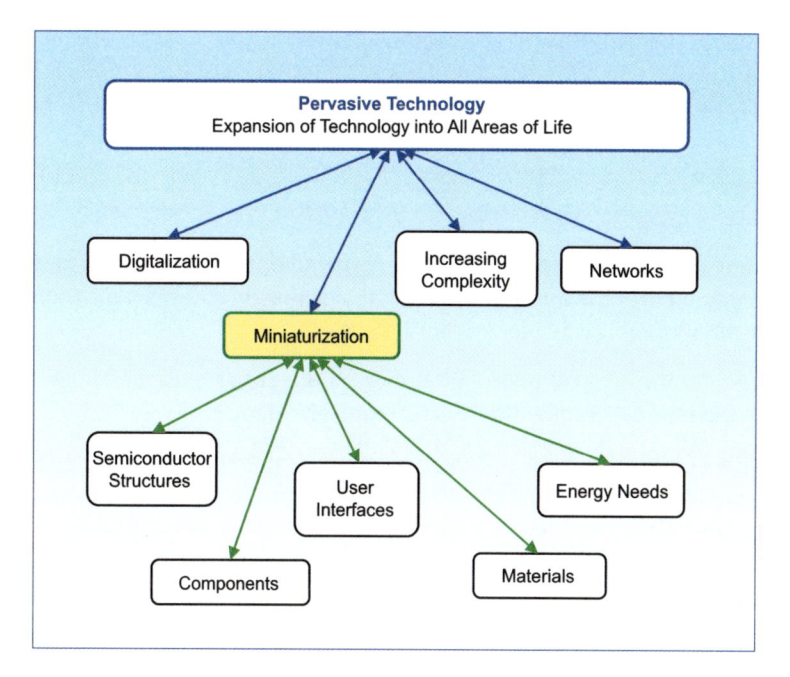

Figure 45 Linking of trends: a high degree of interaction

spread. In addition to providing an array of interesting examples, Gladwell makes an important observation when he suggests that the task of propagating information is primarily a social problem. He refers to it as the "law of the few." There are a few who are better able to compellingly and convincingly present information in a manner that leads to a spark and ensures broader dissemination. The media play an equally important role. Figure 46 offers an illustration of how the number of media reports about a subject leads to reactions at organizational and political levels.

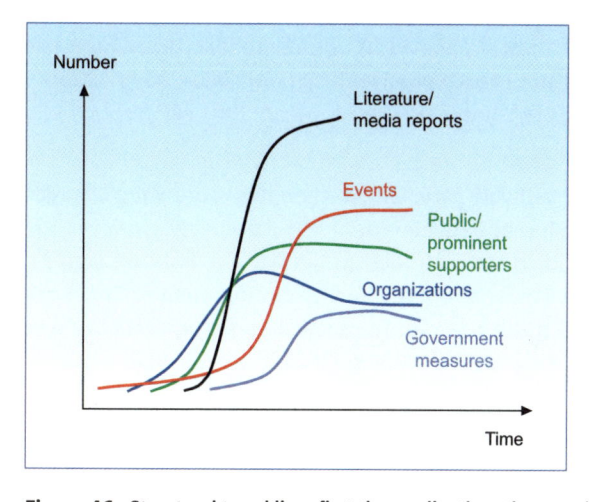

Figure 46 Structural trend line: first the media, then the reactions [Molitor 1979]

3.3 Changes – Trends

Excluding the trends directly influenced by human beings, we can assume that the laws of nature also apply to the emergence and spread of trends. Global warming, for instance, can be traced to high levels of greenhouse gases, and therefore also to human beings.

Projecting Trends

The form of a trend is reflected in the course of its development. We can gain an idea of the course of a trend over time by representing its functional values in a diagram (Figure 47). The reference is applied to the coordinates.

If the trends are referenced to volumes and numerical quantities (e.g. market and product trends), then the task is quantitative and relatively simple.

The situation is different in the case of value and political trends. How does an increased awareness of quality manifest itself? And satisfaction? What trend form can be used to best represent the often cited trend towards increased terrorist activity? Is it really a trend, or just an increasing fear of terror in the population? But how does this fear manifest itself?

Clarity with respect to the formulation and referencing of trends is crucial to their validity. Many "weak" trends can only be ascertained in the context of a representative survey. The efforts involved, however, are almost always justified. In case of doubt, one should operate on the assumption that less is more.

The obvious facts that we only have data concerning the previous development of a trend, and we can merely estimate its future development at best, makes the task even more difficult.

We humans tend to look for easy solutions to complex problems. This is why we often assume, when confronted with problems, that the development seen in the past will repeat itself in the present (i.e. by extrapolation). Here, we forget that the past development represents only one of many possible developments, and that an unchanging development is, in point of fact, less likely owing to complex and dynamic economic and market structures. This is amply supported by the many inaccurate forecasts made by market analysts! The future course of a trend can only be reliably extrapolated in the case of self-contained and simple problems. We are thus advised to take a systematic approach.

The form of a trend can only be positively ascertained when it is over (when changes cease to appear and a stable state has been achieved) or retrospectively. However, the very purpose of considering trends centers on their projection, i.e. forecasting their future course. The assumptions we make about the further development of trends are supposed to be a core element of trend analysis. In practice, however, there is a tendency to place a greatest emphasis on the reasons supplied for the conclusion that we have indeed identified a trend.

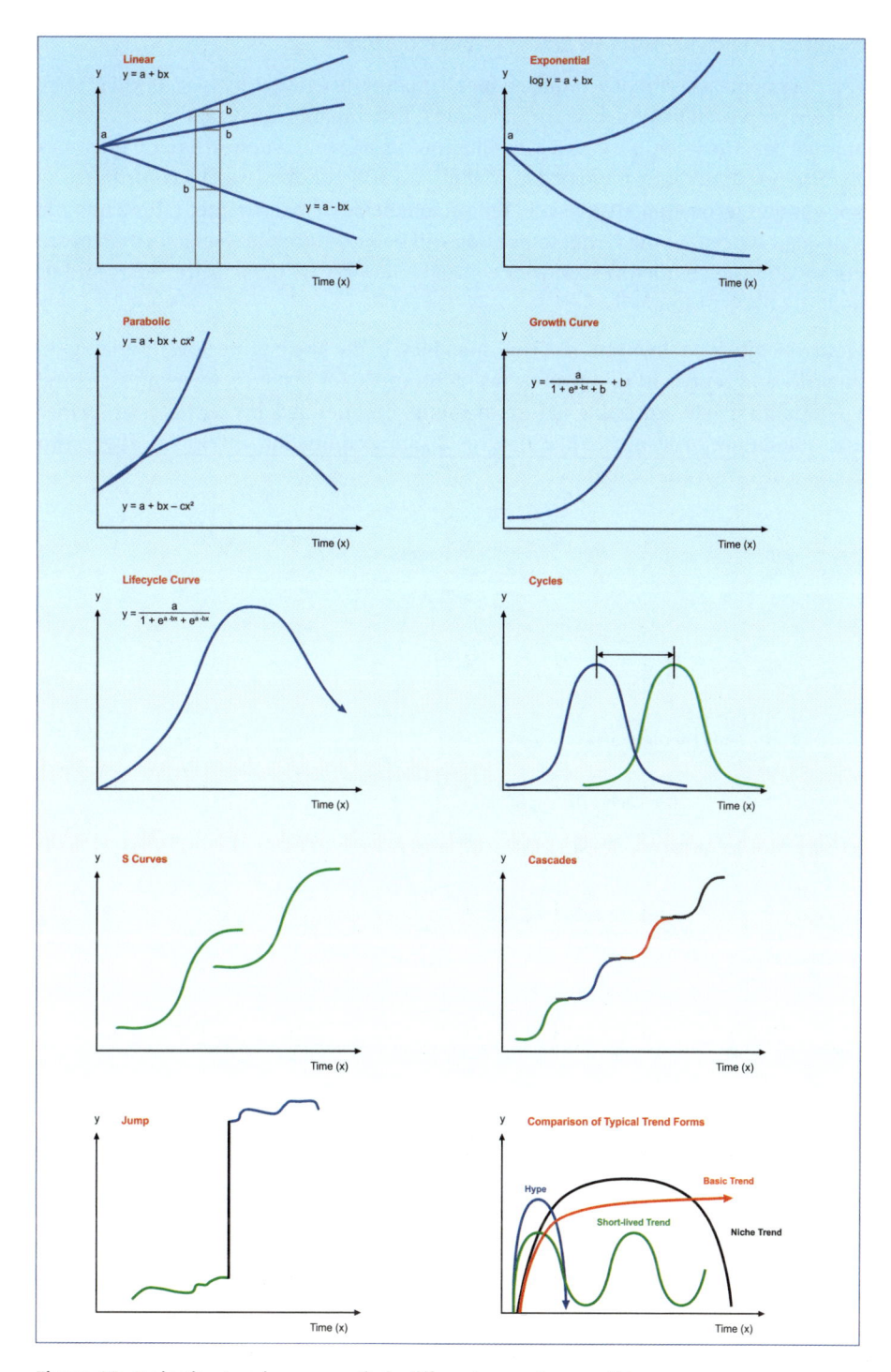

Figure 47 Projecting trends: many entirely different curves are possible

3.3 Changes – Trends

Qualitative and Quantitative Analyses and Projections

A system of measurement is required for all quantitative investigations. It will first be necessary to establish the relevant measures, benchmarks, totals and measurement approaches. However, if we recall the illustration shown in Figure 10 in Chapter 1 as we attempt to account for new knowledge, we will see that we are confronted by notions and terms that are new and not yet amenable to measurement. If we assume that eight percent of the technologies that will be introduced in the next 10 years are not yet known – neither by name nor concept – how are we to measure and record or quantify these technologies?

Figure 48 offers an illustration of this quandary. In the present, we usually attempt to quantify and represent things in terms of numbers, for instance, by using statistics. The quantitatively accessible nature of things declines steadily as we gaze further into the future. The qualitative nature of our examination increases. These two approaches are complementary!

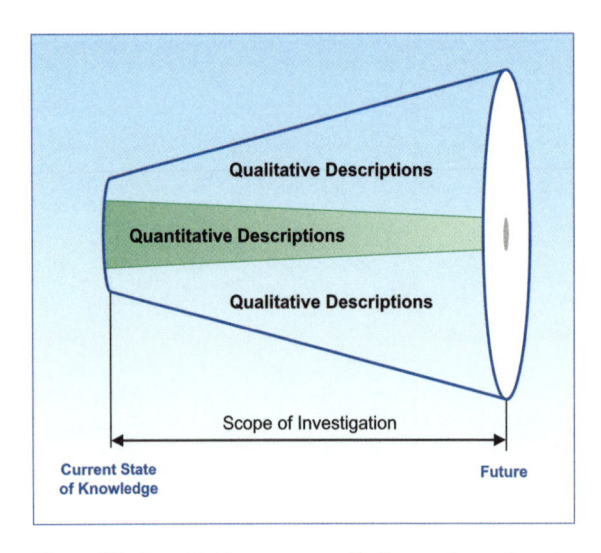

Figure 48 Quantitative versus qualitative analyses: time-dependent projection

Quantitative methods are usually based on economic models that determine future target figures as precisely as possible. Based on the methods of the hard sciences, they also convey the impression that the forecasts themselves are precise, which can lead to inaccurate interpretations. On the other hand, it is entirely legitimate to question the degree to which exact measurements about the future are helpful for our own endeavors in light of the fact that we have to regard the assumptions as subject to change. Figure 49, for instance, shows a projection – with relatively precise figures – of population development in Germany up to the year 2160. But what is the value of such a projection when it is not even certain that Germany will exist (in its present form) in 150 years? After all, the German Empire was founded less than 150 years ago – in the year 1871!

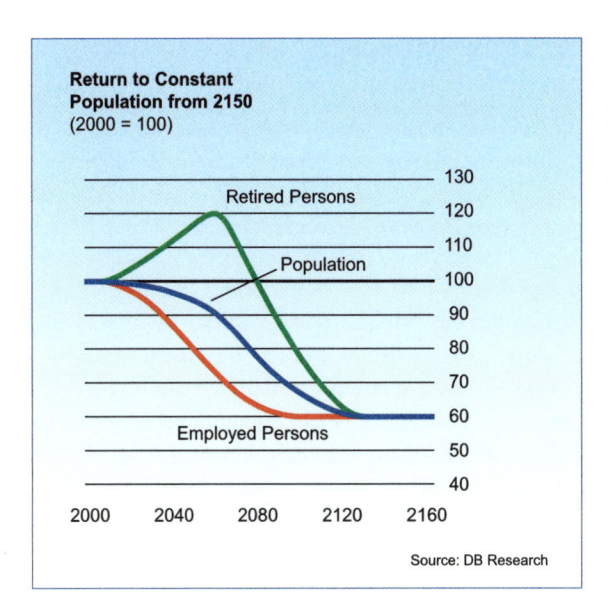

Figure 49 Quantitative Forecasts: population development in Germany until the year 2160 [Source: DB-Research]

This is why only qualitative investigations come into question for longer term projections.

As illustrated in Figure 50, the degree of forecast accuracy decreases dramatically and that of forecast inaccuracy increases dramatically as the scope of our projections extends further into the future. The initial predetermined nature of forecasts can be ascertained using causal connections and derivable changes. Owing to the sometimes nebulous link between trends and connections associated with change, second,

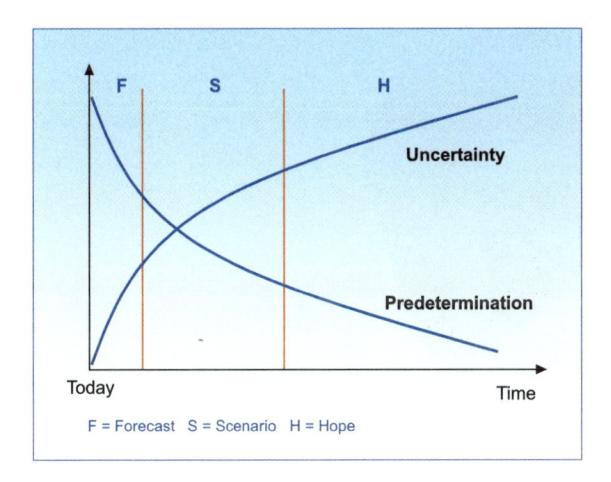

Figure 50 Uncertainty and prior determination: a pair of scissors [Heijden 2005]

3.3 Changes – Trends

third and fourth-order dependencies remain unclear and are usually not considered in examinations of development.

Qualitative descriptions of changes and trends (e.g. increasing, skyrocketing, decreasing, stable, changing, and alternating) are sufficient for long-term projections and usually more serious.

Trend Breaches

In addition to their simple, uninterrupted continuation, skips and breaches in the development of trends are significant. In contrast to trends that show continual development, trend breaches often signify radical change and offer both opportunities and risks. This is why every trend or hypothesis is to be examined in terms of whether it harbors potential for abrupt change (jump function, Figure 47).

Describing and Representing Trends

Templates have proven especially helpful when it comes to describing trends. Their use guarantees a homogenous information base and a clear and simple representation.

Identifying and describing trends takes a lot of work. However, it is often crucial to gaining an understanding of a situation. While purchasing completed trend analyses can save a lot of time and effort, it will not lead to the insight that is achieved when we perform the work ourselves (it is said that we retain 10% of the total information available when we read, around 30% when we listen and more than 60% through the active gathering of information). If trends are identified and described in a team, then the team opinion about the product will be a very good indicator of its quality

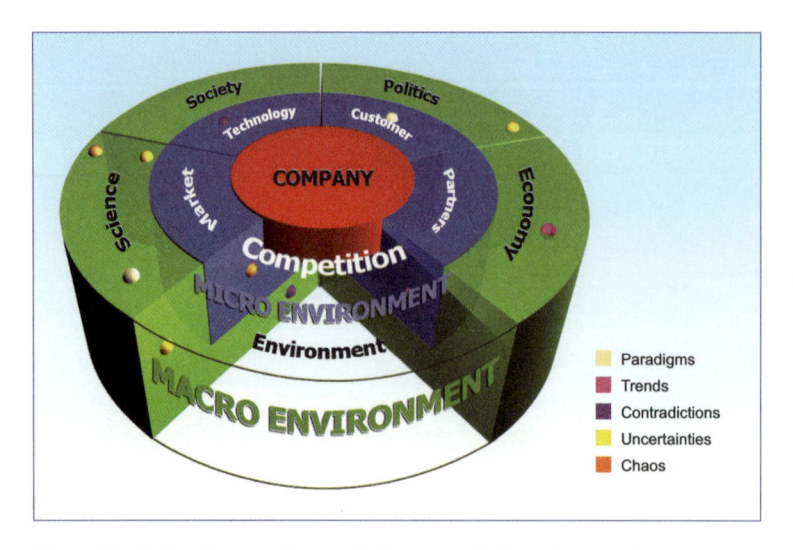

Figure 51 Radar diagram: changes in the enterprise's environment

and the overall understanding of the trend. When it comes to subsequent analysis, the team opinion is also authoritative.

Diagrams are usually used to provide a visualization of trends. Radar diagrams are well-suited to the collective depiction of all trends, paradigms and wildcards. They serve primarily to provide an overview and to facilitate communication. Multiple criteria that are the focus of an evaluation can be placed in a radar diagram. Figure 51 offers an example. A more detailed explanation in this regard can be found in the following section on trend evaluation.

Evaluating Trends

The strict separation between the gathering of information and the evaluation of information is essential to preserving objectivity.

Experience has shown that it makes sense to undertake the evaluation phase only after one has gathered and prepared all of the relevant information. This often proves difficult in practice because a level of evaluation is involved from the very outset, namely, as one gathers information (see Chapter 1). Nonetheless, an honest effort to maintain the separation will help to secure transparency and reproducibility and to avoid preconceptions as far as possible. Beyond this, it warrants pointing out that the various sources of the available information will introduce various points of view. Here, it is important to bear in mind that the evaluation always proceeds from the perspective of the enterprise!

Evaluations have two main goals:

- To prioritize the elements that have so far had an equal status. The idea here is that while all elements will continue to develop, not all elements will have the same significance for the enterprise.

- To consider the interrelations among the elements. For this purpose, the information base is broken down into the following elements: "paradigms," "trends" and "wildcards," with each element being considered and analyzed separately.

What are we looking to accomplish by undertaking to evaluate trends? As the leader of an enterprise or as a manager, we will be interested in knowing what impact a trend has or could have on our business. Moreover, trends are not self-generating. All trends are shaped in terms of their direction and strength by drivers and forces. This means that they can be influenced.

Evaluating trends is a very challenging undertaking. After all, it is a matter of forecasting their future development. While a good evaluation will pay off, there is no way to get around the fact that evaluations will never offer a kind of ultimate proof. In light of the fact that this issue is a matter of heated debate among scholars, permit me to make a brief detour here to assess the various scientific assessments of trend evaluation.

The Available Models of Trend Evaluation

The simple approaches are largely based on two dimensions of evaluation: influence and uncertainty.

In the context of environment analysis, Wilson deploys the "issues-priorities matrix." The aim of environment analysis is to detect approaching issues at an early stage so as to be in a position to develop the appropriate proactive strategies [Wilson 1983]. Wilson uses the term "issue" in this context to refer to a significant external or internal trend (or development) that will have a significant impact on the future success of the enterprise.

As a tool for identifying issues, Wilson first deploys issue mapping. In addition to this, a connection is drawn between trends detected in the macro world and the micro world of the enterprise in the framework of scanning and monitoring. Using this juxtaposition as a basis, issues are then derived that can be evaluated on the basis of the issues-priorities matrix. A matrix is then devised that shows the two dimensions "development probability" and "enterprise impact" (cf. Figure 52). The first step is to assign a value to each trend that is to reflect the probability that the trend will develop into a significant issue. The second step is to give an indication about how strong the possible impact on the enterprise might be (i.e. on the assumption that an issue develops). Although Wilson suggests that a system of evaluation used to estimate probability and impact may exhibit any degree of complexity or simplicity, he never fleshes out this claim. In the end, he suggests that the categories "high," "medium" and "low" are sufficient for an evaluation of both dimensions.

Various priorities are assigned to the issues depending on their particular position in the matrix. If the degree of probability that a trend will develop into an issue is assessed as high and the trend can be expected to have a high impact on the enterprise, then it is assigned the highest priority. In contrast, low priority is assigned to trends whose probability of developing into issues is assessed as low and whose impact on the enterprise is also assessed as low. Between these two levels are trends that are assigned medium priority.

The two approaches to evaluation presented by Schwartz [Schwartz 1991] and van der Heijden [Heijden 2005] do without the use of probabilities. Both methods are closely tied to scenario-based techniques. Scenario-based techniques can be seen as instruments of strategic early detection and involve "... the drafting of various scenarios (i.e. hypothetical views of the future of a socioeconomic area) that take account of the various possible developments of various factors as well as the connections between these factors." [Götze 1993] Schoemaker links the procedure to Ansoff's concept of weak signals by suggesting, "It [scenario planning] institutionalizes the hunt for weak signals." [Schoemaker 1997] Huss and Honton identify three types of scenario analysis: intuitive logic, the trend-impact analysis and the cross-impact analysis [Huss 1987]. While intuitive logic does entirely without mathematical algorithms, the other two procedures qualify as quantitative methods. The methods introduced by Schwartz and van der Heijden belong to the first category. Both concern themselves

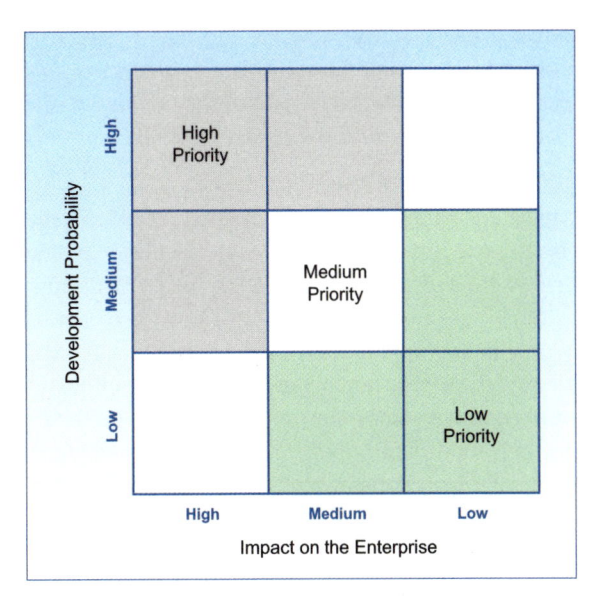

Figure 52 Issues-priorities matrix: evaluation based on probability [Wilson 1983]

explicitly with the use of trends in the development of scenarios. The evaluation of trends then plays a role when it comes to establishing a framework for the scenarios.

Although he suggests that they cannot be entirely demarcated, Schwartz draws a rough distinction in this connection between three categories [Schwartz 1991]. These include "driving forces," "predetermined elements" and "critical uncertainties." The term "driving forces" refers to societal, technological, economic, political and environmental developments. These determine the outcome of scenarios. In outlining this notion of driving forces, Schwartz expressly recommends looking for trends and trend breaches, without omitting to point out the difficulty that results when one attempts to foresee the latter. In contrast, "predetermined elements" are already known and their development qualifies as certain, irrespective of which scenario actually results. Schwartz is less specific when it comes to "critical uncertainties," other than to suggest that their consideration is closely tied to the predetermined elements. They are identified by calling our assumptions about the predetermined elements into question.

Given that the scenarios are expected to represent very different pictures of the future, their development will focus on precisely those elements that can be expected to have a considerable impact on the enterprise and whose future forms are very uncertain. This is why trends are to be evaluated on the basis of their significance and their uncertainty. It is deemed important to devise multiple scenarios for the two to three trends that have been assessed as the least certain and as having the greatest impact potential. These are then used to determine the dimensions of the scenario framework. The scenarios can then be fleshed out with the remaining trends.

Van der Heijden takes a similar approach to that of Schwartz. He, too, uses terms such as "driving forces" and "critical uncertainties." In addition to this, however, he also considers megatrends. The latter distinguish themselves in terms of being the observable results of individual forces in the environment (cf. Heijden, 2005 on this and other definitions).

While Schwartz says little about critical uncertainties, van der Heijden introduces the concept of predictability, which I briefly explain in what follows. Predictions become harder to make as their target periods are shifted further into the future. This suggests that classical forecasting methods are more suited to short-term projections and the use of scenarios is more suited to making medium-term projections. For the long term, we will have to content ourselves with hope. Van der Heijden points out that, in addition to considerable uncertainties, there may also be certain predetermined elements about which it may be very difficult to make an accurate prediction. It follows that while the basic direction of a development can be determined, the exact outcome is extremely uncertain.

The "impact-predictability matrix" (Figure 53) developed by van der Heijden is comparable to Wilson's issues-priorities matrix. Like Schwartz, he selects the elements that can be expected to have a significant impact on the enterprise and that also exhibit a high degree of uncertainty when considering the subsequent scenario dimensions (Chapter 4).

Van der Heijden points out that the selection is ultimately relative, i.e. that everything is essentially important or unpredictable, but that some elements can be expected to have more influence or are easier to predict. When facing the task of selecting scenario dimensions, van der Heijden and Schwartz concentrate on the lower right

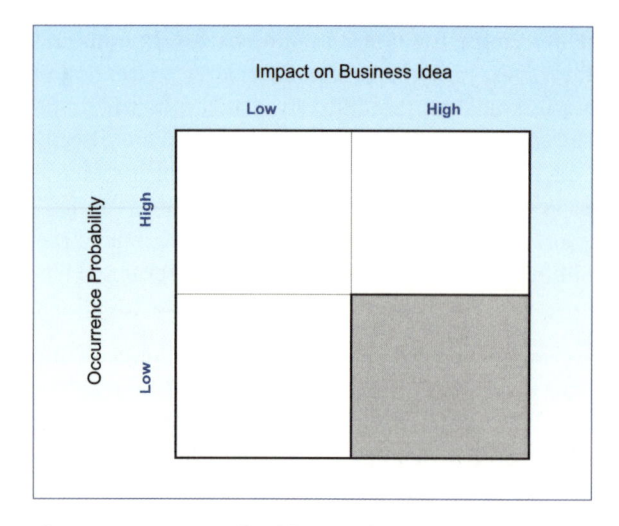

Figure 53 Impact-predictability matrix: a classification of themes (scenario dimensions) [Heijden 2005]

quadrant of the matrix where the elements exhibiting a high degree of impact and development uncertainty are located.

Van der Heijden warns against interpreting the fleshed out matrix (i.e. filled with subjects and trends) in a way that leaves the future exhaustively accounted for. This is because the unexpected events that could not have been considered by the team will be missing. For this reason, he recommends continuous monitoring, and repeating scenario projects instead of carrying out new ones episodically.

While the focus has primarily been on the evaluation of individual elements, the interaction among the various elements is also of great interest because it gives one a sense of which elements are especially active and which are largely passive.

Network-oriented approaches represent a further variation of the complex approaches to trend evaluation. Here, we can distinguish between the impact matrix [Gomez 1997] and cross-impact analysis [Porter 1991]. Both methods make use of matrices in which the mutual relations between various factors are represented.

When working with impact and cross-impact matrices, it is important to determine the intensity of the relations between all of the factors in a network (1 = weak impact, 2 = medium impact and 3 = strong impact). The values in the impact matrix are added together line by line to yield an active total for each factor. Similarly, the passive total is yielded by adding together the values column by column. The factors are then placed in the matrix on the basis of these two totals. The ultimate positions can then be noted to determine which elements are sluggish, reactive, active, and critical (see Figures 89 and 90 in Section 4.8).

In contrast to the impact analysis, the cross-impact analysis [Porter 1991] is based on degrees of probability and is primarily deployed for scenario-based techniques (cf. Chapter 4). Here, the investigation focuses on how the conditional probability of an occurrence changes in the face of a second occurrence whose probability was previously estimated.

A network-oriented approach – the morphological box – is explained in greater detail in the Annex (Section 10.4.1).

Trend Application

Being prepared for the future and being in a position to anticipate developments introduces options and possibilities of actively influencing developments.

Trends are among the few instruments that allow us to see the direction in which changes are going. The attention they are given is accordingly considerable. Alternatives for intervening in the development of trends depends on the forces affecting the trends and their degree of impact. As shown in Figure 34, the possibility of influencing trends from the perspective of the enterprise decreases as their distance to the enterprise increases. Significant room for exerting influence offers an enterprise an opportunity to proactively shape trends and thus to shape its own future. In contrast, independent trends can merely be observed as a means of preparing appropriate responses. In light of this, we can apply trends as follows:

- *Trends as a means of communication*

  Trends are frequently used when changes are to be described. They allow us to develop a common understanding of a problem. The substantive discussion and understanding of trends helps us to form opinions.

- *Trends as a marketing instrument*

  Creating trends (trendsetting) and promoting certain developments can actively drive change. This enables us to influence purchasing decisions and even, given the right handling, manipulate consumer decision making. Here, it is especially important to exercise great care in setting trends.

- *Trends as a basis for strategic work*

  Working systematically with trends is a fundamental component of strategic analysis and a useful instrument. A proper understanding of trends and an appropriate way of deploying them form a basis for the development of scenarios.

3.4 Uncertainty

Although all future elements are theoretically uncertain, certain areas can be identified in the spectrum of possible change and our knowledge about change that can be described as stable (e.g. paradigms and constants) or that constitute changes that have a certain recognizable direction (trends). As a future element, the term "uncertainty" is applied to those changes that are identified as indeterminate: a direction or tendency cannot be detected and several outcomes are conceivable. Most uncertainties are linked to decisions. For instance, "How will the enterprise develop with the new CEO at the helm?" Genuine uncertainties are rarely seen in nature ("Is the volcano going to erupt?"). We can delimit the actual uncertainty in situations that appear nebulous and complex by breaking the situation down into its various future elements until we reach the future element "uncertainty."

3.5 Contradictions

The world is full of contradictions. However, this does not mean that the aim of our investigations of the future should be to resolve these contradictions. On the contrary, what is important in the context of investigating the future comes down to the naming and describing of developments.

Contradictions result from the submission or utterance of opposing views that relate to one and the same object. The question as to which, if any, of the opposing views is right cannot be clarified at the time of our investigation.

Even the Bible contains contradictions. For instance, we find different claims about the number of pairs Noah is instructed to take aboard the ark. Is it one pair of each kind of animal or seven pairs? We also find disparate accounts of the events leading up to the crucifixion of Jesus. According to one account, Jesus is the one who carries the cross. In another account, it is carried for him:

"And he bearing his cross went forth into a place called [the place] of a skull, which is called in the Hebrew Golgotha:" (John 19, 17).

"And after that they had mocked him, they took the robe off from him, and put his own raiment on him, and led him away to crucify [him]. And as they came out, they found a man of Cyrene, Simon by name: him they compelled to bear his cross." (Matthew 27, 31-32).

While we cannot resolve or simply ignore contradictions when considering the future, an early naming of them makes it easier to combine future elements and to develop views of the future.

3.6 Indeterminate Elements – Chaos and Wildcards

Some developments are highly indeterminate and seem to occur out of nowhere. Negative examples of such include terrorist attacks, the reactor meltdown in Chernobyl and the tsunami of December 2004. Positive examples – from the point of view of an enterprise – include an upswing in the economy and surprising inventions or discoveries. As indeterminate as they are, such developments must be accounted for when drafting analyses of the enterprise environment and when developing enterprise strategies.

In light of the fact that it is not possible to consider all cases, it is advisable to at least gather and keep track of possible wildcard events that are largely beyond our sphere of influence.

In addition to natural catastrophes, Steinmüller sees innovations as possible wildcards [Steinmüller 2003]. While Steinmüller regards wildcards as "unlikely, although they cannot be ruled out," Cornish refers to a wildcard as "a surprising and extremely consequential event" [Cornish 2003]. He suggests further that we should assume that wildcards will occur in the future because the past has shown us that they occur.

The Limits of Perception

Even enterprises are not in a position to secure themselves against all eventualities. Here, we can recall the story of the mayor and the clairvoyant in Chapter 1. The mayor learns that his city will be destroyed – an epic wildcard. We are naturally forced to concede that there are situations we cannot protect ourselves against and that would entail an utter inability to act. The question as to whether we can prepare for wildcards is a subject of much debate. As early as the 1970s, Ansoff introduced the notion of weak signals to support the view that momentous events are indeed preceded by evidence of their coming. The problem is, who is really in a position to analyze and appropriately arrange such an immense volume of signals? No one. Many enterprises, institutes and governments have more than their hands full when it comes to ordinary changes whose emergence is plain for all to see. We only need to recall the continuing discussions about the German retirement scheme or the lack of young employees in China. But in the end, the frog in the jar of water dies when the temperature of the water is increased gradually. If it were increased suddenly, the frog would react to the change by jumping out.

It has been observed that the capacity to react and make decisions increases significantly in the wake of the occurrence of wildcards.

3.7 From Hypothesis to Future Element

While change may simply emerge – as outlined in the previous section – it is knowledge about the change alone that is significant for its analysis. In other words, the world will continue to develop and change even if we personally fail to take account of the change.

We have already seen in Chapter 2 how information about a subject is gathered and structured. This available information base is now described in terms of elements such as paradigms, trends, chaos, uncertainty and contradictions. This process leads to a further abstraction and tangible structuring of the information. One starting point is to consider the ways in which the various components will change:

- What changes can be represented as trends?
- What are paradigms?
- What are constants?
- Are there any contradictions?
- What might cause chaos, and what wildcards are imaginable?
- Are there any clearly identifiable uncertainties?

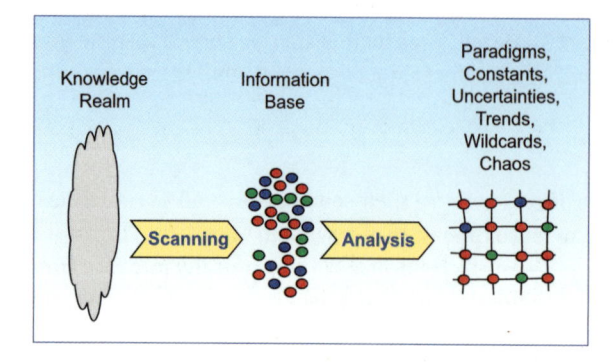

Figure 54 Hypotheses, trends, paradigms, uncertainties, contradictions and wildcards are derived from the information base

The purpose of this classification and homogenization primarily is to make the available elements significantly more amenable to analysis and general handling than a raw, unstructured information base whose various levels may also exhibit considerable differences. Figure 54 offers an illustration of the path taken from the knowledge space to the information base and onwards to hypotheses and their subsequent structuring into various future elements. Figure 55 shows the corresponding process. The example at the end of this chapter was conceived to illustrate the sequence.

As shown, a trend hypothesis is derived from the available information. Figure 56 shows an example of an elaborately devised and verified trend. The trend hypothesis

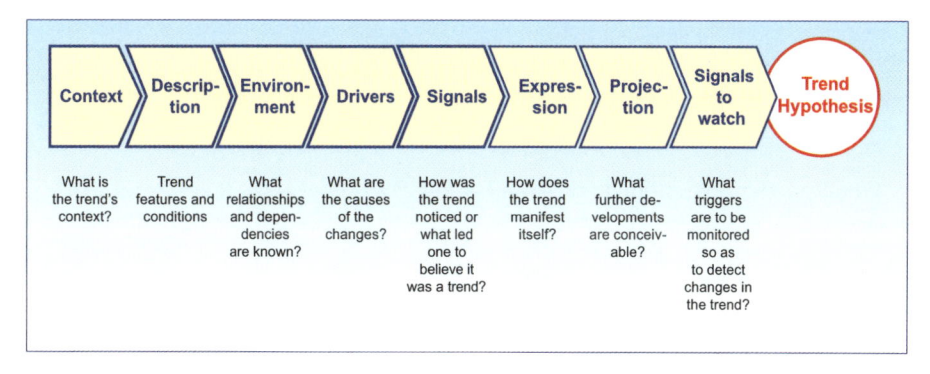

Figure 55 Arriving at a trend hypothesis at the end of a sequence

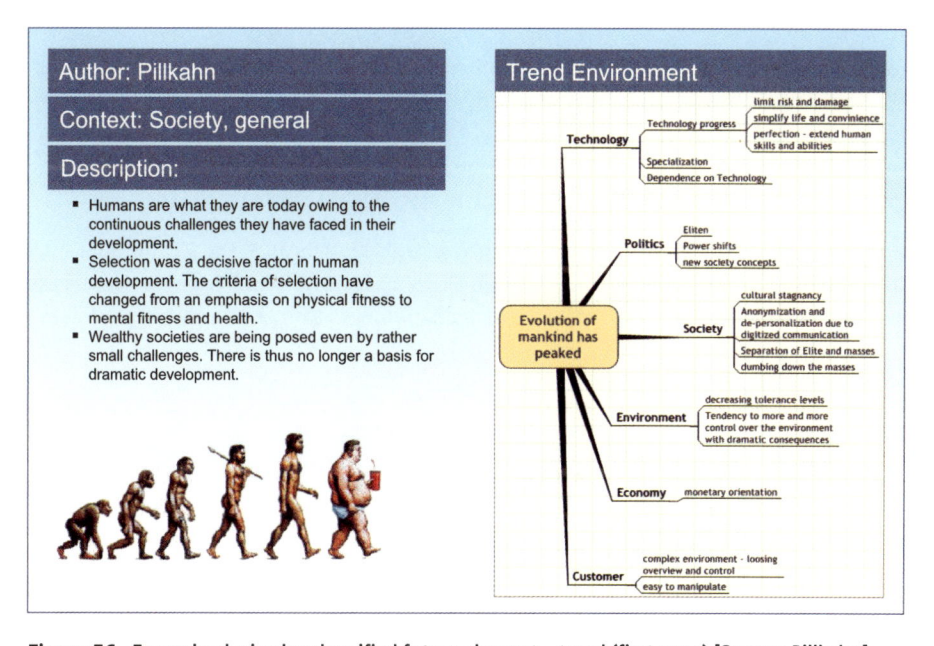

Figure 56 Example: devised and verified future element – trend (first page) [Source: Pillkahn]

3.7 From Hypothesis to Future Element 145

– derived from the information base in the context of a project – can be stated as follows, "Human evolution has reached its zenith."

The description of a future element should include the following items:

- *Context*

  What is the context of the trend's description?

- *Description*

  Features of the trend and basic conditions

- *Environment*

  What connections and dependencies are known?

- *Drivers/Inhibitors*

  What are the causes of the changes?

- *Signals*

  What called our attention to the trend or led us to believe that it is a trend?

- *Expression*

  How does the trend manifest itself?

- *Projection*

  What further development is conceivable?

- *Signals to watch*

  What signals are we to continue to monitor to detect changes?

Experience has shown that it will be helpful in the context of further analysis to classify trend hypotheses, which do not clearly qualify as trends, as uncertainties or contradictions and to treat them separately. Uncertainty applies in this context to the real-world confirmation that hypothesized trend is indeed a trend and not to the question as to how the trend will continue to develop.

Contradictions that turn up when analyzing and describing trends can usually be traced to human inconsistency. For instance, an awareness of the problem of obesity can go hand in hand with its worsening. Such elements cannot be represented using trends.

Future Elements as Instruments of Strategic Planning

Knowledge comes from information. Information was compiled and structured in Chapter 2. This information will now be placed in a context, combined, further structured, formulated, evaluated and described. The issue of who is responsible for uncovering trends, for instance, is therefore crucial. Experience shows that the research and description of trends and their discussion in the context of a team offer an excellent opportunity to gain an understanding of these issues at hand and to acquire knowledge.

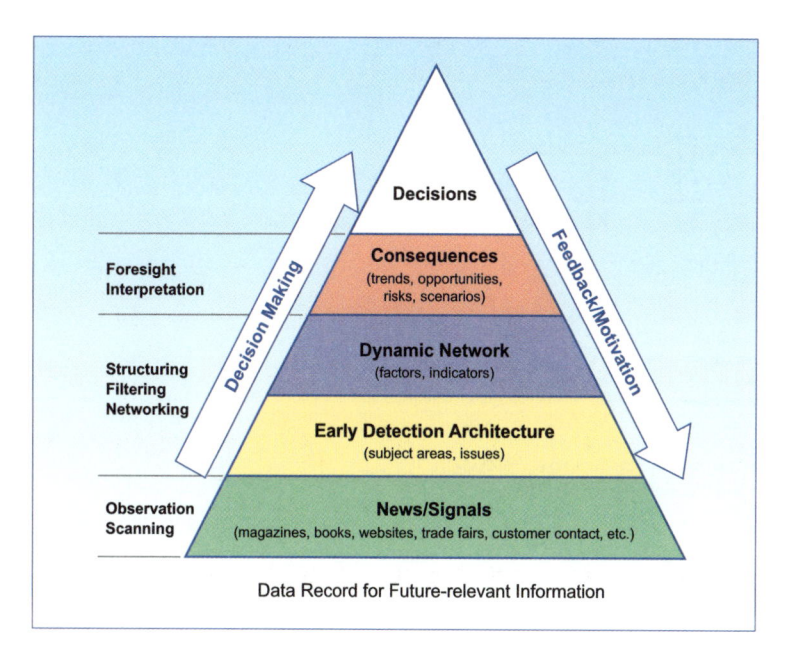

Figure 57 Gathering data and evaluating future elements: the basis of strategy development

Figure 57 shows how the procedure for arriving at future elements can be incorporated into processes of strategy development.

For the sake of illustration, the procedure described here will now be applied to our example "The Future of Television." The example is especially apt given that the developments it involves are dynamic and driven by many technological innovations. The aim in what follows is to use future elements and the structuring of the information gathered in Part 1 to represent the situation.

3.8 The Future of Television (II)

By way of following up on what was accomplished in Chapter 2, I now turn to a further compression and structuring of the available information. Figure 58 shows an overview of the progress made in the research project so far.

Although the available information is presented in tabular form, it still exhibits a certain degree of arbitrariness and heterogeneity. We will begin by establishing elements – statements and individual pieces of information – that will make it much easier to move on to further processing tasks. Signals, breaches, facts, speculations, opinions and changes are reconfigured into elements. As shown in Figure 59, it will be helpful to first organize the information in a mind map. This mind map serves as a template for establishing elements. From the available information, we will then use the questions in Table 15 to develop hypotheses (Table 16) that will then be researched and verified. Figure 60 shows the result based on trend T5.

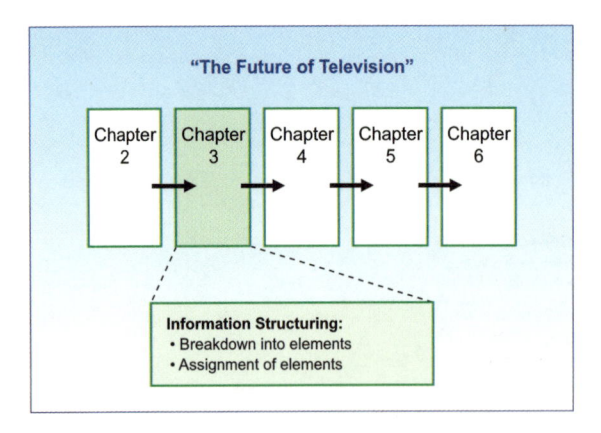

Figure 58 Research project "The Future of Television,"
Part 2: the structuring of information

From the point of view of "change," each of the generated elements has an impact on the subject of our inquiry, namely, the future of television. In accordance with the scheme, all of the future elements are assigned to one of five categories (Figure 41, Table 15). Table 16 shows the compiled result. Figure 61 shows the assignment of the elements to a radar diagram.

It is here at the latest that we will notice that unequivocal assignments are not always given. Our initial attempt to preserve neutrality is now gradually replaced or augmented by a liberty to express our opinions. For instance, the element "IPTV will offer television viewers application advantages" (U1) is classified as an uncertain item. This assumption is a matter of my personal judgment, but which can also be derived from the compiled information. Here, it becomes clear that there can be no neutrality with respect to statements concerning the future. This neutrality will always be replaced by a personal opin-

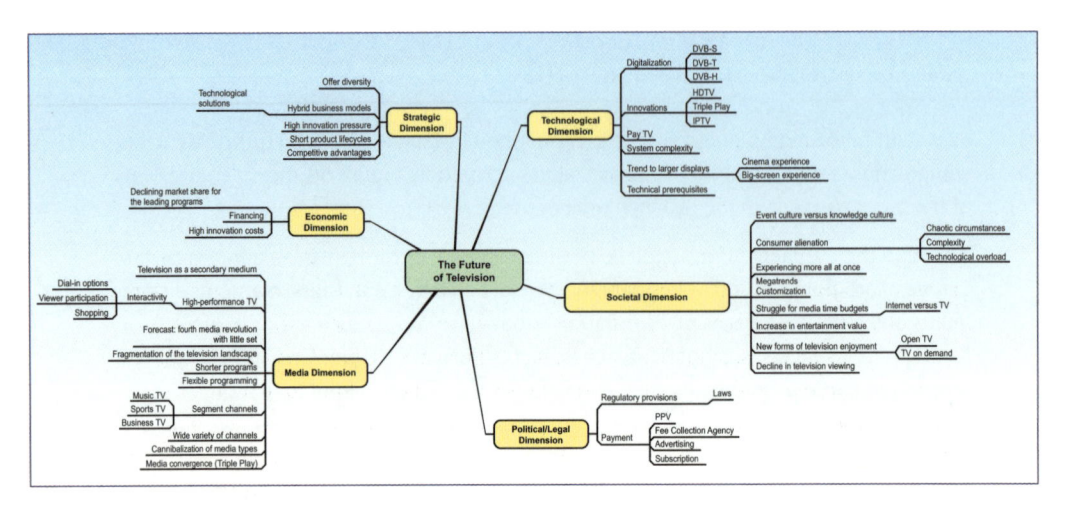

Figure 59 The mind map: medium for initial structuring

Table 15 Future Element Categories

Future Elements	Assignment
Paradigms, constants (P)	What information qualifies as secure and can be described as a fact or a paradigm?
Trends (T)	What can be expected to change in the current situation? What causes or drivers are involved?
Contradictions (C)	What contradictions are contained in the available information?
Uncertainties (U)	What uncertainty factors might play a role in further development?
Paradigms, constants (P)	What information qualifies as secure and can be described as a fact or a paradigm?

ion. As the author, I am aware that there may be (or must be) other opinions with respect to U1 that are based on other information and experiences or that are propped up by wishful thinking.

Having invested in this area, the telecom corporations have a much more positive view of the development and consumers. Assessing the element as a trend would be altogether plausible. As I have already mentioned, working in a team introduces certain forms of decision making. When confronted by differences of opinion, votes can be held to arrive at a team opinion.

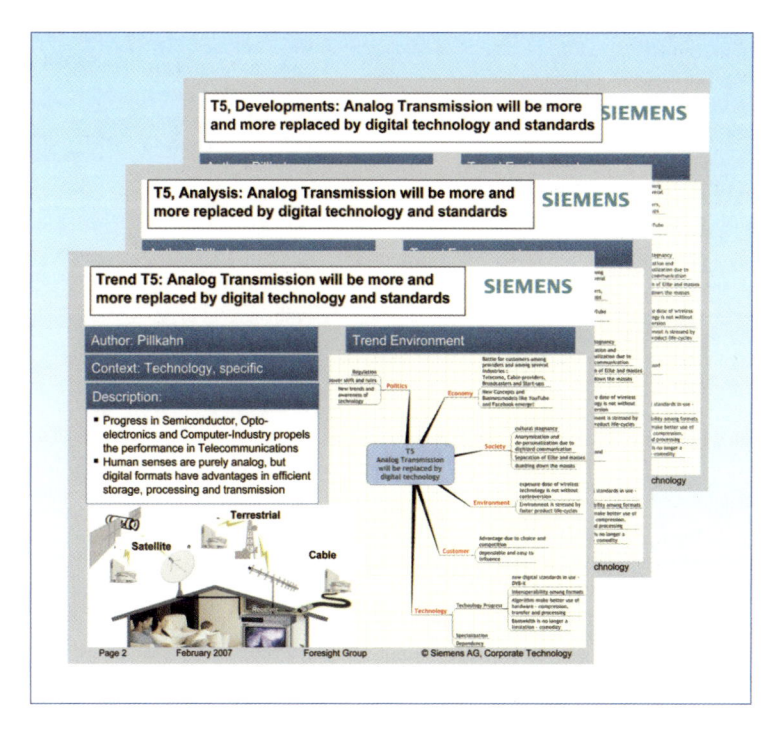

Figure 60 Structuring: the second step in the development of future elements

3.8 The Future of Television (II)

Table 16 Information Structuring: The Future of Television

Paradigms, Constants	Trends	Contradictions	Uncertainty	Chaos, Wildcards
P1: Television is the main entertainment medium. **P2**: "Experiencing more while watching" has become a fixed aspect of TV viewing behavior. **P3**: System complexity can alienate consumers. **P4**: The technology behind the digital transmission of television via satellite and broadband networks is advanced and market-ready. **P5**: Five means of transmission are currently available to viewers in Germany: terrestrial broadcasting (DVB-T), cable, satellite, telephone cable (via DSL), mobile (UMTS, DVB-H). **P6**: TV viewers want a form of passive entertainment. **P7**: The Internet already accounts for 12% of the daily time budget of people between the age of 14 and 49. **P8**: Television viewers have two interests with respect to TV as a medium: entertainment and information. **P9**: Picture quality has improved and the number of reception alternatives has increased.	**T1**: Television is developing into a secondary-focus medium (parallel media use). **T2**: The number of transmission alternatives and technologies has increased excessively. **T3**: Having been replaced to some extent by other media, television viewing, especially among younger individuals, is on the decline. **T4**: Innovative TV technologies are becoming more complex and are associated with high costs for consumers. **T5**: Analog transmission is being replaced by digital transmission. **T6**: As a result of changes in the way consumers spend their free time, TV programs are becoming ever shorter. **T7**: The entertainment value and the makeup of TV programs are gaining in significance at the cost of information content. **T8**: The trend among consumers is towards larger displays. **T9**: Private television is developing into encrypted pay-TV. **T10**: A media convergence is in the making – technologies are melting into one another synergistically (see Triple Play). **T11**: A hard-fought battle is being waged to capture the time budget of television viewers. **T12**: On-demand TV will win out, i.e. consumers will all be able to put together their own programs. TV is becoming more customized. **T13**: The television landscape will be broken down into even more segments (special programs for ever smaller target groups (e.g. MTV, n-TV, CNN, DSF).	**W1**: Technological advances will only penetrate markets if they provide consumers a psychological benefit. **W2**: Can the benefits of the new technologies compensate consumers for the higher costs? **W3**: Contradictory claims about the development of TV viewing (increase or decline).	**U1**: Will IPTV offer TV viewers significant product advantages? **U2**: Do new high-resolution TV programs and formats (e.g. HDTV) have a chance in the future? (chicken-egg problem) **U3**: Are the technological developments compatible with the regulatory landscape and legal provisions? **U4**: What are the effects of the new forms of television viewing? (TV on demand) **U5**: It is doubtful that the segment broadcasters will have the right concepts for positive and sustained earnings development in the long term. **U6**: Some media types and individual channels may be pushed to the verge of extinction (Internet replaces TV / TV replaces cinema) **U7**: To what extent will television suffer a loss of significance as a result of the dominance of the Internet (with respect to news reporting, entertainment, etc.)?	**C1**: The lifecycles of technology products are becoming ever shorter. **C2**: Device manufacturers and media designers are exposed to enormous pressure to innovate. **C3**: Reaction of regulatory agencies and political leaders to the multimedia spread of sex, violence and pornography. **C4**: The TV market currently finds itself in a process of fundamental transformation. The development potential is detectable and presents enormous challenges to the various market players.

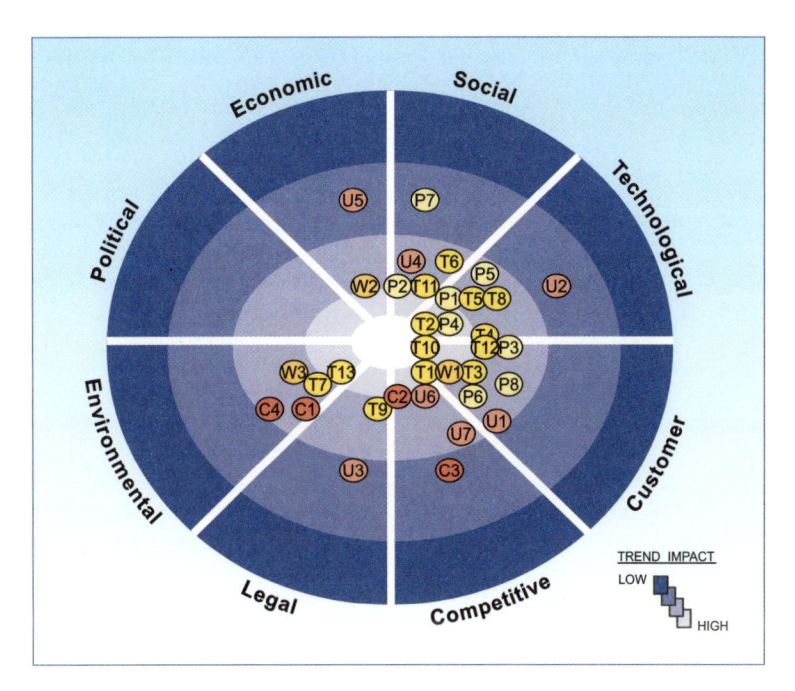

Figure 61 After the structuring: the elements represented in a radar diagram

3.8 The Future of Television (II)

Chapter 4

Understanding

Anticipating the Future

A sense of optimism and excitement prevails among executives at the major oil companies. The economy is growing. Energy demand is on the rise and petroleum plays a vital role in the overall supply of energy. The industry has geared up for a 6 to 7 percent annual increase in demand and has expanded its investments in exploration, drilling, extraction and transport accordingly. Everything seems to be perfectly coordinated. It is the 7 largest oil companies, the 7 sisters, which stand to profit most from the situation. Earning money seems to be no more than a question of efficiently expanding capacities. Everything seems to be going smoothly.

Everything?

A small group of individuals is at work investigating the unimaginable, namely, that the phase of continuous growth could come to a sudden halt. The group studies current developments, takes note of various changes, evaluates the latest news reports and plays out a number of possible developments. Their conclusion is less than euphoric. Indeed, they have identified dramatic changes that could very well interrupt the pattern of even and stable growth. A decision is made to present their findings to the management.

Persistent appeals are voiced "from below" until the management decides to initiate precautionary measures.

As it turns out, the group assembled around Pierre Wack was right in its analysis of the situation, and the persistence of the group is thought to have helped Shell become the second largest and most profitable oil company of the 7 sisters.

The competitive advantage for Shell was derived from the fact that the other oil companies needed up to two years to even realize what had happened in the year 1973. What happened was the first oil crisis in history, and it took most of the major oil companies, whose executives were counting on nothing other than a steady exponential increase in demand, another 5 to 6 years to adjust their capacities to reality.

Figure 62 shows the excess capacities that developed in the wake of the oil crisis and led to enormous investment losses for the oil companies. Shell, however, was prepared for the situation. Thanks to the deployment of scenario techniques, the company was able to introduce strategic and operational measures that allowed for an immediate and effective response to the actual market developments.

(As adapted from: BP Statistical Review; Kees van der Heijden, Scenarios – The Art of Strategic Conversation 1996 [Heijden 1996])

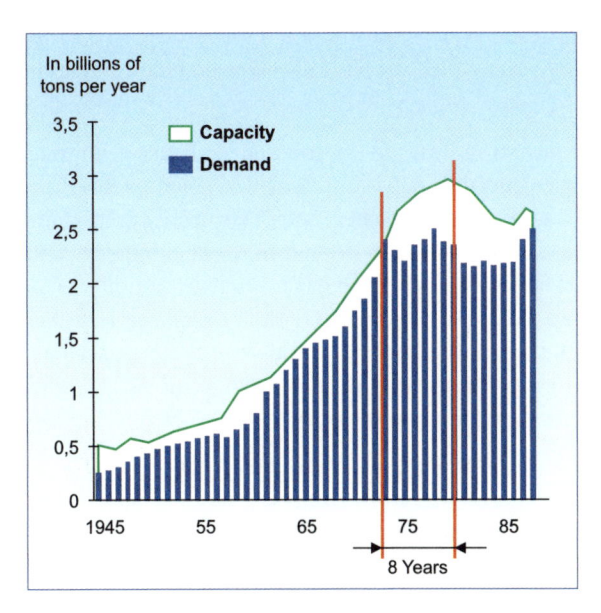

Figure 62 World oil demand and refinery capacity: a lack of correspondence (Source: [Heijden 1996])

4.1 Memories of the Future

It is not only companies and organizations that are exposed to changing environments and are forced to adapt accordingly. Every individual is forced to adapt to changing environments. The Swedish neurobiologist David Ingvar suggests that the human brain is continuously at work processing signals from the environment, both in a conscious and unconscious state [Ingvar 1985]. These signals (or flow of information) are continuously processed in light of the current context as well as of past events, experiences, and acquired knowledge.

We become aware of this processing when a point of correspondence occurs. For instance, when out for a drive, our attention is directed almost exclusively to the road conditions and the traffic around us. Listening to the radio while doing so, however, does not present a problem. An important travel advisory or an unusual noise coming from the engine does not escape our attention because our natural filtering mechanisms are on duty. Beyond this, we tend to project conceivable occurrences into the future by combining our knowledge of past occurrences and our perception of our current situation. Ingvar speaks of "time paths" and suggests that these are not a matter of predictions in a narrow sense of the word. On the contrary, they are strands of possible actions and options. If we hear a travel advisory indicating an accident along our planned route, then we will automatically give thought to our new situation. "Will I be on time for my appointment?" "Should I call ahead?" "Should I expect a detour?" "And how much longer will it take if there is a detour?" Or: "What a nuisance, but that sort of thing happens. I suppose I'll arrive home around 30 minutes late." Ingvar refers to this notion as "memories of the future."

In addition to its use in the literature to describe human foresight, [Geus 1997, Heijden 1996] the notion is ideally suitable for use as a decision-making model for enterprises.

There are certainly big differences when it comes to the concrete daily application of foresight. While people with lower cognitive skills are often described as dull and slow, the very smart among us are said to be able to hear the grass growing. It seems safe to assume that such abilities can be improved by training. And whatever skill works on a small scale – individual human beings – and has been given to humans by evolution as a kind of birthright can plausibly be expected to work on a large scale, i.e. as a concept for enterprises. In contrast to human beings, however, enterprises face the task of arriving at opinions, properly adjusting their sensors and filters, and devising strategies.

What developed in humans in a process of evolution is something that has to be consciously cultivated and installed in an enterprise. In contrast to human beings, an enterprise has no subconscious dimension, no immune system and no conscience. It is thus not capable of spontaneous reaction.

Table 17 Comparison between Humans and Enterprises: Humans Have Natural Immune Systems

	Human Beings	Enterprises
Information gathering	Via multiple sensory organs	Ideally via many employees and numerous sources How is information gathered and documented?
Information filtering	Signals are forwarded from our sensory organs to our brain. Conscious (sunglasses) and subconscious filtering (background noise)	Information flow in the enterprise How is information prepared and compressed (e.g. from many sources of reliable information and reports)? How are decisions made as to what is significant or insignificant? And who makes these decisions? How does the information reach the decision makers?
Information processing	Exclusively in the brain The available information is used to generate time paths and possible actions.	Enterprise management, strategy departments, enterprise planning Depending on the type and form of the organization, information is processed very centrally/decentrally, consciously/subconsciously and explicitly/implicitly. The information leads to an enterprise strategy.
Reactions	Reflexes, actions and plans	Deciders and management initiate strategy implementation. Reactions may take place at all enterprise levels (e.g. avoidance of work accidents).
Breakdowns	We (usually) consult doctors in case of earache or poor vision.	The mere observation that a "sensory organ" is not optimally tuned to changes in the environment and that this could harm the enterprise represents a major challenge. **There is no normal state of health.**

Table 17 shows a comparison of human and enterprise sequences (memories of the future). Although the systems are of the same type, the difference is obvious. The processes that take place in the head of a single human are distributed in the case of an enterprise across many heads. If it is difficult for an individual person to make a decision ("Should I really buy it?") and to compress a lot of information into the form of a decision, it is virtually impossible – especially in large enterprises – to include all the relevantly available heads in a decision-making process. It is understandable that the task of exchanging of information and ideas takes considerable time and effort, i.e. the task of distributing information from one head to the remaining many heads in the enterprise, and then to arrive at a shared opinion.

The comparison between individual human beings and enterprises appears especially apt when we imagine the case of a breakdown in the normal sequence. The human organism is protected by an immune system. To a certain degree this immune system ensures that the processes remain stable. Breakdowns are usually signaled by the body in the form of the sensation of pain. A doctor can then investigate and treat a case of earache, for instance, or write a prescription for a pair of glasses in case of nearsightedness.

What immune responses do we find in enterprises? There is no immune system as we know it in the case of human beings. The only indicator in most cases is the success of the enterprise in the form of growth or profit. If these are not achieved, or if they are on the decline, then emergency programs are implemented. Managers with a sure sense for recovery are in demand. Until then, the only option is the anti anxiety pills. But isn't this just like sending a child to a doctor at the end of the school year on account of bad grades, although the child has had eye problems since the beginning of the school year?

What is it that tells us that a certain form of therapy is appropriate for our enterprise? Do we perform regular fitness checkups?

Coase pointed out as far back as 1937 [Coase 1937] that enterprises are not static constructs and that the explanations provided by the economists for understanding enterprises – which is largely based on the theory of supply and demand – cannot explain why companies arise, change and respond to changes on the market. Working in the context of what was then the developing field of business administration, Jensen and Meckling [Jensen 1976] suggest that enterprises are complex constructions and that the black-box approach is only acceptable at a macro economic level.

These authors suggest that organizations are complex constructions that act in accordance with their own principles and become the objects of scientific curiosity. The claim that information about the environment is gathered continuously and by all employees in enterprises – as in the case of human beings – via the "sensory organs" is uncontroversial. In contrast to human beings, who are capable of responding immediately to certain stimuli, organizations react very sluggishly. Decisions tend to be made by small centralized groups that have direct access to only a small fraction of the information available in the enterprise. The capacity to filter out the important information and to relay this quickly to the decision makers distinguishes enterprises from one another and has an effect on strategy development and its implementation. This is what determines success and failure.

In reporting on a study he conducted about mistakes made in enterprises, Sydney Finkelstein [Finkelstein 2004] uses the data from his numerous company investigations to identify the main causes of "corporate disaster." These main causes include:

- Reality is misinterpreted and misunderstood.

- Important information that should have a decisive impact on an enterprise's worldview fails to make its way to the decision makers or to those who are responsible for processing the information.

- Top managers are so convinced of their skills and talents and so enamored of their own strategies that they defend these to the bitter end.

It follows that mental maps – patterns of thought and worldviews – represent essential components in both the decision-making process and in an enterprise's capacity to act. Actively working on "memories of the future" in the form of an enterprise foresight program will support the procedures for obtaining and processing information, developing appropriate strategies and responding swiftly to change. We can imagine a foresight process for enterprises that ranges from sensory detection to sound decisions and effective action that resembles the time paths of human foresight. The advantage that enterprises have lies in their ability to gather, store and process more information. The challenge for enterprises – their disadvantage compared to human beings – lies primarily in the task of systematically and continuously compressing large amounts of information from many different sources into practicable decisions that are good for the enterprise and refraining from squandering the necessary energy in political, personal, and methodical differences of opinion. It would be ideal if all employees were to function as sensors and filters while the compilation of the information, its analysis and the relevant decisions, were to remain the competence of a central body (as in the case of human beings) such as a central foresight department.

As mentioned above, the state of knowledge of the individual decision makers is marginal compared to the total information available in the enterprise. Nonetheless, decisions must be made. Studies and investigations that cover many different sources of information within the enterprise effectively support the flow of information within the enterprise and help to increase the level acceptance, even if the challenge of effectively including the disparate and variously formatted inflow of information and signals into centralized processing and decision-making procedures remains.

4.2 The Possibilities and Limits of Foresight

Neither theoretical nor empirical approaches alone provide a sufficient means of drafting complete and unequivocal pictures of the future. As pointed out in Chapter 1, the scientific status or legitimacy of statements about the future is unclear. Indeed, this remains a subject of much debate in the literature. Scientific undertakings involve a quest for truth. The truth refers to reality, and independent observation and freedom from contradiction are criteria used in the philosophy of science to assess both methods and conclusions. In light of this, it will never be possible to fully equate investigations of the future with scientific undertakings. After all, observation can begin no sooner than in the present.

Is a mistaken conclusion better when it is scientific?

Even Goethe struggled with these terms:

"Art and science are words that we use so often without really understanding their exact difference that we often use the one for the other. Then we propose other definitions altogether: I think one could refer to science as the knowledge of the general, the derived knowledge, while art, in contrast, would be science used in the service of action. Science would be reason, and art reason's mechanism, which is why one could refer to art as practical science. Science would then at last be theory, and art the problem." [Goethe 2002]

This suggests that science is the theory for the present and past. But what is then used to explain the future? Art? From the perspective of the present, the future is a mixture of truth (science) and assumption (art). There is no right and wrong, only possible and impossible. Nonetheless, there are principles and criteria that prompt people to make statements and formulate assumptions about the future. These can be used as a basis for describing future events, and then generating certain basic rules of inquiry.

Three competencies can be identified as essential for successfully handling the uncertainty that is associated with the future:

- *Coming to terms with a lack of knowledge*

  We cannot know what we will know in the future. The picture loses sharpness as we gaze further into the future.

- *Coming to terms with complexity*

  Future developments are multi-causal results of the interaction of system components and their environments.

- *Coming to terms with dynamic change*

  Given that the dynamics of change cannot be controlled, adaptive skills and flexibility are more important than efficiency.

The right combination of knowledge and assumption allows us to extract important information from the future.

The motivation for undertaking to examine the future can differ significantly from enterprise to enterprise and from branch to branch. The pressure to do so is usually minimal (see the comfort zone in Figure 63) and our focus is adjusted more to the present than to the future. At this phase, the environment appears to be stable and could, from the point of view of the enterprise, remain stable indefinitely. The prob-

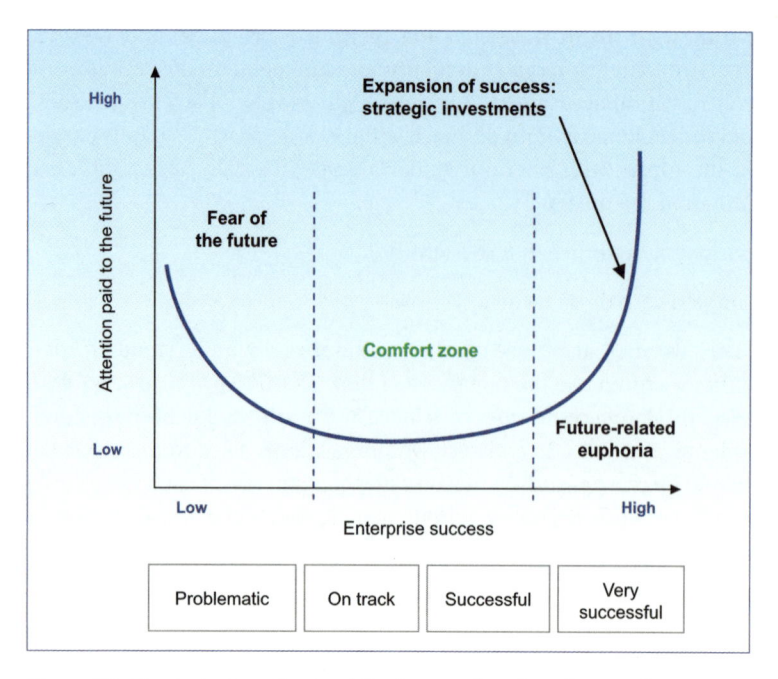

Figure 63 The desire to understand the future: a function of enterprise success

lem is that the enterprise's environment changes continuously (Chapter 1)! The attention we pay to the future tends to peak in two situations: when the deluge is upon us and we fear for our survival; and when significant investments are being considered. The desire for more success arises out of already achieved success – whether this is a matter of size or profit. This success leads to a consideration of secure investments (strategic investments). In contrast, when the very survival of the enterprise is at stake, our desire for a quick solution is understandably pronounced. Here, we are not allowed to underestimate the costs and time associated with a sound analysis. When success elicits a desire for more success, the case is ideal: "money looks for idea." However, it is the many enterprises in the comfort zone that stand to benefit the most from a continuous-duty foresight program. Once they awaken from their slumbers, these enterprises establish new conceptual models, expand their horizons, question their paradigms and actively search for new business opportunities.

An ideal enterprise environment was sketched in Chapter 1. The primary aim for any given enterprise is to survive the present and be successful in the future. Further desires projected by managers onto the future can be subsumed under this aim, including growth, a competitive edge, an efficient enterprise structure, and a stable environment that enables one to plan for the future in the absence of risk. These and other wishes are compiled in Table 18. However, managers will be setting themselves up for a disappointment if they assume that foresight studies containing pictures of the future will fulfill all of these desires. After all, future studies and scenarios do not represent a guarantee for success!

Table 18 Expectations of Pictures of the Future and Foresight Studies

Enterprise Wishes and Hopes	Reality and Possibility
Guaranteed future success	Support, no guarantee
Growth	Identification of opportunities for growth
Planning security	Evaluation and implementation of results creates the actual benefit. No automation!
Minimal risk for strategic decisions and investments	Perceived risks cannot be entirely eliminated. Decision security results from the knowledge acquired.
Increased capacity to compete	Capacity to compete can be increased via the derived strategic measures.
Viable products for the future	Ideas for new products
Efficient enterprise structures	Restructuring is tied to strategy implementation ("structure follows strategy").
Stable environment and new markets	Stable enterprise environments belong to the past. Adaptation is only possible via systematic and continuous foresight.

The following benefits are available to enterprises that have effectively embedded foresight programs in their strategic planning:

- Enterprise flexibility and capacity to respond quickly are increased.
- Enterprise fitness is maintained, and with it, the enterprise's capacity to continually reinvent itself.
- This increases the enterprise's capacity to compete – especially in turbulent environments.
- The detection of dangers turns uncertainty into calculated risk.
- Work on projects involving an examination of the future and the communication of the results throughout the enterprise enable a common understanding of the future and the path into the future.
- The generation of pictures of the future and the stockpiling of knowledge allows one to forestall surprises.
- Scenarios and pictures of the future constitute an instrument of communication that facilitates the exchange of ideas and visions and that allows for the transparent representation of decisions.
- Continuity in the foresight process will lead to the establishment of a business immune system.

The potential for examining the future is limited by an enterprise's strategic capacity. Mintzberg portrays one important roadblock to reaping the benefits of scenarios as follows: "Changing the managerial worldview proved to be a much more demanding task than actually building the scenario." [Mintzberg 1994]

4.3 Origins and Development of Foresight

Although future studies and foresight programs have been around for more than 30 years, their popularity has increased dramatically in recent years, both among scholars and managers. The countless and disparate techniques and methods of examining the future that have been proposed by various scholars enterprises has regrettably led to considerable chaos [Martelli 2001]. This impression is reinforced by the numerous and contradictory definitions, characteristics and principles in the field of future studies.

The procedures used to examine the future essentially derive from four sources:

1. The contributions from practitioners who describe the application of their methods and their experience with them.
2. Those who use scenarios share their experience and issue reports on the design of scenario projects.
3. While scholarly articles in the field of future studies are a source of numerous models for constructing scenarios, many of these, "are impractical and most … have never been adequately tested." [Schmaars 1987]
4. Authors who publish their research results often attempt to demonstrate the benefits of scenarios as a tool for long-term planning.

Origins of Systematic Future Studies

Reviews of the literature and case studies point to a considerable lack of clarity. The very notion of a scenario suggests a multiplicity of uses, including scenario analysis, scenario planning, scenario forecasting, scenario projection methods, and scenario frameworks, to name just a few. Indeed, there appears to be no area relating to scenarios that enjoys a considerable degree of consensus. Definitions, principles, approaches, and characteristics differ from author to author and from publication to publication. Mason suggests that the use of the term "scenario" is often just as misconceived and imprecise as the use of the term "strategy" [Mason 1994]. Martelli describes the situation as "methodological chaos" and expresses doubt that we will overcome the problem in the near future [Martelli 2001].

An attempt to make order out of all the terminological chaos would go beyond the scope of this book. I will therefore limit my discussion to a presentation of the history of scenarios and the vital role they play in examinations of the future.

The concept of scenarios has a long history. Although we can imagine their use at the beginning of civilization, and even as a part of consciousness itself, Plato's "Republic" can be regarded as one of the first attempts to use scenarios to represent the future. In this major philosophical work, Plato describes (roughly 390 years BC) his conception of an ideal republic and addresses problems in the area of justice that are still current today. Plato's theory, which he reveals in the form of dialogues, is regarded among philosophers as an abidingly relevant contribution. The Prussian military strategists von Clausewitz and von Moltke also concern themselves with scenarios in the framework of reflecting on the development of strategies. A comprehensive compilation of visions and scenarios published since 1900 is available in Angela und Karl-Heinz Steinmüller's "Visions 1900-2000-2100" [Steinmüller 1999].

The modern use of the term "scenario" was introduced by Herrmann Kahn. The end of World War II left U.S. politicians and military generals with considerable capacities, including the capacity to consider questions and uncertainties regarding their future aims. It was during this period (1946) that the Rand Corporation was founded as a joint venture involving the U.S. Air Force and the Douglas Aircraft Company. In the years to follow, many techniques and methods were developed exclusively for the U.S. military, as forms of planning and strategy support. It wasn't until after Kahn left the Rand Corporation in 1961 and founded the Hudson Institute that the results of his methods were published. Together with Anthony Wiener, he wrote the book "The Year 2000: A Framework for Speculation on the Next Thirty-Three Years" and published it in 1967 [Wiener 1967]. This book is regarded as a milestone in the area of scenario planning. Kahn defined and used the term "scenario" and thus qualifies as the father of modern scenario analysis.

The origins of the Institute for the Future (IFTF) also go back to the Rand Corporation. Helmer and Gordon – former Rand employees – began to experiment with scenarios in a business environment and belong among the pioneers of future studies in the United States.

These new approaches elicited numerous reactions and developments. Studies were conducted that involved rigorous examinations of the future. Based on the results of these studies, authors published warnings about unchecked development, for instance, the Club of Rome with its report "The Limits to Growth" [Meadows 1970]. Moreover, the Shell Corporation and other companies began to concern themselves with future scenarios.

A chronological list of important examinations of future development is presented in Table 19. The term "scenario" is used rather loosely in these considerations. What used to be referred to as a "vision" or a "utopia" has tended since Kahn to be referred to as a "scenario."

In addition to the broader definitions of the term found in the cited literature, there are also much more focused definitions.

Kahn, who coined the word, defined scenarios as follows, "Scenarios describe hypothetically a succession of events with the objective of drawing attention to causal relationships and working towards decisions." He thereby underscores the significance of scenarios as a tool for arriving at opinions and making decisions. In her definition of the term, Ute von Reibnitz emphasizes the path into the future, "The term scenario refers the description of a future situation and the development or portrayal of the path that leads us out of the today and into the future" [Reibnitz 1992]. Wilms favors scenarios as a systematic approach [Wilms 2006]. Porter emphasizes the distinction between projections and forecasts, "... an internally consistent view of what the future might turn out to be – not a forecast, but one possible future outcome" [Porter 1985].

Table 19 Famous Past and Contemporary Examinations of the Future

No.	Author	Title / content	Year
1	Plato	Republic	Around 390 BC
2	Thomas More	Utopia	1516
3	Tomasso Campanella	The City of the Sun	1602
4	Francis Bacon	The New Atlantis	1626
5	Louis Mercier	The Year 2440	1770
6	Daniel Gottlieb Mehring	The Year 2500 or Alradi's Dream	1794 / 1795
7	Jules Verne	Paris in the Twentieth Century	1864
8	Ferdinand Amersins	The Land of Freedom	1874
9	Kurt Lasswitz	Views of the Future	1878
10	Edward Bellamy [Bellamy 1978]	Looking Backwards	1888
11	Herbert George Wells [Wells 1996]	The Time Machine	1895
12	George Orwell [Orwell 1949]	1984	1949
13	Arthur C. Clarke [Clarke 1958]	Profiles of the Future	1958
14	Herman Kahn / Anthony Wiener [Kahn 1967]	The Year 2000	1967
15	Horst Wagenführ [Wagenführ 1970]	Industrial Future Studies	1970
16	Karl Steinbuch [Steinbuch 1970]	Program 2000	1970
17	Alvin Toffler [Toffler 1970]	Future Shock	1970
18	Ossip K. Flechtheim [Flechtheim 1971]	Futurology: The Struggle for the Future	1971
19	Club of Rome [Meadows 1972]	The Limits to Growth	1972
20	Daniel Bell [Bell 1976]	The Coming of the Post-Industrial Society	1973
21	John Naisbitt [Naisbitt 1982]	Megatrends	1982
22	Michael F. Jischa [Jischa 1993]	The Challenge of the Future	1993
23	Ian Morrison / Greg Schmid [Morrison 1994]	Future Tense	1994
24	Hamish McRae [McRae 1994]	The World in 2020: Power, Culture and Prosperity	1994
25	Joe Coates / John B. Mahaffie / Andy Hines [Coates 1997]	2025: Scenarios of the US and Global Society Reshaped by Science and Technology	1997
26	Michio Kaku [Kaku 1998]	Future Visions	1998
27	Angela & Karl-Heinz Steinmüller [Steinmüller 1999]	Visions 1900-2000-2100	1999
28	Hans Georg Graf [Graf 2002]	Global Scenarios: Megatrends in Worldwide Dynamics	2002
29	Edward Cornish [Cornish 2004]	Futuring: The Exploration of the Future	2004
30	Tom Standage (Publisher) [Standage 2005]	The Future of Technology	2005
31	James Canton [Canton 2006]	The Extreme Future	2006
32	Eric Garland [Garland 2007]	Future, Inc.	2007
33	David Orrell [Orrell 2007]	The Future of Everything	2007

Wack also underscores the intelligent and creative work that goes into the drafting of scenarios, "The scenarios focused less on predicting outcomes and more on understanding the forces that would eventually compel an outcome; less on figures and more on insight" [Wack 1985]. We could easily continue and arrive at fifty definitions that all differ in terms of their frames of reference, demarcation, and methodology [Schnaars 1987, Schwartz 1996, Heijden 1996, Fahey 1998, Marsh 2002, Lindgren 2003, Zürni 2004].

In what follows, the term "scenario" will be used in accordance with the following partial definitions:

Scenarios

- are hypothetical illustrations of the future that describe a cross section in an established context.
- open a realm of possible development alternatives.
- describe development paths and serve as a form of guidance.
- include qualitative and quantitative claims.
- are intentionally applied in multiples to particular situations to show indeterminacy and possible alternatives.

Scenarios are generally to be distinguished from projections owing to their use as alternatives (Table 20).

A classification into various faculties permits a demarcation with respect to the origin and goals of scenarios (Table 21).

Two major philosophies have emerged in the area of future studies. The organic philosophy is essentially based on scenario principles and the mechanistic philosophy assumes that the future is predetermined or can, theoretically, be determined and

Table 20 Definition of "Scenario" as Distinct from "Projection"

	Projection	Scenario
Features	Attempt at an exact prediction of events, oriented to the past	Attempt to represent cross sections of the future as alternatives, oriented to the future
Basis	Based on probabilities	Based on the possible and imaginable
Temporal scope	Short to medium term	Medium to long term
Decision factor	Deterministic	Alternative scenarios as a basis for decision making
Variables	Facts, quantitative, objective, known	Objective and subjective, known and unknown (imaginable), qualitative and quantitative
Risk relation	Suppression of risks	Promotion of risk awareness

Table 21 The Faculties of Scenario Development

Faculty	Description	Proponents / Examples
Artistic, aesthetic	The future is primarily described in books and movies. Artistic freedom or the absence of a claim to scientific legitimacy and utility lead to fantastic portrayals and help to expand our powers of imagination (science fiction).	Books by da Vinci, Francis Bacon, Jules Verne, Orwell Movies: Minority Report, Payback
Military	The conduct of war and strategic advantages in battle are the motive for this faculty. The focus of the work lies in outsmarting one's opponent, anticipating action (active preparation) and reaction.	von Moltke and von Clausewitz RAND Corporation Pentagon
Political	The political faculty sees scenarios as instruments of promoting interests, ranging from the local retention of power to advocating the interests of humanity at a global level.	Herrmann Kahn Club of Rome UNO
Economic-technological	The economic-technological faculty is characterized by competitive advantage, enterprise success and technological advances.	Shell, GE SRI, IFTF

calculated on the basis of current conditions. This latter thereby conforms to the projection model.

Organic Philosophy

The approaches in this area, which were mainly developed in the United States (and which are referred to in Figure 64 as the Anglo-American approaches), tend to be based on qualitative, verbal descriptions. These can be seen both in the formulation and the interpretation of the "imprecision." The focus is on penetrating the situation and generating alternatives and options.

Deterministic Philosophy

Advances in computing technology led to an increase in the use of this technology in the area of scenario development. France, in particular, is seen as an origin for this movement. In Figure 64, these approaches are referred to as continental European.

In addition to these two philosophies, movements of smaller significance emerged, which usually centered on a single method. These include, for instance, Systems Dynamics (developed by MIT [Forrester 1991]) and the matrix-based procedures such as cross-impact analysis (CIA) and trend-impact analysis (TIA).

Beyond this, various methods of drafting scenarios have been developed. I describe some of these in what follows.

Experience Based on Previous Considerations of the Future

Many presentations on the subject of the future begin with a description of mistakes made in the past (see Figure 65).

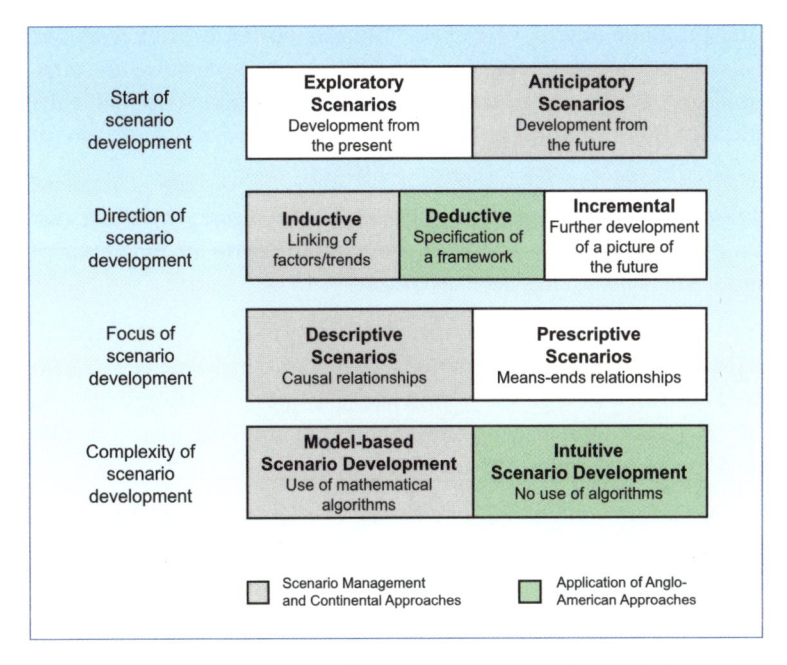

Figure 64 Scenarios: criteria for differentiation (as adapted from [Fink 2001])

A market study conducted by Daimler Benz in 1900 is said to contain the following remark, "Worldwide demand for automobiles will not exceed 1 million, especially on account of the limited number of chauffeurs." Thomas Watson is alleged to have said the following in 1943 when he was the executive director of IBM, "I think there is room on the world market for around five computers." And Ken Olsen is said to have

Figure 65 After a visit to the opera at night in Paris in the year 2000: from the perspective of the year 1902 (Albert Robida, Source: Bridgeman Art Library)

4.3 Origins and Development of Foresight

prophesized in the PC Stone Age of 1977 that, "There is no reason why someone would want a computer in his house." And even Bill Gates, otherwise known as a technology pioneer and prophet is said to have made the following remark about the memory needs for Microsoft programs in 1981, "640 KB should be about enough for everyone."

However, in addition to the often quoted mistakes about the future, there is a vast array of astonishing "predictions." For instance, as shown in Figure 66, the notion of videoconferencing (i.e. television) has been around since 1912!

As early as the year 1626, Francis Bacon described the fantasy island "New Atlantis" as follows, "By art likewise we make them greater or smaller than their kind is, and contrariwise dwarf them and stay their growth ... And we make by art ... trees and flowers, to come earlier or later than their season, and to come up and bear more speedily than by their natural courses they do." [Bacon 1995]

Can this be interpreted as the first warning against genetic engineering? Or an initial glimpse of the pharmaceutical industry? But the issue is: how did people – in the cases mentioned all experts in their fields (more on experts later) – arrive at these findings? It is worthwhile to take a look back and learn from the mistakes made by others and apply what one has learned to one's own practice of examining the future.

The turn of the millennium marks an interesting interval in the calendar. And it is not for nothing that many people in the past reflected on what the world might look like in the year 2000. The difficulty in looking forward is that we can only determine in retrospect whether we were on the right track. Today – having arrived in the new millennium – we can evaluate the projections and derive conclusions for our own future-centered activities.

Isaac Asimov compiled reflections and future visions from the nineteenth century in a book in 1986 [Asimov 1986]. In his extensive dissertation on future visions of the year 2000, Denis List not only compares [List 2004] the predictions with what actually

Figure 66 In the year 2000 people will use the video-telephone: vision from the year 1912

turned out to be the case, he also compares the procedures, methodologies and materials used. His findings, which are briefly described in what follows, will later be considered in the context of developing scenarios.

Many of the investigated materials were not referred to as scenarios because the term wasn't introduced until later. The selection was made on the basis of comparability and focus on the year 2000. Fifteen examples (Table 22) were carefully examined and evaluated. Table 23 shows an overview of the evaluated year-2000 examinations and the relevant scores. This core is essentially a comparison of the described pictures of the future and the year-2000 reality. It warrants mention, however, that the various subjects of investigation make it more difficult to arrive at an evaluation. An objective evaluation is possible only to a limited extent.

Table 22 Year-2000 Predictions [List 2004]

Type of Foresight	Examples Found	Examples Used
Stories	6	2
Collections	5	1
Formal scenarios	64	7
Studies/surveys	8	2
Models	22	3

It is conspicuous that relatively accurate descriptions were also drafted long before the target date. For instance, in "As We May Think" from 1945, Bush describes something like the desktop PC, the Internet, and even digital photography ("dry photography").

Having examined the various scenarios, we can conclude the following:

- While most of the studies were relatively precise in their execution, the details are often clearly inaccurate.
- The scenarios generated better results than the forecasts.
- Normative components play an important role.
- Concerns about self-fulfilling prophecies proved largely unfounded.
- The total effort involved did not necessarily have an impact on the quality of the results.
- Two hypotheses were found in nearly all of the scenarios:
  A belief that technology can solve all problems (see Chapter 6) and a belief in the necessity of protecting the earth and sustainability.

Table 23 A Comparison of Year-2000 Visions

Year	Name	Focus	Method	Region	Reference	Score
1967	Mankind 2000	Comprehensive	Survey of experts and the public	10 countries (rich and poor)	[Jungk 1969] [Ornauer 1976] [Galtung 2003]	*****
1968	Architecture 2000	Architecture and related areas	Expert opinion	World	[Jencks 1971]	****
1945	As We May Think	Information technology	Expert opinion	USA	[Bush 1945]	****
1980	Australia at the Crossroads	Macro economics	2 scenarios (Shell method)	Australia	[Kasper 1980] [Galer 1982]	****
1988	Perspective 2000	Politics, economy and environment	Economy: 3 scenarios (critical uncertainties)	World	[Newton 1990]	***
1987	Norway 2000	Comprehensive	3 normative scenarios	Norway	[Osmundsen 1986] [Nore 1988]	***
1985-89	Poland 2000	Comprehensive	3 normative scenarios	Poland	[Wierzbicki 1991]	***
1975	Telecom 2000	Telephone communication	Modeling, forecasting, various methods, no scenarios	Australia	[Telecom Australia 1975]	**
1974-76	Europe 2000	Society, comprehensive	Various methods	Europe	[Hall 1977]	**
1966	The Year 2000	Comprehensive	1 main scenario + 8 secondary scenarios, forecasting and modeling	World	[Kahn 1967]	**
1976	OECD Interfutures	International economic development	6 scenarios: various methods	World	[Norse 1979]	**
1996	Information Commerce	Internet business applications	4 scenarios (critical uncertainties), 16 drivers	USA	[Randall 1997]	**
1984	Forecast 2000	Comprehensive	Survey of 1,346 experts and youths	USA	[Gallup 1985]	**
1977	Global 2000 (Carter Report)	Economy, environment	Econometric modeling of official statistics	World	[Barney 1980]	*
1893	Today Then	Comprehensive	Survey 74 experts	USA	[Walter 1992]	*

An examination of the scenarios turns up the following problems:

1. Most of the studies do a better job of describing "their" time than the year 2000.
2. No clear connection to 2000 (Why not 1985?).
3. Technological changes are overestimated, social changes neglected (cf. Figure 67).
4. The scenarios resemble one another, and all of them are partially accurate.
5. A number of the scenarios are formulated so vaguely and generally that they are difficult to evaluate, for instance, "The level of public health will be higher in 2000."
6. Most were very externally oriented despite the fact that the future arises in the head.
7. A number of scenarios were compromised by their limited scope ("Europe 2000" was Western Europe 2000 and ignored the Eastern Europe).
8. Experts are seldom in a position to look beyond their expert domains.
9. Famous persons contribute little to the success of scenarios.
10. Only one scenario [Jungk 1969] included reflections on how people in the year 2000 live and think.

Figure 67 This is how peas are eaten in the year 2000: vision from the year 1883

Trends can also be seen in the development of scenarios (see Figure 68):

- Transport issues (including space transport) were the focus of scenarios in the 1960s.

- The environment and environmental pollution were the focus of scenarios in the 1970s.

- Computer technology came into focus in the 1980s, and telecommunication came into focus in the 1990s.

- Ever since the turn of the century, in addition to other subjects, such as climate development, terrorism has been in focus.

- Subjects of abiding interest include artificial intelligence, energy and cosmic reflections.

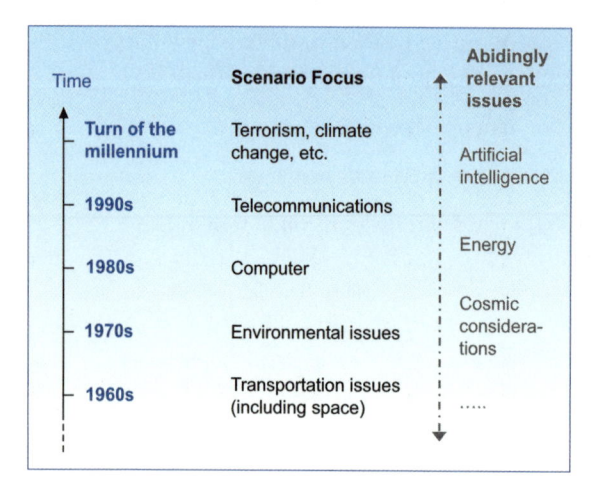

Time	Scenario Focus	Abidingly relevant issues
Turn of the millennium	Terrorism, climate change, etc.	Artificial intelligence
1990s	Telecommunications	
		Energy
1980s	Computer	
		Cosmic considerations
1970s	Environmental issues	
1960s	Transportation issues (including space)	.....

Figure 68 Interest in the future: "Zeitgeist" subjects and evergreens

Visions calibrated to the year 2000 have also been popular in Germany. The book *Program 2000* [Steinbuch 1970] by Karl Steinbuch is probably the most well known among them. The significance of education and its key role in the future is a central aspect of this preview of the future. Steinbuch's criticism of the German educational system has been confirmed by various Pisa studies.

Horst Wagenführ considers the future from the perspective of industry [Wagenführ 1970]. Although his work does not explicitly target the year 2000, it contains many interesting and relevant hypotheses. Future economic development, for instance, is described in the general context of the following prediction, "There will be two types of economies in the coming generation: one of scarcity and one of surplus." This effectively shifts the law of supply and demand to a law of available resources, an interesting prediction, particularly in light of the now foreseeable dependencies and limitations relating to global resources.

Despite his impressive hypotheses, much of Wagenführ's examination of the future can be seen as inspired by the zeitgeist. For instance, he regards the introduction of a 3-day work week by the year 1985 as altogether plausible. This assumption was made at a time when machines, robots and computers were thought certain to reduce the number of hours in a workday. As evidenced by the current abandonment of the 35-hour workweek in favor of longer hours, this has not turned out to be the case. Furthermore, Wagenführ assumes that the future economy will be less oriented towards profit making, an assumption that was likely a matter of wishful thinking.

The following conclusions can be drawn from our investigation of past assessments of the future and brought to bear as lessons learned in our own endeavors:

- We should focus our investigations on societal changes because these are reflective of all changes.
- Technological developments are often overestimated and often inspire wishful thinking. They tend to spread more slowly – if at all – than predicted by the developers.
- It is not necessary to calibrate an investigation to a specific point in time. A number of years, plus or minus, is not likely to make a difference. However, it is important to set the point in time far enough into the future so as to avoid the trap of extrapolation.
- Many imagined developments stem from our subconscious. These should not be neglected.
- It is better to set our scopes too broadly than too narrowly. This will help us to avoid overlooking peripheral developments.
- It is important to create scenarios that are truly distinct.
- When using trends, we should make sure to account for countertrends.

Possible Subjects for the Next 25 Years

- Energy, especially in connection with dwindling supplies of fossil fuels and climate change (see Chapter 7).
- Awareness of issues surrounding climate protection and the protection of our entire ecosystem is growing among world leaders as the evidence mounts suggesting that human activities (industry in particular) are responsible for environmental damage and climate change.
- Food production, particularly with regard to cultivable land. Land area for the world's agricultural needs is limited. Divergent uses of traditional foodstuffs – nutrition and biofuels – will compete in the future.
- Geopolitical realities could change dramatically with Russia as a new energy powerhouse and China emerging as an economic powerhouse; including the United States and Europe, we may see four world powers.

- The issue of genetic engineering in particular, and the general question as to how far humans should intervene in natural processes – especially when the consequences of doing so are largely unknown – will accompany us in the years to come. "Human" experimentation, however, is likely to be outlawed only after it comes to a disaster.

- The world's financial systems could become the focus of our attention. The gap between general societal interests and the interests of financial investors seems to be growing. The role of money could also be called into question. Other models could be proposed for the exchange of goods.

- Technology has always played a major role in speculation about the future, and can be expected to remain immensely significant in the years to come. As in the past, technological possibilities will continue to be overestimated in the future and their long-term impact will receive too little attention. The technical solutions of today are the problems of tomorrow!

4.4 Pictures of the Future

The present section is devoted to a daring shift from individual views of the future to comprehensive pictures of the future, i.e. to the envisioning of coherent cross sections of the future that are comprised of various interconnected elements. This shift is necessary because the analysis of individual elements and their atomistic projection into the future do not adequately account for the interaction, dynamic nature and general complexity of developments.

As emphasized on many occasions so far, we cannot predict the future. We can, however, make assumptions about the future and use these to develop pictures of what the future might look like. In what follows, I explain the development of "pictures of the future" beginning with their basic elements and a number of basic assumptions.

Basic Assumptions

1. The basic idea is that the future will not be a matter of an entirely new and different world. We do not wake up one morning to discover all of a sudden that a majority of automobiles are powered by a new kind of engine. On the contrary, the future emerges in an evolutionary process, forever building upon the state of the present. There is therefore always a part that will not have changed in addition to the part that has changed. The changed part becomes larger and the unchanged part smaller as the reference point in time is moved further into the future.

2. Some changes will occur gradually while others will occur suddenly. As illustrated in Figure 40, mercurial changes in nature and the environment tend to be exceptions (e.g. earthquakes and tsunamis). Radical changes caused by human beings in what would otherwise be a gradually changing environment are either brought about intentionally (the dropping of an

atomic bomb in 1945) or result from mass reactions (e.g. the panic that fuels a stock market crash).

3. All statements concerning the future are necessarily associated with a degree of uncertainty. The degree of this uncertainty is individual, subjective and not measurable. In order to increase transparency, our efforts should be focused from the outset on separating verifiable knowledge and facts from opinion, assumptions and speculation. Whether we apply knowledge or belief can make a big difference when considering the future (cf. Figure 41).

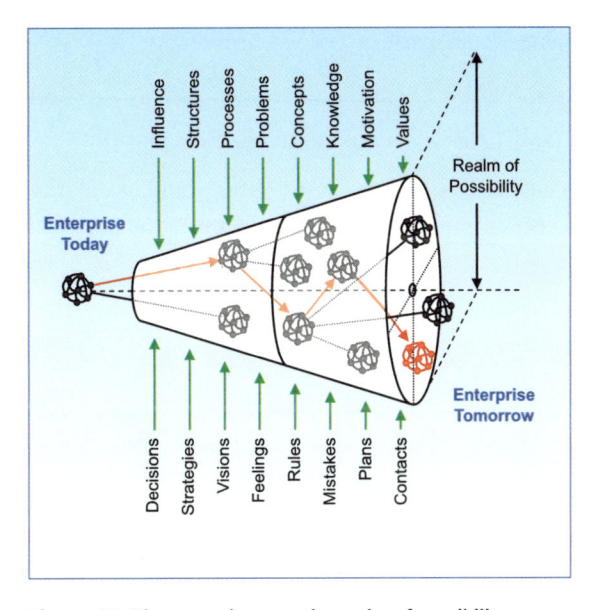

Figure 69 The scenario cone: the realm of possibility

The cone diagram (Figure 69) offers an effective means of illustrating the concept. The cone widens as we move away from the present, thereby illustrating the broadening of the realm of possibility. The realm of possible developments is symbolized in the diagram by a circle or screen. The cone in the figure is used to represent the future development of an enterprise. The factors that could have an impact on the direction that the development takes are represented as arrows. Several alternative paths are indicated. It is necessary to point out, however, that the circle suggests a limitation that does not really exist, i.e. because the future is open. Even the starting situation cannot be exactly demarcated. What does the enterprise consist of? Its premises? Its employees? Its knowledge? Its machines? Its customers? This warrants mention to indicate how difficult it can be – depending on the perspective involved – to clearly demarcate the object of investigation (see the Section entitled "Demarcation and Focus").

4.4 Pictures of the Future

4. The last and most important assumption concerns our manner of dealing with a lack of knowledge. When considering the future, we are unavoidably confronted by conscious and unconscious forms of ignorance. We can do little about unconscious ignorance, and we can therefore never guarantee that future studies are complete. A proper way of dealing with detected ignorance is crucial to the legitimacy of any attempt to understand the future. And the only proper way is to accept and explain it. Otherwise, we will pave the way for speculation and lies.

The most important principles when considering the future include:

- Maintain neutrality as long as possible.
- Proceed in a manner that guarantees transparency and verification.
- Accept unconscious ignorance (in contrast to lies).
- Maintain a strict separation of facts, belief and opinion (future elements).

Adhering to these principles will ensure that the search for stability and orientation will not be controlled by interests (even one's own) and that the future pictures one develops will not be distorted.

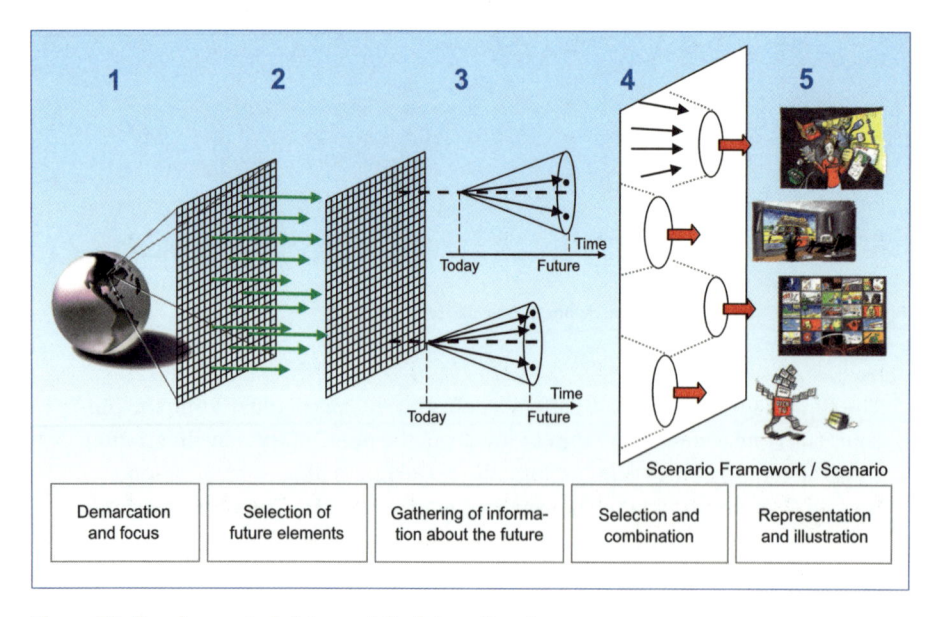

Figure 70 Development of pictures of the future: five steps

Figure 70 offers an illustration of the concept used to generate pictures of the future. Five steps are involved, beginning with the simple question as to what the purpose of the investigation is. What aim is to be achieved by drafting pictures of the future and scenarios and otherwise attempting to research the future (Table 24)?

Table 24 The Five Steps to Developing Pictures of the Future

Step	Question	Focus	Chapter
1	What is the purpose of the endeavor? What are we attempting to explain?	Orientation: From the real world to the object of investigation	4.5
2	How are we to represent the object of investigation?	Gathering of future elements	3.1 4.6
3	What do we know as a matter of fact about the future?	Information about the future	4.7
4	What might the framework of the picture of the future look like?	System architecture, construction of future pictures	4.8
5	How can we represent pictures of the future so as to make them broadly accessible?	Illustration and visualization	4.9

4.5 Demarcation and Focus

The starting point for an examination of the future – for instance, in the context of a project – is a statement of the aim or the scope of the inquiry. Experience shows that aim and expectations do not always correspond. The possible constellations are represented in a matrix in Figure 71. Curiosity is a strong motive and can lead to a broad formulation of the inquiry's scope ("What will the future bring?"). In contrast to this, a very specific formulation can lead to a narrow scope of investigation and a different

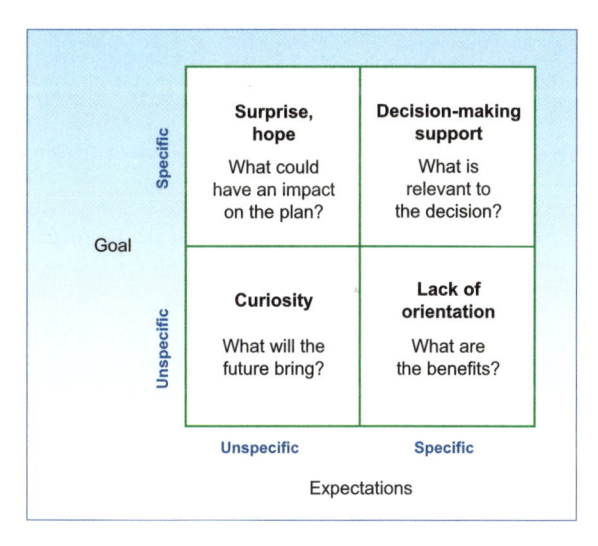

Figure 71 Motives for considering the future: as aligned to the stated aims and expectations

approach ("What will the automobile of the future look like?"). Theoretically, there is no limit to the scope of an investigation (Figure 72).

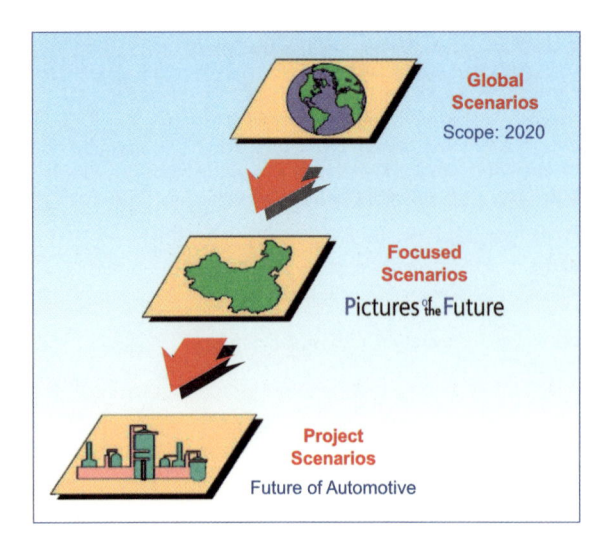

Figure 72 Aims of examining the future: focus (examples drawn from Siemens)

A correspondence between one's expectations and goals is crucial to the success of examinations of the future. Experience shows that an approach characterized by vague goals and high expectations ("We need a new cash cow!") will lead to disappointment. On the other hand, less specific expectations are more likely to lead to results that are promptly filed as "quaint" and that make no contribution to change in the enterprise. This leads to the question about the purpose of the investigation: how are the results to be included in strategy processes or deployed as an instrument of communication? Securing clarity in the context of the first step – for instance, by explaining the goals and expectations and how one plans to use the results – will help to avoid misunderstandings.

Once the subject of investigation has been specified, the examination of the future can begin, for instance, in the context of a project. Although it is latent wishes and inadequately articulated concerns that often lead to the initiation of an examination of the future, clarity must be established from the very outset among all participants about three factors beyond the goals and expectations. These include:

- Focus
- Timeframe
- Geographical scope

The framework for the task at hand is illustrated in Figure 73. We can see that determining the focus of the investigation will also determine how the investigation is to proceed.

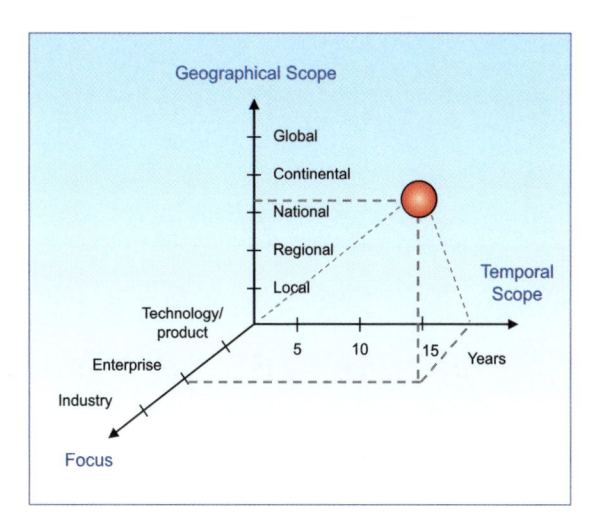

Figure 73 Proper focus: a 3D framework

4.6 Selecting Future Elements

In Chapter 3, I described how changes can be classified according to their degree, ranging from constants and paradigms to focused changes, uncertainties, contradictions, chaos and wildcards (cf. Figure 41). I now wish to describe the subject of investigation representatively in terms of the aim of the examination of the future, the demarcation of the subject area and the focus:

What future elements will allow us to adequately describe and represent reality?

Appropriate selections are typically characterized by low element overlap and a sufficiently comprehensive framing of the problem. While total representation is never possible, the inclusion of more elements in cases of doubt will usually lead to a better picture.

It will be necessary to draft a description of each element (see Chapter 3).

4.7 The Actual "Look" into the Future

The core element of any consideration of the future is the preview. Here, it is a matter of extracting as much information out of the future as possible, i.e. effectively convert the suggestion that "the future cannot be predicted" into "the future cannot be *entirely* predicted."

Reference is often made in the literature to various methods of studying the future [Möhrle 2005, Zürni 2002, Ralston 2006, Millett 1991, Gausemeier 1996]. Figure 74 shows a selection of methods of detecting technologies at an early stage. Figure 75 shows the application frequency of a number of methods based on a survey [Z-Dos-

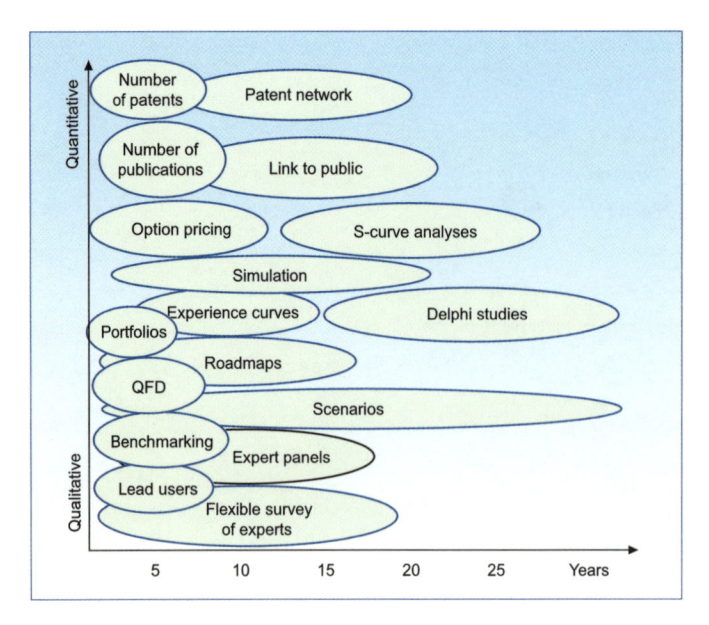

Figure 74 Methods of previewing technologies: various ranges (as adapted from [Lichtenthaler 2005])

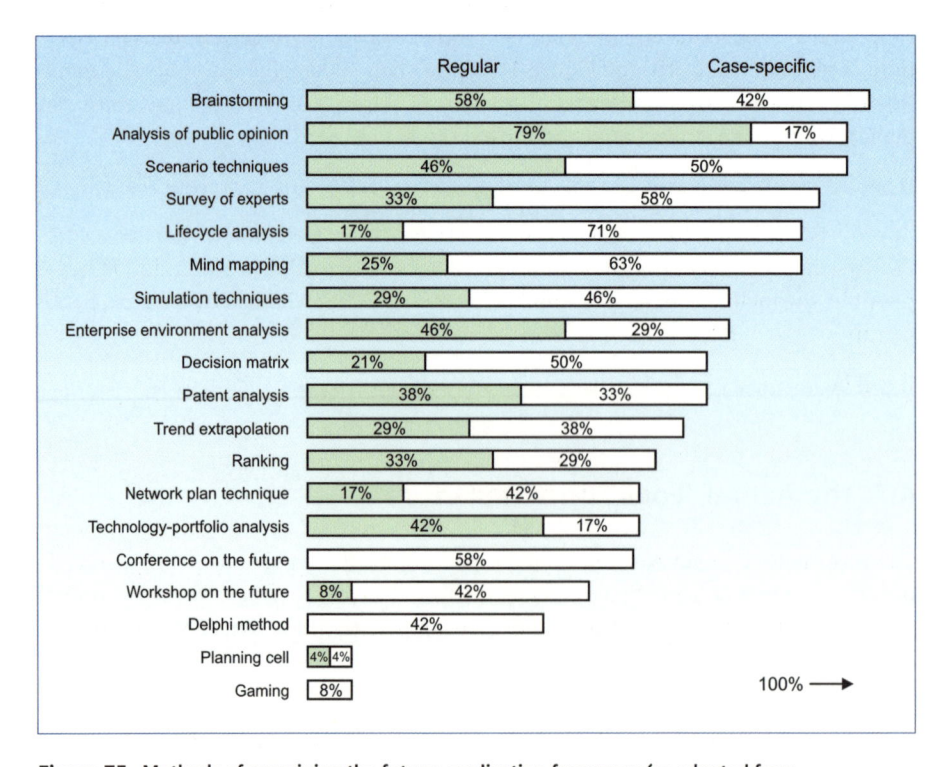

Figure 75 Methods of examining the future: application frequency (as adapted from [Z-Dossier 2002])

180   4 Understanding

sier 2002]. Taking a closer look at the listed methods, we can see that only a few of them really enable us to generate statements about the future. For instance, the often cited patent analysis indicates only that inventions have been made. Registered patents, however, do not tell us whether the inventions in question are pursued further or left unexploited. Offering little information about what might take place in the future, they are usually of only minor significance.

In order to better estimate the utility of the methods for developing pictures of the future, I now turn to a classification of the methods that are usually proposed in the context of future studies:

- Methods of analyzing the future
- Methods of analyzing the present
- Methods of developing opinions and supporting decision making.

Only the methods of analyzing the future are suitable for attempts to look into the future.

4.7.1 Principles and Methods of Analyzing the Future

The most frequently applied principle of analyzing the future is based on the idea of trends and the assumption that identifiable currents will continue well into the future. However, if our considerations of the future are based exclusively on the trend principle, they will lead to one-sided and unsophisticated pictures of the future. In contrast, a systematic approach and the inclusion of further principles will enrich the pictures of the future. The basic principles outlined below are characterized by their capacity to generate new knowledge about a state in the future.

Causal Logic

Causal logic means: the future will be shaped just as the present was shaped by actions in the past. Actions elicit reactions that under certain circumstances will have an effect well into the future. Theories of the future are grounded in a notion of causality. Temporal dependencies arise and certain determining factors have an impact on the future state (Figure 76).

In the case of a pregnancy, we can tell when the birth will take place. A student begins a course of medical studies in the hopes of becoming a certified doctor.

Depending on the system cycles involved, the effects may not be immediately detectable (e.g. climate change and unhealthy diet).

The simplest cases involve the determination of future states via actions in the present. The difficulty now consists in the fact that dependencies change. Determining factors change with respect to their type and strength, and new factors (e.g. disturbances) emerge.

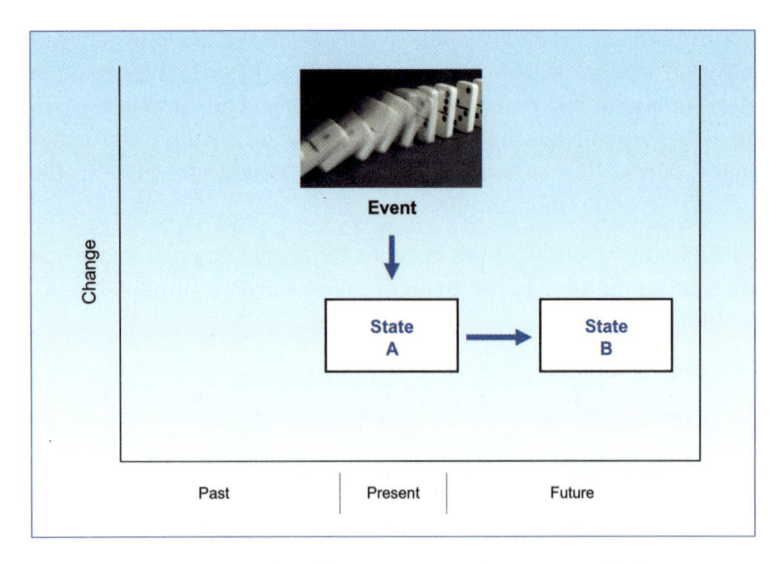

Figure 76 Causal connections: if event X occurs, then state A will change to state B

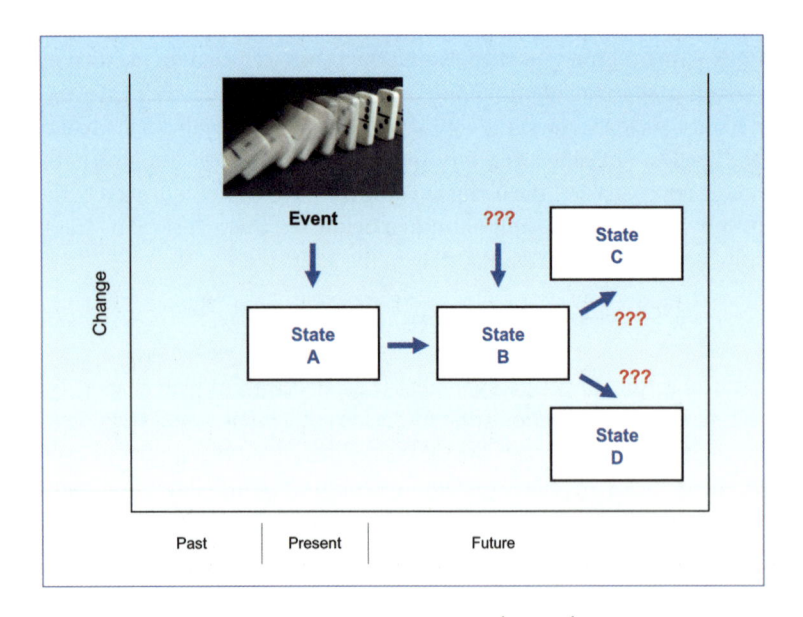

Figure 77 Long-term projections: effects of the 2nd and 3rd order present the real challenge.

The principle of causal logic is particularly suitable for short-term changes, or simple, logical connections. Models are currently being developed for complex situations with alternating dependencies and feedback. However, effects of the second or third order (Figure 77) are often not considered (more about this later in the section entitled "Methods").

Laws

Scientists strive to acquire knowledge and provide explanations. In doing so, they derive theories and laws from observations (Figure 78). In the context of this basic pursuit, the natural sciences yield information about the future: "The sun will also rise in the east fifty years from now;" "Everything that is lighter than air will also continue to rise above the air in fifty years;" and "A fly agaric will be just as fatal when consumed by people in fifty years." The information about the future results from the reproducibility of the observed events and the associated foreseeability. However, it is precisely this reproducibility that is not always available in the social sciences. The fact that exceptions confirm the rule is of little consolation.

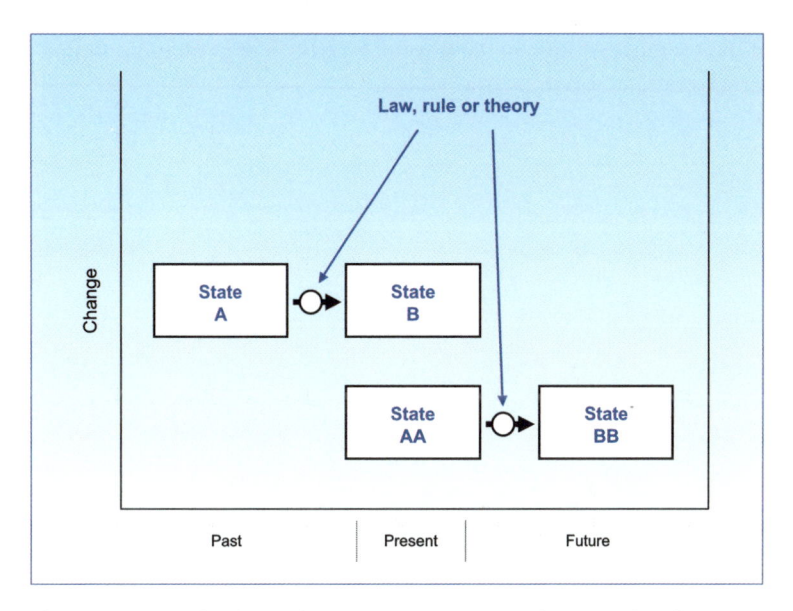

Figure 78 Laws: the change from state A to state B conforms to a law that may also apply to the change from state AA to state BB.

For instance, the manner in which new technologies spread has been thoroughly researched, and their spread can be fairly accurately estimated [Stoneman 2004]. Nonetheless, enterprises are to some extent clueless when it comes to the introduction of new technologies because users do not always act in conformity with the theory. There are also numerous theories about group behavior or group dynamics [Schein 1965]. Little research has been conducted on the application of these theories to future group behavior. Developments are characterized by situation-specific (or even spontaneous) reactions, interactions and feedback and are often difficult to foresee.

Beyond this there are theories based on ideal assumptions. The lifecycle model, for instance, is based on the assumption that the development of products can be represented in equal phases. While the model can undoubtedly be applied to numerous products, there are exceptions. The wave and evolution theories mentioned in Chapter 1 are further examples that underscore the problem of a lack of clarity regarding which law or which theory is applicable.

This basic principle (Figure 78) is suitable for forecasting medium and long-term changes, or for as long as the law is deemed valid by the investigator.

Time Series

Statements about the future that are based on time series are widespread (e.g. in the area of business administration under the name of trend analysis). Whether ascertained quantitatively with the support of statistical instruments or drafted qualitatively via verbal descriptions, trends are based on time series and the assumption that an observed change will continue in the future in the form of a trend, i.e. temporal determinism represented by extrapolation (Figure 79).

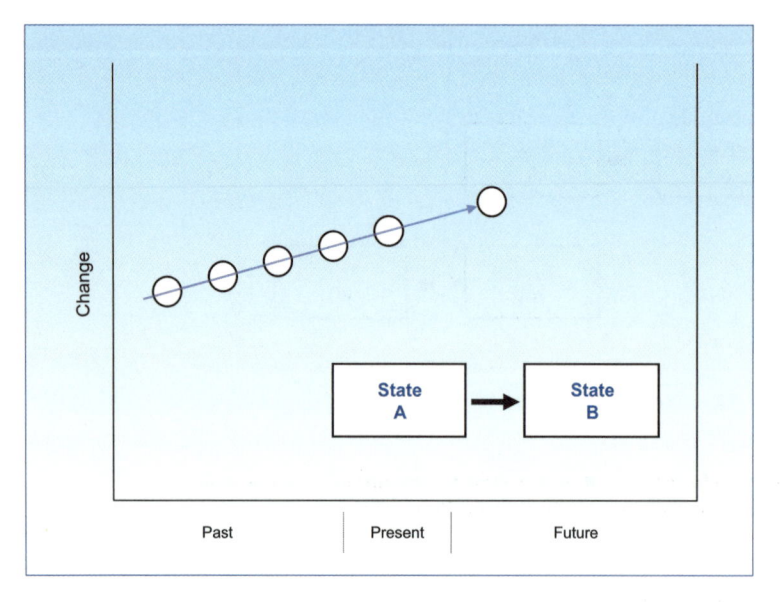

Figure 79 Time series: changes in the past serve as a basis for conclusions about future states

The difficulty with this basic principle consists in determining the scope of its application and the duration of its validity (see Section 1.1). For instance, a trend showing a rise in the number of divorces and a decline in the number of weddings cannot continue indefinitely. The statements "The number of natural catastrophes is increasing steadily" and "The number of traffic-related deaths in Germany is on the decline" can both be represented in a time series. But can we describe both as trends? What information about the future could we derive from doing so? Can we expect the number of traffic-related deaths to fall to zero in around fifty years while deaths related to natural catastrophes increase accordingly? How long do such time series qualify as valid?

The principle of time series is suitable for statements about the medium-term, i.e. statements concerning things in the foreseeable future, so long as we assume constant and clear development for the influencing factors (time-stability hypothesis).

Fantasy and Creativity

The most demanding basic element that goes into our attempt to analyze the future relates exclusively to our powers of imagination. Einstein emphasizes their significance with respect to available knowledge, "Fantasy is more important than knowledge. Knowledge is limited, while fantasy encompasses the entire world." And he pays tribute to the mysterious aspect of the future, "The most beautiful thing we can experience is the mysterious. It is the source of all true art and all science. He to whom this emotion is a stranger, who can no longer pause to wonder and stand rapt in awe, is as good as dead: his eyes are closed." [Einstein 1999]

Only our powers of imagination and the laws of nature can limit fantasy. The information about the future that derives from these is a matter of pictures that are based on evidence (Figure 80) but that do not permit statements about their ultimate occurrence. As outlined in Chapter 1, the crucial thing is to pose many questions because the questions are more important than the answers: properly posed questions establish the direction of further inquiry. The attempt to answer these questions involves a direct testing of speculation, belief and opinion in terms of possible occurrence.

As experience shows, technological developments tend to be overestimated while societal changes tend to be underestimated. The question as to how we will live in the future thus represents a good starting point. What will be important? What will have lost significance? The simple things determine the context. What might appear on the

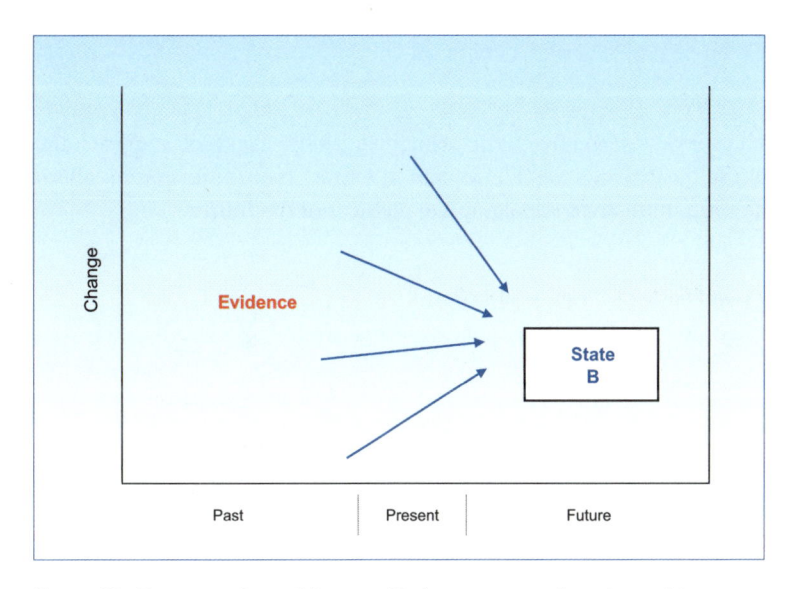

Figure 80 Fantasy and creativity: considering new states based on evidence, independent of the past

front page of a daily newspaper on May 25, 2025? How will we pay for things? Will there still be banks, or will purchases, sales and exchanges be represented on a purely virtual account?

Robert Jungk highlights the significance of fantasy as a basic principle, "It may be that only a small fraction of that which is imagined will become reality. But first we have to imagine something. Then the thought, the idea, the fantasy will draw the reality in its wake. I think of fantasy as a giant magnet that pulls reality in its wake. If I turn the magnet off, then nothing more can happen." [Jungk 1988]

The challenge associated with this basic principle is to establish "enough fantasy to depart from accustomed ways of thinking" without being "so fantastic as to lose the connection to today through science fiction ambition."

Proactive Shaping

The focus in the case of this basic principle is on creating facts and actively shaping the future. In the framework of what is possible, one attempts to influence change and thereby reduce the degree of uncertainty.

Proactive shaping is the only basic principle that includes attempts to influence change. Active shaping arises out of passive observation. The type and extent of influence and shaping correspond to the framework of what is possible. As shown in Figure 25, the degree to which we can have an impact decreases as the distance of the object away from the enterprise increases. However, trendsetters are in a position to have an impact on the direction and orientation of markets and other areas of the micro and macro environment.

In the case of proactive shaping, the information about the future is the result of one's own action.

The Five Basic Principles

Table 25 offers an overview of the five basic principles. As the overview suggests, the combined use of the basic principles allows one to extract more information about the future and develop more vivid and complete pictures of the future.

Table 25 The Five Basic Principles of Future Analysis

Basic Principle	Orientation	Time Scope
Causal logic	Centered on the past	Short to medium term
Time series	Centered on the past	Short to medium term
Laws and theories	Generally valid	Short, medium and long term
Fantasy and creativity	Centered on the future	Medium to long term
Proactive shaping	Centered on the future	Short to medium term

All of the known methods of researching the future can be assigned to one of the basic principles. In what follows, I describe a number of methods and the manner with which we can anticipate knowledge of the future.

Theories and Laws

The danger associated with anticipating future knowledge is the tendency to assume that things will continue to develop as they have. This is the basis, for instance, for Moore's Law according to which the capacity of the semiconductor will double every eighteen months. First proposed by Moore in the year 1965 [Moore 1965], it has retained its validity for more than forty years. However, if we consider the enormous financial efforts that will become necessary as a result of further miniaturization, the question arises as to the further course of development. However, by taking a closer look (instead of blindly accepting the continued validity of this law) it becomes clear that it must be of limited duration. The more interesting question is whether the skyrocketing investments necessary for new chip generations or the reaching of the atomic or subatomic level will lead to a breach in the course of the extrapolated trend.

Other theories include Metcalfe's Law, according to which the value of a telecommunication network is proportional to the square of its users, Gilder's Law, according to which bandwidth doubles at least three times as fast as computer capacity, and the "law of creative destruction," which suggests, "When the rate of external change exceeds the rate of internal change, disaster is imminent." [Pritchett 1995]

A similar assumption is used to support claims about the sine-curve model. While technologies spread very slowly at first, the rate of their spread becomes relatively fast once a certain critical mass has been reached (and in accordance with many multipliers). Once a degree of saturation has been reached, the curve flattens out again. This model has been developed further by Modis who favors its use for analyzing spread dynamics [Modis 1994]. We should not forget, however, that this model, too, represents an ideal state. With the advantage of hindsight, it is relatively easy to

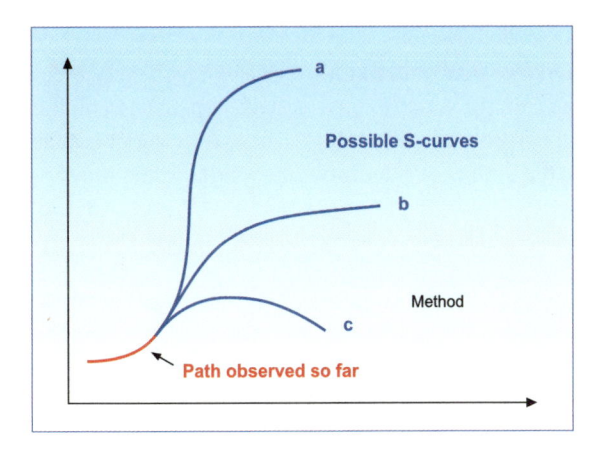

Figure 81 Sine curve concepts: possible development

determine the sine curve. When it comes to a preview of what is to come, we lack reference points.

Figure 81 underscores the problem. The red line represents the observed development of a variable. Optimists tend to believe in the sine curve and assume course a, although courses b and c are also possible. Pessimists may suggest that saturation has already been reached in the case of the red line. As is often the case, it is a matter of interpretation.

Calculations

Assuming a constant flight speed and an absence of interruptions, we can determine a plane's exact time of arrival at its destination airport. The logical piecing together of information available in the present allows us to calculate a future. As in this example, we can draw conclusions about events in the future on the basis of changes in the present. However, this applies only for simple systems and can essentially only be represented for simple events. Such conclusions are always based on the assumption of constant circumstances and the absence of interruption (time-stability hypothesis) [Hansmann 1983]. Travel plans are based on this principle about the future.

Extrapolation

"Extrapolators" assume that the future will look much the same as today. Identifiable currents and trends can be extended into the future. This approach to considering the future is relatively widespread and is frequently applied on account of its simplicity. But extrapolation will deliver accurate statements about the future course of things only if the conditions that applied at the beginning of the observed development continue to apply and only if all other assumptions retain their validity. Despite the widely accepted belief that the rate at which our environment changes has accelerated and will continue to accelerate, we find precisely this dangerous assumption at work again and again in the forecast business, for instance, in the common, overly optimistic analyses of market developments. It is as if we were to drive our cars by looking continuously in the rearview mirror.

"Forecasts are not always wrong; more often than not, they can be reasonably accurate. And that is what makes them so dangerous. They are usually constructed on the assumption that tomorrow's world will be much like today's. They often work because the world does not always change. But sooner or later forecasts will fail when they are most needed." [Wack 1985]

Models and Simulation

One can represent the world in the form of a model – at least the modelers assume this. Circumstances, connections and dependencies are formalized, i.e. processed into forms and systems. Climatologists have been at work for a long time on developing reliable software models of the world's climate – with an unclear degree of success. The decisive advantage associated with this approach is that one is forced to consider very exactly how the individual variables in the model depend on one another, how they change and what remains constant. Nothing is better when it comes to really learning a system and its connections than attempting to reproduce it in the form of a model. However, even in the case of relatively simple systems, the construction of the model can prove to be extremely complex and time consuming. Actual simulation (i.e. the application of the model with concrete values) can quickly turn into a subordinate matter.

Other disadvantages include uncertainty as to whether the model is complete and as to whether it delivers reliable statements. But even if one accepts this shortcoming, one is required to be in the clear on the fact that it is "only" a rigid and inflexible construct – expansions can be very tedious. Even the use of software-based support tools for business purposes is not that widespread.

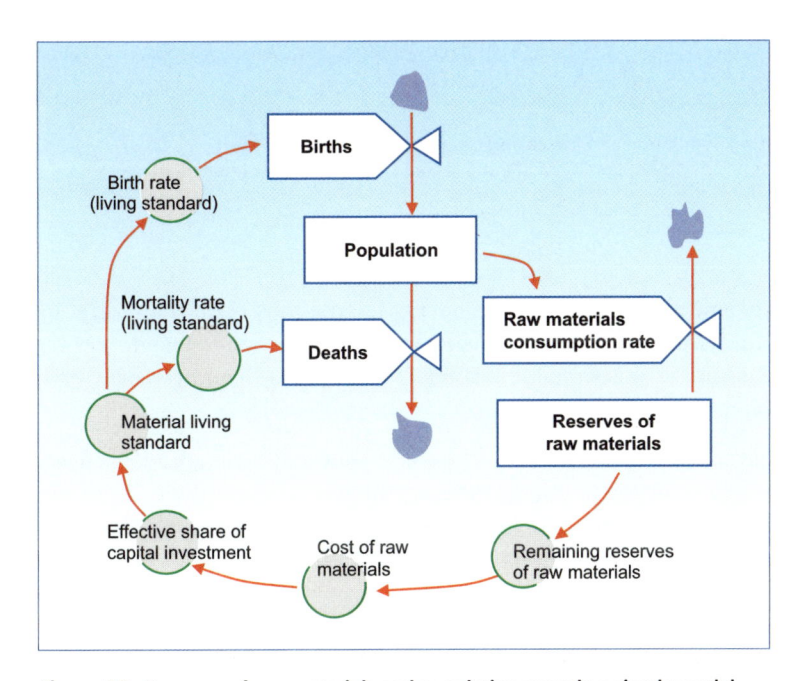

Figure 82 Reserves of raw materials and population growth: a simple model

Forrester is regarded as one of the co-founders of System Dynamics – a modeling tool. While the excessive time and effort associated with the tool's use as well as the difficulties associated with interpreting the results it delivers have probably prevented more widespread use of the tool, it can be very useful when it comes to structuring and representing situations (what-if) and problems [Sterman 2000].

Figure 82 shows a relatively simple model [Forrester 1971]. If we feed the course of development for the initial variables (Figure 83) into this model, we can determine the starting conditions (e.g. population) and we can observe the impact the initial variables have on the overall system as they change.

4.7 The Actual "Look" into the Future

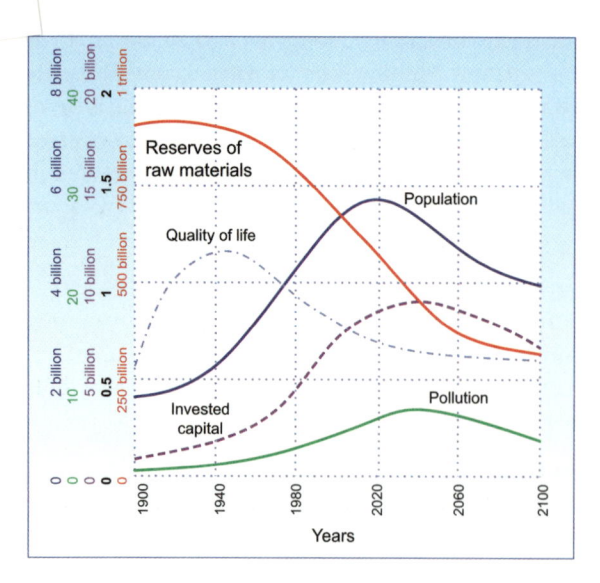

Figure 83 Increasing population and increasing consumption of raw materials: the result is declining quality of life and increasing capital investment

Brainstorming

Human creativity and motivation wind up having a large impact on the future. By writing books, Jules Verne, for instance, has provided tremendous inspiration for generations. According to one estimate, around 300 of his ideas have been converted into inventions and products.

If we assume that the future doesn't simply happen, but that it can also be actively shaped, then we will probably not underestimate the impact of creativity. However, as Teresa Amabile describes in her article "How to Kill Creativity" [Amabile 1998], only a few organizations actively promote creativity. "Serious business" (still) has no room for and no interest in creative approaches. They are too strenuous and too risky. Anyone who conducts a serious consideration of the future, however, will have to conclude that they are indispensable, as I will discuss in more detail in the following section.

Brainstorming is a promising method of expanding our powers of imagination and generating new ideas.

Detecting Recurring Patterns

All cyclical processes, both in nature and civilization, show recurring patterns. These include the seasons and the celebration of Christmas. Every year (even as early as late summer), retailers begin to prepare for the holiday season. It is also a safe assumption that this will still be the case in 50 or 100 years, leaving us with another piece of the future that seems calculable.

On the other hand, caution is advised. Holidays and seasons will certainly occur again, as they have so far or in a similar form. But there are also cycles that are neither predetermined in the manner of the holidays nor linked to the movement of the earth like the seasons. For instance, the chart analysis is recognized as a method of anticipating stock performance. The performance of a stock is analyzed for a certain period. As soon as certain patterns appear, a conclusion is drawn that these patterns will recur. The logic behind this method does not quite hold water. Given that stock performance depends on very many factors (e.g. information about the enterprise, the status of the information and the situation of the market participants) that change rather constantly, it is doubtful whether the method really offers us a reliable way of predicting the course of a stock's further development. Moreover, we can also assume that even if truly reliable methods of determining future stock performance were available and these methods were used by enough market participants, then this would have an impact on the course of stock's development – and the development would be different than anticipated.

This principle based on recurring patterns therefore remains limited to cases involving causal connections.

Decisions

This method allows one to determine and plan for events in the future. The Olympic Winter Games will, as a matter of fact, be held in Vancouver in 2010. The International Space Station (ISS) is to be completed by the year 2010 and is to be operated for at least 10 years. The European Union also has long-term plans. The council presidency is to be taken over by Finland in the year 2020 for a six-month period (from January to June). A pregnancy lasts around nine months and ends with the birth of a child. The future of a human being begins with this conscious decision. The exact date of Easter Sunday is determined by the Catholic Church because it is oriented on the moon (and has seen many exceptions or Easter paradoxes). We thus know that Easter will fall on March 24 in the year 2391. While this determination reaches very far into the future, it compellingly illustrates how the future is shaped by determinations and decisions. This principle effectively reduces uncertainty and increases planning security. However, the fact is that this sort of thing is only feasible in exceptional cases in our continuously changing economic spheres. In contrast to mere planning (i.e. expressing a will to a certain action), determinations create facts.

Weak Signals

Igor Ansoff is the founder of the concept known as "weak signals" [Ansoff 1976]. Even if the concept remains controversial, its introduction by Ansoff effectively created the basis for strategic early detection. Ansoff's approach focuses on discontinuities or events that are difficult to foresee and whose occurrence forces an enterprise to accept the implementation of drastic measures [Ansoff 1981]. The events, or surprises, are thought to be heralded by weak signals. Weak signals can be described as imprecise indications of upcoming events. In contrast, strong signals are sufficiently detectable and specific, thereby allowing enterprises to calculate their impact.

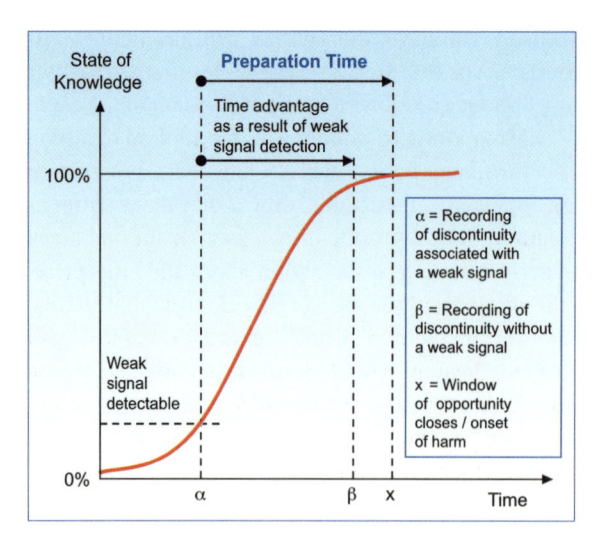

Figure 84 Detecting weak signals: gaining a head start via early detection (as adapted from [Ansoff 1980])

Embracing the concept, however, presents us with a certain dilemma. If the danger is concrete, then it is too late to act. But if the information is vague, then there is no way to foresee discontinuities. In an attempt to avoid the dilemma, Ansoff proposes a phased reaction depending on the emerging strength of the signals. Figure 84 shows the head start that can be won by the early detection of relevant weak signals.

Mintzberg criticizes the increased costs associated with this approach. He suggests that essentially every piece of evidence, no matter how insignificant, can be thought of as a weak signal. What tells us that something is a weak signal? The answer is: the assumption that it will gain in significance. In keeping with Figure 41, a weak signal is thus a prior stage of a trend.

Historical Analogies

In certain circumstances, historical analogies may also provide a way of obtaining information about the future. Although it is known that history can never repeat itself exactly, there are certain constellations that allow one to draw conclusions about the approach of similar developments. Reports on the probability of rain, most common sayings, Kondratieff's wave model, and even certain financial market rules are based on this principle.

Methods Summary

The identified methods of analyzing the future can be arranged as shown in Figure 85. Table 26 offers a further brief characterization. While all of these methods are more or less suitable for generating information about the future, it is also clear that their explanatory power may differ significantly.

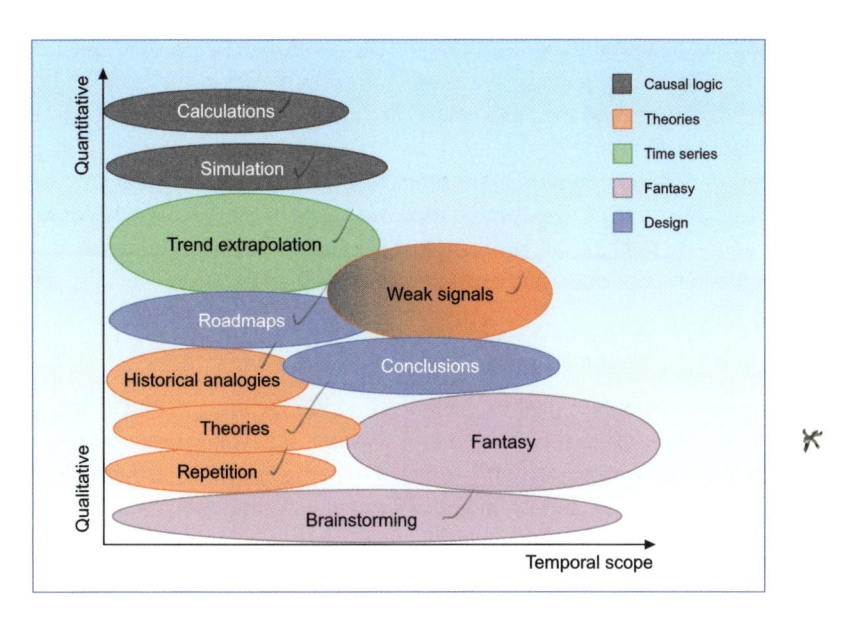

Figure 85 Analyzing the future: most methods do not reach far into the future

Table 26 Methods of Analyzing the Future

	Method	Assumptions	Information about the Future
1	Calculations	Stable development, no interruptions	The forecast is completely accurate.
2	Extrapolation	Initial conditions remain stable, no change in the setting	Developments are foreseeable for short time periods (system time).
3	Models and simulation	Model is incomplete and does not change with respect to reality	What-if information
4	Decisions	Active shaping of the future	Controlled development
5	Weak signals	Weak signals herald change and discontinuity	Evidence and the hunch that the signal will strengthen and gain in significance
6	Historical analogies	Learning from history: assumption that certain developments repeat themselves	What-if information, development according to the historical development
7	Detection of recurring patterns	Events recur under certain (constant) conditions	What-if information
8	Brainstorming	Only limited by powers of imagination	Generation of visions, goals and ideas
9	Theories and laws	Laws and algorithms allow us to foresee developments	Course of a system variable
10	Roadmaps	Planning and shaping the future by establishing fixed events in the future	Future orientation (memories of the future)

4.7 The Actual "Look" into the Future

The scenario analysis has established itself as the most common procedure used to examine the future. Scenario analysis represents more than a set of methods and is better characterized as a process than as a single method. It is thus outstandingly well suited for combination with any of the other basic principles or methods outlined above. The selection depends on personal preference, on the time available and on one's budget. While diversity, i.e. the combination of several of these basic principles, is advisable, it can prove to be rather cumbersome because the information gained is unstructured and heterogeneous – or even contradictory.

4.7.2 Methods of Analyzing the Present

Various methods used to analyze present situations and to facilitate the structuring of information were introduced in Chapter 2 and Chapter 3. Beyond these, however, there are also methods that are persistently referred to in the literature as methods of examining the future although they are not geared to generating information about the future (Table 27) [Wilms 2006, Zürni 2004].

Table 27 Methods of Analyzing the Present

	Method	Assumptions	Information about the Future
1	Patent analysis	Focus of research, description of an invention	None, possible information about the research strategies of competitors
2	Mind mapping	Technique for structuring information	None
3	Cross-impact analysis	Cross connection of development trends and the assumption that these will also apply in the future	Information about cross connections
4	Study of the literature	Information and knowledge about future events	No direct information about the future, only via reflection and inspiration

Further methods for analyzing the micro and macro environment are available in Annex 2.

4.7.3 Methods of Opinion Formation and Decision Making

In addition to the methods outlined above, there is a whole series of methods that are also referred to in the literature as methods of analyzing the future, but which are restricted to the processing and structuring information concerning the present and forming opinions.

While personal opinion will vary, the fact that examinations of the future are often conducted in groups makes it necessary to moderate discussions with a group aim in mind, to be ready for compromise, to consolidate various opinions into a group opinion, and to arrive at decisions that are accepted by the group.

One major flaw in the opinion-forming process is that carefully researched findings about the future are "adjusted" by managers who are authorized to do so in virtue of their higher standing in the enterprise. Instead of reflecting on what the future will mean for the enterprise, they adapt the future to the enterprise and undermine the original intention behind the investigation.

It warrants recalling that we should not allow examinations of the future to be hijacked and turned into opportunities to champion someone's personal views and opinions. On the contrary, the aim is to establish a neutral picture of the future. In addition to the basic principles and the methods of analyzing the future, the methods of forming opinion are therefore of crucial significance.

In what follows, I describe a number of the methods used to form opinions in the context of projects centering on assessments of the future.

The Delphi Method

The Delphi method, for instance, involves an attempt to distill the opinions of the recognized experts down to a substrate that is acceptable for all. The subjective opinions of experts continue to hold sway when it comes to forecasts of technological development [Blohm 1972]. In light of this situation, Delphi method surveys permit a certain inter-subjective selection from the more or less spontaneously and intuitively expressed individual opinions. The method is based on the assumption that a forecast that can be agreed upon by a majority of those surveyed will possess a greater degree of credibility than the opinion of an individual expert. Of course, it follows from this that the composition of the surveyed group will have a considerable impact on the result of the survey. Special caution is warranted when it comes to the role extraneous motives might play in the formation and expression of the opinions held by the experts participating in the survey. Experts may, for instance, present a skewed view (i.e. overly optimistic) of the future prospects of work in their own fields, although a tendency to self-fulfilling prophecies can also not be ruled out.

Observing Trendsetters

There are organizations, institutions and prominent individuals whose capacity to influence the future is undisputed. Opinion formers have a hand in the shaping of the future. One can anticipate developments by studying the relevant trendsetters and considering their influence.

This suggestion is supported by many examples. The influence of Bill Gates and Microsoft (or even Michael Dell with his revolutionary business model) on the computer industry is immense, as is that of Steve Jobs and Apple on the music industry, and Google on the development of the Internet.

However, there are also many counterexamples: Scott McNealy's Net PC still doesn't exist, despite the powerful lobby behind it. WAP technology just doesn't seem to want to go big – despite huge investments and extensive advertising.

While there are considerable risks associated with relying on the opinions of the relevant gurus in the field, taking the time to inform oneself about their motives and latest statements can be very useful when it comes to filling out one's own analysis. It should, however, be clear for the ambitious leaders of enterprises that blindly following a guru is hardly a good way of becoming a market leader.

Expert Opinion

Our faith in experts is unshakeable. But who do we designate as experts? Those who possess special knowledge or skills in a particular field and have also had an opportunity to demonstrate these qualify as experts in the field in question. However, the exceptional domain know-how that characterizes these individuals is also a large burden.

If asked to give their opinions on the role of women in the future, a feminist and the pope (both experts) are likely to give very different answers. The problem is clear. It is important to find the right expert. In other words, we could find a suitable expert for any imaginable future. Our faith in the expertise of the experts is based on the misconception that knowledge about a special area will also entail knowledge about the future.

In his study, "Experts and Foresight: Review and Experience," Denis Loveridge [Loveridge 2004] investigates the role of experts in the foresight process and comes to the conclusion that the opinions of the experts are generally overrated. In particular, the compelling presentation of an expert opinion can lead to bias. In our perception, the opinions of experts are quickly elevated to the status of facts or predetermined elements. "The earnest experts are often bad at forecasting: they propagate their favorite ideas and tend to overestimate the speed with which their own new technologies will spread, and they are often blind to the merits of competing technologies, as well as to the utter complexity of developments. It seems that little has changed in this matter up until the present day." [Steinmüller 2000] However reasonable this assessment may sound, the need for experts is growing continuously. After all, we are living in a time of ever greater specialization.

Group Opinions

It is not only since the publishing of the book, "The Wisdom of Crowds" by James Surowiecki [Surowiecki 2001] that we have known that groups of more than three persons are better at solving problems than individuals. This can also be proven empirically. In contrast to an individual, groups have the option of exchanging their thoughts and views about things. The diversity that is given by the various group members allows for the discussion and development of various ideas and approaches. While groups are also not able to automatically describe the future and to avoid uncertainty, a conception of the future that has been developed by a cohesive group is likely to be more plausible and complete than one reflecting a single opinion.

The magic word is "shared vision." "The practice of shared vision involves the skills of unearthing shared "pictures of the future" that foster genuine commitment and enrollment rather than compliance." [Senge 1990]

Game and Decision Theory

Game theory is a logical-mathematical method of analysis. The metaphor of the game is used to describe and model situations so as to arrive at decisions. Although this sub-area of mathematics has received and continues to receive much attention – not only in the field of mathematics, as is evident in the five Nobel prizes in economics that have been awarded to works in game theory – its suitability as a tool for deriving statements about the future is limited.

Owing to the very simplified representation of situations as games, the results can be applied to reality only to a limited degree. Highly complex situations are reduced to self-contained games involving a fixed number of players and a clear set of rules, with the aim of arriving at optimal decisions. Another disadvantage to this game-theory method is that it assumes rational decisions: the players have all of the relevant information and act logically and rationally. This assumption has largely been replaced by a view of human behavior that includes irrationality – a fact that artists have always known.

However, game theory does allow us to gather evidence for important decisions that could have a large impact on the future. The approach to and the processing of the issues at hand alone expand our mental horizons, and thereby the solution realm as well.

Intuition

Gut decisions are usually made on the basis of feelings, incomplete information and a subconscious analysis and evaluation. Clear, stringent, and logical reasons can usually not be given for such decisions. Why a decision went one way instead of another remains unclear. In the case of decisions that have a bearing on the future, this effectively means that developments are not be pursued and accounted for rationally, but

Table 28 Methods of Forming Opinion and Making Decisions

	Method	Assumptions	Information about the Future
1	*Expert opinion*	Experts know more thanks to their expertise.	Individual
2	*Group opinion*	Groups know more.	Not clear
3	*Game and decision theory*	Rational, logical decisions	If-then analysis
4	*Intuition*	The subconscious knows more.	Feelings, hopes, suppositions

emotionally and nebulously. The result is often a picture of the future that largely reflects the wishes of the gut decider.

This subject plays a large role in investigations of uncertainty and the future. Many assessments are based on intuition and cannot, for the time being, be replaced by sound and rational argumentation. As in the case of the other basic principles, there is no guarantee that such assessments are right. We can only determine after the fact whether the intuitions were helpful as we entered the future.

4.7.4 Selection of Foresight Methods ("Looking into the Future")

In order to minimize the influence of extraneous considerations, the participants in foresight projects are expected to show openness, integrity, a facility with the subject at hand and the ability to take a reasonable approach to considering alternatives.

In the context of introducing the various methods, it was suggested that not all of them are suited to the task of analyzing the future. It would thus be helpful to classify the methods into methods of analyzing the present, methods of analyzing the future and methods of forming opinion. Keeping these separate at all stages of inquiry will help to secure transparency and neutrality. The members of the group should promote a diverse range of opinions and work to reach an agreement on a group opinion.

It is primarily the methods of analyzing the future that are used when the task at hand is to "look into the future." Hypotheses concerning future development are drafted for the previously identified elements. Table 29 shows the possibilities of applying the basic principles to the categories of the elements of the future.

Table 29 Application of the Basic Principles to the Elements of the Future

Elements of the Future	Causal	Laws	Time Series	Fantasy	Shaping
Paradigms/constants	x	x		x	
Trends		x	x		x
Uncertainties	x	x		x	x
Contradictions	x	x		x	
Chaos/wildcards	x			x	

4.7.5 Developing Hypotheses

The factor of time plays a special role in the process of drafting hypotheses. Defining the future-studies project will include the establishment of the timeframe to be considered. Whether the scope extends to five years, ten years or even further into the future usually depends on the definition of the inquiry and the goal of the project. While the desire for such precision is understandable, the establishment of an exact date is of little help.

By way of illustration, let us assume that we have identified, researched and worked out two future elements relating to our example of the future of television. These include P1 "TV is the main medium of entertainment." and T6 "As a result of changes in the way consumers spend their free time, TV programs are becoming ever shorter." From our current perspective, P1 is a paradigm, and therefore very stable, while T6 is a trend. If the scope of our investigation has been set to five or ten years, it will be difficult to detect the difference between the five-year mark and the ten-year mark. Will television still be the main entertainment medium in five years? How short will television programs be in five years? And what changes will occur here between five and ten years? It is therefore almost impossible to hit the target dates exactly.

In view of the various system cycles, it would be better to define the scope in terms of short term, medium term and long term. System cycles are subject-specific. It is estimated to be around seven to eight years for our example of the future of television. This estimate takes into consideration the lifecycle of a television set and expresses how the system "television" can process changes and innovations. A system "notebook" has a shorter system cycle. A system "subway" has a much longer system cycle and a system "earth" has an astronomically longer system cycle. We can thus define our scope as one of the following:

Short term = *immediate future*

Medium term = *the elapsing of around one system cycle*

Long term = *everything that extends beyond the elapsing of a system cycle*

This effectively links the temporal scope of the inquiry to the possibilities of change for the object of the investigation. This is more helpful when it comes to developing hypotheses than abstract points of time in the future.

The hypothesis can be ascertained in the form of a table (see Table 30) for each of the elements. One will have to assume that the element's category will change in the future and that new elements will emerge. This procedure allows one to systematically develop assumptions for each element in keeping with the basic principles and methods of analyzing the future.

Table 30 The Systematic Development of Hypotheses for the Elements of the Future

Elements of the Future	Short Term	Medium Term	Long Term
Paradigms/constants	Complete	No change	Laws
Trends	Complete	Time series, laws	Time series, laws
Uncertainties	Complete	Shaping	Fantasy
Contradictions	Complete	Causal	Causal
Chaos/wildcards	Complete	Speculation	Speculation
New elements	Not applicable	Fantasy, shaping	Speculation

4.8 Development of Scenario Frameworks and Scenarios

The elements of the future will have to be placed in the right combination if we are to arrive at coherent pictures of the future. So far, all of the elements are available as individual building blocks.

The "right" combination is essentially any combination that is plausible. The aim here is to identify combinations with a high degree of inner homogeneity and outer heterogeneity. The arrangement and linking of appropriate pictures yields scenario frameworks that can then be developed into complete scenarios at a later stage.

Number of Scenarios

There is no generally valid response to the question as to how many pictures of the future are optimal. However, depending on the definition of the inquiry and the goal

Table 31 The Number of Scenarios Is Derived from the Definition of the Inquiry and the "Philosophy of the Future"

Number of Scenarios	Evaluation
1	Most likely scenario. Although convenient from the point of view of the strategist, it is nonetheless false. There are no probable scenarios.
2	Two scenarios are usually a matter of two extreme scenarios that will be difficult to handle in the context of evaluation.
3	There is a risk of orienting oneself to the middle scenario.
4	Possible, good cost-benefit ratio
5	Possible
More than 5	Possible, but the cost of drafting and evaluating may increase to a level that is no longer justifiable.

Table 32 Three Approaches to Drafting the Scenario Framework

	Minimal Approach	Standard Approach	Maximum Approach
Number of uncertainties	2	Around 3 to 8	> 8
Deployed tools and methods	Four-quadrants matrix	Wilson matrix, morphological analysis	Wilson matrix, morphological analysis, cross-impact analysis, consistency analysis
Cost	Minimal	Appropriate	Very high
Application	Simple description of the inquiry	Description of the inquiry with a manageable number of uncertainties and elements	Complex subjects with many degrees of freedom and unknown variables

of the project, it should probably be more than two and less than ten. The upward limit in the number of scenarios is set by the necessary time and effort. The lower limit is set by one's understanding of scenarios. Table 31 shows an evaluation of the number of deployed scenarios.

Experience has shown that a number of the methods are well-suited and can be easily combined into a framework. Depending on the situation, motivation, clarity and possible time and effort, one can select from among minimal, standard and maximum approaches (Table 32).

Minimal Approach

The minimal approach is usually suitable when the overview of all elements reveals two criteria that will allow one to determine the further development. A detailed description is available in [Pillkahn 2005]. Such minimal scenarios can be used, for instance, when introducing new products or technologies (Figure 86). One criterion is the demand. The other is the availability. This results in four alternatives from the top down. The elements of the future are adapted and linked according to the particular context.

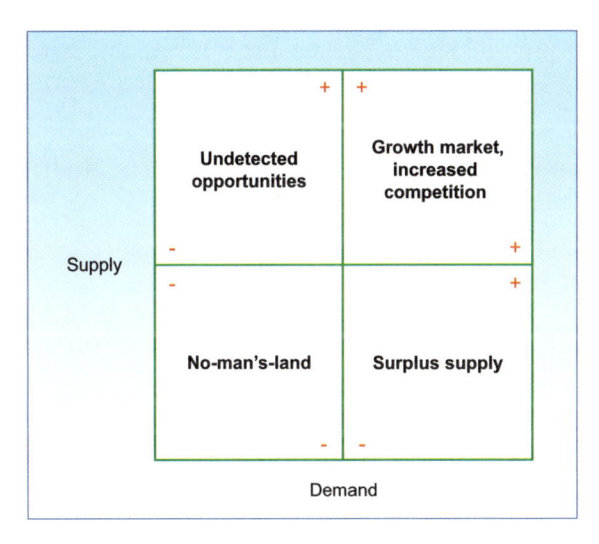

Figure 86 Development of scenarios: the minimal approach

Standard Approach

The standard approach, which allows for a more differentiated assessment of continued development, is recommended if the number of uncertain factors cannot be reduced to two (see Table 30). First, all elements are evaluated separately according to their estimated degree of uncertainty in the context of continued development and their possible impact on the direction of the subject's development (Wilson matrix, Figure 87). The elements that are evaluated as critical distinguish themselves in

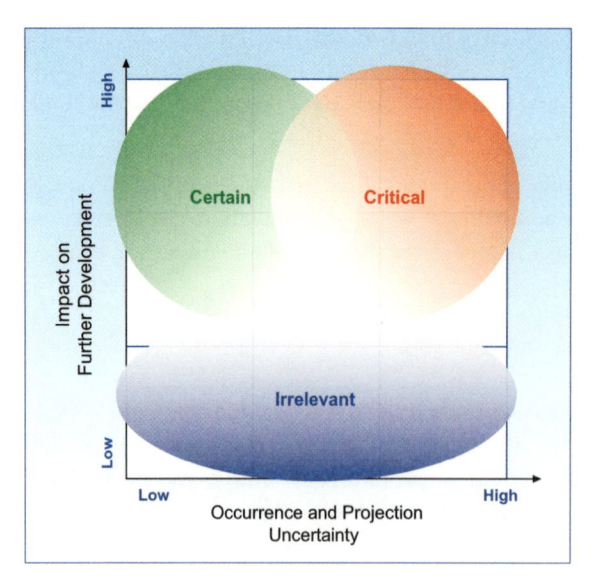

Figure 87 Evaluation of the significance of elements of development: the Wilson matrix

terms of a high degree of uncertainty and high potential impact. This makes them especially interesting. A further investigation is then made of their high degree of uncertainty.

Alternative development variations are yielded for each element that is to be investigated. A chart representation of the procedure is shown in Figure 88:

1. Enter the critical elements at the top of the columns. Note: the example includes space for four elements.

2. Draft a number of conceivable development variations (at least two) and enter these in the corresponding columns.

3. Combine the development variations into plausible strands.

4. Each strand forms the core cell for a scenario. Find an appropriately descriptive name for the scenarios.

Step 3 centers on a combination of those development variations that are not contradictory and that seem to fit together. One is required to take an iterative approach to combining the appropriately matching variations. The number of strands depends on the desired number of scenarios.

The scenario framework results when the developed scenario core is fleshed out with the other elements. The stable ("secure") and irrelevant elements (Figure 87) are the same for all scenarios. The differences lie in the critical elements and the specially ascertained variations.

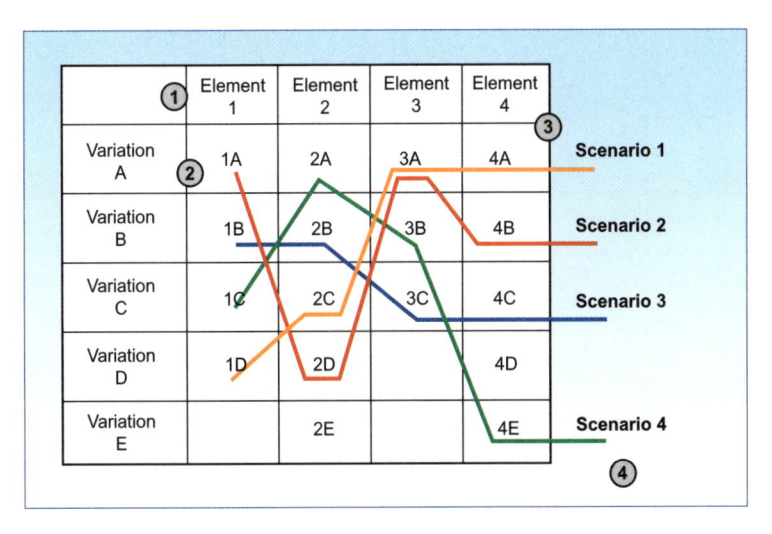

	Element 1	Element 2	Element 3	Element 4	
Variation A	1A	2A	3A	4A	Scenario 1
Variation B	1B	2B	3B	4B	Scenario 2
Variation C	1C	2C	3C	4C	Scenario 3
Variation D	1D	2D		4D	
Variation E		2E		4E	Scenario 4

Figure 88 Morphological analysis: the scenarios are dependent on the variation of the individual elements of the future

Maximum Approach

The maximum approach is used for situations and inquiries that are characterized by an even larger number of elements and uncertainties. Owing to a lack of clarity, the scenario framework cannot – as in the standard approach – be drafted on the basis of the chart alone. A number of additional steps are necessary. One starts by reducing the number of elements with the help of cross-impact analysis.

This involves an analysis of the relationships between the elements and the impact they have on one another (Figure 89). Each combination is investigated separately and assigned a score based on a scale of 0 (independent) to 3 (powerful driver). The active sum allows one to determine the elements that have an especially strong impact on (and essentially drive) the other elements. Note: in the example, these include T1, T4, T7, T8, and T10.

Selecting the elements, as shown in Figure 90, allows one to focus on the factors that show the highest shaping potential. These serve as a basis and starting point for the development of the scenario core.

As in the case of the standard approach, the selected elements are then analyzed using the Wilson matrix (Figure 87) and the morphological chart.

Once the morphological chart has been filled out with the relevant development variations, a consistency analysis is run in the context of the maximum approach using another matrix (Figure 91). The compatibility of the combined variations is checked step by step, resulting in a structuring of the selection of scenario strands. The procedure that was completed in the standard approach with the use of the morphological chart (step 3) is now carried out more comprehensively. As shown in Figure 91, this allows one to secure the consistency of the strands.

	T1	T2	T3	T4	T5	T6	T7	T8	T9	T10	Active Score
T1		3	3	3	2	3	3	2	1	2	**22**
T2	0		3	0	3	0	2	0	1	2	11
T3	1	1		0	0	0	2	1	0	0	4
T4	2	2	3		3	2	3	1	1	2	16
T5	0	2	3	0		0	2	1	1	3	13
T6	2	1	3	1	1		1	0	1	2	13
T7	1	2	2	2	2	1		3	2	3	**18**
T8	2	3	3	1	1	0	3		1	2	16
T9	2	1	0	2	1	2	2	2		1	13
T10	3	3	3	3	3	0	2	2	1		**20**
Score	15	**18**	**23**	12	16	8	**20**	12	9	17	

Active: T1 T7 T10
Passive: T2 T3 T7

0 Independent 2 Dependent
1 Slight impact 3 Strong driver

Figure 89 Cross-impact analysis (example involving 10 trends: T1 to T10): the powerful drivers form the pictures of the future

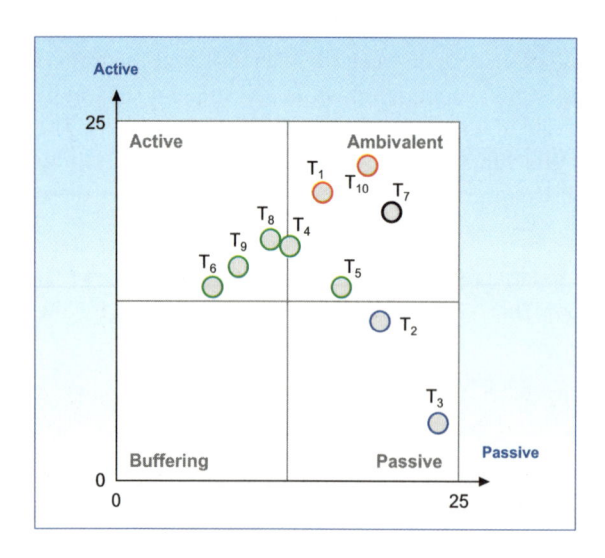

Figure 90 Cross-impact evaluation: identification of crucial elements

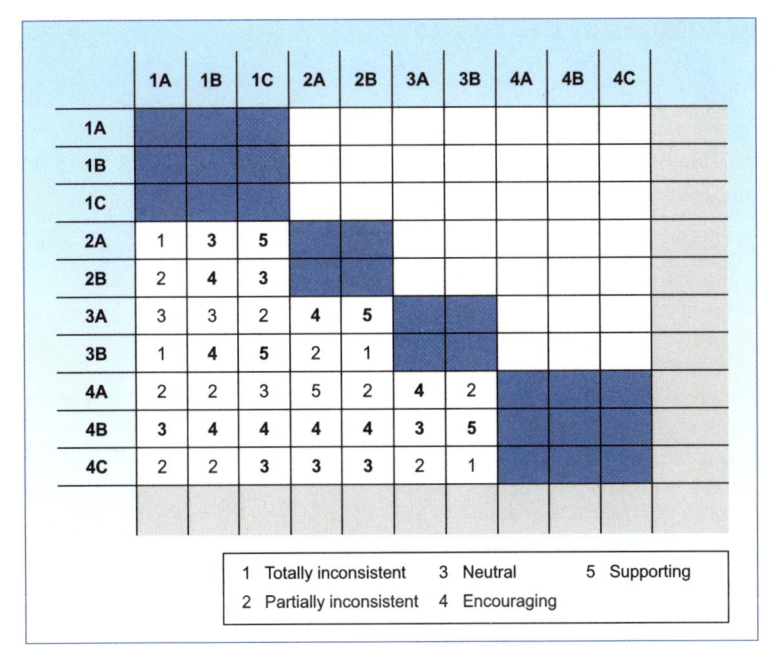

	1A	1B	1C	2A	2B	3A	3B	4A	4B	4C
1A										
1B										
1C										
2A	1	3	5							
2B	2	4	3							
3A	3	3	2	4	5					
3B	1	4	5	2	1					
4A	2	2	3	5	2	4	2			
4B	3	4	4	4	4	3	5			
4C	2	2	3	3	3	2	1			

1 Totally inconsistent   3 Neutral   5 Supporting
2 Partially inconsistent 4 Encouraging

Figure 91 Consistency analysis: what happens and why it happens

The combined variations are evaluated according to the following scheme:

1 – Total inconsistency (impossible combination)

2 – Partial inconsistency (includes contradictions)

3 – Neutral (no cross impact)

4 – Mutual promotion (positive impact)

5 – Mutual dependency (both projections are linked)

This somewhat formalized approach is the most elaborate of all the approaches. A broad array of software products is available for support. However, it warrants bearing in mind that a high degree of quantified consistency is no guarantee for sound and coherent pictures of the future. Both the generation and operative implementation of the elements and the evaluative steps are highly subjective, based on gut feelings, suppositions and wishes. The precise evaluation of imprecise input variables will quickly turn into a purely academic exercise – the quantification of gut feelings. Experience shows that scenarios with fewer but very carefully examined and discussed elements tend to yield better results than scenarios with more elements that have been generated using software tools.

The selection of one of the three approaches is ultimately dependent on the situation at hand and personal preference. The scenario technique represents a framework that offers much room for testing established methods and experimenting. However, the combination of many methods and basic principles guarantees more robust scenarios.

4.8 Development of Scenario Frameworks and Scenarios

4.9 Creating Pictures of the Future

The pictures of the future themselves are then created and described on the basis of the scenario framework. The form that is given to the pictures of the future essentially depends on the aim of the inquiry, on the available design possibilities and on the targeted avenues of communication.

In addition to the representation of the pictures of the future, the conveyance of the core message is especially important: what are the important findings and how are they to be conveyed to recipients whose skills of comprehension and attention spans are limited?

As shown in Table 33, it is easiest to reuse the scenario framework without any additional modifications (e.g. for purposes of internal strategy development). However, if

Table 33 Ways of Creating Pictures of the Future

	Representation	Application
1	Scenario framework	No communication planned
2	Story	Packaging of the elements into a story
3	Visualization	Graphical support in connection with the story, representation of complex circumstances
4	Multimedia presentation	Conveying the messages via movies, suitable for high-level communication and for addressing a large number of recipients

Figure 92 Visualized picture of the future: kitchen showroom 2015 (Jacques Helot 2005)

the findings are to be communicated more broadly – internally and, if appropriate, externally – it is advisable to package the elements in the scenario framework into comprehensible stories. Whether one thinks up a story first, and then packages the

Figure 93 Visualized picture of the future: kitchen scenario 2015 (Jacques Helot 2005)

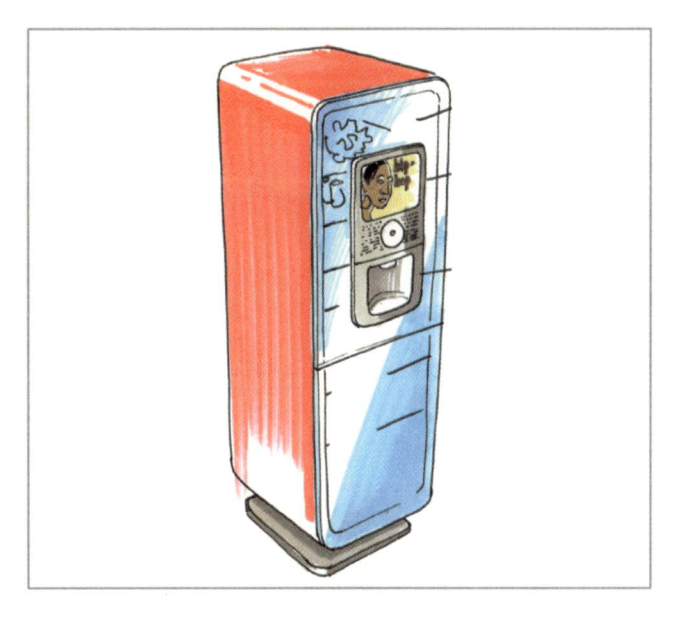

Figure 94 Visualized picture of the future: refrigerator 2010 (Jacques Helot 2005)

4.9 Creating Pictures of the Future

elements in it, or starts with the elements, and then constructs a story around them is a matter of personal preference. Both approaches are possible. The important thing is to make sure that the framework and the story match.

The communication of the scenarios can be supported using any number of simple or elaborate graphical components. Figures 92 to 94 show examples drawn from current projects. However, the best approach is to convey the core messages via movies. If permitted by the available resources (more than just the technical matters can be elaborate), this is certainly the most sophisticated and promising way of communicating the pictures of the future.

4.10 Evaluation of Scenarios

What makes for a good scenario?

One that has an impact!

It's that simple. The scenario's ultimate impact may be owing to any of the following: the suspense in the story told; the new findings themselves; the relevance of the subject matter; or the comprehensibility of the presentation. All of these constitute criteria for evaluating scenarios. The most important thing, however, is the impression that the scenarios make. This overall impression may consist of the following:

- A reconsideration of existing patterns of thought and behavior
- Changed processes
- New beginnings
- Discontinuations
- Initiatives
- Motivation, enthusiasm, etc.

That being said, we also have to bear in mind that scenarios are not sources of miracles. After all, it is the recipients of scenarios who are responsible for their implementation.

Even if we are disposed to move directly from reading a scenario or watching the presentation of a scenario to judging its plausibility or the likelihood of its occurrence, such immediate responses are of little help when it comes to evaluating scenarios: "At first, people refuse to believe that a strange new thing can be done, and then they begin to hope it can be done. Then they see it can be done – then it is done and all the world wonders why it was not done centuries ago." (Francis Hodgson Burnett in [Marsh 2002])

While the inclination to immediately assign a probability to a concept of the future that has been presented may be natural, it warrants bearing in mind that it is not primarily a matter of a prediction or the likelihood of a scenario's occurrence. Good scenarios are thought provoking and inspiring.

4.11 Pictures of the Future

Today, the Siemens Corporation takes a systematic approach to developing "pictures of the future." The term "systematic" here signifies that the pictures of the future are developed "at regular intervals" and "in a specified framework." The unique feature of the process is the combination of extrapolation and "retropolation" [Stuckenschneider 2005]. Based on a concept introduced by Mirow and Linz [Mirow 2000], the methodological approach (Figure 95) has been continuously refined and is today an important component in the company's strategy development program.

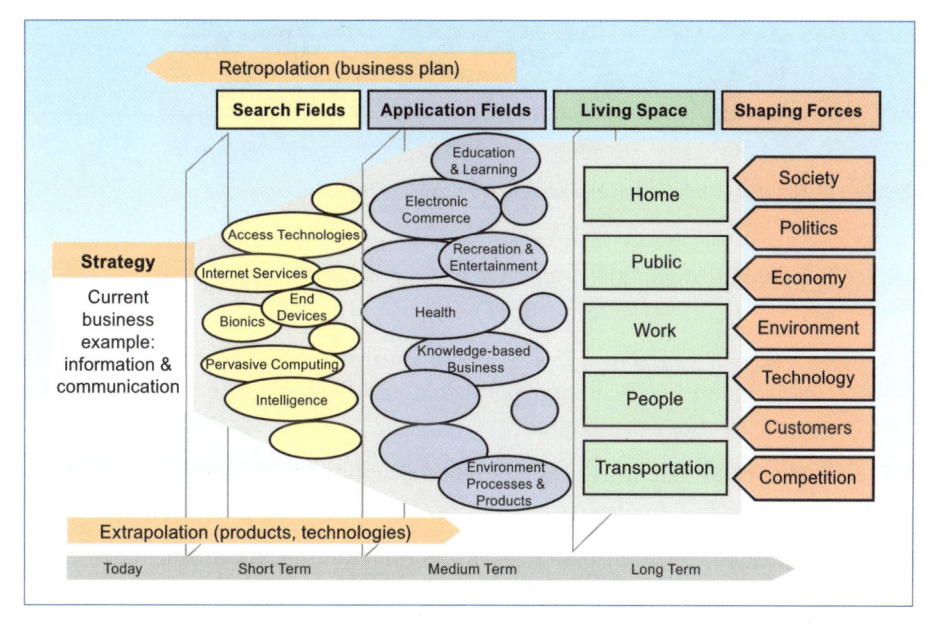

Figure 95 Scenario technique in "Strategic Visioning": extrapolation and "retropolation" [Mirow 2000]

The starting point for an examination of the future is the current business strategy, which is represented in the form of portfolios, product and technology roadmaps and strategic plans. Traditional planning, centering on the further linear pursuit of existing paths of development, is complemented by "strategic visioning." Pictures of the future are developed and strategic plans are expanded, i.e. via additional "new" perspectives.

As shown in Figure 96, findings are indeed rendered in the form of accessible pictures. This is the manner in which pictures of the future are regularly created for all of the relevant units of the Siemens Corporation. These pictures offer a preview of things to come, and serve as a basis for strategic and technological orientation, opinion formation and discussion. They are a vehicle of communication both within the company and between the company and other companies, institutes, universities and

Figure 96 Pictures of the future: an example from the healthcare sector

partners, including Shell, IBM, Coca-Cola, Boeing, Samsung, and IFTF, to name just a few.

The many years of experience in the area of future studies is combined with an intense commitment to continuous methodological improvement. Figure 97 shows an expanded and refined procedure.

The pursuit of continual process enhancement is guided by the following considerations:

- Not all forms of knowledge are equal. As mentioned above, knowledge ranges from speculation and opinion to the grasping of facts. A stronger consideration of the various forms of knowledge in the process would improve the quality of the pictures of the future. The relevant evaluation is a challenge.

- In the context of acquiring knowledge, the question arises as to its intelligent management. Current knowledge management systems, for instance, are not fully capable of accounting for general storage practicability, the exchange of information inside and outside the enterprise, and our need to keep track of the degree to which information is up to date.

- The role of science in the foresight process remains unclear. The issues outlined in Section 1.1 are the focus of activities conceived to reinforce the foundation and magnify the explanatory power of pictures of the future.

- It will also be necessary to secure the continuity and neutrality of foresight activities as well as their integration in the strategy process within the enterprise. High up on the agenda for the further program are questions relating to suitable organizational forms, i.e. forms which guarantee independence and real participation in decision-making processes.

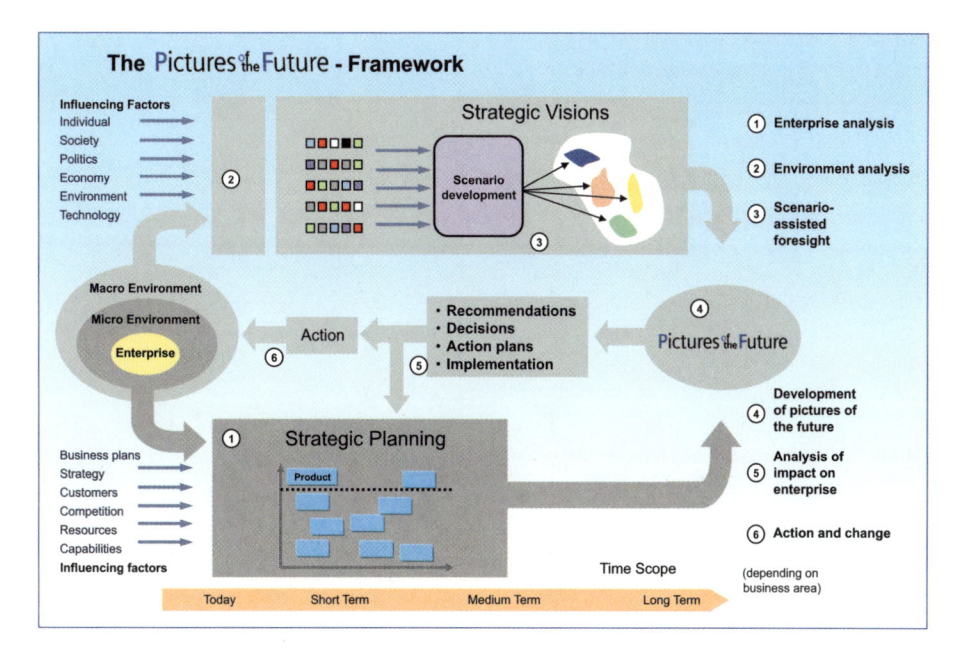

Figure 97 The PoF framework: enhanced procedure

4.12 The Future of Television (III)

The following contributions on the subject of the future of television were worked out in the previous chapters:

- The beginning was a matter of research: information was gathered and an information base was established (Chapter 2).

- This material was then used to identify future elements, draft hypotheses and assign the elements to one of five categories, i.e. depending on their assessed capacity to generate change (Chapter 3).

Figure 98 offers an overview of research progress and the current stage.

Evaluation

The evaluation of the elements (Table 16, Chapter 3) is now carried out using the Wilson matrix (Figure 99). This evaluation can be broken down into an assessment of the impact on the subject in question and an assessment of further development as an uncertainty factor. As described in Chapter 3, one's personal judgment here is a mixture of knowledge and opinion with no claim to accuracy.

In general, all of the elements are used in the drafting of scenarios. The elements in the area framed in red qualify – according to the evaluation – as especially uncertain and as especially important for the further development of television. As described in what follows, these elements receive special treatment.

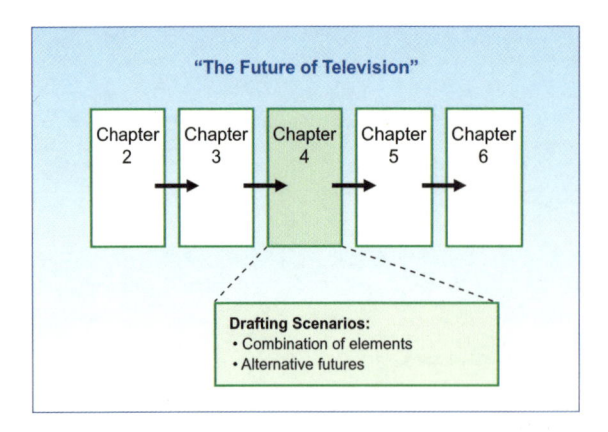

Figure 98 Research project "The Future of Television," stage 3: drafting scenarios

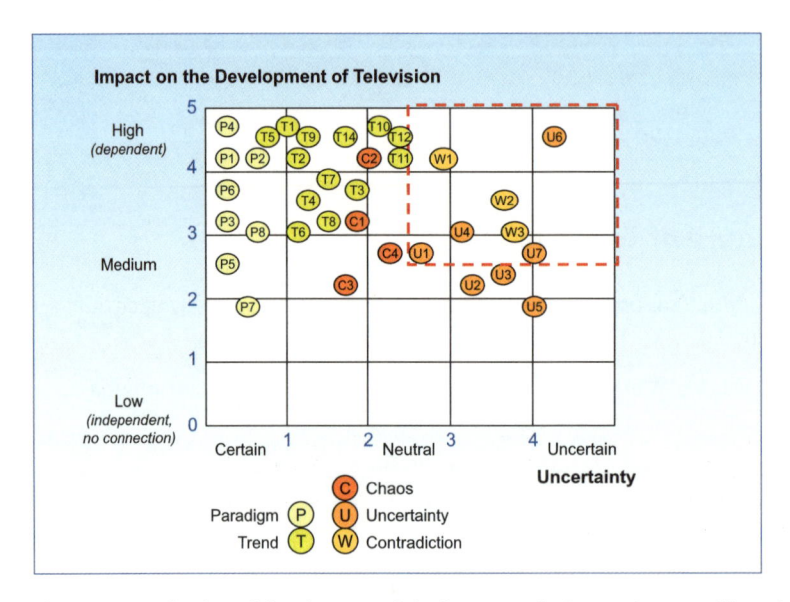

Figure 99 Evaluation of the elements of the future: each element is entered into the scenarios

The specific elements include W1, W2, W3, U1, U4, U6 and U7. The fact that these have been evaluated as very uncertain indicates the existence of several plausible developmental directions. These possible, alternative paths of development – also referred to as variations – are drafted separately for each element. They contain the "view of the future." The information about the future is "generated" with the help of the five basic principles and the relevant methods (as presented in Section 4.7). The possible variations for each selected element – it follows from the classification as uncertain that there must be at least two – are entered into a table. This tool is referred to as the morphological box (or the "Zwicky Box" after its inventor Fritz Zwicky). Possible variations relating to our present example are entered in the table shown in Figure 100.

	W1	W2	W3	U1	U4	U6	U7	Scenario
a	Complex technologies overburden and alienate TV consumers.	On the model of Wiki platforms, open-source TV will see a breakthrough.	Technological overload leads to rejection on the part of TV viewers. Media landscape variety is increasing.	IPTV offers a large variety of services that users are already familiar with (e.g. movies for downloading).	Television viewing is liberated from the constraints of the established program schemes.	Television develops increasingly into a secondary medium.	Internet and television square off in a battle for user attention.	Quo vadis, TV?
b	Users are looking for user-friendly means of operation in the high-tech world.	Triple Play (bundling of TV, cell phone and Internet) enables parallel media use.	Television reception is becoming more flexible (omnipresent television establishes itself).	IPTV enables interactive show formats (viewers can appear in programs).	New offers, business models and formats emerge. Newcomers from other industries enter the TV business.	Highly modern end devices offer users a cinema experience in their living rooms.	Traditional television still needs to establish itself as an interactive medium.	High performance TV
c	TV zapping and parallel watching increasingly establish themselves according to the new paradigm "experience more at the same time."	New household technologies as status symbols.	New formats, contents and distribution mechanisms enable new television experiences.	Viable business models for IPTV still have to be established.	The number of program offers for specific target groups is on the rise.	TV will soon become a channel of social networking; communities use TV to exchange information.	In terms of hours used, the Internet takes over the top spot among youths.	TV à la carte
d	Specialized programs are more important to users than means of transmission.	Digitalization leads to a tremendous increase in program and channel diversity.	The fragmentation of television use continues to increase.	IPTV offers greater variety and customized forms of use.	Consumers become "content creators" and can make content available.	All-round channels targeting mass audiences lose significance.	Television reinvents itself. New formats reach new audience groups.	Open TV

Figure 100 Scenario development: selecting variations to form scenarios

The consideration of alternative developments represents a demanding procedure. After all, it is a matter of projecting the elements into the future. Discussions (with experts and laypersons), brainstorming and other creative methods can be used as forms of support at this juncture. The only limit is one's powers of imagination. Once a number of alternatives have been formulated for each element, the task is to combine and link the variations plausibly and without contradiction. For instance, the combination of W1c and W3a would lead to a contradiction. Given the aim of developing inherently consistent scenarios, the combined elements should be free of substantive contradictions.

As described in Chapter 4, four scenarios make for a good cost-benefit ratio. When attempting to join the variations into four combinations, which then form the basis for the scenarios, it is important to make sure that the strands differ from one another as markedly as possible and include as many of the variations as possible. However, multiple use in this context should be avoided. This guarantees that the four scenarios cover the possible futures to a high degree.

4.12 The Future of Television (III)

The colored lines in Figure 100 link each of the variations to a scenario strand. Once a combination has been identified, a name is found for the scenario (last column). Several iterations are possible and sensible.

The following criteria are to be considered when determining the connecting lines:

- The combinations should be consistent and free of contradiction.
- The combinations should be as clearly distinct from one another as possible and should share few aspects.

The scenarios are now drafted and described:

The starting point is the title of the scenario and the combination of the variations. The elements serve as points of reference and a framework for the actual scenario. Much fantasy, experience, skillful writing and perseverance is necessary to combine the individual parts into a story. Packaging results into a story serves to better communicate the slice of the future in question. More suspenseful and otherwise compellingly written stories will better enable one package and convey the systematically ascertained elements and ideas. It warrants bearing in mind that scenarios are instruments of communication!

Take a look for yourself: a story and a picture is now presented for each scenario. For this book, the details have been evaluated for Germany. Nevertheless, this model works for many countries.

Scenario 1: Quo vadis, TV?

The following scenario framework results for scenario 1:

Component	Element	Description
Title	Quo vadis TV?	Further development is unclear, many possibilities
Main character	Linda Lane	Shortly after breaking up with her boyfriend
Scene	Living room	The plan is to enjoy a quiet evening of television viewing.
Paradigms, constants	P1	Television is the main medium of entertainment.
	P2	"Experience more at the same time" has become a paradigm of viewing behavior.
	P3	Excessive system complexity leads to consumer alienation.
	P4	The technology behind the digital transmission of television via satellite and broadband networks is advanced and market-ready.
	P5	Five means of transmission are currently available to viewers: terrestrial broadcasting (DVB-T), cable, satellite, telephone cable (via DSL), mobile (UMTS, DVB-H).
	P6	TV viewers want a form of passive entertainment.
	P7	The Internet already accounts for 12% of the daily time budget of people between the age of 14 and 49.
	P8	Television viewers have two interests with respect to TV as a medium: entertainment and information.
	P9	Picture quality has improved and the number of reception alternatives has increased.

Component	Element	Description
Trends	T1	Television has developed into a kind of secondary-focus medium (parallel media use).
	T2	The number of transmission alternatives and technologies has increased excessively.
	T3	Having been replaced to some extent by other media, television viewing, especially among younger individuals, is on the decline.
	T4	Innovative TV technologies have become more complex and are associated with high costs for consumers.
	T5	Analog transmission is being replaced by digital transmission.
	T6	As a result of changes in the way consumers spend their free time, TV programs are becoming ever shorter.
	T7	The entertainment value and the makeup of TV programs are gaining in significance at the cost of information content.
	T8	The trend among consumers is towards larger displays.
	T9	Private television is developing into encrypted pay-TV.
	T10	A media convergence is in the making – technologies are melting into one another synergistically (see Triple Play).
	T11	A hard-fought battle is being waged to capture the time budget of television viewers.
	T12	On-demand TV will win out, i.e. consumers will all be able to put together their own programs. TV is becoming more customized.
	T13	The television landscape will be broken down into even more segments; special programs for ever smaller target groups (e.g. MTV, n-TV, CNN, DSF).
Contradictions	W1a	Excessive system complexity leads to consumer overload and alienation.
	W2d	Digitalization leads to an immense increase in program and channel diversity.
	W3a	Technological overload leads to rejection on the part of TV viewers. The diversity of the media landscape is on the rise.
Uncertainties	U1a	IPTV offers a large variety of services that users are already familiar with (e.g. movies for downloading).
	U2	Do new high-resolution TV programs and formats (e.g. HDTV) have a chance in the future (chicken-egg problem)?
	U3	Are the technological developments compatible with the regulatory landscape and legal provisions?
	U4b	New offers, business models and formats emerge. Newcomers from other industries enter the TV business.
	U5	It is doubtful that the segment broadcasters will have the right concepts for positive and sustained earnings development in the long term.
	U6a	Television will increasingly develop into a secondary medium.
	U7a	Internet and television square off in a battle for user attention.
Chaos, wildcards	C1	The lifecycles of technology products are becoming ever shorter.
	C2	Device manufacturers and media designers are exposed to enormous pressure to innovate.
	C3	Reaction of regulatory agencies and political leaders to the multimedia spread of sex, violence and pornography.

4.12 The Future of Television (III)

Component	Element	Description
	C4	The TV market currently finds itself in a process of fundamental transformation. The development potential is detectable and presents enormous challenges to the various market players.
Creativity and fantasy	Individual	Input from the process of joining the elements into a story

Scenario 1

Linda is solo again. Her relationship with John, a relationship that lasted for almost seven years, has come to an end. "It's better this way," she tells herself over and over again. Linda feels the need to get in the clear on what exactly the breakup will mean for her. A number of things will change in her life – that much is certain. This evening, however, she would like to get her mind off of the subject, and simply sit back and relax while spending the evening watching television. Just like the way she used to do when she and John were together.

Linda makes things cozy for herself in the living room, and then turns on the television. While doing so, it occurs to her that it was John who took care of all the technical stuff.

A message appears on the screen. A message from John.

Dear Linda,

You will certainly want to watch television at some point. It wasn't long ago that I installed the HIX system, and I thought you could probably use a few tips on operating it.

It's really pretty simple. The fact that you're reading this message means that the HIX server is on standby. All you have to do is call up the view mode. But before doing that, make sure you know what you want to watch. If you just want to watch television in S-TV or Channel EFG, it's best to activate the TV-Now program guide. It costs a little bit, but all you have to do is click on it. The new standard also allows you to sample a few programs in parallel mode before you really have to make a selection and pay. I set up the A-Box for the payment (the box way at the bottom). There should be some credit left over. Otherwise, you'll have to reload it (at the moment, it seems only to accept the S-TV TV card). The system is being converted from DVB-X to DVB-Y. You'll have to try it out and see if you can still receive it with the HIX extra expansion. Otherwise via cable, although in the case of cable you now have to pay extra for each channel.

Or do you want to watch a movie? There are a number of possibilities. A number of movies are still on the server. If you want to watch one of them, you have to use the xx3 (the box in the middle) to release one of the movies. Or select one from the QLib – but here you might have to download and install the latest decoder. iMovie would also be an alternative, but I don't think it's HIX-compatible, and you would also have to run it using the xx3.

Then there's the option of watching via the Internet. Web 4.8a. I hope you haven't already cancelled the fiber-line. MeTube also shows the sporting events. Enter your key when you're on the website and then adjust the formats. You can do that with the box on top. The orange cable has to be connected to the left outlet. Otherwise, the signal comes from the server and not the modem.

Figure 101 Quo vadis, TV? – a technological jungle (Jacques Helot 2007)

All Linda wanted to do was watch a little television – which used to be a matter of pressing the "ON" button. But that was back in the days of analog television, which was phased out 10 years ago.

The Agency for Exploitation of Musical Rights and the TV Fees Agency now monitor via the implanted eye-scanner. I hope you don't forget that. Otherwise, they send you an eWarning, and you know that can be expensive.

Like I said, it's pretty easy. But if you have any questions, you can give me a call. Just switch over to talk mode.

Linda takes a deep breath. It occurs to her that breaking up with John means breaking up with television. She decides to do something old fashioned – something non-digital – and read one of the books she was planning to get to for a long time. And tomorrow? She figures she could go out and see a movie. She hasn't done that for a long time.

Scenario 2: High Performance TV

The following scenario framework results for scenario 2:

Component	Element	Description
Title	High performance TV	New technologies bring real customer benefits and entertainment pleasure
Main character	Bob Silverman	Technology freak and movie expert
Scene	Home cinema	A normal Friday evening – Bob is manning the remote control
Paradigms, constants	P1	Television is the main medium of entertainment.
	P2	"Experience more at the same time" has become a paradigm of viewing behavior.
	P3	Excessive system complexity leads to consumer alienation.
	P4	The technology behind the digital transmission of television via satellite and broadband networks is advanced and market-ready.
	P5	Five means of transmission are currently available to viewers: terrestrial broadcasting (DVB-T), cable, satellite, telephone cable (via DSL), mobile (UMTS, DVB-H).
	P6	TV viewers want a form of passive entertainment.
	P7	The Internet already accounts for 12% of the daily time budget of people between the age of 14 and 49.
	P8	Television viewers have two interests with respect to TV as a medium: entertainment and information.
	P9	Picture quality has improved and the number of reception alternatives has increased.
Trends	T1	Television has developed into a kind of secondary-focus medium (parallel media use).
	T2	The number of transmission alternatives and technologies has increased excessively.
	T3	Having been replaced to some extent by other media, television viewing, especially among younger individuals, is on the decline.
	T4	Innovative TV technologies have become more complex and are associated with high costs for consumers.
	T5	Analog transmission is being replaced by digital transmission.
	T6	As a result of changes in the way consumers spend their free time, TV programs are becoming ever shorter.
	T7	The entertainment value and the makeup of TV programs are gaining in significance at the cost of information content.
	T8	The trend among consumers is towards larger displays.
	T9	Private television is developing into encrypted pay-TV.
	T10	A media convergence is in the making – technologies are melting into one another synergistically (see Triple Play).
	T11	A hard-fought battle is being waged to capture the time budget of television viewers.
	T12	On-demand TV will win out, i.e. consumers will all be able to put together their own programs. TV is becoming more customized.
	T13	The television landscape will be broken down into even more segments; special programs for ever smaller target groups (e.g. MTV, n-TV, CNN, DSF).

Component	Element	Description
Contradictions	W1c	TV zapping and parallel TV viewing has established itself as a result of the new paradigm "Experience more at the same time."
	W2c	New household technologies as status symbols.
	W3b	Television reception is becoming more flexible (omnipresent television establishes itself).
Uncertainties	U1b	IPTV enables interactive show formats (viewers can appear in programs).
	U2	Do new high-resolution TV programs and formats (e.g. HDTV) have a chance in the future (chicken-egg problem)?
	U3	Are the technological developments compatible with the regulatory landscape and legal provisions?
	U4a	Television viewing is liberated from the constraints of the established program schemes.
	U5	It is doubtful that the segment broadcasters will have the right concepts for positive and sustained earnings development in the long term.
	U6b	Highly modern end devices offer users a cinema experience in their living rooms.
	U7b	Traditional television still needs to establish itself as an interactive medium.
Chaos, wildcards	C1	The lifecycles of technology products are becoming ever shorter.
	C2	Device manufacturers and media designers are exposed to enormous pressure to innovate.
	C3	Reaction of regulatory agencies and political leaders to the multimedia spread of sex, violence and pornography.
	C4	The TV market currently finds itself in a process of fundamental transformation. The development potential is detectable and presents enormous challenges to the various market players.
Creativity and fantasy	Individual	Input from the process of joining the elements into a story

Scenario 2

Yes, Bob Silverman is content. He has set up the 3.20 x 2.10 display in his living room and installed the media hub.

He and his wife are thrilled. While the mega screens have long since replaced the traditional television set, the 3D technology in connection with VHDTV is new. They can now enjoy the cinema experience at home!

Mission Impossible X is set to hit the movie theaters today. As an Alpha Studios premium customer, Bob will receive a single-view copy of the movie. He and his wife are looking forward to this highlight in their evening program.

The selection is not always so easy. On the contrary, it is becoming more and more of a challenge. The offer available on the Internet is overwhelming.

Bob still has a few old DVDs – mostly for reasons of nostalgia. While he will certainly save the one with the movie he saw with his wife on their first date (*The Lord of the Rings III*), he figures he won't need the others anymore. Any time he has an idea for a movie, he activates the movie finder and receives a manageable offer from a worldwide inventory, sorted according to price, rights, etc. The movie he then selects is available for viewing in 10 seconds.

It is now even possible to watch movies in parallel mode. Semi-parallel means that his wife can use the same display to watch a different movie than the one he's watching. A difference of 5 degrees in the viewing angle suffices, a feature that has probably saved quite a few marriages – the solo togetherness experience. Then there is the real-parallel mode: two movies are shown at once for especially savvy viewers. But Bob Silverman and his wife feel too old for such games. They only use this mode for the lottery drawings. Every Saturday evening, they watch one of the last public broadcasting programs. It's a tradition, but this, too, usually runs in parallel mode. It occurs to Bob that *television* should now be called *closevision* or *parallelvision*.

The encroachment of interactive games into the living room sealed the fate of traditional television. While Bob himself is not a fan of the games, he is fascinated by the technical possibilities. A mixture of real and virtual worlds makes for a whole new game experience, and sometimes it is difficult to tell whether they are receiving a normal call or a request to play in a game.

Figure 102 High performance TV: countless options and a high degree of technical comfort (Jacques Helot 2007)

However, Bob has learned to appreciate another media hub function. The hub gives him access to the complete offer, no matter where he happens to be at the moment. Whether he is in his home office, at a hotel, in a car, or plane – he can take his custom media landscape with him wherever he goes. Only the format needs to be adjusted.

Bob now receives the signal that *Mission Impossible X* is ready. His wife hasn't arrived yet. He'll wait for her. After all, they can only see the movie once.

Scenario 3: TV à la Carte

The following scenario framework results for scenario 3.

Component	Element	Description
Title	A la Carte	Large selection, but hardly any time
Main character	Maxwell Bean	Hobby cook
Scene	Living room	On the air with his organic food Internet program
Paradigms, constants	P1	Television is the main medium of entertainment.
	P2	"Experience more at the same time" has become a paradigm of viewing behavior.
	P3	Excessive system complexity leads to consumer alienation.
	P4	The technology behind the digital transmission of television via satellite and broadband networks is advanced and market-ready.
	P5	Five means of transmission are currently available to viewers: terrestrial broadcasting (DVB-T), cable, satellite, telephone cable (via DSL), mobile (UMTS, DVB-H).
	P6	TV viewers want a form of passive entertainment.
	P7	The Internet already accounts for 12% of the daily time budget of people between the age of 14 and 49.
	P8	Television viewers have two interests with respect to TV as a medium: entertainment and information.
	P9	Picture quality has improved and the number of reception alternatives has increased.
Trends	T1	Television has developed into a kind of secondary-focus medium (parallel media use).
	T2	The number of transmission alternatives and technologies has increased excessively.
	T3	Having been replaced to some extent by other media, television viewing, especially among younger individuals, is on the decline.
	T4	Innovative TV technologies have become more complex and are associated with high costs for consumers.
	T5	Analog transmission is being replaced by digital transmission.
	T6	As a result of changes in the way consumers spend their free time, TV programs are becoming ever shorter.
	T7	The entertainment value and the makeup of TV programs are gaining in significance at the cost of information content.
	T8	The trend among consumers is towards larger displays.
	T9	Private television is developing into encrypted pay-TV.
	T10	A media convergence is in the making – technologies are melting into one another synergistically (see Triple Play).
	T11	A hard-fought battle is being waged to capture the time budget of television viewers.
	T12	On-demand TV will win out, i.e. consumers will all be able to put together their own programs. TV is becoming more customized.
	T13	The television landscape will be broken down into even more segments; special programs for ever smaller target groups (e.g. MTV, n-TV, CNN, DSF).

Component	Element	Description
Contradictions	W1d	Special programs are more important to users than the means of transmission.
	W2b	Triple Play (the bundling of TV, cell phone and Internet) enables parallel media use.
	W3d	The fragmentation of television use continues to increase.
Uncertainties	U1d	IPTV offers greater variety and customized forms of use.
	U2	Do new high-resolution TV programs and formats (e.g. HDTV) have a chance in the future (chicken-egg problem)?
	U3	Are the technological developments compatible with the regulatory landscape and legal provisions?
	U4c	The market for specific target group programs is growing.
	U5	It is doubtful that the segment broadcasters will have the right concepts for positive and sustained earnings development in the long term.
	U6d	All-round channels targeting mass audiences lose significance.
	U7c	In terms of hours used, the Internet takes over the top spot among youths.
Chaos, wildcards	C1	The lifecycles of technology products are becoming ever shorter.
	C2	Device manufacturers and media designers are exposed to enormous pressure to innovate.
	C3	Reaction of regulatory agencies and political leaders to the multimedia spread of sex, violence and pornography.
	C4	The TV market currently finds itself in a process of fundamental transformation. The development potential is detectable and presents enormous challenges to the various market players.
Creativity and fantasy	Individual	Input from the process of joining the elements into a story

Scenario 3

Maxwell Bean is a hobby cook. Ever since he and his friends began broadcasting their own program, you might mistake his hobby for his main job. A year ago they founded "Organic Food." Despite the immense competition in the overall media and entertainment sector, they have been surprisingly successful in their niche. They are one of more than 10,000 broadcasters in their country who use the Internet as a television broadcasting platform. Their program is devoted to cooking exclusively with organically produced ingredients.

While the traditional broadcasters were aware of the fact that the Internet was making inroads, they still underestimated the scope of its full impact. Nearly all of the traditional small and niche broadcasters have gone off the air. Only the full programs – including the public broadcasters – managed to survive. The Internet offers many advantages to broadcasters who concentrate on special subjects. The one especially crucial advantage among them is probably the range. But the technology deployed for production and broadcasting is also anything but prohibitive, as it was in the case of traditional television. Starter kits to set up your own broadcasting station are available for 1,000 Euros, and that includes the operating costs for a year.

As so often in life, the idea for the project came by chance. Maxwell had invited someone for dinner and wanted to know two things for sure: whether he needed fenugreek for the chicken vindaloo; and whether he should purée the coriander and turmeric or sprinkle it into the dish. He wasn't able to find out right away, and found himself wishing he had immediate access to such information in his own kitchen. Voila!

There was a time around the turn of the century when the manufacturers of kitchen appliances wanted to sell their refrigerators with built-in screens so that the refrigerators could place orders on their own, i.e. do a bit of virtual shopping. The idea was a terrible flop. There was the case of the refrigerator in Berlin that ordered two pallets of milk. Though the milk was pasteurized, it's shelf life wasn't that long.

Cooking stations and programs like "Organic Food" helped to bring about a renaissance for the idea of a screen in the kitchen. Displays are installed directly above the cooking zone. This enables hobby cooks to follow the program on the screen while they cook for themselves. In contrast to the cooking program broadcast from the television studio, the private cooking program can begin at any given time. Moreover, with more than 100,000 recipes, the selection is more than comprehensive.

A new function is currently being tested. This time it is the hobby cooks who are being targeted. In addition to the cooking presentation, the broadcaster offers remote cooking. Various control parameters such as cooking time and temperature are monitored. This will eliminate the possibility of burning the food!

While Maxwell almost never finds the time to watch television himself, he clearly prefers to broadcast his own program. And that although he only learned how to cook a few years ago.

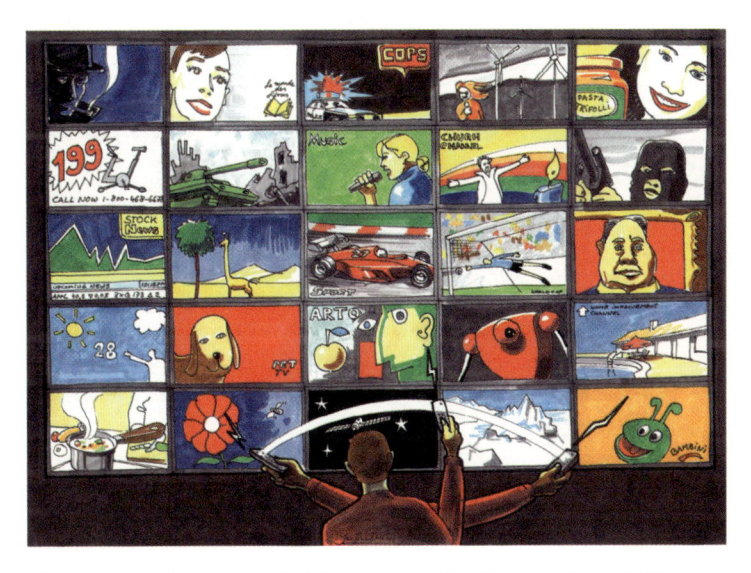

Figure 103 TV à la carte: television for specialists (Jacques Helot 2007)

4.12 The Future of Television (III)

Scenario 4: Open TV

The following scenario framework results for scenario 4:

Component	Element	Description
Title	Open TV	A revolution from below
Main character	Kevin Carter	Program moderator
Scene	Sound studio in Gera	Alive Award (AA)
Paradigms, constants	P1	Television is the main medium of entertainment.
	P2	"Experience more at the same time" has become a paradigm of viewing behavior.
	P3	Excessive system complexity leads to consumer alienation.
	P4	The technology behind the digital transmission of television via satellite and broadband networks is advanced and market-ready.
	P5	Five means of transmission are currently available to viewers: terrestrial broadcasting (DVB-T), cable, satellite, telephone cable (via DSL), mobile (UMTS, DVB-H).
	P6	TV viewers want a form of passive entertainment.
	P7	The Internet already accounts for 12% of the daily time budget of people between the age of 14 and 49.
	P8	Television viewers have two interests with respect to TV as a medium: entertainment and information.
	P9	Picture quality has improved and the number of reception alternatives has increased.
Trends	T1	Television has developed into a kind of secondary-focus medium (parallel media use).
	T2	The number of transmission alternatives and technologies has increased excessively.
	T3	Having been replaced to some extent by other media, television viewing, especially among younger individuals, is on the decline.
	T4	Innovative TV Technologies have become more complex and are associated with high costs for consumers.
	T5	Analog transmission is being replaced by digital transmission.
	T6	As a result of changes in the way consumers spend their free time, TV programs are becoming ever shorter.
	T7	The entertainment value and the makeup of TV programs are gaining in significance at the cost of information content.
	T8	The trend among consumers is towards larger displays.
	T9	Private television is developing into encrypted pay-TV.
	T10	A media convergence is in the making – technologies are melting into one another synergistically (see Triple Play).
	T11	A hard-fought battle is being waged to capture the time budget of television viewers.
	T12	On-demand TV will win out, i.e. consumers will all be able to put together their own programs. TV is becoming more customized.
	T13	The television landscape will be broken down into even more segments; special programs for ever smaller target groups (e.g. MTV, n-TV, CNN, DSF).

Component	Element	Description
Contradictions	W1b	Users are looking for user-friendly means of operation in the high-tech world.
	W2a	On the model of Wiki platforms, open-source TV will see a breakthrough.
	W3c	New formats, contents and distribution mechanisms enable new television experiences.
Uncertainties	U1c	Viable business models for IPTV still have to be established.
	U2	Do new high-resolution TV programs and formats (e.g. HDTV) have a chance in the future (chicken-egg problem)?
	U3	Are the technological developments compatible with the regulatory landscape and legal provisions?
	U4d	Consumers become "content creators" and can make content available.
	U5	It is doubtful that the segment broadcasters will have the right concepts for positive and sustained earnings development in the long term.
	U6c	TV will soon become a channel of social networking; communities use TV to exchange information.
	U7d	Television reinvents itself. New formats reach new audience groups.
Chaos, wildcards	C1	The lifecycles of technology products are becoming ever shorter.
	C2	Device manufacturers and media designers are exposed to enormous pressure to innovate.
	C3	Reaction of regulatory agencies and political leaders to the multimedia spread of sex, violence and pornography.
	C4	The TV market currently finds itself in a process of fundamental transformation. The development potential is detectable and presents enormous challenges to the various market players.
Creativity and fantasy	Individual	Input from the process of joining the elements into a story

Scenario 4

There he is, Kevin. He can't yet comprehend it all and allows it run through his mind yet again:

It all started with Napster. All of a sudden, it was possible to exchange music, just like that. Until the music industry intervened and stopped the experiment. Then came Apple with a new attempt to distribute music legally via iTunes. It was only a matter of time before Internet television and video portals would follow. Today, one can gain access to any kind of medium format via media directories. The borders between videos, television, clips, shows, moderation and communication are becoming ever more blurred.

In the meantime, media designers have taken over the function of designing time blocks, i.e. filling them with available entertainment content in a manner that is harmonized to individual consumers. The buzzword is "balanced entertainment." What used to be the TV guide is now the media designer.

A whole new culture of creating multimedia content has sprung up along with the new technological possibilities. What began in the music scene as "German Idol" inspired the movie producers. They were even daring enough to go a step further by taking control of the competition – as if "German Idol" were not produced by RTL broadcast, but by music students.

Figure 104 Open TV: anyone can join in (Jacques Helot 2007)

And it is exactly on account of this that Kevin is in the sound studio in Gera, a little town and the birthplace of Otto Dix. Kevin is nervous. Today is his big debut. He is actually a lecturer at the university. He knows that his debut today will be compared to those of the professionals on television and that the Alive Award ceremony will decimate the viewing rates of the television companies just like it did last year, although the project has virtually no advertising budget. Kevin also knows that good preparation is everything. He took a good look at all of the 100 candidates for the award in the run-up to the show. Nearly all of the invited guests have taken their seats. The show begins: "Good evening, and welcome to this year's presentation of Alive Award ..."

All of the film projects are works of unknown directors and amateur filmmakers. At first, Kevin was surprised. The movies are comparable to their bigger brothers and sisters from Hollywood and the television studios. The advances in computer animation, movie design and editing software are astounding. Movies are no longer shot, but developed. To start, one has to select the characters and a screen play structure. The software then generates a complete movie based on these. Details and sound are then inserted.

The suspense increases. Kevin's favorite is still in the running. The voting procedure is relatively complicated, but Kevin's friend Bruno is managing that. The result is derived from the votes cast by the theater audience and the votes cast online at the movie portal, where the movies can also be discussed and where producers meet consumers to exchange ideas.

Kevin was almost certain that the documentary "The Last Carboy," a movie about the last cars running on gasoline in Russia, would be among the winners, and he made a bet with Bruno.

The moment has come.

"And the winner is ..."

Reflection on the Scenarios

Developments in the area of the media and television in particular, are without a doubt exciting and turbulent. Many changes can be expected. Suppliers are forcing their way to the marketplace with innovations. Consumers, however, are uncertain. The number of products and options available is on the rise, despite misgivings on the part of consumers. Most consumers don't care whether the television picture is transmitted into their households via cable or IPTV. The main thing is that the service remains reliable and inexpensive. It is a saturated market, and it is becoming difficult to establish new formats, devices, means of transmission, etc.

4.13 Lessons Learned

If we consider the variety of methods, compare origins, procedures and results, we can derive a number of lessons learned:

- There is no single method that is suitable for all areas and requirements.
- Attempts to understand, and the understanding itself, are more important than the methods.
- A variety of methods introduces more security.
- IT support does not lead to better scenarios. A pseudo precision is often "designed" into the system via quantification.
- The group dynamics involved in the drafting of the scenarios is more important than IT support.
- The quality of the input information (rich, diverse, and neutral) plays a crucial role.

Benefits and Applications

The development of scenarios is an especially intense process, a process that includes reflection, speculation, discussion, comparison, rejection, and analysis, to name just a few of the related activities. Logic and scientific methods alone are not enough. Creativity, fantasy, knowledge, experience and powers of imagination are vitally important to shaping the future. It would be more apt to describe the activity behind the development of good, provocative, challenging and refreshing scenarios as an art than as a science.

One should not underestimate the work involved. Compared to a simple hypothesis, a scenario is a complete, carefully thought out and highly consistent picture. By way of justifying the work and expense involved, I turn my attention in the next chapter to the following question: what significance do scenarios have for enterprises?

Scenarios help one to grasp and limit one's own uncertainty as well as to detect the limits of a plausible future. The success of the method depends on the interpretation of the result and the associated course of action. That is the subject of the next chapter.

Chapter 5

Planning

Seizing Opportunities and
Avoiding Hazards

Honda began selling motorcycles on the U.S. market in the year 1959. Only seven years later – in the year 1966 – it had reached a market share of 63%. The share of motorcycles imported from Great Britain fell in the same period from 49% to 10%.

Hoping to come up with an explanation, the British government commissioned the Boston Consulting Group to investigate the case and submit a report.

The report indicated the following:

The export success of the Japanese motorcycle industry was based on strong growth on the domestic Japanese market in the 1950s. "They had developed huge production volumes for small motorcycles on their domestic market, and volume-related cost reductions followed."

The Japanese used this competitive advantage as a springboard for conquering markets around the world.

"The Japanese motorcycle industry and in particular Honda, the market leader, present a [consistent] picture. The basic philosophy of the Japanese manufacturer is that high volumes per model provide the potential for high productivity as a result of using capital intensive and highly automated techniques."

The Boston Consulting Group determined that Honda's marketing strategy was centered on models that were produced in large numbers. This concentration on cost reduction and product engineering was the basis for success.

(Source: Strategy Alternatives for the British Industry, Boston Consulting Group 1975).

Richard Pascale (co-author of the book, *The Art of Japanese Management*, 1981) interviewed the managers who had spearheaded Honda's entry into the U.S. market. Pascale quotes these managers as saying, "In truth we had no strategy other than the idea of seeing if we could sell something in the Unites States."

The crucial difference between this account and the report submitted by the Boston Consulting Group is its conclusion that Honda's success was built in part on hard work and in part on chance. In the beginning, Honda concentrated mainly on large motorcycles. However, the company's higher paid employees and mechanics continued to drive the smaller 50-ccm bikes that were so common in Japan instead of switching over to the 250-ccm bikes made for the macho market. This was noticed by consumers on the domestic market at the beginning of the 1960s – just when oil system problems (leaks) began turning up in the larger motors. This had a negative impact on reliability. A decision was made, more or less out of necessity, to also sell the smaller motorcycles.

This perseverance – a refusal to give up in the face of difficulties – would pay off handsomely for Honda. At the time, no one at Honda was aware of the fact that they had thereby created a new market segment on the U.S. market which was traditionally oriented towards larger bikes.

The opinions presented above concerning strategy development couldn't be more different. On the one hand, we have the conclusion that everything was planned down to the smallest detail, and on the other hand, the suggestion that it was no more than perseverance, alertness, agility, a good business idea and a crisis (i.e. luck) that led to success.

This shows that situations appear different when viewed from different perspectives and that distorted pictures can easily arise when viewing a situation from a great distance. What looks like systematic planning from a distance, turns out to be no more than flexibility and perseverance when viewed from up close. This also demonstrates the crucial importance of changing strategies when confronted with new realities.

(Source: adapted from the article "Perspectives on Strategy: The Real Story behind Hondas Success" by Richard T. Pascale, which appeared in 1984 in the California Management Review XXVI, No. 3 pp. 47-72)

5.1 Planning for the Future: An Insurance Policy

In the previous chapters, I addressed issues centering on enterprise environments. Information was gathered, changes recorded and future developments anticipated. Assuming that this has generated a picture of a given enterprise's future environment, I turn now in the present chapter to the consequences: What can an enterprise do? What do the developments mean for the enterprise? How can one become prepared? What strategic measures are necessary? In the framework of strategic enterprise planning, one attempts to find answers to these questions and to make the enterprise fit for the future.

One alarming investigation of the differences between what is strategically planned and what actually materializes indicates that, "90 percent of carefully planned strategies do not work" [Fox 1982].

Without wishing to address the exact percentages involved, it seems safe to assume that a majority of all planned strategies are destined to fail. A sobering conclusion! But why do enterprises find it so difficult to shape the future to their advantage?

In the present chapter, I will consider how analyses of the enterprise environment (Chapter 2 to 4), analyses of the enterprise itself (Chapter 5) and considerations of the future can be integrated into strategic planning and strategy development. Even if it remains an open question for the time being as to whether this will lead to more successful strategies, the attempt alone is what is important. Recalling our discussion of "memories of the future" in Chapter 2, we can conclude that examinations of the future will help us in terms of our present orientation and the degree to which we are prepared for the future.

To repeat an important question, why do we bother to consider the future at all when we are simply exposed to it and have only limited means of influencing it?

The situation in which we currently live was shaped in the past. When looking to the future, one always assumes that the past is clear and comprehensible, and that it is only the view forward that is veiled. However, the view forward is not entirely veiled and not everything in our history and that of the earth is so clear. For instance, neither the origin of the earth nor the demise of the dinosaurs has been entirely satisfactorily explained.

Through our actions today, we shape the (our) future, at least to a certain extent. However, if we do nothing, we will have to accept the future as it is, or as others shape it for us.

Examining the future is like an insurance policy. If we obtain a fire insurance policy, for instance, and a fire breaks out, then we will know that we did the right thing. If no fire breaks out, we might begin to doubt. Should we have saved the money instead?

Of course not! But the same applies to examinations of the future. A failure to consider the future is a case of negligence. Many enterprises opt to avoid the expense, which is very dangerous and could lead to "learning after the crash" instead of "learning before the crash." A failure to consider the future is perhaps also the reason why such a high percentage of strategies are doomed to fail.

5.2 Strategy Review

A careful plan or method devised to achieve a goal is usually referred to as a strategy. It means doing the right things at the right time to secure future action and success. With an eye to enterprise leaders, this means concentrating on the future survival and success of the enterprise. While it is a relatively simple matter in theory – one is required to guarantee that more money flows in than out – it is, as so often, much more complicated in practice. This is plain to see in company crises and the available bankruptcy statistics.

Traditional concepts assume that adequate strategies can be generated given a systematic and intensive analysis and evaluation of the current situation. These strategies can then be implemented to pave the way into the successful future of the enterprise. Johnson and Scholes offer a basic model of working out strategies (Figure 105) [Johnson 1988]. Based on strategic analysis, one gains a view of the options and selects and implements the right strategy. This idealized representation is oriented towards standard cases.

On the other hand, a vast number of new strategic frameworks, tools and concepts are introduced every year, all promising the ultimate strategy (cf. Figure 16). How are we to navigate our way through this strategy thicket, so full of simplistic solutions and superfluous concepts?

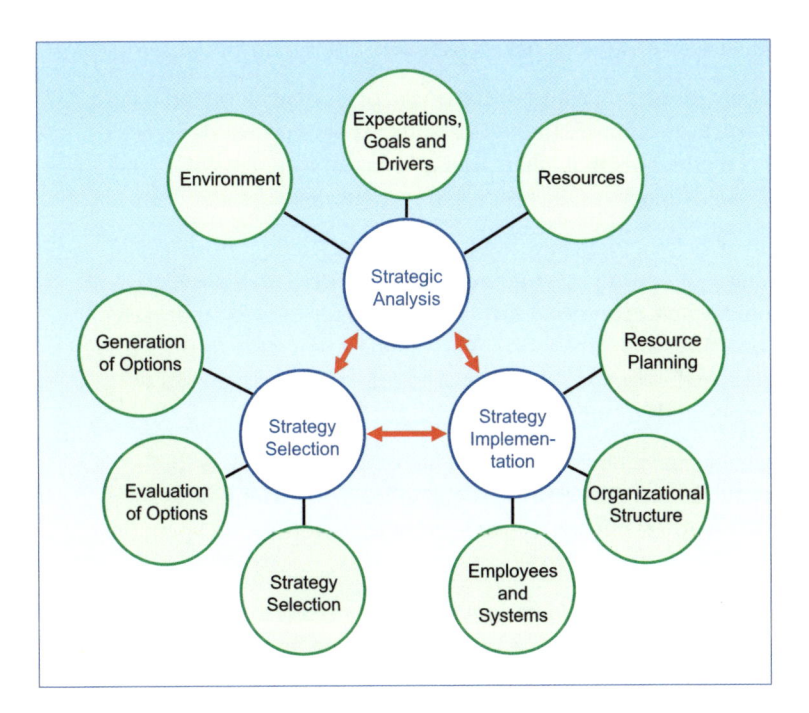

Figure 105 It is not this easy: corporate strategy [Johnson 1988]

History

The notion of a strategy is quite old. People have been considering ways of ensuring survival, success at war and success in politics and trade for thousands of years. Political and military leaders were forced to make decisions about goals, politics, the use of resources, etc. Although the terms "strategic management" and "strategic planning" were introduced only recently by American business schools, all civilizations in the history of humankind have acted in accordance with strategic points of view. Classic texts such as Sun Tzu's *The Art of War* (written in China 2,500 years ago), Machiavelli's *The Prince* (1513) and the already mentioned works on military strategy by von Clausewitz and von Moltke from the 19th century continue to be highly relevant.

It wasn't until the middle of the last century that the notion was applied systematically to companies and organizations.

Historical developments on the subject of "strategy" since 1968 have been compellingly presented by Whittington [Whittington 1993]. Originally referred to as "business policy," the use of the term "business strategy" goes back to ideas presented by Alfred Chandler, Igor Ansoff and Alfred Sloan – the founders of General Motors. Ansoff published his book *Corporate Strategy: An Analytical Approach to Business Policy for Growth and Expansion* in 1965. Ansoff's description of the management approach qualifies as one of the first concepts. Together with Chandler and Sloan, Ansoff created the strategic method, a body of thought that is referred to by Whittington as the "Classical School."

5.2 Strategy Review

ince then, examinations of strategy have developed in three further phases:

- The process-oriented method along with the idea of strategy development as a continuous process appears in the 1970s. Its exponents include Henry Mintzberg. This method distinguishes itself in terms of its emphasis on the inclusion of all stakeholders in the process of strategy development.

- As described by Whittington, the evolutionary method [Heuderen 1989, Nelson 1982] pursues an upward revaluation of market forces as opposed to rational planning, which is assessed as irrelevant. This systematic approach is favored by Gronavetter and Shrivastava. They suggest that strategy primarily depends on the specific context [Shrivastava 1986]. Economic behavior is embedded in social and cultural networks.

- The term "strategic management" has been increasingly mentioned in the literature since the 1980s. This expresses the notion that various subsystems are included in the process of arriving at a strategy [Ansoff 1990, Davenport 2006].

Criticism has frequently been voiced in light of what is perceived as a lack of any real connection to practice – in particular, a lack of knowledge about how strategies are really developed within enterprises, "For nowhere in the planning literature has there been any indication whatsoever that efforts were made to understand how the strategy-making process really does work in organizations. ... In effect, a kind of normative naiveté has pervaded the literature of planning – confident beliefs in what is best, grounded in an ignorance of what really does work." [Mintzberg 1994]

Terminology

Like other terms used in the area of management, the term "strategy" is extremely strained and is used – owing to its secretive and almost mystical connotations – very loosely: "It turns out that 'strategy' is one of those words that we tend to define in a certain way while using it in a different way." [Mintzberg 1999]

It is also not possible to overlook the inflationary tendency to describe things as "strategic" in order to emphasize their significance. We hear of strategic purchases and dialogues that, although undoubtedly important, do not really warrant being referred to as strategic.

So what does "strategy" mean?

- The identification of long-term basic goals and tasks for the enterprise and the adoption and allocation of the corresponding resources [Chandler 1962].

- Strategy is the common theme underlying a set of strategic decisions [Fitzroy 2005].

- Organizations were regarded as efficient, resource-allocating mechanisms that are geared to establishing a competitive advantage [Porter 1985].

- "Strategy is the pattern of activities followed by an organization in pursuit of its long-term purposes." [Open 2000]

What follows is a new definition that accounts for the notion of uncertainty:

- "Strategy is a handful of decisions that drive or shape most of a company's subsequent actions, are not easily changed once made, and have the greatest impact on whether a company meets its strategic objectives." [Coyne 1996]

Hamel and Prahalad [Hamel 1995] suggest that the traditional view of strategy is essentially tied to three factors:

1. The concept of being fit, i.e. the optimal and efficient orientation of the enterprise in its competitive environment
2. The organization of resources as one of many options
3. Long-term orientation and alignment

It seems as if gaining prominence in the area of enterprise strategy is contingent upon having formally proposed at least one definition of strategy. It is otherwise difficult to explain the fact that there is no generally accepted definition of the very subject of inquiry in the area of business administration.

Instead of adding to the list of definitions, I now turn to a brief summary of the available concepts.

Strategy Concepts

The use of numerous concepts today in the area of strategic management suggests that strategy is a complex matter which, owing to constantly changing contexts, cannot be mastered by standard solutions.

"Old fashioned decision making does not meet the needs of a world with too much information and too little time. So-called rational decision making, once the ideal, requires comprehensive knowledge of every facet of a problem, which is clearly impossible today." [Etzioni 1989]

Mintzberg has attempted to group the numerous approaches into schools of thought [Mintzberg 1999] (Table 34, Figure 106).

Each of the concepts involves focusing on the subject of "strategy" from a different perspective, and thereby emphasizing different aspects. By way of summary, however, one is able to gather concurring statements and conclusions for the sake of subsequent analysis (as adapted from [Chaffee 1985]):

- Strategy concerns both the enterprise and its environment.
- The nature of strategy is complex (Figure 107).
- Strategy has an impact on the well-being of the enterprise.
- Strategy concerns both questions of content and procedure.

Table 34 The Mintzberg Model

School of Thought	Features: Strategy as a ...
The Design School	... conceptual process
The Planning School	... formal process
The Positioning School	... analytic process
The Entrepreneurial School	... visionary process
The Cognitive School	... mental process
The Learning School	... educational process
The Power School	... negotiation process
The Cultural School	... collective process
The Environmental School	... reactive process
The Configuration School	... transformation process

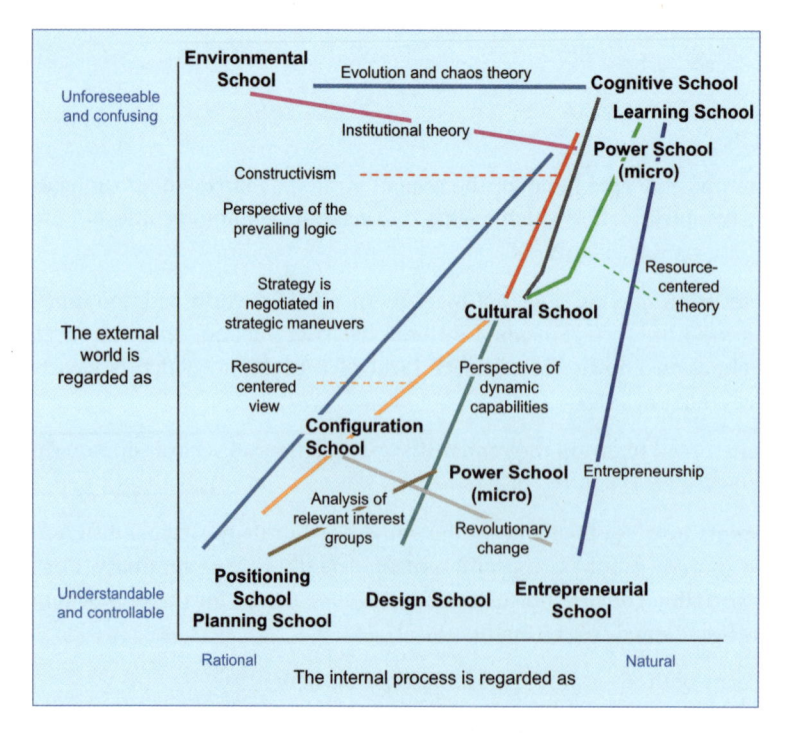

Figure 106 Navigating the thicket: mapping the possibilities of strategic design [Mintzberg 1999]

- Strategies are not established entirely in the framework of conscious processes.
- Strategies exist at different levels.
- Strategies include various processes of thought.

Strategies are first formulated on the basis of analyses of the enterprise and its environment and then implemented. A feedback loop is used to monitor the success of the implemented measures. The results of monitoring are then entered into the analysis of the enterprise. Although this very general model is considerably older, it continues to be no less relevant. Attempts to circumvent, shorten or transfer its altogether logical sequence – consisting of analysis, strategy development, implementation and control – by establishing results arbitrarily will have no more than short-term success. This suggestion is supported by numerous examples (VW, Marconi, Deutsche Telekom). "The trouble starts when an executive decides that the margin is too low," says Arie de Geus [Geus 1997].

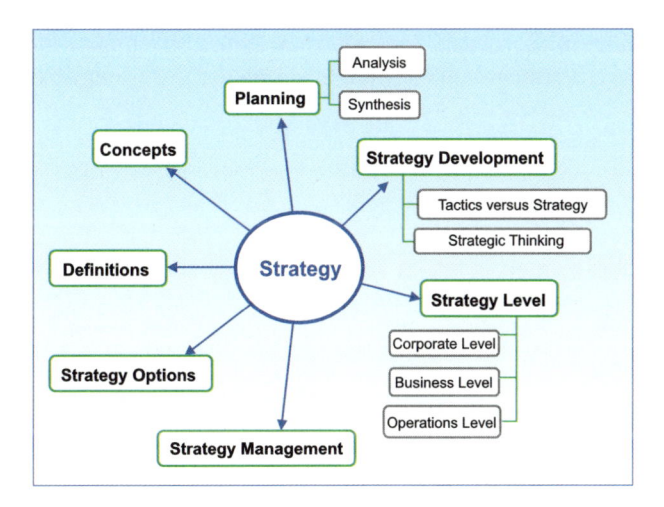

Figure 107 Basic mind map: the nature of strategy

The assumption that synthesis and implementation follow careful analysis – the basic premise of strategy concepts introduced in the past decade – is not a matter of dispute.

Ever since the turn of the century, the focus of attention seems to be the question of how to deal with complexity and uncertainty. Numerous publications devoted to these issues offer support for this suggestion [Day 2006, Ormerod 2005, Rosenzweig 2007, Finkelstein 2004, Taleb 2005, Kelly 2005].

In the following section, I turn to a discussion of strategy in times of turbulence.

5.3 Developing Strategies in Turbulent Environments

Having presented a number of theoretical concepts in the previous section, I now turn my attention to a consideration of complexity, uncertainty, and dynamism in the context of strategy development. When reviewing the many concepts, opinions, views and theories, it is striking that everything appears, at least on the drawing board, to be very simple and plausible. In practice, however, things quickly look very different from the tidy theoretical presentations. It is seldom that textbook strategies apply to the real world.

Beyond this, however, managers are increasingly confronted by situations in which the capacity of conventional approaches to offer assistance is severely limited. The strategies – developed on the assumption of equilibrium conditions – are deployed in an environment marked by complex, chaotic, and nebulous conditions. "In this world, they make reasonable assumptions about the evolution of product markets, capital markets, technology, and government regulation and, in effect, 'assume away' most risk." [Bryan 2002]

We read statements of the following sort every day in the newspaper, "We underestimated our competitors" and "The response of consumers to product XYZ is not what we expected."

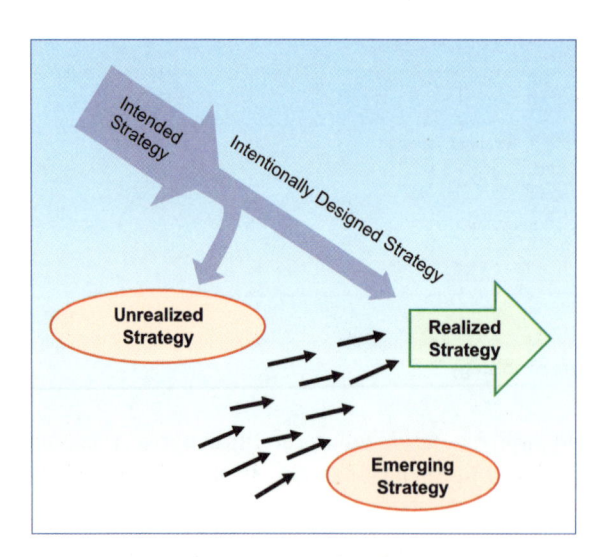

Figure 108 Strategy formation according to Mintzberg: only a part of the plan is implemented

The requirements are much more extensive and demanding in a turbulent environment than those derived from traditional strategic planning. In keeping with this suggestion, Mintzberg drafts a model of various strategy forms [Mintzberg 1989]. As shown in Figure 108, it is by no means the case that strategies are developed in tidy processes and then implemented. In reality – and here it is helpful to recall the notion of "memories of the Future" discussed in Chapter 4 – it turns out that the strategy that is ultimately implemented arises in a process of maturation. The original or planned strategy is subject to the continuous influence of various factors, its viability is then reconsidered and parts of it are discarded. On the other hand, new considerations come into play and have an impact, i.e. in their capacity as emerging strategies, on the existing strategy.

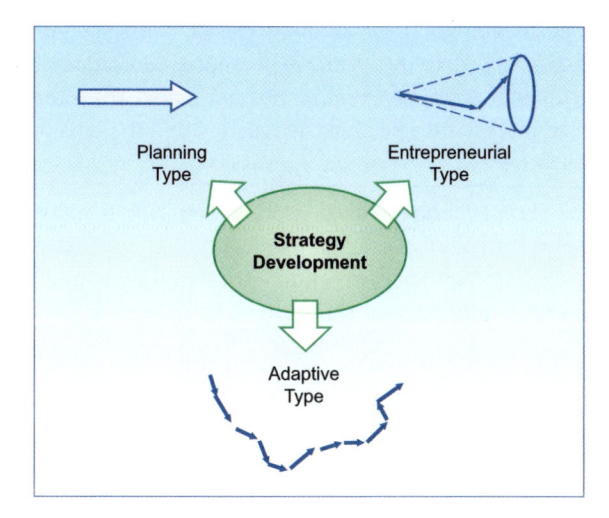

Figure 109 Strategy development: three basic types [Quinn 1988]

Strategy development essentially demands entrepreneurial skills, i.e. astute observation, a capacity to analyze, a readiness to accept risk, a capacity to assert oneself, clear powers of imagination, a willingness to make decisions and, last but not least, energy. While many of the properties mentioned can be learned, they cannot be learned by reading a textbook. They require experience. The challenge is to successfully position the enterprise in an environment that is marked by change, turbulence and uncertainty in a manner that secures long-term success.

As illustrated in Figure 109, strategic approaches can be grouped according to three archetypes. As already mentioned, the first is strategic planning – oriented towards the long term and handed down by the management in a stable environment. The second is the entrepreneurial mode which is also for the long term, but includes a greater degree of flexibility and accommodates sweeping decisions. The third is the adaptive mode which assumes a complex and uncertain environment, is conceived to enable short-term reactions and emphasizes the importance of making incremental steps towards the enterprise's goal.

Even if the classification of strategies into forms or modes has more academic than practical value, it nonetheless gives an indication of our general direction: the exception will become the rule.

The strategy is usually a kind of master plan, carved in stone. Every departure from the holy plan is tantamount to a defeat and must be justified. Examples here include the maiden flights of the Airbus A380 and Boeing's Dreamliner. Irrespective of whether the delays were owing to the ambitious project management or the strategic management, both examples represent cases of plans being confronted by reality, and the participants were forced to learn that one's ability to plan major undertakings in highly complex and interrelated environments is limited.

The strategic requirements faced by enterprises experiencing different degrees of turbulence may be altogether different. For instance, using the classification scheme in Table 12 (Section 3.1) one is inclined to give the scenario presented in Chapter 4 ("The Future of Television") a turbulence score of 4 to 5. As we can gather from the table, the major change for the enterprise is the speed of the reaction and the type of strategy development which is characterized as "strategic aggression."

When the conditions in their environment change – this is usually seen in an increasing degree of turbulence – enterprises are often overloaded, and either fail to react at all or they react in the wrong way. The strategic concepts and instruments are aligned to stable environmental conditions or conditions that change only slightly.

In the context of a study, Wiggins and Rüffli examined 6,772 companies for a period of 23 years [Wiggins 2002]. Depending on their overall fitness, the authors broke down the investigated companies into three different groups, including superior, average and inferior. What the authors determined in their evaluation is indeed astonishing. Only 5% of all companies maintained a status of superior for 10 years or longer. The authors conclude that companies exhibiting a temporarily high degree of fitness tend to be very efficiently and effectively aligned to their environments. However, once the environment changes, they often fail to retool quickly enough. This supports the suggestion that competitive advantages are only temporary and have to be reestablished continuously. Only a very few exceptional enterprises succeed in continuously tapping new sources and in continuously reinventing themselves. Only 0.5% of the companies examined retained a status of superior for a period of more than 20 years and only three companies (American Home Products, Eli Lilly and 3M) or 0.3% succeeded in remaining both efficient and adaptable for a period of 50 years.

What is so difficult about remaining both efficient and adaptable for a longer period of time? We can recall the statistics about the Forbes 100 companies from the year 1917 that were cited in Chapter 1. Only 17 of these companies still existed in the year 2001!

It depends on a balanced attention to both the enterprise and its environment. It follows that knowledge about the enterprise and a proper analysis of the enterprise's environment are crucial when it comes to developing strategies and making strategic decisions. Moreover, it is safe to assume that successful strategies account for more than just the enterprise's environment.

5.4 Enterprise Analysis

It is clear that economic success is not a matter of chance. The position that an enterprise enjoys on the market is determined by its capacity to compete on the market. Direct comparisons show that the position and success of enterprises that operate in similar market environments and that enter their markets having met similar prerequisites can differ significantly.

As was shown in the previous section, knowledge about the enterprise's environment and developments in this environment are immensely important for future success. Extensive knowledge about one's own enterprise is just as important. Without wishing to provide an answer to one of the most discussed issues in the area of business administration, i.e. whether market-oriented or resource-oriented approaches are more successful, I would suggest that a combination of both is what will ensure success. The question is:

What can the enterprise do very well and what distinguishes it from others? In this regard, Andrews suggests, "The distinctive competence of an organization is more than what it can do, it is what it can do particularly well." [Andrews 1971]. What is meant are the things that are really exceptionally good, or so good that other enterprises couldn't imitate them without considerable effort.

What is the basis of success?

If you ask someone from senior management about the strengths that make the enterprise competitive, you will seldom get a satisfactory answer. "We are market leaders," signifies success, but says little about the reasons for the success. Can we conclude that the reason for the success (or lack thereof) of the enterprise in the last quarter (or business year) was that it worked exceptionally well and that the strategy was outstandingly effective?

- Or was it a matter of bad luck (or whatever) on the part of the competition?
- Or was it a matter of favorable market development and strong demand?
- Or was it a matter of shrewd restructuring?

In one case, it is a matter of fortune, and in the other a matter of skill. So long as the numbers are right, there are not that many around who really care. Success, i.e. success in terms of good business figures, is usually attributed to the management. A lack of success is usually attributed to unfavorable markets. This can also apply in times of excellent economic development. But even at this particular time, most managers claim that the success resulted mainly from cost-saving measures from previous years – the result of excellent management.

Success even leads to the assumption that the right path was taken, the right strategy deployed and that all one has to do in the future is to continue to apply the same strategy, only perhaps with a little more effort, i.e. in keeping with the strategy of scales. However, if the success did not stem from the genius of the management, but from napping on the part of one's competitors or temporary market luck, the strategy may end in disaster when one's competitors at last wake up or when demand suddenly tails off.

The assumption that it is the strategy that is behind the success can be deceptive and dangerous. As already mentioned, the explanation for the lack of success is always given. It is explained by most managers either in terms of the market, which has behaved different than expected, or the employees, who have failed adhere to the strategy. Mintzberg puts the point compelling, "If only you dumbbells had appreciated our brilliant strategies, all would be well. But the clever dumbbells might well respond: 'If you are so smart, why didn't you formulate strategies that we dumbbells could implement? You knew who we are: why didn't you factor our incompetence into your thinking?'"

We can conclude that, by definition, a failed formulation of strategy is behind every failed strategy and the lack of success is ALWAYS a result of bad decisions made at management level. It follows that strategy analysis and strategy development are NEVER to be regarded as a routine task or a standard procedure, a matter of pressing a button and checking off the steps to success.

In order to answer the question about a strategy's success or lack of success in advance, there will be no avoiding a meaningful assessment of the enterprise itself – including its strengths and weaknesses. However, "Many companies, especially the large ones, have only the vaguest notion of the nature and degree of the competencies that they may posses." [Mintzberg 1989]

Self-assessment: Enterprise Strengths and Weaknesses

Managers tend to assess enterprises exclusively in terms of performance criteria (growth, profit, and EBIT) and to formulate goals accordingly. While this reductionist approach effectively reduces the complexity of the task of analysis, it is based exclusively on the past and gives little indication as to the reasons for success or the lack of success. An assessment of the enterprise's capacity to perform and its potential is crucial, particularly when it comes to strategy development. It is only with an accurate assessment as a basis that strategic decisions will lead to the desired result.

This should not be construed as a call for greater self-preoccupation in the future. It is much more a call to sketch a realistic picture of the enterprise's potential (its strengths and weaknesses) in addition to identifying the possible changes and uncertainties in the enterprise's environment in the future.

One would expect this to be self-evident. A study carried out by Howard Stevenson [Stevenson 1997] offers an explanation: "... the result of the study brought into serious question the value of formal assessment approaches." The author notes in particular that a heightened sense of optimism prevails at the level of senior management. However, even more interesting is his remark that strengths are essentially based on historical data – primarily competitive success – while weaknesses are based on normative views – personal evaluations. Stevenson concludes that managers are realistic when assessing strengths, but are led by wishful thinking when assessing weaknesses.

Mintzberg goes one step further [Mintzberg 1994], arguing that it is primarily the distance of the managers from the events themselves that leads to inaccurate assessments. He also suggests that strengths and weaknesses are essentially situation-specific. A strength in one case may be a weakness in another. This suggests that general statements are of little help. In Chapter 6, I will also discuss power structures as a factor that prevents neutral self-assessment.

In addition to performance figures and EBIT, the number of patents, the number of employees with academic qualifications, the number of new products, current market share, growth, technological sophistication and similar values could be drawn upon for purposes of a superficial analysis. The relevant values are usually relatively easy to determine, and given that they can be quantified, they come with the added bonus of being comparable and implying precision. But it is exactly this implied precision that also leads to the assumption that one has indeed established an overview of the enterprise or the business field. However, a look at the obvious success factors does not qualify as an adequate analysis of the enterprise because it merely presents the results of activities in the past.

Ansoff has presented a rather comprehensive list of potential strengths and weaknesses [Ansoff 1965] that was later expanded by Porter in the form of the value chain [Porter 1980] (Figure 165, Section 10.3.2). These works can be seen as having inspired a trend towards more sophisticated assessments of enterprise capabilities. The introduction of key performance indicators and balanced-scorecard systems has enabled a quantification of performance data.

Thompson, for instance, proposes evaluating enterprises on a scale of 1 to 10, according to criteria such as manufacturing capabilities, technological skills, quality/product performance and reputation/image. This score is then compared to those of the enterprise's competitors. Furthermore, there is also an "unweighted overall strength rating." It is thus possible to express enterprise potential in the form of a number. What we again see here is the strong and widespread tendency to assume that information expressed in numbers is precise [Thompson 2004].

This may be sufficient for administrative purposes. One should not, however, forget that the resulting data are merely an expression of performance capabilities, and are expressly not a statement about the reasons or causes. Such data are an insufficient basis for analyses whose objective is to generate strategic decisions and initiate improvements within an enterprise. What is called for here is a far more systematic and profound approach.

Enterprise Assessment

The 7S model can be used to assess the organizational effectiveness of an enterprise (Table 35, Figure 110). "Organizational change is really the inter-relationship between structure, strategy, systems, style, skills, staff and ... superordinate goals."

[Waterman 1980] It is based on the knowledge that enterprises are more than a structure and a strategy, and that they can be characterized by seven elements that are closely tied to one another. A change in any one element will have an impact on the remaining elements and on the overall enterprise system. The model thus contravenes the widespread and naive belief that there is a secret adjustment screw somewhere in the enterprise whose adjustment will lead to more success.

It is time to reconsider and expand upon the often cited remark made by Chandler, namely, that "structure follows strategy." Capabilities, values, culture, human resources, systems and structures follow strategy.

Table 35 The 7S Approach to Assessing Enterprises

	Element	Explanation
Hard Ss	Strategy	The measures planned by an enterprise in response to changes and expected changes in its environment.
Hard Ss	Structure	As the framework for the specialization, coordination and cooperation of individual enterprise units, the structure is essentially determined by the strategy, the size of the enterprise and the diversity of its products and services.
Hard Ss	Systems	The formal and informal processes used to implement the strategy in the given structures.
Soft Ss	Style/culture	The culture of the enterprise, consisting of two components: The leadership approach taken by the management. More a question of how the management acts than what it says. What does the management spend its time doing? What does it focus its energy on? The enterprise's overall operating approach. The dominant values and norms that have developed in the course of time and that are reflected in the way the employees present themselves.
Soft Ss	Staff	The enterprise's human resources: Refers to how people are trained, socialized, guided, integrated, motivated, promoted and evaluated.
Soft Ss	Skills	What the enterprise does best, its distinctive capabilities and competencies, as well as measures used to expand upon and develop these essential capabilities and competencies.
Soft Ss	Shared values	Formerly referred to as superordinate goals; the enterprise's guiding concepts and principles, as well as its vision, usually expressed in simple words at an abstract level and usually vital to the internal and external image the enterprise projects.

Enterprises that work effectively show an even balance of these seven elements. This is also the origin of the model's characterization as a diagnostic model for assessing enterprise effectiveness.

A change in any one of the elements will have an impact on all of the other elements. For instance, changes to components in the HR system (e.g. internal career planning, opportunities for promotion, and professional training) will trigger changes in the enterprise culture and leadership style, and thereby also lead to changes in its structures and processes and, ultimately, in its distinctive capabilities and competencies.

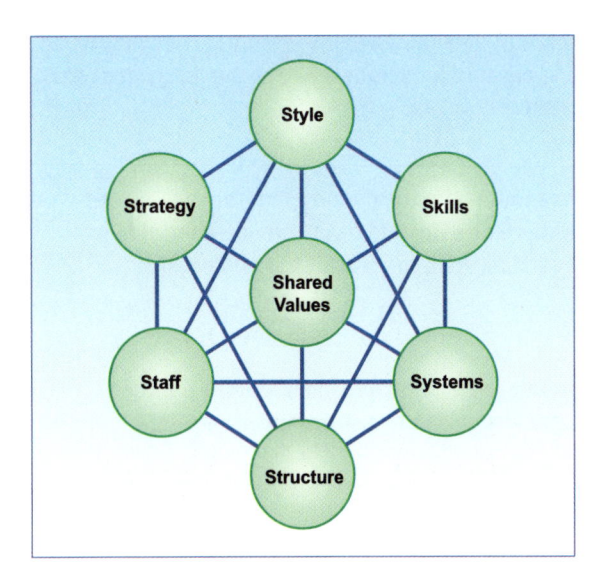

Figure 110 The 7S model: all things are interdependent
[Quinn 1988, Waterman 1980]

Once we have completed an assessment of the enterprise as a system, we can move forward to establishing an overview of the available resources, capabilities and competencies. In keeping with Grant [Grant 1998], we can draw a distinction between material and immaterial resources.

Resources, Capabilities and Competencies

The material resources can be divided up into:

- *Financial resources*

    These refer to the possibility and magnitude of financial action, as well as to existing monetary reserves.

- *Organizational resources*

    These include the enterprise's formal structure: planning, control, coordination, implementation.

- *Physical resources (assets)*

    These include buildings, machines and equipment as well as access to materials and components.

- *Technological resources*

    These essentially include the available technologies, some of which may be protected by patents or copyrights.

The immaterial resources, which are often responsible for the operation of the (material) production facilities, are described by Mintzberg as follows, "... while hard data may inform the intellect, it is largely soft data that generate wisdom. They may be difficult to analyze, but they are indispensable for syntheses – the key to strategy making." These include [Mintzberg 1999]:

- *Human resources*

    It is not the number of employees that is significant here, but the capabilities of the employees. The resources here also include trust and other social factors such as loyalty, assertiveness, management capabilities and organizational routines.

- *Innovation potential*

    The crucial elements of innovation potential include ideas and the ability to create new things, generate knowledge and transform inventions into products.

- *Reputation*

    This essentially refers to the value of the brand, and the trust of customers and employees in the enterprise.

This gives a good indication as to how difficult it is to assess the soft factor. How are we to assess innovation capacity, or the motivation of employees, or the nature of cooperation? And in particular: WHO is to assess these attributes? In the case of small enterprises, the managers can establish an opinion and update this opinion as appropriate on the basis of their proximity to daily activities. Large enterprises have a considerable disadvantage here. Given that the expense associated with finding out is considerable, the task itself – as mentioned earlier – is often neglected.

As illustrated by the account of the 7 sisters at the beginning of the chapter, it is primarily "soft" information that is important crucial to assessments. "This is why the alignment between a strategy and a company's real strengths is a critical, though often neglected, factor in determining whether strategies succeed." [Apesi 1999]

Enterprise Strengths and Weaknesses

Strengths mainly refer to those things that introduce competitive advantages, other features that make an enterprise unique and competencies that distinguish an enterprise from its competitors and make a decisive contribution to success.

Weakness refers to an organizational inability to detect certain developments or to implement measures to the necessary degree. However, one might also refer to functional deficiencies as weaknesses (e.g. elements in the value chain proposed by Porter) [Porter 1980].

The fact is: most attempts to systematically analyze the strengths and weaknesses of enterprises remain "in an embryonic stage" [Jain 2004].

One of the few thorough investigations of this subject can be found in a dissertation by Stevenson [Stevenson 1963]. Stevenson's work offers a number of recommendations for incorporating strengths and weaknesses into the relevant enterprise analyses. He proposes the following evaluation criteria:

- Organizational structure
- Formalities and rules
- Senior management capabilities
- Information systems [and the ability to use them]
- Sequences and procedures
- Manager behavior and attitude
- Relationship to labor unions
- Technological capabilities
- Research potential
- New product ideas
- Production facilities and capacities
- Demographic composition of the staff
- Distribution system
- Sales capabilities
- Product line diversity
- Quality and quality control
- Stock market reputation
- Understanding of consumers
- Market domination

It is not my aim here to develop a comprehensive framework for evaluating the strengths and weaknesses of an enterprise. I am much more concerned with the task of getting in the clear on the enterprise's potential, and to question whether self-assessments are realistic. Here, it is helpful to bear in mind that many strategic mistakes derive from inaccurate assessments of one's own capabilities and potential – usually a matter of overestimating these. Nutt estimates that half of all the decisions made by a given enterprise are mistaken [Nutt 1999].

The following questions can help us to obtain the information we need to better understand and accurately assess the enterprise or the business area:

- *Management*
    - What is the nature of the management's capabilities?
    - Are entrepreneurial approaches promoted?
    - Does the notion of *shaping* enjoy greater esteem than *administering*?

- Are the managers good role models for the employees?
- Is the power that comes with managerial positions deployed in the interest of the enterprise?
- Are there any means of intervening in management processes? (And by whom?)
- Are certain leadership styles prevalent? What role is played by openness and trust and power and fear?
- How does the management arrive at decisions?

In addition to complexity and uncertainty, conflicts within the enterprise also have an impact on management developments [Amit 1993]. The capacity to arrive at decisions in circumstances characterized by an incomplete information base, uncertainty, and a vast array of options has become an indispensable management competence for strategy development.

- *Knowledge*
  - How is knowledge generated in the enterprise?
  - How is knowledge shared in the enterprise?
  - What are the incentives that employees have to share their knowledge within the enterprise?
  - What are the available ways of communicating or reporting knowledge?
  - While knowledge management systems are regarded as modern, they are not capable of generating knowledge. They are merely used to represent or store information. How are they deployed in the enterprise?
  - How is knowledge valued in the enterprise?
  - What is the enterprise's capacity to learn?
  - How can one evaluate the knowledge status achieved by an enterprise?

  The immaterial resources and competencies are difficult to evaluate. The task itself is subjective and a challenge for the management. "Part of the problem is that 'information' is generally a fact, whereas 'knowledge,' which focuses on linkages and relationships, is subjective." [Hauschild 2001]

- *Competencies*
  - Does the enterprise have capabilities and competencies that distinguish it from its competitors and that are difficult to copy?
  - Are certain capabilities promoted in a focused manner?
  - Are the competencies of employees known?

- *Innovation*
  - Has an innovation culture been established?
  - Is innovation promoted and demanded?
  - What is the motivation for promoting innovation?

- Is the enterprise prepared for revolutionary innovations or are only "secure" innovations promoted?
- How does one deal with failure?
- What volume of resources is allocated to innovation projects, i.e. in terms of time and budget?
- How are ideas evaluated and innovation projects selected?
- Could personal matters and matters of internal enterprise politics hinder important innovations?

- *Information*
  - How is important information forwarded in the enterprise?
  - How and where is information generated, processed and forwarded?
  - Is communication within the enterprise limited to reports from below and evaluation and instructions from above?
  - How are decisions made?
  - Have feedback loops been established?
  - Are there any means of cross-hierarchy communication?

- *Culture*
  - How might one describe the enterprise culture?
  - Are there any paradigms and unwritten laws?
  - How are differences of opinion dealt with? Does status within the hierarchy take precedence or do arguments have weight?
  - What symbols are associated with the power structures?
  - How is the power in the enterprise distributed?

- *Motivation and loyalty*
  - What motivates the employees and managers to give their best?
  - Is the enterprise loyal to its employees? Are the employees loyal to the enterprise?
  - How do employees work (cross-departmentally) together?

- *Organization*
  - What is the enterprise's organizational structure?
  - Has it proven effective?
  - What are its advantages and disadvantages?
  - What reasons are there to justify this structure?
  - Is the structure oriented towards tasks, markets, processes, employees and customers?
  - Can the organizational structure be adapted quickly to new circumstances?
  - How are the stakeholders and their needs accounted for?

- Is the organization capable of learning?
- Are results questioned in the interest of improvement or to identify a responsible party?

- *Capacity to change*
  - How are changes within the enterprise initiated?
  - Who is responsible for driving changes?
  - Are changes initiated and driven from top down or bottom up?
  - Could self-satisfaction prevail, with the result that further development is brought to a halt?
  - How does the enterprise behave in situations of crisis?
  - How do new business fields arise?
  - What has the organization learned from past changes?

- *Response times*
  - How quick can the enterprise respond to changed situations?
  - How are changes detected and accounted for by the enterprise and how are changes within the enterprise initiated?

  In addition to the enterprise's general capacity to perform effectively, an ability to respond quickly is regarded as especially significant. The response time is the time it takes the enterprise to initiate a change in strategy, make relevant decisions and introduce specific measures and actions after detecting a strong or weak signal (cf. Figure 34).

The account of the 7 sisters' response to the oil crisis of 1973 at the beginning of Chapter 4 illustrates the significant impact that an enterprise's capacity to respond quickly can have on its performance. It is not only the knowledge that change has occurred that is decisive, it is also a capacity to quickly implement appropriate measures.

For instance, a telecom provider may regard its traditional business as threatened by the new VoIP technology that allows consumers to place calls for significantly less. Although there has been an awareness of this technology and its impact on the market at all of the relevant levels of the company for a long time, it has nonetheless taken years for any sort of response.

Sony is known as an innovative company. Still, as the inventor of the Walkman, Sony failed to recognize the potential of digital music, and left the market almost entirely to Apple.

The list could be extended indefinitely, whether it is a matter of products (the particle filter), societal change (healthcare reforms) or economic changes (the production of photo technology has disappeared almost entirely from Germany because the Japanese competition was first ignored and then simply accepted). This phenomenon of paralysis seems to be very widespread (Figure 111).

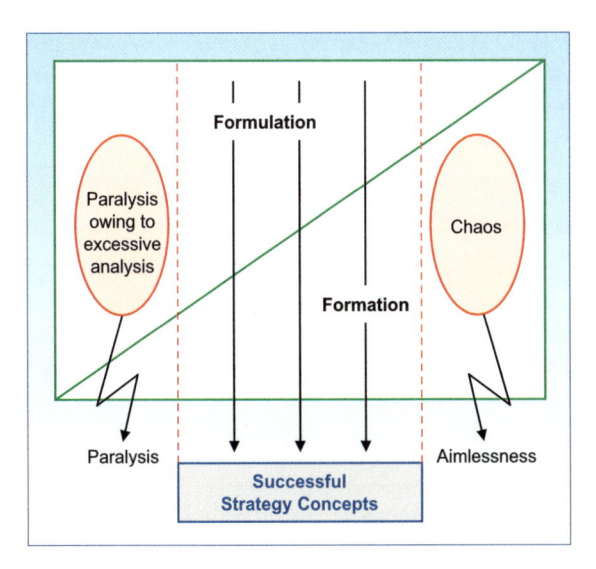

Figure 111 The continuum of strategy development: the right weighting of formulation and formation (as adapted from [Weidler 1997])

It also warrants mention in this context that the analysis of the enterprise can be just as extensive and costly as that of the enterprise's environment – especially in the case of enterprises with large organizational structures. Knowledge about the enterprise itself can help the enterprise to reduce uncertainty, particularly when it is confronted by turbulence in its environment. In other words, attempts to develop strategy in the absence of knowledge about the enterprise's environment AND the enterprise are like driving blindfolded. Knowledge about the enterprise and the capacity to act and have an impact increase strategic security and reduce degrees of freedom.

5.5 Strategy Synthesis

"And now?" The most important step in the development of strategy is synthesis, with the aim of generating new strategic options, drafting strategic plans and preparing decisions. However, experience shows that the tasks of interpreting and reflecting on the results of the relevant analyses tend to be neglected. It is usually the pressure to meet deadlines that leads to no more than the obvious strategic proposals at this stage, which naturally leads to the question as to whether the costs of analysis were at all justified.

Take your time. Sit back and give yourself a chance to reflect on the results presented so far. Given that the development of strategies is a creative process, it can also be helpful to view things from a different perspective or to spend a day concerning yourself with other things.

You now have an opportunity, before it becomes very serious, to again call to mind your strategic goals, visions and basic understanding of the enterprise. Equipped with an assessment of the enterprise, i.e. knowledge about its resources, capabilities, core competencies and competitive advantages, and an assessment of both the enterprise's micro and macro environment (e.g. in the form of scenarios), you are now in a position to consider the enterprise's strategic orientation.

5.5.1 Basic Understanding of Strategy and Strategic Goals

Ken Andrews is regarded as the pioneer of the SWOT analysis. He was also one of the first scholars who described the significance of "strategic fit" as a combination of operational strength/weakness and opportunities and risks appearing outside the operational sphere [Andrews 1971]. The procedure originally proposed by Andrews (Figure 112) differs from the SWOT matrix as it is known today. In contrast to its current form, the original matrix considers the orientation and the mission of the enterprise.

Having already considered the questions: "What can we do?"; "What should we do?"; and "What do others expect us to do?", let us now turn to the question, "What do we want to do?" before moving on to strategy development.

Let's start with a subject that at first glance appears to be very simple: every enterprise should be able to answer the question as to why it exists. The reason is often linked to the enterprise's mission or vision. The particular missions may vary considerably. We can imagine that smaller family enterprises exist simply because they have already existed for generations. Others have an obligation to enhance shareholder value. Others, still, are simply committed to implementing their ideas or perceive a certain societal responsibility.

Even if most people are less mindful of these things, calling them to mind and promoting a common understanding of them can be immensely important when it comes to reflecting on strategic goals. This is the basis of one's understanding of the company and also of its strategic orientation.

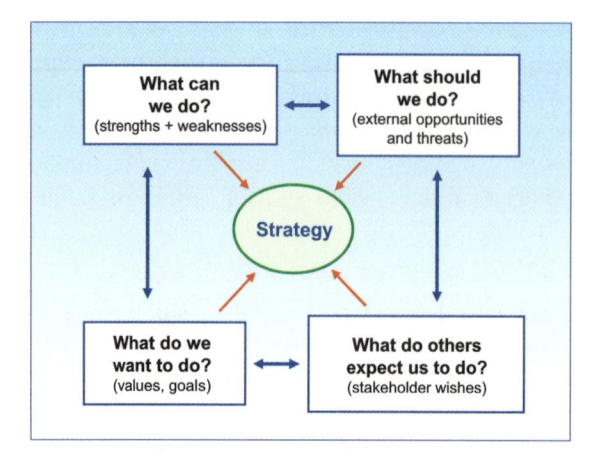

Figure 112 Strategic tool: the SWOT analysis presented by Andrews

Existing strategic goals are evaluated and new strategic goals are formulated in the framework of strategic analysis. This includes an examination of the enterprise's goals, mission and vision.

The Mission Statement

Does the enterprise have a mission statement? Mission statements usually account for the following:

- The enterprise's global business policy, especially its supply policy
- The enterprise's relationship to customers and employees
- The enterprise's relationship to the state and the overall economy
- The enterprise's management principles

The capacity of the enterprise's mission statement to function as a model or set of guidelines depends on its credibility. The enterprise's managers have a special role when it comes to the mission statement's application.

Visions

Does the enterprise have visions? While I intentionally omit to cite examples of visions because they require individual development, visions should have the function of motivating individuals and engendering a sense of enthusiasm. Challenging goals are often suitable to establish identification with the enterprise.

In contrast, key figures from the repertoire of business administration are ill-suited. Dividend or profit targets have a minimal to negative impact on employee motivation. Nothing succeeds more in increasing the gap between the management and the employees than dividend targets. And nothing can unify an enterprise more than challenging and motivating visions (e.g. the vision of being the first to land on the moon).

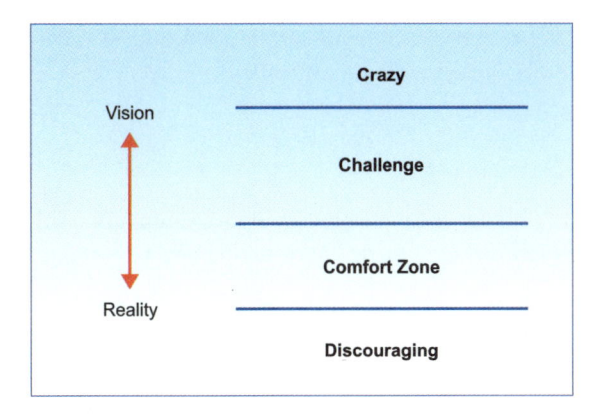

Figure 113 The vision: usually far away from enterprise realities

5.5 Strategy Synthesis

Do the results of analysis obtained so far match the enterprise's visions – which are usually established from the top down? Do any contradictions appear? For instance, cuts in research funding are not likely to be compatible with an enterprise's vision of becoming a technology leader. Figure 113 offers a look at a possible spectrum of considerations that can be incorporated into the formulation of visions.

Enterprise Goals

A goals statement must reflect the enterprise's market and societal orientation. We can thus distinguish among the following:

- Performance goals
- Market share
- Quality
- Research goals
- Employee qualifications
- Promotion of employee participation in decision making
- Success goals
- Profitability
- Cost reduction
- Avoiding employee terminations
- Promotion of female employees
- Financial goals
- Liquidity

The goals that take precedence in a particular enterprise will depend on the following:

- Ownership (private versus public)
- The economic system (market economy versus state-controlled)
- The attitude of the managers
- The strength of the employee representatives

Here, too, the question arises as to whether the enterprise goals are compatible with the enterprise? In the interest of credibility and image, there should be no discrepancies here.

Example: Deutsche Telekom

T-Spirit is the motto of Deutsche Telekom (http://www.telekom3.de/de-p/konz/1-ko/5-ko/inha/031017-leitbild-ar.html). It stands for:

Strengthening the value of the corporation: "We strive to increase the value of Deutsche Telekom for the long term."

Partner for our customers: "We win the loyalty of our customers with excellent products and services."

Innovation: "We create a climate that fosters innovation and excellence."

Respect: "We use, respect and support our cultural diversity."

Integrity: "We communicate openly and honestly, and keep our promises."

Top excellence: "We think and act resolutely. We aim to become ever more efficient with the right people at the right place. We consistently reward excellence and sanction inappropriate behavior."

The six values make it clear that T-Spirit is not just a philosophical superstructure. T-Spirit is a behavioral model that applies to all of the corporation's employees. The senior management at Deutsche Telekom has committed itself to acting in accordance with the enterprise values in the capacity of role models. The goal is to achieve an outcome whereby all of the corporation's employees adhere to the code.

In light of one's experience as a customer of Deutsche Telekom and former reports about the company (€ 5 billion in cost cutting, cutting of 32,000 jobs and the cancellation of 2 million fixed network connections per year), it is difficult to believe that much regard is really paid to the mission statement.

While the reminder that one should not lose sight of the enterprise's goals may sound trivial, the example of Deutsche Telekom shows that orientation and goals are immensely important. These are used to evaluate enterprises both internally and externally as well as to develop strategies.

5.5.2 Strategic Options and Strategic Fit

In addition to a self-concept, each enterprise should have a clear understanding of its role in the industry in which it is active. Is it an active shaper in this industry, capable of exploiting opportunities, or a passive observer? "Depending on the extent of its ambition, a company can adopt one of three strategic postures: adopting, shaping, or reserving the right to play." [Kauffman 1995]

The question as to which approach is more promising has long been a subject of research among economists, and it is not possible to give a clear and simple answer. Such investigations have largely been conducted with respect to stable environments or have failed to adequately account for the enterprise environment. [Grant 1998]. If we also take account of the environment, we will arrive at considerations of the sort outlined in Table 36.

The basic approach that an enterprise takes may change over the course of time as it discards old roles and assumes new roles. There are also examples of enterprises that take both active and passive approaches. Samsung started in the electronics industry as a typical adopter. The aim was simply to implement the specifications of others,

Table 36 Archetypical Behavior in the Spectrum of Change (cf. Figure 41)

Turbulence Level	Adopter	Shaper
General	Tries to adapt to the changed environment. Necessary: very good observation of the market, consumers, competitors and the environment as well as of all relevant changes. Flexible organizational structure. Core competencies are acquired if necessary. Orientation: outwards. Cautious investments.	Tries to change or reinvent the rules of the game. Necessary: courage, strength, orientation, conviction, willpower and market influence. Stable organizational form. Core competencies are expanded. Orientation: inwards.
Paradigms	Both archetypes behave similarly.	
Trends	Recognizes trends and follows them from a safe distance.	Sets trends via new products, services or business models.
Contradictions	Are ignored or repressed.	Are exploited.
Uncertainties	Observe, wait and see. Avoid risks.	Take a stand, trumpet claims, exploit opportunities.
Chaos	Passive	Active

only better. Having achieved success, a desire took hold in the company to shape the market, with the result that the company's own concepts and product ideas were pursued.

Once a shaper, the Microsoft Corporation has developed into a typical adopter that is concerned to defend its status and success. Innovation is now largely driven by other companies such as Google while Microsoft reacts.

In order to avoid falling gradually into an extremely passive adopter role – which can happen if there is no one in the enterprise to introduce new ideas for shaping – it can be useful to reflect upon one's own role from time to time.

"You have to run faster and faster, just to stay in the same place." [Kauffman 1995]

The paradox is that the shaping influence that an enterprise has on the industry should increase as it remains inflexible in an environment characterized by ever increasing turbulence. In other words, if the role of the shaper is often associated with considerable risk, self-confident action may be more advantageous in turbulent situations than taking a wait-and-see approach.

In the context of a study of 50 companies conducted from 1985 to 1995, McKinsey determined that 86% of the more successful companies pursued a market-shaping philosophy. This may be an indication that merely observing the market and adapting accordingly also leads to "merely" average results. In other words, adaptation involves orienting oneself to the average.

5.5.3 Developing Enterprise Scenarios

The future of one's own enterprise is usually thought of as a given, and something that can be described using strategic plans and roadmaps. However, plans often involve a degree of wishful thinking and tend to reflect no more than the realm of the possible. In exceptional cases, we find action programs that are indeed connected to perceptions of future development. It is not least on account of this that Mintzberg doubts whether managers orient themselves on such plans at all [Mintzberg 1999].

The assumption that it is only the environment that is exposed to change and that the enterprise itself is essentially a constant is mistaken. Enterprises sometimes change faster than their environments. Like scenarios depicting the future of the environment change within the enterprise can be detected on the basis of signals, trends and other information (see Table 37). In light of this, I now wish to present the concept of "enterprise scenarios."

Owing to the many degrees of freedom associated with the diversity, potential and dynamism within enterprises, it will be helpful, like in the case of scenarios depicting the future of the enterprise's environment, to develop scenarios of the future enterprise. An enterprise's development as it moves into the future is likely to be determined by people acting both rationally and emotionally, and is therefore very unlikely to proceed in a linear fashion. The inclusion of all known sources of change in the analysis will help to make the scenario more vivid.

As outlined in Chapters 3 and 4, changes in the enterprise environment can be classified as paradigms, trends, contradictions, uncertainties and chaos. Changes in the enterprise can be described and analyzed similarly.

This requires considerable knowledge about the enterprise and an approach that is similarly disciplined and neutral as that taken with respect to scenarios of the future of the enterprise's environment. An awareness of the strengths and weaknesses of an

Table 37 Relation of the Changes to the Environment and the Enterprise

Element	Environment	Enterprise
Paradigms	Stable, constant features, e.g. physical constants, pursuit of happiness	Reliable starting points, e.g. enterprise goals and philosophies
Trends	Foreseeable change, e.g. societal aging	Clear change that may be welcome or unwelcome, e.g. outsourcing
Contradictions	Dilemmas (e.g. "Tragedy of the Commons") and differences of opinion	Mutually defeating efforts, e.g. team spirit versus measurement of personal performance
Uncertainties	Change whose further development is unclear, e.g. scarcity of raw materials	Change whose further development is unclear, e.g. enterprise culture, continuity
Chaos	Unpredictable wildcards, e.g. catastrophes	Surprising events, e.g. damage claims owing to defective products, hostile takeover

enterprise – as described above – leads to logical conclusions. Logical conclusions and actual reactions may differ considerably owing to an array of irrational factors that are present in all enterprises. A number of reasons were presented in Chapter 2. Envy and ambition, for instance, can motivate illogical actions.

How is power distributed within the enterprise? Who makes decisions? Where is decision making neglected? What areas are considered sluggish? What areas are considered dynamic? Where is active shaping at work? Where are things dutifully performed as expected?

Take a look at your enterprise's business report. Does the report offer an accurate view of reality or have things been made to look better than they are? How large is the difference between the inner perspective and the perspective from above? (I will say more about this in the section entitled "Unwritten Laws" in Chapter 6.)

These aspects are considered in the enterprise scenarios and are to be regarded as a crucial supplement to previous practice along the way to strategy development. The sequence followed to generate enterprise scenarios is largely the same as that followed for environment scenarios, for instance, as seen in our example of the "Future of Television" (Section 5.8).

5.5.4 Developing Strategic Options

Building upon the results of the analysis of the enterprise – and also after having analyzed the changes, established the normative goals, and developed the enterprise scenarios – we can now turn to the development of strategic options and the drawing up of spheres of action and possible actions.

The following questions now present themselves: What possibilities of initiating change in the enterprise, i.e. both intervening in the organizational structure and conscious shaping, do we have at all? How can we influence the enterprise or, if necessary, the environment? The range of options is large. Alternative strategic measures include the following:

- Do nothing.
- Make appropriate staff changes.
- Make appropriate investments.
- Enter into or terminate partnerships.
- Make appropriate acquisitions.
- Sell appropriate enterprise units.
- Establish new competencies and phase out others.
- Promote projects, programs and other actions.
- Initiate or terminate programs.
- Change goals specifications.

- Implement changes in financial systems, information systems, and related structures and processes.

- Implement operational changes (e.g. shift or transfer the value added chain).

- Implement measures to increase employee motivation and to otherwise influence the enterprise culture.

- Etc.

This list represents an excerpt from the comprehensive repertoire of strategic measures. If we examine the possibilities of change purely quantitatively, we wind up with exactly four alternatives (Figure 114), consisting of reducing or expanding with or without external help.

As shown in the above list, there is much more room for maneuver in the case of qualitative assessment. The variations differ largely with respect to the degree of risk involved. Are we prepared to make large investments with a high degree of risk or is it enough to retain the right to play via smaller investments or partnerships? Protecting ourselves against attacks would also be possible, for instance, by establishing the right competencies.

This provides a basis for generating strategic options. Ideally carried out in a team, the approach one takes to processing the considerable information and generating options is largely a matter of intelligence. The process itself – the exchange of information about the environment (general and specific), the flow of information (top down and bottom up) within the enterprise and the continual development of strategy – is illustrated in Figure 115.

Nothing should be considered taboo when it comes to developing strategic options. The overly ambitious aims of the management should not be allowed to hinder an accurate estimation of the enterprise's strengths and weaknesses. Similarly, one

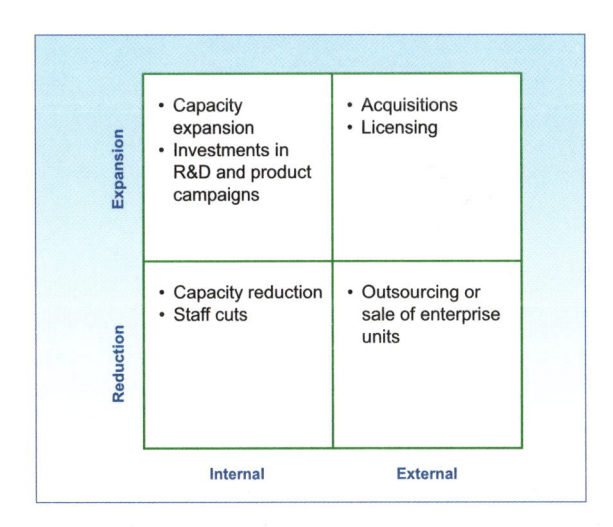

	Internal	External
Expansion	• Capacity expansion • Investments in R&D and product campaigns	• Acquisitions • Licensing
Reduction	• Capacity reduction • Staff cuts	• Outsourcing or sale of enterprise units

Figure 114 Enterprise change: the quantitative approach

5.5 Strategy Synthesis

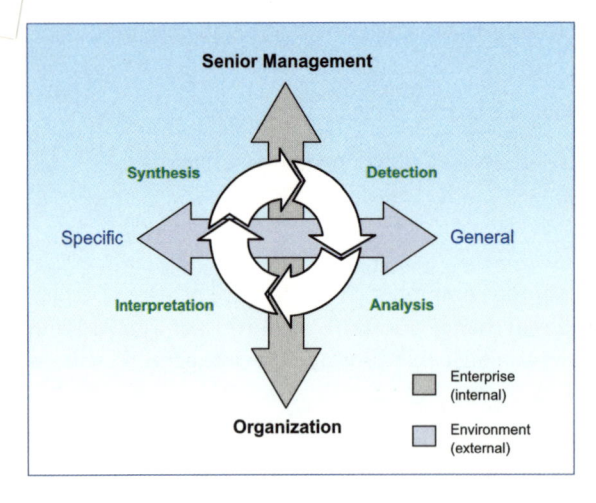

Figure 115 Enterprise change: the qualitative approach

should be prepared to jettison the goals in the face of clear weaknesses. Strategic options must be realistic and consistent. This is often a spot where grave mistakes are made – especially when the gap between what one wishes and what one can deliver is too wide, forcing the organization into turmoil.

5.5.5 Strategic Fit

A "strategic fit" has been established when the enterprise's capabilities and resources are deployed in a manner that optimally meets the needs of the market (the customer), both in stable environments and environments marked by turbulence and uncertainty.

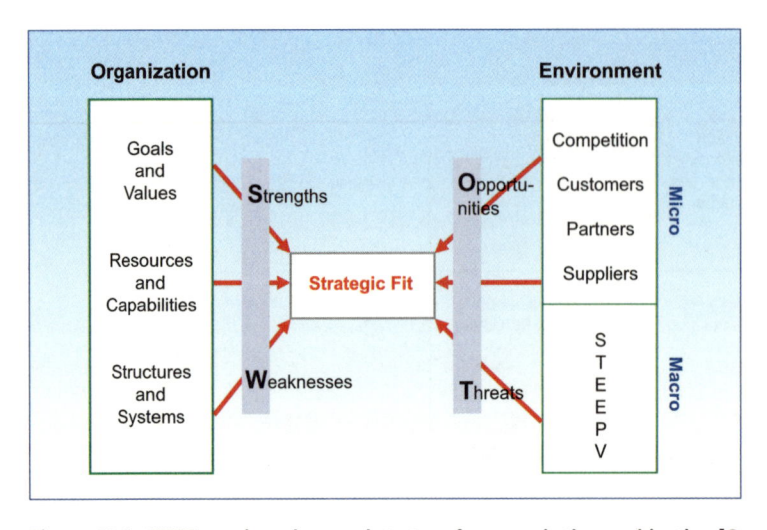

Figure 116 SWOT matrix and general strategy framework: the combination [Grant 1994]

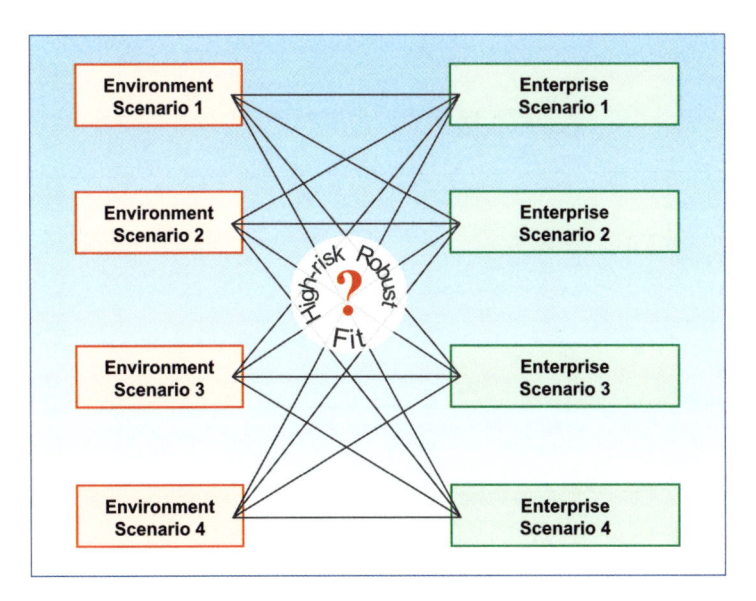

Figure 117 Strategic fit: comparison of scenarios

Building upon the progress made so far, it is now important to consider the future strategic fit. The starting point for this consideration is the expanded SWOT diagram. The disadvantage of the SWOT matrix is its rigidity. The simplification reduces the concept to the structuring and arrangement of information (Figure 116).

The fact that many scenarios are available and that none of them has been selected as "most likely" makes it more difficult to proceed and to arrive at an answer to the question as to what one is now to do with the scenarios and the related findings. As illustrated in Figure 117, the environment scenarios and the enterprise scenarios are now juxtaposed and inspected for proper alignment.

5.5.6 Robust Strategies

The primary goal of an enterprise is to survive. This means that its strategy must be robust. It is only after this has been secured that one can move on to consider new business opportunities. Regrettably, this is often overlooked on account of the available opportunities and ambition on the part of the management. As trivial as it may sound, a check of robustness should be carried out regularly within the enterprise – whether or not one would like to initiate change.

It will become clear that juxtaposing environment scenarios and enterprise scenarios introduces an excellent basis for further discussion. This enables one to test various options, consider their advantages and disadvantages and – ideally in the context of a team – select preferred strategies from the scenarios and options. Figure 118 shows examples of evaluation based on the wind tunnel proposed by Schwartz [Schwartz 1991]. The enterprise's environment is represented as a wind tunnel and the enter-

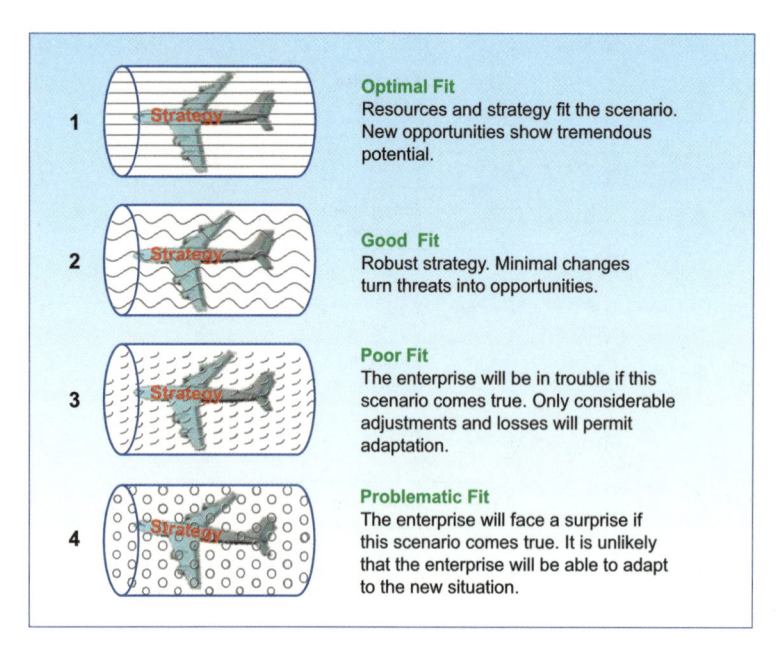

Figure 118 Wind tunnel metaphor: the aerodynamics (strategy) must fit in with the environmental conditions

1 Optimal Fit
Resources and strategy fit the scenario. New opportunities show tremendous potential.

2 Good Fit
Robust strategy. Minimal changes turn threats into opportunities.

3 Poor Fit
The enterprise will be in trouble if this scenario comes true. Only considerable adjustments and losses will permit adaptation.

4 Problematic Fit
The enterprise will face a surprise if this scenario comes true. It is unlikely that the enterprise will be able to adapt to the new situation.

prise strategy as an airplane. The resistance is least and the aerodynamics best when the strategic fit has been optimized.

A strategy qualifies as robust when it focuses on the stability of the enterprise and includes a consideration of alternative developments and how to respond to them. Growth strategies are always associated with a higher degree of risk.

If one evaluates the enterprise scenarios according to the two criteria "stability" and "potential" and transfers the result to a matrix, one will arrive at a representation of the kind seen in Figure 119. The arrows point towards the goal: this is where one should wind up, namely, with strategies that are robust and exhibit high growth potential. Given that the enterprise and its environment change constantly, the position of the scenarios will also change constantly. This underscores the fact that strategy development is a continuous task and that any given evaluation of a strategy is no more than a snapshot.

The planned strategy will certainly be influenced by changed circumstances. As was shown in Figure 107, the strategy that is ultimately realized will certainly not correspond to the originally planned strategy. It is thus indispensable to familiarize oneself with various "triggers" in the context of scenario development. These include events whose occurrence would require a change in the strategy: triggers are anticipated events or changes that will have an impact on the enterprise's strategy.

Taking triggers into consideration in the context of realizing a strategy enables one to pursue a higher risk strategy. One keeps an eye on the triggers and remains ready in

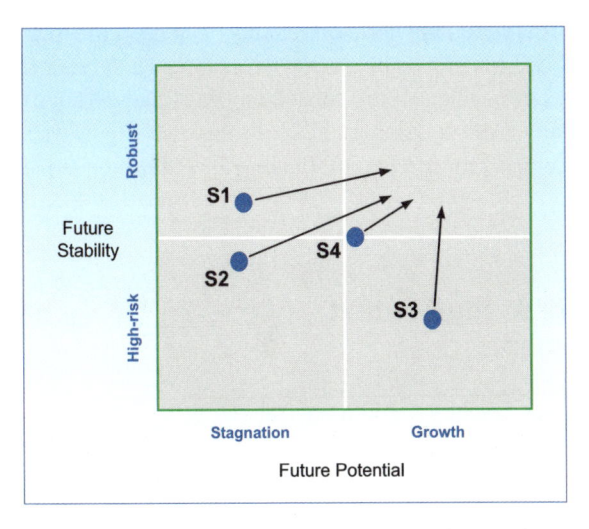

Figure 119 Potential and stability: a steep path upwards

case of their real-world occurrence to implement corresponding measures immediately. The advantage of this method is that it essentially anticipates decisions. One has already secured options in case the projected event actually occurs. This enables one to respond more quickly. Triggers should be a fixed feature of all strategic planning.

5.6 Strategic Decisions

Strategic decisions are made in the period between the end of analysis and the beginning of action. Decisions are necessary to initiate changes.

But it appears to have become more difficult to make precisely these decisions. While managers are also judged on the basis of their decisions, we can only determine in retrospect whether the decisions were good or bad. Refraining from making any decision so as to avoid making a bad decision appears in many cases to be a reasonable compromise. A decision is made in favor of doing nothing so as to keep the risk as low as possible.

Ideally, however, every form of analysis should lead to a decision. Conscious decisions and their proper communication promote transparency and predictability. They help to reduce internal operational uncertainty and increase flexibility. Indecision often leads to sluggishness and paralysis. Given that it is generally not possible to make optimal decisions, we can regard a capacity to draw reasonable conclusions on the basis of incomplete information as a sign of a good manager.

"The justification for the prestige, high prices, and attention lavished on strategy seems straightforward: doing the right thing, even if it isn't done perfectly, is more important than doing the wrong thing exceptionally well." [Pfeffer 2006]

Circumstances and the bases we use for making decisions change. The flexibility that is so crucial to enterprises is determined in part by an eagerness to make decisions. Neither our desire for perfection nor our fear of the consequences of bad decisions should qualify as a reason for delays in the decision-making process. Careful analysis and swift decision making are the basis for intelligent, flexible and future-oriented enterprises.

5.7 Examining the Future in the Context of Strategy Development

Strategy departments in enterprises usually enjoy a special status. These are the institutions that are responsible for processing huge volumes of information so as to establish a basis for decision making, all the while keeping an eye on the big picture and the details and also meeting the challenge of effectively communicating important messages within the enterprise. Along with the increase in the rates of internal and external change that I have described throughout this book, the challenges facing strategy departments can be expected to grow.

Frederick Taylor coined the term "scientific management"" [Taylor 1911] and is regarded as the founder of "work sharing." The application of his methods enabled the achievement of considerable improvements in production. The revolutionary aspect of his work sharing proposal is that it turns on a separation of work planning and control on the one hand and the performance of work on the other. The role of the manager gained increased significance in the wake of the introduction of this still highly relevant principle.

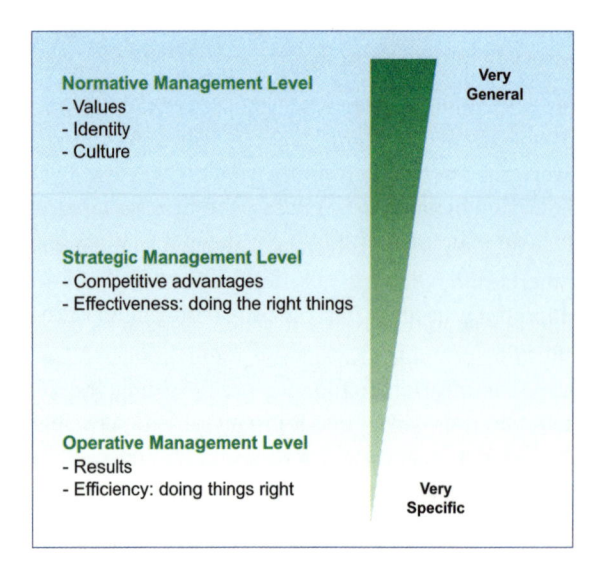

Figure 120 Sankt Gallen Model of strategic levels: strategy as a midlevel activity

The separation of "thinking" and "acting" has established itself in many areas within enterprises. While such strict separation may still promise success in very small enterprises, the borders between the two begin to fade (and other challenges emerge) as the enterprises and structures in question become larger and more complex.

The fact that employees reflect more broadly on the work they perform (e.g. in the interest of improvement) has come to be self-evident. This, however, may introduce a certain dilemma or lead to discontent because discrepancies can emerge between planning and a will on the part of employees to "contribute" in the ways they deem best. Many companies continue to operate on the assumption that there are specifications for work activities that are to be followed and employees need only to report results – just as was proposed by Taylor almost 100 years ago. A willingness to contribute is regarded as desirable only to a certain degree. The deployment of knowledge management systems that include mechanisms for taking account of new ideas and suggestions, which may or may not be assessed and adopted on the management side, will also fail to compensate for a lack of appropriate feedback channels in an enterprise's communication structure.

Strategy development in large companies with several business areas is often handled at multiple levels. The Sankt Gallen Model [Stürm 2003] is based on three levels (Figure 120):

- The normative level is responsible for the values, the identity and the self-concept of the enterprise. Here, much value is placed in continuity. This then proves to be a source of stability in the face of all the changes and uncertainties – one of the enterprise's few constants.

- The strategic level is responsible for orienting the enterprise for an optimal strategic fit – today and in the future. Strategic fit in this context means deploying the enterprise's capabilities and resources in the best possible manner, and thereby achieving competitive advantages. While it is a matter of doing the right thing, the right thing is subject to constant change.

- The operative level is responsible for ensuring that things are done right. Optimal (not necessarily efficient!) processes play a decisive role when it comes to implementing specifications and plans and reaching goals.

In addition to the strategic levels – which represent a vertical extension in the management and which also indicate increasing complexity within the enterprise – one can also extend the strategic development procedure horizontally in the manner proposed by Johnson and Scholes [Johnson 1988].

A distinction is made in the corporate strategy model between "strategic analysis," "strategy selection" and "strategy implementation." Each of the three functions is carried out by different individuals and is also accompanied by different personal and group goals that follow from the respective positions in the enterprise (Table 38).

In order to make the right decisions, the management needs the relevant information and analyses. The strategy departments handle the investigation of the enterprise and its macro and micro environment and take account of the goals and expectations

Table 38 Strategy Functions According to Johnson and Scholes [Johnson 1988]

Function	Execution	Goal
Strategic analysis	Strategy department / planning	Comprehensive analysis
Strategy selection	Management	Right decisions
Strategy implementation	Middle management and organization	Efficient implementation

established by the management. The management is responsible for selecting strategies. Here, the management depends on the strategy departments to provide the right information. Ideally, the strategic decisions are made for the enterprise on the basis of the analysis. The various organizational units are then responsible for implementing the established strategies.

That is the ideal case. "In reality, however, investment dollars often flow to projects favored by people who hold political power or who generated yesterday's revenues rather than tomorrows possibilities." [Beinhocker 1999]

Indeed, it should come as no surprise that 90% of all planned strategies do not work. Why? The reasons preventing a higher rate of success include the following:

1. *Unfavorable task assignment*

   The task assignment specifies that the analysis is to be carried out by the strategists, the decisions are to be made by the management, and the execution is to be handled by the organization.

   The management – known for its chronic lack of time – prefers a brief and compressed representation. But what is the optimal way of preparing the results of an analysis? It is like the squaring of the circle: to represent the results on a single page, and that although the details can be of crucial significance and a preparing of the mind should be the focus (Louis Pasteur: "Chances favor only the prepared mind"). The representation is often tied to a loss of information that usually undermines any eagerness to make a decision.

   In case of a decision, the relevant organizational units are informed of the corresponding measures.

   While the first two paths of interaction are rather transparent, the third path, i.e. from the organization to the management and to the strategists, is relatively undeveloped. Experience shows that strategy workshops that include all of the three responsible parties are significantly more effective when it comes to bridging the communication gaps caused by the task distribution.

   "Senior managers need to be involved in designing the total strategy package, not piecemeal approaches." [Mass 1996]

2. *Focus of Strategy Work*

   Enterprises clearly put great effort into analyzing markets, ascertaining success factors and studying their competitors. However, when the task is to formulate possible strategies, consider options, and arrive at a strategy, there are suddenly few resources and little time. This phenomenon is apparent in both the projects initiated by enterprises and publicly financed studies.

Value is placed on examining the details in the first part. But then it proves easy to lose sight of the way forward on account of the many details. Then the effort is reduced during the crucial part of the process. The interpretation and synthesis deserves far more consideration. What do the circumstances mean for the enterprise? What options are available? What are we going to do? These questions will have to be aired and discussed. The options will have to be considered in detail. And what-if analyses will have to be carried out. Figure 121 highlights the problem, which is exacerbated by IT support tools. Again and again, it turns out that the procedure and execution of strategy projects are determined by the availability and the deployment of IT tools. Here, another apt remark by Mintzberg: "For data to be 'hard' means that they can be documented unambiguously, which usually means that they have already been quantified. That way planners and managers can sit in their offices and be informed … The point is that much information important for strategy making never does become hard fact." [Mintzberg 1994]

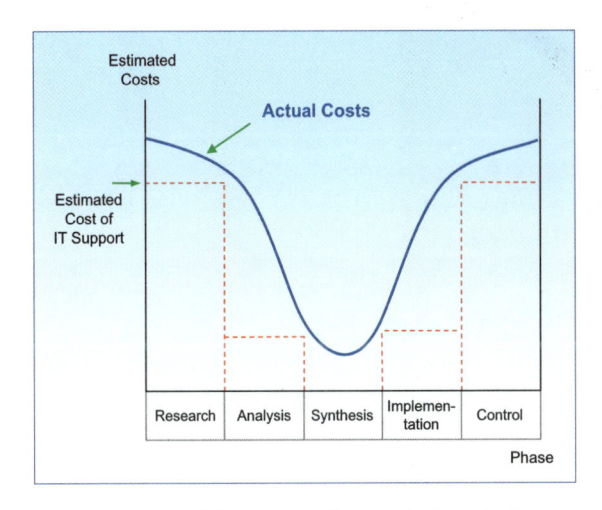

Figure 121 The decision gap: one invests the least in the most crucial area

3. Strategic Planning

When do enterprises become strategically active? Strategic planning is usually determined by the business year. With regard to this annual planning, Beinhocker and Kaplan remark, "Yet the extraordinary reality is that few executives think this time-consuming process pays off, and many CEOs complain that their strategic-planning process yields few new ideas and is often fraught with politics." The authors go on to suggest that "real-time-strategy making" should be supported and "creative accidents" should be expressly promoted [Beinhocker 2002].

4. Top-down Sequence

As compellingly illustrated by the example presented at the beginning of the chapter, business opportunities arise via gains in knowledge and only exceptionally by chance. "But in the case of emergent strategy, because big strategies can grow from little ideas (initiatives), and in strange places, not to mention at unexpected times, almost anyone in the organization can prove to be a strategist." [Mintzberg 1994]

All big business opportunities start off small. However, top-down strategy processes are neither geared to chance nor gains in knowledge. This means that paralysis in times of turbulence is effectively preprogrammed.

5. *While strategy is primarily a decision and an expression of a commitment, the difficult part is the implementation.*

The Belgian painter and surrealist René Magritte drew a pipe and named the drawing, "Ceci n'est pas une pipe" or "This is not a pipe" (Figure 122).

Figure 122 Rene Magritte 1928/29: Ceci n'est pas une pipe
[Source: akg-images]

The idea is clear. He wanted to illustrate that the representation of an object is not the same as the object itself. The same applies to the strategy, the structure and the organization. An organizational chart is not an organization – it is only a model! It follows that a change in the organization is not the same as a simple shifting of boxes in the organizational chart.

"It was very clear, among the best practice companies we studied, that those who carry out strategy must also make it." [Beinhocker 2002]

Summary:

There is no such thing as THE strategy. *Strategy* is a dynamic process that must be continuously called into question and adapted accordingly (e.g. in the context of a monthly review that accounts for evidence of triggers). The basic condition for a successful enterprise is that goals, strategies, actions and structures fit together.

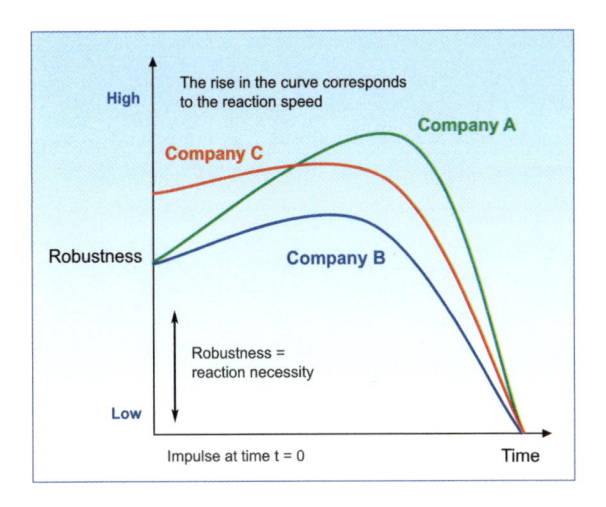

Figure 123 Reaction time: robust versus quick-response enterprises

The potential for improvement is immense – a suggestion that probably applies to most enterprises. The division of tasks leads to an increase in complexity and neutralizes the advantages targeted by Taylor. Instead of seeking to formalize and program the process even more, one should strive for common learning, reflection and shaping.

One should focus on reaction speed (Figure 123). This will entail a streamlined flow of information, permit intense discussions, allow for an even more intensive synthesis of the strategies, and enable a flow of information from the bottom up. This includes a decentralization of decision making which will enable higher reaction speeds, and thereby serve the goal of making the enterprise fit for the future.

Remark on Figure 123: Richard Bettis and Michael Hitt developed the concept of "strategic response capability" [Bettis 1995]. The idea is based on the biological approach of stimulating and then observing the response of an organism. "Because of the dynamism in the new competitive landscape, firms cannot remain static even if they operate in mature industries." They identify two components of fitness for survival: the ability to respond to threats and the ability to position oneself better by actively searching for new opportunities. The figure offers a comparison of the performance of 3 companies: A, B and C. A stimulus is triggered at time t = 0. Company C proves to be more robust than A and B, which are equally robust (high robustness means that the company has more or less anticipated the stimulus with the result that it does not become an immediate threat). Company A proves in the course of time to be a quick responder and increases its robustness via suitable measures (e.g. resource reconfiguration) while Company C, which was very robust at the beginning, shows a decline in its response speed over the course of time. Robustness and response speed help to increase the intelligence of the organization (cf. the intelligence test in Chapter 1).

5.8 The Future of Television (IV)

The question now arises as to the nature of the support the scenarios drafted in Chapter 4 can offer when it comes to the further development of strategy in the run-up to its implementation. Figure 124 illustrates progress on the way "from foresight to insight to action."

Further considerations and developments will be explained using the example of the fictional enterprise "Channel A" (Table 39). The example centers on a description of the business case "MTV versus Channel V" [Hitt 2005].

The television broadcaster has kept itself aware of the latest developments of its environment and is concerned about the future. There is support within the enterprise for different views concerning the enterprise's orientation and the best strategy to pursue. The

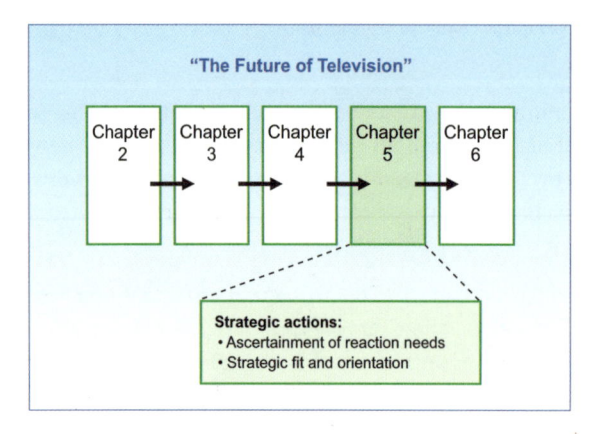

Figure 124 Research project "The Future of Television," step 4: strategic actions

Table 39 The Media Enterprise "Channel A"

Criterion	Channel A
Target group	Viewers between the ages of 15 and 40
Range	German-speaking countries (Germany, Austria, Switzerland)
Business model	Financed via advertising
Current strategy	Growth – new advertising customers, new markets, new products, new channels
Substantive orientation	Music
Image	Cool
Formats	Clips, moderated shows, concerts, charts
Distribution	Satellite, cable, broadcasting, webcasting
Company headquarters	Hamburg

current strategy is directed to ensuring further growth. The enterprise itself is still rather young and has a relatively simple organizational structure. The enterprise is privately owned and the owner views solidity as more important than growth. An IPO is regarded exclusively as an emergency measure, for instance, in case an infusion of capital is needed to secure growth. That being said, the owner makes no qualms about expressing his preference for smaller growth and independence over a complicated ownership structure. Spontaneous actions, new offers and innovative formats as instruments of provocation in the media sector are among the enterprise's stated goals.

Table 40 Structure of Scenario Development for the Fictional Enterprise "Channel A"

Paradigms and Constants	Trends	Contradictions	Uncertainty	Chaos and Wildcards
P1: Television broadcaster's mission statement.	T1: Outsourcing of expensive production activities.	W1: Knowledge management versus individual performance evaluation.	U1: Continuity: will the still small enterprise be able to assert itself in the turbulent TV landscape?	C1: Product lifecycles become ever shorter.
P2: Television broadcaster's vision: high quality programming – extensive information, some entertainment, no sex and violence.	T2: Benchmarking: price comparisons are leading to lower prices and diminished profile.	W2: Ability to work in a team versus individual performance evaluation.	U2: How will the enterprise respond to new channels of distribution and broadcasting technologies?	C2: Device manufacturers and media shapers face immense pressures to innovate.
P3: Target group: informed and interested viewers.	T3: Innovation: the broadcaster is constantly attempting to set trends via new formats and innovative reporting.	W3 Creativity versus efficiency.	U3: Will the broadcaster be able to further reinforce its profile?	C3: Takeover, sale, bankruptcy or break-up.
P4: Viewing rates are not the measure of all things.	T4: Introduction of administrative tools on the Intranet is leading to system dependencies.	W4: Quality versus quantity.	U4: Image: will the broadcaster be able to enhance its image as a modern information channel?	C4: Entirely new media landscape.
P5: Enterprise headquarters are to remain in Hamburg.	T5: Regional aspects are playing an ever greater role in programming.	W5: Promoting innovation versus expecting innovation.	U5: Are the broadcaster's enterprise structures flexible enough to permit an appropriate response to changes?	C5: Media laws block broadcasting.
P6: Television is to remain the broadcaster's main medium.	T6: Technology: the broadcaster is committed to new means of distribution and would like to invest.			C6: Damage claims.
P7: The new key medium Internet already accounts for 12% of the daily time budget of 14 to 49-year-olds.	T7: Financing via premium contents.		U6: Growth: will the broadcaster succeed in achieving solid growth without high risk financing?	C7: Employee strike.
P8: Television viewers have two needs: entertainment and information.	T8: The broadcaster has expanded its range. Nationwide reception is set for the end of 2007.		U7: Will the broadcaster be able to retain its spirit in a larger environment?	C8: Viewer boycott motivated by political or religious reasons.
P9: The quality and the number of television sets has increased.	T9: Strategic decisions are increasingly being transferred from the owner to the strategy department.		U8: Will the broadcaster be able to preserve an atmosphere in which its stakeholders have a sense of being in the same boat?	

5.8 The Future of Television (IV)

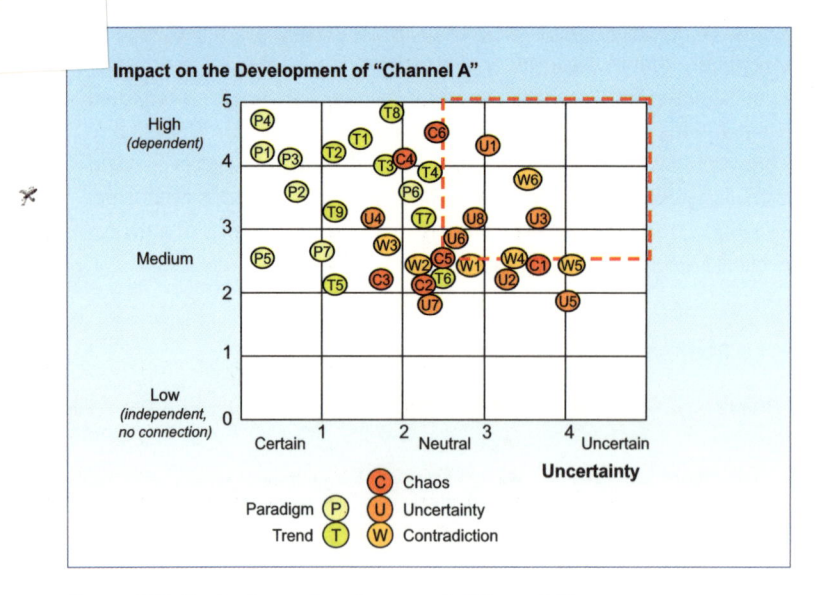

Figure 125 Evaluation: enterprise scenario "Channel A"

	T1	W1	W2	W3	W5	U2	C8	Scenario
a	Production is outsourced completely.	No individual performance evaluation.	Teamwork is emphasized.	Focus on creativity.	Innovation?	DVB – an effort is made to go forward with digital transmission.	Fully exploit creative options while avoiding boycotts.	Creative
b	Expensive production activities are outsourced.	Individual performance evaluation with proportional payment	Promotion of high performers and individual performance evaluation.	Focus on efficiency.	Promote innovation (e.g. via monthly idea market and budget supplements).	Certain contents are made available on homepage.	Uncompromising support for broadcast opinion.	Conservative
c	Partnerships with broadcasters in Austria/Switzerland.	Evaluation of group performance and bonus system	Evaluation of project teams based on results + individual evaluation.	Efficient production and routine sequences plus creative liberty.	Issue innovation reports and promote only the best ideas (fast benefit).	The broadcaster sticks with traditional broadcasting technologies.	No high risk contents.	TV 2.0
d	Vertical integration – all programs are produced in-house.	Knowledge marketplace.	Balanced performance evaluation: team and individual evaluation.		No extra programs or initiatives. Securing of the enterprise's natural development.	IPTV is used both for broadcasting and distributing "external" content.	Provocative issues and viewer participation.	Fire Fighter
e		Bonus system for knowledge workers.				Radio program is regarded as an option.		
f						On-demand services as an expansion (music + movies).		

Figure 126 Scenario development on the future of television: enterprise scenario for "Channel A"

Internal opinions about the broadcaster's future range from "expanding the offer through the addition of a music platform (on the model of iTunes)" to "embracing a pay-per-view business model" and "focusing on the Internet as a channel." The executive committee is uncertain, and takes the step of commissioning an extensive analysis.

The four environment scenarios from Chapter 4 are to be applied. Beyond this, four enterprise scenarios are to be drafted and juxtaposed to gain a view of how things may develop.

Table 40 offers a representation of the enterprise's situation. Figure 125 offers a general evaluation. Figure 126 shows the variations for the elements that are characterized by considerable impact potential and uncertainty as well as the enterprise scenarios derived from these. This is followed by a direct comparison of the four enterprise scenarios and the four environment scenarios from Chapter 4.

Scenario 1: "Creative"

Component	Element	Description
Title	"Creative"	
Main character	–	Not applicable
Scene	Headquarters	Not applicable
Paradigms, constants	P1	Television broadcaster's mission statement.
	P2	Television broadcaster's vision: high quality programming – extensive information, some entertainment, no sex and violence.
	P3	Target group: informed and interested viewers.
	P4	Viewing rates are not the measure of all things.
	P5	Enterprise headquarters are to remain in Hamburg.
	P6	Television is to remain the broadcaster's main medium.
	P7	The new key medium Internet already accounts for 12% of the daily time budget of 14 to 49-year-olds.
	P8	Television viewers have two needs: entertainment and information.
	P9	The quality and the number of television sets has increased.
Trends	T1c	Partnerships with broadcasters in Austria and Switzerland.
	T2	Benchmarking: price comparisons are leading to lower prices <u>and</u> diminished profile.
	T3	Innovation: the broadcaster is constantly attempting to set trends via new formats and innovative reporting.
	T4	Introduction of administrative tools on the Intranet is leading to system dependencies.
	T5	Regional aspects are playing an ever greater role in programming.
	T6	Technology: the broadcaster is committed to new means of distribution and would like to invest.
	T7	Financing via premium contents.
	T8	The broadcaster has expanded its range. Nationwide reception is set for the end of 2007.

Component	Element	Description
	T9	Strategic decisions are increasingly being transferred from the owner to the strategy department.
Contradictions	W1e	Bonus system for knowledge workers.
	W2c	Evaluation of project teams based on results + individual evaluation.
	W3a	Focus on creativity.
	W4	Quality versus quantity.
	W5b	Promote innovation (e.g. via a monthly idea market and budget supplements).
Uncertainties	U1	Continuity: will the still small enterprise be able to assert itself in the turbulent TV landscape?
	U2b	Certain contents are made available on homepage.
	U3	Will the broadcaster be able to further reinforce its profile?
	U4	Image: will the broadcaster be able to enhance its image as a modern information channel?
	U5	Are the broadcaster's enterprise structures flexible enough to permit an appropriate response to changes?
	U6	Growth: will the broadcaster succeed in achieving solid growth without high risk financing?
	U7	Will the broadcaster be able to retain its spirit in a larger environment?
	U8	Will the broadcaster be able to preserve an atmosphere in which its stakeholders have a sense of being in the same boat?
Chaos, wildcards	C1	Product lifecycles become ever shorter.
	C2	Device manufacturers and media shapers face immense pressures to innovate.
	C3	Takeover, sale, bankruptcy or break-up.
	C4	Entirely new media landscape.
	C5	Media laws block broadcasting.
	C6	Damage claims.
	C7	Employee strike.
	C8a	Fully exploit creative options while avoiding boycotts.
Creativity and fantasy	Individual	Input from the process of joining the elements into a story.

Scenario 2: "Conservative"

Component	Element	Description
Title	"Conservative"	
Main character	–	Not applicable
Scene	Headquarters	Not applicable
Paradigms, constants	P1	Television broadcaster's mission statement.
	P2	Television broadcaster's vision: high quality programming – extensive information, some entertainment, no sex and violence.

Component	Element	Description
	P3	Target group: informed and interested viewers.
	P4	Viewing rates are not the measure of all things.
	P5	Enterprise headquarters are to remain in Hamburg.
	P6	Television is to remain the broadcaster's main medium.
	P7	The new key medium Internet already accounts for 12% of the daily time budget of 14 to 49-year-olds.
	P8	Television viewers have two needs: entertainment and information.
	P9	The quality and the number of television sets has increased.
Trends	T1b	Expensive production activities are outsourced.
	T2	Benchmarking: price comparisons are leading to lower prices and diminished profile.
	T3	Innovation: the broadcaster is constantly attempting to set trends via new formats and innovative reporting.
	T4	Introduction of administrative tools on the Intranet is leading to system dependencies.
	T5	Regional aspects are playing an ever greater role in programming.
	T6	Technology: the broadcaster is committed to new means of distribution and would like to invest.
	T7	Financing via premium contents.
	T8	The broadcaster has expanded its range. Nationwide reception is set for the end of 2007.
	T9	Strategic decisions are increasingly being transferred from the owner to the strategy department.
Contradictions	W1b	Individual performance evaluation with proportional payment.
	W2b	Promotion of high performers and individual performance evaluation.
	W3b	Focus on efficiency.
	W4	Quality versus quantity.
	W5c	Issue innovation reports and promote only the best ideas (fast benefit).
Uncertainties	U1	Continuity: will the still small enterprise be able to assert itself in the turbulent TV landscape?
	U2c	The broadcaster sticks with traditional broadcasting technologies.
	U3	Will the broadcaster be able to further reinforce its profile?
	U4	Image: will the broadcaster be able to enhance its image as a modern information channel?
	U5	Are the broadcaster's enterprise structures flexible enough to permit an appropriate response to changes?
	U6	Growth: will the broadcaster succeed in achieving solid growth without high risk financing?
	U7	Will the broadcaster be able to retain its spirit in a larger environment?
	U8	Will the broadcaster be able to preserve an atmosphere in which its stakeholders have a sense of being in the same boat?

Component	Element	Description
Chaos, wildcards	C1	Product lifecycles become ever shorter.
	C2	Device manufacturers and media shapers face immense pressures to innovate.
	C3	Takeover, sale, bankruptcy or break-up.
	C4	Entirely new media landscape.
	C5	Media laws block broadcasting.
	C6	Damage claims.
	C7	Employee strike.
	C8c	No high risk contents.
Creativity and fantasy	Individual	Input from the process of joining the elements into a story.

Scenario 3: "TV 2.0"

Component	Element	Description
Title	"TV 2.0"	
Main character	–	Not applicable
Scene	Headquarters	Not applicable
Paradigms, constants	P1	Television broadcaster's mission statement.
	P2	Television broadcaster's vision: high quality programming – extensive information, some entertainment, no sex and violence.
	P3	Target group: informed and interested viewers.
	P4	Viewing rates are not the measure of all things.
	P5	Enterprise headquarters are to remain in Hamburg.
	P6	Television is to remain the broadcaster's main medium.
	P7	The new key medium Internet already accounts for 12% of the daily time budget of 14 to 49-year-olds.
	P8	Television viewers have two needs: entertainment and information.
	P9	The quality and the number of television sets has increased.
Trends	T1d	Vertical integration – all programs are produced in-house.
	T2	Benchmarking: price comparisons are leading to lower prices <u>and</u> diminished profile.
	T3	Innovation: the broadcaster is constantly attempting to set trends via new formats and innovative reporting.
	T4	Introduction of administrative tools on the Intranet is leading to system dependencies.
	T5	Regional aspects are playing an ever greater role in programming.
	T6	Technology: the broadcaster is committed to new means of distribution and would like to invest.
	T7	Financing via premium contents.
	T8	The broadcaster has expanded its range. Nationwide reception is set for the end of 2007.

Component	Element	Description
	T9	Strategic decisions are increasingly being transferred from the owner to the strategy department.
Contradictions	W1d	Knowledge marketplace.
	W2a	Teamwork is emphasized.
	W3c	Efficient production and routine sequences plus creative liberty.
	W4	Quality versus quantity.
	W5d	No extra programs or initiatives. Securing of the enterprise's natural development.
Uncertainties	U1	Continuity: will the still small enterprise be able to assert itself in the turbulent TV landscape?
	U2f	On-demand services as an expansion (music + movies).
	U3	Will the broadcaster be able to further reinforce its profile?
	U4	Image: will the broadcaster be able to enhance its image as a modern information channel?
	U5	Are the broadcaster's enterprise structures flexible enough to permit an appropriate response to changes?
	U6	Growth: will the broadcaster succeed in achieving solid growth without high risk financing?
	U7	Will the broadcaster be able to retain its spirit in a larger environment?
	U8	Will the broadcaster be able to preserve an atmosphere in which its stakeholders have a sense of being in the same boat?
Chaos, wildcards	C1	Product lifecycles become ever shorter.
	C2	Device manufacturers and media shapers face immense pressures to innovate.
	C3	Takeover, sale, bankruptcy or break-up.
	C4	Entirely new media landscape.
	C5	Media laws block broadcasting.
	C6	Damage claims.
	C7	Employee strike.
	C8b	Uncompromising support for broadcast opinion.
Creativity and fantasy	Individual	Input from the process of joining the elements into a story.

Scenario 4: "Fire Fighter"

Component	Element	Description
Title	"Fire Fighter"	
Main character	–	Not applicable
Scene	Headquarters	Not applicable
Paradigms, constants	P1	Television broadcaster's mission statement.
	P2	Television broadcaster's vision: high quality programming – extensive information, some entertainment, no sex and violence.
	P3	Target group: informed and interested viewers.

Component	Element	Description
	P4	Viewing rates are not the measure of all things.
	P5	Enterprise headquarters are to remain in Hamburg.
	P6	Television is to remain the broadcaster's main medium.
	P7	The new key medium Internet already accounts for 12% of the daily time budget of 14 to 49-year-olds.
	P8	Television viewers have two needs: entertainment and information.
	P9	The quality and the number of television sets has increased.
Trends	T1a	Production is outsourced completely.
	T2	Benchmarking: price comparisons are leading to lower prices <u>and</u> diminished profile.
	T3	Innovation: the broadcaster is constantly attempting to set trends via new formats and innovative reporting.
	T4	Introduction of administrative tools on the Intranet is leading to system dependencies.
	T5	Regional aspects are playing an ever greater role in programming.
	T6	Technology: the broadcaster is committed to new means of distribution and would like to invest.
	T7	Financing via premium contents.
	T8	The broadcaster has expanded its range. Nationwide reception is set for the end of 2007.
	T9	Strategic decisions are increasingly being transferred from the owner to the strategy department.
Contradictions	W1c	Evaluation of group performance and bonus system.
	W2d	Balanced performance evaluation: team and individual evaluation.
	W3b	Focus on efficiency.
	W4	Quality versus quantity.
	W5a	Innovation?
Uncertainties	U1	Continuity: will the still small enterprise be able to assert itself in the turbulent TV landscape?
	U2e	Radio program is regarded as an option.
	U3	Will the broadcaster be able to further reinforce its profile?
	U4	Image: will the broadcaster be able to enhance its image as a modern information channel?
	U5	Are the broadcaster's enterprise structures flexible enough to permit an appropriate response to changes?
	U6	Growth: will the broadcaster succeed in achieving solid growth without high risk financing?
	U7	Will the broadcaster be able to retain its spirit in a larger environment?
	U8	Will the broadcaster be able to preserve an atmosphere in which its stakeholders have a sense of being in the same boat?
Chaos, wildcards	C1	Product lifecycles become ever shorter.
	C2	Device manufacturers and media shapers face immense pressures to innovate.

Component	Element	Description
	C3	Takeover, sale, bankruptcy or break-up.
	C4	Entirely new media landscape.
	C5	Media laws block broadcasting.
	C6	Damage claims.
	C7	Employee strike.
	C8d	Provocative issues and viewer participation.
Creativity and fantasy	Individual	Input from the process of joining the elements into a story.

The enterprise scenarios shown in Figure 127 can be positioned according to their stability and potential. The goal is a position with robust growth.

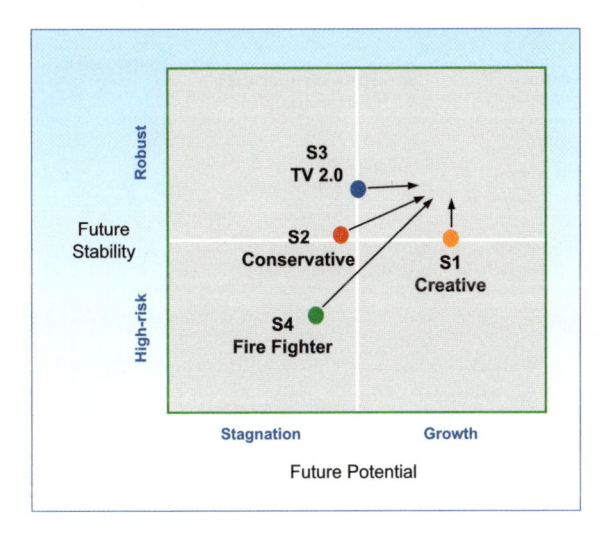

Figure 127 Potential and stability: scenario positioning

Analysis of the Strategic Fit

The environment scenarios and the enterprise scenarios are juxtaposed in Figure 128. Each of the four enterprise scenarios is compared with each of the four environment scenarios for strategic fit.

Table 41 shows how the environment scenario for "Quo vadis, TV?" is compared to the enterprise scenario "Conservative." The principle at work resembles that of the SWOT analysis. The risks and opportunities that result from the scenario are identified for the enterprise environment.

What is important for the enterprise is to ascertain its strengths and weaknesses from the scenario. One gains a sense for the possible developments by filling out the matrix. These developments can then be compressed into an evaluation of the strategic fit. The possi-

5.8 The Future of Television (IV)

Enterprise scenarios \ Environment scenarios	Quo vadis, TV?	High Performance TV	TV à la carte	Open TV	Evaluation
Creative	Robust	Robust	Robust	Robust	Robust strategy
Conservative	Inflexible	Missed opportunities	Missed opportunities	Insignificance	Too conservative for the dynamic market
TV 2.0	Shaping and influencing	Growth opportunity	Risky	Threat	Big opportunities along with big risks
Fire Fighter	Overloaded	Follower	Follower	Threat	Lack of "future fit," strategic preparation indispensable

Figure 128 A juxtaposition of the environment and enterprise scenarios

Table 41 Analysis of Future Strategic Fit

	Environment Scenario "Quo vadis, TV?"	Enterprise Scenario 2 "Conservative"	
Opportunities	Many new business ideas arise with the development of new technologies	Well-positioned in the existing market, stable structures	*Strengths*
Dangers	Departure from traditional television, technological frustration	Very static and inflexible, one-sided orientation	*Weaknesses*

ble, attractive and robust strategies as well as the risk associated with certain strategies can be ascertained by evaluating all of the 16 possible applications.

The present investigation indicates that the enterprise scenarios "Creative" and "TV 2.0" come closest to the aim of achieving a robust strategy and high growth potential. These two scenarios thus provide a basis for the future strategy. In the specific case, one could describe the planned strategy as follows:

- Focus on creativity.
- Aim for increased efficiency in the area of routine tasks.
- Place greater emphasis on team spirit in the system.
- Establish an Internet platform.

In addition to this, planning activities are to take account of the relevant triggers (e.g. technological developments).

Chapter 6

Implementation

Managing Change

At the beginning of the last century, milk was delivered directly to homes in milk canisters and bottles.

Tetra Paks had not yet been invented and milk, not yet homogenized (i.e. processed using high pressure to break the fat globules in milk down into small particles of uniform size so as to increase digestibility and shelf life), was typically delivered raw to the customer's door in an open container with its cream portion on the top.

It was of course a nuisance for consumers that birds often discovered this rich source of nutrition. In Great Britain, for instance, titmice, finches and other birds were often observed feeding on the upper layer of cream.

The dairy industry reacted by sealing the milk bottles with an aluminum seal which was still in use up until a few years ago. They believed they had thereby solved the problem. In the years to follow, however, birds were observed deftly picking off the aluminum seal to get at the cream they had come to like so much. Ornithologists soon determined that some types of birds had mastered the art of removing the new seals better than others. One investigation indicated that titmice were particularly good at opening the seals while finches were observed to do so only sporadically. The researchers found themselves faced with a mystery. Why were titmice in Britain generally able – in the span of just a few years – to deftly open the milk bottles while only individual finches were able to do so?

There was much speculation and debate among the experts. Investigations centering on beak shapes, dietary preferences, digestibility, behavioral traits and other bird characteristics were carried out in order to determine what was behind the difference.

As it turns out, the type of communication that takes place between birds was ultimately identified as the reason behind the different propagation rates for the ability in question. Titmice move about in groups and frequently change their whereabouts. In contrast, finches have a fixed territory that they seldom leave. Titmice are therefore much better at broadly sharing their capabilities among their fellow titmice. The lack of interaction among finches means that their knowledge tends to remain localized.

The same question – concerning the phenomenon of knowledge sharing – is also immensely relevant to enterprises. Some are in a position to effectively share knowledge and have internalized the notion of a learning organization. Others wonder why knowledge remains localized – despite the fact that high-power IT tools have been acquired to ensure sharing.

In the present chapter, I present one possible answer.

(Source: as adapted from a passage in Arie de Geus' book, "The Living Company" [De Geus 1997])

6.1 The Dimensions of Change

The aim of this book is to increase a capacity for strategic thought and to make this capacity more secure in the face of uncertainty. In seeking to achieve this aim, it is my intention to distance myself from the cookbook approach one finds in most strategy and management books. The task at hand is to implement the lessons learned so far.

Instead of reciting the many golden rules of strategy implementation, I will discuss the factors that tend to undermine strategy implementation and a number of commonly accepted myths drawn from management practice.

Why do enterprises have such a hard time when it comes to implementing their strategies? Bringing about change in an enterprise is clearly a difficult matter. This suggestion is born out by the poor rates of success. Major efforts to initiate change at Fortune 100 companies between 1980 and 1995, for instance, were shown in one Harvard study to have largely failed [Isaksen 2006]. Almost all of the companies had initiated change programs during the period in question and funded these programs with an average of 1 billion U.S. dollars. The results of the study are sobering: in only 30% of the cases were the companies able to recoup their investments by the changes that were introduced and only around half of all initiatives led to an increase in company stock.

The change itself is usually not the problem; the problem lies in the approach taken:

"Social change and economic impact are not things that can be extrapolated out of a piece of hardware." [Rosenberg 1995] Strategy planning and implementation programs usually take too little account of economic reforms and the social and human elements of change. If surprises, signs of departure from and resistance to the plan are then ignored during the plan's implementation, then failure is preprogrammed. "Much of what we refer to as 'resistance to change' is really 'resistance to uncertainty.' Thus the resistance derives from the process of handling and managing change, not from the change as such." [Carnall 2003]

At the beginning of this book, I pointed out that there is likely to be no super process whose consistent implementation will always lead to extraordinarily positive results.

A number of standard dilemmas faced by nearly all enterprises were discussed in Chapter 1. The inclusion of analyses of the future, trends, scenarios and strategy into enterprise practice introduces still more traps that are to be avoided.

There are many factors that discourage change in enterprises. While the aim of each form of analysis is change and improvement, there is always an associated cost. In order to ensure that the cost is really worth paying, the focus should be on the changed state and not the analysis/synthesis in the form of a document. Picking up on the theory introduced in Chapter 4 as to what makes for a good scenario, I would suggest that the success of a plan to initiate change is entirely dependent on the way in which it is implemented. The purpose of scenarios is to inspire change. They encourage one to intentionally depart from the comfort zone. They are provocative and they serve as a basis for discussion. The question as to the evaluation of scenarios is therefore misplaced. Like strategies, it doesn't matter how good individual scenarios are – if they do not have an effect and lead to action, then they are pointless.

Change and Transformation

There are various types of change, and none of them is the same as a formalized procedure. Figure 129 shows some of the dimensions in the spectrum of change. Restructuring may be precisely localized, directed to many areas within an enterprise or directed to the enterprise as a whole. The number of enterprise units and the degree of process complexity will increase as the targeted level within the enterprises increases. This introduces degrees of freedom and the possibility of 2nd and 3rd order effects that were not considered during the planning stage and that could present a risk or become a source of surprises. The same applies to the number of affected functional areas: is the restructuring limited to the marketing department or are all main units affected? Whether a restructuring initiative arises internally (e.g. owing to a study of the future), "externally" or is ordered from "above" will also have an effect on the shape that the relevant change processes take. Two examples are highlighted in Figure 129. The one (red box) is a strategic measure: the establishment of a think tank to help secure the enterprise's fitness in the future. The other, an operative (reactive) change (green box), might involve a new approach to the issue of information management owing to the limited benefits for the enterprise from previous attempts.

The state that enterprises find themselves in may be stable or instable (i.e. subject to fundamental change). Most enterprises go through continuous processes of incremental change.

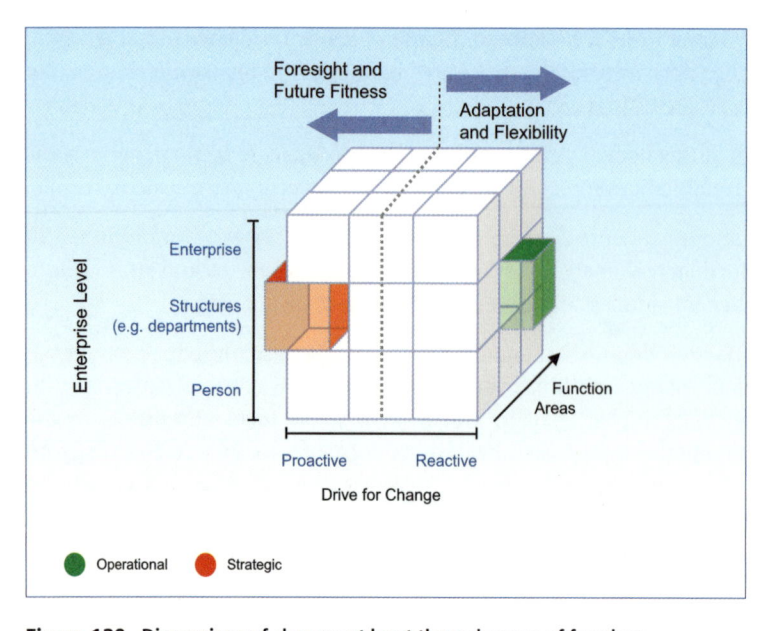

Figure 129 Dimensions of change: at least three degrees of freedom

The popular science literature generally reflects the assumption that strategy is "planned" and "implemented" from the top down. It is not unusual, however, when efforts to implement strategy are driven from below (consider the example of the submarine below). This path of change cannot be planned in the traditional sense and cannot be represented as a part of the planning efforts. It thus represents an uncertainty or a planning uncertainty.

Why is it so difficult for enterprises to derive concrete measures and to implement these measures in practice? What can one do to get around this difficulty? In what follows, I will first describe the optimal implementation process (i.e. according to the textbook) and then discuss the practical hurdles that stand in the way of successful change.

Tips on how to clear these hurdles are offered in the interest of more successful implementation projects.

6.2 The Logic of Change

Decisions mark the point of transition from understanding to action. Once one has established clarity in the matter of the goal and the path to it, one gains a view of the possible means and a sense of duty.

The difficulty initially consists in identifying concrete measures that will allow one to gain room to maneuver. Consistency in the matter of implementation is necessary to move from an abstract plan to a factual change. For instance, if an enterprise has resolved to become a technology leader, it will be essential to flesh out this strategy with research projects, new development, innovation initiatives and other measures.

Figure 130 shows a format for devising an action plan. Depending on the strategy level (enterprise or department level) involved and the scope of the strategy itself, the plan of action can be driven by individual measures or entire packages of measures. Individual actions, programs, initiatives, projects and the establishment of new processes or structures for long-lasting changes are suitable for facilitating the implementation of strategies. The operative phase and the involvement of daily business sequences begins with the allocation of resources, the assignment of responsibilities and the establishment of a timeframe and expectations.

The capacity of any given organization to change is limited. Business operations centering on the customer can withstand only a certain degree of change at any given time. The most important measures in the action plan are implemented first. These are then followed by the more elaborate and longer term actions.

Surprisingly enough, it is exactly this that appears to be a major challenge for enterprises, and not a few accurately formulated strategies fail in the implementation phase because the transition from "architect" to "site manager" proves problematic. The concepts described in the professional and popular science literature (e.g. in [Doppler 2005] and [Carnall 2003]) often prove to be too theoretical in practice. In

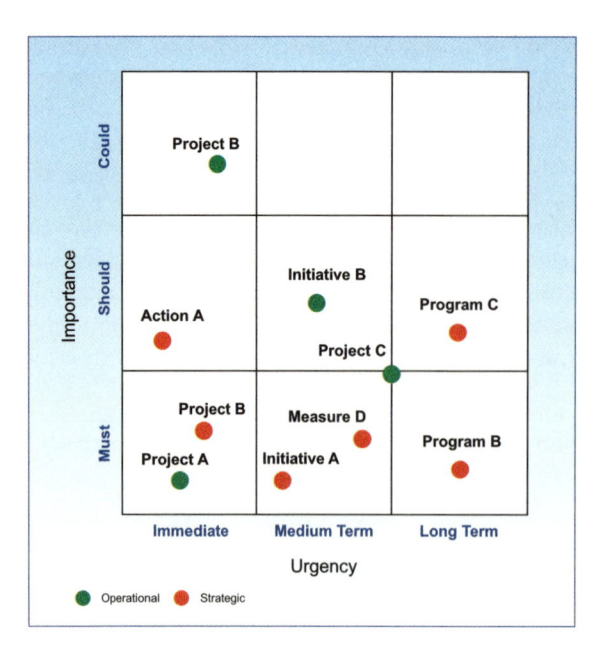

Figure 130 The result of strategy analysis: the action plan

what follows, I describe a number of factors that can prevent simple and smooth implementation.

More than 1,700 business books were published in the United States in the year 1996. This invites the question as to why so many mistakes are made despite the apparent availability of knowledge. The dilemma lies with the enterprises themselves. While managers try to do things right, it would be far more important for the enterprises if the right things were done.

6.3 The Reality of Change in Enterprises

A desire for change and renewal does not automatically mean that one is ready for change. On the contrary, a desire for improvement often contradicts a will to change. But how can something change when the systems, the culture, the people, and the processes are to remain as intact as possible? This is the first implementation trap.

Einstein defined madness as "doing the same thing again and again, but expecting different results." In other words, "If you always do what you have always done, you will always get what you have always gotten!" Vacillators often present any number of excuses and reasons that speak against a change. Success in the enterprise's process of change therefore crucially depends on the will and the attitude of the management. Are the changes at issue profound changes and are these being driven uncompromisingly and shaped proactively or are half-hearted actions involved that are being carried out spontaneously and superficially with the aim of short-term success? The threshold to "change fatigue" is quickly reached in the face of a thoughtless action-at-all-costs approach. The credibility of and the confidence in the management's leadership skills can also evaporate quickly.

The second trap consists in emphasizing the following message: change means additional costs! It is obvious enough that any manner of change or transformation – whether a transformation of an entire enterprise or a mere local initiative – will entail additional (long-term) costs that were probably not taken account of during the planning phase. The seriousness of efforts to initiate change can be directly measured in terms of the existing willingness to allocate resources to them.

It is altogether advisable to determine the degree to which a willingness to implement changes really exists within an enterprise before initiating investigations, analyses and projects concerned with the future. If it is clear right from the outset that the client within the enterprise has neither the power nor the motivation to implement change, success will be very modest and will likely be limited to mini projects. In all likelihood, the result will be a further study for one's files.

The third trap is the "paper tiger." It would be possible to divide up enterprises in terms of paper and action: the larger enterprises are – and enterprises tend to grow – the stronger will be the necessity of exchanging information (a corollary of Metcalfe's law: the number of interactions will increase exponentially if the number of participants increases linearly). This reinforces the shift from well-focused actions to paper-based exchange. This is reinforced even further in that our perception and evaluation of paper and action are different. Actions and real changes require great effort and tenacity. They tend to take place – almost unnoticed – in the background. This is not the case for the exchange of information in the form of presentations.

"An even more extreme form of substituting talk for action occurs when managers act as if talk, writing, and analysis are the main tasks that they, or anyone else in the firm, ever need to do. This problem seems to be particularly acute in large organizations, especially where many senior executives are financially oriented and out of touch with how work is done in their firms. Managers in such firms seem to spend much of their time preparing, delivering, and listening to flashy and well-rehearsed presentations that are designed to impress one another. Executives devote a great deal of time to presentations, but they often spend little or no time 'on the ground.'" [Pfeffer 1999]

Analyses are explained, strategies are derived, and recommendations for action are given in front of larger audiences. While the exchange of information is vital, it is also essential to avoid the illusion that the presentation of information alone will lead to some sort of change. Young and talented individuals learn quickly how tedious it can become to insist on action, what a negative impact it can have on their careers and how lucrative it can be to maintain a high degree of visibility in the enterprise. It can be more promising to concentrate on one's personal visibility, to speak in the subjunctive case and to compellingly represent and present information. As paradoxical as it sounds, the recognition one receives for eloquently presented visions and concepts is far greater than what one receives for actually implementing changes. In most cases, it pays more to remain nothing but eloquent.

"Talk is also valued because ... the quantity and 'quality' of talk can be assessed immediately, but the quality of leadership or management capability, the ability to get things done, can be assessed only with a greater time lag." [Pfeffer 1999]

Motivation for Change

Would an enterprise be capable of surviving and remaining competitive for a period of time if it were to undergo no changes? Yes, but probably not for very long. The American quality guru Deming puts it this way, "It is not necessary to change; survival is not mandatory." [Juran 2000] He thereby sheds light on a widespread misconception: enterprises must change and adapt primarily in order to survive and NOT because it pleases them or because of a certain mood or trend!

The transformation of the enterprise's environment (macro environment) and changes in business conditions (micro environment) force the enterprise to change and adapt. If the enterprise is not capable of changing at least as fast as its environment, problems will arise sooner or later. Johnson and Scholes describe this effect as "strategic drift." Figure 131 illustrates the gap that can arise between strategic change in the enterprise and change in the enterprise's environment. The detection of such drift and the corresponding adaptation of the enterprise is the responsibility of the management. Who else can be expected to have an overview of both the enterprise and its position on the market?

The motivation for implementing change arises out of one's concern to secure the enterprise's ability to compete. It would be naive to also try to derive such motivation from the responsibility of the management. We can assume such motivation unconditionally only in the case of family enterprises, private unincorporated companies and other very small companies. Otherwise, managers and other employees can be seen as subject to a conflict of interest, namely, between their personal interests and those of the enterprise. While this dichotomy has received great attention in the liter-

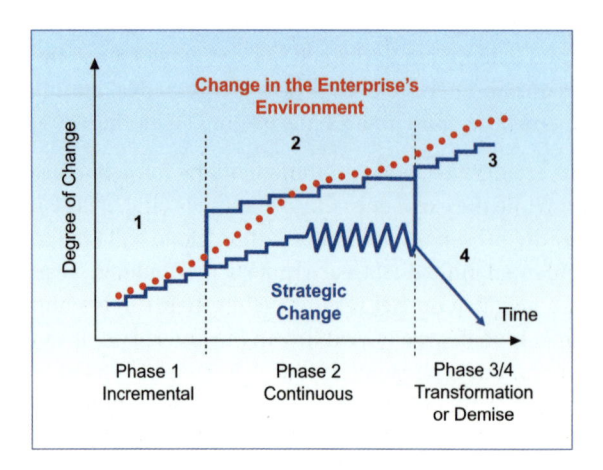

Figure 131 Model of strategic change: the aim is to prevent a gap between the enterprise and its environment (as adapted from [Johnson 1988])

ature (e.g. [Milgrom 1992]), this does not diminish the doubts one might have with respect to the motivation of managers and employees to work towards the benefit of the enterprise that is assumed in the concepts of change in enterprises. Examples from the recent history of many corporations confirm that greed (Enron, VW), personal ambition (Airbus, Daimler Chrysler) and the desire for public recognition often lead to different vectors of interest. While this conflict is usually not in the interest of enterprises, "Most executives won't admit it." [Pfeffer 2006]

There is therefore a general discrepancy between reality and the motivation for change presented in many textbooks. This can lead to major conflicts when, for instance, the real reasons for implementing change are obviously tied to the ambition of individual managers competing for recognition and success.

The other extreme appears when the pressure to change that is present at the moment in the enterprise is too weak to suggest any necessity to change. It is then likely that the results of analysis have had no effect. The expression "they don't know what they are doing" then becomes "they are not doing what they know they should."

Studies of the future in such constellations tend to be relegated to weekend reading and alibi events. Change is resisted and occurs only in the face of pressure, "better wait and see and avoid risks, better do nothing than do something wrong."

One further implementation trap arises when the quality of the relevant investigations is called into question. A widespread, but nonetheless false assumption is that investigations focusing on the future must generate new ideas and that proposals for improvement must be as far-reaching as possible and, ideally, also solve all current problems. The disappointment is readily apparent when everything that results from the investigation was already known. However, knowledge does not automatically imply action. It thus may be that nothing happens. Change is difficult, especially when it is a matter of the future. It is important for the future of any given enterprise to apply knowledge quickly.

A Strategy for Developing Strategy

Inadequate communication combined with a lack of an awareness of the necessity of change may also represent a barrier along the way to a changed state. An awareness at the level of senior management is necessary, but not sufficient. Major change projects effect large parts of the enterprise or the entire enterprise. The task of arriving at mutual decisions tends to be underestimated, particularly in the case of cross-divisional undertakings. Resistance is provoked at an early stage and one's own power is overestimated: "Leaders are sometimes shocked to discover how little power they have to push changes through an organization." [Pfeffer 2006] Political power games and competency struggles can nip entire initiatives in the bud. Things turn into a struggle to retain power. Change in the interest of the enterprise? Such sober-sounding recipes for success exist only in textbooks.

As soon as emotions, feelings, desires, will, assertiveness, motivations (i.e. all of the various human properties that are neither quantifiable nor constant for long periods) come into play – and they will come into play given that organizations are primarily comprised of people – efforts to bring about change also take on an unpredictable character. As in the case of enterprise scenarios, many factors have an impact on the direction things take. It is thus more important – as in the case of physical systems when these are struck by an impulse – that the system has the capacity to first gain its bearings and muster a reaction before yet another change is triggered by an impulse. However, this demand for a period in which to react should not be tantamount to a rejection of the suggestion that change in the enterprise is necessary. After all, change in organizations must be executed with levelheadedness and foresight. Moreover, despite all efforts to initiate change, the center of all activities must remain an organization capable of action. A fundamental question arises at this juncture: what actually prevents organizations from changing continuously (according to an action plan) and not only after they have been forced to do so?

Having addressed the many hindrances and barriers, I turn in the following section to a description of a number of success factors.

6.4 Elements of Change

Enterprise structures are significantly more complex than is often supposed. A knowledge of the relevant connections can be very useful when it comes to the task of successfully implementing change. As outlined in Chapter 5, enterprises can be effectively described using the 7S model. A crucial success factor for bringing about change in enterprises lies in the inclusion of all of the enterprise's elements in the process. In what follows, I address the interrelationships and dependencies among the elements in greater detail.

The 7S model goes back to a publication in the year 1980 [Waterman 1980]. Both the field of business management and the requirements faced by enterprises have continued to develop since then. In light of the new findings, I would propose expanding the 7S model through the addition of the following new components, which I will refer to collectively as E, F and I (or EFI):

- In keeping with the essence of the previous chapter, a "Foresight" component is added. This component symbolizes an enterprise's capacity to understand and shape the future.

- The component "Entrepreneurship" is a property that is essential for the existence of any enterprise. It can be described as business sense combined with an ability to detect and exploit opportunities at the right moment.

- The component "Intelligence" stands for competence in managing information. How can we generate key knowledge from information and make it available in the enterprise to support strategic decisions?

The expanded 7S model is shown in Figure 132.

Table 42 offers a representation of the interrelationships and dependencies that exist among the ten elements. 0 signifies "no influence", 1 "minimal influence" and 2

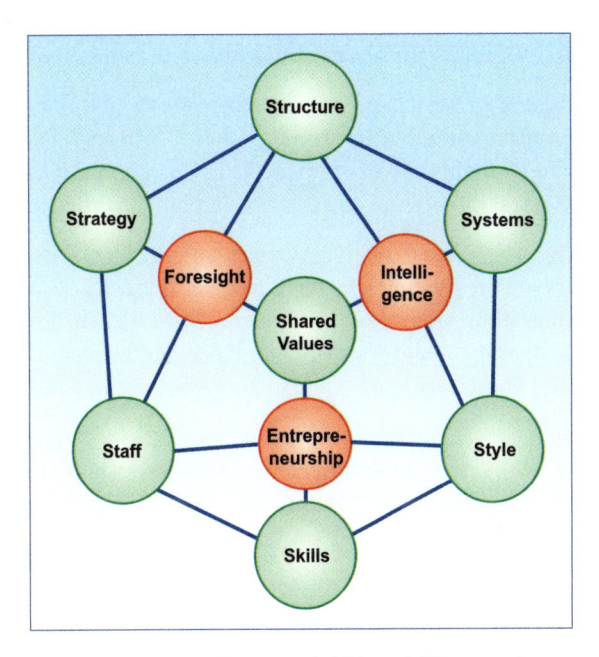

Figure 132 7S+EFI: the expanded 7S model for assessing organizations

Table 42 The Interdependency of Enterprise Elements

	1.	2.	3.	4.	5.	6.	7.	8.	9.	10.
1. S: Strategy	☒	1	2	0	1	2	2	2	2	1
2. S: Structure	2	☒	2	0	1	2	1	1	1	2
3. S: Systems	1	2	☒	1	1	1	1	1	0	2
4. S: Style	1	1	0	☒	2	1	0	1	1	1
5. S: Staff	1	1	1	2	☒	2	1	1	2	2
6. S: Skills	1	1	2	1	2	☒	1	1	1	2
7. S: Shared values	2	1	1	0	1	1	☒	2	2	2
8. F: Foresight	2	1	1	0	1	1	2	☒	2	2
9. E: Entrepreneurship	1	2	2	0	2	2	2	2	☒	2
10. I: Intelligence	2	2	2	1	1	2	2	1	2	☒

6.4 Elements of Change

295

"strong influence." The evaluation is based on a large company. The strong dependencies are quite conspicuous. For instance, the impact of the strategy on the enterprise structure is estimated as strong (column 1, line 2). The enterprise structure can also be seen to influence the strategy (e.g. when an overly rigid enterprise structure would prevent a flexibility strategy), although not as strongly (column 2, line 1).

Change processes are usually initiated by strategic decisions, and efforts to implement change usually concentrate on changing the "structure" and the "systems" (see red frame in table). The remaining elements are often neglected. This approach is based on the assumption that structural integration and system adaptation suffice to bring about successful integration.

Roughly 60 percent of all mergers and acquisitions in the European finance sector fail on account of inadequate integration: "About 60 percent of all M&A deals are unsuccessful because they approached the deal with overconfidence and instead of taking into account all the facts, they chose to pursue their goal of global expansion." [BI 2004]

There are various reasons for this failure: late integration of employees, inadequate communication, overestimation of synergies, underestimation of cultural differences and wrangling over who is to receive what position. The case of DaimlerChrysler can be expected to rekindle discussion of this matter.

Despite being prepared for an accelerated rate of change, it is clear that not all aspects of an enterprise can be changed equally quickly, as if at the press of a button. While

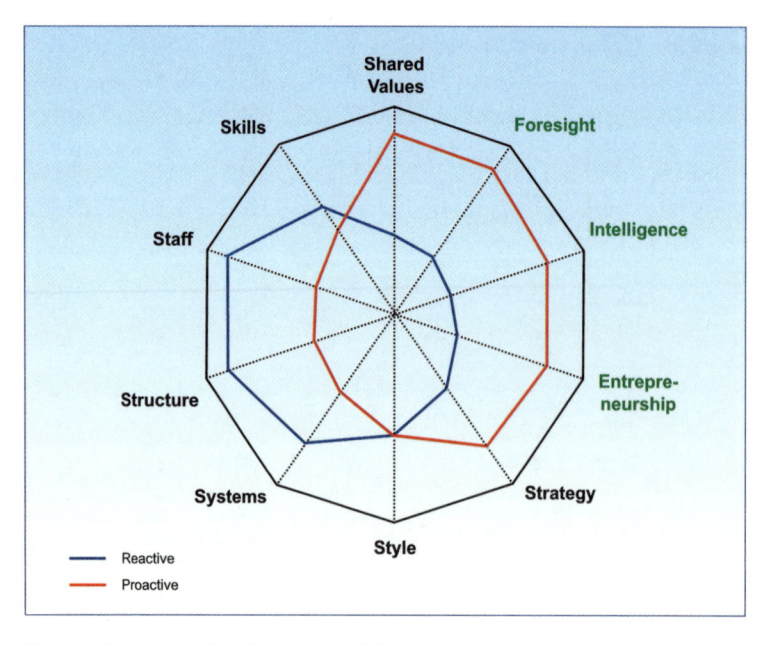

Figure 133 Enterprise elements: their impact on reactive and proactive measures

strategic decisions can rapidly lead to new enterprise strategies, the impact on the enterprise culture – whether it has been intentionally shaped or not – can last for years. This shows how important it is to carefully prepare for change and to consider its impact on all of the relevant components, both in advance and during implementation.

However, this also means that there is no magic formula. Every change is situation-dependent.

Motivations for change can differ. While motivation usually arises as a reaction to a changed environment, it can also arise from foresight and an interest in retooling the enterprise so as to make it more competitive and better prepared for the future. The significance of the ten elements in the change process is different in these two cases. When in reactive mode, a premium is placed on the speed with which one adapts the enterprise structures and systems to the new conditions. In proactive mode, the focus is on the soft factors. Figure 133 offers an illustration of the difference.

I will now consider the role of the elements in relation to change and the two perspectives within the enterprise before moving on to describe individual aspects and success factors for avoiding operational blindness and for increasing an enterprise's fitness for the future.

6.4.1 The First S: Strategy

The possibilities outlined in Chapters 2 to 5 represent only an excerpt from the repertoire of strategic instruments and possibilities. Analysis procedures for the areas market, consumer, industry, competition and technology play a role that is equally important as that of the procedures geared to foresight.

In previous chapters, I have also highlighted the fact that strategy is only partly a matter of planning. The remaining part is reaction. Again, the question arises as to the extent to which strategic planning is at all capable of determining the fate of an enterprise.

Socialist systems failed in part because they embraced planned economies, rigid five-year plans. On the other hand, going entirely without a plan is the same as having no means by which to orient oneself. The important thing is to achieve a balance between a core strategy that ensures stability and orientation and a high degree of flexibility so as to retain a capacity to respond quickly to changes in the environment and to appropriately adapt the enterprise.

If we consider the many significant changes that have occurred – globalization, increased complexity, and acceleration to name just a few – it becomes clear that flexibility in the development of enterprise strategy will assume even greater significance in the future. Strategy plans will take on the significance of guidelines and orientation tools. These will be expected to prevent a hindering of quick responses on account of an overly rigid adherence to plan specifications.

The separation between thinking and acting that was introduced by Taylor and the associated worker and process specialization is still largely accepted as valid today. However, in order to prevent the emergence of two isolated levels (i.e. their intentional removal), the exchange of information and feedback is necessary. This will the more be the case as the following increase: complexity, complication, interdependence and uncertainty.

6.4.2 The Second S: Structures

Enterprises are grown-up organizations. They continue to develop. Enterprise structures are supposed to regulate the energy and forces within the system. They are formal and determine the way that work is performed. They also formalize who is to report to whom.

Today's enterprise structures are often restricted to administration. This is because processes, structures, sequences and systems are oriented towards stable circumstances. An intentional change in a structure is usually carried out on the assumption that the new form will permit one to pursue the strategy better, to cooperate better, to work more efficiently thanks to synergies, to respond quicker and more effectively to change, etc.

However, there is no such thing as an ideal structure. The requirements that are to be met by the structure are different owing to the different strategies, business orders and the industry environment. Any particular structure represents a compromise between efficiency and flexibility. The organizational structure can be described in terms of several opposing criteria:

- Centralized versus decentralized
- Efficient versus effective
- Control versus commitment
- Change versus stability
- Functional structure versus project structure (i.e. matrix structure)
- Bureaucratic versus unbureaucratic
- Steep hierarchy versus flat hierarchy

A lack of trust in the "periphery" often prevents a stronger downward transfer of responsibility and a more consistent implementation. The assumption here is that bad decisions are mainly associated with lower levels in the hierarchy. Why this assumption persists remains a secret guarded by the senior management. Personal management styles, experience and preferences have a hand in shaping structures. Rigid control and management will undermine attempts to become an intelligent enterprise. Strictly speaking – and as Gunter Dueck suggests in his book *Lean Brain* – an enterprise will lose its intelligence as it becomes more process-oriented and bureaucratized [Dueck 2006]. Why does one need highly qualified employees for routine tasks? The freedom to decide is reduced to a minimum, every move is regulated.

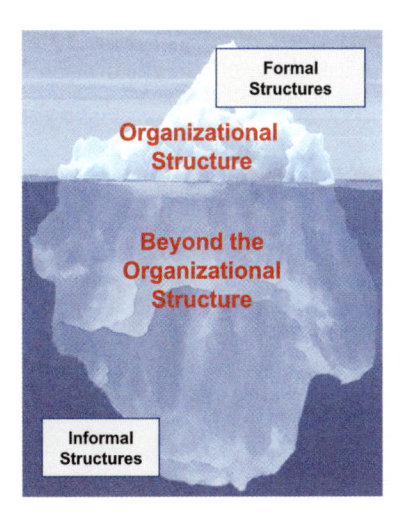

Figure 134 Formal and informal structures: one system

This situation is often described using the metaphor of a machine. In the face of increasing acceleration, an enterprise that is oriented towards the metaphor of an organism will certainly be better prepared for the future. Here, change is not the exception or the interim state between stable periods, it is the rule.

Management books deploy auspicious terms to describe the implementation of measures in enterprises: "anchor," "optimize," "improve," "address," etc. All of these terms are primarily aligned to formal structures. However, if the structure of an enterprise is changed, it is not only the structural chart and the number of employees that will change. While there are no plans that account for informal structures, these structures are destroyed in the process of restructuring and need to be created anew (Figure 134).

If an enterprise is to become or remain functional and to achieve the benefits of restructuring, the implementation of the restructuring must be carried out rapidly.

It may sound exaggerated, but the actual implementation – the adjustment of reality to the specifications in the plan – often drags on for months in overly bureaucratic environments.

The Magic 150

"We'll have to do something when people start parking on the lawn."

What at first sounds like a parking problem is in reality a statement made by a senior manager about the enterprise structure. It is based on an astonishingly simple concept – "the magic 150."

As an anthropologist, R. Dunbar has determined in the context of his research that the neocortex in humans is especially pronounced when compared to other mammals. Dunbar suggests that this is related to the capacity of human beings to enter into social relationships. He concludes that the size ratio of the neocortex to the entire brain will increase as the capacity of a species to manage social contacts and relationships increases.

Dunbar has determined an ideal group size of around 148 for humans. In other words, humans are (on average) capable of actively maintaining around 150 personal relationships.

What is so astonishing in connection with this theory is that military organizations have determined on the basis of their own studies – trial and error – that a company strength of less than 200 makes for an optimal structure in terms of the communication that takes place between the soldiers. If the group is larger, other forms and structures become necessary, i.e. hierarchies, formalities (rules, guidelines) and chains of command.

Wilbert Gore, founder of the company of the same name, is convinced that personal contacts are immensely important and that many rules, guidelines, and formalities are superfluous. The lack of anonymity leads to increased reliability, more effective channels of communication, and a very flexible and efficient organizational structure. The success of the Gore Company – one of the most innovative companies in the world – appears to confirm Gore's theory. "We found again and again that things get clumsy at a hundred and fifty," says the company founder in an interview.

When the first employees in a business unit start parking on the lawn, then the time has come to divide it. If the unit has gotten too big and cumbersome, then the administrative tasks will also have gotten too costly. In order to prevent this outcome, two separate units are formed on the basis of special skills or products.

This approach is also remarkable in that it introduces creative space (e.g. for innovation) by reducing the need for an administrative and regulatory apparatus. It is surprising that enterprises do not experiment more with such organizational forms. The reaction to poor business development usually focuses on capacity adjustments, although every manager should realize that each employee lost means a reduction in the likelihood that new ideas and innovations will appear.

Markets will continue to change – and even faster. Capacity adjustments in the traditional sense will prove to be too inflexible. It is already the case that many enterprises are playing catch up with their demand for capacity – "capacity" here referring somewhat pejoratively to employees. EADS is desperately looking for engineers – after firing them a few years ago.

Why not combine available employees into think tanks or innovation reactors? Not more than 150 at once and with the sole task of creating something new?

It is precisely a matter of generating uncertainty! At best, by creating something new, similar to Google where almost no day passes without the presentation of a new service or product. And those in the branch watch as if dumbstruck and simply continue to adjust capacities.

This is another reason why it is necessary to deal with uncertainty.

6.4.3 The Third S: Systems

The third "hardware" element encompasses the systems and the processes of an enterprise (e.g. bookkeeping, human resources development, planning systems, budget systems and evaluation systems). Systems constitute the backbone of an enterprise. They ensure stability and the optimal execution of routine tasks.

"Organizational change involves the intervention in existing processes of interaction, i.e. using them accordingly." [Müller-Stewens 2005]

Optimal enterprises find the right balance between efficiency and flexibility. Efficiency can be easily measured and verified. A lack of flexibility is usually only detectable with the advantage of hindsight (learning after the crash). Preventive learning and measures to increase flexibility are usually sacrificed in favor of efficiency. The benefits of flexibility are usually not immediately perceivable and it is thus hard to make a case for flexibility when faced by efficiency-minded managers – in particular when the environment and enterprise analysis could prove to be very expensive: "By the time an organization has perfected its systems and structures, it has invested tremendous energy and everyone in the organization is loath to change anything because of all the effort sunk into the status quo." [Harris 2002]

However, strategic investigations and their implementation are very situation-dependent procedures. Attempts to represent strategy development via formal processes leads to a situation in which today's problems are addressed and solved with yesterday's instruments. The desire for greater efficiency has led to the paradox of an ever more formalized approach to strategy development. Chandler's theory that "structure follows strategy" is effectively reversed. Strategy becomes a byproduct of structure. One analyzes, evaluates, qualifies, compares and compresses, and in the end one winds up with recommendations for action that – once implemented in the framework of the specified structure – are supposed to lead to success.

All the while one forgets that strategic thinking cannot be taken over by systems. It is a unique and highly complex matter that depends on many factors and participants. Even the desire to have a share in the success of other enterprises by copying certain behaviors is suitable as a replacement strategy only to a very limited degree and for a very short period of time.

Processes

Formal processes are lined up against individual, tailor-made actions. Formal processes are optimal for routine tasks (e.g. bookkeeping, purchasing, etc.). They establish clear rules, reduce error rates and increase efficiency.

Here, one should not forget that all systems are tools and that no added value will be created if they are not wielded properly. Intelligence is located in the heads of employees.

IT Systems

One of the original hopes expressed in connection with information technology was to liberate people from the necessity of having to repeat the same tasks. Another hope was that IT would facilitate the exchange of information.

According to one estimate, 60 billion e-mail messages are transmitted via Internet every day. They compete with a volume of around 15 billion SMS messages. The phenomenon is called information overload. Time is a finite good and it seems safe to assume that more information must come at the price of diminished attention (information volume times attention is constant). The suspicion that more is not necessarily better is gathering weight every day. This has hardly undermined our belief in IT. New technologies are constantly turning up that promise to eliminate the shortcomings of the previous technologies.

The authors of the study "How IT Enables Productivity Growth" [McKinsey 2002] on the role of information technology in enterprises come to the following conclusion, "We found that the productivity acceleration of the mid to late 1990s, the so called 'new economy,' was concentrated in only six sectors and that the role of information technology (IT) was only one of several factors at work in the productivity jump. Innovation (including but not limited to IT and its applications), competition, and, to a lesser extent, cyclical demand factors were the most important factors." Thorp sketches a similarly differentiated picture [Thorp 2003].

The time has come to reconsider the role of IT. Without a doubt, there are areas in which information technology has led to the automation of tasks and thus to immense increases in productivity. However, the attempt to simplify studies of the future, foresight and strategy development via IT technology and to make the corresponding results more clear is bound to fail. The above-mentioned study involved an

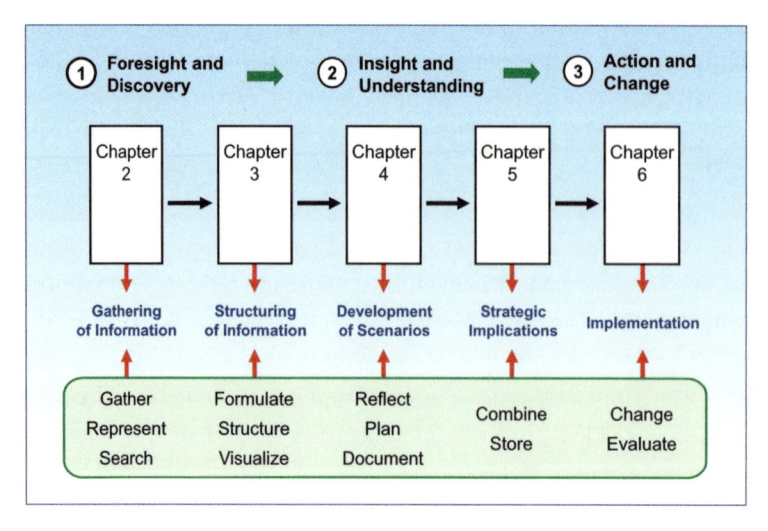

Figure 135 Process phases in Foresight: where does it make sense to make use of IT support?

investigation of the various processing phases, beginning with information gathering and extending to implementation and the control (Figure 135) of the benefits of support based on information technology. The result is presented in Table 43.

For each phase an evaluation is given of the degree to which it would appear to make sense to make use of IT support and thus to exploit possible increases in productivity. It quickly becomes clear that the benefit of IT tools is limited.

It is only in the case of searching for, structuring and representing information that the utility is uncontroversial. However, IT support is assessed as very doubtful both in the case of strategic planning and decision making. After all, the quantification of gut feelings increases neither the security nor the quality of decisions. No tool can help when it comes to understanding the content of information and its evaluation.

If we factor in the expenses associated with introducing and maintaining software, the utility balance looks even less favorable. Further disadvantages result from the fact that the available tools (e.g. Eidos by Parmenides) support only certain steps in the process and that any expenses that have been saved may be neutralized by the need to adapt formats to meet the specifications of the tools. Even if Parmenides claims that its Eidos tool supports thinking itself, the conclusion remains that one has to do one's thinking on one's own.

The fact that trust in software leads to a situation in which systems and tools determine processes and work methods also speaks against software and for common sense. Something similar can be observed today in operational bookkeeping. Once systems have been installed and introduced, it is difficult to initiate change.

Employees mutate into system-controlled enforcement officers – this phenomenon is also referred to as "New Taylorism" – independent thinking and acting is prevented by processes and systems. What gets lost in the management system is sound thinking, imagination, innovation, risk-readiness – intellectual assets: "Organizations rush to purchase IT 'silver bullets' in the form of customized business solutions, enterprise application packages and other ready-to-wear IT solutions in the naive belief that they come neatly packaged and stamped 'benefits inside.' Again, the idea is that all you have to do is plug in the technology and, magically, the benefits will flow." [Thorp 2003]

Enterprises seem to allocate far more resources to measuring productivity than to foresight activities. Moreover, it also seems that many enterprises drift away from robust enterprise strategies as they become ever more preoccupied with measurement and the short-term fulfillment of specifications, a tendency that can ultimately prove fatal.

Stephen Denning of the World Bank assesses the balance in knowledge based enterprise units as "80% brainpower and 20% information technology" [Denning 1999]. The advantage of information technology is and remains the organization and representation of information. "Formal systems can't store knowledge that isn't easily described or codified but nonetheless essential for doing the work, called 'tacit knowledge.'" [Aldag 2002]

Table 43 Process Phases in Foresight: Where does it make sense to make use of IT support?

Phase	Support/Limit	Instruments/Tools	Evaluation
Gathering information (Chapter 2)	Searching for information Orderly storage of information	Search engines (Google) Research on the Internet	Very sensible
		Libraries (also electronic)	Very sensible
	Compression of information Compilation of information Generation of new knowledge Experience	Databases (special or standardized, office-based) Personal contacts and …	Sensible
		… conversations – no known tool	Would be sensible
Structuring of information (Chapter 3)	Structuring of information Documentation of information Exploration and visualization	Structuring with mind maps (mind managers)	Sensible
		Breakdown, abstraction, clustering of elements – in substantive terms	Impossible
		Breakdown, abstraction, clustering of elements – visualization	Sensible
	Comprehension of content	No known tools	Impossible
Drafting of scenarios (Chapter 4)	Drafting of scenario framework	Tools for drafting scenarios: www.zukunftsgipfel.de	Scarcely sensible
	Development of scenarios	Creativity tools and visualization tools	Partly sensible
	Reflection on the future	No known tools	Impossible
Strategic implications (Chapter 5)	Representation of the possibilities	Strategy tools	Scarcely sensible
	Evaluation of options	Strategy tools	Partly sensible
	Generation of new options	Combination, abstraction, creativity	Impossible
	Decision making	Existing analysis tools merely break problems down into sub-problems	Impossible
Implementation (Chapter 6)	Drafting of structures Planning of changes Visualization of implementation	Project management, planning tools Standard office tools	Sensible
	Change and impact on values, culture, respect, recognition, style, capabilities	No known tool except for project management	Partly sensible
Control	Measurement of business indicators Performance evaluation	Balanced scorecard, SAP	Sensible
	Evaluation of soft factors (e.g. motivation, satisfaction, etc.)	Quantification of qualitative indicators	Scarcely sensible

Evaluation Systems

If enterprises wanted to depart from the paper orientation described above and return to an action-oriented enterprise culture where actions really count more than transparencies and presentations, then they would have to investigate their own values systems and systems of recognition and make the necessary adjustments, "One of the main barriers to turning knowledge into action is the tendency to treat talking about something as equivalent to actually doing something about it." [Pfeffer 1999] The task is to implement the ideas that are presented – a task that is ideally performed by the presenters themselves. Conclusions about the future of the enterprise can then be derived from the nature of the motivation and inspiration and from the performance evaluation.

It is paradoxical that monetary, extrinsic motivation is the only known form of performance recognition in many enterprises. A willingness to perform at a higher level is then pegged to the evaluation system. Recognition that is exclusively monetary leads to "trained monkeys" who are willing to perform for a reward and are not willing to perform in the absence of a reward. Individual promotion, respect and esteem with respect to the performance and a high degree of intrinsic motivation are better suited to exploiting the future potential in the interest of the enterprise.

In the following section (Fourth S – Style), I will take a closer look at the differences between the official rules and the unwritten laws and the impact these have on the enterprise.

6.4.4 The Fourth S: Style

The style or culture of an enterprise – "the way we do things here" – is a crucial element for its success. While style and culture put their stamp on the enterprise, they can be difficult to analyze.

One can gain an impression of an enterprise upon one's first contact with it – whether this is a visit or an employment interview. How do the employees interact with one another? What do the offices look like? What status symbols are visible? Is there a dress code? How are mistakes dealt with?

In addition to these plainly visible features, there are also invisible mechanisms that are difficult to understand from the outside and difficult to copy. They form the basis of the enterprise's success.

Given its clear significance for enterprise success, one can readily understand the desire to influence the latent culture as much as possible for the benefit of the enterprise.

Attempts to strategically influence enterprise culture are common:

For instance, a German bank announced that all of its employees were to address one another using a familiar salutation, effective immediately. What was originally a decision made by individuals was taken over by the enterprise. Attempting to convey a sense of flat hierarchies, open discussion and startup flair in this manner leaves one with a funny feeling. Although the Bank's CEO emphasizes that it is not a matter of a familiar form of address signifying friendship, but an expression of modernity and professionalism as in the use of "you" in English speaking countries, it contributes to an atmosphere of confusion. Can one expect to increase a commitment to professional standards by introducing the equivalent to an English form of address? IKEA is more honest in this matter.

Cosmetic approaches miss the point. More appearance than reality, the parroting of a certain enterprise culture is destined to lead to confusion, resistance, a loss of trust and even derision. Enterprise cultures cannot be dictated from above and an order to address one's colleagues in the familiar voice usually will neither lead to more innovation and enthusiasm nor to more success.

Table 44 Official Rules and Unwritten Laws

Desire	Official Rule	Unwritten Law	Result
Promotion of the most capable and deserving	Experience in the enterprise, performance and success determine promotion.	Visibility: make sure that your top performance is visible and distinguishes you from the rest. Success: send only positive messages to your superior. Experience: switch as quickly as possible to the next best position.	It is not the most capable and deserving who are promoted, but those who present themselves the best.
High performance organization	Employee performance evaluations	Performance: concentrate only on the measured criteria. Teamwork: only the minimum	An organization should be more than the sum of its members. But not that way!
Entrepreneurship	Promotion of self-reliance among employees	While well-intended, it is doomed to fail in reality. High risk, costly, minimal support and minimal chances of success.	The paying of lip service and a sluggish organization are the result.
Knowledge as a basis of success	Knowledge management to secure knowledge sharing in the enterprise	While transferring knowledge may benefit the enterprise, it brings no personal advantage and has no effect on the performance evaluation.	Information and knowledge are transferred only in exceptional cases or only to the right colleagues.
Innovation	Demanding innovation	Innovation is sexy, especially talking about it and analyzing it. Radical innovation is much too risky.	A lot of administration, innovation management systems, but no innovators in sight.
Learning enterprise	We learn from our mistakes.	No experiments, no mistakes. They have a negative impact.	Enterprise sluggishness. A lack of courage for new things.

Enterprise decision makers have the following four alternatives when it comes to dealing with change [Scott-Morgan 1994]:

- Accept and resign in the face of the (too) slow pace of change.
- Attempt to circumvent the existing enterprise culture and "force" change.
- Wait until the enterprise is facing a crisis because quick changes will only be possible then.
- Take the long and difficult route of coming to understand the culture and then change it.

However, when attempting to make the enterprise fit for the future, ignoring, waiting and forcing do not represent serious options.

The low hanging fruits have all been picked. It is time to concern oneself with the higher hanging fruits of greater value.

Table 44 offers a number of examples that show the results of attempting to fulfill wishes and achieve goals with the wrong instruments. All official rules will have side effects and take on a life of their own in the enterprise. A lack of feedback and the unbridgeable gap between the management and the rest of the enterprise can lead to unpredictable results.

It is clear that the fate of the enterprise is tied to more than an understanding of the outer world and the future. The most important inside-the-box assets are an understanding of the enterprise itself, a knowledge of the possibilities of intervention and feedback relating to the results.

6.4.5 The Fifth S: Staff

Changes in enterprises always have an impact on people. Employees are often fully unprepared for these changes. Successful change processes distinguish themselves in terms of their tendency to soften the moment of surprise and helplessness with a view of new opportunities and freedoms.

"What incentive do I have to work in your enterprise?" One would like to think of this as a trivial question.

In a study conducted at George Mason University, 1,000 employees and 100 managers were asked what motivated employees to work [Nelson 1994]. The astonishing result was that while the employee and manager responses included similar factors, employees and managers differ considerably when it comes to top motivation. While managers were of the opinion that employees were motivated primarily by a good salary and a secure job, employees indicated that interesting and meaningful work and recognition were the most important. This result has been confirmed by other authors, "It is not money alone that attracts an employee or manager but the challenge of work. It is the possibility of learning new skills, of extending oneself, and of feeling that one is doing something useful and meaningful in the world." [Peat 2002]

Figure 136 shows Abraham Maslow's pyramid representation of human motivation [Maslow 1954]. Probably the most important insight we can gather from Maslow's theory is that while the items in the lower levels do not alone generate motivation, their absence can lead to demotivation. They are necessary, but not sufficient conditions. Real motivation – and thus the basis for top performance – comes exclusively from self-realization, a sense of meaningfulness, and responsibility, i.e. the items at the top of the pyramid.

Frederick Herzberg expands upon this model and draws a distinction between so-called hygienic factors and real motivators [Herzberg 1959]. Although the models presented by Maslow and Herzberg are a number of years old and quite widely accepted, we continue to find considerable misunderstanding and conflict between managers and their employees.

These tend to come to the fore in the context of change projects. Structures and strategies do not automatically ensure employee motivation. A large part of one's attention is given to determining the optimal number of employees. It is either the case that talented individuals are sought or that – usually on account of a perceived need to cut costs – employees are fired. The far more interesting question, however, is: why do newly hired, motivated, curious and enthusiastic employees (i.e. those who are closest to the top level of the pyramid) begin to show signs of resignation within a few years and ultimately turn into demotivated laborers? "Not-so-great companies take talented people and manage to lose the benefits of their talent, insight and motivation." [Pfeffer 1999]

Once again, we see the tight connection to the other elements. Human resources planning is directly connected to "strategy" and "skills." In the following section, I address the skills in greater detail.

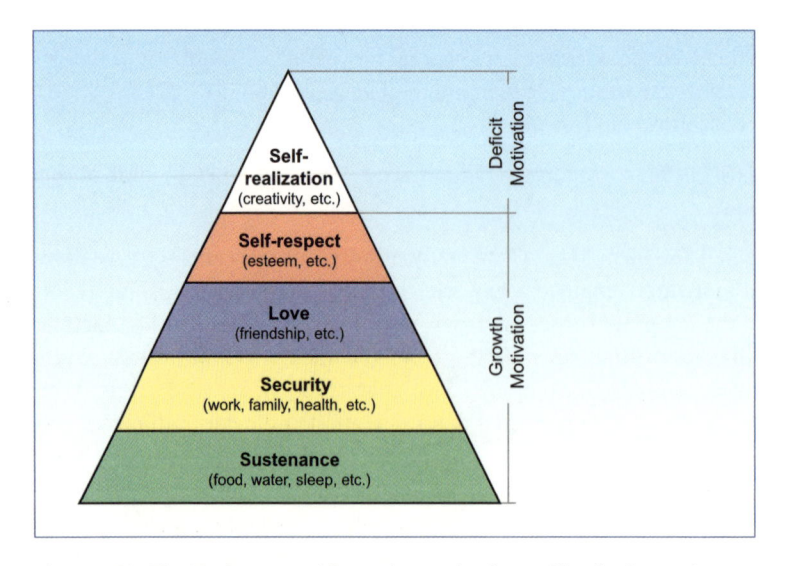

Figure 136 The Maslow pyramid: creative motivation and inspiration at the top

"This is the difference between leadership and management. Management works within existing paradigms while leadership moves between them." [Harris 2002]

6.4.6 The Sixth S: Skills

The competencies available within an enterprise are summarized in the "skills" element. Skills are the foundation for solving problems, performing routine tasks and meeting challenges.

The direct influence on key enterprise factors such as efficiency and productivity is apparent. Unsatisfactory work results can have different causes. In addition to inadequate qualification, the obvious reasons include a lack of motivation or the right attitude, an inadequate description of the tasks involved a lack of support and a lack of the proper means of work. The existence of ideal circumstances in which a precisely formulated task is performed by a person with exactly the right qualifications is an exception. The importance of a contribution on the part of the employee, learning and active shaping increases when the description of the task at hand is less clear. Self-reliance and motivation are becoming ever more important qualities – especially in times of increasing complexity and uncertainty, and as environments, tasks and competencies change.

However, it is safe to assume that many enterprises are not sufficiently aware of their own core competencies and of the kind of knowledge and skills that allow the enterprise to distinguish itself. Do you suspect that your enterprise does not know these things? Ask one of your superiors the following questions:

- What is the enterprise's core competence, i.e. that which distinguishes it from its competitors and is worth developing?

- What competencies will play an important role for the enterprise in the future and what is the plan to develop these competencies and capabilities?

It is a matter of the enterprise's future. It is always the right time to do something about it! And the acquisition of knowledge – generating knowledge stockpiles – is a very promising option.

Information and Knowledge

The terms "information" and "knowledge" are often mistakenly used as synonyms. What is the difference?

If we can define information as data in a meaningful form, then knowledge is information placed in a meaningful context. At the traffic light, the information is that the light is red (or green). The knowledge that we are required to wait when the light is red is the knowledge that we all learn as children. The capacity to interpret is the crucial difference between knowledge and information. Red on the gas gauge means something different than red at the traffic light.

This capacity distinguishes human beings from machines. Knowledge can be codified, formalized and written down. One could teach a robot to react properly to the red light. But such a machine is not in a position to generate new knowledge. Detecting relationships between concepts, generating ideas and proposing hypotheses are (still) the exclusive domain of human beings. And this works best, as researchers have determined, when a lot of knowledge comes into contact with a lot of information (Louis Pasteur: "Chance favors only the prepared mind.").

Enterprises have recognized this and invested huge sums of money in new technologies in recent years. Technologies that "manage" information. While the fact that the systems are called "knowledge management systems" certainly provides a sales boost, it is a clear misnomer and contributes to the illusion that knowledge can be managed. Although managers have made knowledge out to be the fabric of future business, a certain misconception persists: knowledge management "begins and ends with building sophisticated information systems" [Hauschild 2001]. As is so often the case, simplified solutions do not work for complex problems.

Knowledge is the raw material of innovation. However, in contrast to information – which consists essentially of facts – knowledge is subjective, scarcely graspable, and often defies articulation. The largest part of knowledge lies like an unexcavated treasure in the heads of employees. Somewhat greater efforts are required to reach this treasure. The work to excavate this treasure begins with creating the right attitude towards knowledge – and here it becomes very clear that it takes far more than the introduction of a modern instrument to initiate a change in an enterprise. Efforts to measure and compare the performance of employees in ever greater detail will prove to be a mistake, as will the belief that knowledge and creativity are for free and simply emerge. What motivates people to share their knowledge? Recognition and idealism. Both of these get lost in the so-called high-performance organizations.

It is now the right time to consider the skills that will be necessary in ten years.

6.4.7 The Seventh S: Shared Values – Visions

The soul of an enterprise is comprised of its values, traditions and philosophies. These supply an answer to the question: What is the reason for enterprise's existence and what is its self-concept? In contrast to the other components, common ideals and a binding enterprise culture can be planned, but not so easily inculcated or changed. Much patience is necessary to reconfigure deeply rooted traditions and internalized goals. It is often the impatience of managers who ignore the enterprise culture that most undermines efforts to change.

The visions and values clearly reveal how finely one must tune the various components of change to one another. No matter how ambitious, a strategy will fail in the implementation phase if the interaction of the various components is left unconsidered. The capacity of enterprises to perform can be seen in the degree to which one succeeds at finely tuning their various parts. Visions bind, offer orientation and motivate.

Enterprise Intelligence

The intelligence of an enterprise is not a constant factor and it cannot be meaningfully reduced to a figure such as the human intelligence quotient (IQ). The fact is that changes in the enterprise's organization have an impact on its intellectual capabilities.

"It doesn't take much intelligence! But the intelligence that one needs is apparently in ever shorter supply," says Gunter Dueck ironically, picking up on the tendency in many enterprises to increasingly reduce intelligence to system features (e.g. data bases and processes) [Dueck 2006].

Where is the intelligence of an enterprise hidden? Enterprise intelligence can best be captured by two criteria: foresight and flexibility. The term "learning organization" has come into use as a synonym for intelligent enterprises (see "Enterprise Intelligence Test," Section 1.5).

Learning Organizations

"Not surprisingly most organizations are reluctant learners – and one strategy that they adopt is to try to short cut the process by borrowing ideas from other organizations. While there is enormous potential in learning from others, simply copying what seems to work for another organization will not necessarily bring any benefits and may end up costing a great deal and distracting the organization from finding its own ways of dealing with a particular problem." [Isaksen 2006]

There are a number of different learning models available [Carnall 2003]:

- *Learning by doing*

   The most efficient method and the one promising the best retention. Attempting to do things, experimenting and working things out on one's own results in a steep learning curve and high rates of retention.

- *Learning by using*

   Learning from others – copying and benchmarking

- *Learning from failure*

   While this can lead to greater retention than learning by doing, the desired effect is brought about only when one makes an effort to identify the reasons that led to failure.

This is illustrated in the following three areas: technology evaluation, communication and benchmarking.

Technology Evaluation

For the first time, radio frequency identification (RFID) technology was used for ticket identification at the World Cup Soccer Championships in Germany in 2006. A number of reasons were cited in the run-up to the event for using the new tickets. These included a desire to prevent black market ticket trade and to identify and separate potentially violent fans. The aim was to establish a "scalable and flexible security concept."

The World Championships are over. The RFID ticket technology turned out to be "technocratic nonsense" because it was too bureaucratic, prone to error, and complex while offering few benefits. "If a signal rocket is launched from block 17, row 12, seat 35, then we'll know immediately who it was who did the launching," said Wolfgang Niersbach, Vice President of the WC Organizing Committee, by way of giving the rationale for using the technology. Although signal rockets were fired during the matches between Croatia and Brazil and between Sweden and Paraguay, the perpetrators were never identified. They probably weren't sitting in block 17, row 12, seat 35. The black market trade in tickets flourished. Altogether a debacle. In an article entitled "The Big High-Tech Bluff," the Financial Times Deutschland (page 30, issue from 6/21/2006) offered the following comment, "The World Championships went well despite and not on account of the high-tech ticketing." The chip tickets offer a textbook example of the introduction of useless novelties. One can often win support for such technology by merely claiming that it offers a benefit ("scalable and flexible security concept") or will enable cost savings or increased effectiveness.

The European Championships in 2008 will see a return to the good-old paper tickets.

The question is: could Philips, the manufacturer, have seen the disaster coming or was it simply accepted? Put more generally, what distinguishes successful technologies from less successful technologies? Although this question is highly significant for manufacturers and technology developers, the many failures show that the learning curve is quite flat.

Christensen describes how utterly serious the situation is, "Despite the best efforts of remarkably talented people, most attempts to create successful new products fail. Over 60 percent of all new-product development efforts are scuttled before they ever reach market. Of the 40 percent that do see the light of day, 40 percent fail to become profitable and are withdrawn from the market. By the time you add it all up, three-quarters of the money spent in product development investment results in products that do not succeed commercially." [Christensen 2003]

We know that the world is changing ever more quickly. Technology is an important driver of change. That is the good news – for technology firms. The bad news is that such a small percentage of new technologies and products survive. It even seems as if the failure rate were on the rise.

We also know that the processes of change are very complex and only partially foreseeable. This uncertainty is a stumbling block for enterprise planners. Their efforts to formalize, automate and increase the efficiency of processes are also directed to product development. Countless dissertations have been written on how technologies are to be evaluated or how they spread [Pawlowski 1999, Day 2000, Bürgel 1996] – always with the aim of unburdening the decision-making process, i.e. formalizing it and turning it into a routine. However, the problem is not the technology, but the human factor. More trust is placed in a computer-assisted analysis than common sense (which may be in need of exercise after losing a number of battles with the computer).

Let us consider the introduction of a new technology, for instance, a micro fuel cell for cellular telephones.

The situation appears as follows from the perspective of the manufacturer:

While the fuel cell is a little bit larger than a conventional battery, it powers cell phones for around one month. A technological breakthrough! The fuel itself is methanol and it comes in exchangeable cartridges. The relevant individuals at the enterprise believe that it will lead to economic success because the benefit for the user is obvious – longer operating times and independence from electrical networks and loading cycles. A decision is made to develop and market the fuel cell.

The situation appears as follows from the perspective of the average user:

Although the performance of cell-phone batteries has been disappointing, the situation has improved significantly in recent years. Operating times of one whole week are no longer unusual. Users have more or less accepted the necessary routine of charging their cell-phone batteries once per week. Battery technology also continues to advance, a fact that promises longer operating times in the future. The handling involved is simple and self-explanatory. While cartridge systems are comfortable enough, they have a reputation (e.g. in the case of printers) for being expensive and for creating a dependency.

Discussion:

The user has apparently gotten used to the situation. It would be nice if the batteries offered longer operating times, but this does not represent a big problem. Here, the manufacturer may be attempting to solve a problem that does not exist.

Complicating the situation even more is the fact that the user would be expected to get used to a new system. Handling, operation, and charging routines have to be learned. While this may be trivial for a technology freak, it would entail a loss of time for most users – and would thus present a hurdle for the new product's introduction.

I know of three companies working on micro fuel cells for cellular telephones. A commercial success can scarcely be expected (except among outdoor enthusiasts with extreme demands and no access to electrical outlets). The added value brought by such a substitute product is too small compared to the market introduction problems. The Iridium Company experienced similar difficulties with its satellite telephones.

Technologies are often evaluated by manufacturers in terms of their "technology appeal" and "market appeal" [Brockhoff 1999]. Consumers often use criteria such as the burden associated with switching technologies and the pain thresholds associated with not using new technologies. Enter your new technologies in the diagram shown in Figure 137 and you will gain an immediate idea of their prospects for market success!

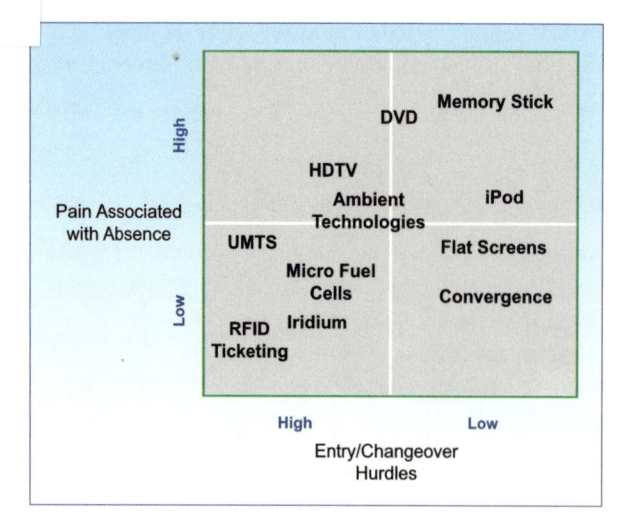

Figure 137 Technology evaluation: the user's perspective on new products

The examples outlined above are only meant to present a snapshot. The actual situation could change rapidly – depending on how effectively manufacturers are able not only to meet consumer needs, but also to awaken consumer needs. However, manufacturers often believe they are responsible for what winds up being successful on the market. This is a misconception. It is the consumer and it will also remain the consumer in the future.

Communication

Learning success is especially high when learning and the application of what is learned can proceed without hierarchies and decision makers. "The increasing complexity of problems requires new ways of solving them. Top-down decision making doesn't work anymore." [Harris 2002]

Figure 138 illustrates how one can transcend the dilemma "employees generate knowledge and managers evaluate it from above" by including the management in the process of generating knowledge.

"... as news travels up the hierarchical levels, each messenger changes a bit to tell the boss a happier story. This so-called mum effect helps explain what Nobel Prize-winning physicist Richard Feynman learned when investigating the 1986 explosion of the Challenger space shuttle. Feynman asked a group of engineers to estimate the probability that the shuttle's main engine would fail. Their estimates ranged from 1-in-200 to 1-in-300. When Feynman asked NASA's boss to make the same estimate, he proposed a failure rate of 1-in-100.000 ... isolation from reality." [Pfeffer 2006]

Benchmarking

Enterprises like to compare their performance data with those of other enterprises – competitors and partners alike. As outlined in the Annex, a comparison is also made

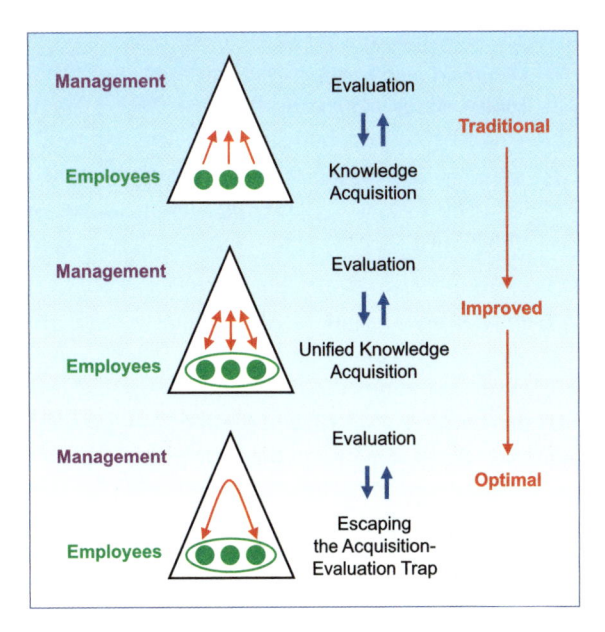

Figure 138 Communication: overcoming communication barriers by including the management in the process of generating knowledge

of processes, systems, results and other apparently important parameters. While this may appear quite sensible at first glance, closer examination reveals that such comparisons legitimate an orientation towards average performance. The explanatory power is thus limited and the impact on strategy dubious.

Enterprises A and B agree to a benchmarking process. It turns out that A has shorter development times and B has a more effective sales department. One result might be that B shortens its development process, which would prove to be tragic because A's competitiveness lies primarily in its engineering excellence.

A desires a sales department that is similarly effective as that of B. Given that growth in new markets can currently be ruled out, its sales department is restructured, i.e. staffing adjustments are made. The result is a short-term increase in performance thanks to reduced staffing costs. However, the increased load per employee leads to compromises in customer support that are simply accepted.

In the end, benchmarking has proven to be of little service to A and B.

It warrants emphasizing that benchmarking is not the same as strategy development and it is not a strategic instrument. In light of a world in which the rate of change is accelerating and uncertainty is growing, it would be better to invest more in the acceleration of processes and response times.

The danger associated with benchmarking lies primarily in the interpretation of its results. It is too often the case that enterprises copy concepts without having understood them and without having a clue as to how they might be integrated. Much has been written about the success of Toyota. The fact that the cause of success is tied to the company's human resources policies is typically suppressed, with the result that Toyota's success remains inimitable. Delta Airlines was so impressed by the success of Southwest Airlines that it decided to establish its own budget brand. The copy-and-paste mentality meant that SONG (the name of Delta's budget liner) simply copied many of Southwest's concepts. Even the bright uniforms were the same. Operations were then halted on April 30, 2006. Colorful jackets were apparently not the secret to success for Southwest Airlines.

A further danger is that comparison soon becomes a method. As if endowed with nothing more than a herd instinct, attention is always paid to the enterprises that are presumed to be the best. Somehow it never dawns on the decision makers that this approach will guarantee that no disruptive innovations will emerge and that the enterprise will never become better than the best – at least not in the benchmarked area.

"Benchmarking is an important way to improve operational efficiency, but it is not a tool for strategic decision making. When competitors all try to play exactly the same game, declining margins are bound to follow." [Nattermann 1999]

The situation is similar when it comes to best-practice efforts. Taking a look beyond the edge of one's own nose is certainly vital. Learning, however, means avoiding the mistakes of others and adapting (not copying) the successes of others to one's own enterprise. "This conclusion means that although knowledge creation, benchmarking, and knowledge management may be important, transforming knowledge into organizational action is at least as important to organizational success." [Pfeffer 1999]

6.4.8 F – Foresight

"However good our future research may be, we shall never be able to escape from the ultimate dilemma that all our knowledge is about the past, and all our decisions are about the future." [Wilson 1975]

Enterprises spend a lot of time evaluating, portraying and publishing the results of their work. The future is accorded the same value in only the fewest of enterprises. On average, senior managers spend "less than three percent of their overall time on drafting a view of the future from the perspective of the entire enterprise. And in some enterprises, it is not even one percent. Both are far too little to generate clear predictions about the future [Hamel 1995].

If enterprises were to allocate the same resources to studies of the future that they allocate to evaluating the past, the number of enterprises that remain successful over long periods of time would be significantly higher. How would it be, for instance, if enterprises would hold "summits on the future" or similar events devoted to learning about and understanding the future as a complement to annual general meetings?

"Driving at high speed in fog is a metaphor for organizations today ... Seemingly healthy companies that can't recognize and respond quickly to change may be dead but not know it yet." [Harris 2002]

6.4.9 E – Entrepreneurship

Entrepreneurship is one of the most important components of enterprises and enterprise cultures. However, it is undoubtedly also one of the most underestimated and neglected components. Entrepreneurship can be characterized by the independent recognition of business opportunities – at all enterprise levels – and continuous renewal. The lack of entrepreneurship turns enterprises into administrative bodies.

Like motivation, entrepreneurial spirit is a property that is difficult to measure – a horror for bureaucrats. But it is exactly this that distinguishes visionary enterprises from average enterprises. Freedom is permitted, one's own business uncertainty is accepted and regarded as a source of energy. Favoring chance, recognizing opportunities and solid business implementation are hallmarks of intelligent enterprises.

6.4.10 I – Innovation Management versus Innovation

Innovation has become a buzzword. It is seen as the stuff that fuels technological advances. Not surprisingly, it is vehemently demanded by senior managers. However, as in the world of politics, the difficulty lies in real promotion and implementation.

Promoting a cause often means supporting it without having a final result in sight. One simply expects it more or less. However, this contradicts the widespread results-oriented enterprise philosophy. While demanding something is easy, promoting it is another story. Innovations always interrupt routines, and thus look rather suspicious.

"Despite all the management books about embracing innovation and thinking outside the box, business executives are basically a conservative lot. They embrace new ideas reluctantly – and only if there is an abundance of proof, or pressure." [Frankel 2004]

In contrast to invention, innovation is an invention (or idea) coupled with business success. Put simply, the chances of success for a business idea are highest when brilliant ideas and inventions pair up with lots of money ("lots of money" as in "a desire to invest"). If one of the two components makes a solo appearance on the stage, nothing is likely to come of it. The idea withers and the "willing" capital looks for other means of compounding itself. It follows that if one wants to do more than merely demand innovation, but also promote it, one will have to join the two components.

However, the most common reason behind the failure of solid innovations is that no one is found who is willing to invest in them. Investing presupposes making a decision. Decisions are seldom made because those who have the money at their disposal are preoccupied with daily business matters. No time for new ideas is the one reason and the other reason is the risk. Companies are quite aware of this dilemma, and as it turns out so often in such cases, attempts are made to solve the problem via systems and technology so that it can be managed: innovation management systems represent an attempt to institutionalize innovation. The aim is to very systematically convert experience and ideas into products and business via a formal process. While the systems themselves will thrive when one takes this approach, the ideas and inventions will perish.

Striving for systematic, formal and stable processes leads to the administration of ideas. This approach even supplies an alibi for the result that no one wants to assume responsibility and make a decision. While there can be no doubt that decisions as to which ideas or inventions are worth supporting are difficult, enterprises lack entrepreneurs who recognize the potential wrapped up in ideas and inventions and are willing to actively promote them.

The best innovation process is one that concentrates on advancing the idea: "idea meets visionary" is the secret. Ask around in your enterprise to find out who is ready to make a contribution to promoting an undeveloped, but promising idea.

Enterprises strive for planning security and stability in order to make business, products and services calculable. Fitness is to be planned. Operational systems are introduced in the context of such striving and then represented in the form of processes. This means an increase in efficiency and the avoidance of errors in the case of routine tasks. However, processes quickly turn into traps for inherently chaotic endeavors.

The starting point for the process drift is the correct assumption that a lot of unexploited potential in the form of ideas is available in the enterprise – in the heads of the employees. These ideas are then to be gathered and evaluated, with the best among them being pursued and hopefully converted into new products and services that make a substantial contribution to earnings. It thus follows that the introduction of innovation management systems is based on the assumption that it is possible to measure and compartmentalize an inherently chaotic and to some extent mysterious process.

Figure 139 shows a typical innovation process (or innovation management process) planned in laboratory conditions. Such an approach raises the following questions:

1. Innovation need: if one can precisely formulate one's need for innovation, one moves intentionally in the direction of evolutionary innovation. How then are revolutionary innovations to be represented?

2. Idea generation: although ideas can be consciously generated, most of them arise during one's activities or spontaneously. How are these ideas to be gathered? What motivation does one have to share such ideas?

3. Evaluation and selection: who is to evaluate the ideas? According to what criteria? How can one ensure that the ideas are understood?

When one considers the selection criteria for innovation projects – typically consumer utility and enterprise fit – then it becomes clear why it is so difficult for enterprises to develop good ideas. As already mentioned in Chapter 1, ideas are supported when the risk of doing so is low and the benefits are high. While this is understandable from the perspective of the management, i.e. because it enables one to avoid mistakes, it is fatal for the enterprise.

In order to avoid subjecting good ideas to such administrative processes and to bring about their realization, it is necessary to bring them into contact with entrepreneurs. Try to find out which decision makers in your enterprise are willing to invest in good

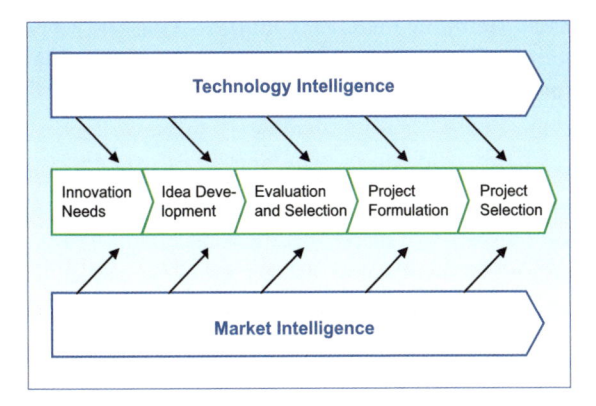

Figure 139 An ideal innovation process: the exception

ideas. Organize a kind of marketplace where ideas can meet capital and bring your enterprise forward!

This approach offers the following advantages:

- First, only those decision makers will respond who are really willing to take a risk and invest.
- Second, you will enjoy the benefit of an immense speed advantage over the usual management process.
- Third, decisions will be made immediately.

You will never be able to see through the realization of an idea if it is subject to only half-hearted and unmotivated consideration. If you are convinced by the idea and no one else within the enterprise recognizes its potential, then approach others. That is the way that the Intel Corporation was born!

4. Project formulation: how and when are decisions made? Most ideas cannot be formulated precisely. If they could be, then it would be merely a matter of solving a problem. New ideas often lead to uncertain results and findings. They arise during analysis and development. How does one ensure that the selection of ideas and the formulation of projects do not end in the formulation of problems and the rejection of ideas with potential?

5. Project selection: what criteria are used to select projects?

A common method of evaluating and selecting future investment projects is the net-present-value method [McAfee 2002]. "Net present value" refers to the present value of future investment returns, discounted at the marginal cost of capital, minus the present value of the investment. If the value is positive, one may assume that the investment will pay and that the return on investment (RoI) will be positive. This allows one to compare several investment projects in terms of their contribution to the value of the enterprise. The disadvantage of this method is that the specifications of future returns are purely subjective or worse in that they can be arbitrarily

6.4 Elements of Change

adjusted (cf. the article on Franz-Josef Bierbrauer in [Eberl 2007]). This method is not suited to the evaluation of innovation projects. Qualitative assessments of potential from the perspective of the enterprise represent a far more sensible approach to sizing up innovations than quantitative approaches.

As was shown in Figure 137, the aim in the classical innovation process – as described above – is exclusively directed towards the market-pull quadrants and one restricts oneself in the context of innovation activities to a search for solutions to known problems. However, revolutionary innovations involve a search for problems and solutions. Innovation involves a good measure of luck, chance and possibility. Those who are unwilling to accept this should ask themselves why post-it notice blocks were not discovered earlier. This shows that the error lies in the system.

If the implementation of an idea fails on account of enterprise structures ("We can't represent and incorporate this idea in our IT landscape!"), then we have a clear sign that the structures have begun to hinder the enterprise's further development.

It warrants mentioning at this point that revolutionary innovations always lead to changes in the conditions of life for human beings, i.e. in contrast to evolutionary innovations that introduce, for instance, functional improvements that do not change behavior.

Here, too, we can conclude that it is people who decide what takes place in an enterprise. People are influenced by the system and its environment. Enterprises don't have the option of suddenly becoming innovative. The culture, the systems, the spirit, the motivation, the values, the structures and the strategy must fit and conspire. It will not suffice to change one element.

The difficulty in the case of innovations lies in their detection and rapid implementation. All formal processes tend to prevent detection and implementation. Motivation is more important than process! "Innovation doesn't have anything to do with perfection. It may take a few failures before you learn how it works." [Kelley 2001]

Given that the task of dealing with uncertainty often turns out to be quite difficult (as outlined in the previous chapters), it may be a promising approach to cause a little uncertainty of one's own. The advantage to this approach is clear: one remains a step ahead of one's competitors and can, to some extent, steer development.

Submarines

What are submarines and what do they have to do with innovation?

This subject was touched upon in the context of standard enterprise dilemmas (Section 1.4). Inertia, risk aversion and inflexibility offer good reasons for submarines. The metaphor comes from the fact that dedicated, creative and motivated employees start secret projects below the surface. A lack of funding and other support is compensated for by much enthusiasm.

The BMW X3 is said to have been developed in a garage in Munich. This is one way to convince and convert even the most disinclined of managers.

An enterprise couldn't have anything better happen to it. Go ahead and start submarine projects and participate in the motivation and enthusiasm of your employees.

Experiments

How does the enterprise deal with mistakes?

If no mistakes are made, then your enterprise isn't innovative enough!

This is not a call for the making of mistakes, but to have the confidence to experiment more. Those in learning organizations know that one can usually learn more from mistakes than from successes.

6.5 Orientation in the Process of Change

The sayings "planning replaces chance with error" and "the more one plans, the harder one is hit by chance" are (regrettably) justified to a certain extent. This dilemma is made worse in the face of increasing uncertainty and rigid planning processes. However, a move to give up on planning altogether would lead to chaos – which is really not worth striving for. The crucial question is thus: "How much planning is necessary and sensible for the enterprise?" Planning offers guidance, particularly in times of turbulence. What is missing is the connection among the uncertain, turbulent environment (environment scenario), the enterprise strategy and its concrete implementation, i.e. the implementation of the strategy under consideration of the findings from scenario and strategy development.

Roadmapping and Roadmaps

Roadmaps introduce a temporal reference to planning and they help to visualize the milestones that have to be reached. Typical roadmap concepts are based on extrapolation into the future – the existing product or technology portfolio will be developed further [Möhrle 2005]. This normative-extrapolative approach can be very helpful in the case of technology visions. The roadmap represents an expression of a willingness to proceed (see Figure 140). The derivation of technology developments and research projects proceeds here in harmony with market developments, product functions and the technology strategy.

Roadmaps can generally be applied to all areas and segments for which components, elements and actions can be gathered in a specific timeframe. Figure 141 shows a further example of a kind of roadmap, a vision of technology extending to the year 2055 presented by the Institute of the Future (IFTF). In contrast to the technology roadmap, it serves primarily as a source of orientation and a sketch of the possibilities.

The formal drafting of a roadmap is relatively simple. There is a time axis and an object axis. The challenge lies in placing the elements, i.e. in the right granularity, in the right spot and with the right designation. Experience shows that a considerable need for discussion arises at this phase. The participants are often made aware at this

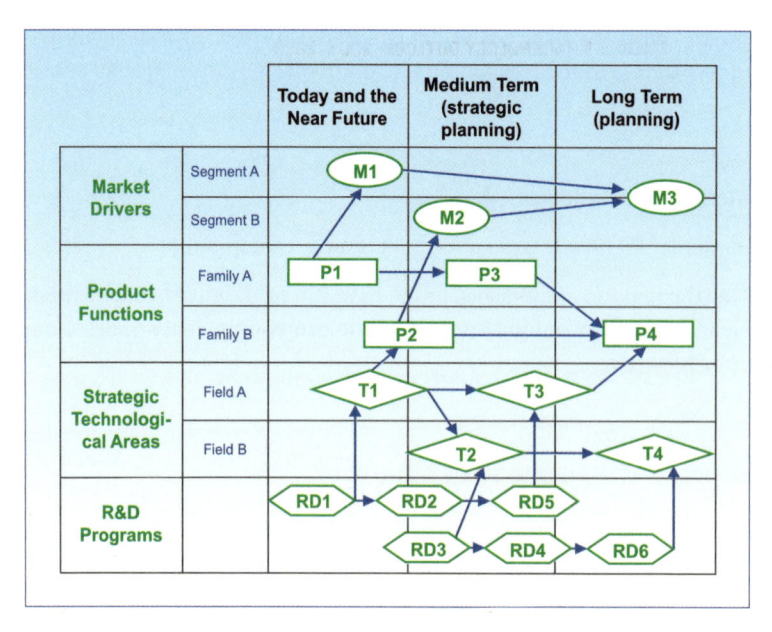

Figure 140 Technology roadmap (Generic Technology Road Map): navigation basis for innovation (as adapted from [Tschirky 2003])

juncture of the implications of considering the future. An object on the roadmap is usually associated with follow-up activities. Responsibility is assigned and a measurable procedure easily arises out of a previously formulated idea or concept. The ensuing discussion thus represents an initial test of the acceptance of the findings gained in the preceding phases.

Product roadmaps represent a special case: they differ from technology roadmaps in that they make statements about products and are thus required to consider the consumer as a user of the products.

The drafting of the scenarios gives one a sketch of the future. The task is now to expand the existing roadmap concept and to incorporate the new knowledge into the process of fleshing out the roadmap.

As mentioned in Chapter 1, it is people who are the causes and drivers of change in most areas. What could be more obvious than to examine the scenarios in terms of the motivations for the changes in question? Motivations for changes are not, however, to be mistaken for consumer utility. "What motivates the users and buyers of products to change themselves?" This must be the central question for a product roadmap. The current product portfolio is merely a starting point for investigation.

As we have witnessed in many failed product innovations, a utility introduced by a product is necessary, but not sufficient for change or the success of the product. However, if we have understood the motivations of the users, we can accept development directions. As shown in Figure 142, users are essentially motivated to change their

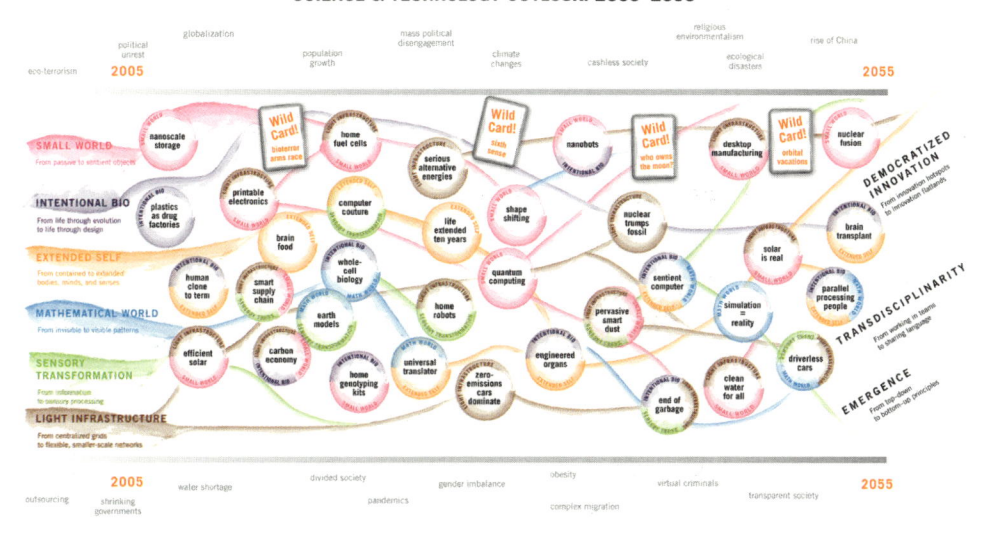

Figure 141 Roadmap: technology vision (Source: IFTF 2005)

present behavior by time savings, cost savings and reductions in complexity (the illustration derives from a scenario of "Mobile Communication").

The roadmap is expanded so as to allow for the placement of the product portfolio to the left of and above the time indicator – the current state. The factors that motivate users are entered to the right on the outside. Products already in the planning are also entered. The gaps that arise are bridged by the ideas and concepts that have been

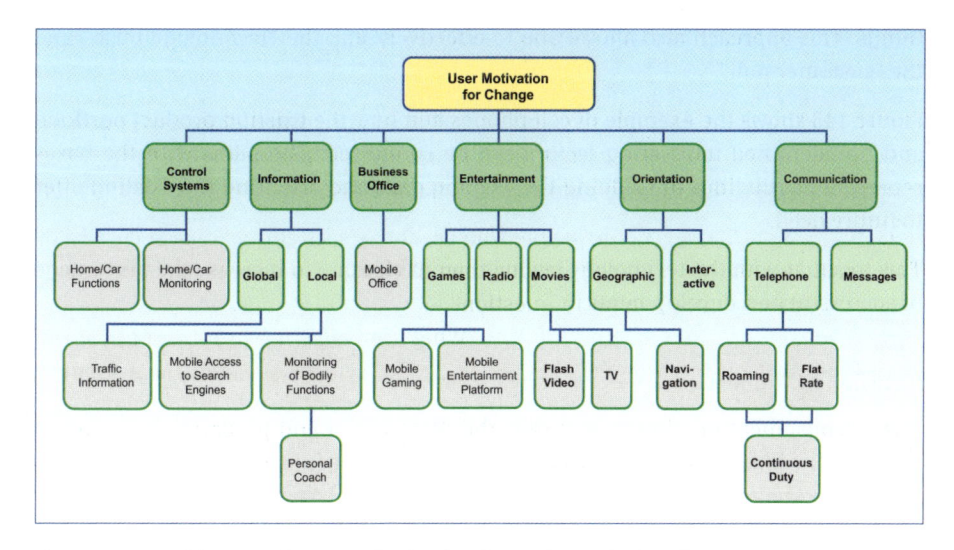

Figure 142 Drafting a roadmap: motivation for change (e.g. cell phone)

6.5 Orientation in the Process of Change

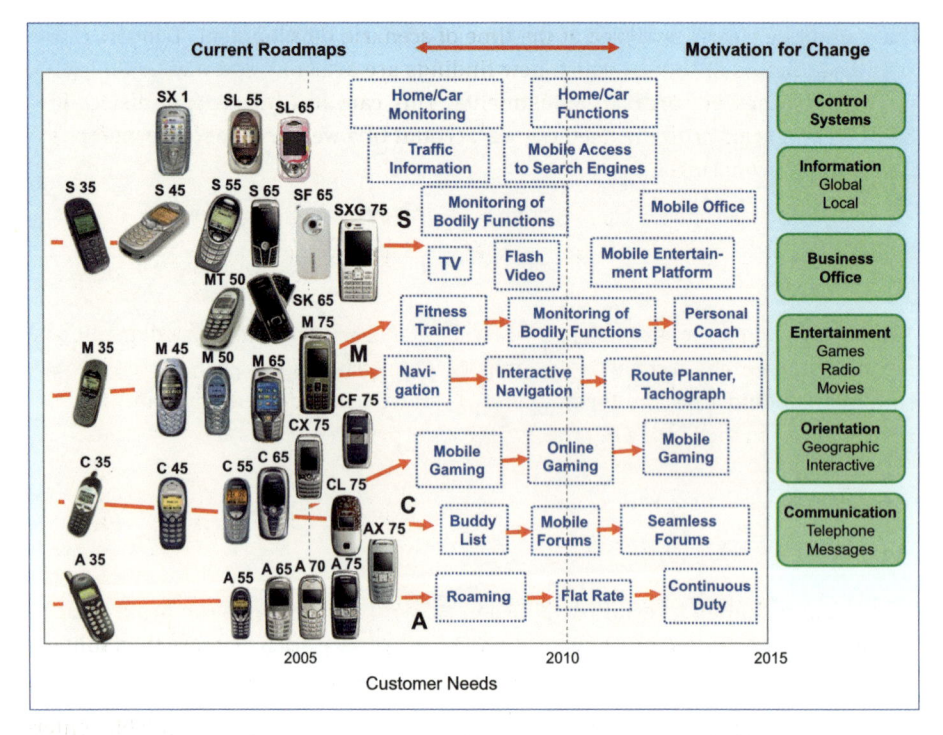

Figure 143 A roadmap for cell phones: the link between existing products (left) and user motivation for change (right)

worked out. Compared to traditional concepts, this approach gives the roadmap procedure a greater focus on the goal. The main aim of the roadmap is to generate discussion and inspire new ideas so as to help in the development of a common view of things. This approach also allows one to effectively link the "technology push" and the "customer pull."

Figure 143 shows the example of cell phones and how the existing product portfolio and the identified motivating factors can be connected. The paths with the boxes represent possibilities of bridging the existing gaps and orienting the existing offer to future need.

This together with the technology evaluation enables one to increase the percentage of successful new developments.

Inclusion of Triggers

The establishment of triggers and thus the detection of and preparation for future events is one important benefit from examinations of the future. Along with the roadmap, the scenarios and the developed strategies, it is advisable to consider the various triggers that could signal the direction that the identified uncertainties will ultimately take and that could thus have a bearing on strategy. Options that are identified in the context of developing scenarios are often dependent on certain developments that cannot be clearly analyzed at the time of scenario development. Triggers represent those points in time at which new findings are available and that could lead to strategy changes or roadmap adjustments. This can, in turn, lead to dislocations between scenarios or to the need (i.e. on account of a wealth of new information) to redesign the scenarios.

A trigger in the case of our example of the future of television would be the establishment of a new standard or the passage of new laws to regulate "killer games" and pornography.

The use of triggers in an enterprise's strategy makes planning more dynamic and flexible. One thereby accepts the fact that the enterprise and its environment change continuously and that any formulation of strategy that does not account for new information can turn into a big risk for the enterprise.

6.6 Including the Results of Analysis

The task of including foresight activities in enterprise procedures can prove difficult and usually does proceed systematically. Such efforts are often no more than solitary, spontaneous initiatives that derive from a certain pressure to act.

While a desire to preserve enterprise stability is altogether understandable, enterprises of the future will be forced to contend with uncertainty more than they have so far and it is advisable to begin to consider today how uncertainty can be included in planning and budgeting without leading to chaos.

Assuming that most of the decisions made in enterprises continue to be based on precise, numerical predictions, it will remain a challenge to make the switch to scenario-based strategy development. In many cases, this will mean more than a reassessment of the factors that go into strategy development, but a complete, philosophically-oriented change in attitude – a new mindset, as it were. Instead expecting someone to tell them what the future looks like, deciders will expect a presentation of alternative scenarios and options, and will then demand time to consider these before making decisions.

Scenarios deliver alternative views of the future and force one to reflect. This may be uncomfortable for many, but there will be no way of avoiding it in the future.

Changes can represent crisis situations. Imagine the case of an employee being transferred from one department within an enterprise to another. This might run quite smoothly and without excess formality in small enterprises. In large enterprises characterized by complex, rigid structures, it can be an elaborate and ultimately exhausting procedure. Mail, telephone, office, accounting systems and other systems all need to be updated. If we assume rapidly changing environments, it is clear that enterprises will have to become more flexible to handle such cases. Change should be normal and should not hinder enterprise processes. Stability will turn into the crisis and organizational changes will become normal.

Table 45 The Status of Foresight Activities

Today	Tomorrow
• Annual planning and budgeting	• Continual strategy adjustment
• No or only sporadic foresight with non-binding consequences	• Regular, continuous foresight with binding implementation
• Advisory, informing character, supplementary information	• Basis of strategic planning

As indicated in Table 45, future processes of strategy development will have to take much greater account of foresight activities. In seeking to achieve this, it will be crucial to find the right balance between shaping and adapting.

Consistent implementation will indeed require radical changes:

6.7 Reflection, reflection, reflection ...

One crucial finding that I hope to have made clear in this book is that while the world can be expected to become ever more turbulent, and change ever faster, it will remain necessary to reflect. In light of rapid change, the increase in complexity, the increasing degrees of freedom and growing uncertainty, one would expect that managers, strategists, analysts and observers of the future would take more time for reflection. The evidence suggests the opposite is the case.

Go into any given office and you will see people sitting at computers, busily entering data. In the face of such time constraints, who among us can afford to take the time

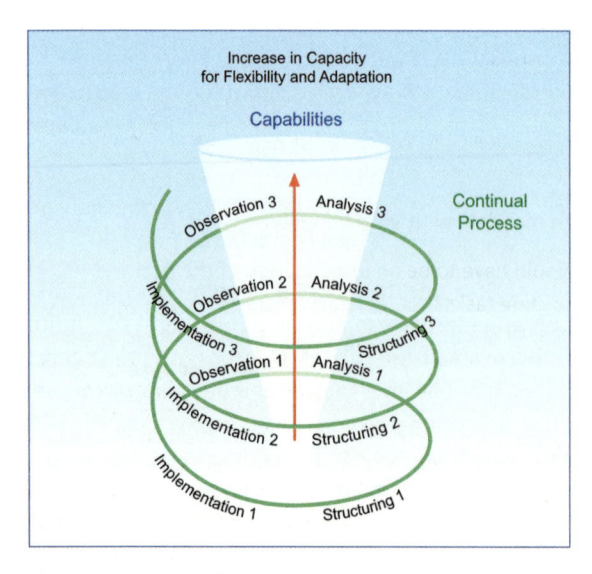

Figure 144 Future fitness: hardly a chance without continuous improvement

to gather their thoughts? Aren't we overcome by the feeling of being unproductive as soon as we attempt to do so? Results count, deadlines are pressing, studies have to be brought to completion, presentations drafted. As a filler between data entry and output, as an interruption when switching from one tool to another, reflection has become secondary. Reflection has become a luxury even for those who want to take the time. But wait, is it really so? The best tool for looking into the future is one's own mind. No tool can predict the future as precisely as the strategists would like. But the more intensively and longer we consider how information is to be interpreted and how knowledge is to be acquired, the better we will be prepared for the future. Trends, scenarios and tools for strategy development represent forms of support that accompany us along the way. Software tools are only capable of processing and representing – in another form – the thoughts that we enter. These tools cannot relieve us of the task of reflection – as a continuous process (Figure 144) – and if we don't understand what these tools do, then we should refrain from using them anyhow.

6.8 The Future of Television (V)

The evaluation of the presented scenarios and analyses with respect to the future of television will lead to the following mandates:

- Promote creativity because it will play a greater role in the added value generated by the broadcaster.
- Establish a means of handling routine tasks more efficiently.
- Change the organizational structure to account for teamwork as a source of renewal.
- Pursue the idea of an Internet platform as an additional medium.

While this will make the strategy somewhat more concrete, it essentially still represents a wish list. The task at hand is now a matter of really changing the enterprise by implementing the strategy and to deriving actions from knowledge and insight ("from foresight to insight to action").

The first step will be to back up each mandate with an action plan.

One measure in this specific case would have to be an investigation of the business processes with the aim of identifying routine tasks that are really characterized by recurring sequences and thus can be automated or redesigned for greater efficiency. A project can be defined for this mandate and resources, responsibilities, timelines and expectations can be formulated in the framework of this project. A prioritization of the specific measures will allow one to stagger the additional resources (beyond those for daily business activities) in accordance with the implementation schedule.

Every change in one enterprise component will have an impact on the remaining components. Successful change processes distinguish themselves in terms of permitting careful

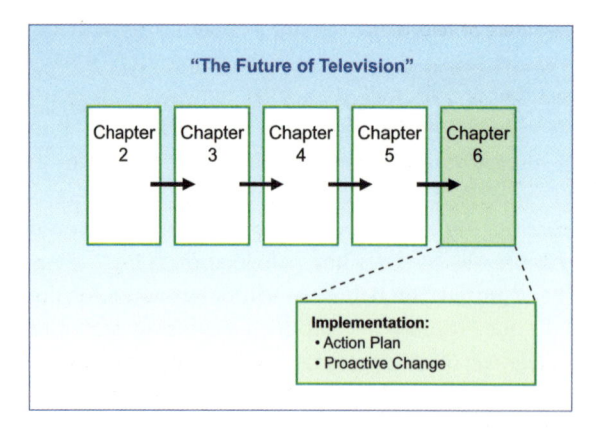

Figure 145 Research project "The Future of Television," step 5: implementation

preparation of the sort outlined in Table 46. An attempt is to be made to determine the impact within the enterprise of each measure that is to be taken as well as to make the preparations that will be necessary for successful implementation.

In order to foster creativity in the enterprise, one might consider the measure of giving employees the liberty to get involved in submarines projects, experiments and other projects that are assessed as interesting.

Table 46 Examples of Measures for "The Future of Television"

	Current Situation	Change Goal	Planned Actions	Preparation and Next Steps
1 *Strategy*	No clear strategy formulated	To firmly anchor strategy development in the enterprise (continuously and systematically)	Analyze the results of the study "The Future of Television." Draft measures catalogue, develop roadmap, and define projects.	Organize workshop. Goal: basic decision and its communication in the enterprise.
2 *Structure*	Rigid structures, low degree of flexibility	To quickly adapt enterprise structures to current requirements	Review of the organizational structure	Project kickoff: "Flexible Organizational Structures"
3 *Systems*	The installed systems block the further development of the enterprise. The system-related strain on employees is too high (hidden costs)	Systems are supposed to unburden and not burden. The aim is to find the best solution for the enterprise. Improvements are to be checked for the flaws of being temporary or lopsided!	Phased approach: 1. Focus on routine tasks: efficient processes and unburdening of employees 2. Focus on creativity and innovation: enabling freedoms (see staff)	Project: "Analysis of the Task Spectrum from the Perspective of the Enterprise"

Table 46 Examples of Measures for "The Future of Television" *(continued)*

	Current Situation	Change Goal	Planned Actions	Preparation and Next Steps
4 *Style*	No clear enterprise culture	To establish a mission statement expressing the relevant values To establish a creative, inspiring work atmosphere	Initial work on the subject of project definition	Commissioning of a scholarly dissertation: "Development of a Mission Statement on the Basis of the Given and Targeted Cultural Values"
5 *Staff*	Room for employee development is limited	To improve employee motivation, and to better promote potential	Establishment of freedoms and the necessary time Pilot projects for motivating employees via transfer of more responsibility	Start of project: "Filling Out Core Competency Form" by the human resources department
6 *Skills*	Advanced training and support are individual measures	Support and advanced training for ALL – continuous and systematic	Provision of adequate funding for advanced training	Expand cooperative endeavors with universities.
7 *Shared values*	Not available	A guiding vision is to be developed in consultation with the corporate foresight unit.	Draft proposal.	Organize a workshop in consultation with corporate foresight unit.
8 *Foresight*	Not available	Introduction of a corporate foresight system and its inclusion in strategy development (see strategy development)	Establishment of a think tank assigned to independently and objectively conduct surveys of the future and to communicate the results throughout the enterprise	Drafting of a foresight concept on the basis of the study "The Future of Television"
9 *Entrepreneurship*	Hardly any chance of development	Promotion of entrepreneurship at all levels of the enterprise Focused support for individual initiatives	Establishment and firm installation of an internal "marketplace for innovations" Provision of a budget for individual initiatives	Organization of the "1st Marketplace for Innovation"
10 *Intelligence*	No statement	Focused support for capacity for early-stage detection and fast response at all levels of the enterprise	A concept is to be developed in consultation with the corporate foresight unit which ensures the optimal flow of signals and information until decisions are made and implemented.	Draft concept proposal.

The measures catalogue shown in Table 46 represents a first step towards change. One is required to recognize that the simultaneous start of all of the proposed mandates would overload the organizational structure. A prioritization and a linking of actions are necessary. The establishment of triggers effectively expands the representation of all measures in a roadmap or action plan. For instance, the existing strategies will be constrained by the availability of new transmission technologies or standards or the entry of new competitors – which will also have an impact on the enterprise strategy and the action plan.

For the time being, this implementation marks the end of the strategy project "The Future of Television." However, the ultimate success of the project will require a continuous investigation of the future, regular analyses of the current situation and the direct infusion of new findings into the strategy development process, ideally via the corporate foresight unit proposed in the example.

Chapter 7

Learning

Applications and Examples

Tommy the tortoise lived in a marsh just outside of town. There was nothing especially fancy about his life, and he wasn't known for being an adventurous sort, but he was altogether content and felt safe and secure in his marshy home.

One day, the animals in the neighborhood organized yet another sports competition. Tommy was very good at a number of sports – such as diving and hiding – but he was rather bad, and quite perplexed, when it came to running.

Quite sure that he would come in last place in both the cross-country event and the 100-meter dash, Tommy was suddenly discontent and unsure about what he should do. Like many who are undecided about what they should do, Tommy turned to a reputable consulting firm for advice.

Within a few days, Tommy was surrounded by consultants with MBA degrees from the best universities. The consultants interviewed many other tortoises, surveyed the track and field facilities, measured Tommy up and down and listened carefully as he related all of his problems and worries.

Having completed their investigations, the consultants withdrew to complete an evaluation of the data they had gathered and to prepare a recommendation.

A senior consultant appeared at the presentation and explained to Tommy why he was so slow by comparing him to the other animals. "Harry the hare," the senior consultant pointed out, "had much longer legs than Tommy and weighed far less besides." Tommy was impressed. Then one of the junior consultants used a diagram to illustrate the relationship between body weight and leg length, ultimately (and quite convincingly!) concluding that Jeremy the jaguar could be expected to be even faster than Harry – hence the firm's recommendation that Tommy should turn into a jaguar in order to be rid of his problems.

Tommy was very impressed indeed, even if he viewed the recommendation as rather theoretical. A few days after the consultants had packed up and gone, Tommy, feeling again quite unsettled, called the firm again to find out whether there was really a way for tortoises to turn into jaguars? The consultant reassured him that there were other consultants he could turn to who specialized in exactly such transformations. "Yes, they use a process known in the field as change management," the consultant said. Tommy was not averse to the notion, but decided to confer with his friend Owen the owl on account of the exorbitant price. Once Tommy had related to Owen all the details of the case, Owen pointed out that tortoises and hares have adapted quite well to their respective environments and that it would be best to simply accept that. "The competitive advantages that tortoises have are related to the water while those of hares are related to the open fields," Owen continued. "Adaptation represents an inherent compromise and no manner of analysis is going to change the situation. Striving for other competitive advantages may come at the cost of losing those that one has, for instance, the ability to swim and dive.

Owen's reflections made a lot of sense to Tommy. It was as if Owen had related something to him that he was already aware of deep down inside.

(Source: the above discussion has been adapted from the article "The Tortoise and the Hare: A Fable for Senior Executives" by John Kay, published in the Financial Times on September 5, 1997)

7.1 Dealing with Uncertainty in Practice

The steps that are necessary to conduct future-oriented strategy analyses were discussed in Chapters 1 to 6. I will now use an example to show how the theoretical knowledge involved can be applied to practice. The example relates to an issue that has received a great deal of media coverage of late and that is a source of considerable controversy – namely, the future of petroleum.

In using the example, my intention is to demonstrate how the methods introduced in previous chapters can be applied and to provide food for thought in connection with one's own work, enterprise and worldview. As I have emphasized on a number of occasions, the aim is not to offer an exact prediction of the future, but to use the available information and analyses to gain an understanding of the subject itself. It is this that will allow a decision maker to draft pictures of the future and to thereby establish a foundation for strategic decisions.

The focus in this endeavor is learning. But what does learning mean? Learning essentially involves an ability to detect and reflect upon one's own successes and mistakes as well as those of the competition and to effectively change one's actions so as to become more competitive and successful.

How can an enterprise improve its capacity to do this?

It is safe to assume that the future will be characterized by turbulence. Merely concentrating on gains in efficiency could lead to unpleasant surprises. Those who are able to adapt the fastest to changes and remain efficient while doing so – i.e. those who are capable of learning – will be successful.

7.2 The Future of Petroleum – Introduction

Petroleum is a special kind of fluid. As crucial and controversial as petroleum is – the world's industries are virtually unthinkable without it, with 95% of all transport services being directly or indirectly dependent on it – there are serious doubts about its further development and availability. Many experts suggest that scarcity is imminent and that this could trigger global crises. Others suggest that there are still ample reserves and that these will provide a basis for stability (Figure 146). Much attention has been drawn of late

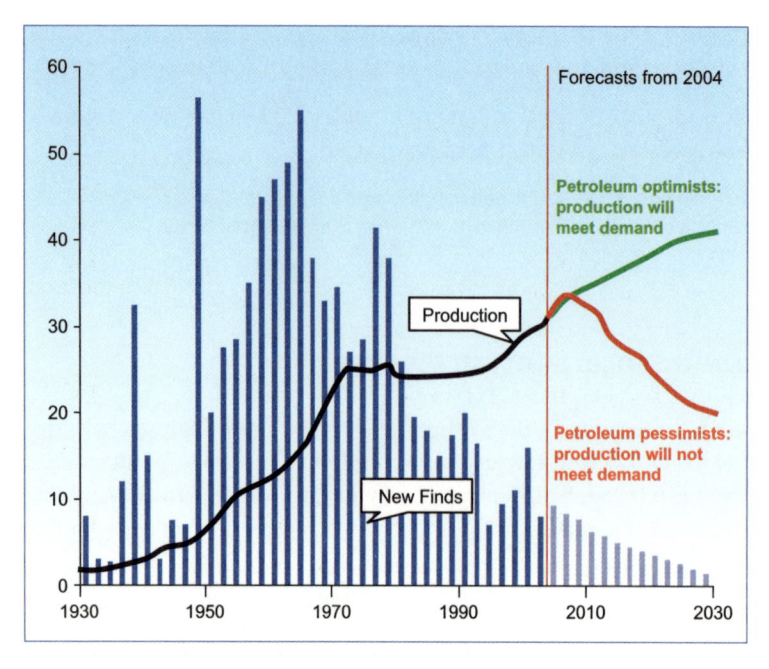

Figure 146 Worldwide oil production (in billions of barrels): according to ASPO, subsequent reserve corrections relating to existing fields were backdated to the year of their initial exploitation; figures from 2004 are estimates (Source: BP, IEA, ASPO)

to the subject of climate change and its relationship to the use of fossil fuels, including petroleum, coal and gas.

Our relationship to oil is highly ambivalent. Conflicting and even diametrically opposed points of view – which are not only based on our perceptions of our own interests – make oil an interesting subject of investigation. Moreover, its importance and the uncertainty of its further development make it an excellent subject of future scenarios. In proceeding to introduce this subject, I will consider conclusions drawn in the previous chapters of this book.

What might the future of petroleum look like? It will surely affect us all – as private individuals and as stakeholders in enterprises. What impact will changes in supply, demand, speculation and prices have on our daily lives and the economy?

Focusing and Demarcation

- The aim of this analysis is to reach a better understanding of and an ability to form an opinion about the subject of oil in light of the uncertainty that surrounds it. The resulting four scenarios of the future of petroleum constitute a basis for strategic considerations and decision making.

- The subject of oil is of global significance. The known reserves are distributed around the world, although not evenly. Demand can also be regarded as global – with various regional and local dimensions and development.

- The analysis assumes a global consideration of the subject and focuses only in individual cases on regional peculiarities.

- A decision was made to refrain from setting a precise temporal scope so as to avoid a discussion of whether sufficient oil will still be available at a given point in time. The scope is selected so as to suggest that the impact of increasing scarcity will be significant and tangible (i.e. 20 to 30 years).

- In order to be able to derive the robustness of the strategy from the comparison of the enterprise scenarios and the environment scenarios and to make a selection, a fictional enterprise will be used as a basis for the enterprise scenario (see section 7.6).

The Future of Energy Supply

The development of humankind can be traced back to around 50,000 years ago. With time, people learned how to use other sources of energy in addition to their own. The wind was used for sailing and fire was used as a means of cooking and keeping warm. The use of coal dates back to the Middle Ages. In addition to wood, it was used for heating and to process metal.

Technological advances and broad industrialization were spurred by the discovery of petroleum and its use as a convenient source of energy. The link between consumption and the development of civilization and wealth is uncontroversial.

Petroleum offers many advantages. Its high energy density, easy extraction and processability make it a coveted commodity. These advantages, however, are increasingly turning into disadvantages.

Petroleum's easy accessibility led to an explosion in demand.

People soon grew accustomed to and ultimately dependent on the easy accessibility of energy, especially that of petroleum. As a natural resource, the supplies of petroleum are limited. While it took nature millions of years to create the earth's petroleum reserves, they will have been consumed in a period of less than 200 years (Figure 147).

The questions are:

- What happens when the low-hanging fruits, easily accessible petroleum, have been entirely transformed into movement, warmth and CO_2? What will we then be able to use to secure wealth?

- How will people respond to the consequences of climate change?

It seems quite certain that people will be disinclined to change their ways voluntarily or in keeping with the principles of reason. Life in affluent societies has become too comfortable. All attempts to change will be immediately met with warnings about the economic consequences and the impact on general living standards.

Something will be done about the situation only after the pain associated with energy scarcity or climate change forces us to do something about it.

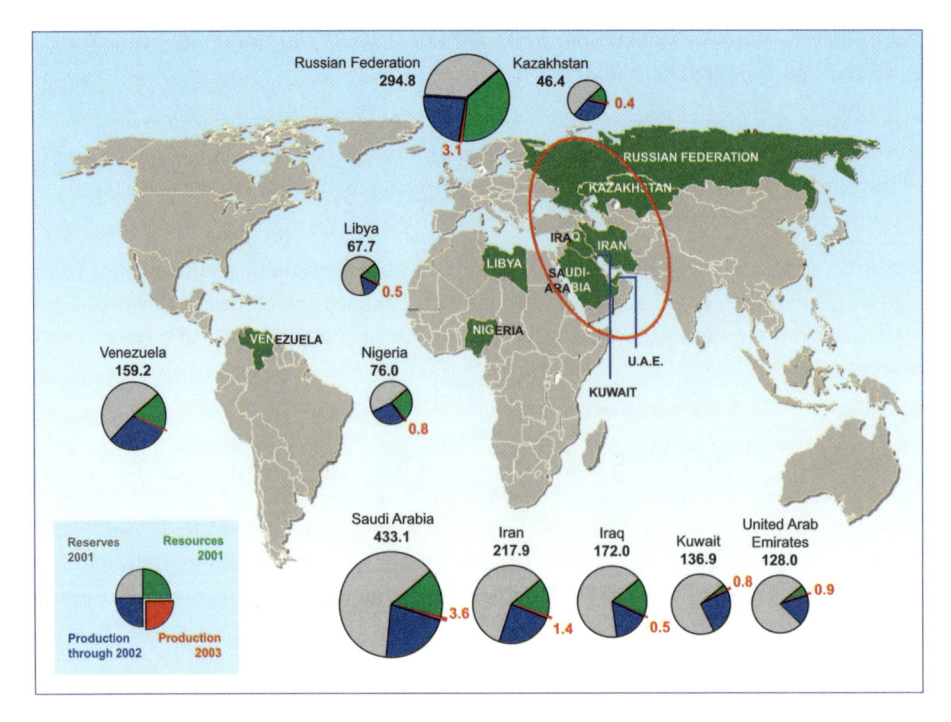

Figure 147 The world of petroleum: depleted reserves, resources and reserves (in billions of barrels, Source: BP)

The predicament will give rise to a reevaluation of goods and values. The current conditions of life and trade are taken for granted. Wealth is associated with the possession of lots of money. But money will not protect us against climate change and energy scarcity.

7.3 The Future of Petroleum – An Information Base

The first step is to gather information. As described in Chapter 2, it is essential to gather information from a sufficiently diverse array of sources. This alone will enable an objective assessment. In establishing an information base for the subject "The Future of Petroleum," 85 sources were drawn upon, including sources from the oil industry (8), financial institutes (2), conservationists (2), geologists (5), relevant experts (9), economists (6), climatologists (3), relevant organizations (4), scholars and futurologists (6). The results are compiled in Table 47.

When seeking to arrive at an opinion of the subject, it is essential to examine the information in a manner that is as objective and dispassionate as possible. As described in Chapter 2, it is important to first gain an overview of the material and then use this overview as a basis for analysis, interpretation and evaluation.

While this initial effort is considerable, it will prove to be a tremendous advantage when it comes to subsequent processing.

The aim of the initial investigation is to establish an overview of the situation and then to create scenarios that can be incorporated into the process of strategy development and thereby make a contribution to efforts to shape the future.

Table 47 The Future of Petroleum: Information Base (Pages 339 to 358)

No.	Information Source	Core Statement	Indicators and Signals	References and Remarks
1	Book Werner, Fritz: "Petroleum: The Most Valuable Raw Material of Our Time" 1971	• Episode from the long history of petroleum. • Petroleum has been used by human beings in various forms for thousands of years – Bible: construction of Noah's ark with pitch (a petroleum residue). • The various uses of oil are shown. • Petroleum as a source of nutrition – proteins! • "Energy cells" for electricity driven by oil?	• Petroleum as a diversely applicable raw material • View of the future from the 1970s: new materials, energy cells, space travel …	"Petroleum has not only become the most valuable raw material, it will retain this status well into the future!"
2	Book Keppner, Gerhard: "Explosive Material – The End of the Oil Era" 1979	• A history of oil: Incas and Aztecs used oil, beginning of industrial mining in the USA and later spread throughout the world. • Future impact of oil scarcity on the economy and wealth, possible alternatives.	• Significance of oil • Historical development • Early warning signals	Figures: the path of oil, photos.
3	Book Banks, Ferdinand E.: "Energy Economics: A Modern Introduction" 2000	• The connection between energy and the economy. • Background, theories and calculations, how oil gas, and coal work. • Volatile market. • Oil's applications: synthetics, textiles, pesticides, pharmaceutical products. • Alternatives: coal, gas, nuclear energy … • Financial instruments in connection with energy (options, swaps futures…). • Many mathematical calculations and theoretical background information (e.g. reserve-production ratio).	• Examination of the energy markets from the perspective of micro economics and finance. • More methods than facts!	"It doesn't make a difference when it comes – anytime will be too soon."
4	Brochure Vision 2000: Energy as an Adventure 1992	• Status of energy technology at the beginning of the 1990s. • Climate change is already an issue – goal: more energy, less CO_2. • Analysis of the various forms of energy. • The electric car is a big issue – superseded by hydrogen. • Oil, gas and coal are too inexpensive, i.e. to permit the development of alternative forms of energy – lack of political will. • Much idealism surrounding new forms of energy, but they are – for various reasons – often not suitable for mass application.	• The future of energy from the perspective of the 1990s. • The burning of 5,931.3 kcal is necessary to bake a pizza with 1,000 kcal for human consumption.	
5	Book Deffeyes, Kenneth S.: "Hubbert's Peak" 2001	• Analysis of the "oil issue." • Geology, exploration, mining, drilling, transport and production. • Geological origin of oil ≈ 100 million years, consumption ≈ around 200 years. • "Peak oil" is expected between 2004 and 2008 – oil companies are more optimistic. • Overestimate of oil reserves by OPEC.	• Focus of book: determining Hubbert's peak – academic, theoretical discussion. Debates about whether the peak is reached in 2008 or 2010 are academic.	"In 1980 it was a problem of distribution; the oil was there, but it wasn't getting to the corner gas station. In 2008, the oil won't be there." (p.186)

Table 47 The Future of Petroleum: Information Base (Pages 339 to 358)

No.	Information Source	Core Statement	Indicators and Signals	References and Remarks
		• Possible new oil fields: South China Sea – high exploration and drilling costs. • Discussion of "Hubbert's Peak" – what methods deliver optimal results? • Alternatives: geothermal, nuclear, solar, and wind energy.		"In a sense, the oil crises of the 1970s and 1980s were a laboratory test." (p.10)
6	Study "The Energy Review" Cabinet Office, UK 2002	• Energy policy in the UK: challenges, certainties, scenarios, trends ... • Focus of future policy should include: attaching high priority to energy security (sufficient availability of energy); ensuring long-term perspective; increasing investments in the energy sector; promoting of innovations and greater efficiency in the area of environmental protection. • 5 scenarios were drafted: world markets, business as usual, global sustainability, provincial enterprise and local stewardship. • 2050 will be characterized by energy services, focus on carbon dioxide reduction, a wide array of fuels is available, no hydrogen economy. • Not very much will change by 2020, oil will remain number 1 (80% imported).	• Extensive study (218 pages) commissioned by the UK government. • Contains medium (2020) and long-term (2050) scenarios.	"The future context for energy policy will be different." "Are there enough reserves globally to meet the UK's potential demand?"
7	Book Rifkin, Jeremy: "When there is no more oil ... the hydrogen economy" 2002	• Most of the book is a description of the role played by energy in civilization and development, oil dependency and the "Islamic wildcard." • Only around 30 pages are actually devoted to the hydrogen revolution. • Hydrogen and fuel cells are described as a new economic revolution (trade, social matters, political matters). • What triggers the revolution is the world's dependency on oil reserves in the Middle East.	• Hydrogen is proposed as an alternative to petroleum. The problem, however, is that hydrogen is an energy carrier and not a primary source of energy.	Euphoric tone. Danger of hype! "The next great economic revolution?"
8	Book Rethfeld, Robert; Singer, Klaus: "Worldviews and Broad Views, a Look at the Future of the World's Economy" 2004	• Snapshot of the world's current state – view of further development. • Treatment of the following subjects: progress, climate, environment, economy, finance, society, world politics, democracy, high culture, wave theory, etc. • In addition to global connections, one chapter is devoted to the subject of fossil fuels and their limited supply. • Population growth, projection of future population declines. • Petroleum is the most coveted of fossil fuels. • Assuming a continuation of current trends, a continuous decline in living standards may begin in the next 50 to 100 years ("The Limits of Growth"). Cause: depletion of energy reserves. • 80% of the available reserves are located in a single region that extends from the Caspian Sea to the Persian Gulf (gas, petroleum, coal). • The largest oil fields are located in the Middle East (old finds). • 80 million barrels are currently produced every day. The demand in the year 2050 will be around 120 million barrels a day. • The increasing scarcity of petroleum will inspire the oil-producing countries to attempt to secure control over energy. • Population increases and increasing wealth will soon lead to a depletion of fossil fuels.	• Attempt at a holistic examination of the development of the world, including many issues. • 2 scenarios: each author presents a scenario that is considered probable. • Description of connections and dependencies	Experts suggest that the "limits of growth" for the fossil fuels petroleum and gas have nearly been reached; significant production increases can already be ruled out.

Table 47 The Future of Petroleum: Information Base (Pages 339 to 358)

No.	Information Source	Core Statement	Indicators and Signals	References and Remarks
9	Magazine Mare; Oil, Fuel for Myths and Motors: "The Impure Conscience" April 1, 2004	• Oil catastrophes destroy the environment and living creatures (environmentally hazardous, destructive impact on nature, sea birds and ocean dwellers). • Oil testing: consistency, temperature, composition.	• Side effects of petroleum • Destruction of the environment	
10	Magazine Mare; Oil, Fuel for Myths and Motors: "The Treasure from the Jura Lake" April 1, 2004	• History of petroleum. • Sandstone: mushroom-shaped salt mines that contain vast amounts of oil (10 to 20%). • The large oil fields were discovered quickly. At the moment, it seems that only small fields remain. • The newest technology enables one to extract the last drops from the storage facilities.	• Reporting from the Shetland Islands – largest North Sea oil fields	Cross-section illustrations Oil platforms
11	Magazine Mare; Oil, Fuel for Myths and Motors: "The Friendly Bacteria" April 1, 2004	• Thought experiment: our oil reserves are endangered by microorganisms (globacter benevolens) that feed on the valuable raw material deep under the surface of the earth. • Petroleum: highly toxic substance. One is required to either fight oil spills or build double-layered tankers.	• Thought experiment: microorganisms feed on petroleum, just as they do after oil spills. • Idea based on the novel "Sexy Sons" (Kegel, B.).	
12	Magazine Mare; Oil, Fuel for Myths and Motors: "Sparks Over the Fuel Reserves" April 1, 2004	• Caspian Sea: discovery of new oil reserves of > 1 billion tons, "Golf of the 21st Century." • Interested parties: Russia and energy-hungry China. • The oil is located miles below the surface + inferior quality + tectonic phenomena to consider. • Sea is located on the strategic ellipse, which ranges from the Persian Gulf, the Caucasus and Central Asia to the Bering Sea and contains 3/4 of the world's oil and gas deposits. • The various oil and gas pipeline projects.	• New oil field discovered. • Initial estimates: 200 billion barrels • Realistic estimates: < 35 billion barrels • Great political tension among countries and oil companies.	Map: Caspian Sea and the oil pipelines
13	Book Peterson, Peter G.: "Running on Empty" 2004	• The USA is the world's largest debtor. • The financial future of the USA turns into a threat for future generations.	• Description of the desolate financial situation of the USA	
14	Study International Energy Agency, "World Energy Outlook 2004" 2004	• Extensive energy-related statistics and projections to the year 2030. • Analysis of oil price phenomenon. • Russia as an emerging energy super power. • Alternatives for a sustainable energy supply. • Relationship between energy use and development. • Energy resources are sufficient; everything is a matter of price. • Oil market outlook (Chapter 3). • Demand for oil increases 1.6% per year to 121 million barrels a day in 2030. • "Peak oil" in the year 2030. • Challenge = energy security => urgent political measures to be taken. • High oil price case: $35 per barrel! (the current price is more than $70) – need is 15% less than projected.	• IEA is a political organization – part of OECD, active in the capacity of an observer and consultant in 26 of the 30 OECD countries. • Very optimistic. • CO_2 emissions will increase 60% by 2030.	"New energy investments will cost over $ 500 billion per year." Many diagrams, tables, maps and statistics.

Table 47 The Future of Petroleum: Information Base (Pages 339 to 358)

No.	Information Source	Core Statement	Indicators and Signals	References and Remarks
		• Outlook for gas, coal, electricity needs, renewable sources of energy. • Energy trends and regional differences (Russia: Chapter 9).		
15	Magazine Greenpeace Magazine "The Dirtiest Business in the World: Exploiting the Last Oil Reserves" April-May 2005	• Environmental damage: oil spills and climate change. • Differing opinions about available reserves. • Problem: increasing demand and declining reserves. • Environmental pollution (e.g. Alaska). • Oil industry is in an increasingly desperate situation. • Search for new reserves has become more difficult and large finds are no longer expected. • Daily global need = 82.4 million barrels! • Peak = maximum production capacity (between 2015 and 2020). • Many countries remain poor despite considerable resources. • Petroleum has diverse applications: furniture, fittings, bitumen, synthetic fertilizers, detergents, drugs, fertilizers, etc (50% is used for fuel). • Oil companies and U.S. government have different opinions about the future of petroleum. • Consequences: greenhouse gas effect is to be considered => catastrophic climate change.	• Consideration of various aspects of petroleum (from the perspective of the environmental organization!): exploration, drilling, transport, consumption and balance. • Even if there were enough petroleum, that would be bad news for the planet! • Every year the world burns as much oil as it took nature one million years to create.	"It was the biggest party the world ever saw. Now, the oil party is coming to an end and we can expect a big hangover." Diagrams and maps (based on Exxon, BP, IEA)
16	Study GBN "The Future of Energy: A Flawed Consensus" March 11, 2006	The various consequences of oil scarcity in case alternatives are not secured by the time the oil runs out: • Change and drop in living standards • Increased demand for coal and gas => increase in prices • Increasing price of petroleum • Declining competitiveness of dependent countries • Conflicts between countries	• GBN Global Business Network: futurists • Difference between supply and demand • Surprising consequences of oil scarcity	www.gbn.com Video web conference "Perspective of the Future" Diagrams and scenarios
17	Magazine National Geographic "What Comes After Oil?" August 2005	• Researchers around the world are looking for alternatives to oil as a source of energy. Germany has assumed a leading role in the development. • The experts suggest that oil will last for another 30 years. • Oil regions from the Persian Gulf to Nigeria and Venezuela are politically unstable. • Alternative: gas = scarcity, coal = finite resources, tar sand and oil shale reserves = small amounts, coal power plants without carbon dioxide emissions = technological utopia, solar power = depends on weather => time to step up our efforts to find the next fuel. • Possible alternatives: renewable sources of energy, agricultural products and atomic energy (inexhaustible and emission-free). • When the reserves of coal, oil and gas are depleted, there will be no (adequate) replacement in sight by which to maintain current living standards. • All forms of energy are associated with advantages and disadvantages. There is no ideal form of energy: fossil: cheap, but CO_2; alternatives: expensive, but sustainable.	• Popular science investigation of the subject of petroleum. • Many compelling comparisons (e.g. use) • Global energy consumption per day: 320 billion kwh • CO_2 emissions 2002: 2.6 billion tons, 2030: 4.2 billion tons (assuming constant development)	"We save 225 kilograms of coal for every light bulb that is replaced by an energy-saving light bulb." "One would have to double the extent of existing cultivation to run all of the world's vehicles on biodiesel."

Table 47 The Future of Petroleum: Information Base (Pages 339 to 358)

No.	Information Source	Core Statement	Indicators and Signals	References and Remarks
18	Magazine SZ – Knowledge "The Search for the Last Drop" January 2005	• Debate among oil experts: from pessimistic to optimistic. • The end of cheap oil results in monumental changes in the world's economy. • Technological advances fail to satisfy the growing demand for petroleum – improved mining techniques and increased energy efficiency can only slow consumption. • The economy is dependent on oil, which covers an estimated 35% of our energy needs. • Continuously increasing demand leads to higher prices. • "Extent" as an expression of remaining reserves is illusory because the data are based on current supply and demand, which is subject to change. • Reference: 41 to 48 years (including oil sand). • Peak sometime between 2008 and 2020 – followed by an escalation in tension. • Are non-conventional oil sources (sand, shale and heavy oil) sufficient?	• Article addresses the question of the extent of supplies and presents arguments of optimists (oil companies, IEA, American Geological Agency) and pessimists. • Technological progress is limited and can only delay the end of oil. • Environmental damage increases along with enhanced technology.	"The gap between supply and demand will widen by 2020 at the latest – with extreme consequences for the world's economy." Diagram of new finds and production – shows that more oil has been consumed than discovered for the last 20 years.
19	Book Boetius, Henning: "The Hydrogen Shift: A New Form of Energy Supply" 2005	• Energy as civilization indicator: increases in societal development are tied to higher demand for energy. • The transitions between energy carrier eras were always associated with tremendous social tension and an enormous boost in technology. • The hydrogen economy will replace the oil and gas economy => more effective, economical and environmentally friendly. • Description of how hydrogen is produced and how a future hydrogen economy might work. • Hydrogen: production, transport, hazards, fuel cells, advantages & disadvantages of the hydrogen economy. • Fuel-cell technology. • It is clear that existing petroleum reserves are finite and that the end of petroleum will have an impact on all areas of life.	Reserves: • "Fossil Lobby": 50 to 100 years • "Experts": 10 to 20 years • Iceland as a model: fossil fuel independence in 10 years? • Very visionary. Just where the hydrogen is to come from is not explained.	"At some time in the foreseeable future, we will witness a growing hydrogen economy and a declining oil and gas industry."
20	Book Preuß, Olaf: "Energy for the Future" 2005	• The limits of today's energy economy, potential and problems of individual energy carriers and how an energy shift could happen. • Gas: less damaging to the environment, versatile, increasing demand, Europe draws more than 1/3 of its need from Russia (gas world power). • Oil: 2/3 of reserves are in the Persian Gulf, world consumption: 82 million barrels per day (2004). • Atomic energy accounts for 17% of world electrical production. • Coal: coal reserves are expected to last another 180 to 200 years, trend towards clean coal-based energy without CO_2. • Renewable sources of energy: low economic feasibility, but tremendous potential. • Long transport routes and complex transformation processes take away 2/3 of the power of oil, coal and gas. • Increased gas imports from Russia => dependency (unstable country), 2/3 of all petroleum reserves are in unsafe/unstable countries. • Increasing demand from China and India.	• Good overview of the current state of energy supply – limited. • Sustainability requires the commitment of consumers. • Scarcity will reintroduce the subject of efficiency and thrift.	"Our energy supply will not suffice for the future." "One of the most important sources of energy in the future is called: energy conservation."

Table 47 The Future of Petroleum: Information Base (Pages 339 to 358)

No.	Information Source	Core Statement	Indicators and Signals	References and Remarks
21	Book Seifert, Thomas: "The Black Book of Oil" 2005	• Description of how petroleum, the global economy and power politics are related, why the major powers are directing their attention to new locations, and what alternative energy carriers will come into question. • The oil era is coming to a close, 50% of global reserves have been depleted, and we have already gone over the peak. • Little hope for the discovery of new reserves, Canadian oil sand reserves are finite, overestimation of reserves in OPEC countries. • Increasing demand for oil: China the "hungry dragon" (6 million barrels per day), China's energy need is increasing twice as fast as the Chinese economy. • Alternatives: fuel cells (not before 2020), hybrid (=saving), gas-to-liquid (synthetic fuel made from gas), biogas, energy saving.	• Very polemic – a typical example of the "patchwork publishing" genre. • Countries without oil enjoy higher degrees of democracy. • The energy demand in China is increasing twice as fast as its economy.	"The sun and wind can not be as easily monopolized as an oil field." Oil is "nothing other than a highly concentrated, viscous instrument of power."
22	Online document Brown, Jim: "Profiting from the Coming Oil Crisis" 2005	• Existence of oil > consumption of oil (temporally). • Oil exists only in a few geological types. • Earlier: primary technology is used to produce oil. Today: complex technology used to find oil in difficult zones. • Most reserves (including the most important) have already been discovered. • Increasing demand, declining production, higher costs, increasing price => discrepancy between supply and demand. Demand increases at a slower rate than expected on account of economic turndown. • Lack of new types of energy. • World dependency on Saudi Arabia and OPEC. • Hubbert's peak scenario (U.S.). • U.S. consumption: 22 barrels per person – representing only 5% of the world's population, it consumes 26% of available oil. China consumption: 1.6 barrels. • "Global peak will not peak over the projection period 2003-2030 as long as the necessary investments in supply infrastructure are made." • Peak oil is expected between 2030 and 2050 => very grave consequences for the global economy. • Possibility of a new oil crisis. • Oil production will double by 2030. • 3 scenarios, 1 difference = the time. • Oil: 95% transport, 40% trade energy (percentage). • Analyses from USGS, Shell, BP, Exxon.	• Analysis of a finance expert • Metastudy: analyzes many sources of information, many quotes and posing of critical questions. • New capacities cost between $3,000 and $6,000 per "daily barrel." • Huge investments will be necessary to meet the increasing demand.	www.100dollaroil. com A number of diagrams – usually from other sources of information
23	Online article SAM Sprott Asset Management, Inc. "Market at a Glance: A Crude Awakening" August 22, 2005	• Problem of peak oil: declining oil reserves, increasing global demand (insatiable demand), end of cheap energy, increasing price, population growth and few resources, etc. • After peak oil => back to the Stone Age, the oil era is a short span in the history of human beings. • Technological advances are largely based on cheap energy: oil. • Globalization will revert to localization. • The world is not prepared for this phase of regress.	• Interesting article – represents the development of civilization in connection with petroleum in an evolutionary dimension. • Demand for oil follows market principles.	http://www.sprott. com/pdf/marketsata glance/08-22-2005.pdf Diagram: "The Short Span of Industrial Civilization" "... the world is, for the most part, clueless."

Table 47 The Future of Petroleum: Information Base (Pages 339 to 358)

No.	Information Source	Core Statement	Indicators and Signals	References and Remarks
24	Study Energy Information Administration (EIA): Annual Energy Outlook 2006	• Very extensive study (236 pages), many statistics, trends, issues, regulation. • Forecast based on assumptions relating to growth, supply, demand and price development, is described in the study report. • Includes a comparison to other forecasts.	Long-term energy forecast concerning energy supply and demand.	www.eia.doe.gov/oiaf/aeo/ "... are not statements, of what happens but of what might happen."
25	Article Leng, R. A.: "Implications of the Decline in World Oil Reserves for the Future of Livestock Production" 2005	• Far-reaching impact on the further development of civilization: environmental damage, climate change, lack of water for 60% of humanity by 2025, population growth, etc. • There is a direct connection between cheap oil and cheap food. • Petroleum reserves will not keep pace with demand. • It is not a matter of the end of oil, but the end of cheap oil. • USA produces 5% of the world's oil while using 30%. • Global demand for oil increases every year => fewer resources and increasing oil prices. • Agricultural dependency on oil => necessity of diversification (e.g. biofuels). • There is a connection between the increasing BIP and increasing demand for energy.	• Paradigms • Trend hypotheses	"The greatest issue in the world appears to be how to use oil efficiently from now on." "There is no cheap fix for the energy of the future."
26	Book Goodstein, David: "Out of Gas: The End of the Age of Oil" 2005	• Declines in oil production and increasing consumption => economic crisis. • Modern civilization finds itself without a replacement energy. • Ever more carbon dioxide in the atmosphere. • Decline in the conventional cheap oil. • Inflation.	• Professor at California Institute of Technology • Dilemma	"One certain effect will be steep inflation, because gasoline, along with everything made from petro-chemicals and everything that has to be transported, will suddenly cost more."
27	Magazine Spiegel Spezial: "The Future of the Earth" October 1998	Civilization going full speed ahead: • CO_2 levels in the atmosphere have increased from 270 to 360 ppm in the last 100 years. • An increase of 1.5 ppm per year (current value) "normally" took at least 200 years. • Climate developments are thought to be extremely complex. • Climate-relevant processes can have an impact on one another, decline, increase and, in certain circumstances, also lead to catastrophe – extreme climate changes in the past suggest this is the case.	The analysis is around 10 years old and has largely been confirmed. A number of forecasts were too optimistic.	"Every future has a past." "Climate change impacts the earth like a hammer." "People like to ignore pessimistic forecasts."
28	Magazine Technology Review: "Dirty Oil from Canada" March 3, 2006	• One million barrels of oil are produced per day. Over 80 million are consumed around the world every day. • Around 2 tons of sand is processed to produce 1 barrel of oil. • The reserves are estimated to be around 174 billion barrels. • Estimates suggest that the emission of greenhouse gases is 2 to 3 times higher than in the case of conventional oil production.	Description and documentation showing how oil is extracted from oil sand.	Diagrams and photos
29	Newspaper Financial Times Deutschland: "The Gas Givers" March 17, 2006	• Liquid gas will be the petroleum of the 21st century. • Liquefied natural gas (LNG), gas cooled to a temperature of -162. • More cost-effective than a pipeline beyond a transport distance of 3,000 km.	Liquid gas as an alternative to pipeline transport	"Liquid gas will move from being a niche product to a mass product."

Table 47 The Future of Petroleum: Information Base (Pages 339 to 358)

No.	Information Source	Core Statement	Indicators and Signals	References and Remarks
		• Qatar as driver and exporter. • Liquefaction processes are still relatively costly. • Percentage of overall energy consumption is still minimal.		Diagram: "Distribution of the World's Gas Reserves as of 2005 in %"
30	Financial Times Deutschland: "USA Reconsidering its Energy Mix" March 29, 2006	• U.S. energy supply according to energy carrier: petroleum: 40.2%; gas: 23.0%; coal: 22.4%; nuclear power: 8.3%; bio: 2.7%; hydroelectric: 2.7%; wind, solar, geothermal: 0.5%; other: 0.2% • More dependent on oil than Europe, primarily on account of gasoline consumption. • Pennsylvania is soliciting investments from abroad for the development of alternative sources of energy. • $ 1 billion available.	Alternative sources of energy have arrived in the political arena.	While president Bush would like to see long-term reduction in U.S. oil imports, he says little about his strategy for achieving this.
31	Magazine Technology Review "Goodbye, Hydrogen!" April 2006	• Many individual attempts to develop hydrogen car and bus prototypes • Much enthusiasm (Rifkin – see [7]), little reality. • Hydrogen is a future technology without a future – it could never be competitive. • The Green Party is positive ("The system is great technology"). • Problem: can hydrogen solve the problem of increasing energy consumption and the increasing scarcity of oil? • Where is the revolutionary hydrogen to come from? Many procedures for producing hydrogen – all are elaborate and not sustainable. • Comparison between gasoline and hydrogen: gasoline and diesel engines cost 30 to 40 Euro per kilowatt of engine power. Fuel cells cost 5,000 Euro per kilowatt. • Further problem: hydrogen storage.	Critical examination of hydrogen as the energy of the future. • In order to operate 100% of traffic needs in Germany, one would need three times the current electricity consumption in Germany. • Very unfavorable balance.	"The relevant ministries have already given up their faith in the hydrogen economy and promotion has been reduced to almost zero." "We have no reason to expect fuel cell cars even in 15 to 20 years."
32	Newspaper Financial Times Deutschland: "Gas Pressure" April 25, 2006	• Germany is too dependent on Russian gas supplies. • Energy supply as a tool of political pressure. • A new energy policy is necessary (energy diversification).	35% of gas comes from Gazprom – high dependence.	"We must further diversify our sources of energy."
33	Newspaper Financial Times Deutschland Dossier Renewable Energy: April 28, 2006	• Renewable sources of energy create supply security (economic and environmental) and they strengthen medium-sized enterprises in Germany. • Increasing prices for petroleum, gasoline, gas, electricity. • Growth stimulus for renewable forms of energy. • Renewable forms of energy as a percentage of primary energy consumption in Germany = 4%. • Renewable forms of energy as a percentage of electricity = 10%. • Risks drive oil prices : growing demand (China + USA), crisis on account of the Iranian nuclear program, etc. • Peak oil theory (the zenith of conventional oil production has already been reached). How quickly it will decline remains unclear. • Germany: world leader in technology for renewable forms of energy. • Efficiency: wind power is now profitable: geothermal energy and solar energy will follow. • Energy derived from manure and plant matter will compete with gas.	• Description of various renewable forms of energy. • The giant global need for energy and increasing demand cannot currently be met by renewable forms of energy. • In light of climate change, these represent an important source of hope.	–

Table 47 The Future of Petroleum: Information Base (Pages 339 to 358)

No.	Information Source	Core Statement	Indicators and Signals	References and Remarks
34	Study The Future of the Hydrogen Economy: Bright or Bleak? Bossel, Ulf 2003/2005	• Efficiency of electricity: up to 90%, with hydrogen transformation it sinks to around 30%. • Fuel cells are energy converters, not sources of energy. • Hydrogen production, transport, and storage reduce efficiency. • Use of methanol, gas, etc. is better – hydrogen is not necessary.	• Critical examination of the subject of hydrogen as an alternative for fossil fuels • Physical basis and comparisons	www.efcf.com/reports "For a secure sustainable energy future, mankind needs new energy sources, not new energy carriers."
35	Study Clean Edge: Clean Energy Trends 2006	Trends on the clean energy market: 1: Clean energy is becoming a security issue. 2: Innovations are driving solar. 3: Renewable energies are at the tipping point. 4: Flexible fuels will succeed (larger potential than hybrid technology). 5: China and India join in! (China has the largest potential for wind parks – 2000 GW, leading role in solar-thermal energy). • Data: venture capital investments in the U.S.: 36% energy distribution, 30% intelligent energy production and use, 13% reliability of energy production, 11% new materials, and 11% related services.		http://www.cleanedge.com/reports-trends2006.php "For the first time in modern history, clean-energy technologies are becoming cost-competitive with their 'dirtier' counterparts." "China to Spend $180 Billion to Boost Renewable Energy Use."
36	Le Monde Diplomatique: "L'après-pétrole a déjà commencé" May 1, 2006	• Politicians and experts are aware of the problem with oil. It is time to implement measures to become less dependent on fossil fuels. • Political instability in those countries that are leaders in the energy sector, e.g. the Middle East (oil), Russia (gas). • Price spiking on account of geopolitical factors (political instability in the Middle East, Iranian nuclear program, conflicts in Nigeria, etc.) and a volatile supply and demand ratio. (OPEC: price/barrel: $24.36 (2002), $50.58 (2005), >$75 today). • Demand for oil on the rise: e.g.: China +7.6% in 2003 and +15.8% in 2004. Global consumption: +50% in the next 25 years, i.e. an increase from 83.2 million barrels (2005) to 115.4 million barrels (2030). • Unreliable data on reserves and production capacities (e.g. gap between OPEC and ASPO data on account of assumed constancy despite changed conditions over a long period.) • A lack of investments to establish new capacities. • Political conflicts between countries with high needs and few reserves and oil-rich countries.	Politicians recognize the need for action.	
37	Magazine Technology Review: "The New Twist" May 2006	• New technologies for efficient production: vertically mounted wind rotors. • Efficiency: around 50% (not confirmed). • Cheap production, scalable and deployable in case of strong wind.	Presentation of new technologies for efficient production.	–
38	Study ifp (Institut français du pétrole): "Quels nouveaux paradigmes énergétiques?" May 11, 2006	• Energy needs, the new paradigms, and what is to be done. • Various paradigms in connection with transport.		Diagram: "Demography," "3 Different Paradigms"

Table 47 The Future of Petroleum: Information Base (Pages 339 to 358)

No.	Information Source	Core Statement	Indicators and Signals	References and Remarks
39	Study ifp (Institut français du pétrole): "Quelles réserves de pétrole et de gaz?" May 11, 2006	Reserves, resources, scenarios and consequences.		Diagrams of reserve development
40	Newspaper Financial Times Deutschland, Insert: "Energy of the Future" May 16, 2006	• Upswing for renewable forms of energy on account of European Union law (fixed tariffs). • Renewable energy = high costs. However, owing to the increasing number of facilities and technological innovation, the renewable forms of energy will become ever more cost-effective – in contrast to oil, gas and coal. • Use of renewable forms of energy is not only ecologically sound; it is economically sound (job creation + development of market factor). • 20 to 25% annual growth in the solar branch. • German wind rotor manufacturers = technology and global market leaders. • Electricity production at bioplants has more than doubled since 2004.	• Time is working on behalf of renewable forms of energy. • These are becoming ever more efficient and cost-effective – oil ever more expensive.	"Boom in company startups in the solar branch" "High demand for wind rotors made in Germany" Graphic: "German Energy Balance 2005"
41	Study PoF Energy 2003 "Picture of the Future"	–	–	Internal company documents
42	Study Prognos Energy Report IV: "The Development of the Energy Market to the Year 2030" 2005	• Reference forecast: enables analytic view (whatever that is). • The evaluation of development takes place on the basis of basic conditions and assumptions (resource availability, consumption, price development, technological progress, etc.) • Kyoto obligations will be fulfilled in 2030 (emissions drop by 18.6% since 2002). • Interesting: comparison with other investigations – heterogeneous picture depending on goals, methods and temporal scope is conceded (not neutral!). • Conspicuous: WEA estimates oil price in 2030 to be $35 [2004], Prognos sees $37 [2005]? (see information source [14])	Forecasts of the development of global energy markets	http://www.prognos.ch/pdf/Energiereport%20IV_Kurzfassung_d.pdf "The present reference forecast enables an analytic view of energy market development in Germany up to 2030."
43	Presentation OECD Seiichi, K.: 23rd Oil & Money Conference, London, November 6, 2002	• 62% of increased demand up to 2030 will come from developing countries. • Demand for gas will increase the most. • Oil needs in 2030: around 120 million barrels per day. • High prices will cool demand.	World Economy and Energy Outlook (to 2030)	"Reforms are essential to make markets work."
44	Study U.S. Congress, Office of Technology Assessment: "Energy Technology Choices: Shaping Our Future" 1991	• 6 scenarios – growth, efficiency and alternatives as coordinates: Scenario 1: Baseline Scenario 2: High Growth Scenario 3: Moderate Emphasis on Efficiency Scenario 4: High Emphasis on Efficiency Scenario 5: High Emphasis on Renewable Energy Scenario 6: High Emphasis on Nuclear Power	• Overview (152 pages) of the available energy options – roadmap. • Includes scenarios – Focus 2015. • Scenario 6: 374 new nuclear reactors by 2015!	"Improved technology is a major reason for the present lull in attention to energy."

Table 47 The Future of Petroleum: Information Base (Pages 339 to 358)

No.	Information Source	Core Statement	Indicators and Signals	References and Remarks
45	Book Alt, F.: "War for Oil or Peace for the Sun" 2004	• Regenerative sources of energy solve energy supply problems. • Switch to regenerative sources of energy secures peace. • 90% of petroleum reserves have already been discovered (estimate). • Ever higher costs for exploration, drilling and transport. • Distribution wars over scarce oil have already begun. • Decentralized energy comes with many advantages.	Describes the connection between war, oil and energy supply.	"Global climate change is a test for world politics." "80% of our environmental problems are energy problems."
46	Newspaper Financial Times Deutschland Dossier: "Greenhouse Effect Doubles Its Speed" August 3, 2006	• The effects of global warming will be more dramatic than previously assumed. • Germany, too, will be expected to make infrastructure changes (e.g. power plants). • We are currently experiencing climate change – the earth is warming much faster than previously assumed. • The only solution is to reduce greenhouse gas emissions.	Article based on an interview (?) with Achim Steiner (Head of the U.N.'s Environmental Program).	"Climate is thus no longer a reliable partner for the economy."
47	Study National Energy Policy: Report of the National Energy Policy Development Group 2001	• Increase in demand outstrips the production of energy. • Focus: energy efficiency, environmental protection, efficient infrastructure.	Extensive assessment of current energy situation in the United States.	G.W. Bush: "America must have an energy policy that plans for the future while meeting the needs of today."
48	Newspaper Handelsblatt: "Solar Energy without Silicon" June 1, 2006	• Boom in solar energy. • Petroleum reserves are becoming scarce. • New generation of solar cells that does without silicon.	New technologies.	
49	Newspaper The Independent: Leggett, Jeremy: "What they don't want to you to know about the coming oil crisis" January 20, 2006	• U.S. government estimates that demand will have increased by the year 2025 to 120 million barrels per day and 43 billion barrels per year. • It is doubtful that oil companies will be able to meet this demand. • The United States currently consumes 20 million barrels per day, with 5 million of these coming from the Middle East. • The oil trap is difficult to understand because it is known that oil is a finite resource. • Late toppers: 2 trillion barrels of remaining reserves: oil companies, governments, most financial analysts and economic journalists. • Early toppers: 1 trillion barrels: geologists, small number of journalists. • Just-in-time principles make the economy vulnerable. • Tanker and refinery capacities represent a problem. • Point in time of market realization is referred to as "peak panic point."	• First oil drilling: 1859 • Oil consumption today: more than: 80 million barrels per day 29 billion barrels per year • Since 2003, no oil field has been discovered with more than 500 million barrels (average size)! (Ghawar: 87.5 billion barrels).	"Ninety per cent of all our transportation, whether by land, air or sea, is fuelled by oil. Ninety-five per cent of all our food products require oil use." (p.2)
50	Study Simons & Company International: "Investment Bankers to the Energy Industry"	• Discussion of peak oil. • Refers to the highest level of oil production after which the production rates can only decline (not the end of oil). • Demand will increase to 85 million barrels per day in 2006.	Financial analysts. Analysis of peak oil and petroleum availability.	www.simmonsco-intl.com "21st century's future will hinge on how crisis is addressed."

7.3 The Future of Petroleum – An Information Base

Table 47 The Future of Petroleum: Information Base (Pages 339 to 358)

No.	Information Source	Core Statement	Indicators and Signals	References and Remarks
		• Appeal for data reform because the currently available data do not correspond to reality and distort the situation.		
51	Online Article Swenson, R. "Solar Meets the Peak Oil Challenge" July 2006	[Graph: Oil Supplies curve from 1900 to 2050 showing Growth in Demand, with scenarios: Conservation, Life Style Change, Substitution, Deprivation?] Oil consumption rates will change depending on reaction. • Conservation: higher need, higher efficiency • Life style change: e.g. telecommuting • Substitution: e.g. walking, solar • Deprivation: suffering	• 4 scenarios of the course of energy supply in relation to petroleum • EROEI – energy returned on energy invested: coal: 1: 80 petroleum (1930): 1:120 petroleum (today): 1:25 solar: 1:45 biomass: 1:70 nuclear: 1:17	http://www.hubbertpeak.com/swenson/ Bartlett, R.: "It might seem possible to 'fill the gap' in the short term. However, in the long term, this will be impossible. For one thing, it will hasten the exhaustion of other finite resources. That will make the inevitable transition to renewable sources more difficult and more painful."
52	Study BGR (German Agency for Geological Sciences and Raw Materials) Hannover, Dr. Gerling, Peter, J.: "Petroleum Reserves, Resources and Range" 2004	• Extensive study of the current role of petroleum. • Geology experts suggest that petroleum supply is assured for 1 to 2 decades. • There are numerous uncertainties: reserves, heavy oil, price development, emissions. • Explanations of how reserves are calculated – storage facility parameters. • Estimates of commercially extractable amounts of oil: BGR: 1,172 Giga barrels (GB); Campbell: 871 GB (2002); Oil & Gas Journal: 1,266 GB. • New oil field discoveries have been on the decline since 1960. • A total of 139 GB had been produced by 2004, reserves: around 159 GB, resources: 82 GB. • Testimony of the experts shows significant discrepancies. • Finance sector uses its own gauges. • Percentage of non-conventional oil is increasing – oil sand, heavy oil and shale. • Peak is expected to be reached in 2025.	Neutral examination of current situation and careful forecasts.	www.bgr.de Reserves: technologically and commercially extractable. Resources: proven, either not technically or commercially extractable, or geologically possible, but not proven. Informative diagrams
53	Study BGR: "Reserves, Resources, Availability of Energy Types" 2002	• Examination of current primary energy situation. • Global change and regional developments. • Fossil fuel reserves and renewable sources of energy.	–	–
54	Online Wikipedia	• Peak oil, scenarios, calculation of reserves, questioning of official expectations, consequences for the economy, geopolitical consequences, etc. • While peak oil is already in the past for around 60 countries, the date of global peak oil remains an unknown. • Reality: conventional and unconventional oil. • 96% of the energy consumed for transport comes from petroleum.	• Very extensive source of information with further links. • Neutral, unevaluated information	http://de.wikipedia.org/wiki/Peak_oil

350　　　　　　　　　　　　　　　　　　　　　　　　　　　　7 Learning

Table 47 The Future of Petroleum: Information Base (Pages 339 to 358)

No.	Information Source	Core Statement	Indicators and Signals	References and Remarks
		• Alternatives for home supply, agriculture, synthetics industry … • The 3 largest importers are the United States, China and Japan.		
55	Online Wikipedia: Dossier l impasse énergétique: "Le „peak oil", bombe à retardement du XXe siècle" ("Peak Oil: The 20th Century Time Bomb")	• End of cheap conventional oil. • 4 zones have already gone over the peak: United States, Canada, Venezuela and the North Sea.	Additional details	http://fr.wikipedia.org/wiki/Pic_pétrolier
56	Book/Study Shell Global Scenarios to 2025: "The Future Business Environment: Trends, Trade-offs and Choices" 2005	• The various scenarios for 2025 consider three market aspects: incentives, communities, and coercion and regulation (global business environment). These pursue different goals: efficiency, social cohesion and justice and security. • Three global scenarios are developed: 1) low trust globalization – a legalistic "prove it to me" world 2) open doors: a pragmatic "know me" world 3) flags: a dogmatic "follow me" world. • Many aspects of future development are considered in detail: energy security, climate change, biodiversity, global power situation, productivity and growth, corporations, business, politics, etc. • New oil finds have replaced only 45% of production since 1999 (p.194).	• An attempt to introduce clarity and simplicity to a complex world. • In addition to statements about developments in the energy sector, an extensive view of the future is provided. Very critical and independent of Shell.	"Energy companies, more than most businesses, need to take a long term view." "National decisions made now and in the long-term future will influence the extent of any damage suffered by vulnerable populations and ecosystems later in the century."
57	Study MIT: "The Future of Nuclear Power" 2003	• Nuclear energy is regarded as an option for limiting the greenhouse effect. • Four critical points: cost: too high compared to fossil fuels. Safety: high uncertainty and risk. Waste: long-term storage of atomic waste is a problem. Proliferation: international security regime is unsuitable for proliferation. • Four options for reducing CO_2 emissions: greater efficiency in energy production and use, expanded efforts to tap renewable sources of energy, CO_2 bonding, more nuclear power.	Interdisciplinary study conducted at MIT – investigates the possibilities of nuclear power as an alternative.	http://web.mit.edu/nuclearpower/ "In our view, it would be a mistake at this time to exclude any of these four options […] from an overall carbon emission management strategy."
58	Magazine Spiegel-Spezial: "Struggle for Raw Materials" May 2006	• Biofuel: 1st generation – rape seed oil is scarcely feasible owing to its poor energy balance, 2nd generation – biomass. • Despite efforts in the 1930s to develop alcohol into a commercial fuel, petroleum won out – except for Brazil (40% of fuel need is met by bioethanol). • Biofuel: production corresponds to 1,650 liters of fuel per hectare. • Sunfuel: carbon V procedure for deriving fuel from organic matter; Choren Company: 4,000 liters of SunDiesel per hectare. • Biofuel is the only alternative to petroleum. The electric car has failed. • Methane derived from biomaterials – biomethane is very rich in energy. • Alternative fuels could gradually replace petroleum. There is much current experimentation.	• Examination and discussion of the raw materials situation in the world – from petroleum to diamonds. • The spread of biofuels is being examined by the tax authority, which sees its tax monopoly in danger.	http://www.spiegel.de/spiegelspecial/0,1518,,00.html "In the case of transportation, there are still no effective alternatives to fossil fuels except for biofuels."

Table 47 The Future of Petroleum: Information Base (Pages 339 to 358)

No.	Information Source	Core Statement	Indicators and Signals	References and Remarks
		• Interview with Yergin: oil has not become scarce for the first time, people underestimate technology, cycles of scarcity and surplus are normal. The peak-oil theory is misleading – what will be reached by 2040 or 2050 is much more a plateau. There will be both calculable and incalculable interruptions in supply. • Rebirth of raw materials nationalism and the power of the oil-producing countries. • China: immense need for energy + new players in the global economy. • Question of energy security => diversification of supply and sources + investment in new technologies + securing of pipelines. • Gas and oil develop in tune with the foreign policies of the countries in question.		
59	Newspaper Guardian: "Sweden plans to be world's first oil-free economy" August 2006	• Sweden has become one of the first countries to strive to eliminate its dependence on petroleum – and without building new nuclear plants! • Goal: replace fossil fuels via renewable sources of energy. • And thus become independent of petroleum and fight climate change. • Preparation for peak oil (technologically and mentally). • 32% of energy is derived from petroleum toady – 77% in the year 1977! • The UK and Brazil have great potential in the area of renewable sources of energy (wind and wave power, ethanol from sugarcane).	No other country is as well prepared for peak oil as Sweden.	"The decision to abandon oil puts Sweden at the top of the world green league table."
60	Magazine Technology Review: "Special Report: It's Not Too Late" Articles: "The Messenger" (climate) "The Oil Frontier" (petroleum) "The Dirty Secret" (coal) "The Best Nuclear Option" "Brazil's Bounty" (alcohol) "Redesigning Life to Make Ethanol" "It's Not Too Early" (Big Picture) August 2006	• Climate change can be traced to CO_2 emissions and human activities. • Dilemma: energy demand will double by 2050 leading to a doubling of CO_2 emissions! The rate of climate change will accelerate. • 24% of coal is used for energy and 40% is used for electricity. • Burning coal "generates" the greatest CO_2 emission levels. • Development of "A Super Clean Coal Plant" with zero emissions (USA), integrated gasification combined cycle (IG-CC) – however, the cost is more than that of conventional burning. • It used to be coal gasification in countries that have no available oil. • Nuclear power: alternative for reducing CO_2 emissions and stopping climate change. • Controversial on account of the risk associated with radio-active waste. • Number of nuclear power plants is on the rise. • Ethanol: alcohol as an alternative to oil. Advantage: previously bonded CO_2 will be released. • Search for innovative production process for ethanol. • Search for a practical and competitive ethanol. • Ethanol is produced from biomass and its production is still too expensive (i.e. compared to petroleum). • New methods: bio/genetic engineering to boost efficiency.	• Very extensive treatment of the subject of energy, also in connection with climate change and possible alternatives. • The world uses 13 terawatts of energy, 80% comes from fossil fuels. • In order to come close to maintaining current conditions in the world (climate, sea level, etc.), between 10 and 30 terawatts of power will have to come from CO_2-free sources of energy by 2050! This assumes annual economic growth of 3%. • The time has come for a carbon-free era. • Promotion of a research program on the scale of Apollo.	"It's time to stop waffling so much and say that the greenhouse effect is here and is affecting our climate now." Diagram: relationship between CO_2, average planet temperature and sea levels (p. 40-41)

Table 47 The Future of Petroleum: Information Base (Pages 339 to 358)

No.	Information Source	Core Statement	Indicators and Signals	References and Remarks
61	Book Tetzakian, Peter: "A Thousand Barrels a Second" 2006	• Oil supply is regarded as self-evident (p. 23). • Energy cannot be produced (Helmholtz), it has to be converted. • Development of energy use (history). • Industrial revolution began with James Watt's steam engine. • Energy efficiency. • Possession of oil means power. • Oil versus coal. • Energy roadmaps (p. 176). • Outlook: change in behavior. Transition in 2007/2008. Focus on efficient use. Russia becomes number one oil supplier. • 4 dimensions: cheap, clean, safe, discrete.	• South Korea is becoming independent of oil. • Governments, USA, China • Struggle between businesses, entrepreneurs, individuals • => the largest enterprises were developed in times of great change. • Shift in energy mix.	"Low cost produces win." (p. 233) "... behemoth energy companies like ExxonMobil, Shell, General Electric, and Siemens. These are leaders and entities made their fortunes during the break points of the past, as the world cowered around them. While economies of scale remain important in energy, don't be misled into believing that only titans and giants will thrive in the world of tomorrow. In fact, as with the digital revolution, many fortunes will be made by the smaller players who recognize early on the opportunities of a rapidly evolving new game ..." (pp. 244-245) Energy Evolution Cycle (p. 249)
62	Book Heinberg, Richard: "The Party is Over" 2004	• Can free-market economies avoid a resource war? • "Paradox of Scale": age of fossil fuels – growth is tied to higher energy needs. • Party time: surplus of cheap oil – cause of dependency • Transition: oil is becoming scarce – however, the end of oil has often been predicted. • Successors: petroleum, coal, nuclear power – all have disadvantages. • Last one standing: competition for remaining resources. • Waiting for a magic elixir: false hope, wishful thinking. • Alternatives are non-alternatives (elaborate explanation). • Consequences of energy shortage: financial crises, diminished mobility, hunger.	• Very critical, very gloomy! • Catastrophe: connection between growth, energy, and consumption • There are currently no alternatives to petroleum! No energy carrier, not even regenerative ones, can replace oil! • Many facts! Holistic consideration.	"The increase in agricultural production that was based on cheap energy reserves enabled the feeding of a global population that grew from 1.7 billion to more than 6 billion in a single century."
63	Book Roberts, Paul: "The End of Oil" 2004	• Oil reserves will be effectively depleted in 30 years at the latest. • The world is dominated by energy concerns (p. 5). • The oil industry belongs among the most stable of industries. • Signals of change: oil companies invest in other forms of energy (BP). • Energy system transitions were associated with turbulence in the past => focus should be on energy efficiency instead of more energy. • Energy security. • Developing countries take the easiest path: high environmental pollution. • Energy security will not only become a problem for the developing countries.	Many problems in the hydrocarbon system: • Pollution • Climate • External costs • Discussion of energy-political consequences and connections (1st World – 3rd World)	Proposes an overall cost-benefit analysis and has an idea of how to undertake such an analysis. External – internal costs (p. 275)

Table 47 The Future of Petroleum: Information Base (Pages 339 to 358)

No.	Information Source	Core Statement	Indicators and Signals	References and Remarks
64	Book/Study Glenn, J.C. / Gordon, T.J.: "The State of the Future" 2006	• The starting point consists of 15 global challenges facing civilization (from water supply to disease and criminality). • Essentially 4 scenarios of the future of energy: business as usual – the skeptic environmental backlash high-tech economy – technology pushes off the limits of political turmoil Outlook in scenario 3 – oil reserves (economic and technological)	• Millennium Project at UN University • Annual publication of a report and a calculation of a global and country-specific state of the future index (SOFI). • Interesting scenarios	http://www.acunu.org/millennium/sof2006.html "The World Cup is on TV now, so let's worry about all this tomorrow." (Scenario 1)
65	Magazine Spiegel Online, Traufetter, Gerald: "Sweden Plans Wood Fueled Future" 22.03.2006 and Spiegel 12/2006 Wüst, Ch.: "Wood in the Tank"	• Sweden would like to become independent of oil by 2020. • Regenerative raw materials: wood, grain, sugarcane, etc. Most of these still come from Brazil, the goal is to meet most of one's needs via one's own production. • Volvo, Saab and Ford are pushing the development of flexible fuel vehicles (FFVs) – several fuel alternatives. • Gas as fuel is too complex for tanking.	The only reason that car engines do not run on ethanol is that petroleum was once so cheap.	http://service.spiegel.de/cache/international/spiegel0,1518,406937,00.html "That cars haven't been running on ethanol for a long time is, in fact, simply a historical accident." "In the 1920s, car magnate Henry Ford was in favor of ethanol-powered engines. But the Rockefeller oil dynasty was able to push through the use of gasoline motors."
66	Magazine McKinsey Quarterly: "Securing India's Energy Needs" 2005	• The country's energy needs will increase 40% by 2010. • India imported 70% of its oil supply. • Invests in sources (e.g. in Russia and Sudan). • High investment need.	McKinsey recommends privatization and liberalization => increased competition.	–
67	Magazine McKinsey Quarterly "What Next for Big Oil?" 2004	• Many of the remaining reserves for oil and gas are in countries with a high degree of political instability or where conditions make drilling and excavation difficult (Middle East, Antarctic). • China and India invest large sums in developing new fields. • Oil companies have the technology, money, expertise while countries have the oil. • Many of the oil fields of the 5 biggest producers (ExxonMobil, BP, Royal Dutch Shell, ChevronTexaco, Total) are older and supply less than during peak times. • Increasing production costs (average cost of North Sea production increased 42% between 2000 and 2005). • The average size of new oil-field finds is declining.	• The replacement rate of the major oil companies dropped to below 80% in 2004. • Tough international competition for new sources! • Technological head start for the oil companies.	–

Table 47 The Future of Petroleum: Information Base (Pages 339 to 358)

No.	Information Source	Core Statement	Indicators and Signals	References and Remarks
		• Shell replaced only 15-25% of its production in the year 2004. • State-run oil companies are expanding internationally. • Production capacities dropped from 10 million barrel per day in the ten year period between 1970 and 1980 to 3-5 million barrels per day.		
68	Magazine McKinsey Quarterly: "Meeting China's Energy Needs through Liberalization" 2006	• Energy need is increasing along with affluence. • In addition to an increasing need for petroleum, the need for larger production capacities for refineries and transport is also on the rise. • China is the second largest automobile market (5 million new cars per year). • The number of registered vehicles could increase to 100 million in 2015. • Demand for fuel is expected to increase around 6% per year. • The import of petroleum could increase from its current level of 3 million barrels per day to 10 million barrels per day by 2020 – as much as the U.S. imports today.	• China has invested $15 billion in foreign oil fields since 2001 • => Mc Kinsey proposes liberalization with regard to oil price development and an opening of markets => necessary step, but also increases global demand!	–
69	Online Essay Harding, Gary W. "The Way Things Are Going To Be" 1998	Discussion of energy problems: • Hubbert's peak is reached at 1,600 billion barrels of oil. A total of 900 billion have already been consumed. • Energy costs will increase as soon as the peak has been reached – and not only for oil. • Much capital will flow from developed countries to oil countries.	The approaching dilemma is being denied – for various reasons.	http://members.aol.com/trajcom/private/oilcris.htm "We are not running out of oil, just the cheap and abundant oil that has fueled our recent economic prosperity."
70	Magazine Bild der Wissenschaft: "Energy, Energy, Energy" 10/2005	• Germany is Europe's largest energy market. • Petroleum: 36.4%; gas: 22.4%; hard coal 13.1%; nuclear power 12.6%; brown coal: 11.4%; water: 0.5%; wind: 0.4%; rest: 0.29% (2004). • Very high degree of uncertainty – everything is being discussed. • Energy is also a political arena. • Efficiency: more evolution than revolution. • Interview with Hilmar Rempel on the subject of petroleum (BGR see [52, 53]).	• More status quo in the energy situation in Germany than novelty. • Everything the same, nuclear power is controversial.	"This decoupling of primary energy consumption and economic growth will continue in the future."
71	Book Simmons, Matthew R.: "Twilight in the Desert" 2005	• Investigation of the case of Saudi Arabia. • Detailed compilation of history, politics and oil reports. • Three quarters of Saudi oil comes from 5 large and well-exploited oil fields. • This dependence is concealed by optimistic information policies.	• Reserve estimates are too optimistic! • Investment bankers	–
72	Study DB Research: "Energy Prospects after the Oil Age" 2004	• Energy security is in danger: oil price development, blackouts, etc. • Only broad-based measures can secure energy supply. This must be pushed through both nationally and internationally (e.g. EU). • Energy mix of the future will include a smaller percentage of fossil fuels. • Germany and Europe should have the courage to develop their own energy policies. • Huge need for investment – for modernization and expansion of the energy infrastructure.	• Analysis of possible measures as a reaction to oil scarcity. • Concrete proposals: Energy efficiency, energy conservation, technologies: new generation of power plants.	www.dbresearch.de "Conclusion: it is time to act." "R&D efforts centering on secure power plants (including nuclear energy) and grids, renewable sources of energy and hydrogen are to be developed."

Table 47 The Future of Petroleum: Information Base (Pages 339 to 358)

No.	Information Source	Core Statement	Indicators and Signals	References and Remarks
		• Long-term increases in the price of energy are preprogrammed although the range specifications have always been exceeded. • "Appropriate prices" carry security and environmental conditions.		
73	Study DB Research: "Bioenergy for the Time after Oil" 2005	• Biofuels are no longer niche products. • Promotion can secure a technological head start. • Bioenergy already accounts for 60% of the renewable forms of energy. • Advantage of CO_2 neutrality – reproducible raw materials. • Larger expansion is limited by available agricultural space.	• Description of the advantages and disadvantages of the different forms of bioenergy. • Could increase by 2030 to 10% (today: 2.3%).	www.dbresearch.de "Biofuels would be competitive given the current state of technology at an oil price of $100 per barrel."
74	Magazine Business Week: "The Future of Oil: Four Scenarios" August 8, 2006	• Uncertainty in the Middle East, many conflicts: Iran, Iraq, Israel, Lebanon. • U.S. economy is very sensitive to oil price, more so than before 2005. • More money for energy, increasing inflation and fear of recession. • Scenario 1: Conflict contained Oil price falls despite conflicts to below $60, U.S. economic growth at 2.5%, Europe accelerates, Asia stable. • Scenario 2: Iran shuts taps For various reasons, Iran stops sypplying oil; oil price increases to more than $100, and then stabilizes at $95 before sinking to $66 at the end of 2008. • Scenario 3: The Gulf goes dry Iran closes the Strait of Hormuz to tanker transit. World deliveries fall by 20%. Oil price increases to more than $250, world recession as in 1980. U.S. inflation at 10%, economy shrinks by 5.2%. • Scenario 4: The US gets off Embargo against the US, but it does not last for long. Impact remains minimal.	• BW and Standard & Poor's analyze oil price development and its impact on the U.S. economy with the help of 4 scenarios. • Scope: up to 2008, only U.S. • Typical wish scenario: scenario 1 is the best and most likely – let's hope that this one really comes. • Interesting: the estimate of vulnerability of oil supply.	www.businessweek.com/investor/content/aug2006/pi20060808_648271.htm "Again, worse cases than any of these are entirely possible, with resulting impacts on the U.S. and world economy that are nearly impossible to model. The best hope is for a diplomatic breakthrough – and a little luck – to help limit the outcome to Scenario One."
75	Chapter Cordeiro, J.L.: "Energy 2020: A Vision of the Future" WFS August 28, 2006 "Creating Global Strategies for Humanity's Future"	• Optimistic outlook concerning petroleum. • Nearly 4 trillion barrels in oil reserves including conventional oil, Arctic oil, heavy oil, shale and oil sand. • The end of oil has been predicted five times in the past: 1880, after WWI, after WWII, 1970 (oil crisis) and around 2000. • Stronger increase in gas as a source of energy, decline in nuclear energy. • A new energy source – no specifications here – will emerge by 2020. • An energy Internet will arise and bioenergy will play an important role. • Bacterium "petroleum artificiali" generates fuel from CO_2 and H_2O.	Interesting vision – the earth has enough energy, what is missing is the right technology.	"The earth, the sun, the galaxy, and the universe have more than enough energy resources to power our civilization for the following decades, centuries, and millennia. With enough technology, it is basically a matter of costs and priorities."
76	Online Source British Petrol		Carbon footprint calculator	www.bp.com
77	Online Source: Royal Dutch Shell	• The large oil companies control only a small percent of the crude oil market. • World production in 2005 was 83.80 million barrels per day.	Activities in the area of hydrogen, solar and wind	www.shell.com

Table 47 The Future of Petroleum: Information Base (Pages 339 to 358)

No.	Information Source	Core Statement	Indicators and Signals	References and Remarks
		• Of this, Shell produced 2.14 million, ExxonMobil 2.54 million, BP 2.59 million, Chevron 1.79 million, Total 1.66 million (Total: 10.72 million barrels per day). • OPEC produced around 33 million barrels per day. • The rest produced around 40 million barrels per day.		
78	Online Source: Total	Pursuing technological advances.		www.total.com
79	Online Source ChevronTexaco			www.chevron.com
80	Online Source ExxonMobil	Report: The Outlook for Energy – A View to 2030.	• Exxon drafts an annual long-term forecast – contains data on the global economy and energy needs. • Works together with IEA and U.S. Department of Energy.	www.exxon.com "We will need approximately 60% more energy in 2030 than in 2000."
81	Online Source Esso	• Many reports, studies and statistics available, e.g.: Oildorado 2005, energy trends, energy forecast 2003. • Oil and gas will remain the most important sources of primary energy until 2020. • Investments made by the oil and gas industry come in at an annual $200 billion. • Comparison with its competitors.	• Consumption increase 2005: 120 million tons • Reserve increase 2005: 1,600 million tons	www.esso.de "Energy demand is very high around the world and continues to grow. Meeting this demand represents a major challenge."
82	Intergovernmental Panel of Climate Change (IPCC): 4th Assessment Report	Scenarios of climate change:		"The atmospheric concentration of carbon dioxide in 2005 exceeds by far the natural range over the last 650,000 years (180 to 300 ppm) as determined from ice cores." http://www.ipcc.ch/index.html http://www.ipcc.ch/SPM2feb07.pdf
83	Book Rahmstorf, S.; Schellnhuber, H.: Climate Change	Climate change: overview of research, consequences and possible solutions.		
84	Study Tyndall – Center for Climate Change Research: Linking Air Pollution with Climate Change. 2007	Outlook to 2020: Compared to 1995, potential for reducing CO_2 emissions is seen in the areas of "power generation," "field combustion" and "residential" whereas the volume related to "transport" will quadruple!		http://tyndall.webapp1.uea.ac.uk/publications/tech_reports/tr53.pdf

7.3 The Future of Petroleum – An Information Base

Table 47 The Future of Petroleum: Information Base (Pages 339 to 358)

No.	Information Source	Core Statement	Indicators and Signals	References and Remarks
85	Book Kara Mikko, et.al.: Energy Visions for 2030 for Finland VTT EDITA Helsinki 2003	Contains 3 scenarios for Finland 2030: Kyoto: orientation on Kyoto Protocol / Save: focus on energy conservation / Technology: technological solutions for the problems	Very detailed description of the situation, alternatives, technologies and prospects (refers largely to Finland).	"In the Kyoto-Scenario the total amount of emissions is not very much reduced after the year 2010, whereas in the Save and Technology scenarios the longer-term goal of an additional 20% reduction is reached."

7.4 Compression and Operation

The present information base is the result of extensive research. However, despite its relatively broad scope, the information base is no where near complete. Heterogeneous sources of information were intentionally selected in the interest of increasing diversity and accounting for many perspectives and interest groups.

When conducting research, one soon determines that certain data – for instance, concerning oil reserves (see Figures 148 and 149) – begin to repeat themselves and that these can probably be traced to the same source. The task at hand now is to process the gathered information so that it can be used. It is apparent that interest in the subject is

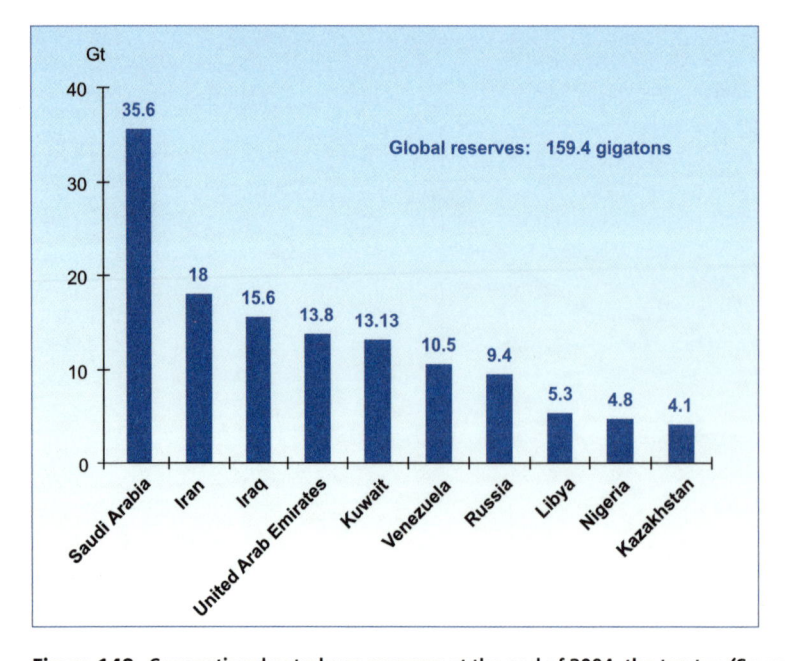

Figure 148 Conventional petroleum reserves at the end of 2004: the top ten (Source: BP)

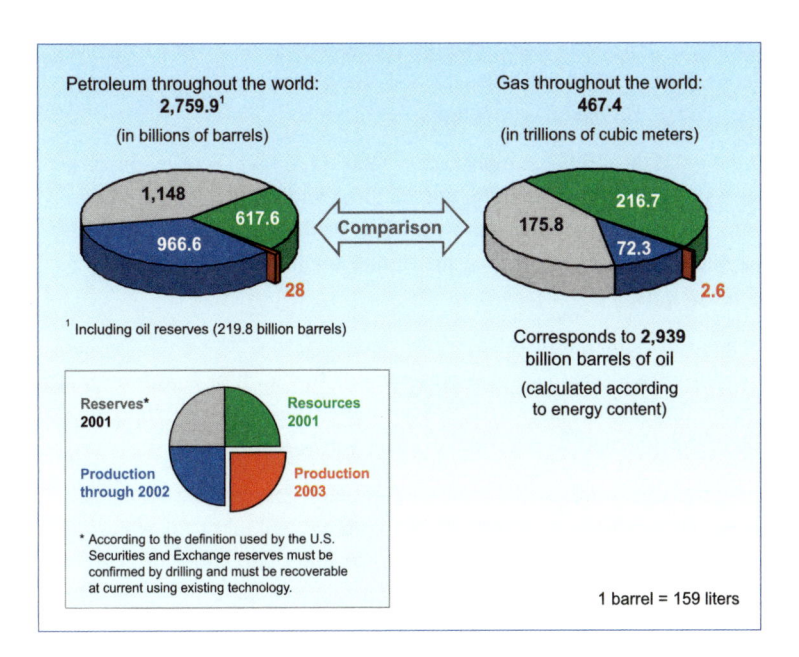

Figure 149 An overview of energy reserves: more gas than oil
(Source: SZ-Knowledge, January 2005: "The Search for the Last Drop")

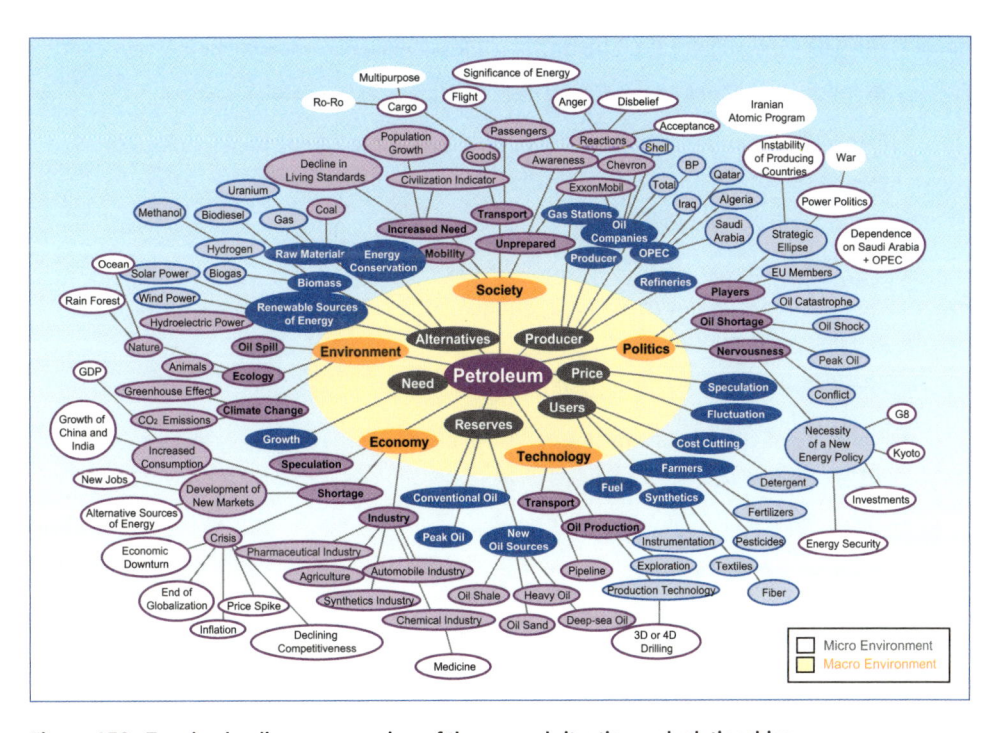

Figure 150 Trend radar diagram: overview of the general situation and relationships

7.4 Compression and Operation

growing – at all levels of society. The notion that it is time to act has reached a high level of general acceptance. That being said, however, it is also apparent that a number of governments continue to be untroubled by the future.

Having examined the material and the compilation in Table 47, one is faced by the challenge of sorting and structuring the disparate, unstructured and to some extent contradictory information. The representation of the elements in the radar diagram (Figure 150) can help one get a start with the task of structuring the information according to segments and degree of impact.

The radar diagram helps to highlight the relationships between the items (as represented by the lines). However, the special advantage presented by this form of representation emerges during its drafting. Signals and trends are positioned, discussed and then repositioned. The result offers help both in terms of structure and orientation.

The following hypotheses were developed using the information base in Table 47. As mentioned above, the information is assigned (and thereby compressed) to the following five categories: paradigms, trends, contradictions, uncertainties and chaos and wildcards (cf. Figure 41). The standard approach will be used for the present example (cf. Section 4.8).

Paradigms: Constants, Facts and Assumptions that Qualify as Certain

What information qualifies as certain and can be referred to
as a matter of fact or paradigm?

- The earth's reserves of fossil fuels, and petroleum in particular, are finite.
- When used, all forms of energy will have an impact on the environment.
- Petroleum currently accounts for more than 90% of the energy used for mobility and transport!
- The burning of fossil fuels releases CO_2 – a greenhouse gas that leads to global warming.
- The selection of energy sources will continue in the future to be determined by costs and not by the principles of reason.
- Private and societal wealth depends on the availability of energy.
- The forms of energy that we typically use in our daily lives essentially include electricity (electrons) and fuels (molecules).
- Dependence on petroleum is unmistakable.
- The three largest importers of petroleum are the United States, China and Japan.
- The convenient accessibility of cheap energy drives progress and productivity.
- The supply of petroleum is prone to disruption and markets are accordingly volatile.
- While hydrogen is regarded as an *energy source* of the future, it is merely an *energy carrier* – it will thus not play a significant role in the future of petroleum.

- There are numerous applications for petroleum.
- It took around 100 million years for nature to create the world's petroleum reserves – it will take less than 200 years to deplete these reserves (CO_2 emissions!).
- 80% of all petroleum reserves are located in what is referred to as the "strategic ellipse" (cf. Figure 147).

Trends: Changes That Take a Certain Direction

What will change in the current situation? What will be the causes and drivers?
Do any patterns emerge?

- Energy needs (electricity, fuel) are increasing (although at different rates in different regions).
- The price of energy and petroleum will increase in the long run owing to increasing demand.
- Technological advances enable more effective recovery of petroleum and more efficient use of energy.
- The search for and the recovery of petroleum is becoming ever more elaborate.
- The percentage of overall consumption that is accounted for by alternative forms of energy is (slowly) increasing.
- The dependence of the industrialized countries on imported oil will continue to increase (assuming constant behavior and rates of growth).
- The cost of maintaining energy security will increase.
- In addition to the traditional sources of oil (crude oil), oil sand and shale are playing a bigger role.

Contradictions: Cannot Be Completely Settled

What contradictions are contained in the available information?

- Conflicting statements about petroleum reserves (intentional or unintentional).
- Date of peak oil – between 2005 and 2040.
- Energy awareness – conservation and wastefulness (increasing average miles per gallon for cars in the United States).
- Climate awareness and environmental awareness – "Tragedy of the Commons" dilemma of divergent vectors of self interest: one's individual interest and those of society and the world at large.
- Large discrepancies among data on capacities and possibilities of expanding production of fuels.

- The issue of the availability of alternative forms of energy – as a substitute for petroleum – is largely unsettled.
- The attempt to prevent climate change (e.g. by storing CO_2) is another attempt to solve problems with technology. This would seem to contravene long-term climate protection – which requires a radical reconsideration of the matter. History has often shown that the technological solutions of today are the problems of tomorrow.

Uncertainties: Multiple Possible Versions of Development

What are the uncertain factors that can be expected to determine development?

- Will society remain focused on short-term economic success or long-term development in the energy sector? (Will the world be influenced by a bad conscience?)
- Political activities: provisions and reactions?
- Economic development in the face of dependence and uncertainty?
- Alternative forms of energy: availability and mass deployment?
- Power shift at the global level: will Russia become a new world power owing to its energy reserves?
- The role of petroleum: increasing dependence or the beginning of independence?
- Assessment of the energy situation by business and political leaders?
- Further development of globalization: will worldwide resource procurement be based on the lowest cost and optimal availability?
- Will oil companies be able to reinforce their power and assert themselves in the face of political and societal pressure?
- Will the opportunities that arise on account of uncertainty in the energy sector lead to innovation and to new forms of energy?
- What role will human reason play at a global level (humans regard themselves as intelligent creatures)?

Chaos/Wildcards: Surprises, Development Breaches and Radical Changes

What surprises and development breaches could lead to radical changes and disruptions?

- Natural catastrophes of all kinds.
- Wars, violence, terror – in relation to resources and reserves.
- Abrupt stop in oil delivery.
- Reduction in reserves (e.g. owing to microorganisms).
- Sudden climate changes (Gulf Stream) with a significant impact on our way of life.
- Financial market crises and stock market turbulence.

- Discovery of the new super energy – cheap and with no known impact on the environment.
- Changed business models that lead to other requirements and uses of energy.
- Radical societal changes.

Table 48 Compressed and Verified Theories Concerning the Future of Petroleum

Paradigms and Constants	Trends	Contradictions	Uncertainties	Chaos and Wildcards
P1: The world's fossil fuel reserves (petroleum) are finite. **P2:** Oil offers a diverse range of applications (fuel, synthetics, textiles, pesticides, pharmaceutical products). **P3:** It took nature around 100 million years to create the world's petroleum reserves. Their depletion will take less than 200 years (CO_2 emissions). **P4:** The supply of petroleum is prone to disruption and markets are accordingly volatile. **P5:** The "strategic ellipse" accounts for 80% of global reserves (gas, petroleum, coal). **P6:** The 3 biggest importers of oil are the United States, China and Japan. **P7:** There is a vital link between technological progress, population growth, GDP, living standards and the availability of energy (oil). **P8:** Petroleum accounts for 90% of the energy used for mobility and transport.	**T1:** Energy needs and consumption are increasing, especially in developing countries. **T2:** The price of petroleum will continue to rise along with the rise in demand. **T3:** Alternative sources are gaining in significance (gas, nuclear, solar, bio, etc). **T4:** Dependence on petroleum continues to rise. **T5:** Instability in many petroleum rich countries and regions continues to rise. **T6:** Climate change (temperature increases linked to CO_2 emissions) and other environmental consequences are becoming more pronounced (hurricanes, extreme weather). **T7:** The cost of maintaining energy security is increasing. **T8:** Drilling and recovery conditions have become more difficult and expensive. **T9:** Technological advances and improved methods of recovery are compensating for some production losses. **T10:** Nervousness relating to availability is increasing.	**W1:** Conflicting statements about remaining petroleum reserves. **W2:** Conflicting statements about the speed with which alternative sources of energy will be available (solar, wind, nuclear, ecological solutions, other). **W3:** Peak oil: Hubbert's Peak – conflicting statements about the time it will take to reach the peak. **W4:** Our awareness and concern about energy is increasing, but there is also blindness to the issue. **W5:** Conflicting statements about the development oil demand. **W6:** Conflicting statements about refineries and oil production capacities. **W7:** Conflicting private and societal interests.	**U1:** Are alternatives available and can these compensate for shortfalls? **U2:** What form will the transition to a post-oil era take and what will be its effects? **U3:** What impact will a significant energy scarcity have on living standards? **U4:** Will the globalization paradigm (low wages and low transport costs) be reversed? **U5:** What impact will political activities have on further development? **U6:** What will be the reaction of the various industries (energy-dependent industries)? Will we see alternative materials and products? What will be the impact on economic development? **U7:** How will economies develop in the face of dependence and uncertainty? **U8:** Will new economic and geopolitical power centers emerge? **U9:** How will the price of petroleum develop in the face of changing demand? **U10:** Will innovative enterprises be able to seize the opportunities associated with an uncertain energy situation?	**C1:** Microorganisms "consume" oil reserves. **C2:** Impact of shortfalls on industry and civilization. **C3:** Collective awareness and behavior (1st world vs. 3rd world?). **C4:** War, violence and terror in connection with remaining resources. **C5:** Natural catastrophes of all kinds. **C6:** Climate shock and its effects. **C7:** Abrupt stop in oil delivery. **C8:** Discovery of a "super" energy.

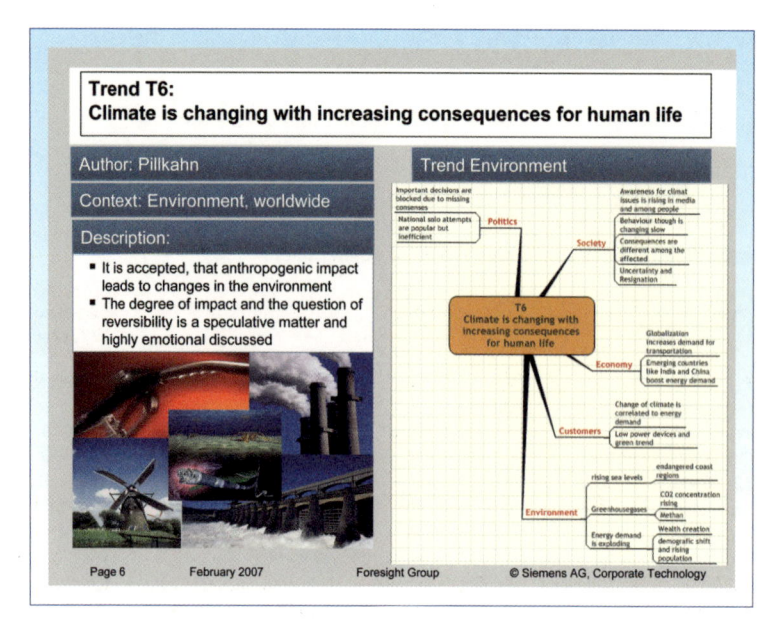

Figure 151 Trend: climate change

Thorough research becomes especially necessary when a lack of clarity results while developing the elements from the hypotheses. Experience shows that it is helpful to complete a detailed analysis for each of the featured hypotheses. This ensures a greater degree of clarity and constitutes an investigation of the statements. Figure 151 offers an example.

Those claims that prove to be false or only partially accurate are removed from the list of hypotheses and are not included in the list of elements. This leads to a further compression of the information. Table 48 offers a view of the result.

7.5 Generating Environment Scenarios

As outlined in Chapter 4, the verified hypotheses (the elements of the future) are now used to draft the scenario framework. The individual elements are first evaluated in terms of their uncertainty (or the likelihood of their occurrence) and their potential impact on petroleum supply and the future of petroleum in general (Figure 152).

This is then followed by the investigation of the trends' cross impact using trend-impact analysis (Figure 153). Each of the trends is then investigated to determine its relationship to the other trends. This enables one to identify those trends that can be regarded as actively driving development and those whose behavior is more or less passive. We can infer from the matrix that T6, T8 and T9 are primarily driving the situation (climate change and technological progress) while T2 and T3 (demand and alternatives) are being driven and show no independent momentum. While there are no buffering elements, there is a whole series of ambivalent trends – which can be regarded as a sign of high uncertainty. Figure 153 offers a representation of the active and passive scores. The activity scores that are assigned to the individual elements will be considered later in the context of creating the pictures of the future.

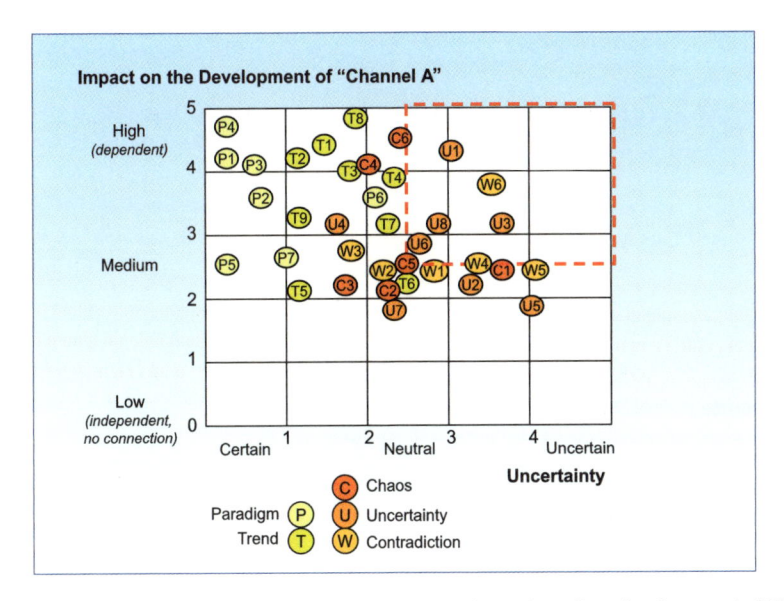

Figure 152 Environment scenario "The Future of Petroleum": evaluation matrix (Wilson matrix)

	T1	T2	T3	T4	T5	T6	T7	T8	T9	T10	Active Score
T1		3	3	3	2	3	3	2	1	2	**22**
T2	0		3	0	3	0	2	0	1	2	11
T3	1	1		0	0	0	2	1	0	0	4
T4	2	2	3		3	2	3	1	1	2	16
T5	0	2	3	0		0	2	1	1	3	13
T6	2	1	3	1	1		1	0	1	2	13
T7	1	2	2	2	2	1		3	2	3	**18**
T8	2	3	3	1	1	0	3		1	2	16
T9	2	1	0	2	1	2	2	2		1	13
T10	3	3	3	3	3	0	2	2	1		**20**
Passive Score	15	**18**	**23**	12	16	8	**20**	12	9	17	

Active: T1 T7 T10
Passive: T2 T3 T7

0 Independent 2 Dependent
1 Slight impact 3 Strong driver

Figure 153 Environment scenario "The Future of Petroleum": trend-impact analysis

7.5 Generating Environment Scenarios 365

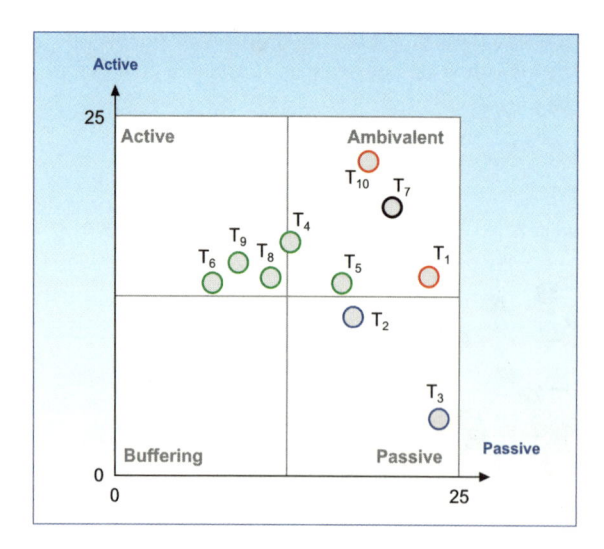

Figure 154 Environment scenario "The Future of Petroleum": representation of the results of the trend-impact analysis

A scenario framework can now be developed based on the compilation in Table 48 and the evaluation (Figure 152). This framework is then used to develop the pictures of the future. Figure 155 shows the process which involves the use of the morphological box, just as it was used in the previous examples.

In what follows, each of the scenario drafts (the compilation of elements, the formulated short scenario and a graphical implementation) is presented in a separate section.

In contrast to the drawings used to illustrate the scenarios of the future of television, collages are used to illustrate the present scenarios of the future of petroleum. Here, it warrants bearing in mind that utility and effectiveness take precedence over beauty. It is essential to express the ideas and core messages.

	W1	W2	W6	U1	U2	U8	C1	C4	Scenarios
a	The abundantly available oil sand represents a new option.	Wind, sun, atoms, and water are available and can to some extent compensate for shortfalls.	Production capacities are just barely sufficient.	While several energy alternatives are available, they are regarded as too expensive.	No more than a gradual transition.	Russia advances to the status of a new super power.	Microorganisms threaten to decimate reserves.	Oil scarcity leads to animosity and wars.	"Empty"
b	Overestimated reserves and production decline.	Hardly any investments in alternative sources because these are regarded as too expensive.	Capacity shortfalls are only temporary.	No alternatives in sight that could entirely replace petroleum.	Shock oil shortage and far-reaching societal disruptions trigger urgent search for alternatives.	China's development comes to a halt.	Protection and guarding of reserves (very costly).	Successful protection of reserves and delivery thanks to the deployment of considerable staff.	"Transition"
c	Improved technology for exploiting sources.	New forms of energy production and storage as a result of intensified research.	Oil-producing countries force scarcity by reducing production.	Partial replacement (e.g. alcohol as a fuel).	Oil-independent countries enjoy economic upswing.	The United States loses geopolitical influence and economic power.	Climate change: CO_2 changes have an impact on petroleum.	Terrorist organizations attempt to disrupt oil supply and trigger chaos.	"Fight"
d	Price fluctuation owing to conflicting accounts of remaining reserves.	Coal regains significance.	The recovery of petroleum becomes so elaborate that it is no longer profitable.	Politically driven active search for and use of alternatives.	Energy users gear up for oil scarcity. Many countries achieve oil independence. World is divided into oil-dependent and oil-independent countries. Demand for oil declines.	After initial difficulties, oil-independent countries begin to flourish.	Not relevant because oil independence has been achieved.	Decline in the economic significance of oil.	"Independence"

Figure 155 Environment scenario "The Future of Petroleum": the scenario framework is developed using the morphological box

7.5.1 Scenario 1: "Empty"

Component	Element	Description
Title	"Empty"	The tank is empty.
Main character		Reporter covering a summit of the European Union
Scene	Press conference	Summit of the European Union
Paradigms, constants	P1	The world's fossil fuel reserves (petroleum) are finite.
	P2	Oil offers a diverse range of applications (fuel, synthetics, textiles, pesticides, pharmaceutical products).
	P3	It took nature around 100 million years to create the world's petroleum reserves. Their depletion will take less than 200 years (CO_2 emissions).
	P4	The supply of petroleum is prone to disruption and markets are accordingly volatile.
	P5	The "strategic ellipse" accounts for 80% of global reserves (gas, petroleum, coal).
	P6	The 3 biggest importers of oil are the United States, China and Japan.
	P7	There is a vital link between technological progress, population growth, GDP, living standards and the availability of energy (oil).
	P8	Petroleum accounts for 90% of the energy used for mobility and transport.
Trends	T1	Energy needs and consumption are increasing, especially in developing countries.
	T2	The price of petroleum will continue to rise along with the rise in demand.
	T3	Alternative sources are gaining in significance (gas, nuclear, solar, bio, etc).
	T4	Dependence on petroleum continues to rise.
	T5	Instability in many petroleum rich countries and regions continues to rise.
	T6	Climate change (temperature increases linked to CO_2 emissions) and other environmental consequences are becoming more pronounced (hurricanes, extreme weather).
	T7	The cost of maintaining energy security is increasing.
	T8	Drilling and recovery conditions have become more difficult and expensive.
	T9	Technological advances and improved methods of recovery are compensating for some production losses.
	T10	Nervousness relating to availability is increasing.
Contradictions	W1b	Overestimated reserves and production decline.
	W2d	Coal regains significance.
	W3	Peak oil: Hubbert's Peak – conflicting statements about the time it will take to reach the peak.
	W4	Our awareness and concern about energy is increasing, but there is also blindness to the issue.
	W5	Conflicting statements about the development oil demand.

Component	Element	Description
	W6d	The recovery of petroleum becomes so elaborate that it is no longer profitable.
	W7	Conflicting private and societal interests.
Uncertainties	U1b	No alternatives in sight that could entirely replace petroleum.
	U2b	Shock oil shortage and far-reaching societal disruptions trigger urgent search for alternatives.
	U3	What impact will a significant energy scarcity have on living standards?
	U4	Will the globalization paradigm (low wages and low transport costs) be reversed?
	U5	What impact will political activities have on further development?
	U6	What will be the reaction of the various industries (energy-dependent industries)? Will we see alternative materials and products? What will be the impact on economic development?
	U7	How will economies develop in the face of dependence and uncertainty?
	U8b	China's development comes to a halt.
	U9	How will the price of petroleum develop in the face of changing demand?
	U10	Will innovative enterprises be able to seize the opportunities associated with an uncertain energy situation?
Chaos and wildcards	C1a	Microorganisms threaten to decimate reserves.
	C2	Impact of shortfalls on industry and civilization.
	C3	Collective awareness and behavior (1st world vs. 3rd world?).
	C4a	Oil scarcity leads to animosity and wars.
	C5	Natural catastrophes of all kinds.
	C6	Climate shock and its effects.
	C7	Abrupt stop in oil delivery.
	C8	Discovery of a "super" energy.
Creativity and fantasy	Individual	Input from the process of joining the elements into a story.

Live from Brussels

The various ministers of the European Union (EU) member states have come together to consider the latest developments in the oil supply and energy situation.

What led to the present meeting was Norway's announcement that it intended to suspend all oil deliveries in light of its own increasing demand and dwindling reserves.

While the EU regards its petroleum imports from Norway as highly significant, they account for only around one-fifth of its total oil need. The unsettling aspect of the matter is that it could send a signal to other oil-producing countries to follow suit. This includes especially those countries that no longer depend on petro dollars. In the wake of these developments, the current dependence on Russian supply as well as Europe's vulnerability can be expected to grow. In the past, Russia has often responded to price and delivery

Figure 156 Environment scenario "The Future of Petroleum": visualization of scenario 1 "Empty"

disputes with its European clients by turning off the pipeline. If this happens again, Europe will be faced by unprecedented energy problems.

No one dares to articulate what everyone is thinking: "What happens if the oil scarcity worsens and no alternatives are in sight?"

Prices for virtually all commodities – naturally including gasoline – would spike. The ghost of inflation would have returned. The financial markets would spin out of control. The consequences would be unimaginable. Transport costs and the costs of mobility would skyrocket. Globalization itself, which was essentially driven by the cheap transport of goods, would come to a standstill. Locally manufactured products would suddenly be competitive. The transport costs would clearly outstrip the difference in wages. China, too, would have some hard thinking to do about how it intends to preserve its future growth, that is, how it intends to get the energy to support it.

Many models of economics would need to be exchanged. A society of surplus could quickly revert to a society of scarcity. Energy costs will spike in the near future – that much is certain.

The various heads of state have debated the issues the whole night without reaching any significant resolutions. The fact that the EU has proven incapable of reaching an agreement on action in this dire situation again underscores the serious limitations it faces as a political institution, an institution that will be called upon to grapple with yet more far-reaching changes. Energy conservation is clearly essential, but the response has to be more than an outlawing of traditional light bulbs.

7.5.2 Scenario 2: "Transition"

Component	Element	Description
Title	"Transition"	There are many signs of a steady transition to the post-oil era.
Main characters	Mr. and Mrs. Hobbel	Hilda and Herman Hobbel
Scene	On their way home …	… discussing the purchase of a new car
Paradigms and constants	P1	The world's fossil fuel reserves (petroleum) are finite.
	P2	Oil offers a diverse range of applications (fuel, synthetics, textiles, pesticides, pharmaceutical products).
	P3	It took nature around 100 million years to create the world's petroleum reserves. Their depletion will take less than 200 years (CO_2 emissions).
	P4	The supply of petroleum is prone to disruption and markets are accordingly volatile.
	P5	The "strategic ellipse" accounts for 80% of global reserves (gas, petroleum, coal).
	P6	The 3 biggest importers of oil are the United States, China and Japan.
	P7	There is a vital link between technological progress, population growth, GDP, living standards and the availability of energy (oil).
	P8	Petroleum accounts for 90% of the energy used for mobility and transport.
Trends	T1	Energy needs and consumption are increasing, especially in developing countries.
	T2	The price of petroleum will continue to rise along with the rise in demand.
	T3	Alternative sources are gaining in significance (gas, nuclear, solar, bio, etc).
	T4	Dependence on petroleum continues to rise.
	T5	Instability in many petroleum rich countries and regions continues to rise.
	T6	Climate change (temperature increases linked to CO_2 emissions) and other environmental consequences are becoming more pronounced (hurricanes, extreme weather).
	T7	The cost of maintaining energy security is increasing.
	T8	Drilling and recovery conditions have become more difficult and expensive.
	T9	Technological advances and improved methods of recovery are compensating for some production losses.
	T10	Nervousness relating to availability is increasing.
Contradictions	W1c	Improved technology for exploiting sources.
	W2b	Hardly any investments in alternative sources because these are regarded as too expensive.
	W3	Peak oil: Hubbert's Peak – conflicting statements about the time it will take to reach the peak.
	W4	Our awareness and concern about energy is increasing, but there is also blindness to the issue.

Component	Element	Description
Uncertainties	W5	Conflicting statements about the development oil demand.
	W6a	Production capacities are just barely sufficient.
	W7	Conflicting private and societal interests.
	U1a	While several energy alternatives are available, they are regarded as too expensive.
	U2a	No more than a gradual transition.
	U3	What impact will a significant energy scarcity have on living standards?
	U4	Will the globalization paradigm (low wages and low transport costs) be reversed?
	U5	What impact will political activities have on further development?
	U6	What will be the reaction of the various industries (energy-dependent industries)? Will we see alternative materials and products? What will be the impact on economic development?
	U7	How will economies develop in the face of dependence and uncertainty?
	U8a	Russia advances to the status of a new super power.
	U9	How will the price of petroleum develop in the face of changing demand?
	U10	Will innovative enterprises be able to seize the opportunities associated with an uncertain energy situation?
Chaos and wildcards	C1b	Protection and guarding of reserves.
	C2	Impact of shortfalls on industry and civilization.
	C3	Collective awareness and behavior (1st world vs. 3rd world?).
	C4b	Successful protection of reserves and delivery thanks to the deployment of considerable staff.
	C5	Natural catastrophes of all kinds.
	C6	Climate shock and its effects.
	C7	Abrupt stop in oil delivery.
	C8	Discovery of a "super" energy.
Creativity and fantasy	Individual	Input from the process of joining the elements into a story.

The Ride Home

After fifteen years, it is time to think about a new car. Herman and Hilda Hobbel own an SUV – very large, very comfortable, very high sticker price, very large gasoline tank, and very thirsty. They seldom drive it anymore, and no one would be interested in buying it. Worthless. When they bought it, size wasn't a consideration. Big was important and the SUV reflected a certain lifestyle and was a status symbol. A lot has changed since then. Today, cars are again a luxury item. Not the cars themselves, but actually driving them. In addition to the cost of gasoline and upkeep, it is the many fees and taxes that have taken the fun out of driving. Environment tax, emissions tax, petroleum tax, parking fees, highway tolls and the normal automobile tax have made driving one's own car almost prohibitively expensive for average citizens. A number of alternative concepts have been developed out of this "mobile predicament" – as one well-known automobile association described the situation. The signs of this revolution from below had been apparent for a long time. Carmakers in Europe reacted too slowly to the changed conditions. They had apparently devised a strategy based on hope – the hope that not much would change in the "car system" in the future and that they could concentrate on earning money. The "car system" worked as follows: the carmakers made the cars and the government took in a lot of money on the operation of cars. But now the system is on the verge of collapse and the stakeholders are in denial. Their reactions speak of helplessness and a complete loss of orientation.

Herman and Hilda Hobbel are unsure. Herman says, "Actually, an electric car would be an alternative." Hilda responds, "Yeah, but you know how they drive. I've never heard of the company that makes them. And I doubt that eDriving is going to be tax free for very much longer." Herman says, "You may be right about that, but the hybrid cars are much too expensive and the hydrogen cars aren't even really on the market yet. What other choice do we have?" Herman would really like to avoid a big discussion.

"Well, there are still the solar cars and the biogas cars," says Hilda, resuming the discussion after a pause and then going on to point out that both are and will remain tax free when run on self-generated energy to meet one's own needs because the government has no centralized way of collecting other than at gas stations. Herman broods as they approach a hill.

Naturally, governments around the world confirm that energy security and environmental protection are the most important political issues of the times, and even the United States and China have indicated their support for the Kyoto Protocol – but apparently only until their budgets are no longer in danger. Given that Germany did not want to refrain from taxing biofuels, around ninety percent of this energy comes from Poland.

Figure 157 Environment scenario "The Future of Petroleum": visualization of scenario 2 "Transition"

7.5 Generating Environment Scenarios

The head start that Germany had at the beginning of the century in bioenergy technology quickly evaporated. It has failed to meet the EU's ecological criteria for years and has been forced to pay Brussels regular and painful penalties.

Europe continues to invest heavily in protecting the existing oil supply systems. Government statements offer as little guidance when it comes to purchasing a new car as those of the manufacturers and the oil companies.

Having arrived home, Herman and Hilda park their bicycles in the garage. Herman is happy to have their conversation interrupted. He doesn't understand Hilda. Just like her he would like to buy another nice car. But they don't really need one. Given that they only use their car occasionally – on the weekends – buying a new car now would be too much of a risk. They'll cancel the registration for their SUV and wait and see how the situation develops. In the meantime, they'll continue to use their bicycles.

When buying a new car before, brand, color and size were the deciding factors. Now it is independence and flexibility with regard to fuel.

7.5.3 Scenario 3: "Fight"

Component	Element	Description
Title	"Fight"	The fight for the remaining accessible oil reserves has begun.
Main character	Karen	Gas station owner
Scene		Gas station in Calgary
Paradigms and constants	P1	The world's fossil fuel reserves (petroleum) are finite.
	P2	Oil offers a diverse range of applications (fuel, synthetics, textiles, pesticides, pharmaceutical products).
	P3	It took nature around 100 million years to create the world's petroleum reserves. Their depletion will take less than 200 years (CO_2 emissions).
	P4	The supply of petroleum is prone to disruption and markets are accordingly volatile.
	P5	The "strategic ellipse" accounts for 80% of global reserves (gas, petroleum, coal).
	P6	The 3 biggest importers of oil are the United States, China and Japan.
	P7	There is a vital link between technological progress, population growth, GDP, living standards and the availability of energy (oil).
	P8	Petroleum accounts for 90% of the energy used for mobility and transport.
Trends	T1	Energy needs and consumption are increasing, especially in developing countries.
	T2	The price of petroleum will continue to rise along with the rise in demand.
	T3	Alternative sources are gaining in significance (gas, nuclear, solar, bio, etc).
	T4	Dependence on petroleum continues to rise.
	T5	Instability in many petroleum rich countries and regions continues to rise.

Component	Element	Description
	T6	Climate change (temperature increases linked to CO_2 emissions) and other environmental consequences are becoming more pronounced (hurricanes, extreme weather).
	T7	The cost of maintaining energy security is increasing.
	T8	Drilling and recovery conditions have become more difficult and expensive.
	T9	Technological advances and improved methods of recovery are compensating for some production losses.
	T10	Nervousness relating to availability is increasing.
Contradictions	W1a	The abundantly available oil sand represents a new option.
	W2a	Wind, sun, atoms and water are available and can to some extent compensate for shortfalls.
	W3	Peak oil: Hubbert's Peak – conflicting statements about the time it will take to reach the peak.
	W4	Our awareness and concern about energy is increasing, but there is also blindness to the issue.
	W5	Conflicting statements about the development oil demand.
	W6b	Capacity shortfalls are only temporary.
	W7	Conflicting private and societal interests.
Uncertainties	U1c	Partial replacement (e.g. alcohol as a fuel).
	U2c	Oil-independent countries enjoy economic upswing.
	U3	What impact will a significant energy scarcity have on living standards?
	U4	Will the globalization paradigm (low wages and low transport costs) be reversed?
	U5	What impact will political activities have on further development?
	U6	What will be the reaction of the various industries (energy-dependent industries)? Will we see alternative materials and products? What will be the impact on economic development?
	U7	How will economies develop in the face of dependence and uncertainty?
	U8c	The United States loses geopolitical influence and economic power.
	U9	How will the price of petroleum develop in the face of changing demand?
	U10	Will innovative enterprises be able to seize the opportunities associated with an uncertain energy situation?
Chaos and wildcards	C1c	Climate change: CO_2 changes have an impact on petroleum.
	C2	Impact of shortfalls on industry and civilization.
	C3	Collective awareness and behavior (1st world vs. 3rd world?).
	C4c	Terrorist organizations attempt to disrupt oil supply and trigger chaos.
	C5	Natural catastrophes of all kinds.
	C6	Climate shock and its effects.
	C7	Abrupt stop in oil delivery.
	C8	Discovery of a "super" energy.

Component	Element	Description
Creativity and fantasy	Individual	Input from the process of joining the elements into a story.

At the Gas Station

Karen loves these sunny mornings and today is a special day: because she'll again be getting a delivery of gasoline. Karen has run her private gas station here in Calgary for more than twenty years, but she never experienced anything like this. She used to get her deliveries from the United States, directly from the refinery in Seattle. But that's not an option anymore. Fuel exports from the United States have been banned. Oil has become too expensive to permit export. While the United States may have been the first, other countries have begun to prepare for the oil scarcity and to emphasize national interests. This has led to tremendous unease. Karen had to increase the price of regular three times last week, and if the delivery doesn't arrive today as planned, she'll have to charge a few cents more tomorrow.

In Alberta, the mining of oil sand and shale has been stepped up recently and processing capacities expanded. Canada now processes everything on its own and has also banned exports. This makes Canada – in terms of its oil supply – relatively independent. Other countries – especially the United States – are confronted by more severe supply problems. Europe, though, has it the worst. There, the governments have agreed to dramatically lower carbon dioxide emissions and have given highest priority to promoting alternative forms of energy to compensate for the shortfalls in imported oil and gas. Ever since Russia and China reached extensive cooperative agreements, trade between the countries – oil for products – has been intense and both countries are showing consider-

Figure 158 Environment scenario "The Future of Petroleum": visualization of scenario 3 "Fight"

able vitality. In geopolitical terms, two power blocks have emerged, with Russia and China on one side and Europe and North America on the other.

Karen knows that running a gas station might prove to be a dead-end in the long run, and that leaves her worried about the future. While business is relatively good at the moment, she can't be certain that delivery will be reliable. In addition to general worries about energy scarcity – especially petroleum – she is concerned about the increase in climate terrorism. While terrorism used to be known as a form of political-ideological warfare, it has been increasingly used to mark out territorial claims. Environmental activists from Cameroon have claimed responsibility for the recent attacks on the oil refineries in Nevada. The string of bombings at the GM plant in Detroit have disrupted production for months. Inuit spokesmen seemed strangely less than determined to deflect the suspicions that have been directed against various Inuit groups. In ecologically-minded Europe, resistance against climate sinners has turned violent. In the Netherlands, protests have been organized to force the closure of the Rotterdam oil harbor. Power companies are complaining that acts of sabotage have led to damage at coal plants that equals ten percent of annual turnover. It seems to Karen that it is only a matter of time before radical environmentalists have identified gas stations as targets. Maybe she should quit while she can. Maybe it would be better to sell the station now while she can still get something for it.

Karen decides to talk about it with her husband in the evening. Then she sees the tanker approaching out of the distance.

7.5.4 Scenario 4: "Independence"

Component	Element	Description
Title	Independence	Independence as an opportunity
Main character	Carl	Development worker
Scene		On assignment in Morocco
Paradigms and constants	P1	The world's fossil fuel reserves (petroleum) are finite.
	P2	Oil offers a diverse range of applications (fuel, synthetics, textiles, pesticides, pharmaceutical products).
	P3	It took nature around 100 million years to create the world's petroleum reserves. Their depletion will take less than 200 years (CO_2 emissions).
	P4	The supply of petroleum is prone to disruption and markets are accordingly volatile.
	P5	The "strategic ellipse" accounts for 80% of global reserves (gas, petroleum, coal).
	P6	The 3 biggest importers of oil are the United States, China and Japan.
	P7	There is a vital link between technological progress, population growth, GDP, living standards and the availability of energy (oil).
	P8	Petroleum accounts for 90% of the energy used for mobility and transport.

Component	Element	Description
Trends	T1	Energy needs and consumption are increasing, especially in developing countries.
	T2	The price of petroleum will continue to rise along with the rise in demand.
	T3	Alternative sources are gaining in significance (gas, nuclear, solar, bio, etc).
	T4	Dependence on petroleum continues to rise.
	T5	Instability in many petroleum rich countries and regions continues to rise.
	T6	Climate change (temperature increases linked to CO_2 emissions) and other environmental consequences are becoming more pronounced (hurricanes, extreme weather).
	T7	The cost of maintaining energy security is increasing.
	T8	Drilling and recovery conditions have become more difficult and expensive.
	T9	Technological advances and improved methods of recovery are compensating for some production losses.
	T10	Nervousness relating to availability is increasing.
Contradictions	W1d	Price fluctuation owing to conflicting accounts of remaining reserves.
	W2c	New forms of energy production and storage as a result of intensified research.
	W3	Peak oil: Hubbert's Peak – conflicting statements about the time it will take to reach the peak.
	W4	Our awareness and concern about energy is increasing, but there is also blindness to the issue.
	W5	Conflicting statements about the development oil demand.
	W6c	Oil-producing countries force scarcity by reducing production.
	W7	Conflicting private and societal interests.
Uncertainties	U1d	Politically driven active search for and use of alternatives.
	U2d	Energy users gear up for oil scarcity. Many countries achieve oil independence. World is divided into oil-dependent and oil-independent countries. Demand for oil declines.
	U3	What impact will a significant energy scarcity have on living standards?
	U4	Will the globalization paradigm (low wages and low transport costs) be reversed?
	U5	What impact will political activities have on further development?
	U6	What will be the reaction of the various industries (energy-dependent industries)? Will we see alternative materials and products? What will be the impact on economic development?
	U7	How will economies develop in the face of dependence and uncertainty?
	U8d	After initial difficulties, oil independent countries begin to flourish.
	U9	How will the price of petroleum develop in the face of changing demand?
	U10	Will innovative enterprises be able to seize the opportunities associated with an uncertain energy situation?

Component	Element	Description
Chaos and wildcards	C1d	Not relevant because oil independence has been achieved.
	C2	Impact of shortfalls on industry and civilization.
	C3	Collective awareness and behavior (1st world vs. 3rd world?).
	C4d	Decline in the economic significance of oil.
	C5	Natural catastrophes of all kinds.
	C6	Climate shock and its effects.
	C7	Abrupt stop in oil delivery.
	C8	Discovery of a "super" energy.
Creativity and fantasy	Individual	Input from the process of joining the elements into a story.

Made in Sweden

It is unbearably hot in the burning sun. Carl still finds it difficult to live and work in this kind of heat.

He came here two years ago from Sweden. His country is one of the few that succeeded in eliminating all oil imports in a relatively short span of time (10 years). It was a difficult process. Most Swedes saw no compelling reasons for the government's action, and were bitterly opposed to it. Scuffles broke out at gas stations across Sweden on the day the price was increased by 500%. However, an understanding of the situation's urgency and the government's action then developed gradually. The public transport systems were expanded and the prices cut in half. Today, all Swedes are a little bit prouder of their country. The Scandinavians have once again shown the world a more responsible path.

Figure 159 Environment scenario "The Future of Petroleum": visualization of scenario 4 "Independence"

7.5 Generating Environment Scenarios

Sweden's environmental balance sheet is the best in the world. It is the first industrialized country to remove more carbon dioxide from the atmosphere than it produces.

Other countries have invested heavily in the development of technologies to store carbon dioxide. Sweden has taken the approach of planting trees, a lot of young trees. It turns out that young trees, i.e. those that are in a more intense growth phase, are especially good at binding atmospheric carbon dioxide and emitting oxygen. All of Sweden's inhabitants and all of its private enterprises are obligated to submit an annual environmental balance sheet to the government. One kilogram of carbon dioxide must be bound for every kilogram produced, for instance, by planting trees or other plants for biofuels. Cultivatable land is gradually becoming scarce. Those who report a negative environmental balance are required to pay a tax and the government is obligated to channel this revenue into environmental projects – mainly in the interest of the climate.

The change in policy on the part of the government is owing to the fact that Sweden is the world's leader in the area of biotechnology. Despite the successes so far, the search for clean energy continues at research facilities in Sweden's Energy Valley north of Göteborg. New technologies are being developed – such as Organic2Fuel technology whose aim is to make virtually any organic material efficiently convertible into fuel. One special feature of research in this area is the notion of independent, small-scale fuel production facilities. Instead of being produced in giant refineries, fuel is produced by small-scale "farm" units, with fuel stations mainly selling the fuel they have produced themselves. Other fuel is hardly available anymore on account of the environmental balance sheets. One further promising research project is "artificial photosynthesis." Here, sunlight is used to bind large amounts of carbon dioxide and to form carburets. The first prototypes, which combine the benefits of solar cells and carbon dioxide sequestration, are already in operation.

The government in Sweden is naturally aware of the fact that Sweden does not account for significant production in global terms. Nonetheless, it is sparing no efforts in its attempts to export its successful model. Development workers such as Carl are helping other countries to shore up their environmental balance sheets. There is plenty of interest in the Swedish model, as is evidenced by the fact that the European Union is currently considering proposals to levy import fees on goods from countries with especially negative environmental balance sheets. This would hit China, the world's biggest environmental delinquent, very hard.

Demand for petroleum and petroleum prices continue to decline. The temptation to move away from clean energy in favor of "cheap" energy is growing. The government in Sweden has even set up a special police department for environmental enforcement, again proving how committed it is to environmental protection.

Other countries can be expected to follow suit. The EU in particular is preparing the necessary legal framework. There seems to be a clear mandate in the EU, despite the claims of critics who fear that it will block growth.

Carl smiles. He is proud of his country now that the world no longer associates it only with IKEA.

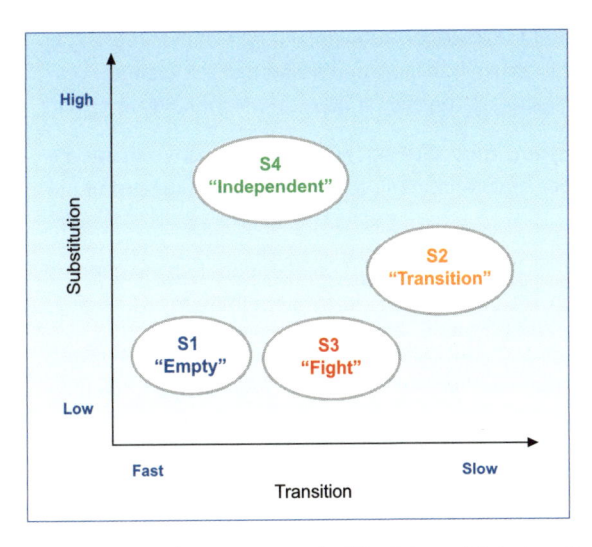

Figure 160 Environment scenario "The Future of Petroleum": scenario evaluation

Assuming that the world's petroleum reserves are finite and that its use as a primary energy carrier is also limited, the developed scenarios clearly indicate that further development is essentially tied to two criteria:

- The availability of substitute sources, i.e. sources of energy that could compensate for shortfalls in the supply of petroleum.

- The speed of the transition: will the coming scarcity emerge under market conditions that will permit a gradual transition? Or will we be confronted by sudden scarcity that then leads to chaotic circumstances?

An evaluation of the scenarios can be found in Figure 160. Scenario S1 "Empty" represents the crash scenario.

7.6 Generating Enterprise Scenarios

I have selected a fictional airline by the name of "Andromeda" to illustrate the impact of changes in the environment on an enterprise. Any similarities to existing airlines are merely coincidental.

"Andromeda" was founded in Europe in the wake of the deregulation of air traffic in the 1990s. The airline has experienced peaks and valleys since its founding fifteen years ago. The terrorist attacks of September 11, 2001 and the downturn in air traffic that followed almost pushed the airline into bankruptcy. It was only a consistent orientation towards the high-price segment and a quick and across-the-board recovery of passenger volumes that allowed the airline to survive. Today, "Andromeda" is one of the most successful carriers in Europe.

The enterprise is divided into three units: Passenger Transport, Freight Transport & Logistics, and Technology. At 55%, the Passenger Transport unit accounts for the largest portion of sales, followed by Freight Transport & Logistics at 30%, and Technology at 15%.

Andromeda is a publicly traded company. Thirty-five percent of the company's shares are owned by one family, which describes its commitment as "long term," and the rest of the shares are spread widely.

The company's aim is to continue to grow despite the stiff competition, to build upon its excellent market position and to branch off into related areas that promise to be lucrative.

The fleet has so far consisted exclusively of Airbus A320 models. However, in light of the Airbus record, Andromeda is reconsidering the issue of Airbus's reliability as a business partner and the option buying Boeing planes.

Table 49 Elements of Evaluation for Enterprise Scenario "Andromeda"

Paradigms and Constants	Trends	Contradictions	Uncertainty	Chaos and Wildcards
P1: No compromises when it comes to the safety and maintenance of the airplanes. **P2:** Andromeda can be expected to remain focused on flying. **P3:** Maintenance of high employee satisfaction. **P4:** No foreseeable changes in basic airplane technology. **P5:** Propulsion will continue to be based on turbine engines. The relevant fuel is kerosene. **P6:** The assumption is that globalization will continue and will lead to increasing demand in both the passenger and cargo/logistics areas. **P7:** The specifications in air traffic are as follows: budget segment (inexpensive); business segment (comfortable and fast); logistics segment (fast and reliable).	**T1:** Consolidation in the air traffic sector continues. **T2:** Downward pressure on prices continues – especially in budget sector. **T3:** Asian airlines have emerged as tough competitors on long routes, especially routes involving North America. **T4:** All-inclusive packages will become established in the high-price segment: "business class from door to door." **T5:** Customer loyalty programs will also play a more important role in the future when it comes to airline selection. **T6:** Customers in the logistics area will show an increased interest in end-to-end solutions. **T7:** Direct flights are clearly preferred on account of the time delays associated with more elaborate security measures. **T8:** All indications suggest that air traffic volume will continue to increase. **T9:** Technological advances in navigation, propulsion systems, service, etc.	**W1:** Unwillingness to sacrifice mobility conflicts with willingness to heed climate change warnings. **W2:** Demand for ever faster and more comfortable travel is undermined by ever new conditions (e.g. security). **W3:** Burgeoning regulations – national and international – make it more difficult to ensure efficient air traffic planning. **W4:** Automation (e.g. ticket sales) versus a desire for high service standards. **W5:** Exposure to many higher powers (e.g. weather and traffic) reduces Andromeda's reliability and punctuality. **W6:** Desire to grow versus profitability.	**U1:** How will the enterprise respond to the strategies of the budget airlines? **U2:** Will the concentration on Airbus turn into risk? How reliable will Airbus be as a partner in the future? **U3:** How will the company deal with fluctuation in the cost of jet fuel? **U4:** Would it make sense to expand the range or increase the density of the carrier's flight network? **U5:** What impact will further security regulations have on air traffic? **U6:** How will the enterprise's culture develop? **U7:** How will flight routes and takeoff/landing permits be affected by regulations? **U8:** What will be the impact of reorganization and restructuring on the airline?	**C1:** New terrorist attacks lead to declines in passenger volume. **C2:** Introduction of additional taxes. **C3:** Natural catastrophes of all kinds. **C4:** Climate shock and its impact. **C5:** Strikes by air-traffic controllers or pilots. **C6:** Hostile takeover of Andromeda. **C7:** Change in management.

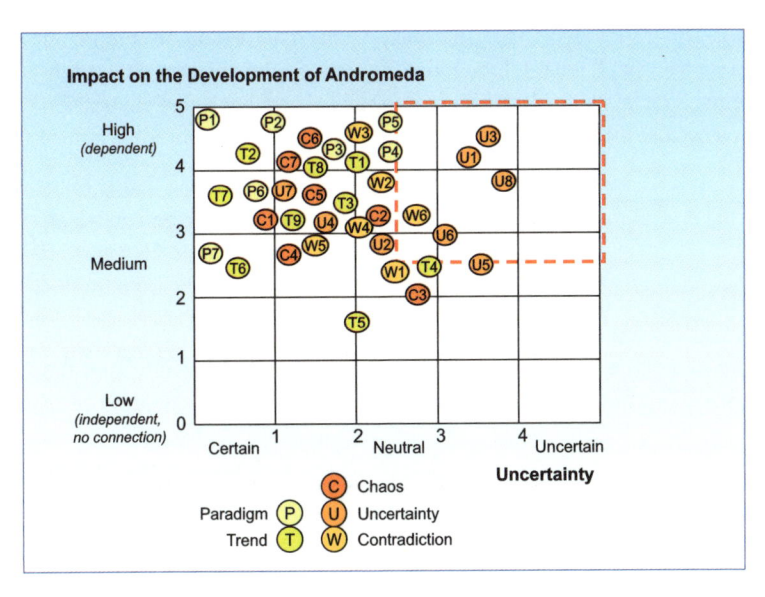

Figure 161 Evaluation – enterprise scenario "Andromeda"

	U1	U3	U6	U8	W6	Scenarios
a	Strident public confrontation with budget airlines interrupts scheduling and forces delays.	Investments in the development of new propulsion technologies.	Management strives to turn the airline into a learning enterprise.	Enterprise experiences restructuring fatigue on account of too many measures.	Balanced management helps to generate solid growth and maintain profitability.	Cautious Innovation
b	Sitting out the budget airline phase.	Enterprise enters into long-term supply agreements and strategic partnerships with suppliers.	Consistent promotion of innovation leads to an inspiring work atmosphere.	Proven organizational structure is maintained.	Expansion into related business areas allows the enterprise to grow, but at the cost of profitability.	
c	Highlighting of the enterprise's existing strengths and enhanced customer support.	Tough cost-cutting measures and transfer of savings to customers.	Status quo – no significant efforts to improve or maintain the culture.	The organization is turned into a machine via strict controlling and ambitious goals. Employee participation in decision-making is unwelcome.	Exclusive focus on core business leads to business contraction.	No Experiments
d	Differentiation via introduction of new offers and improved services.	Hope!	Employee motivation drops on account of incomprehensible management decisions.	The organization hindered by the emergence of "fiefdoms" – no effective exchange of information and knowledge within the enterprise.	Outsourcing of business areas.	No Plan
e				The focus of strategic shaping is on the delegation of responsibility and the promotion of entrepreneurship.	Andromeda degenerates into a "corporate monopoly" owing to its pursuit of a portfolio strategy.	Aggressive

Figure 162 Scenario framework: the future of "Andromeda"

7.6 Generating Enterprise Scenarios

The female CEO is known for demanding accuracy while maintaining an altogether friendly tone. She is held in high regard throughout the company and beyond. She is convinced that customer satisfaction is essentially to be reached via employee satisfaction and is also personally committed to maintaining a friendly atmosphere within the enterprise.

As in the case of the environment scenario, the description of the future elements – paradigms, trends, uncertainties, contradictions and wildcards – is the basis for selecting scenario elements and operation (Table 49). The standard approach will be used for this example (cf. Section 4.8).

We can begin by evaluating all of the elements in terms of their "uncertainty" and the extent of their possible "impact on the further development of Andromeda" (Figure 161).

Figure 162 shows the resulting scenario framework for "Andromeda."

7.6.1 Scenario 1: Cautious Innovation

Component	Element	Description
Title	Cautious Innovation	
Main character	–	Not applicable
Scene	–	Not applicable
Paradigms and constants	P1	No compromises when it comes to the safety and maintenance of the airplanes.
	P2	Andromeda can be expected to remain focused on flying.
	P3	Maintenance of high employee satisfaction.
	P4	No foreseeable changes in basic airplane technology.
	P5	Propulsion will continue to be based on turbine engines. The relevant fuel is kerosene.
	P6	The assumption is that globalization will continue and will lead to increasing demand in both the passenger and cargo/logistics areas.
	P7	The specifications in air traffic are as follows: budget segment (inexpensive); business segment (comfortable and fast); logistics segment (fast and reliable).
Trends	T1	Consolidation in the air traffic sector continues.
	T2	Downward pressure on prices continues – especially in budget sector.
	T3	Asian airlines have emerged as tough competitors on long routes, especially routes involving North America.
	T4	All-inclusive packages will become established in the high-price segment: "business class from door to door."
	T5	Customer loyalty programs will also play a more important role in the future when it comes to airline selection.
	T6	Customers in the logistics area will show an increased interest in end-to-end solutions.
	T7	Direct flights are clearly preferred on account of the time delays associated with more elaborate security measures.

Component	Element	Description
	T8	All indications suggest that air traffic volume will continue to increase.
	T9	Technological advances in navigation, propulsion systems, service, etc.
Contradictions	W1	Unwillingness to sacrifice mobility conflicts with willingness to heed climate change warnings.
	W2	Demand for ever faster and more comfortable travel is undermined by ever new conditions (e.g. security).
	W3	Burgeoning regulations – national and international – make it more difficult to ensure efficient air traffic planning.
	W4	Automation (e.g. ticket sales) versus a desire for high service standards.
	W5	Exposure to higher powers (e.g. weather and traffic) reduces Andromeda's reliability and punctuality.
	W6a	Balanced management helps to generate solid growth and maintain profitability.
Uncertainties	U1d	Differentiation via introduction of new offers and improved services.
	U2	Will the concentration on Airbus turn into risk? How reliable will Airbus be as a partner in the future?
	U3a	Investments in the development of new propulsion technologies.
	U4	Would it make sense to expand the range or increase the density of the carrier's flight network?
	U5	What impact will further security regulations have on air traffic?
	U6b	Consistent promotion of innovation leads to an inspiring work atmosphere.
	U7	How will flight routes and takeoff/landing permits be effected by regulations?
	U8e	The focus of strategic shaping is on the delegation of responsibility and the promotion of entrepreneurship.
Chaos and wildcards	C1	New terrorist attacks lead to declines in passenger volume.
	C2	Introduction of additional taxes.
	C3	Natural catastrophes of all kinds.
	C4	Climate shock and its impact.
	C5	Strikes by air-traffic controllers or pilots.
	C6	Hostile takeover of Andromeda.
	C7	Change in management.
Creativity and fantasy	Individual	Input from the process of joining the elements into a story.

While the enterprise will certainly not change its business model or reinvent the rules of air traffic, it remains open for innovation, both from within and from without. In addition to its carefully organized routines, which help to ensure continual success, the enterprise grants its employees a significant degree of freedom for "experimentation." The staff is largely creative and motivated.

7.6.2 Scenario 2: No Experiments

Component	Element	Description
Title	No Experiments	
Main character	–	Not applicable.
Scene	–	Not applicable.
Paradigms and constants	P1	No compromises when it comes to the safety and maintenance of the airplanes.
	P2	Andromeda can be expected to remain focused on flying.
	P3	Maintenance of high employee satisfaction.
	P4	No foreseeable changes in basic airplane technology.
	P5	Propulsion will continue to be based on turbine engines. The relevant fuel is kerosene.
	P6	The assumption is that globalization will continue and will lead to increasing demand in both the passenger and cargo/logistics areas.
	P7	The specifications in air traffic are as follows: budget segment (inexpensive); business segment (comfortable and fast); logistics segment (fast and reliable).
Trends	T1	Consolidation in the air traffic sector continues.
	T2	Downward pressure on prices continues – especially in budget sector.
	T3	Asian airlines have emerged as tough competitors on long routes, especially routes involving North America.
	T4	All-inclusive packages will become established in the high-price segment: "business class from door to door."
	T5	Customer loyalty programs will also play a more important role in the future when it comes to airline selection.
	T6	Customers in the logistics area will show an increased interest in end-to-end solutions.
	T7	Direct flights are clearly preferred on account of the time delays associated with more elaborate security measures.
	T8	All indications suggest that air traffic volume will continue to increase.
	T9	Technological advances in navigation, propulsion systems, service, etc.
Contradictions	W1	Unwillingness to sacrifice mobility conflicts with willingness to heed climate change warnings.
	W2	Demand for ever faster and more comfortable travel is undermined by ever new conditions (e.g. security).
	W3	Burgeoning regulations – national and international – make it more difficult to ensure efficient air traffic planning.
	W4	Automation (e.g. ticket sales) versus a desire for high service standards.
	W5	Exposure to higher powers (e.g. weather and traffic) reduces Andromeda's reliability and punctuality.
	W6c	Exclusive focus on core business leads to business contraction.

Component	Element	Description
Uncertainties	U1c	Highlighting of the enterprise's existing strengths and enhanced customer support.
	U2	Will the concentration on Airbus turn into risk? How reliable will Airbus be as a partner in the future?
	U3b	Enterprise enters into long-term delivery agreements and strategic partnerships with suppliers.
	U4	Would it make sense to expand the range or increase the density of the carrier's flight network?
	U5	What impact will further security regulations have on air traffic?
	U6a	Management strives to turn the airline into a learning enterprise.
	U7	How will flight routes and takeoff/landing permits be effected by regulations?
	U8b	Proven organizational structure is maintained.
Chaos and wildcards	C1	New terrorist attacks lead to declines in passenger volume.
	C2	Introduction of additional taxes.
	C3	Natural catastrophes of all kinds.
	C4	Climate shock and its impact.
	C5	Strikes by air-traffic controllers or pilots.
	C6	Hostile takeover of Andromeda.
	C7	Change in management.
Creativity and fantasy	Individual	Input from the process of joining the elements into a story.

We could summarize the guiding principle for Andromeda as it approaches the future in this scenario as, "It can't be wrong to apply what has worked in the past to the future." While this policy gives the enterprise sufficient stability and the necessary internal comprehensibility, it will work against the enterprise when it comes to recognizing changes on its markets and in its business environment. This could make the enterprise vulnerable in turbulent times.

7.6.3 Scenario 3: No Plan

Component	Element	Description
Title	No Plan	
Main character	–	Not applicable.
Scene	–	Not applicable.
Paradigms and constants	P1	No compromises when it comes to the safety and maintenance of the airplanes.
	P2	Andromeda can be expected to remain focused on flying.
	P3	Maintenance of high employee satisfaction.
	P4	No foreseeable changes in basic airplane technology.
	P5	Propulsion will continue to be based on turbine engines. The relevant fuel is kerosene.

Component	Element	Description
	P6	The assumption is that globalization will continue and will lead to increasing demand in both the passenger and cargo/logistics areas.
	P7	The specifications in air traffic are as follows: budget segment (inexpensive); business segment (comfortable and fast); logistics segment (fast and reliable).
Trends	T1	Consolidation in the air traffic sector continues.
	T2	Downward pressure on prices continues – especially in budget sector.
	T3	Asian airlines have emerged as tough competitors on long routes, especially routes involving North America.
	T4	All-inclusive packages will become established in the high-price segment: "business class from door to door."
	T5	Customer loyalty programs will also play a more important role in the future when it comes to airline selection.
	T6	Customers in the logistics area will show an increased interest in end-to-end solutions.
	T7	Direct flights are clearly preferred on account of the time delays associated with more elaborate security measures.
	T8	All indications suggest that air traffic volume will continue to increase.
	T9	Technological advances in navigation, propulsion systems, service, etc.
Contradictions	W1	Unwillingness to sacrifice mobility conflicts with willingness to heed climate change warnings.
	W2	Demand for ever faster and more comfortable travel is undermined by ever new conditions (e.g. security).
	W3	Burgeoning regulations – national and international – make it more difficult to ensure efficient air traffic planning.
	W4	Automation (e.g. ticket sales) versus a desire for high service standards.
	W5	Exposure to higher powers (e.g. weather and traffic) reduces Andromeda's reliability and punctuality.
	W6d	Outsourcing of business areas.
Uncertainties	U1b	Sitting out the budget airline phase.
	U2	Will the concentration on Airbus turn into risk? How reliable will Airbus be as a partner in the future?
	U3d	Hope!
	U4	Would it make sense to expand the range or increase the density of the carrier's flight network?
	U5	What impact will further security regulations have on air traffic?
	U6d	Employee motivation drops on account of incomprehensible management decisions.
	U7	How will flight routes and takeoff/landing permits be effected by regulations?
	U8a	Enterprise experiences restructuring fatigue on account of too many measures.

Component	Element	Description
Chaos and wildcards	C1	New terrorist attacks lead to declines in passenger volume.
	C2	Introduction of additional taxes.
	C3	Natural catastrophes of all kinds.
	C4	Climate shock and its impact.
	C5	Strikes by air-traffic controllers or pilots.
	C6	Hostile takeover of Andromeda.
	C7	Change in management.
Creativity and fantasy	Individual	Input from the process of joining the elements into a story.

The development of the company can indeed be described ungoverned and chaotic. Frequent changes at the level of the management board lead to numerous changes that are reflective of conflicting goals. No clear direction has been established. The enterprise is clearly not among the shapers on the market. The enterprise's success is solely a matter of increased demand.

7.6.4 Scenario 4: Aggressive

Component	Element	Description
Title	Aggressive	
Main character	–	Not applicable.
Scene	–	Not applicable.
Paradigms and constants	P1	No compromises when it comes to the safety and maintenance of the airplanes.
	P2	Andromeda can be expected to remain focused on flying.
	P3	Maintenance of high employee satisfaction.
	P4	No foreseeable changes in basic airplane technology.
	P5	Propulsion will continue to be based on turbine engines. The relevant fuel is kerosene.
	P6	The assumption is that globalization will continue and will lead to increasing demand in both the passenger and cargo/logistics areas.
	P7	The specifications in air traffic are as follows: budget segment (inexpensive); business segment (comfortable and fast); logistics segment (fast and reliable).
Trends	T1	Consolidation in the air traffic sector continues.
	T2	Downward pressure on prices continues – especially in budget sector.
	T3	Asian airlines have emerged as tough competitors on long routes, especially routes involving North America.
	T4	All-inclusive packages will become established in the high-price segment: "business class from door to door."
	T5	Customer loyalty programs will also play a more important role in the future when it comes to airline selection.

Component	Element	Description
	T6	Customers in the logistics area will show an increased interest in end-to-end solutions.
	T7	Direct flights are clearly preferred on account of the time delays associated with more elaborate security measures.
	T8	All indications suggest that air traffic volume will continue to increase.
	T9	Technological advances in navigation, propulsion systems, service, etc.
Contradictions	W1	Unwillingness to sacrifice mobility conflicts with willingness to heed climate change warnings.
	W2	Demand for ever faster and more comfortable travel is undermined by ever new conditions (e.g. security).
	W3	Burgeoning regulations – national and international – make it more difficult to ensure efficient air traffic planning.
	W4	Automation (e.g. ticket sales) versus a desire for high service standards.
	W5	Exposure to higher powers (e.g. weather and traffic) reduces Andromeda's reliability and punctuality.
	W6e	Andromeda degenerates into a "corporate monopoly" owing to its pursuit of a portfolio strategy.
Uncertainties	U1a	Strident public confrontation with budget airlines interrupts scheduling and forces delays.
	U2	Will the concentration on Airbus turn into risk? How reliable will Airbus be as a partner in the future?
	U3c	Tough cost-cutting measures and transfer of savings to passengers.
	U4	Would it make sense to expand the range or increase the density of the carrier's flight network?
	U5	What impact will further security regulations have on air traffic?
	U6c	Status quo – no significant efforts to improve or maintain the culture.
	U7	How will flight routes and takeoff/landing permits be effected by regulations?
	U8c	The organization is turned into a machine via strict controlling and ambitious goals. Employee participation in decision-making is unwelcome.
Chaos and wildcards	C1	New terrorist attacks lead to declines in passenger volume.
	C2	Introduction of additional taxes.
	C3	Natural catastrophes of all kinds.
	C4	Climate shock and its impact.
	C5	Strikes by air-traffic controllers or pilots.
	C6	Hostile takeover of Andromeda.
	C7	Change in management.
Creativity and fantasy	Individual	Input from the process of joining the elements into a story.

The enterprise has been too rigidly aligned to success. The new CEO has a habit of referring to the company as a "high-performance enterprise." Success is almost exclusively a matter of the right data. Andromeda is forced to learn the painful lesson that this model can only offer temporary success.

If we assume that all of the scenarios have an equal chance of occurring (i.e. the future is likely to contain elements from all four scenarios), then it seems clear that myopia, a lack of knowledge, false hopes and ignorance will play an important role – in politics, society, and enterprises alike. The hope that a cheap and clean new source of energy will appear on the scene just in time could prove disastrous.

If we consider the strategic fit that results from the cross comparison of the enterprise and environment scenarios (Figure 163), we can conclude that the fictional airline Andromeda is not prepared for future changes in fuel supply. The enterprise can, however, gain important room to maneuver by orienting itself on the robust constellations.

	"Empty"	"Transition"	"Fight"	"Independence"	Evaluation
"Cautious Innovation"	Attempt to compensate for sudden scarcity via price adjustments and energy conservation. (risk)	Long-term supply agreements, retooling with more energy efficient engines. (risk)	Pursuit of two strategies: accept the situation and replace existing engines (flexible and partly stable)	Active search for alternatives, investments and cooperative endeavors. (robust)	The most promising scenario.
"Aggressive"	Considerable operational cost cutting is to compensate for higher costs. (risk)	Fuel surcharges and reorganization are to preserve competitiveness. (risk)	Intense global search for suppliers offering acceptable conditions. (risk)	Securing of available fuel. (risk)	The intense focus on performance is associated with the risk of failing to recognize the new situation or recognizing it too late.
"No Experiments"	Andromeda prefers to copy the responses of the other airlines. (risk)	Slow response owing to the slow response of other airlines. (risk)	Scarcity management. (high risk)	Holdout and wait for new concepts. (risk)	High risks: conservative policies make it more difficult to adapt to new situations.
"No Plan"	Many hasty measures, including energy conservation and cost-cutting programs. (high risk)	No clear direction. (high risk)	Reduction in flights in accordance with the availability of fuel. (temporarily robust)	No concept. (high risk)	Absence of foresight and preparation imperil the very existence of the enterprise.

Figure 163 Strategic fit for Andromeda Airlines: a juxtaposition of the enterprise scenarios and the environment scenarios for "The Future of Petroleum"

7.6 Generating Enterprise Scenarios

The scenario "Cautious Innovation" offers direction. No matter what, the long-term plan will have to account for shortfalls in the availability of fuel. The existence and vitality of the enterprise will depend on its response to scarcity and the severity of the scarcity involved.

Based on its investigation, Andromeda Airlines decides in favor of an action plan containing the following elements:

- *Drafting of a crisis plan for each of the environment scenarios and identification of triggers that can be interpreted as indicators of certain developments.*
- *Installation in the enterprise of a continuous foresight program assigned to monitor changes and submit regular reports to the management.*
- *Working out of possible investments that could secure the supply of fuel. The focus here is on the development of alternatives to the existing concept and to examine their technological feasibility.*
- *Preparation of emergency measures whose aim is to immediately replace the engines of all existing aircraft with more fuel-efficient alternatives.*
- *Possible triggers include legal changes with regard to emissions and taxes as well as new technological developments in the area of jet propulsion.*

The drafting of the scenarios and their presentation ensure that an awareness of the danger of fuel scarcity makes its way to the level of senior management. Initial measures have been agreed upon. Given that the development of new propulsion concepts usually takes more than ten years, the enterprise has made it a goal to actively support the development of new jet engine technology and to enter into strategic joint ventures.

7.7 Strategic Implications

The realization that the time of low-hanging fruits is likely to be over in the near future is probably the most important conclusion that can be drawn from the scenarios. However, given that we cannot assume that civilization is ready to change its ways (or is only ready to do so very gradually), enterprises will be faced by new problems. Problems also represent opportunities for positive change, influence and growth.

The emergence of closed energy circuits on the order of photosynthesis would certainly be welcome because only such offer a truly sustainable solution. As long we refuse to include environmental damage and the risks of climate change in the equation, oil will be regarded as a cheap source of energy. However, such global considerations are often eagerly pushed to the back burner by competition-minded enterprises. Such enterprises tend to regard the inclusion of scenarios into the process of strategy development as a kind of exception.

If we consider the results of the scenario analysis in a larger context, we will see that the question of energy supply – and thus also the role of petroleum – is one that touches on the destiny of our civilization. As noted while introducing this example, the importance of economic success, wealth and growth in large portions of society is ranked higher than environmentally friendly energy supply whose aim is to avert a climate catastrophe. Personal, regional, national and entrepreneurial interests can undermine the protection of the environment and our own habitat. The damage to public property that has occurred under the aegis of market economics and the drive to gain competitive advantages in particular (e.g. the earth's climate) is a threat to the very existence of humanity.

"... the dinosaurs did manage to survive over a hundred times longer than human beings have so far." [Senge 2004] The question therefore arises as to whether a market economy is ultimately capable of survival. Mounting evidence suggests that problems of a global scale cannot be solved by the existing systems. Democracy and market economics represent achievements in our history and have made an immense contribution to progress and wealth. Time will tell whether they are equal to the challenges of the future.

One question is: will we face a gradual transition to an oil-free future or an abrupt transition? Petroleum accounts for 95% of our mobility!

Another question is: what is the real potential of the technology behind renewable forms of energy?

The uncertainty associated with the further development of petroleum can thus be reduced to three essential questions:

1. How abrupt will oil scarcity, i.e. the transition to a post oil era, be?
2. How applicable will alternative forms of energy be once the oil scarcity is upon us?
3. What role will the increased media coverage of climate change play in the future of petroleum?

If we imagine the earth as a closed system, it seems clear that a clear shift of system variables will lead to system instability. The following equation represents a direct means of providing wealth for humanity:

(1) Burning: carbon + oxygen ⇨ warmth + carbon dioxide

Although it is a very simplified representation, the equation identifies the cause of the increase in carbon dioxide in the atmosphere. The emission of carbon dioxide (and other gases) into the atmosphere, however, is regarded as a cause of climate change. Carbon is in coal, petroleum and other fossil fuels.

The following also applies:

(2) Photosynthesis: carbon dioxide + sunlight ⇨ biomass

Equation 2 contributes only indirectly to wealth (e.g. agriculture). While forests, as places of photosynthesis and sources of oxygen, can be construed as public assets, they are often sacrificed for purposes of profit.

The imbalance between equations 1 and 2 could be mitigated by a reduction in the burning of fossil fuels (equation 1) or the expansion of photosynthesis (equation 2). This suggests that an intensive, global reforestation campaign would present an answer. Such a campaign would certainly not be cheap, but the assessment of such proposals according to monetary criteria alone is highly dubious. The assessment "too expensive" is always an assessment of the moment. What qualifies as too expensive today, may appear very cost-effective in retrospect. The answer "too expensive" seems ludicrous when we imagine its utterance in the year 2020 as a response to the question as to why such a reforestation program wasn't introduced in the year 2007.

Returning to the question posed in Chapter 1 about the next Kondratieff cycle, it would not be absurd to suggest that the next cycle will be the energy cycle – or, more precisely, the sustainable energy cycle.

7.8 Example Summary

The scenario example above underscores the importance of including considerations of the future in strategic analysis and the role of trends and scenarios in strategy development.

While the subject is not new, it has again come to the attention of consumers, managers and politicians thanks to the current media coverage, particularly associated with climate change. The existence of diverging vectors of self interest and the associated differences of opinion make the subject especially suitable for illustrating the conclusions drawn in previous chapters.

It warrants pointing out again that there is no master plan. There are many sound ways of approaching the task of strategic analysis and implementing strategic foresight. The important aspects include neutral analysis and hardnosed conclusions about any necessary actions. The procedure shown here is based on many years of experience in the area of strategic analysis on behalf of the Siemens Corporation and other enterprises.

With the exception of standard office and Internet applications, no special IT or software tools were used in drafting the scenarios. A clear head, a willingness to learn, ample time for careful reflection and experience in dealing with uncertainties are sufficient prerequisites.

The future of petroleum was developed as an example with regard to the strategy options for an enterprise – an airline. The creation of scenarios – both enterprise scenarios and environment scenarios – leads to an expansion of one's reflective horizon. If we widen the scope even further to include subjects beyond petroleum and events beyond a 10-year horizon, then the questions and perspectives will shift accordingly. This will allow one to approach an overall context, i.e. the big picture.

The world's forests are currently being reduced at a rate of around 200 square kilometers per day. According to the World Forest Report, the overall surface area of forested land was reduced by 3% between 1995 and 2000. If we extrapolate on the basis of this figure, then...

Chapter 8

Homework

What You Should Do

The Philosophical Component

Although it is clear that knowledge of what the future holds in store would give enterprises a tremendous advantage, it is equally clear that there can be no absolute certainty in this regard.

It is also doubtful whether we would really want such certainty. For one, preventive measures would be introduced, i.e. attempts to intervene in the course of things so as to prevent certain events. This would then trigger attempts to prevent the impact of the preventive measures, etc., with the result that the phenomenon of acceleration takes on a new dimension. It is an open question whether such certainty would really be desirable, for instance, when one considers the resignation that would follow from the predetermined nature of events – resignation of the sort that might have overcome the mayor in our example of the mayor and the clairvoyant.

As it stands, all enterprises profit from a level playing field with respect to the future. It is up to the enterprises themselves just how seriously they wish to study the future and the extent to which such investigations are accorded a rightful place in the framework of strategy development. That is the good news.

The not so good news (i.e. from the perspective of goals and results-oriented planners) is that a study of the future is a continuous and never-ending journey. The benefit of operative foresight programs is that they offer a basis for strategic planning and strategy development. The challenge consists in including all of the sources of information that are available in the enterprise in the process of studying the future in order to arrive at balanced opinions, make informed decisions and secure a capacity to act.

Examinations of the future require objective and dispassionate analyses. First, one conducts an objective analysis. Then one reflects and evaluates in a context-specific manner in order to ultimately go forward with the necessary implementation and thereby reach the beginning of a new cycle. During this process, examinations of the future and strategic planning are characterized by explorative, unconventional and creative considerations. Accepting this is the first step to a new way of dealing with uncertainty.

Ways of approaching the future will consist of two essential components: orientation – what one hopes to achieve and a realistic plan for getting there – and a capacity to respond – alertness with regard to change and the ability to react and adapt quickly. A balanced interplay between orientation and response makes for a solid strategy.

While orientation is often a given in many enterprises, a capacity to respond is often lacking. This is why enterprises will have to pay much more attention than they typically do to internal processes. The cost factors and questions of efficiency in this connection only account for half of what is necessary. Intelligence should take precedence over efficiency!

How does your enterprise respond to opportunities? Would an idea on the scale of a Google search engine or an Apple iPod have found the necessary nurturing environment in your enterprise? How does your enterprise respond to risks? Imagine the case of an important product in the enterprise's portfolio being replaced by a new technology. How would your enterprise respond? Would it first deny the legitimacy of the new technology? Would it be prepared?

If your enterprise is not in a position to shape its future, then you will have to accept the way that it is shaped by others. Undertaking to study the future in an enterprise is like practice sessions for a football team, only different in that the rules of football remain largely the same whereas the rules in the world of business change on a daily basis. In either case, winning decisive games depends on intelligent training.

The benefits of foresight activities for your enterprise can be condensed down to three key competitive advantages:

- More robust strategies thanks to an enhanced capacity to deal with uncertainty
- Access to a more vibrant source of innovations and new business
- Enhanced communication of viable ideas for the future and thus the availability of partners for shaping the future

Outlook: What will the world look like in a thousand years or more?

In an article in the magazine GEO [GEO 2006] an author ventures a look at the world in five to two-hundred million years. "It is the logic of life that evolution never ceases." What is astonishing in this view is that human beings no longer exist. However, other living creatures – that are based on the biomechanical, physiological and ecological principles of existing organisms – do exist. Only a few species will survive the global catastrophes, and new species will emerge – such as giant turtles, 8-ton octopuses and desert lizards.

If there happens to be creatures with an intelligence that is comparable to that of human beings, these creatures might ask themselves why human beings died out back then, so many years ago. Everything will be clear in retrospect: human beings systematically destroyed their habitat. But why? Scientists will consider this question, perhaps with the aim of deriving something important lesson for their own future. Maybe some will wonder why individual human intelligence was so high, while combined human intelligence was so frightfully low. Perhaps a discovery will also be made that money played an important role in the advance of human civilization. Paradoxically, these creatures may one day determine that it was the monetary insignificance of the essential human habitat that led to its neglect and final destruction.

What You Have to Do

As formulated at the very beginning, the aim of this book is to give you, the reader, support when it comes to the following: studying the future; developing an enhanced capacity for foresight; and becoming more independent and effective at dealing with uncertainty. What is learned should be more than just ready for application, it should actually be applied.

The learning curve enabled by books is primarily oriented on the individual reader:

Buy book:	Communicate interest and give expression to this interest via the investment.
Read:	Assess the subject matter as important and take the time to read.
Understand:	Introduce new ideas to one's repertoire of concepts and ideas (one's knowledge).
Reflect:	Relate the concepts and ideas to one's own situation (privately or within one's enterprise) and gain new insights.
Use:	Bridge the knowing-doing gap with concrete action.

It is now your turn:

Think about your enterprise! Describe your enterprise and consider possible scenarios for it:

- What aspects do regard as stable (paradigms)?
- Do you see any gradual changes (trends)?
- Where do you see conflicts, paradoxes and dilemmas (contradictions)?
- What do you regard as uncertain (uncertainties)?
- Are there any threats (wildcards)?

Once you have answered these questions, then:

- Generate elements and evaluate these elements with the help of the Wilson matrix.
- Draft a scenario framework and derive possible scenarios from it. Then place the scenarios in the table. The cross comparison will then yield necessary actions and options.
- Formulate an enterprise strategy in the form of various courses of action.
- Draft an action plan and consider what you can begin with immediately.
- Identify the relevant triggers so that you will be in a position to strategically consider trend breaches and any other new situations.

Should you determine that your enterprise is not sufficiently prepared, then do something! Set something in motion! Don't rest – make others feel uncomfortable.

Chapter 9

Appendix I

100 Sources of Information

This section offers a list of 100 sources of information that may prove helpful as you work on your own projects. A score has been assigned to each source. These scores are based on a scale of 1 to 5, with 1 signifying an excellent source and 5 signifying a poor source. The scale itself is ultimately based on experience and makes no claim to universal or perpetual validity. The individual scores can be interpreted as follows:

1. Excellent source of information, comprehensive, up-to-date, material available either directly or when ordered
2. Good source of information, some irrelevance and limited availability of the material
3. Partly good, partly irrelevant
4. Unclear, little relevant information, expensive
5. Inaccurate information, not up-to-date, expensive, irrelevant or useless information

No.	Source	Link	Focus	Remarks	Score
1	APEC, Asia Pacific Economy Cooperation International Agency	http://www.apecsec.org.sg	Focus on the Asia-Pacific region: education, energy, finance, health, investment, science and technology, trade, transport, etc.	Reports are often available free of charge.	2
2	AT&T Corporation	http://www.business.att.com	Focus on technology and related areas: Networks, artificial intelligence, broadband access, human-computer interface, mobile wireless, photonics, security – VoIP / IP telephony, VPNs, etc.	Newsletter available upon registration.	4
3	Australian Foresight Institute (AFI) Institute	http://www.swin.edu.au/afi	Focus on Australia: General future-related topics	Complicated website, but research reports and monographs are accessible free of charge.	3
4	BAT Recreation Research, Institute Questions Concerning the Future Institute	http://www.bat.de	Focus on Germany: Work, education & child-raising, citizens & state, adventure centers & recreational parks, recreation & sports, generations & demographics, consumer issues, culture, media & data protection, tourism & mobility, values and & social issues, etc.	Website of the British American Tobacco Group in Germany. Public attention was drawn to the institute via "Deutschland 2010" by Horst W. Opaschowski.	3
5	Battelle Institute	http://www.battelle.org	Focus on technology: Innovation and technology forecasts.	Worth reading, many ideas, explanations, descriptions and comments.	2

No.	Source	Link	Focus	Remarks	Score
6	Bell Labs Corporation (Alcatel-Lucent)	http://www.bell-labs.com	Focus on technology: Innovation, network technologies, convergence, optical networks, software development, algorithms, etc.	Overview and links to developers, related issues and details.	3.5
7	Bertelsmann Foundation Institute	http://www.bertelsmann-stiftung.de	Focus on "Sustainable Society" (Germany): Very broad spectrum of societal issues: politics, society, business, education, health, culture.	Much material available and much free of charge.	2
8	Bley und Schwarzmann AG, Future Business Group, Schorndorf Corporation	http://www.bleyundschwarzmann.de	No focus	Sees itself as pathbreaker, little substantive information, mainly self-promotion.	4.5
9	BrainStore, Biel, Switzerland Corporation	http://www.brainstore.com	Focus: generating ideas to-go.	Little content, mainly self-promotion.	5
10	British Telecom Corporation	http://www.btplc.com/ http://www.groupbt.com/innovation	Focus on technology and society: Innovation, network technologies, gadgets, "on the move," service, social and environment report, etc.	Good source of information, many ideas, and many reports and studies available. E.g.: "Changing Values," "Technology Timeline"	1.5
11	German Federal Department of Education and Research German Agency	http://www.bmbf.de	Focus on Germany: Selected issues: nanotechnology, information society, production research, climate-protection research, microsystem technology, medicine, etc.	Many reports are available.	2.5
12	Office for Estimating the Impact of Technology (TAB) of the German Parliament German Agency	http://www.tab.fzk.de	Focus on selected issues such as risk, innovation and knowledge.	Discussion papers, background papers and reports available (some are not up-to-date).	2.5
13	Cato Institute, Washington Institute	http://www.cato.org	Focus: U.S. public policy debates: current issues.	Much material available, often politically motivated.	3.5
14	Census Bureau Government Agency	http://www.census.gov	Focus on U.S., statistics: People & household, business & industry, geography, special topics.	Very extensive source of data, including links to further U.S. agencies (e.g. Center of Economic Studies), hardly any issues relating to the future.	2
15	Center for Applied Political Research (CAP) Munich University	http://www.cap-lmu.de	Focus on political issues of the future: European integration, modern government, transformation research, issues relating to the future, political education, etc.	Many studies and reports available free of charge.	2

9 Appendix I

No.	Source	Link	Focus	Remarks	Score
16	Centre for Future Studies (CFS), Canterbury, Kent Company	http://www.futurestudies.co.uk	Focus: consulting services relating to the future for selected industry sectors.	Company profile, hardly any material available.	4
17	CIA Factbook Government Agency	https://www.cia.gov	Profile of all countries (geography, politics, economy, population) – current data.	The Factbook is available (in book or digital form).	2
18	CIFS – Copenhagen Institute for Future Studies Institute	http://www.cifs.dk	Future studies on selected issues for members.	Few articles available free of charge.	4
19	DARPA Government Agency	http://www.darpa.mil	Focus on military: various programs.	Research institute of the U.S. Department of Defense, program information available.	4.5
20	DB Research Institute	http://www.db-research.de	Focus on global macroeconomic developments.	Broad selection of issues, much material is interpreted and most material is available free of charge, very good source.	1
21	Demos, London Company	http://www.demos.co.uk	Focus on Great Britain: general interest issues.	"The Think Tank for Everyday Democracy." Most articles are available in digital form free of charge or in print form for a fee.	3
22	German Institute for Economic Research DIW Institute	http://www.diw.de	Focus on economic development in Germany: Economic reports and forecasts, productivity, capacity, population development	Extensive material available, numerous links to other sources	2
23	Department of Trade and Industry (DTI) Future and Innovation Unit (FIU), UK Government Agency	http://www.dti.gov.uk	Focus on economic development in Great Britain: Trade, business, employees, consumers, innovation, science and energy	Most of the reports are available free of charge.	1.5
24	Drivers of Change Arup Foresight + Innovation + Incubation Initiative	http://www.driversofchange.com	Focus on drivers of change: Society, technology, the environment, economics, politics.	Maps (available for a fee) and blog.	3.5
25	Portal of the European Commission International Agency	http://www.europa.eu http://www.eurofound.euro pa.eu	Focus: Information on all EU matters.	Very extensive source of information, mostly neutral presentation.	1.5
26	European Information Technology Observatory International Agency	http://www.eito.com	Focus on technology in Europe: Statistics on ICT and consumer markets.	A number of statistical reports are available free of charge, EITO appears annually, can be ordered on website.	3

No.	Source	Link	Focus	Remarks	Score
27	Faith Popcorn BrainReserve, New York Company	http://www.faithpopcorn.com	Focus on marketing: Consulting services in trends, consumers, marketing, visions, etc.	Hardly any substantive material available.	4.5
28	FCL – Future Concept Lab, Milan Institute	http://www.futureconceptlab.com	Focus: Marketing issues and trends in consumption.	Hardly any substantive material available.	4
29	FiBS – Research Institute for Education and Social Economics Institute	http://www.fibs-koeln.de	Focus on Germany: Education & economics, social economics.	Articles appearing in the FIBS Forum are available free of charge.	3.5
30	Finland Futures Research Centre Institute of the "Turku School of Economics"	http://www.tukkk.fi/tutu	Focus on Finland at regional and national levels, some global reporting: Society, environment, innovation, economics, technology, culture, knowledge, etc.	Some material is available, much in the Finnish language.	4
31	Forecast Center, LLC Website	http://www.forecastcenter.com	Focus: USA, international: Demographics, economy, energy, environment, health, lifestyles, politics, technology, etc.	Some material is available free of charge, registration is sometimes required. Coverage of U.S. only	3
32	Foresight Institute, Palo Alto, USA Institute	http://www.foresight.org	Focus on technology: Nanotechnology.	Some material is available.	3
33	Foresight International	http://foresightinternational.com.au	Focus on societal development "Help create and sustain social foresight." Politics, strategy, organization, innovation, etc.	Papers available free of charge; books and publications can be ordered online.	3
34	The Fraunhofer Institute for Systems and Innovation Research (ISI) Institute	http://www.isi.fhg.de	Focus on innovation: Energy, environment, production, communication, biotechnology, sustainable economies	Hardly any material available free of charge, may be ordered.	3.5
35	The Fraunhofer Institute for Natural Science and Technology Trend Analyses (INT) Institute	http://www.int.fhg.de	Focus on technology: Technology analysis and technology outlook.	Hardly any material available free of charge, strong military reference.	4,5
36	Friedrich Ebert Foundation, Germany Institute	http://www.fes.de	Focus on politics and society: Societal justice, innovation and progress, active democracy.	Large archive with search function, most material available free of charge.	1.5
37	Future Management Group AG Company	http://www.micic.com	Focus on "future management": Trend research, future studies (society, economics, technology), and selected (current) issues.	Description of the "future factors," glossary and published articles are available free of charge.	3

No.	Source	Link	Focus	Remarks	Score
38	Futuribles Group, Paris, France Non-profit Consulting Firm	http://www.futuribles.com	Focus on Western Europe: Society, politics, future, methodology (look-out system).	Little material available free of charge, most material in the French language.	3.5
39	Gartner, Inc. Consulting Firm	http://www.gartner.com	Focus on technology and markets: specialized in IT technology.	Various products and programs, ranging from short analyses to detailed market studies. For paying customers only.	4.5
40	Gottlieb Duttweiler Institut (GDI), Rüschlikon/Zurich, Switzerland Institute	http://www.gdi.ch	Focus on end customer: Marketing, market and consumer analysis for many branches.	Study reports can be ordered online.	3
41	Global Business Network (GBN), USA Consulting Firm	http://www.gbn.com	Focus on the future in general: Politics, economics, society, values, etc.	Large selection of current issues and new ideas.	2.5
42	Society for Future Models and System Criticism (GZS), Münster, Germany Association	http://www.zukunft-gzs.de	Focus on a "better future": Future studies, peace studies, the future of work, peace work, etc.	Publisher of "Focus on the Future" – available online in German free of charge. Online publications available	4
43	Hawaii Research Center for Future Studies (HRCFS) Research Center	http://www.futures.hawaii.edu	Focus on Hawaii, North America, South East Asia, Pacific: Politics, institutions, society, population, etc.	Extensive collection of material available (e.g. Hawaii 2050).	2.5
44	Horizon Site	http://horizon.unc.edu/onramp	Focus on environmental changes: STEEP approach	Good source of information and many links to further sources.	2
45	IAF – Institute for Alternative Futures – Institute	http://www.altfutures.com	Focus on future-related issues: Education, society, politics, technology, knowledge, etc.	Some project material and reports are available. E.g.: Rural Futures: Scoping Social Science Research Needs.	2.5
46	ICEBERG Consulting, Society for Applied Trend Research GmbH, Bremen, Germany Consulting Firm	http://www.iceberg-consulting.de	Focus: Management and sales, information technologies, scenarios, trend research, TIME industries, CRM, HR, strategies & implementation, automobile industry, consumer products.	Selected reports are available, but to some extent out-of-date.	4

No.	Source	Link	Focus	Remarks	Score
47	Institute for Work and Technology (IAT) Institute	http://www.iatge.de/iat	Focus on change processes: Organizations, economics, politics and society.	Access to manuscripts and presentations on focus subjects (via search function).	2.5
48	Institute for the Future (IFTF), Palo Alto USA Institute	http://www.iftf.org	Focus on technology and society: Nonprofit, subjects are determined on an annual basis.	Current reports only available for members, older reports available free of charge, well-maintained blog.	1.5
49	Institute of Ideas, London/UK Institute	http://www.instituteofideas.com	Focus on current societal issues: Freedom, culture, society, health, politics, etc. (also UK).	Many articles available online.	3
50	Institute for Futures Studies and Technology Assessment (IZT), Berlin Institute	http://www.izt.de	Focus on future studies relating to current issues, Germany, Europe and the world: "Interdisciplinary Drafting of Future-related Project Studies of Issues with Long-term Significance for Society."	Material on selected issues is available.	2
51	International Institute for Strategic Studies (IISS), UK Institute	http://www.iiss.org	Focus on politics and military: Investigations of eight regions and eight issues: conflict, terrorism, defense, etc.	Books on sale. Registered users can obtain more information about the books and reports.	3.5
52	International Institute for Applied Systems Analysis (IIASA) Institute	http://www.iiasa.ac.at	Focus on environment, economics, technology and society: 3 main issues: environment and natural resources, population and society, energy and technology.	Documents on many subjects available.	2
53	The Institute of Policy Studies (IPS), Singapore Institute	http://www.ips.org.sg	Focus on the development of Singapore: Population, family, economics, environment, information, society, law, politics, etc.	Extensive publications list.	2
54	Institute for Prospective Technological Studies (IPTS) Institute	http://www.jrc.es	Focus on technological development: Innovation, energy, transport, information society, etc.	Study reports on many subjects available – via database	2
55	IST, Information Society Technology, EU International Agency	http://www.cordis.lu/ist	Focus on societal and economic challenges: Innovation, computer technologies, communication technologies, etc.	Publications on research subjects project results available.	2.5
56	Institute for Technology Assessment and Systems Analysis (ITAS), Karlsruhe, Germany Institute	http://www.itas.fzk.de	Focus on human behavior in connection with new technologies: "Systematic Relationships between Processes of Societal Change and Developments in Science, Technology and the Environment."	Extensive material available (since 1985).	2

9 Appendix I

No.	Source	Link	Focus	Remarks	Score
57	Leading Futurists Consulting Firm	http://www.leadingfuturists.biz	Focus on general future studies: Scans and trend insights to build a picture of the emerging environment – keynote presentations – foresight workshops.	Little substantive material available.	4.5
58	Ministry of Economy, Trade and Industry (METI), Japan Government Agency	http://www.meti.go.jp/english	Focus on the development of Japan: Industry, economics and trade, statistics, technology development and science.	Good source of information (difficult navigation).	2.5
59	Massachusetts Institute of Technology (MIT), Cambridge / USA University	http://web.mit.edu	Focus on new technologies and scientific developments: Environment, economics, technology, etc.	Very extensive information with different degrees of availability.	2
60	Max Planck Institute for Demographic Research Institute	http://www.demogr.mpg.de	Focus on demographic change: Societal and economic influence.	Extensive information – some dissertations and books are available online.	1.5
61	MIT Media Lab University	http://www.media.mit.edu	Focus on computer and communication technology: Research, trends, innovations, etc.	Very extensive information with different degrees of availability (to some extent excessive).	3
62	National Academies Institute	http://www.nationalacademies.org	Focus USA: "Advisers to the Nation on Science, Engineering und Medicine."	Publications on featured subjects.	3
63	National Environmental Policy Plan Netherlands (NEPP) Government Agency	http://www.sharedspaces.nl	Focus on city development: City planning, city development and the environment.	Reports are available.	3
64	National Institute of Science and Technology Policy (NISTEP) Institute	http://www.nistep.go.jp	Focus on research and technology in Japan: Research processes, energy, nanotechnology, communication technology, etc.	Material on many subjects available, e.g. "Trends Quarterly Review."	2.5
65	National Science Foundation Government Agency	http://www.nsf.gov	Focus on science and development: Material sciences, nanotechnology, the environment, robotics, etc.	Extensive material available.	3
66	Nomura Research Institute (Nomura Group), Japan Consulting Firm	http://www.nri.co.jp	Focus on future development in Japan: "Dream up the Future" Economics, science, finance, etc.	Some study reports available.	2.5

No.	Source	Link	Focus	Remarks	Score
67	Northern Great Plains Inc., Canada Non-profit Research Organization	http://www.ngplains.org	Focus on agriculture and natural resources: Economics, health, agriculture in North America and Europe.	Most of the reports are available.	2.5
68	OECD International Agency	http://www.oecd.org	Focus on global economic development: Statistics, economics, economic factors, innovation, etc.	News available, study reports can be ordered online.	2.5
69	Potsdam Institute for Climate Impact Research (PIK) Institute	http://www.pik-potsdam.de	Focus on climate and environmental issues: Analysis of the ecological, geophysical and socioeconomic aspect of global environmental changes, climate impact research – climate change, sustainable development.	Selected reports are available.	2.5
70	PricewaterhouseCoopers Consulting Firm	http://www.pwc.com	Focus on industry analyses: Activities in most industry sectors	A number of White Papers are available (The Technology Center).	3
71	Prognos AG, Basel, Switzerland Consulting Firm	http://www.prognos.com	Focus on market and societal issues of the future: Life, learning & work, economics & population, health & social concerns, energy & water, future of various regions, waste disposal & environment, innovation policies, management & organizational consulting, etc.	Material on selected subjects available (e.g. "Future Atlas 2007").	3
72	RAND Corporation, Santa Monica, USA Institute	http://www.rand.org	Focus on the future in general: Terrorism, the environment, energy, education, demographics, etc.	Hardly any material available.	4
73	Rheingold – Institute for Qualitative Market and Media Analyses Institute	http://www.rheingold-online.de	Focus on market and media analyses: Women, internal affairs, youth, children, culture, markets, brands, media, Internet, seniors, sports, sponsoring, trends, advertising, etc.	Articles on selected subjects available.	3.5
74	Robert Jungk Library for Questions Concerning the Future	http://www.jungk-bibliothek.at	Focus on general questions involving the future: "Collects and documents interdisciplinary future-relevant publications from numerous subject areas."	Little material available.	3.5
75	St. Gallen Center for Future Studies (SGZZ) Institute	http://www.sgzz.ch	Focus on market development, branch forecasts, scenario management: Enterprise strategies, branch analyses, economic policies.	The name is misleading, inaccurate information, and little material available.	4.5
76	Santa Fe Institute, USA Institute	http://www.santafe.edu	Focus on critical, current issues: Physics, nature, biology, the environment, economics, technology, etc.	Access to material on a broad array of subjects.	2.5

No.	Source	Link	Focus	Remarks	Score
77	Scenario Management International AG, ScMI – Paderborn, Germany Consulting Firm	http://www.scmi.de	Focus on consulting: Basis is the scenario management method.	Hardly any material available, lists of published articles and books.	4
78	SCP – Social and Cultural Planning Office of the Netherlands, Netherlands – Government Agency	http://www.scp.nl/english	Focus on European development: Health, societal development, social security, job market, demographics.	Good source of information, many documents available.	2
79	SFZ – Secretariat for Future Studies, Dortmund, Germany Institute	http://www.sfz.de	Focus on general future issues: Society, technology, politics, economics, sustainability	Hardly any material available.	4
80	Sinus Sociovision GmbH, Heidelberg, Germany Company	http://www.sinus-sociovision.de	Focus on market research: Psychological and socio-scientific research and consulting, division of society into milieus and the (controversial) attempt to explain societal and market developments on the basis of these defined milieus.	Description of the concepts and a number of selected study reports available.	3
81	Social Technologies Consulting Firm	http://www.social-technologies.com	Focus on the future: Foresight, strategy and innovation.	Little useful material except for the company profile.	4.5
82	SRI Consulting Business Intelligence (SRC-BI) Consulting Firm	http://www.sric-bi.com	Focus on technology: Monitoring of a "Technology List," e.g.: biosensors, fuel cells, nanomaterials, etc. contract research in various programs, e.g. Explorer, Scan.	Essentially contract research, little material available except for examples. Some programs seem interesting.	3.5
83	SRI International – Policy Division, USA Non-profit Institute	http://www.sri.com	Focus on technology: Analyses concentrate on 5 segments: Engineering & Systems Division, Policy Division, Information and Computing Sciences Division, Biosciences Division, Physical Sciences Division.	A number of recent articles are available under the rubric "Publications."	3
84	TechCast Institute	http://www.techcast.org	Focus on technology: Analysis of future technologies and forecasts about their actual development.	Access to (expert-based) "Strategic-Breakthrough Analysis."	2
85	Technology Information, Forecasting and Assessment Council (TIFAC), India Government Agency	http://www.tifac.org.in	Focus on technology in India: Biotechnology, Communication and Information, Energy, Science & Technology in India, Environment and Habitat, Water – Environment, Electronics & Instrumentation – Foods and Agriculture, Control, Automation, Communication, Transport, etc.	Extensive source of information (e.g. Vision 2020), to some extent out-of-date.	2.5

No.	Source	Link	Focus	Remarks	Score
86	The Futurist – Website	http://www.futurist.com	Focus on general future issues: Trends, economics, technology, the environment and energy, society and culture, global issues, demographics, transport, traffic, values, family, etc.	Extensive source of information, many comments.	2
87	Time, Visions of the 21st century Website	http://www.time.com/time/reports/v21	Focus on visions of the 21st century: Work, life and technologies in the 21st century, outlook and discussions, questions and answers concerning the future.	Interesting source of information (including further sources).	3
88	Trendbüro Consulting Firm	http://www.trendbuero.de	Competencies: Trend Research, Consumer Insight, Branding & Communication, Innovation & New Product Development, Business Development (Language: German!).	A number of study reports are available free of charge, also organizes trend conferences.	3.5
89	UN – United Nations International Agency	http://www.un.org	Focus on global situation and development: Peace, civilization, economic development, climate change, etc.	Extensive offer of study reports and statistics, most can be ordered online.	3
90	UN – Industrial Development Organization International Agency	http://www.unido.org	Focus on global industrial development Energy, the environment, trade, productivity and fighting poverty.	Extensive source of information and statistics, most material available free of charge.	1.5
91	United Nations University Tokyo, Japan International Agency	http://www.unu.edu	Focus on global problems facing humanity: Land, peace, food, energy, etc.	Extensive information, including a lecture series.	2.0
92	USA, Office of Science and Technology Policy Government Agency	http://www.ostp.gov (Executive Office of the President)	Focus on technology in the U.S.: Analyses of U.S. competitiveness in the areas of technology development, telecommunications and information technology, the environment, the sciences in general, societal development, etc.	Reports (some out-of-date) are available free of charge.	3.5
93	Scientific Institute for Communication Services (WIK) Institute	http://www.wik.org	Focus on infrastructure in Germany: Regulation & competition, market structure and enterprise strategies, communication and innovation, postal system and logistics, cost models and Internet economy, energy markets and energy regulation.	Successor to a Deutsche Post think tank. Many study reports are available free of charge.	3.5
94	Science Center Berlin (WZB) Institute	http://www.wz-berlin.de	Focus on societal development in Germany: Main subject: "Development Tendencies, Adaptation Problems and Innovation Opportunities of Modern Democratic Societies" Job market and economic development, innovation and science policies, intercultural and international conflicts, etc.	Discussion papers and lectures available free of charge.	2.5

No.	Source	Link	Focus	Remarks	Score
95	World Global Trends Website	http://t21.ca	Focus on international development: Trends, population development, the environment, politics, health, culture, economics, etc. "Accurate representation of world issues is crucial."	Extensive source of information.	2
96	World Future Society (WFS) Association	http://www.wfs.org	Focus on global future studies: Globally organized platform for handling questions concerning the future Forecasts, trends, ideas about future developments.	Annual conference, various publications (e.g. Futures Research Quarterly) Some material is available free of charge, some can be ordered online.	2
97	Wuppertal Institute Institute	http://www.wupperinst.org	Focus on climate, the environment, energy: Resources, transportation, climate, the environment, sustainability, etc.	Reports available free of charge, books can be ordered.	2
98	Xerox PARC Institute	http://www.parc.xerox.com	Focus technology development: Biomedicine, mobile & wireless, image processing, materials, processes, micro-devices, human-machine interface, ubiquitous computing.	Comments, articles and analyses available free of charge. Books and publications can be ordered.	2.5
99	Z-Punkt The Foresight Company Consulting Firm	http://www.z-punkt.de	Focus on economics, technology and innovations Future issues, megatrends, technologies, developments, etc.	Some articles, reports, and dossiers available free of charge; books and publications can be ordered.	2.5
100	Zukunfts-institut GmbH Institute	http://www.zukunftsinstitut.de	Focus on society, marketing, economics, politics Markets, consumers, braches, trends.	Study reports and books can be ordered, most material is available only to members.	3.5

Chapter 10

Appendix II

Short Profiles of Selected Methods

In what follows, I describe a number of methods that can be usefully deployed in connection with trends and scenarios. The methods that have been used throughout the book are assigned to their respective contexts in Table 50. Elaborate and comprehensive descriptions of the methods of analysis are available, for instance, in [Have 2003; Fleisher 2003; Chernev 2006] and particularly in [Kerth 2007]. It warrants bearing in mind once again that there are no ultimate tools or methods. All such instruments entail a certain compromise. If applied appropriately, they can make a contribution to an effective sorting of information, the establishment of a greater degree of clarity, and the analysis of problems.

Table 50 Methods of Analysis and Their Contexts

Context	Section	Method
Macro environment analysis	10.1.1	Environment analysis (STEEPV) (cf. Section 2.2)
	10.1.2	Trend analysis (cf. Section 3.3)
	10.1.3	Issue management (cf. Section 2.3)
Micro environment analysis	10.2.1	Stakeholder analysis (cf. Sections 1.4, 5.2)
	10.2.2	Customer profile analysis (cf. Section 1.4)
	10.2.3	Branch analysis (5F) (cf. Section 1.4)
Enterprise analysis	10.3.1	7S model (cf. Section 5.4)
	10.3.2	Value-chain analysis (cf. Section 5.4)
	10.3.3	Benchmarking (cf. Section 6.4.7)
Foresight	10.4.1	Morphological analysis (cf. Section 4.8)
	10.4.2	Trend extrapolation/forecast (cf. Section 1.1)
	10.4.3	Weak-signal analysis (cf. Section 2.4)
Strategic analysis	10.5.1	BCG matrix (cf. Chapter 5)
	10.5.2	SWOT analysis (cf. Section 5.5)
	10.5.3	Ansoff matrix (cf. Section 5.2)
Change management	10.6.1	Eight-phase model according to Kotter (cf. Chapter 6)
	10.6.2	Balanced scorecard (cf. Sections 1.4, 5.4)

10.1 Macro Environment Analysis

10.1.1 Environment Analysis (STEEPV)

Description

The STEEPV analysis essentially offers a form of structural help when it comes to assessing an enterprise's environment. The method involves a breaking down of the environment into six segments.

STEEPV stands for:

S	Social	Social issues
T	Technological	Scientific and technological issues
E	Economic	Economic issues
E	Environmental or Ecological	Environmental, habitat and sustainability issues
P	Political	Political issues
V	Values	Consideration of values

The significance of the individual segments may differ according to the focus and the perspective of the particular inquiry. Descriptions of other bases for analysis offering similar structural support, such as PEST and PESTL, are also available in the literature. The **L** in these acronyms stands for "legal" issues.

Application

It is essential when it comes to the practical application of these methods of analysis to establish clarity with regard to the subject of inquiry. For instance, in the case of economic issues, the focus may be local, regional, national or international, i.e. for any given segment in the complex "Economic" (Table 51). The segments are then analyzed in detail using such further specification. Moreover, other methods of analysis may also be applied.

Table 51 Examples of Issues Featured in STEEPV Segments

Social	Technological	Economic	Environmental	Political	Values
Population	Progress	Macro Economics	Climate	Stability	Culture
Wealth	Innovation	Finance Market	Species Protection	Power Distribution	Ideals

Aim

STEEPV represents a first step in many investigations, a point of entry for a more extensive analysis. STEEPV can be used to establish an overview or a big picture of the current situation and to set the course for further investigation.

Limits

The establishment of segments entails a certain investigative limitation. One should make sure to consider (or intentionally filter out) any relevantly related issues or issues that simply do not correspond to the structure (e.g. the issue of research).

While the method clearly offers valuable structuring support, the quality and the completeness of the information itself remains a general problem.

10.1.2 Trend Analysis

Description

Trend analysis involves a longer-term identification and description of specific changes. The basic assumption is that changes detected in the past will have an impact on the future according to a certain pattern.

A distinction is made here between quantitative and qualitative procedures.

Application

Establishing a subject of inquiry will necessarily limit the search. While systematically monitoring and scanning the environment, one gathers information (and reevaluates information that is already available) that is then examined for the presence of development patterns. Tendencies that are identified are formulated as hypotheses and then verified or discarded.

Aim

Knowledge about the development of changes in the enterprise environment constitutes a basis for subsequent strategic considerations. Both the strategic planning of an enterprise and its capacity to respond to detected risks and opportunities is enhanced via continuous trend analysis.

Limits

Looking into the future is not an exact science and trend analysis is also caught in the force field between theory and practical necessity. As I have suggested throughout this book, surprises are a part of our future. The challenge when applying this method is to identify and demarcate trends. A trend is not a change that takes place in ideal conditions and that is amenable to exact demarcation. It follows that, in addition to projecting a trend into the future, it is essential for effective trend analysis to come up with a workable description or formulation of the trend. An improved understanding of the relationships between and interactions among change phenomena will lead to more sound strategic decisions. A lack of knowledge here can lead to poor strategic decisions. However, it is naturally not possible to obtain and evaluate all of the relevant information. Accordingly, one should beware of falling into the trap of "paralysis through analysis."

10.1.3 Issue Management

Description

The term "issue management" refers to an early warning/early reaction system that is used to observe and analyze the enterprise's environment so as to enable both crisis prevention and the communication of opportunities. By ensuring the early detection of critical issues and the demands of stakeholders that threaten to restrict an enterprise's room to maneuver, issue management provides a basis for taking an active approach to such issues. Issue management is based on the notion that enterprises (as parts of society) are offered a certain arena in which they can pursue business and that the esteem enjoyed by an enterprise correlates to the degree to which it assumes an active role within this arena. Issue management is to ensure that certain issues do not "escalate" and damage the reputation of the enterprise.

Application

Issue management has an early warning function and is supposed to enable one to develop strategies to influence the public treatment of relevant issues or, if this is not possible, to appropriately adapt enterprise policy. Issue management thus centers on the following activities:

- The identification, observation and analysis of social, technological, political and economic forces and trends that could have an impact on the enterprise
- The identification of the implications of such forces and trends and the identification of the enterprise's response options
- The selection and implementation of strategies for dealing with these issues.

Aim

Issue management is more of a strategic instrument – involving the continuous participation of all of an enterprise's departments – than a communication-intensive instrument. The aim of issue management is to detect risks and opportunities (both with respect to business and the media) at an early stage and to respond accordingly.

Limits

Opinions as to what constitutes an opportunity and what constitutes a risk are subjective and their accuracy can only be evaluated in retrospect. While the method itself is to be assessed as helpful, caution is to be exercised with respect to its political placement within the enterprise. Moreover, efforts to integrate it into strategic management have shown little success so far. Managers often prefer to stick to the plan until it's too late (e.g. when the Mercedes A-Class failed the high-speed swerve test).

10.2 Micro Environment Analysis

10.2.1 Stakeholder Analysis

Description

The stakeholder analysis permits an initial differentiated look at the most important players in the enterprise and their interests with respect to the enterprise. The stakeholder analysis has a number of goals:

- First, it is to facilitate the identification of the relevant claims groups.
- Second, it is to clarify the significance of these groups to the enterprise.
- Third, it is to work out suggestions for properly dealing with the needs and demands of these groups.

The stakeholder analysis is to account for the following items:

- The interests and expectations stakeholders have with respect to the actions taken by the enterprise
- The opinions of stakeholders relating to enterprise issues, the arguments they use, and how they attempt to influence the way such issues are handled
- The existing relationships between the individual stakeholder groups
- The extent of the various claims groups' influence

Application

The stakeholder concept assumes a mutually beneficial relationship between the enterprise and its stakeholders (interest groups). A stakeholder analysis can be carried out to determine the following:

- To identify the potential stakeholders at the time of the enterprise's formation
- To establish an overview of the claims groups that are relevant to specific enterprise projects (e.g. customers, employees, owners, and lenders involved in a marketing project).

Aim

The stakeholders and their interaction with one another have a significant impact on the general situation and competitiveness of enterprises. It follows that knowledge of who makes decisions within an enterprise and of the way they behave and interact can offer managers an enhanced capacity to influence the course of things within an enterprise.

Limits

Enterprises are not rigid constructs. On the contrary, they change continuously and are continuously subject to both internal and external sources of influence. A stakeholder analysis is therefore to be regarded as a continuous process and not as a one-time analysis. Moreover, one should also bear in mind that enterprises are made up of people and are thus subject to (capricious) human behavior. Like most instruments, the stakeholder analysis is more a form of support for developing a more intricate understanding of situations than a method of generating reliable hypotheses.

10.2.2 Customer Profile Analysis

Description

The needs of customers are becoming ever more specific and individual. For an enterprise, it is important to understand customer requirements in order to remain competitive. An awareness of the fact that customers differ in terms of their contribution to the success of the enterprise can help one to appreciate the challenge, for instance, of increasing one's competitive advantage by orienting oneself towards the premium-customer segment. Identifying these customers and offering them special segment-specific treatment reflect the core of segmentation theory.

Application

The customer analysis should provide answers to the following questions:

- Will newly acquired customers be more profitable than existing customers?
- What is the lifetime value of one's top customers?
- What customer group uses what product and with what frequency?
- What customer group is very likely to react positively to a certain product?

The first step in the customer analysis is to identify and demarcate customer groups, i.e. break customers down into subsegments. The customers within each segment have similar needs and exhibit similar behavior. This is represented by various criteria. These criteria should be measurable and have a clear relationship to the needs or behavior of the customers. Various customer segments are then presented as the result of this analysis.

The next step is to assess the attractiveness of the customer segment for the enterprise and to develop specific measures for addressing this segment.

Aim

An improved understanding of customers is always an advantage. In addition to knowledge of customer needs, it can be especially worthwhile for enterprises to identify the customers who contribute most to the success of the enterprise and to offer these customers more intensive support.

Limits

Both customer-relationship-management systems (CRMSs), which focus on the automated recording of customer contacts and the drafting of customer profiles, and milieu profiling based on general attributes such as gender, age and income represent further developments of this model. One should not forget, however, that an understanding of customers and their needs can only be won by intensive contact with customers. This is a prerequisite for any form of customer analysis, and it cannot be replaced by automated systems or the recording of statistics.

10.2.3 Industry and Market Analysis

Description

Markets distinguish themselves in terms of their products, innovation cycles, regulatory status, industry structure, development speed and many other factors. From an entrepreneurial or investment perspective, they may be variously attractive, depending on the various business opportunities they offer.

Porter proposes the use of the five-forces framework (Figure 164) to ascertain the attractiveness of an industry from the perspective of competition. The model is based

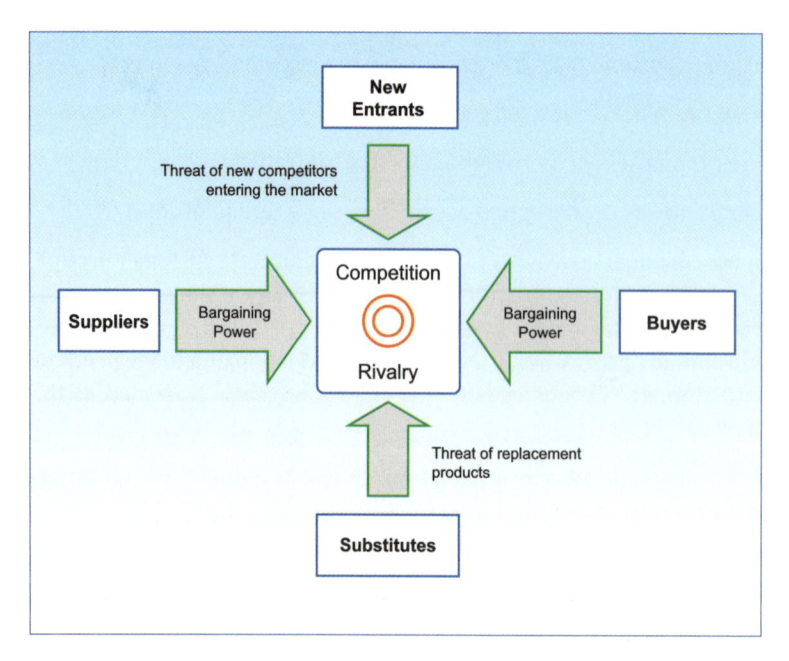

Figure 164 Porter's five-forces framework: pressure from all sides

on the notion that the intensity of competition is essentially determined by the nature of the five forces of competition:

- Rivalry among extant competitors
- Bargaining power of the buyer
- Bargaining power of the supplier
- Threat created by substitutes
- Threat created by new entrants

Application

The five forces proposed by Porter that determine the attractiveness of specific markets are assessed individually and compressed into an overall opinion of how attractive the market is. The evaluation is usually qualitative. While we could imagine a scheme for quantification, such could scarcely be expected to lead to a more precise evaluation. This sort of systematic and comprehensive examination of the factors relevant to competition can be particularly helpful when it comes to developing an understanding of a specific market in the initial phases of a strategic analysis.

The model permits one to assess risks and opportunities and offers one the option of taking a structured approach to examining and evaluating complex interaction between competitors on particular markets.

Aim

This instrument gives one an overview of particular markets and a better understanding of the force structure it is based on. This enables a strategic evaluation of future activities.

Limits

Numerous examples offer testimony to the fact that enterprises can also be very successful and earn lots of money on apparently unattractive markets. The evaluation of the attractiveness of a market therefore does not represent a comprehensive basis for strategic decisions. The essential weakness of the model is related to the historical context in which it was developed. The world economy at the beginning of the 1980s was characterized by fierce competition and cyclical growth. The primary enterprise goal consisted of securing survival and profitability. One basic condition for this was an optimization of strategy with respect to the competitive environment. Compared to the developments on many markets today, developments back then were relatively stable and predictable.

This is another reason why the application of Porter's framework of the five forces of competition to today is limited. The model cannot be used to examine new business models and dynamic market development. The utility of the model today is that it enables one to gain an initial structured and comprehensible overview of the situation on a given market.

10.3 Enterprise Analysis

10.3.1 The 7S Model

Description

Enterprises are complex entities. One instrument used for analyzing the organizational structure of enterprises is the 7S model that was described in Section 5.4. It represents a management model with a special focus on the integration of soft factors into enterprise development, an area that is typically characterized by strategy planning.

Application

The seven components (also referred to in the literature as factors or elements) of the model can be divided into 2 categories: "hard" (i.e. tangible factors such as strategy, structure and systems) and "soft" (i.e. flexible factors such as vision, employees, capabilities and enterprise structure). After all, the success of an enterprise depends on more than just rational, explicit and quantitative (hard) factors. Soft factors, which are more implicit, emotional and qualitative also play an important role. In any case, all factors should be considered together.

Aim

The aim of the method can be seen primarily in connection with change processes. As experience shows, the success of operative change initiatives depends on the inclusion of all relevant factors. Unsuccessful initiatives can often be explained by the fact that although the factors "strategy" and "structure" were revamped, the remaining five factors were not considered. The method can therefore be regarded as a form of support when it comes to implementing change. All factors are related to one another and any change in one factor will have an impact on the other factors.

Limits

The model is to be regarded as a framework or a source of orientation. Each factor should be comprehensively examined. This may involve the deployment of additional models and instruments. This represents a considerable improvement over traditional change processes in enterprises. That being said, it does not represent a guarantee for the successful implementation of change. As outlined in Section 5.4, a case-specific expansion of the model through the addition of other elements (factors) may prove helpful, particularly in dynamic business environments.

10.3.2 Value-chain Analysis

Description

This instrument is used to examine internal business in terms of its contribution to value creation. The model – also developed by Porter – is based on the assumption that the processes within an enterprise can be broken down into functional units and analyzed separately. Each individual value-creating activity can have an impact on costs and the degree of differentiation. One may therefore question whether the resources involved have optimally allocated or whether there are any alternatives in case the value contribution is minimal.

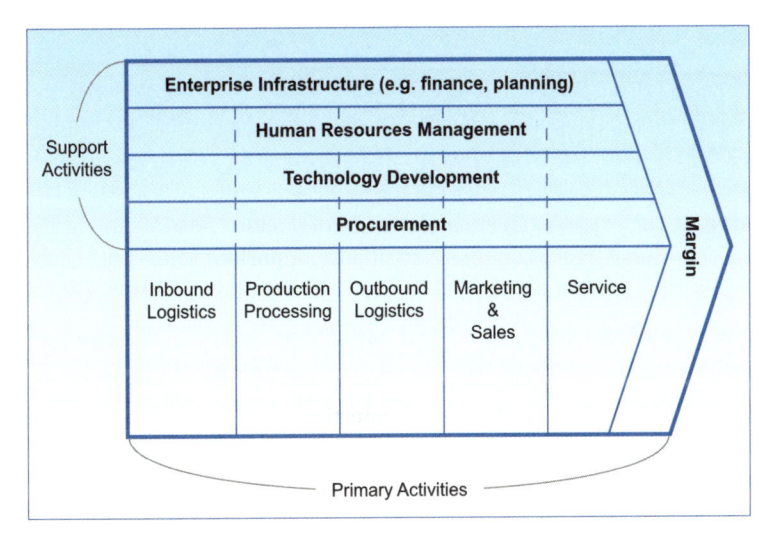

Figure 165 The value chain according to Porter: should be applied carefully

The model breaks down the activities in an enterprise into primary and support activities. The sequential work steps count as main activities and include clearance inwards, operations (production), clearance outwards, marketing & sales and customer service. Infrastructure development, human resources management, technology development and procurement are categorized as auxiliary or support activities and enable cooperation within the enterprise and general enterprise functioning.

Application

Using a simple input-output model, business sequences are broken down into functional blocks. These areas are then analyzed in terms of their cost position, differentiation potential and contribution to value.

Aim

The aim of value-added chain analysis is to increase the enterprise's competitiveness via increased effectiveness. This enables one to get clear on the individual functional blocks and their position in the overall scheme of operations, with decisions then being related to the overall scheme.

Limits

The model of the value-added chain is based on the notion of an ideal sequence with respect to the manufacturing of a product. This process is likely to be an exception on today's markets. Service-oriented industries are organized differently. Owing to the principle of division into individual activities, the representations can be expected to be quite specialized. With increasing complexity things will quickly lose clarity.

A further disadvantage associated with this model is the competition (us against them instead of joining forces) that can develop between the functional blocks owing to the pronounced departmentalization.

10.3.3 Benchmarking

Description

Benchmarking involves a comparison of the strengths of one's own enterprise (i.e. the whole enterprise or parts of it) with those of one's competitors. The typical object of comparison is the market leader.

Application

The comparison can be applied at various levels:

- Financial strength
- Process efficiency
- Market strength
- Strategic strength and decision strength
- Innovation strength
- Etc.

The enterprise establishes the area that is to be benchmarked and defines the relevant indicators that are to be used as a basis for comparison. Gaining access to the competitor's data can represent a challenge.

Aim

The aim of benchmarking is to expand one's horizons and exploit an opportunity to learn from the competition. One may discover room for improvement in one's business operations. It is an instrument of continuous quality and improvement management.

Limits

Benchmarking alone is not enough if one wants to become the market leader. Indeed, it can even be seen as a method of pegging oneself to the average. This is because no necessity is seen for discarding the status quo in favor of going off ahead of the competition. Benchmarking is often no more than a replacement for original strategy development and sound strategy management.

10.4 Foresight

10.4.1 Morphological Analysis

Description

The morphological analysis is a creativity technique that is oriented towards generating answers to a certain questions. The core of the method is a matrix containing a list of the various parameter elements. This matrix represents the "answer realm" in which logical combinations of element variations can be ascertained (see Figure 88).

Application

First, a matrix is drafted. The headers of the columns are filled with parameters that are characterized by various possible answers and that yield an answer to a question when combined. A search is then conducted for variations for each established parameter. Each variation is then entered in the relevant matrix column. If enough variations have been generated for each parameter, then these are combined into a strand or several strands. It is important to make sure that each strand remains free of contradiction and that each strand is different from all the other strands. Each strand represents a possible solution to the question.

Aim

This instrument has proven especially effective in the development of scenarios. A search is conducted for alternative variations and these are then combined into one or more possible solutions to a question relating to the ascertained uncertainties (see Section 4.8) that represent the parameters for the case in question. These variation strands then represent the basis for a scenario.

Limits

This method is essentially limited by the number of manageable parameters. More than ten parameters tends to be confusing. Software solutions are available as an alternative for such cases. In order to ensure greater insight into the nature of the problem, however, such solutions should be avoided.

10.4.2 Forecast

Description

Decisions are always based on expectations and forecasts. Trend extrapolation is a widespread procedure for projecting the development of trends. The procedure is based on the assumption that developments are determined by laws and causal connections that are at work in all historical developments.

Application

The basis for every projection is a model that orders the data in a temporal and causal connection. Simple cases can be represented in a time series:

Time series = trend + economic development + season + remainder

The time series is therefore defined by the trend function, an economic component, a seasonal component and a remainder. Although no limits to the complexity of forecasts apply, it is important to bear in mind that every development is also characterized by chaos and surprises that cannot be accounted for in a forecast and that therefore limit explanatory power.

A distinction is made between short-term (< 3 months), medium-term (3 months to 2 years) and long-term (> 2 years) forecasts.

Aim

The aim of time series in stable environments is obvious. The method can be used to forecast indicators. This enables a more precise planning of resources and stringent strategy planning, which supports an enterprise's ability to compete.

Limits

The question as to whether the application of extrapolation to determine further development is justified can only be clearly answered in retrospect. It follows that results are always to be interpreted first before being used – unfiltered – in decision making. The method is not suitable for long-term forecasts because the variance is already too big within the parameters in order to permit sound results at all. The assumption of the time stability hypothesis (i.e. that the conditions for the development remain constant throughout the reference period) is no longer given.

10.4.3 Weak-signal Analysis

Description

The weak-signal method can be assigned to early strategic detection. The weak-signal approach introduced by Ansoff assumes that unexpected exogenous disruptions are not entirely unforeseeable. On the contrary, such events are always preceded by harbingers, i.e. early indicators of possible change. It is thus possible to detect structural breaches and crises at a sufficiently early stage.

Application

In order to be able to use this instrument, one is first required to determine what exactly one means in a given context when one refers to weak signals so that one can then examine the enterprise environment for the presence of such signals. Each period of harbingers is derived from the assumption that the early indicators signify the development of monumental changes.

Aim

The aim is to help enterprises become prepared. The early detection of possible changes will afford an enterprise more room to maneuver and an enhanced ability to respond.

Limits

Increasing the focus of observation to include weak signals will also increase the costs of observation and analysis. The challenge consists in distinguishing these signals from any old event on the landscape. Theoretically, any indication, no matter how apparently insignificant, could be a weak signal. This would quickly bring one up against the limits of one's processing capacity. Often it is a matter of premonition or a gut feeling, that is to say, very subjective assessments that then lead to the determination of a weak signal.

10.5 Strategic Analysis

10.5.1 BCG Matrix

Description

One of the most well-known management tools is the BCG matrix. Named after the Boston Consulting Group (BCG), this approach involves placing an enterprise's products in a portfolio. The evaluation of the products in terms of their relative market share and market-growth rate then allows one to represent the competitive position and the foreseeable product lifecycle of the product compared to other products. The

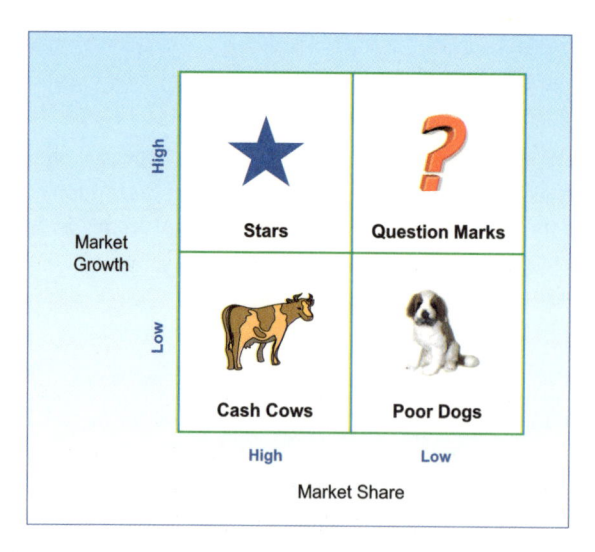

Figure 166 The BCG matrix: the clear, but risky classic of portfolio representation

relative market share is determined via the relationship of the product's market position to that of the strongest competitor. Market growth is ascertained on the basis of the change in sales over time.

The two criteria yield four possible assignments (Figure 166):

- Stars

    The dream constellation, excellent position both respect to competitiveness and the future.

- Question Marks

    Owing to a weak market position, only a limited degree of growth in the product segment can be achieved.

- Cash Cows

    Low rates of growth indicate that today's market position will not last.

- Poor Dogs

    Neither the rates of growth nor the market position give cause for optimism.

Application

The functional values for both criteria are ascertained for each product or for each product group. The key figures determine the position in the matrix. The position is usually indicated by a point. Color-coding or form and size attributes (e.g. "size corresponds to sales") allow one to represent further criteria.

The four fields yield a certain recommendation (norm strategy) about further procedure with the objects. The assumption is that the ideal lifecycle runs from "Question Marks" to "Stars" to "Cash Cow" and then to "Poor Dog."

Aim

The aim of the matrix is to offer an overview of the product portfolio and thus a basis for strategic discussion. The BCG matrix offers information about the product situation and is therefore an analysis instrument that can be used to support strategic orientation at a product level.

Limits

The advantage of portfolios – their clear representation – is at the same time the instrument's limitation. Every simplification is associated with a loss of information. The key figures conceal complex structures and relationships. As so often in the case of strategic tools, the benefits of the matrix here have less to do with the matrix itself than with the analysis and interpretation of the information. The challenge thus consists in interpreting the results and to appropriately consider the assumptions without simply accepting them as given. It is an open question whether market share, for instance, is a suitable criterion for representing the success of the product. Given the fact that the model represents a snapshot of the current situation and that new developments and innovations, for instance, are not considered, the forecast strength remains limited.

10.5.2 SWOT Analysis

Description

The SWOT analysis (**S**trengths, **W**eaknesses, **O**pportunities and **T**hreats) is an instrument of strategic management. It enables one to analyze and juxtapose an enterprise's internal operational performance – divided into strengths and weaknesses and external developments – divided into opportunities and threats (cf. Figure 113).

Application

The model offers a framework for further investigations and more extensive analyses. The SWOT analysis is the starting point and terminal point for determining the enterprise's strategic fit, i.e. the alignment of the enterprise's products to the demands of the market. Smooth enterprise activities are a sign of an optimal fit. This results from an intelligent alignment of internal and external features (cf. Figure 117).

One goal of the analysis is to identify possible sources of competitive advantages and needs for internal actions on the basis of the (internal) strengths-weaknesses analysis and the (external) opportunities-threats analysis. Important indicators for enterprise strategy are given when the strengths of an enterprise converge with opportunities or when weaknesses are detected.

Aim

The main aim of this method is to establish a clear representation of key data and features in a structured form. The results of further methods of analysis can then be compressed into core statements. A careful SWOT analysis can be a basis for decision making in the area of strategic management.

Limits

Every threat is simultaneously an opportunity. In light of this, an assignment is not always easy. The few strategy recommendations one finds in the literature such as the S-T strategy (use strengths to meet threats) are little helpful in this context because it is a matter of an overall view.

10.5.3 Ansoff Matrix

Description

The purpose of the Ansoff matrix (Figure 167) is to generate generic product strategies in accordance with the newness of the market and product.

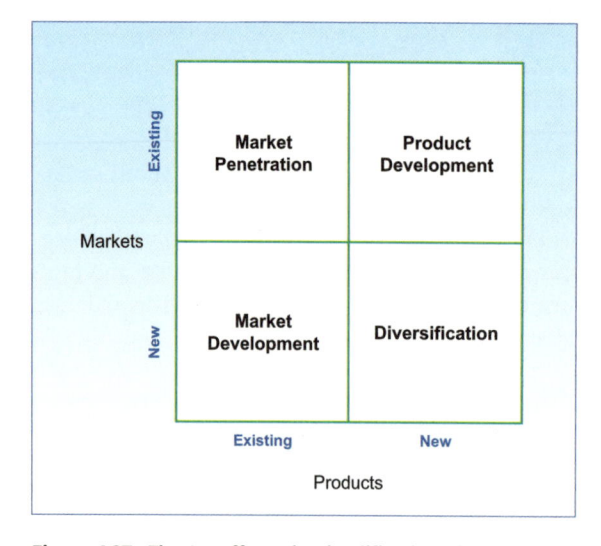

Figure 167 The Ansoff matrix: simplification of strategy proposals

Application

One can begin assigning the existing or planned products to one of the four quadrants once one has established a distinction between existing and new markets and characterized the products accordingly.

The model's core function consists in generating suitable strategies for the combinations. The diversification strategy, for instance, is suitable for the introduction of a new product to a new market. This may involve vertical integration or horizontal diversification or other possibilities. In contrast, methods of market penetration (e.g. vertical, regional) are suitable for placing existing products in existing markets.

Aim

The aim of this strategic instrument is to enable one to quickly identify a strategy in ideal circumstances and to elegantly represent possibilities.

Limits

While the Ansoff matrix is suitable for generating strategic options when deployed in the process of strategy development, it largely fails to account for market peculiarities and fast changes.

10.6 Change Management

10.6.1 Eight-phase Model According to Kotter

Description

The eight-phase process – conceived as a guideline – was developed as a promising method by John Kotter on the basis of an analysis of more than 100 case studies of attempts on the part of enterprises to implement change.

Application

The eight phases of change include:

Phase 1	Create a sense of urgency.
Phase 2	Establish a leadership coalition.
Phase 3	Develop a vision and strategies.
Phase 4	Communicate the vision of change.
Phase 5	Secure a broad empowerment base.
Phase 6	Generate short-term wins.
Phase 7	Consolidate successes and derive further changes.
Phase 8	Anchor new approaches in the culture.

Aim

The aim of the model is to significantly increase the chances of success for change projects via a systematic approach.

Limits

This model is also not to be regarded as a blueprint for change. It will be necessary to adapt and deploy it in accordance with the circumstances involved.

10.6.2 Balanced Scorecard

Description

The main task that is to be performed with the balanced scorecard is to transform the enterprise's strategy in measurable and quantifiable figures. This top-down approach offers managers the possibility of establishing an overview of the enterprise's current capacity to compete.

Application

The strategic goals are typically viewed from various perspectives: financial, customers, processes (internal sequences) and employees (learning and development). Indicators are selected for each of the perspectives. These are to measure the enterprise's approach to the strategic goals. The challenge is to select fewer, but more relevant indicators that – ideally – influence one another directly. For instance, a customer indicator should be selected so as to ensure that its achievement will have a positive impact on superordinate financial indicator.

Aim

The aim of the method is to create greater transparency for far-reaching changes and improvements through the implementation of the strategy and new procedures.

Limits

The tool focuses on the implementation and harbors the risk of excess bureaucracy. Rigid structures are created that are then difficult to change. Once it has been introduced, the balanced scorecard can lead to the professional implementation of misguided strategies.

References

[Albers 2005] Albers, S.; Gassmann, O. (Eds.): Handbuch Technologie-und Innovationsmanagement. Strategie – Umsetzung – Controlling. Wiesbaden: Gabler 2005.

[Aldag 2002] Aldag, R.J.; Kuzuhara, L.W.: Organizational Behavior & Management, An Integrated Skills Approach. Cincinnati, OH: South-Western Thomson Learning 2002.

[Amabile 1998] Amabile, Teresa: How to kill Creativity. Harvard Business Review, September 1998. Boston: Harvard Business School Publishing 1998.

[Amit 1993] Amit, R.; Schoemaker, P. (1993) 'Strategic Assets and Organizational Rent', Strategic Management Journal, Vol. 14, 33–46.

[Andrews 1971] Andrews, K.R.: The Concept of Corporate Strategy. Homewood, IL: Dow Jones-Irwin 1971.

[Ansoff 1965] Ansoff, H.I.: Corporate Strategy. New York: McGraw Hill 1965.

[Ansoff 1976] Ansoff, H.I.: Managing Surprise and Discontinuity – Strategic Response to Weak Signals, in: Schmalenbachs Zeitschrift für betriebswirtschaftliche Forschung, 28th year 1976.

[Ansoff 1981] Ansoff, H.I.: Die Bewältigung von Überraschungen und Diskontinuitäten durch die Unternehmensführung – Strategische Reaktion auf schwache Signale, in: Steinmann, H. [Ed.]: Planung und Kontrolle: Probleme der strategischen Unternehmensführung. München 1981.

[Ansoff 1990] Ansoff, I.; McDonnell, E.: Implanting Strategic Management (2nd edition). Hertfordshire, UK: Prentice Hall International 1990.

[Asimov 1986] Asimov, I.; Cote, J.-M.: Futuredays: A Nineteenth Century Vision of the Year 2000. New York: Henry Holt & Co. 1986.

[Backhouse 2002] Backhouse, R.E.: The Penguin History of Economics. London: Penguin Books 2002.

[Bacon 1995] Bacon, F.: Neu-Atlantis. Stuttgart: Reclam 1995.

[Barney 1980] Barney, G.O.: The Global 2000 Report to the President. New York: Pergamon Books 1980.

[Bea 2001] Bea, F.X.; Haas, J.: Strategisches Management. Stuttgart: Lucius & Lucius 2001.

[Beardsley 2006] Beardsley, S.C.; Bradford, C.J.; Manyika, J.M.: Competitive Advantage from Better Interactions. The McKinsey Quarterly 2006 Number 2. New York.

[Beck 1996] Beck, D.E.; Cowan, C.C.: Spiral Dynamics: Mastering Values, Leadership and Change. Malden, MA: Blackwell 1996.

[Becker 2006] Becker, W.M.; Freeman, V.M.: Going From Global Trends to Corporate Strategy. The McKinsey Quarterly 2006 Number 3.

[Beinhocker 1997] Beinhocker, E.D.: Strategy at the Edge of Chaos. The McKinsey Quarterly 1997 Number 1.

[Beinhocker 1999] Beinhocker, E.D.: On the Origins of Strategy. The McKinsey Quarterly 1999, Number 4.

[Beinhocker 2002] Beinhocker, E.D.; Kaplan, S.: Tired of Strategic Planning? The McKinsey Quarterly 2002 Special Edition: Risk and Resilience. New York.

[Bell 1973] Bell, D.: The Coming of the Post-industrial Society. New York: Basic Books 1973.

[Bellamy 1978] Bellamy, E.: Ein Rückblick aus dem Jahr 2000. Frankfurt (Main): Fischer Taschenbuch Verlag 1978.

[Berner 2004] Berner, G.: Management in 20XX. A holistic look into the future. Erlangen: Publicis Corporate Publishing 2004.

[Berth 2003] Berth, R.: Auf Nummer sicher. Harvard Business Manager, Juni 2003.

[Bettis 1995] Bettis, R.; Hitt, M.: The New Competitive Landscape. Strategic Management Journal 16, 1995.

[BI 2004] Business Insights Ltd.: Mergers and Acquisitions in European Financial Services. London: MBA Group Limited 2004.

[Blohm 1972] Blohm, H; Steinbuch, K. (Eds.): Technische Prognosen in der Praxis. Methoden, Beispiele, Probleme. Düsseldorf: VDI-Verlag 1972.

[Bolz 1997] Bolz, N.: Komplexität und Trendmagie. In: Ahlemeyer, H.W.; Königswieser, R. (Ed.): Komplexität managen. Strategien, Konzepte, Fallbeispiele. Wiesbaden: Gabler 1997.

[Bretz 2001] Bretz, M.: Zur Treffsicherheit von Bevölkerungsvorausberechnungen. In: Wirtschaft und Statistik. Nr.11, 2001.

[Brockhaus 2000] Brockhaus-Redaktion (Ed.): Die Zukunft unseres Planeten. Brockhaus Mensch – Natur – Technik. Leipzig: Brockhaus 2000.

[Brockhoff 1999] Brockhoff, K.: Forschung und Entwicklung. Planung und Kontrolle. München: Oldenbourg 1999.

[Brockman 2002] Brockman, J.: The Next Fifty Years. Science in the First Half of the Twenty-First Century. New York: Vintage Books 2002.

[Brown 2005] Brown, J.S.; Hagel III, J.: The next Frontier of Innovation. The McKinsey Quarterly 2005 Number 3. New York.

[Bruckner 1999] Bruckner, K.; Leithner, S.; McLean, R.; Taylor, C.; Welch, J.: What Is the Market Telling You about Your Strategy? The McKinsey Quarterly 1999 Number 3. New York.

[Bryan 2002] Bryan, L.L.: Just-in-Time Strategy for a Turbulent World. The McKinsey Quarterly 2002 Special Edition: Risk and Resilience. New York.

[Bryan 2004] Bryan, L.L.: Making a Market in Knowledge. The McKinsey Quarterly 2004 Number 3. New York.

[Bryan 2005] Bryan, L.L.: Strategy in an Era of Global Giants. The McKinsey Quarterly 2005 Number 4. New York.

[Buck 1998] Buck, A.; Herrmann, Ch.; Lubkowitz, D.: Handbuch Trend-Management. Innovation und Ästhetik als Grundlage unternehmerischer Erfolge. Frankfurt am Main: Frankfurter Allgemeine Zeitung 1998.

[Bürgel 1996] Bürgel, H.D.: F&E Management. Vahlen, München 1996.

[Burmeister 2004] Burmeister, K.; Neef, A.; Beyers, B.: Corporate Foresight. Unternehmen gestalten Zukunft. Hamburg: Murmann 2004.

[Burmeister 2005] Burmeister, K.; Neef, A. (Eds.): In The Long Run. Corporate Foresight und Langfristdenken in Unternehmen und Gesellschaft. München: Oekom 2005.

[Bush 1945] Thorp, J.: The Information Paradox. Realizing the Business Benefits of Information Technology. Toronto: McGraw-Hill 2003.

[Canton 2006] Canton, J: The extreme Future. The Top Trends That Will Reshape the World for the Next 5, 10, and 20 Years. New York: Penguin 2006.

[Carnall 2003] Carnall, C.A.: Managing Change in Organizations (4th edition): Harlow, England: Pearson 2003.

[Celente 1997] Celente, G.: Trends 2000. How to Prepare for and Profit from the Changes of the 21st Century. New York: Warner 1997.

[Chaffee 1985] Chaffee, E.E.: Three Models of Strategy. Academic Management Review 1985, Vol.10. New York.

[Chalmers 1999] Chalmers, A.F.: Grenzen der Wissenschaft. Berlin: Springer 1999.

[Chalmers 2001] Chalmers, A.F.: Wege der Wissenschaft. 3. Auflage. Heidelberg: Springer 2001.

[Chandler 1962] Chandler, A.D.: Strategy and Structure: Chapters in the History of the Industrial Enterprise. Cambridge, MA: MIT Press 1962.

[Chernev 2006] Chernev, A.: Strategic Marketing Analysis. Brightstar Media 2006.

[Choo 1995] Choo, Ch.W.: Information Management for the Intelligent Organization: The Art of Scanning the Environment. Medford, NJ: Information today (for the American Society for Information Science) 1995.

[Christensen 2000] Christensen, C. M.: The Innovators Dilemma. New York: Harper Business Essentials 2000.

[Christensen 2003] Christensen, C.M.; Raynor, M.E.: The Innovators Solution. Creating and sustaining successful growth. Boston: Harvard Business School Press 2003.

[Clarke 2005] Clarke, C.A.: Profiles of the Future. New York: Bantam Books 1958.

[Cleary 2006] Cleary, S.; Malleret, T.: Resilience to Risk. Business Success in Turbulent Times. Cape Town: Human & Rousseau 2006.

[Clements 2002] Clements M.P; Hendry D.F.: A Companion to Economic Forecasting. Oxford: Blackwell Publishing 2002.

[Coase 1937] Coase, R.H.: The Nature of the Firm. Economica, Vol. 4, November Oxford: Blackwell Publishers 1937.

[Coates 1997] Coates, J.F.; Mahaffie, J.B.; Hines, A.: 2025: Scenarios of U.S. and Global Society Reshaped by Science and Technology. Greensboro, NC: Oakhill Press 1997.

[Coates 2001] Coates, J.F.: Futures Research Quarterly Fall 2001, Volume 17, Number 3. Special Issue. Bethesda, MD: World Future Society 2001.

[Cohen 2006] Cohen, D.S.: Inside the Box. Leading with Corporate Values to Drive Sustained Business Success. Mississauga, Ontario: Jossey Bass 2006.

[Collins 1994] Collins, J.C.; Porras J.I.: Built to Last. Successful Habits of Visionary Companies. New York: Harper Business 1994 (3rd edition. 2000).

[Cooke 1991] Cooke, R.M.: Experts in Uncertainty. Opinion and Subjective Probability in Science. New York: Oxford University Press 1991.

[Cornish 2003] Cornish, E.: The Wildcards in Our Future. The Futurist, July-August 2003 pp 18-22. Bethesda, MD: World Future Society 2003

[Cornish 2004] Cornish, E.: Futuring. The Exploration of the Future. Bethesda, MD: World Future Society 2004.

[Courtney 1997] Courtney, H.; Kirkland, J.; Viguerie, P.: Strategy Under Uncertainty. Harvard Business Review, November/December. Boston: Harvard Business School Publishing 1997.

[Courtney 2001] Courtney, H.: Making the Most of Uncertainty. The McKinsey Quarterly 2001 Number 4.

[Coyne 1994] Coyne, K.P.; Subramaniam, S.: "Bringing Discipline to Strategy". The McKinsey Quarterly 1996 Number 4. New York: McKinsey & Company 1996.

[Davenport 2006] Davenport, T.H.; Leibold, M.; Voelpel, S.: Strategic Management in the Innovation Economy. Erlangen: Publicis Corporate Publishing 2006.

[Davis 1989] Davis, S.M.: Future Perfect. Massachusetts: Addison-Wesley 1989.

[Day 1998] Day, J.D.; Wendler, J.C.: The New Economics of Organization. The McKinsey Quarterly 1998 Number 1.

[Day 2000] Day, G.S.; Schoemaker, P.J.H.; Gunther, R.E.: Managing Emerging Technologies. New York: John Wiley & Sons, 2000.

[Day 2006] Day, G.S.; Schoemaker, P.J.H.: Peripheral Vision. Harvard Business School Press, Boston 2006.

[De Geus 1997] Geus, A.: The Living Company. Habits for Survival in a Turbulent Business Environment. Boston: Harvard Business School Press 1997.

[Denning 1999] Denning, S.: The Knowledge Perspective: A New Strategic Vision. In: Ruggels, R.; Holtshouse, D.: The Knowledge Advantage. Oxford: Capstone Publishing 1999.

[Doppler 2005] Doppler, K.; Lauterbach, C.: Change Management. Den Unternehmenswandel gestalten. 11th edition. Frankfurt am Main: Campus 2005.

[Dorgan 2006] Dorgan, S.; Dowdy, J.; Rippin, T.: The Link Between Management and Productivity. The McKinsey Quarterly (February 2006).

[Dörner 1992] Dörner, D.: Die Logik des Misslingens. Strategisches Denken in komplexen Situationen. Reinbek: Rowohlt 1992.

[Dueck 2006] Dueck, G.: Lean Brain Management. Erfolg und Effizienzsteigerung durch Null-Hirn. Heidelberg: Springer 2006.

[Eberl 200] Eberl, U.; Puma, J.: Innovative Minds. Erlangen: Publicis Corporate Publishing 2007

[Einhorn 1987] Einhorn, H.J.; Hogarth, R.M.: Decision Making. Going forward in Reverse. Harvard Business Review Jan/Feb 1987. Boston.

[Einstein 1999] Einstein, A.; Calaprice, A.: Einstein sagt. Zitate, Einfälle, Gedanken. München: Piper 1999.

[Eisenhardt 1998] Eisenhardt, K.M.; Brown, S.L.: Time Pacing: Competing in Markets That Won't Stand Still. Harvard Business Review, March 1998.

[Etzioni 1989] Etzioni, A.: Humble Decision Making. Harvard Business Review Vol. 67 (July - August 1989) pp. 122-6. Boston: Harvard Business School Publishing 1989.

[Fahey 1986] Fahey, L.; Narayanan, V.K.: Macroenvironmental Analysis for Strategic Management. St. Paul, MN: West Publishing Company 1986.

[Fahey 1998] Fahey, L.; Randall, R.M.: Learning from the Future. Competitive Foresight Scenarios. New York: John Wiley & Sons 1998.

[Fink 2001] Fink, A.; Schlake, O.; Siebe, A.: Erfolg durch Szenario-Management – Prinzip und Werkzeuge der strategischen Vorausschau. Frankfurt: Campus 2001.

[Finkelstein 2004] Finkelstein, S.: Why Smart Executives Fail. And What You Can Learn from Their Mistakes. New York: Portfolio Publishing 2004.

[FitzRoy 2005] FitzRoy, P.; Hulbert, J.: Strategic Management. Creating Value in Turbulent Times. Chichester, UK: John Wiley & Sons 2005.

[Flechtheim 1971] Flechtheim, O.K.: Futurologie. Der Kampf um die Zukunft. Köln: Wissenschaft und Politik 1971.

[Fleisher 2003] Fleisher, C.S.; Bensoussan, B.E.: Strategic and Competitive Analysis. Methods and Techniques for Analysing Business Competition. Upper Saddle River: Pearson Education 2003.

[Forrester 1971] Forrester, J.W.: Der teuflische Regelkreis. Kann die Menschheit überleben? Stuttgart: Deutsche Verlags-Anstalt 1971.

[Forrester 1995] Forrester, J.W.: The Beginning of System Dynamics. The McKinsey Quarterly 1995, Number 4.

[Foster 2001] Foster, R.N.; Kaplan, S.: Creative Destruction. The McKinsey Quarterly 2001 Number 3.

[Fouke 2000] Fouke, J. (Editor): Engineering Tomorrow. Today's Technology Experts Envision the Next Century. New York: IEEE Press 2000.

[Fox 1982] Fox, H.W.: Monitoring Internal Support of Strategies. Mid-South Business Journal. July 1982.

[Frank 2001] Fank, M.: Einführung in das Informationsmanagement: Grundlagen, Methoden, Konzepte. München: Oldenbourg 2001.

[Frankel 2004] Frankel, C.: Earth we have a Problem. In: Kurtzman, J.; Rifkin, G.; Griffith, V.: MBA in a Box. Practical Ideas from the Best Brains in Business. New York: Crown Business 2004.

[Fraser 2006] Fraser, C.H.; Strickland, W.L.: When the Organization Isn't Enough. The McKinsey Quarterly 2006 Number 1.

[Galer 1982] Galer, G.; Kasper, W.: Scenario Planning for Australia. Long Range Planning 15 (4) 50-55.

[Gallup 1985] Gallup, G.; Proctor, W.: Forecast 2000: George Gallup, J., Predicts the Future of America. New York: William Morrow 1985.

[Galtung 2003] Galtung, J.: What did people predict for the year 2000 and what happened. Futures 35 (2) p. 103-121.

[Garland 2007] Garland, E.: Future,Inc. How Business Can Anticipate and Profit from What's NEXT. New York: AMACOM 2007.

[Gausemeier 1996] Gausemeier, J.; Fink, A.; Schlake, O.: Szenario-Management. München: Hanser 1996.

[GEO 2006] Vision: Die bizarre Welt von übermorgen. GEO kompakt Heft 8. Hamburg: Gruner & Jahr 2006.

[Gigerenzer 2002] Gigerenzer, G.: Reckoning with Risk. Learning to Live with Uncertainty. London: Penguin 2002.

[Gladwell 2001] Gladwell, M.: The Tipping Point. How Little Things Can Make A Big Difference. Boston: Little, Brown & Company 2001.

[Goethe 2002] Goethe, J.W.: Wilhelm Meisters Wanderjahre oder die Entsagenden. Frankfurt: Insel 2002.

[Gomez 1997] Gomez, P.; Probst, G.: Die Praxis des ganzheitlichen Problemlösens: Vernetzt denken, unternehmerisch handeln, persönlich überzeugen, 2nd edition, Bern 1997.

[Götze 1991] Götze, U.: Szenario-Technik in der strategischen Unternehmensplanung. Wiesbaden: Deutscher Universitäts-Verlag 1991.

[Graf 1999] Graf, H.G.: Prognosen und Szenarien in der Wirtschaftspraxis. München: Carl Hanser 1999.

[Graf 2002] Graf, H.G.: Global Scenarios. Megatrends in Worldwide Dynamics. Zürich: Rüegger 2002.

[Graf 2005] Graf, H.G.: Economics & Management: Zusammenhänge der Wirtschaftswelt. Zürich: Rüegger 2005.

[Grant 1998] Grant, R.M.: Contemporary Strategy Analysis. Oxford: Blackwell Publishers 1998.

[Graves 1974] Graves, C.W.: Human Nature Prepares for a Momentous Leap. The Futurist, Vol. 8 No. 2, April 1974. Bethesda, MD: World Future Society 1974.

[Gribbin 2005] Gribbin, J.: Deep Simplicity. Chaos, Complexity and The Emergence of Life. London: Penguin 2005.

[Hadeler 2000] Hadeler, T.; Winter, E.: Gabler Wirtschaftslexikon – Die ganze Welt der Wirtschaft: Betriebswirtschaft, Volkswirtschaft, Recht und Steuern, Wiesbaden 2000.

[Hall 1977] Hall, P.: Europe 2000. London: Gerald Duckworth 1977.

[Hamel 1995] Hamel, G.; Prahalad, C.K.: Wettlauf um die Zukunft. Wie Sie mit bahnbrechenden Strategien die Kontrolle über Ihre Branche gewinnen und die Märkte von morgen schaffen. Wien: Überreuter 1995.

[Händeler 2005] Händeler, E.: Die Geschichte der Zukunft. Brendow 2005.

[Hansmann 1983] Hansmann, K.-W.: Kurzlehrbuch Prognoseverfahren. Wiesbaden: Gabler 1983.

[Harris 2002] Harris, J.: Blindsided. How to spot the next breakthrough that will change your business forever. Oxford: Capstone 2002.

[Hauschild 2001] Hauschild, S., Licht, T.; Stein, W.: Creating a Knowledge Culture. The McKinsey Quarterly 2001 Number 1. New York.

[Hauschild 2004] Hauschild, J.: Innovationsmanagement. 3rd edition. München: Vahlen 2004.

[Have 2003] ten Have, S.; ten Have, W.; Stevens, F.; van der Elst, M.: Key Management Models. London: Financial Times Prentice Hall 2003.

[Heijden 1996] Heijden, K. van der: Scenarios: The Art of Strategic Conversation. Chichester, UK: John Wiley & Sons 1996.

[Herbst 2001] Herbst, D.: Erfolgsfaktor Wissensmanagement. Berlin: Cornelsen 2001.

[Heuer 1999] Heuer, R.J.: Psychology of Intelligence Analysis. Washington: United States Government Printing 1999.

[Hitt 2005] Hitt, M.A.; Ireland, R.D.; Hoskisson, R.E.: Strategic Management. Competitiveness and Globalization: Concepts and Cases. Mason: Thomson Learning 2005.

[Hölscher 1999] Hölscher, L.: Die Entdeckung der Zukunft. Frankfurt (Main): Fischer Taschenbuch 1999.

[Horx 1996] Horx, M.; Wippermann, P.: Was ist Trendforschung? Düsseldorf: Econ 1996.

[Horx 1997] Horx, M.: Trendforschung – Pro: Matthias Horx. Forschung & Lehre. 12 / 1997. Deutscher Hochschulverband. 1997.

[Horx 2005] Megatrend Dokumentation. Zukunftsinstitut Kelkheim 2005.

[Hurst 1995] Crisis & Renewal. Meeting the Challenge of Organizational Change. Boston: Harvard Business School Press 1995.

[Huss 1987] Huss, W.R.; Honton, E.J.: Scenario Planning – What Style Should You Use?, in: Long Range Planning, Vol. 20, No. 4, August 1987.

[IFO 2003] Innovationsaktivität in der Industrie 2001/2002: Leichter Rückgang auf hohem Niveau. In: ifo Schnelldienst Nr. 2, 56th year, 2003.

[Ingvar 1985] Ingvar, D.H.: Memory of the Future: An Essay on the Temporal Organization of Conscious Awareness. Human Neurobiology. Heidelberg: Springer 1985.

[Isaksen 2006] Isaksen, S.G.; Tidd, J.: Meeting the Innovation Challenge. Leadership for Transformation and Growth. Chichester, England: John Wiley & Sons 2006.

[Jain 2004] Jain, S.C.: Marketing, Planning and Strategy. Cincinnati: South Western College Publishing 2004.

[Jantsch 1967] Jantsch, E.: Technological Forecasting in Perspective. Paris: Organization for Economic Co-Operation and Development (OECD) 1967.

[Jencks 1971] Jencks, C.: Architecture 2000: Predictions and Methods. London: Studio Vista 1971.

[Jensen 1976] Jensen, M.C.; Meckling, W.H.: Theory of the Firm: Managerial Behaviour, Agency Costs and Ownership Structure. Journal of Financial Economics, Volume 3 No. 4. 1976. Amsterdam: North-Holland 1976.

[Jischa 1993] Jischa, M.F.: Herausforderung Zukunft. Technischer Fortschritt und ökologische Perspektiven. Heidelberg: Spektrum Akademie 1993.

[Johnson 1988] Johnson, G.; Scholes, K.: Exploring Corporate Strategy. Englewood Cliffs, NJ: Prentice-Hall 1988.

[Jungk 1969] Jungk, C.; Galtung, J.: Mankind 2000. London: Allen and Unwin 1969.

[Jungk 1988] Jungk, R.: Im Interview mit Jürgen Streich. Politische Ökologie, Vol. 65, 1988.

[Juran 2000] Juran, J.M.; Godfrey, A.B.: Juran's Quality Handbook. New York: McGraw-Hill 2000.

[Kahn 1967] Kahn, H.; Wiener, A.J.: The Year 2000. New York: Hudson Institute 1967.

[Kaku 1998] Kaku, M.: Zukunftsvisionen. Wie Wissenschaft und Technik des 21. Jahrhunderts unser Leben revolutionieren. München: Lichtenberg 1998.

[Kant 2005] Kant, I.: Kritik der reinen Vernunft. Wiesbaden: Marixverlag 2005.

[Kano 1984] Kano, N.: Attractive Quality and Must-be Quality. Journal of the Japanese Society for Quality Control. No. 4, 1984.

[Kasper 1980] Kasper, W.; Blandy, R.; et al.: Australia at the Cross Roads: Our Choices to the Year 2000. Sydney: Hardcourt Brace Jovanovich 1980.

[Kauffman 1995] Kauffman, S.A.: Technology and Evolution. Escaping the Red Queen Effect. The McKinsey Quarterly 1995 Number 1.

[Kelly 2006] Kelly, E.: Powerful Times: Rising to the challenge of our uncertain world. Wharton School Publishing Upper Saddle River 2006.

[Kerth 2007] Kerth, K.; Asum, H.; Nührich, K.P.: Die besten Strategietools in der Praxis. München: Hanser 2007.

[Keynes 1936] Keynes, J. M.: General Theory of Employment, Interest, and Money. London: Macmillan Cambridge University Press 1936.

[Kiesel 2001] Kiesel, J.: Szenario-Management als Instrument zur Geschäftsfeldplanung. Marburg: Tectum 2001.

[Knight 1921] Knight, F.H.: Risk, Uncertainty and Profit. Boston: Hart, Schaffner & Marx; Houghton Mifflin 1921.

[Kreibich 2002] Kreibich, R.; Schlaffer, A.; Trapp, C.: Zukunftsforschung in Unternehmen. Vol. 33. Berlin: Sekretariat für Zukunftsforschung 2002.

[Krystek 1993] Krystek, U.; Müller-Stewens, G.: Frühaufklärung für Unternehmen: Identifikation und Handhabung zukünftiger Chancen und Bedrohungen. Stuttgart: Schäffer-Poeschel 1993.

[Kuhn 1996] Kuhn, T.S.: The Structure of Scientific Revolutions. Third Edition. Chicago: University of Chicago Press 1996.

[Kunze 2000] Kunze, C.W.: Competitive Intelligence. Ein ressourcenorientierter Ansatz strategischer Frühaufklärung. Dissertation. Aachen: Shaker 2000.

[LeGault 2006] LeGault, M.R.: Think: Why Crucial Decisions Can't Be Made in the Blink of an Eye. New York: Simon & Schuster 2006.

[Liebl 2000] Liebl, F.: Der Schock des Neuen. München: Gerling Akademie Verlag 2000.

[Liebl 2003] Liebl, F.: Woher kommt der Trend? Kolumne brand eins, Dezember 2003/ Januar 2004, Hamburg: brand eins 2003.

[Lindgren 2003] Lindgren, M.; Bandhold, H.: Scenario Planning. The Link Between Future and Strategy. Basingstoke: Palgrave Macmillan 2003.

[List 2000] List, D.: Reviewing hindsight to sharpen foresight: scenarios of 2000. Dubrovnik Conference 2004: Innovation and Social Development in the Knowledge-Based Economy/Society. Dubrovnik: 7-9 May 2004.

[List 2004] List, D.: Scenario network mapping: the development of a methodology for social inquiry. Dissertation. Adelaide: University of South Australia 2004

[Little 1997] Little, A.D. (Ed.): Management von Innovation und Wachstum. Wiesbaden: Gabler 1997.

[Lovallo 2006] Lovallo, D.P.; Sibony, O.: Distortions and Deceptions in Strategic Decisions. The McKinsey Quarterly 2000 Number 1.

[Loveridge 2004] Loveridge, D.: Experts and foresight: review and experience. International Journal of Foresight and Innovation Policy (IJFIP) 2004.

[Low 2002] Low, J.; Kalafut, P.C.: Invisible Advantage. How Intangibles are Driving Business Performance. Cambridge, MA: Perseus 2002.

[Lutz 1955] Lutz, F.A.: Das Problem der Wirtschaftsprognosen. Tübingen: Mohr 1955.

[Lyman 2003] Lyman, P.; Varian, H.R.: How much Information 2003? School of Information Management and Systems, University of California, http://www.sims.berkeley.edu/research/projects/how-much-info-2003 (May 2006).

[Mansfeld 1983] Mansfeld, J.: Die Vorsokratiker I. Ditzingen: Reclam 1983.

[Marsh 2002] Marsh, N.; McAllum, M.; Purcell, D.: Strategic foresight. The power of standing in the future. Melbourne: Crown Content 2002.

[Martelli 2001] Martelli, A.: Scenario Building and Scenario Planning: State of the Art and Prospects of Evolution, Futures Research Quarterly, Vol. 17 No. 2, WFS Maryland Summer 2001.

[Marti 1996] Marti, I.-M.: A Typology of Information Needs. Greenwich: JAI Press 1996.

[Maslow 1954] Maslow, A.: Motivation and Personality. New York: Harper and Row 1954.

[Mason 1994] Mason, D.H.: Scenario-based Planning: Decision Model for the Learning organization, Planning Review March/April 1994.

[Mass 1995] Mass, N.J.; Berkson, B.: Going Slow to go Fast. The McKinsey Quarterly 1995 Number 4.

[McAfee 2002] McAfee, R.P.: Competitive Solutions. The Strategist's Toolkit. Princeton: University Press 2002.

[McKinsey 2002] McKinsey Global Institute: How IT Enables Productivity Growth. Washington DC: November 2002.

[McRae 1994] McRae, H.: The World in 2020. Power, Culture and Prosperity. London: Harper Collins 1994.

[Meadows 1972] Meadows, D.H.; Meadows, D.L.; Randers, J.; Behrens, W.W.: The Limits to Growth. New York: Universe Books 1972.

[Meyers 2003] Meyers Großes Taschenlexikon. Mannheim: Bibliographisches Institut 2003.

[Micic 2003] Micic, P.: Der ZukunftsManager. Wie Sie Marktchancen vor Ihren Mitbewerbern erkennen und nutzen. 3rd edition. Freiburg: Haufe 2003.

[Micklethwait 2003] Micklethwait, J.; Wooldridge, A.: The Company. A Short History of a Revolutionary Idea. New York: Random House 2003.

[Milgrom 1992] Milgrom, P.; Roberts, J.: Economics, Organization and Management, London: Prentice-Hall 1992.

[Millett 1991] Millett, S.M.; Honton, E.J.: A Manager's Guide to Technology Forecasting and Strategy Analysis Methods Columbus, Ohio: Battelle Press 1991.

[Mintzberg 1994] Mintzberg, H.: The Rise and Fall of Strategic Planning. Reconceiving Roles for Planning, Plans, Planners. New York: The Free Press 1994.

[Mintzberg 1999] Mintzberg, H.; Ahlstrand, B.; Lampel, J.: Strategie-Safari. Eine Reise durch die Wildnis des strategischen Managements. Wien: Ueberreuter 1999.

[Mintzberg 2005] Mintzberg, H.; Ahlstrand, B.; Lampel, J.: Strategy bites back. It is far more and less, than you ever imagine. Harlow, England: Pearson 2005.

[Minx 2006] Minx, E.; Böhlke, E: Denken in alternativen Zukünften, in: Zukunftsfragen, Internationale Politik (Zeitschrift der DGAP) December 2006.

[Mirow 2000] Mirow, M.; Linz, C.: Planung und Organisation von Innovationen aus systemtheoretischer Perspektive, in: Häflinger, G.E., Meier, J.D. (Eds.): Aktuelle Tendenzen im Innovationsmanagement. Heidelberg: Physica-Verlag 2000.

[Modis 1994] Modis, T.: Die Berechenbarkeit der Zukunft. Warum wir Vorhersagen machen können. Basel: Birkhäuser 1994.

[Möhrle 2005] Möhrle, M.G.; Isenmann, R. (Eds.): Technologie-Roadmapping. Zukunftsstrategien für Technologieunternehmen. 2nd edition. Berlin, Heidelberg: Springer 2005.

[Molitor 1979] Molitor, G.T.: The hatching of public opinion. In Allio, R.J.; Pennington, M.W. (Eds.): Corporate planning techniques and applications (pp. 53-62). New York: American Management Association 1979.

[Moore 1965] Moore G.E.: The density of transistors assembled on a micro chip doubles every 12 month! Electronics, Volume 38, Number 8, April 19, 1965.

[Morrison 1994] Morrison, I.; Schmid, G.: Future Tense. The business realities of the next ten years. New York: William Morrow and Company, 1994.

[Müller-Stewens 2005] Müller-Stewens, G.; Lechner, C.: Strategisches Management. Wie strategische Initiativen zum Wandel führen. 3rd edition. Stuttgart: Schäffer-Poeschel 2005.

[Naisbitt 1982] Naisbitt, J.: Megatrends: Ten New Directions Transforming Our Lives. New York: Warner Books, Inc. 1982.

[Nattermann 2000] Nattermann, P.M.: Best Practice Best Strategy. The McKinsey Quarterly 2000 Number 2.

[Nelson 1994] Nelson, B.: 1001 Ways to reward Employees. New York: Workman Publishing 1994.

[Neubauer 1977] Neubauer, F.F.; Solomon, N.B.: A Managerial Approach to Environmental Assessment. Long Range Planning (LRP), International Journal of Strategic Management. London: Elsevier 1977.

[Newton 1990] Newton, K.; Schweitzer, T.; Voyer, J.P. (Eds.): Perspective 2000: Proceedings of a Conference sponsored by the Economic Council of Canada. Ottawa: Economic Council of Canada 1990.

[Nicolis 1989] Nicolis, G.; Prigogine, I.: Exploring Complexity: An Introduction.
New York: W. H. Freeman 1989.

[Nore 1988] Nore, P.; Osmundsen, T.: Three scenarios for Norway towards the year 2000. Futures 20 (5) 568-577.

[Norse 1979] Norse, D.: Scenario Analysis in INTERFUTURES. Futures 11 (5) 412-422.

[Nutt 1999] Nutt, P.: Selecting Tactics to Implement Strategic Plans, Strategic Management Journal, 10, 145-161 1999.

[O'Hara 2004] O'Hara-Devereaux, M.: Navigating the Badlands: Thriving in the Decade of Radical Transformation. San Francisco: Jossey-Bass 2004.

[Open 2000] MBA-Kurs "Strategy", Book 1, Open University Milton Keynes 2000.

[Ormerod 2005] Ormerod, P.: Why Most Things Fail: Evolution, Extinction and Economics. New York: Pantheon Books 2005.

[Ornauer 1976] Ornauer, H.; Wilbert, H.; Sicinski, A.J.; Galtung, J.: Images of the World in the Year 2000: A Comparative Ten Nation Study. The Hague: Mouton 1976.

[Orrell 2007] Orrel, D.: The Future of Everything. The Science of Prediction. New York: Thunder's Mouth Press 2007.

[Osmundsen 1986] Osmundsen, T.: Scenarios for Norway year 2000. Futures 18 (4) 549-552.

[Pascale 1990] Pascale, R.T.: Managing on the Edge. London: Penguin 1990.

[Pascale 2004] Pascale R.T.; Millemann, M.; Gioja, L.: Surfing the edge of chaos. The laws of nature and the new laws of business. Great Britain: Thomson 2004.

[Pawlowsky 1999] Pawlowsky, C.: Bewertung konkurrierender Technologien. Ph.D. Thesis, München 1999.

[Peat 2002] Peat, F.D.: From Certainty to Uncertainty. The Story of Science and Ideas in the Twentieth Century. Washington, D.C.: Joseph Henry Press 2002.

[Pfeffer 2000] Pfeffer, J.; Sutton, R.I.: The knowing-doing gap. How smart companies turn knowledge into action. Boston: Harvard Business School Publishing 2000.

[Pfeffer 2006] Pfeffer, J.; Sutton, R.I.: Hard Facts. Dangerous Half-Truths & Total Nonsense. Boston: Harvard Business School Publishing 2006.

[Pillkahn 2005] Pillkahn, U.: Technology Intelligence: Basis for smart Business Strategies. Futures Research Quarterly, Vol. 21 No. 3, WFS Maryland 2005.

[Pillkahn 2007] Pillkahn, U.: Wissenschaftliche Grundlagen der Zukunftsforschung. LMU München 2007.

[Pine 1999] Pine, B.J. II; Gilmore, J.H.: The Experience Economy. Boston: Harvard Business School Press 1999.

[Popcorn 1991] Popcorn, F.: The Popcorn Report. New York: Harper Business 1991.

[Popcorn 1996] Popcorn, F.; Marigold, L.: Clicking. New York: Harper Business 1996.

[Popper 1969] Popper, K.R.: Das Elend des Historizismus. 2nd edition. Tübingen: Mohr Siebeck 1969.

[Porter 1980] Porter, M.E.: Competitive Strategy: Techniques for Analyzing Industries and Competitors. New York: Free Press, 1980.

[Porter 1985] Porter, M.E.: The Competitive Advantage: Creating and Sustaining Superior Performance. New York: Free Press, 1985.

[Porter 1991] Porter, A.L.; Roper, A.T.; Mason, T.W.; Rossini, F.A.; Banks, J.: Forecasting and Management of Technology. New York: John Wiley & Sons 1991.

[Pritchett 1995] Pritchett, L.: Stop Paddling and Start Rocking the Boat. New York: Harper Collins 1995.

[Quinn 1988] Quinn, J.B.; Mintzberg, H.; James, R.M.: The Strategy Process. Concepts, Contexts and Cases. Englewood Cliffs, NJ: Prentice-Hall 1988.

[Ralston 2006] Ralston, B.; Wilson, I.: The Scenario Planning Handbook. Developing Strategies in Uncertain Times. Mason, OH: Texere, Inc. 2006.

[Randall 1997] Randall, D.: Consumer strategies for the Internet: Four Scenarios. Long Range Planning 30 (2) 157-168.

[Raschke 2005] Raschke, M.: Mittendrin. Brand eins Magazin 08 / 2005. Hamburg: Brand eins 2005.

[Reibnitz 1992] Reibnitz, U.: Szenario-Technik. Instrumente für die unternehmerische und persönliche Erfolgsplanung. Wiesbaden: Gabler 1992.

[Rescher 1985] Rescher, N.: Die Grenzen der Wissenschaft. Stuttgart: Reclam 1985.

[Rescher 1997] Rescher, N.: Predicting The Future. An Introduction to the Theory of Forecasting. Albany: State University of New York Press 1997.

[Rethfeld 2004] Rethfeld, R.; Singer, K.: Weltsichten-Weitsichten. München: FinanzBuch 2004.

[Rhynne 1971] Rhynne, R.F. et al: "Projecting wholebody Future patterns – the field anomaly relaxation (FAR) method," SRI Educational Policy Res. Center, EPRC 6747-10 prepared for National Center for Res. and Dev., US Office of Education 1971.

[Rifkin 2003] Rifkin, J.: The Hydrogen Economy: The Creation of the Worldwide Energy Web and the Redistribution of Power on Earth. New York: Tarcher/Penguin 2003.

[Ringland 1998] Ringland, G.: Scenario Planning. Managing for the Future. New York: John Wiley & Sons 1998.

[Ringland 2002] Ringland, G.: Scenarios in Business. Chichester, United Kingdom: John Wiley & Sons 2002.

[Rosenberg 1995] Rosenberg, N.: Innovation's Uncertain Terrain. The McKinsey Quarterly 1995 Number 3.

[Rosenzweig 2007] Rosenzweig, P.M.: The Halo Effect… and the Eight other Business Delusions. New York: The Free Press 2007.

[Rushkoff 2005] Rushkoff, D.: Get back in the box. Innovation from the Inside Out. New York: Harper Collins 2005.

[Rust 1997] Rust, H.: Trendforschung – Contra: Holger Rust. Forschung & Lehre. 12/1997. Deutscher Hochschulverband. 1997.

[Rust 2002] Rust, H.: Zurück zur Vernunft. Wenn Gurus, Powertrainer und Trendforscher nicht mehr weiterhelfen. Wiesbaden: Gabler 2002.

[Sawhney 2001] Sawhney, M.; Zabin, J.: The Seven Steps to Nirvana. Strategic Insights into e-Business Transformation. New York: McGraw-Hill 2001.

[Schein 1965] Schein, E.H.: Organizational Psychology. Englewood Cliffs, N.J.: Prentice-Hall 1965.

[Schnaars 1987] Schnaars, S.P.: How to Develop and Use Scenarios, in: Long Range Planning (LRP) 20. Jg., Nr. 1. London: Pergamon 1987.

[Schoemaker 1997] Schoemaker, P.J.H.: Disciplined Imagination: From Scenarios to Strategic Options, In: International Studies of Management & Organization, Vol.27, No. 2, 1997.

[Schüll 2006] Schüll, E.: Zur Wissenschaftlichkeit von Zukunftsforschung. Tönning: Der Andere Verlag 2006.

[Schwartz 1991] Schwartz, P.: The art of the long view: the path to strategic insight for yourself and your company. New York: Doubleday 1991.

[Schwarz 2005] Schwarz, B.: The paradox of choice. Why more is less. How the culture of abundance robs us of satisfaction. New York: Harper Collins 2005.

[Scott-Morgan 1994] Scott-Morgan, P.: The Unwritten Rules of the Game. New York: McGraw-Hill 1994.

[Senge 1990] Senge, P.M.: The Fifth Discipline. The Art and Practice of the Learning Organization. New York 1990

[Shrivastava 1986] Shrivastava, P.; Lamb, R. (Eds.): Advances in strategic management. Greenwich, CT: JAI Press, 1986.

[Simon 1972] Simon, H.A.: Theories of Bounded Rationality. In McGuire, M.C. and Radner, R. (eds.). Decisions and Organizations, North Holland: Amsterdam, 1972.

[Spierling 2006] Spierling, V.: Kleine Geschichte der Philosophie. München: Piper 2006

[Standage 2005] Standage, T.: The future of technology. Wales: Profile Books Ltd. 2005.

[Steinmüller 1999] Visionen. 1900 2000 2100. Eine Chronik der Zukunft. Hamburg: Rogner & Bernhard 1999.

[Steinmüller 2000] Steinmüller, K.: Wie weiter mit der Zukunftsforschung? In: Zukünfte. Zeitschrift für Zukunftsgestaltung und vernetztes Denken. Heft 33, 2000.

[Steinmüller 2003] Steinmüller, K.: Ungezähmte Zukunft. Wildcards und die Grenzen der Berechenbarkeit. München: Gerling Akademie 2003.

[Stermann 2000] Sterman, J. D.: Business Dynamics: Systems Thinking and Modeling for a Complex World. Boston: McGraw-Hill 2000.

[Sternberg 1999] Sternberg, R.: Handbook of Creativity Cambridge: Cambridge University Press 1999.

[Stevenson 1963] Stevenson, C.L.: Facts and Values: Studies in Ethical Analysis. New Haven, CT: Yale University Press 1963.

[Stevenson 1976] Stevenson, H.H.: Defining Corporate Strength and Weaknesses". Sloan Management Review, Spring 1976.

[Stoneman 2001] Stoneman, P.: The Economics of Technological Diffusion. Oxford: Blackwell 2002.

[Stuckenschneider 2005] Stuckenschneider, H.; Schwair, T.: Strategisches Innovations-Management bei Siemens, in: Albers, S.; Gassmann, O. (Eds.): Handbuch Technologie- und Innovationsmanagement. Wiesbaden: Gabler 2005.

[Stürm 2003] Rüegg-Stürm, J.: Das neue St.Galler Management Modell. Bern: Haupt 2003.

[Surowiecki 2005] Surowiecki, J.: The Wisdom of Crowds. New York: Anchor Books 2005.

[Taleb 2005] Taleb, N.N.: Fooled by Randomness: The hidden Role of Chance in Life and in the Markets. Texere, New York 2005.

[Taylor 1911] Taylor, F.W.: The Principles of Scientific Management. New York: Harper & Row 1911.

[Telecom Australia 1975] Telecom 2000: An Exploration of the Long-Term Development of Telecommunications in Australia. Melbourne: Australian Telecommunications Commission.

[Thorp 2003] Thorp, J.: The Information Paradox. Realizing the Business Benefits of Information Technology. Toronto: McGraw-Hill 2003.

[Tidd 2001] Tidd, J.; Bessant, J.; Pavitt, K.: Managing Innovation. Chichester, United Kingdom: John Wiley & Sons 2001.

[Toffler 1970] Toffler A.: Future Shock. New York, Bantam Books 1970.

[Tsoukas 2004] Tsoukas, H.; Shepherd, J.: Managing the Future: Strategic Foresight in the Knowledge Economy. Oxford: Blackwell 2004.

[Twain 1984] Twain, M.: Life on the Mississippi. New York: Penguin 1984.

[Ulbrich 2004] Ulbrich, S.: Möglichkeiten und Grenzen der Szenarioanalyse. Eine Analyse am Beispiel der Schweizer Energieplanung. Berlin: WiKu 2004.

[Underwood 2004] Underwood, J.: What's your Corporate IQ? How the smartest Companies learn, transform, lead. Chicago: Dearborn Trade Publishing 2004.

[Wack 1985] Wack, P.: Scenarios: Uncharted Waters Ahead. Sept-Oct 1985, Boston: Harvard Business School Publishing 1985.

[Wacker 2001] Wacker, W.; Taylor, J.; Means, H.: Kursbuch für Visionäre. Landsberg: Moderne Industrie 2001.

[Wacker 2002] Wacker, W.; Ryan, M.: The Deviants Advantage: How Fringe Ideas Create Mass Markets. London: Crown Business 2002.

[Wagenführ 1970] Wagenführ, H.: Industrielle Zukunftsforschung. München: Moderne Industrie 1970.

[Walter 1992] Walter, D.(Ed.): Today then: America's Best Minds Look 100 Years into the Future on the Occasion of the 1893 World's Columbian Exposition. Helena, USA: American and World Geographic Publishing 1992.

[Watermann 1980] Waterman, R. Jr.; Peters, T.; Phillips, J.R.: "Structure Is Not Organization" Business Horizons, 23, 3 June 1980, 14-26.

[Weick 1985] Weick, K.E.: Making Sense of the Organization. Oxford: Blackwell Publishing 1985.

[Weidler 1997] Weidler, A.: Entwicklung integrierter Innovationsstrategien. Frankfurt am Main. Peter Lang 1997.

[Wells 1996] Wells, H.G.: Die Zeitmaschine. München: Deutscher Taschenbuchverlag 1996.

[Whittington 1993] Whittington, R.: "What is Strategy: Does it Matter?" New York: Routledge. 1993.

[Wiener 1967] The Year 2000: A Framework for Speculation on the Next Thirty-three Years. New York: Macmillan Publishing Company 1967.

[Wierzbicki 1991] Wierzbicki, A.J.: Poland's development dilemmas on the verge of the 21st century. Futures 23 (4) 392-401.

[Wiggins 2002] Wiggins, R.R.; Ruefli, T.W.: Sustained competitive advantage: Temporal dynamics and the incidence and persistence of superior economic performance. Organization Science Vol. 13, 2002.

[Wilber 2000] Wilber, K.: A Theory of Everything: An integral Vision for Business, Politics, Science and Spirituality. Boston: Shambala 2000.

[Wilms 2006] Wilms, F.E.P.: Szenarien sind Systeme. In: Wilms, F.E.P.: Szenariotechnik. Zürich: Haupt 2006.

[Wilson 1983] Wilson, I.: The benefits of environmental analysis, in: Albert, K. (Ed.): The strategic management handbook. New York 1983.

[Wind 1982] Wind, Y.J.: Product Policy: Concepts, Methods, and Strategy. Addison-Wesley 1982.

[Worthington 2003] Worthington, I.; Britton, C.: The Business Environment. Essex, United Kingdom: Pearson Education 2003.

[Z-Dossier 2002] Z-Punkt (Ed.): Zukunftsforschung in Unternehmen. Praxis, Methoden, Perspektiven. Essen 2002.

[Zürni 2004] Zürni, Ulbrich, S.: Möglichkeiten und Grenzen der Szenarioanalyse (Ph.D. Thesis). Stuttgart: Wiku 2004.

Index

A
Acceleration 40, 54-55, 315
Alcmaeon 31
Analysis
 qualitative 115, 134, 429
 quantitative 33, 134, 430
Analysis of the present 181, 194, 198
Ansoff matrix 418, 434-435
Ansoff, Igor 191-192, 235-236, 245
Antiquity 25
Apple 53, 108, 195
Aristotle 31
Augustine 39

B
Bacon, Francis 166, 168
Balanced scorecard 53, 245, 304, 436
BCG matrix 418, 431-433
Benchmarking 311, 428
Bolz, Norbert 66
Boston Consulting Group 232, 431
Bottle deposit 58
Bounded rationality 93
Brainstorming 190, 193, 213

C
Calculations 38, 188, 193, 339
Capital 61, 317, 319, 355
Capitalism 60
Celente, Gerald 27
Chandler, Alfred 235-236, 246
Change
 classification of 117-119
Change management 334, 418, 435
Chaos 29, 32, 119, 143-144
Chaos research 31
Chaos theorists 29
Club of Rome 26, 163-164
Collins, Jim 49
Competition 46-48, 61, 127, 320
Competitor analysis 83
Complexity 117

Complexity, the dilemma of 92, 315
Constant state 29, 119
Consumer 62-64, 314
Content analysis 27
Cornish, Edward 143, 164
Corporate disaster 158
Corporate foresight 24, 69, 329
Costs 47
Creativity 185-186, 190
Cross-impact analysis 138, 141, 166, 194, 200, 203-204
Customer 423-424
Customer focus 52
Customer profile analysis 418, 423

D
Daimler Benz 167
Data 64, 91, 93-94
Data gathering 147
Decision making 24, 43, 93, 104, 115, 158, 163, 181, 194, 197, 430
Decision theory 197
Decisions 87, 157-158
Dell 61, 195
Delphi-Methode 195
Delta Airlines 316
Deutsche Bank 60
Deutsche Telekom 256-257
Dueck, Gunther 298, 311
Dunbar, Robin I.M. 299

E
Effectiveness 67, 246, 312, 428
Efficiency 67, 121, 298
Eight-phase model 435
Einstein, Albert 37, 185, 290
Engelbart, Douglas C. 58
Enterprise
 assessment 245
 development 45
Enterprise analysis 243, 426
Enterprise blindness 53-54, 297

Enterprise goals 47, 255-257, 259
Enterprise intelligence test 72
Entrepreneurship 249, 294-295, 317, 329
Environment analysis 82, 143, 242
Environment observation 54, 96, 103
Environment, changes in 115, 259, 411
Experiment 31, 80, 174, 225
Expert opinion 195-196
Experts 170-171, 196
Extrapolation 132, 184, 188

F
Fantasy 28, 185-186
FAR method 84
Feedback 251, 307
Filter 89-90, 93, 156, 158
Finkelstein, Sydney 158, 239
Five-forces framework 61, 424
Flechtheim, Ossip K. 164
Forbes 100 companies 48, 242
Ford, Henry 45, 354
Forecast 33, 134, 166, 430
Foresight 158, 160-162, 198, 316, 326, 429
Foresight study 160-161
Forrester, Jay W. 166, 189
Four-quadrants approach 85
Frog, example of change 42, 144
Future
 dilemma 51
 look into 179
 prediction 29
 research 326
 strategy 54
 studies 23-25, 30, 34, 162
Futurist 27, 342
Futurology 164

G
Game theory 197
Gartner, Market Research Institute 35, 408

G

Gates, Bill 168, 195
General Motors 235
GetAbstract 101
Geus, Arie de 23, 67, 156, 239
Gladwell, Malcolm 122, 130
Globalization 42, 81, 129
Globalnomic® Method 27
Goethe, Johann-Wolfgang 159
Google 195, 258, 300, 304
Gore, Wilbert 300
Group opinion 121, 197-198
Growth 59, 157, 160-161
Guidance 27-28, 159

H

Hamel, Gary 47, 51, 53, 67, 69, 237, 316
Heijden, van der Kees 135, 138, 140-141, 156, 165
Heraclitus of Ephesos 41
Herzberg, Frederick 308
Hodgson, Francis B. 208
Honda 232-233
Hypothesis 144, 199, 420

I

IFTF 163, 321, 323, 409
Ignorance 66, 391
Industry and market analysis 83, 424
Information 66, 72, 82-87, 89-95, 97-98, 100, 102-105
Information filter 101
Information gathering 104-105, 137
Information pathologies 91-92
Information processing 84, 90, 93
Information structuring 150
Ingvar, David 155
Innovation 68
Innovation capacity 66, 248
Innovation management 69, 74, 317-318
Innovation need 318
Intuition 28, 87, 197-198
Issue 138, 347, 418, 421
Issue management 418, 421
Issue mapping 138
IT support 94, 227, 302, 304

J

Jobs, Steve 108, 195, 257
Jungk, Robert 170-171, 186, 411

K

Kahn, Herrmann 26, 163-164, 166, 170
Kano, Noriaki 64-65
Kissinger, Henry 81
Knowledge 30-31, 35, 196, 250
Knowledge management 45, 91, 210
Kondratieff cycle 44-45, 56, 394
Kondratieff, Nikolai D. 44-45, 56, 192, 394

L

Law of creative destruction 187
Laws 24, 35, 85, 185-187, 193, 198, 251, 260, 306, 370
Limits of perception 143
List, Denis 168-169, 412
Little, Arthur D. 55
Logic, causal 31, 181-182, 289
Loveridge, Denis 196

M

Market 46, 61, 243-245
Market domination 249
Martelli, Antonio 162
Maslow pyramid 308
Maslow, Abraham 308
Maximum approach 200-201, 203
McKinsey 258, 302
McTaggart, John E. 39
Measurability 65, 72, 259
Methods 179-182, 192-195, 418
Microsoft 65, 168, 195, 258
Milieu studies 62
Mind map 147-148, 239
Mindset 93, 325
Minimum approach 200-201
Mintzberg, Henry 236-238, 240, 269-270
Mission statement 255
Model 35, 39, 188
Modis, Theodore 187
Monitoring 96-97, 102
Moore, Gordon 121, 187
Morphological box 212
Motivation 23, 159
Motivation for change 292-293, 297

N

Naisbitt, John 26-28, 164

Naming 27
Net PC 195
New Economy 43, 55

O

O_2 51
Oil 336
Oil crisis 154
Oil price 341, 346, 348
Olsen, Ken 167
Opinion formation 194-195, 197-198, 209
Opportunity 67-68

P

Paley Commission 66
Paradigm 117, 119-121
Paradigm change 122
Parmenides 31, 303
Patent analysis 181, 194
Peer-to-peer 53
Petroleum 67, 100, 335-337
Philosophy
  deterministic 165-166
  dialectical 42
  organic 165-166
Physical constants 121, 259
Physical laws 121, 183
Pictures of the future 160-161, 174, 203-204, 206, 348
Pisa study 172
Planning 70, 233, 235-236
Plato 31, 42, 120, 162
Pollard, Roger D. 65
Popcorn, Faith 26, 28, 407
Pope 196
Popper, Sir Karl 31, 36, 68, 94
Porras, Jerry I. 49
Prahalad, Coimbatore K. 47, 67, 69, 237
Predictability 31, 140
Principle about the future 188
Probability 35-38, 138-139

Q

Quality 52, 66

R

Radar 137
Radar diagram 148, 360
RAND Corporation 26, 166, 411
Recurring pattern 190-191
Reengineering 52
Regionalization 129

Reibnitz, Ute von 163
Research 28, 32, 34
  formal 96-99, 102, 104
  informal 16, 94-98, 100, 102-103
Restructuring 52, 243, 382
Risk 38
Roadmaps 193, 321-322, 325
Rumors 93

S

Saint Exupéry, Antoine de 58
Samsung 210, 257
Scanning 27-28, 96-98, 138
Scenario 15, 162-163, 165
Scenario analysis 138, 392
Scenario cone 175
Scenario evaluation 208, 287
Scenario framework 200, 202-203, 206, 366-367, 384, 400
Schimanek, Uwe 56
Schwartz, Barry 64, 84, 138-140, 165, 263
Scientific integrity 30
Scientific management 266
Search agents 94-95
Shared vision 197
Shell 26, 163
Shrivastava, Paul 236
Siemens 178
Siemens Corporation 2, 6, 108, 209, 353, 394
Signal 125, 192, 217, 431
Signals, weak 191, 431
Simulation 188, 193
Sine-curve model 187
Sinus milieu 62
Sloan, Alfred 235
Smith, Adam 49
Socrates 31
Sony 60, 70, 252
Source of information 89, 98-99
Southwest Airlines 316
Spiral Dynamics 85
Stakeholder analysis 418, 422-423
Standard approach 201, 203, 360, 384
Stanford Research Institute 26
STEEPV 84, 418-419
Steinbuch, Karl 164, 172
Stevenson, Howard 244, 248
Stora 49
Strategic drift 292
Strategic fit 262-263
Strategic visioning 209
Strategie review 234
Strategy concepts 234, 237, 239
Strategy development 239-242, 264, 266, 301-302
Strategy of scales 243
Submarines 320-321, 328
Sumitomo 49
Surowiecki, James 196
SWOT analysis 82, 254, 281, 418, 433-434
SWOT diagram 263
System Dynamics 189

T

Taylor, Frederick 266-267, 271, 298
Technology 84-85, 209, 311-313
Technology evaluation 311, 314, 324, 409
Technology foresight 180, 407
Television, the future of
  I 104
  II 147
  III 211
  IV 272
  V 327
Terror 37, 132, 362-363
Theories 31, 183, 186-187
Theory of evolution 44
Time series 184-186, 198, 430
Toyota 316
Trend 122, 124, 127, 129-130, 132, 144-146
Trend analysis 132, 418, 420
Trend breaches 28, 136, 400
Trend radar diagram 359
Trend researchers 26-28
Trend scout 15
Trend speculation 27
Trend strength 127
Trend-impact analysis 166, 364-366
Trendsetter 52, 74, 130, 186, 195
Trendstrength 127
Triggers 146, 264, 282, 324-325, 392, 400
Twain, Mark 40

U

Uncertainty 38
User friendliness 56

V

Value-chain analysis 418, 427
Verne, Jules 164, 166, 190
Visions 253, 255, 310

W

Wack, Pierre 154, 165, 188
Wacker, Watts 37
Wagenführ, Horst 164, 172-173
Watson, Thomas 167
Wave theory 44
Weak-signal analysis 97, 418, 431
Weather report 29, 35
Weihenstephan, Brewery 49
Whittington, Richard 235-236
Wildcards 118-119, 137, 143-144
Wilms, Falko E.P. 163, 194
Wilson matrix 200-202, 211, 365, 400
Work sharing 266, 268, 271
World view 31, 40, 115

X

Xenophanes 31

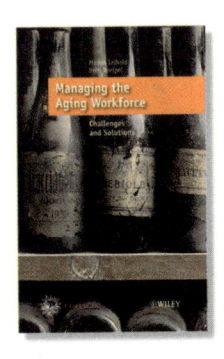

Marius Leibold, Sven Voelpel

Managing the Aging Workforce

Challenges and Solutions

2006, 244 pages, 24 illustrations,
12 tables, hardcover
ISBN 978-3-89578-284-8
€ 32.90 / sFr 53.00

Managing the Aging Workforce is one of the crucial topics for many of the world's enterprises. Where experts are needed, the workforce's age may even increase between 5 and 10 years in only one decade. The challenges arising from this include leadership, health management, knowledge management and learning, as well as to drive ideas for diversity and innovation. For executives and HR managers, this book presents an analysis of the present and upcoming situation, and an introduction into the concepts enterprises will need to survive in aging societies.

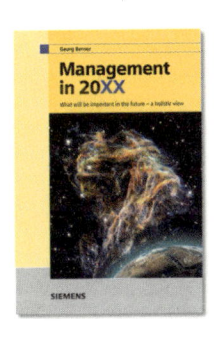

Georg Berner

Management in 20XX

What will be important in the future – a holistic view

2004, 224 pages, 141 colored
illustrations, hardcover
ISBN 978-3-89578-241-1
€ 39.90 / sFr 64.00

The whole world is witnessing radical economic changes. Traditional markets are stagnating; global markets are emerging. Business processes are becoming more mobile, more flexible, and much more streamlined. The boom companies of yesterday have disappeared from the scene. Such an environment calls for innovative ideas - for new ways of doing business, for new products and services, and for a totally new world.

The book lays out some remarkable scenarios and ambitious visions for the future. It helps readers to formulate ideas and plot new directions for their business and points out the changes needed to meet challenges that lie ahead. The new role people will play in the evolving world of business also receives attention in this book that is at once informative and inspiring.

www.publicis-erlangen.de/books

Marius Leibold, Gilbert J.B. Probst, Michael Gibbert

Strategic Management in the Knowledge Economy

New Approaches and Business Applications

2nd updated edition, 2005,
355 pages, hardcover
ISBN 978-3-89578-257-2
€ 39.90 / sFr 64.00

Due to the dramatic shifts in the knowledge economy, this book provides a significant departure from traditional strategic management concepts and practice. Designed for both advanced students and business managers, it presents a unique combination of new strategic management theory, carefully selected strategic management articles by prominent scholars such as Gary Hamel, Michael Porter, Peter Senge, and real-world case studies.

On top of this, the authors link powerful new benchmarks in strategic management thinking, including the concepts of Socio-Cultural Network Dynamics, Systemic Scorecards, and Customer Knowledge Management with practical business challenges and solutions of blue-chip companies with a superior performance (Lafite-Rothschild, Who's Who, Holcim, BRL Hardy, Kuoni BTI, Deutsche Bank, Unisys, Novartis).

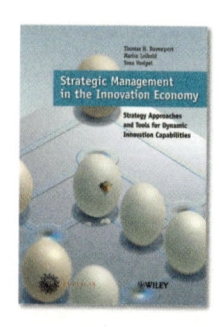

Thomas H. Davenport, Marius Leibold, Sven Voelpel

Strategic Management in the Innovation Economy

Strategy Approaches and Tools for Dynamic Innovation Capabilities

2006, 441 pages,
38 illustrations, hardcover
ISBN 978-3-89578-263-3
€ 32.90 / sFr 53.00

For both advanced students and business managers, this book presents a well-balanced combination of leading-edge theory, published articles by prominent scholars, and case studies & examples, all designed to substantiate a new strategic mindset, innovative tools, and practical applications for significantly increased innovative capabilities.

This is the first book dealing comprehensively with innovation from a strategic point of view, matching the know-how of leading experts on strategy, innovation and practical business.

www.publicis-erlangen.de/books

Ulrich Eberl, Joerg Puma

Innovative Minds
A Look Inside Siemens' Idea Machine

2007, 259 pages, 73 colored
illustrations, hardcover
ISBN 978-3-89578-299-2
€ 34,90 / sFr 56,00

Innovative Minds: A Look Inside Siemens' Idea Machine tells the story of 30 innovations – the large and the small, the rapid and the slow-moving, the disruptive and the evolutionary – and covers the entire spectrum of people and processes involved in their development.

The book provides a unique insight into the multi-dimensional process of innovation development at Siemens. All of the innovations were shaped not only by complex organizational forces and strategies, but also by a host of factors, including bold visions, creative freedom, conflicts, internal and external networks, customer orientation, teamwork – and an ample measure of luck.

Every innovation story yields many valuable lessons, for companies and for each individual involved.

With this in mind, the authors offer a wealth of experiences for all readers who are involved in the process of innovation – whether in a strategic or hands-on capacity – in fields such as research and development, marketing, production and sales, strategy and innovation management, organization and management.

www.publicis-erlangen.de/books

Nicolai Andler

Tools for Project Management, Workshops and Consulting

A Must-Have Compendium of Essential Tools and Techniques

August 2008, ca. 300 pages,
107 illustrations, hardcover
ISBN 978-3-89578-302-9
ca. € 39.90 / sFr 64.00

Written by a professional consultant and executive coach, this book is a unique reference work and guide for those wanting to learn about or who are active in the fields of consulting, project management and problem solving in general. As such, it presents cookbook-style access to more than 100 most important skills.

Nicolai Andler's work differs from many other consulting and project management textbooks. While these primarily concern themselves with the art of running a consulting practice or managing a project, Andler's work focuses mainly on the tools and techniques of the trade. Its power lies in acknowledging that these form part of today's management competencies.

Each tool or technique is broken down into the following components:

- Intention: Why and when to use it?
- Purpose: What does the tool achieve?
- Instruction: How do I do it?
- Tips and suggestions
- Examples or ready-to-use templates
- Cross-reference to related tools described in the book

To make personal use of the tools as easy as possible, they are grouped into task-specific categories entitled Define Situation, Gather Information, Creativity, Goal Setting, Organisational Analysis, Technical Analysis, Strategic Analysis, Decision Making, Project Management, Checklists and Questions as well as Scenarios. In addition, Andler provides a rating of each tool in terms of applicability, ease of use and effectiveness.

"This book is the kind you always wanted to have and didn't think would and could ever exist: the universal field theory of problem solving." *(Prof. Dr. Tom Sommerlatte)*

www.publicis-erlangen.de/books